The Descendants of George Abbott of Andover and Hannah Chandler

Complete Descendants Following Both Male and Female Lines to the Fifth Generation

Compiled by:

Patricia A. Abbott

© 2018 Patricia A. Abbott. All rights reserved.

ISBN-13: 978-0692132845 (Patricia A. Abbott)
ISBN-10: 0692132848

Dedication: To Stephen Edward Abbott, one step toward his goal of documenting every Abbott in America.

Introduction

What do Robert Frost, Eleanor Hallowell Abbott the creator of *Candyland*, and Dorcas Doyne the victim of a sensationalized 1836 murder have in common? They are all descendants of George Abbott of Andover and his wife Hannah Chandler. This compilation is an attempt to provide as complete information as possible of the descendants of George Abbott and Hannah Chandler including complete families through four generations. This includes the listing of the fifth-generation children of those families and their spouses. Both the male and female lines are included so there are many Chandlers, Holts, Ingalls, and Fryes.

Within these pages you will find the full range of human behavior: individuals with great accomplishments, those with humble, ordinary lives, and those who faced incredible hardship and tragedy. There are personal struggles including poverty and reliance on almshouses for subsistence, out-of-wedlock children, and persons who wrestled with alcoholism, depression, and other mental illness. There are also Harvard graduates, attorneys, physicians, and clergymen. There are women pioneers persevering in the face of tremendous challenges. There are the first settlers of many communities in Massachusetts, Connecticut, New Hampshire, Maine, Vermont, Pennsylvania, and upstate New York. There are even several descendants in these first four to five generations who made their way to Canada and into Ohio and Michigan and one or two who relocated to the southern colonies.

Although this is a genealogical compilation, I hope that the presentation of the individual families will allow at least some sense of the humanity of these individuals and their contributions to the founding and development of the country.

Why this book?

There have been previously published genealogies of the descendants of George Abbott of Andover, so why this book? There were several motivations for creating this new genealogy. First, earlier genealogies, for the most part, do not follow the female lines of descent. Not only does this result in an incomplete consideration of the descendants, it prevents a full appreciation of the degree of inter-connectedness of this kinship network. Next, although prior genealogies are very detailed, some information is omitted (e.g., not all the birth or death dates are provided, some names of spouses are not included). As far as possible, this work attempts to provide a more complete detailing of the individual descendants. Prior genealogies are, on a whole, remarkably accurate, but there are some errors. This work also likely has inaccuracies, but when there are areas of disagreement with other genealogies, I have attempted to lay out the reasoning for making one decision over another. One further consideration: an easier to read format. Hopefully, you will be able to read the information without a magnifying glass.

I have attempted to verify each piece of information with documents (birth, death, and marriage records; wills and probate records; and land transactions) to the degree that these could be accessed online. Admittedly this is a quite limited record access, but even within these limits, a large amount of information was able to be verified. Vital records present their own problems as what are mostly available are transcriptions of records, not original records. There are doubtless errors that crept in to the transcriptions. I imagine I also made errors entering my data from the transcriptions. There are inconsistencies in records. For example, there are birth records for a single family in which one child is listed as born in April and a second child is recorded as being born in October of the same year. Often, birth records were recorded in more than one location, so it is not possible to *really* know where the person was born. But within the limits of available records, I have done my very best to be accurate.

Of course, there are not available records for all events (certainly not yet online), or even any records for some persons. For that, I have relied on previously published and unpublished genealogical material and town and county histories. Chief among these were the 1847 "Genealogical Register of the Descendants of George Abbot of Andover. . ." prepared by Abiel Abbot and Ephraim Abbot and the unpublished family notes documents prepared by Charlotte Helen Abbott. There were many other sources and you will find a complete list of these at the end of the book. Sources are also noted in footnotes. Even in those cases in which previously published work was used, I attempted to verify the information contained in those documents. In several cases, there was information that conflicted with available vital records or wills and I have noted those discrepancies and how they were resolved.

One "t" or two?

Some Abbott members use the double "t" and some use one. The patterns of use are often confusing. The original George Abbott of Andover used both; he signed his will with the double "t", so he is a double "t" in this book. Other individuals switched back and forth. Sometimes, members of the same family unit used one while others used two. So, what do we have in this book? When using my database, as I have several thousand Abbott's in there, it became confusing having the two spellings and resulted in people being duplicated and not being able to find who I was looking for. Consequently, I made every Abbott a double "t". When transferring this information into the genealogy, I have attempted to switch those persons who were consistent with the single "t" to a single "t", but I am sure that some were missed. Please do not be offended if you are from the single "t" line. When "Abbott" or "Abbot" was used as a first name or a middle name, I did use the version contained in the records.

How the book is organized

The book is divided into chapters based on generations. When an individual is first introduced, if that person married and had children, you will see a number at the start of the entry that will allow you to know where to look for the next generation for that person. For example, you will see this type of entry when a person is first introduced:

2)   i   JOHN ABBOTT, b. 1648; d. 19 Mar 1720/1; m. at Andover, 17 Nov 1673 SARAH BARKER, b. at Andover, 23 Nov 1647 daughter of Richard and Joanna (-) Barker; Sarah d. 10 Feb 1728/9.

The "2" indicates that you will find follow-up information later in the book. (The "i" indicates that this is the first child in that family.) Of course, there are complications. There are more than a few instances in which descendants of the immigrant George Abbott married each other. In those cases, I have cross-referenced the information, so you hopefully will be able to find what you are looking for from either side of the couple.

The book is organized by generations. All the second generation, followed by all the third generation, then all the fourth. There are some complications with this, for example when a descendant from the second generation married a descendant from the third generation. In those cases, that couple and their children are included in the generation that appears first.

When moving down the generations, you will find in parentheses the track back to George Abbott the original. For example, Hannah Chandler, the daughter of Hannah Abbott and John Chandler, married Daniel Abbott, the son of George Abbott and Dorcas Graves. When the family of Hannah Chandler and Daniel Abbott is introduced, you will see this:

22)   HANNAH CHANDLER (*Hannah Abbott Chandler², George¹*) and DANIEL ABBOTT (*George², George¹*)

From this, you can see that Hannah Chandler was the daughter of Hannah Abbott Chandler who was the daughter of George Abbott. You will also see that Daniel Abbott was the son of George Abbott who was the son of George Abbott. When just the first name is given, the last name is Abbott.

Note: Families numbered 289 and higher will be covered in Generation Five in a planned Volume II.

Table of Contents

Generation One 1

Generation Two 5

Generation Three 29

    Section I: The Children of John Abbott and Sarah Barker 29

    Section II: The Children of Hannah Abbott and John Chandler 45

    Section III: The Children of George Abbott and Dorcas Graves 54

    Section IV: The Children of William Abbott and Elizabeth Geary 62

    Section V: The Children of Sarah Abbott and Ephraim Stevens 75

    Section VI: The Children of Benjamin Abbott and Sarah Farnum 84

    Section VII: The Children of Timothy Abbott and Hannah Graves 92

    Section VIII: The Children of Thomas Abbott and Hannah Gray 97

    Section IX: The Children of Nathaniel Abbott and Dorcas Hibbert 106

    Section X: The Children of Elizabeth Abbott and Nathan Stevens 120

Generation Four 129

    Section I: The Grandchildren of John Abbott and Sarah Barker 129

    Section II: The Grandchildren of Hannah Abbott and John Chandler . 187

    Section III: The Grandchildren of George Abbott and Dorcas Graves . 218

    Section IV: The Grandchildren of William Abbott and Elizabeth Geary 251

    Section V: The Grandchildren of Sarah Abbott and Ephraim Stevens . 313

    Section VI: The Grandchildren of Benjamin Abbott and Sarah Farnum 345

    Section VII: The Grandchildren of Timothy Abbott and Hannah Graves 376

    Section VIII: The Grandchildren of Thomas Abbott and Hannah Gray 391

Section IX: The Grandchildren of Nathaniel Abbott and Dorcas Hibbert 421

Section X: The Grandchildren of Elizabeth Abbott and Nathan Stevens 492

Master List of Families 521

Data Sources 531

References 536

Name Index 551

Descendants of George Abbott and Hannah Chandler of Andover

Generation One

1) GEORGE ABBOTT baptized 22 May 1617 Bishops Stortford, Hertfordshire son of George and Elizabeth (-) Abbott;[1] d. at Andover, 24 Dec 1681; m. 12 Dec 1646 at Roxbury

HANNAH CHANDLER; baptized 22 May 1630 Bishops Stortford, Hertfordshire daughter of William and Annis (Bayford) Chandler. Hannah Chandler Abbott m. 2nd at Andover about 1690, Francis Dane. Hannah Chandler d. at Andover, 2 Jun 1711.

George Abbott and Hannah Chandler were both from Hertfordshire. Although the exact dates of emigration are not known, they likely both arrived sometime in the mid 1630's. Hannah traveled as a young child to New England with her parents William and Annis Chandler, and it is probable that George arrived as a single young man and may have been sponsored by the Chandler family or the family of John Dane. In any event, the Chandler family was first in Roxbury before settling in Andover in 1643. George Abbott settled in Andover also as a first proprietor in 1643.[2]

Although William Chandler and George Abbott were both first proprietors in Andover, they were not among the largest landholders. Each of them received a 4-acre home lot in the first

---

[1] Moriarty, G. Andrews, "Ancestry of George Abbott of Andover," *The New England Historic and Genealogical Register,* 85 (1931): 79-86
[2] Marjorie W. Otten (2000), "The Two George Abbots of Andover, Massachusetts," *The Essex Genealogist*, 20 (2000): 19-23.

division of land and both had lots of still 4 acres just prior to 1662.³ The four largest original land owners in Andover were Simon Bradstreet (who received 20 acres in the first division), John Osgood (20 acres), Nicholas Holt (15 acres), and Joseph Parker (10 acres).

But what the Abbott family lacked in terms of the size of the original property, they made up for in the sheer size of their families and the tendency of the Abbott family members to stay in Andover rather than move on to other locations. In 1730, there were 23 Abbott males on the tax rate lists out of a total of 199 males on the list. They accounted for 11.5% of the males paying taxes in the town. As comparison, the next highest number was the Holt family with 15 males on the tax rate lists in 1730.⁴

George Abbott and his family lived originally in what was North Parish in Andover. In 1663, George Abbott obtained property from Richard Sutton in the area of the current Central Street in Andover. It was here that George Abbott built his garrison house in the South Parish. This was one of twelve garrison houses in Andover at that time. It is believed that it is in this area that on 8 April 1676, Joseph, the 24-year old son of George and Hannah, was killed by Indians and another son, 13-year old Timothy, was taken captive for several months.⁵

George Abbott wrote his will on 12 December 1681 and signed his last name with the double-t (Gerog Abbott). It begins "To all christen people to hom this presont righting may com." After making the customary statements related to giving his soul to god, he continues (in modernized version here) *And as for that portion of worldly goods that god has given me, considering the great love and affection I have unto my loving wife Hannah Abbott, and considering*

---

³ Philip J. Greven, *Four Generations: Population, Land, and Family in Colonial Andover, Massachusetts.* (Ithaca, NY: Cornell University Press, 1970).
⁴ Greven, *Four Generations*
⁵ Claude Moore Fuess, 1959, *Andover, Symbol of New England: Evolution of a Town*, (Andover, MA: Andover Historical Society, 1959), 70.

her tender love and respect she had to me, and also considering her care and diligence in helping to get and save what god has blessed us with. . . leave my whole estate to her.[6]

The total value of the estate in the inventory was 587 pounds, 12 shillings, 5 pence. This inventory excludes portions of the property that had previously been given to the eldest son, John Abbott, as his portion of the estate. Hannah was left the responsibility of disposing of the property she and George Abbott and acquired. She did this 10 February 1706/7 when she conveyed property to her sons Timothy, Thomas, and Nathaniel.[7]

George Abbott and Hannah Chandler had thirteen children all born at Andover.[8]

2) i JOHN ABBOTT, b. 1648;[9] d. 19 Mar 1720/1; m. at Andover, 17 Nov 1673 SARAH BARKER, b. at Andover, 23 Nov 1647 daughter of Richard and Joanna (-) Barker; Sarah d. 10 Feb 1728/9.

ii JOSEPH ABBOTT, b. 11 Mar 1649; d. 24 Jun 1650.

3) iii HANNAH ABBOTT, b. 9 Jun 1650; d. 2 Mar 1740/1; m. at Andover, 20 Dec 1676 JOHN CHANDLER, b. at

---

[6] *Essex County, MA: Probate File Papers, 1638-1881.* Online database. AmericanAncestors.org. New England Historic Genealogical Society, 2014. (From records supplied by the Massachusetts Supreme Judicial Court Archives.) Probate of George Abbot, file #43

[7] Sarah Loring Bailey, *Historical Sketches of Andover*, (Boston: Houghton, 1880), 85-86

[8] All vital records from *Early Vital Records of Massachusetts from 1600 to 1850*, http://ma-vitalrecords.org/ unless otherwise noted.

[9] Massachusetts: Legislators of the General Court, 1691-1780 (Online database: AmericanAncestors.org, New England Historic Genealogical Society, 2002), (Orig. Pub. by Northeastern University Press, Boston, MA. John A. Schutz, *Legislators of the Massachusetts General Court 1691–1780 A Biographical Dictionary*, 1997.)

                Andover, 14 Mar 1655 son of Thomas and Hannah (Brewer) Chandler; John d. 19 Sep 1721.

        iv   JOSEPH ABBOTT, b. 3 Mar 1652; d. 8 Apr 1676, a casualty of conflict with the Indians. Death record transcription reads Joseph, s. George and Hannah (Chandler), "killed by ye Indians," Apr. 8, 1676.

4)   v   GEORGE ABBOTT, b. 7 Jun 1655; d. 27 Feb 1736; m. 17 Apr 1678 DORCAS GRAVES, b. at Lynn, about 1655 daughter of Mark and Amy (-) Graves; Dorcas d. 19 Feb 1739/40.

5)   vi   WILLIAM ABBOTT, b. 18 Nov 1657; d. 24 Oct 1713; m. at Roxbury, 19 Jun 1682 ELIZABETH GEARY, b. at Roxbury, 10 Jul 1661 daughter of Nathaniel and Anne (Douglas) Geary; Elizabeth d. 26 Nov 1712.

6)   vii   SARAH ABBOTT, b. 14 Nov 1659; d. 28 Jun 1711; m. 11 Oct 1680, EPHRAIM STEVENS, b. about 1649 son of John and Elizabeth (Parker) Stevens; Ephraim d. 26 Jun 1718.

7)   viii   BENJAMIN ABBOTT, b. 20 Dec 1661; d. 30 Mar 1703; out-of-wedlock relationship with Naomi Hoyt in 1683; m. 22 Apr 1685 SARAH FARNUM, b. 14 Jan 1661 daughter of Ralph and Elizabeth (Holt) Farnum; Sarah d. before 1726.[10]

8)   ix   TIMOTHY ABBOTT, b. 17 Nov 1663; d. 9 Sep 1730; m. 27 Dec 1689 HANNAH GRAVES, b. at Lynn, 14 Dec 1657 daughter of Mark and Amy (-) Graves

---

[10] Charlotte Helen Abbott, "Early Notes and Records of the Farnum Family of Andover," undated manuscript. Retried from https://www.mhl.org/sites/default/files/files/Abbott/Farnum%20Family.pdf

(sister of Dorcas who married George); Hannah d. 16 Nov 1726.

9)   x   THOMAS ABBOTT, b. 6 May 1666; d. 28 Apr 1728; m. 7 Dec 1697, HANNAH GRAY, b. at Salem 30 Jan 1674/5 daughter of Robert and Hannah (Holt) Gray; Hannah d. 25 Jan 1763.

       xi   EDWARD ABBOTT; b. abt. 1668; died young when drowned.[11]

10)   xii   NATHANIEL ABBOTT, b. 4 Jul 1671; d. 1 Dec 1749; m. 1 Nov 1695, DORCAS HIBBERT, b. about 1675 daughter of Joseph and Elizabeth (Graves) Hibbert of Salem and Beverly; Dorcas d. 17 Feb 1742/3.

11)   xiii   ELIZABETH ABBOTT, b. 9 Feb 1673; d. 4 May 1750; m. 24 Oct 1692, NATHAN STEVENS, b. 5 Apr 1665 son of John and Hannah (Barnard) Stevens; Nathan d. 25 Sep 1740.

Generation Two

2)   JOHN ABBOTT (*George¹*), b. 1648[12] son of George and Hannah (Chandler) Abbott; d. 19 Mar 1720/1; m. at Andover 17 Nov

---

[11] Abiel Abbot and Ephraim Abbot, *Genealogical Record of the Descendants of George Abbot of Andover, George Abbot of Rowley, Thomas Abbot of Andover, Arthur Abbot of Ipswich, Robert Abbot of Branford, CT, and George Abbot of Norwalk, CT*, (Boston: James Munroe and Company, 1847). (available at archive.org)

[12] Massachusetts: Legislators of the General Court, 1691-1780 (Online database: *AmericanAncestors.org*, New England Historic Genealogical Society, 2002).

1673, SARAH BARKER, b. at Andover 23 Nov 1647 daughter of Richard and Joanna (-) Barker; Sarah d. 10 Feb 1728/9.

John Abbott wrote his will 16 May 1716. The will includes bequests to "my well-beloved wife Sarah" who receives £10 and all the moveable estate, and after Sarah's death, the moveable estate will be divided between his two daughters Sarah Chandler and Priscilla Abbott. Well-beloved son John Abbott receives one part of the homestead, with the other part of the homestead going to well-beloved son Joseph Abbott. To his well-beloved son Stephen Abbott, he grants one-half of a property that he purchased, the other half going to well-beloved son Ebenezer. Well-beloved son Ephraim receives £40 (which he has already received) and a 3-acre plot near Ephraim's house and another 2.5 acres that are part of the common land. Beloved son Joshua is granted £45 (which he has already received). Well-beloved daughter Sarah Chandler receives two cows and six sheep as does well-beloved daughter Priscilla Abbott. Sons John Abbott and Joseph Abbott are named executors.[13]

John Abbott and Sarah Barker had nine children born at Andover. Some of the sons used the double-t and some did not.

12) i JOHN ABBOT, b. 2 Nov 1674; d. 1 Jan 1754; m. 6 Jan 1702/3 ELIZABETH HARNDEN, b. at Wilmington 25 Sep 1672 daughter of Richard and Mary (-) Harnden; Elizabeth m. 2nd Zebadiah Chandler 29 Mar 1756; Elizabeth d. 9 Aug 1756.

13) ii JOSEPH ABBOT, b. 29 Dec 1676; d. 9 Jan 1757; m. 4 Apr 1722, HANNAH ALLEN, b. 12 Sep 1690 daughter of John and Mercy (Peters) Allen; Hannah d. 4 Mar 1755.

---

[13] *Essex County, MA: Probate File Papers, 1638-1881.* Probate of John Abbot, 10 Apr 1721, Case number 66.

14)	iii	STEPHEN ABBOT, b. 16 Mar 1678; d. 27 May 1766; m. 22 Jul 1708, SARAH STEVENS, b. 28 Oct 1681 daughter of Ephraim and Sarah (Abbott) Stevens; Sarah d. 28 Dec 1750.
15)	iv	SARAH ABBOTT, b. 26 Nov 1680; d. 6 Mar 1754; m. 9 Jan 1707, ZEBADIAH CHANDLER, b. 1 Apr 1683 son of John and Hannah (Abbott) Chandler. Zebadiah m. 2nd, Elizabeth Harnden Abbott (see above, Family #12); Zebadiah d. 20 Jun 1766.
16)	v	EPHRAIM ABBOT, b. 6 Aug 1682; d. 3 Jun 1748; m. 6 Jan 1714/5 Sarah Hunt (a widow most likely SARAH CROSBY the widow of Thomas Hunt, identity discussed with Family #16 below), b. 12 Jun 1694 daughter of Joseph and Sarah (French) Crosby. Sarah m. 3rd John Dane; Sarah d. about 1760.
17)	vi	JOSHUA ABBOTT, b. 17 Jun 1685; d. at Billerica 11 Feb 1769; m. 1st, 10 Jun 1710 REBECKAH SHED, b. at Billerica, 21 May 1685 daughter of John and Sarah (Chamberlain) Shed; Rebeckah d. 7 Apr 1720. Joshua m. 2nd, 2 Mar 1720/1, DORCAS WHITING, b. at Billerica, 21 Mar 1692 daughter of Oliver and Anna (Danforth) Whiting; Dorcas d. 23 Dec 1765.
	vii	MARY ABBOTT, b. 9 Jan 1687; d. 22 Dec 1688.
18)	viii	EBENEZER ABBOT, b. 27 Sep 1689; d. 14 Jan 1761; m. 5 Apr 1720, HANNAH TURNER, widow of Francis Dane; Hannah was b. at Charlestown about 1694 daughter of James and Hannah (Lazell) Turner; Hannah d. 1788.

ix   PRISCILLA ABBOT, b. 7 Jul 1691; d. 24 May 1791. Priscilla did not marry. According to the genealogy by Abiel Abbot and Ephraim Abbot, she often nursed the sick, was meek and cheerful. An anecdote is that her nephew Barachias, when he was aged, sent Priscilla a message via his son: "Tell my aged aunt Priscilia, that I am likely to shoot the gulf before her." Her answer was "Ah! I wish I was as fit to shoot the gulf as I think he is."[14]

3)   HANNAH ABBOTT (*George¹*), b. 9 Jun 1650 daughter of George and Hannah (Chandler) Abbott; d. 2 Mar 1740/1; m. at Andover 20 Dec 1676 JOHN CHANDLER, b. at Andover, 14 Mar 1655 son of Thomas and Hannah (Brewer) Chandler; John d. 19 Sep 1721.

Hannah Abbott and John Chandler were first cousins, John being Hannah Chandler Abbott's nephew.

The will of John Chandler was written 16 July 1721 and proved 4 December 1721. He made the following bequests: dear and loving wife Hannah Chandler received eight bushels of Indian corn plus two bushels each of rye, wheat, and ground meal, plus some sheep's wool, 100 pounds of good pork, 50 pounds of good beef (and other provisions too numerous to mention here); son John receives all the living from the property he is already working including the housing, orchards, and pastures; son Zebadiah receives some additional land beyond what has already been given to him (this land lying near that of "son" Daniel Abbott who is the husband of Hannah Chandler); daughters Hannah Abbott and Sarah Wright receive some household goods beyond what they have already received; he gives his daughter-in-law Hephzibah Chandler two cows, some other provisions and household items,

---

[14] Abbot and Abbot, *Genealogical Record of Descendants*, p 2

and the use of the back house as long as she is a widow; and his granddaughter Abial Chandler is the receive £50.[15] (Hephzibah is the widow of John's son Abiel.)

Hannah Abbott and John Chandler had six children whose births are recorded at Andover. Some sources list another son, Josiah, in this family. However, there are no records related to him and he is not in the will.

        i   JOHN CHANDLER, b. 23 Oct 1677; d. 10 Jul 1679.

19) ii   JOHN CHANDLER, b. 14 Mar 1679/80; d. 3 May 1741; m. 4 Jun 1701, HANNAH FRYE, b. 12 Apr 1683 daughter of Samuel and Mary (Aslett) Frye; Hannah d. 1 Aug 1727.

15) iii ZEBADIAH CHANDLER, b. 1 Apr 1683; d. 20 Jun 1766; m. 9 Jan 1707, SARAH ABBOTT (Same as Family #15 above); Zebadiah and Sarah were first cousins.

20) iv ABIEL CHANDLER, b. 9 Jan 1686/7; d. 1 Sep 1711; m. 22 Mar 1711, HEPHZIBAH HARNDEN, b. at Reading 19 Sep 1688, daughter of Richard and Mary (-) Harnden. Hephzibah m. 2nd Timothy Chandler; Hephzibah d. 17 Mar 1783.

21) v   HANNAH CHANDLER, b. 12 May 1690; d. at Woodstock, CT, 3 Mar 1755; m. 1st DANIEL ABBOTT, b. 10 Jan 1687/8 son of George and Dorcas (Graves) Abbott; Hannah and Daniel were first cousins; Daniel d. Aug 1731 at Woodstock. Hannah m. 2nd John Bartholomew.

---

[15] *Essex County, MA: Probate File Papers, 1638-1881.* Probate of John Chandler, 4 Dec 1721, Case number 4939.

22) vi SARAH CHANDLER, b. 8 Oct 1693; d. at Woodstock, CT 15 Mar 1737;[16] m. 12 Jan 1712/3 as his 1st wife, JOSEPH WRIGHT, b. 29 Oct 1693 son of Walter and Elizabeth (Peters) Wright. Joseph m. 2nd Elizabeth Chamberlain and m. 3rd Hannah Ashley.[17] Joseph d.? (a Joseph Wright of Norwich with a wife Hannah has a will probated in 1753; the will requests the division of his estate equally "among all my children" but they are not named).

4) GEORGE ABBOTT (*George¹*), b. 7 Jun 1655 son of George and Hannah (Chandler) Abbott; d. 27 Feb 1736; m. 17 Apr 1678, DORCAS GRAVES, b. at Lynn, about 1655 daughter of Mark and Amy (-) Graves; Dorcas d. 19 Feb 1739/40.

The will of George Abbott was written 7 February 1735/6. His will includes a bequest to his dearly beloved wife Dorcas, beyond the customary widow's third, "the use of all my silver money, and the liberty to spend it so far as she shall have need of" for her support and comfort during her widowhood. He makes a bequest to the children of his son Daniel late of Woodstock who is deceased "besides the money and lands I have given to my said son in his lifetime to the value of many hundred pounds," an additional gift of 20 pounds in bills of credit to be paid when they come of age. Well-beloved "eldest surviving" son George receives an additional grant of land beyond what has been given him. There are also bequests for well-beloved son Henry, well-beloved daughter Hannah, grandchild Sarah who is the daughter of Elizabeth who is deceased, and to "youngest well-beloved son Isaac" who receives

---

[16] Vital Records of Woodstock 1686-1854 (accessed through archive.org)
[17] Vital Records of Woodstock 1686-1854 (accessed through archive.org)

an additional money bequest beyond what he has already been given for his "learning."[18]

George Abbott and Dorcas Graves had ten children whose births are recorded at Andover.

    i   SARAH ABBOTT, b. 26 Aug 1679; d. 17 Nov 1679.

    ii   JOSEPH ABBOTT, b. 7 Oct 1680; probably died young.

    iii   NATHAN ABBOTT, b. 12 Feb 1682; probably died young.

    iv   MARTHA ABBOTT, b. 12 Feb 1682; d. 4 Dec 1683.

23)   v   HANNAH ABBOTT, b. 27 Feb 1684; d. 25 Dec 1774; m. 16 Sep 1708, JOHN OSGOOD, b. 28 Jun 1683 son of John and Hannah (Eires) Osgood; John d. 22 Nov 1765.

21)   vi   DANIEL ABBOTT, b. 10 Jan 1687/8; d. at Woodstock, CT, Aug 1731; m. 12 Sep 1711, HANNAH CHANDLER, b. 12 May 1690, daughter of John and Hannah (Abbott) Chandler (the same as Family #21 above).

24)   vii   ELIZABETH ABBOTT, b. 25 Jul 1690; d. 3 Sep 1718; m. 24 Dec 1716, BENJAMIN ABBOTT, b. 11 Jul 1686 son of Benjamin and Sarah (Farnum) Abbott; Elizabeth and Benjamin were first cousins. Benjamin m. 2nd Mary Carleton and 3rd Abigail Abbott (his second cousin and great granddaughter of the

---

[18] *Essex County, MA: Probate File Papers, 1638-1881*. Probate of George Abbott, 15 Mar 1736, Case number 46.

immigrant George Abbott of Rowley). Benjamin died before 5 Dec 1748 the date of probate of his estate.

25) viii GEORGE ABBOTT, b. 22 Dec 1692; d. 19 Mar 1768; m. 29 Nov 1721, MARY PHILLIPS, b. at Salem 5 Aug 1694, daughter of Samuel and Mary (Emerson) Phillips; Mary d. 4 Oct 1785.

26) ix HENRY ABBOTT, b. 12 Jun 1696; d. Feb 1776; m. 27 Oct 1721, MARY PLATTS, b. at Rowley 5 Sep 1700, daughter of James and Lydia (Hale) Platts; Mary d. Aug 1784.

27) x ISAAC ABBOTT, b. 4 Apr 1699; d. 9 Aug 1784; m. 1st, 29 Nov 1739, PHEBE LOVEJOY, b. 20 Jan 1715 daughter of William and Sarah (Frye) Lovejoy; Phebe d. 17 Dec 1751. Isaac m. 2nd, 3 Jan 1754, LYDIA STIMSON, b. at Charlestown, 10 Oct 1703 daughter of Andrew and Abigail (Sweetser) Stimson;[19] Lydia d. 28 Feb 1791. Lydia Stimson was the widow of Robert Calley.

5) WILLIAM ABBOTT (*George¹*), b. 18 Nov 1657 son of George and Hannah (Chandler) Abbott; d. at Andover, 24 Oct 1713; m. at Roxbury, 19 Jun 1682 ELIZABETH GEARY, b. at Roxbury, 10 Jul 1661 daughter of Nathaniel and Anne (Douglas) Geary; Elizabeth d. 26 Nov 1712.

The estate of William Abbott entered probate 16 November 1713. His will includes bequests to the following persons: beloved wife Elizabeth, son William, son Ezra, sons James and Paul, son Philip, son Caleb, daughter Elizabeth, daughter Hannah, son Nathan, and son Zebadiah. The will was written 2 January 1711/12

---

[19] The 1726 will of Abigail Sweetser Stimson includes a bequest to her daughter Lydia Calle. Lydia was the widow of Robert Calley when she married Isaac Abbott.

and son Ezra died in 1712. The property division in 1716 includes "Joseph Phelps and his wife."[20]

William Abbott and Elizabeth Geary had twelve children born at Andover.

28)   i   ELIZABETH ABBOTT, b. 29 Apr 1683; d. 18 Jul 1762 at Pomfret, CT;[21] m. 13 Mar 1710/1, JOSEPH PHELPS, b. 8 Feb 1688/9 son of Samuel and Sarah (Chandler) Phelps; Joseph d. about 1773 at Pomfret when his will was probated.

     ii   WILLIAM ABBOTT, b. 16 Mar 1684/5; d. 28 Oct 1713.

     iii   GEORGE ABBOTT, b. 19 Mar 1686/7; d. 16 Nov 1690.

     iv   EZRA ABBOTT, b. 7 Jul 1689; d. 19 Nov 1712.

     v   GEORGE ABBOTT, b. 21 Dec 1691; d. 30 Dec 1691.

     vi   NATHAN ABBOTT b. 10 Dec 1691; d. 9 Jan 1712/3.

29)   vii   JAMES ABBOTT, b. 12 Feb 1694/5; d. 27 at Concord, NH, possibly in 1778;[22] m. 6 Jan 1713/4, ABIGAIL FARNUM, b. 3 May 1692, daughter of Ralph and Sarah (Sterling) Farnum; Abigail's date of death is not known.

---

[20] *Essex County, MA: Probate File Papers, 1638-1881.* Probate of William Abbott, 16 Nov 1713, Case number 148.
[21] Connecticut Town Death Records, pre-1870 (Barbour Collection). The vital records for Connecticut are from the Barbour Collections unless otherwise noted.
[22] The death date for James Abbott is not certain. Published genealogies, including the Abbott genealogy by Abiel Abbot and Ephraim Abbot list a date of 27 Dec 1787, but I cannot locate a record that supports this. There is a transcription of a death record for a James Abbott in Concord, NH for 1778 that lists the age at death as 83 which would be the right age for this James Abbott.

30) viii PAUL ABBOTT, b. 28 Mar 1697; d. at Hampton, CT, 8 May 1752; m. 8 Feb 1719/20, ELIZABETH GRAY, b. 28 Mar 1700 daughter of Henry and Mary (Blunt) Gray; Elizabeth d. at Pomfret, CT 9 Jul 1765.[23]

31) ix PHILIP ABBOTT, b. 3 Apr 1699; d. 4 Nov 1748 at Hampton;[24] m. 8 Oct 1723 at Windham, ABIGAIL BIGFORD whose origins are not known; Abigail's date of death is not known although it is after 1748 as she was living at the time of the codicil to Philip's will that was written 1 Nov 1748.[25]

32) x HANNAH ABBOTT, b. 5 Apr 1701; d. 11 Feb 1751/2 at Windham; m. 21 Feb 1721 ABIEL HOLT, b. 28 Jun 1698 son of Nicholas and Mary (Russell) Holt. Abiel m. 2nd Sarah Downer; Abiel d. 11 Nov 1772 at Willington.

33) xi CALEB ABBOTT, b. 8 Oct 1704; died at Union, CT, 31 Jan 1778; m. at Pomfret 3 Dec 1730,[26] ELIZABETH PAINE, b. 9 Aug 1710 at Pomfret daughter of Samuel and Ruth (Perrin) Paine; Elizabeth d. 1 Apr 1772 at Union, CT.

xii ZEBADIAH ABBOTT, b. 1706; he was living at the time of his father's will in 1713. According to the Abbot genealogy he married a woman named Hannah and had one daughter named Hannah who died at age 12. There were no records located related to this family.

---

[23] Connecticut Town Death Records, pre-1870 (Barbour Collection).
[24] Connecticut, Hale Collection of Cemetery Inscriptions and Newspaper Notices, 1629-1934
[25] Connecticut, Wills and Probate Records, 1609-1999 (accessed through ancestry.com)
[26] New England Historical and Genealogical Register, 1913, volume LXVII, Marriages at Pomfret, Conn., p. 372

6) SARAH ABBOTT (*George¹*), b. 14 Nov 1659 daughter of George and Hannah (Chandler) Abbott; d. 28 Jun 1711; m. 11 Oct 1680, EPHRAIM STEVENS, b. about 1649 (based on age at time of death) son of John and Elizabeth (Parker) Stevens; Ephraim d. 26 Jun 1718.

Ensign Ephraim Stevens was a selectman of Andover and he was also charged with the security of the town's supply of weapons and ammunition. Town records for 20 February 1712/13 state "we have left the keas of the Town Stock of Ammunition with Ensign Ephraim Stevens, to be at ye selectmen's service, when they shall have ocation for them, and there is two dry casks of the Towns left standing on ye chest that the Amonition is locked up in."[27]

Ephraim Stevens wrote his will 11 June 1718 and his estate entered probate 7 July 1718.[28] To his son-in-law Robert Swan and daughter Hannah, he left his buildings and lands except one-half of the house being reserved for the use of his younger daughters while they are unmarried. He bequeaths to the other five daughters, Sarah, Elizabeth, Mary, Mehitabel, and Deborah, £20 each. The three younger daughters are to receive amounts equal to the amounts the three older daughters received at the time. His six daughters receive his stock of cattle and all the household goods. The daughters also receive £55 to be divided equally among them. Son-in-law Robert Swan was named executor.

Sarah Abbott and Ephraim Stevens had eight children all born at Andover.

---

[27] Bailey, "Andover in the Indian Wars," *Historical Sketches of Andover*, 185.
[28] *Essex County, MA: Probate File Papers, 1638-1881,* Probate of Ephraim Stevens, 7 Jul 1718, Case number 26333.

14)	i	SARAH STEVENS, b. 28 Oct 1681; d. 28 Dec 1750; m. 22 Jul 1708, STEPHEN ABBOTT son of John and Sarah (Barker) Abbott; the same as Family #14 above.
34)	ii	ELIZABETH STEVENS, b. 7 Aug 1683; d. 28 Apr 1763; m. 20 Mar 1706/7, JOSEPH ROBINSON, b. about 1678 son of Joseph and Phebe (Dane) Robinson; Joseph d. at Andover, 9 Apr 1761.
35)	iii	HANNAH STEVENS, b. 18 Nov 1685; d. before 28 Sep 1773 when her will was probated; m. 17 Mar 1708/9, ROBERT SWAN, b. at Haverhill 28 May 1686 son of Robert and Elizabeth (Storie) Swan; Robert died before 4 Sep 1770 when his estate was probated.
	iv	MEHITABLE STEVENS, b. 29 Sep 1691; died young.
36)	v	MARY STEVENS, b. 10 Feb 1693/4; d. at Pomfret, 9 Mar 1773; m. 5 Nov 1719, JAMES INGALLS, b. 9 Aug 1695 son of James and Hannah (Abbott) Ingalls; Hannah Abbott Ingalls is from the Rowley Abbott line; James d. at Pomfret 6 Mar 1767.
	vi	EPHRAIM STEVENS, b. 13 Jul 1698; d. 9 Nov 1702.
37)	vii	MEHITABLE STEVENS, b. 31 Aug 1700; d. probably in NH; m. 4 Dec 1729, EBENEZER HOLT, b. 8 Apr 1705 son of Samuel and Sarah (Farnum) Holt; Ephraim probably died in NH.
38)	viii	DEBORAH STEVENS, b. 4 Oct 1704; d. 17 Jun 1748 at Salem; m. 20 Jun 1726, SAMUEL CARLETON, b. 3 Jun 1696 son of John and Hannah (Osgood) Carleton; Samuel d. at Salem 9 Mar 1767.

7) BENJAMIN ABBOT (*George¹*), b. 20 Dec 1661 son of George and Hannah (Chandler) Abbott; d. 30 Mar 1703; out-of-wedlock relationship with NAOMI HOYT 1683; m. 22 Apr 1685 SARAH

FARNUM, b. 14 Jan 1661 daughter of Ralph and Elizabeth (Holt) Farnum; Sarah d. before 1726.[29]

Although Benjamin made important contributions to his community, he is also known as being the accuser of Martha Carrier for witchcraft. There was a property dispute that may also have been a factor in the accusations of witchery. Martha Carrier and her husband Thomas owned a property adjacent to Benjamin Abbot. There was dispute about the property line and, during an argument between Martha and Benjamin, she cursed him for seven years. At some point following this, Benjamin developed a series of maladies including a swollen foot and a pustule on his side. He attributed this to Martha's witchery. Martha was arrested and jailed, the first accused witch from Andover. She was also accused of witchcraft by the infamous Salem girls who fell in hysterics during her trial. Martha was tried, convicted, and hanged in Salem on August 19, 1692.[30]

Benjamin Abbot was the builder of what is now one of the two oldest houses in Andover located at 9 Andover Street. The house was placed on the National Register in 1976.[31]

Benjamin Abbot's estate entered probate 26 April 1703.[32] He did not leave a will. Sarah Abbott was administrator of the estate. Sarah Abbott was named guardian for the minor children Benjamin,

---

[29] Abbott, Charlotte Helen, "Early Notes and Records of the Farnum Family of Andover," undated manuscript. Retried from https://www.mhl.org/sites/default/files/files/Abbott/Farnum%20Family.pdf

[30] Information summarized from Bill Dalton, 2010, Witches and Switches: The Benjamin Abbot House, The Andover Townsman Online, Retrieved from http://www.andovertownsman.com/community/dalton-column-witches-and-switches-the-benjamin-abbot-house/article_6954f4c3-c022-5274-814e-a15d94ac99d5.html

[31] Andover Historic Preservation, 9 Andover Street, Retrieved from https://preservation.mhl.org/9-andover-st

[32] *Essex County, MA: Probate File Papers, 1638-1881*, Probate of Benjamin Abbot, 26 Apr 1703, Case number 21.

David, Jonathan, and Samuel Abbott. (Although records for the father Benjamin Abbot are most often the one "t", the records for Sarah and the children are most often two "t's".)

Benjamin Abbot had a relationship with Naomi Hoyt Lovejoy when he was about age 22 and she was a young widow about age 28. There was a daughter born of this relationship recorded in the Andover vital records: "Abbot, Ben Naomie, d. illegitimate, Benjamin and Naomie Lovejoy, 1684." It is not known what became of this child.

Benjamin Abbot and Sarah Farnum had four children whose births are recorded at Andover.

24) i BENJAMIN ABBOTT, b. 11 Jul 1686; d. before 5 Dec
39) 1748; m. 1st, 24 Dec 1716 ELIZABETH ABBOTT, b. 25 Jul 1690 daughter of George and Dorcas (Graves) Abbott. BENJAMIN m. 2nd, 23 Oct 1722 MARY CARLETON, b. 7 Apr 1700 daughter of John and Hannah (Osgood) Carleton; Mary died 19 Jan 1725/6. BENJAMIN m. 3rd 1729, ABIGAIL ABBOTT, b. 7 Oct 1699 daughter of Nehemiah and Abigail (Lovejoy) Abbott. Abigail Abbott is from the George Abbott of Rowley line; Abigail d. 8 Dec 1753. Benjamin Abbott and his families with his three wives are covered in Families #24 and #39.

40) ii JONATHAN ABBOTT, b. Sep 1687; death reported as 21 Mar 1770 although record was not located;[33] m. 6 May 1713, ZERVIAH HOLT, b. 24 Mar 1688/9 daughter of Henry and Sarah (Ballard) Holt; Zerviah d. 26 Mar 1768.

41) iii DAVID ABBOTT, b. 18 Jan 1688/9; d. 14 Nov 1753; m. 20 Mar 1717/8, HANNAH DANFORTH, b. at

---

[33] Holt Association of America, *First Three Generations of Holts in America*, (Newburgh, NY: Moore, 1930), 316

Billerica, 20 Aug 1698 daughter of Samuel and Hannah (Crosby) Danforth; Hannah d. 8 Jan 1788.

 iv SAMUEL ABBOTT, b. 19 May 1694; d. 29 Oct 1762; m. 8 Aug 1735, MARY PRESTON, widow of Christopher Lovejoy; Mary b. 31 Mar 1699 daughter of Samuel and Sarah (Bridges) Preston; Mary d. 15 Apr 1754. Samuel and Mary had no children. In his will, Samuel makes bequests to his three "sons-in-law" (stepsons) who were the sons of his deceased wife Mary (the sons of Mary with first husband Christopher Lovejoy): Christopher, Nathan, and Isaac Lovejoy, and a bequest to Nathan's wife Apphia. He also makes bequests to the six daughters of his deceased brother Benjamin (Sarah, Mary, Abigail, Elizabeth, Anna, and Dorcas), three sons of his brother Benjamin (Benjamin, Daniel, and Abiel), the sons of his brother Jonathan (Jonathan, David, Nathaniel, and Samuel), three sons of his deceased brother David (David, Solomon, and Jonathan), Zuriah daughter of brother Jonathan, Hannah and Sarah daughters of brother David, and the children of deceased Job Abbott (Job being a son of Samuel's brother Jonathan).

8) TIMOTHY ABBOTT (*George[1]*), b. 17 Nov 1663 son of George and Hannah (Chandler) Abbott; d. 9 Sep 1730; m. 27 Dec 1689 HANNAH GRAVES, b. at Lynn, 14 Dec 1657 daughter of Mark and Amy (-) Graves (sister of Dorcas who married Timothy's brother George); Hannah d. 16 Nov 1726.

 Timothy was taken captive by the Indians on 8 April 1676, an attack in which his older brother was killed. Timothy was returned the following August in nearly starved condition.

According to Fuess in his *Andover: Symbol of New England*, there is story tradition that as an adult Timothy never allowed his three children to complain of hunger as they did not know what true hunger was.[34]

Timothy Abbott wrote his will 3 March 1730 and his estate entered probate 21 September 1730. Timothy bequeaths to his only and well-beloved son Timothy, husbandman of Andover, several parcels of land including a parcel that was formerly owned by the elder Timothy's brother William who is now deceased. Eldest and well-beloved daughter Hannah receives £43 and youngest and well-beloved daughter Dorcas receives £21. These money amounts are in addition to payments previously made to them and constitute their whole portion. The two daughters also receive all the household items. In addition, after any debts are paid from the estate, any other money or bills of credit are to be equally divided among the three children. Son Timothy Abbott is named sole executor of the estate.[35]

Timothy Abbott and Hannah Graves had three children all born at Andover.

42) i TIMOTHY ABBOTT, b. 20 Jun 1693; d. 10 Jul 1766; m. Dec 1717, MARY FOSTER, b. at Boxford, 2 Aug 1698 daughter of William and Sarah (Kimball) Foster; Mary d. 31 Aug 1784.

43) ii HANNAH ABBOTT, b. 8 Oct 1695; d. 22 Apr 1769; m. 16 Mar 1732 as his 2nd wife, JOHN LANE, b. 20 Oct 1691 son of John and Susannah (Whipple) Lane; John d. 23 Sep 1763.

---

[34] Fuess, *Andover: Symbol of New England*, 71.
[35] *Essex County, MA: Probate File Papers, 1638-1881*, Probate of Timothy Abbott, 21 Sep 1730, Case number 143.

44) iii DORCAS ABBOTT, b. 25 Apr 1698; d. 25 Oct 1758; m. 12 Apr 1717 as his 2nd wife, NICHOLAS HOLT, b. 21 Dec 1683 son of Nicholas and Mary (Russell) Holt; Nicholas d. 1 Dec 1756.

9) THOMAS ABBOTT (*George¹*), b. 6 May 1666 son of George and Hannah (Chandler) Abbott; d. 28 Apr 1728; m. 7 Dec 1697 HANNAH GRAY, b. at Salem 30 Jan 1674/5 daughter of Robert and Hannah (Holt) Gray; Hannah d. 25 Jan 1763.

A probate record for Thomas Abbott was not located. Thomas Abbott and Hannah Gray had ten children all born at Andover.

45) i THOMAS ABBOTT, b. 3 Jan 1698/9; d. 11 Jul 1774; m. 28 Jan 1724/5, ELIZABETH BALLARD, b. 14 Jan 1700/1 daughter of Joseph and Rebecca (Johnson) Ballard; Elizabeth d. 31 Jul 1782.

ii HANNAH ABBOTT, b. 11 Sep 1700; d. at Rumford, NH, 22 Jul 1746; Hannah did not marry but accompanied some of her siblings to New Hampshire.

46) iii EDWARD ABBOTT, b. 9 Jun 1702; died at Concord, NH, 14 Apr 1759; m. 15 Jul 1728, DORCAS CHANDLER, b. about 1705 daughter of Thomas and Mary (Peters) Chandler; Dorcas d. 16 May 1748. Edward married 2nd, 23 Jan 1748/9, MEHITABLE EASTMAN, b. at Haverhill 17 Nov 1707 daughter of Jonathan and Hannah (Green) Eastman.

47) iv DEBORAH ABBOTT, b. 1 Dec 1704; d. at Concord, NH, 25 Oct 1801; m. at Andover 5 Jul 1736, JOSEPH

HALL, b. 15 Dec 1707 son of Joseph and Sarah (Kimball) Hall; Joseph d. 8 Apr 1784 at Concord.[36]

48) v GEORGE ABBOTT, b. 7 Nov 1706; d. at Concord, NH, 6 Oct 1785; m. 1 Feb 1737, SARAH ABBOTT (who was his first cousin, once removed), b. Oct 1711 daughter of Samuel and Sarah (Stevens) Abbott and granddaughter of John and Sarah (Barker) Abbott; Sarah d. at Concord 14 Jun 1769.

vi ZEBADIAH ABBOTT, b. 25 Jan 1708/9; d. 17 May 1745 in the siege of Louisbourg.

49) vii BENJAMIN ABBOTT, b. 31 Mar 1710; d. at Concord, NH, 8 Mar 1794; m. 23 Jun 1742, HANNAH ABBOTT (who was his first cousin once removed), b. 30 Jul 1716 daughter of Samuel and Sarah (Stevens) Abbott and granddaughter of John and Sarah (Barker) Abbott; Hannah d. at Concord 27 Jul 1786.

viii CATHERINE ABBOTT, b. 31 Mar 1710; d. at Andover, 14 Sep 1744; Catherine did not marry.

ix AARON ABBOTT, b. 8 Aug 1714; d. 9 Apr 1730.

x ISAACK ABBOTT, b. 13 Feb 1715/6; d. 3 Nov 1745 in the siege of Louisbourg from illness; Isaac, s. Thomas and Hannah, "sickness in ye Kings Service at Lewisburg," Nov. 3, 1745, a. 28 y. 8m. 21 d.[37]

10) NATHANIEL ABBOTT (*George¹*), b. 4 Jul 1671 son of George and Hannah (Chandler) Abbott; d. 1 Dec 1749; m. 1 Nov 1695 DORCAS HIBBERT, b. about 1675 daughter of Joseph and Elizabeth (Graves) Hibbert of Salem and Beverly; Dorcas d. 17 Feb 1742/3.

---

[36] New Hampshire Death and Disinterment Records, 1754-1947, accessed through ancestry.com
[37] Massachusetts: Vital Records, 1620-1850

Nathaniel Abbott and Dorcas Hibbert had ten children all born at Andover. There are two daughters, Sarah and Hannah, for whom there are no birth records, but these daughters are included in published genealogies including the Abbot genealogy.[38] For the daughter Hannah, there is no further record. The is a marriage reported for Sarah and that information is included here.

50)   i   MARY ABBOTT, b. 28 Jan 1697/8; d. unknown; m. 29 Dec 1718, BENJAMIN BLANCHARD, b. 14 Feb 1693 son of Jonathan and Anne (Lovejoy) Blanchard; Benjamin d. perhaps at NH.

51)   ii   NATHANIEL ABBOTT, b. 9 Jun 1700; d. at Concord, NH 1770;[39] m. 23 Nov 1726, PENELOPE BALLARD, b. 1705 daughter of Joseph and Rebecca (Johnson) Ballard; Penelope d. at Concord, date unknown (there is a death record transcription that gives the place of death, but not the date).

52)   iii SARAH ABBOTT, b. about 1702 (based on age of 56th year at time of death); d. 11 Nov 1757; m. 4 Apr 1722, JOSEPH BLANCHARD, b. 19 Feb 1701 son of Thomas and Rose (Holmes) Blanchard. Joseph m. 2nd the widow Mary Frost.

53)   iv   JOSEPH ABBOTT, b. 22 Jan 1704/5; d. 23 Aug 1787 at Wilton, NH; m. 12 Aug 1731, DEBORAH BLANCHARD, b. 18 Apr 1712 daughter of Thomas and Rose (Holmes) Blanchard; Deborah d. at Andover 21 Jul 1773.

---

[38] Abbot and Abbot, *Genealogical Record of Descendants*, p 144
[39] New Hampshire Death and Disinterment Records, 1754-1947

54)   v   TABITHA ABBOTT, b. about 1707; d. at Concord, NH date unknown, but before her husband; m. 5 Jan 1726/6, her first cousin once removed and George Abbott descendant, JOHN CHANDLER, b. May 1702 son of John and Hannah (Frye) Chandler; John d. at Concord 26 Jul 1775.

55)   vi   JEREMIAH ABBOTT, b. 4 Nov 1709; d. at Billerica 28 Aug 1748; m. 2 Jan 1734/5, HANNAH BALLARD, b. 27 Jun 1714 daughter of Hezekiah and Rebecca (Davis) Ballard. Hannah m. 2nd William Stickney; Hannah d. 11 Feb 1789 at Billerica.

      vii   JOSHUA ABBOTT, b. 3 Feb 1712. The Abbot genealogy[40] lists Joshua the son of Nathaniel and Dorcas (Hibbert) Abbott as marrying Lydia in Ashford, CT. However, there is another Joshua Abbott born 22 Feb 1711/2 in Ashford who is the son of Nathaniel and Mary (Hutchinson) Abbott. It would seem the Joshua born in Ashford is the more likely choice to marry Lydia in Ashford. Nathaniel Abbott who married Mary Hutchinson is from the George Abbott of Rowley line (through the "son" Thomas, Jr.). *Descendants of George Abbott of Rowley* lists Joshua of the Rowley line marrying Lydia and that is supported with land records and seems a sound case.[41] There is no further record that I could locate for this Joshua the son of Nathaniel and Dorcas.

56)   viii ELIZABETH ABBOTT, b. 1 Feb 1713; d. 25 Jul 1799; m. 26 May 1741, TIMOTHY MOOAR, b. 16 Jun 1713

---

[40] Abbot and Abbot, *Genealogical Record of Descendants*, 143
[41] Lemuel Abbott, *Descendants of George Abbott of Rowley*, 912

son of Timothy and Anne (Blanchard) Mooar; Timothy d. 20 Jan 1787.

57)   ix   REBECCA ABBOTT, b. 24 Apr 1717; d. 13 Feb 1803 at Concord, NH; m. 18 Mar 1741/2, ABIEL CHANDLER, b. 14 Mar 1717 son of John and Hannah (Frye) Chandler; Abiel d. abt. 1752 at Concord. Rebecca m. 2nd by 1754, her first cousin, once removed, AMOS ABBOTT, b. 18 Feb 1725/6 son of James and Abigail (Farnum) Abbott.

          x   HANNAH ABBOTT; she is listed in the Abbot genealogy, but I cannot find any record.

11)   ELIZABETH ABBOTT (*George¹*), b. 9 Feb 1673 daughter of George and Hannah (Chalder) Abbott; d. 4 May 1750; m. 24 Oct 1692 NATHAN STEVENS, b. 5 Apr 1665 son of John and Hannah (Barnard) Stevens; Nathan d. 25 Sep 1740.

Nathan Stevens wrote his will 13 May 1740.[42] Beloved wife Elizabeth is to receive one-third of the produce of his tillage lands, two cows to be at her disposal, plus other provisions needed for her care and support. His grandchildren, who are the children of his daughter Elizabeth who is deceased who was the wife of Timothy Pearl, receive six pounds to be divided among them. Daughter Hannah the wife of Samuel Eams receives five pounds by the end of three years after his decease. Daughter Pheby the wife of Nicholas Steel receives ten pounds. There is an interesting bequest to granddaughter "Eunos Ginnins" (or perhaps Germin, but it is not

---

[42] *Essex County, MA: Probate File Papers, 1638-1881.* Probate of Nathan Stevens, 6 Oct 1740, Case number 26408.

clear in the will) who is the oldest daughter of his daughter Pheby who is to receive ten pounds when she reaches the age of 21. This granddaughter is not from Phebe's marriage to Nicholas Steel and this will be addressed with Phebe's family (Family #61). Daughter Lydia Stevens receives 60 pounds, and if she remains single will receive the use of the portion of the house that her mother occupies after mother's decease, as well as some other considerations. Son Nathan, who is named executor, receives all the lands and the remainder of the estate not otherwise distributed.

On 27 September 1746, Elizabeth Abbott Stevens signed a quit claim releasing her dower portion in exchange for a settlement of a payment to her of 40 pounds per year. This allowed grandson Nathan Stevens to take full control of the real property. Elizabeth's son Nathan died just a few months after his father. In 1746, grandson Nathan Stevens was 22 years old and ready to assume his adult responsibilities.

The births of six children of Elizabeth Abbott and Nathan Stevens are recorded at Andover.

58) i NATHAN STEVENS, b. 22 Sep 1693; d. 20 Sep 1741; m. 3 Nov 1715, HANNAH ROBINSON, b. 29 Jan 1694/5 daughter of Dane and Mary (Chadwick) Robinson; Hannah d. possibly at Boxford in 1753 (see discussion in Family #58 in Generation Three).

59) ii ELIZABETH STEVENS, b. 14 Oct 1697; d. at Windham, CT, 28 Aug 1736; m. 24 Aug 1722, TIMOTHY PEARL, b. at Bradford 23 Feb 1695 son of John and Elizabeth (Holmes) Pearl. Timothy m. 2nd Mary Leach; Timothy d. at Windham 9 Oct 1773.

60) iii HANNAH STEVENS, b. 1701; d. after 1782; m. 13 Jan 1720/1 as his 2nd wife, SAMUEL AMES, b. 6 Feb

Generations One and Two 27

1695/6 son of Robert and Bethia (Gatchell) Ames; Samuel d. at Groton 1784.

61) iv PHEBE STEVENS, b. 1704; date of death is unknown, although she is perhaps the Phebe Steel who is the head of household in the 1790 U.S. Census for Andover;[43] m. 7 Nov 1734, NICHOLAS STEEL whose origins are unknown, but described as a laborer.[44] The births of six children are recorded at Andover, but there are no death records in Massachusetts for either Phebe or Nicholas.

v LYDIA STEVENS, b. 1 Aug 1706; d. before 6 Jul 1790 when her estate entered probate;[45] m. 9 Jan 1744 as his 2nd wife, FRANCIS INGALLS, b. 20 Dec 1694 son of Henry and Abigail (Emery) Ingalls; Francis d. 26 Jan 1759. Lydia and Francis did not have children. In her will, Lydia left her estate to her son (step-son) Francis Ingalls, his wife Eunice, and their children Eunice and Asa.

vi Unknown child STEVENS, b. and d. 30 May 1709.

---

[43] 1790 United States Federal Census; Year: 1790; Census Place: Andover, Essex, Massachusetts; Series: M637; Roll: 4; Page: 20; Image: 35; Family History Library Film: 0568144. Household headed by Phebe Steel and household consists of two females.

[44] Charlotte Helen Abbott, Notes on the Steele Family

[45] *Essex County, MA: Probate File Papers, 1638-1881.* Probate of Lydia Ingalls, 6 Jul 1790, Case number 14537.

Generation Three

Section I: The Children of John Abbott and Sarah Barker

12)   JOHN ABBOT (*John², George¹*), b. 2 Nov 1674 son of John and Sarah (Barker) Abbott; d. 1 Jan 1754; m. 6 Jan 1702/3 ELIZABETH HARNDEN, b. at Wilmington, 25 Sep 1672 daughter of Richard and Mary (-) Harnden. Elizabeth m. 2nd Zebadiah Chandler, 29 Mar 1756; Elizabeth d. 9 Aug 1756.

John Abbot remained in Andover his entire life. He served as deacon of the church at Andover for 34 years. He was active in other town affairs including serving as selectman.[46]

John and his wife Elizabeth had six children, one of whom died in infancy. Another son, Abiel, attended Harvard College graduating in 1737. However, he died just two years later cutting short a promising career as a minister. The Reverend J. Barnard delivered a sermon at the funeral of Abiel lamenting the loss of a young life.[47]

Elizabeth was widowed in 1754. That same year, her brother-in-law Zebadiah Chandler was widowed when his wife Sarah Abbot (sister to John Abbot) died. Elizabeth and Zebadiah married in 1756, but Elizabeth died about five months after the marriage.

John Abbot wrote his will 12 August 1747 and it was proved 21 January 1754.[48] His will included bequests to the following persons: "Elizabeth, my dear and well-beloved wife" who received

---

[46] Abbot and Abbot, *Genealogical Record of Descendants*
[47] William B. Sprague, *Annals of the American Pulpit, Volume 1*. (New York: Robert Carter, 1859).
[48] *Essex County, MA: Probate File Papers, 1638-1881.* Probate of John Abbot, 21 Jan 1754, Case number 67.

a fairly typical widow's bequest of the use of the west end of the house and a detailed list of requirements for her son to meet for her continued maintenance; eldest and well-beloved son John received all the homestead lands and some other property and livestock including "one-quarter part of my stock of brute creatures"; second and well-beloved son Barachias received the full deed to the land on which he currently lived; "well-beloved and only daughter Elizabeth" received another quarter of the brute stock and a bequest of money which is to offset a bill of credit that she owes to her father; and youngest and well-beloved son Joseph gets the last quarter of the brute stock and the deed to land on which he has been living. John made additional dispositions of his silver money, paper money, and bills of credit among his wife and his four children.

The children of John and Elizabeth Abbot were all born at Andover.

        i   JOHN ABBOT, b. 1 Sep 1703; d. 10 Sep 1703.[49]

62)   ii   JOHN ABBOT, b. 3 Aug 1704; d. 10 Nov 1793; m. 28 Sep 1732, PHEBE FISKE, b. at Boxford 4 Aug 1712 daughter of John and Abigail (Poore) Fiske; Phebe d. 7 Dec 1802.

63)   iii   BARACHIAS ABBOT, b. 14 May 1707; d. 2 Oct 1784; m. 22 Mar 1733, HANNAH HOLT, b. 18 Dec 1709 daughter of Timothy and Rhoda (Chandler) Holt; Hannah d. 2 Aug 1775.

64)   iv   ELIZABETH ABBOT, b. 28 Oct 1711; d. 4 Jul 1758; m. 26 Oct 1732, ASA FOSTER, b. 16 Jun 1710 son of William and Sarah (Kimball) Foster; Asa d. 17 Jul 1787.

---

[49] *Early Vital Records of Massachusetts from 1600 to 1850*

      v   ABIEL ABBOT, b. 7 Jan 1715/6; d. 18 May 1739. He graduated from Harvard in 1737.[50]

65)   vi   JOSEPH ABBOT, b. 24 Apr 1719; d. 30 Jan 1790 at Chester, MA; m. 12 Nov 1741 his first cousin, HANNAH ABBOTT, b. 29 Dec 1721 daughter of Ebenezer and Hannah (Turner) Abbott; Hannah d. 2 Jun 1805 at Chester.

13)   JOSEPH ABBOT (*John², George¹*), b. 29 Dec 1676 son of John and Sarah (Barker) Abbott; d. 9 Jan 1757; m. 4 Apr 1722 HANNAH ALLEN, b. 12 Sep 1690 daughter of John and Mercy (Peters) Allen; Hannah d. 4 Mar 1755.

There is little known from the records for Joseph Abbot and Hannah Allen. Hannah Allen was orphaned by the time she was three months old as both her parents died in the 1690 smallpox epidemic. There are just two children recorded for this family, one of whom died in early infancy. A probate record could not be located for Joseph. The children were born at Andover.

66)   i   JOSEPH ABBOT, b. 31 May 1724; d. 10 Dec 1766; m. 9 Feb 1748/9 ANNA PEABODY, b. at Boxford 21 Jul 1723 daughter of Jonathan and Alice (Pearl) Peabody; Anna d. 20 May 1766. Joseph married 2nd, 1 Nov 1766, EDNA PLATTS, b. 15 Nov 1737 at Bradford. Joseph died just one month after his second marriage.

      ii   WILLIAM ABBOT; b. 3 Dec 1730; d. 17 Dec 1730.

---

[50] Harvard University, *Quinquennial Catalogue*, 119

14)   STEPHEN ABBOT (*John², George¹*), b. 16 Mar 1678 son of John and Sarah (Barker) Abbott; d. 27 May 1766; m. 22 Jul 1708, SARAH STEVENS (*Sarah Abbott Stevens², George¹*), b. 28 Oct 1681 daughter of Ephraim and Sarah (Abbott) Stevens; Sarah d. 28 Dec 1750.

Stephen Abbot and Sarah Stevens were first cousins and both descendants of George Abbott. Stephen and Sarah had nine children whose births were recorded at Andover. One of these children died in infancy. Son Samuel Abbot died at Lake George, New York during the French and Indian War.

Stephen had considerably less land than his older brothers having an estate of 150 to 190 acres at the time of his death. He made provisions for each of his three sons to settle on this single estate. Two of his sons died before Stephen. As a result, nearly all his lands were bequeathed to his remaining son Stephen, Jr. Stephen, Sr. had retained legal control of all his land until his death at the age of 88.[51]

The will of Stephen Abbot was written 3 November 1759 and proved 8 July 1766.[52] In his will, Stephen made bequests to the following persons: well-beloved son Stephen receives lands and buildings; daughter Elizabeth receives half of whatever grain and corn is on hand at the time of his death; beloved son Ephraim the son of Ephraim who is deceased receives a portion of land; his grandson Ephraim is to make a money payment to each of his five sisters from his bequest, those granddaughters being Hannah, Mehitable, Sarah, Abiel, and Rhoda; beloved daughter Sarah receives one-fifth of the moveable estate as do beloved daughter Hannah and beloved daughter Priscilla and beloved daughter Elizabeth. The last fifth of the moveable estate is granted to his granddaughters Sarah and Mary who are the children of his

---

[51] Greven, *Four Generations*
[52] *Essex County, MA: Probate File Papers, 1638-1881.* Probate of Stephen Abbot, 8 Jul 1766, Case number 132.

daughter Mary who is deceased. On the other hand, his two granddaughters Elizabeth and Hannah who are the children of his deceased son Samuel receive a bequest of land.

67)   i   EPHRAIM ABBOTT, b. 1710; d. 14 Apr 1745; m. 14 Feb 1733/4 HANNAH PHELPS, b. 1709 (est. based on age at death) daughter of Samuel and Hannah (Dane) Phelps; Hannah m. 2nd John Chandler; Hannah d. 5 Aug 1781.

48)   ii   SARAH ABBOTT, b. Oct 1711; d. at Concord, NH 14 Jun 1769;[53] m. 1 Feb 1737, GEORGE ABBOTT her first cousin, once removed, b. 7 Nov 1706 son of Thomas and Hannah (Gray) Abbott; George d. at Concord 6 Oct 1785.[54] (This is Family #48 in Generation Two.)

68)   iii   MARY ABBOTT, b. 4 Aug 1713; d. at Lunenburg, 5 Aug 1748; m. 14 Aug 1742, JOSEPH HOLT, b. 28 Feb 1715/6 son of Thomas and Alice (Peabody) Holt. Joseph m. 2nd Dorcas Frost; Joseph d. at Lunenburg 1754 (based on date of probate 26 Sep 1754).

49)   iv   HANNAH ABBOTT, b. 30 Jul 1716; d. at Concord, NH 26 Jul 1786;[55] m. 23 Jun 1742, BENJAMIN ABBOTT her first cousin, once removed, b. 31 Mar 1710 son of Thomas and Hannah (Gray) Abbott; Benjamin d. at Concord 8 Mar 1794. (This is Family #49 in Generation Two.)

---

[53] Abbot and Abbot, *Genealogical Record of Descendants*
[54] Confirmed by probate date 16 November 1785
[55] New Hampshire Death and Disinterment Records, 1754-1947, accessed through ancestry.com

Children of John Abbott and Sarah Barker

69)   v   STEPHEN ABBOT, b. 2 Mar 1717/8; d. 8 Nov 1768; m. 24 May 1743, MARY ABBOTT, his second cousin, b. 12 Mar 1722/3 daughter of George and Mary (Phillips) Abbott. Mary m. 2nd as his second wife, her second cousin Jonathan Abbott son of Jonathan and Zerviah (Holt) Abbott; Mary d. 8 Aug 1792.

vi   PRISCILLA ABBOTT, b. 20 Feb 1719/20; d. 28 Dec 1796; m. 28 Mar 1771 as his 2nd wife, JACOB FOWLE of Lancaster; there were no children from this marriage; Jacob d. 6 Mar 1774 at Lancaster.

vii   ELIZABETH ABBOTT, b. 29 Dec 1721; d. about 1786;[56] she does not seem to have married.

70)   viii   SAMUEL ABBOT, b. 23 Jun 1726; d. 1758 at Ft. George, NY during the French and Indian War; m. 14 Dec 1754, ELIZABETH WYMAN probably born about 1730, described as "of Pelham" but not further information has been located on her origins. Elizabeth m. 2nd Joseph Dane; Elizabeth d. 26 Sep 1778.

ix   MEHITABLE ABBOTT, b. 17 Mar 1727/8; d. 16 Apr 1728.

15)   SARAH ABBOTT (*John²*, *George¹*), b. 26 Nov 1680 daughter of John and Sarah (Barker) Abbott; d. 6 Mar 1754; m. 9 Jan 1707 ZEBADIAH CHANDLER (*Hannah Abbott Chandler²*, *George¹*), b. 1 Apr 1683 son of John and Hannah (Abbott) Chandler. Zebadiah m. 2nd Elizabeth Harnden Abbott (widow of John Abbott); Zebadiah d. 20 Jun 1766.

    Sarah and Zebadiah Chandler were members of the South Parish church in Andover. Zebadiah held some positions in the

---

[56] Abbot and Abbot, *Genealogical Record of Descendants*

town including surveyor 1721-1726 and was chosen constable 3 Mar 1734/5.[57] Sarah and Zebadiah had five daughters. The estate of Zebadiah Chandler was probated 8 July 1766. He made bequests to the following persons: beloved daughter Sarah Chandler (who married Joshua Chandler), beloved daughter Joanna Shaddock, beloved daughter Priscilla Phelps, beloved daughter Mehitable Lovejoy, beloved daughter Elizabeth Lovejoy, and beloved grandson Joshua Chandler son of daughter Sarah. Grandson Joshua Chandler was the executor.

71) i SARAH CHANDLER, b. 1707 (based on age at time of death); d. 28 Mar 1768; m. 18 Feb 1728/9, JOSHUA CHANDLER, her 1st cousin (and a descendant of George Abbott), b. 1705 son of John and Hannah (Frye) Chandler; Joshua d. 24 Mar 1734; Sarah did not remarry.

72) ii JOANNA CHANDLER, b. 1710 (based on age at time of death); d. 12 Sep 1791; m. 3 Jun 1728, JOSEPH SHATTUCK, b. 1707 (based on age at time of death); Joseph d. 21 Mar 1772.

73) iii PRISCILLA CHANDLER, b. 26 Apr 1713; d. 4 Jan 1778; m. 29 Jan 1735/6, SAMUEL PHELPS, b. 5 Feb 1712/3 son of Samuel and Hannah (Dane) Phelps; Samuel d. 17 Apr 1795.

74) iv MEHITABLE CHANDLER, b. 1717; d. 26 Jan 1786 (reported, but no record found); m. 26 Jan 1738, CALEB LOVEJOY, b. 28 Dec 1716 son of Henry and

---

[57] George Chandler. *The Chandler family: The descendants of William and Annis Chandler who settled in Roxbury, Mass 1637.* (Worcester, MA: Charles Hamilton, 1883).

Sarah (Farnum) Lovejoy. The family relocated to Suncook, NH and Caleb is reported to have died there 1781 (this is the date used by the Daughters of the American Revolution and Carter's *History of Pembroke*).

75)   v   ELIZABETH CHANDLER, b. 5 Feb 1721; d. probably in NH, date unknown; m. 26 Mar 1741, DAVID LOVEJOY, b. 10 Oct 1715 son of Henry and Sarah (Farnum) Lovejoy. The family relocated to Suncook, NH. The DAR gives the death date of David as 18 Feb 1819, although I believe this to be the death date of his son David Lovejoy.

16)   EPHRAIM ABBOT (*John²*, *George¹*), b. 6 Aug 1682 son of John and Sarah (Barker) Abbott; d. 3 Jun 1748; m. 6 Jan 1714/5 Sarah Hunt (a widow most likely SARAH CROSBY the widow of Thomas Hunt; identity discussed below), b. 12 Jun 1694 daughter of Joseph and Sarah (French) Crosby. Sarah m. 3rd John Dane; Sarah d. about 1760.

On 6 January 1714/5, Ephraim Abbot married Sarah Hunt, widow of Billerica. The Billerica records show that Thomas Hunt, the husband of Sarah and son of Samuel, Sr., died 16 September 1709. Thomas Hunt is recorded as marrying Sarah Crosby, although the date of the marriage did not survive in the records; there is just a record that a marriage occurred. There is one child born to Thomas and Sarah Hunt, a daughter Sarah born 20 November 1709. In the Billerica records, there are two potential Sarah Crosbys who might be the wife of Thomas Hunt. First is Sarah Crosby born in 1684 the daughter of Simon and Rachel Crosby. The second is Sarah the daughter of Joseph and Sarah Crosby. These two Sarah's were aunt and niece, the older Sarah being the sister of Joseph. However, the elder Sarah Crosby was married to a man named Rawson established by the 1724 will of Simon Crosby which includes a bequest to his daughter Sarah

Rawson. The only real concern about this identification of Sarah daughter of Joseph being the wife of Thomas Hunt is her very young age (either 15 or 16) at the time of her first marriage. However, Thomas Hunt was born in 1689 making him a quite young husband in 1709. No death record or guardian record could be located for the child Sarah Hunt born to Thomas and Sarah.

In his will, Ephraim Abbot has bequests to the following persons: dearly and well-beloved wife Sarah, eldest and well-beloved son Ephraim, second and well-beloved son Joshua, and his other well-beloved sons Daniel, Josiah, Ebenezer, and Peter, and well-beloved daughters Sarah, Mary, Elizabeth, and Martha. Daniel is the executor of the estate.[58]

Ephraim Abbot and Sarah Crosby had eleven children all born at Andover.

76) i SARAH ABBOTT, b. 25 Jan 1715/6; d. at NH; m. 8 Sep 1736, SAMUEL GRAY, b. Jul 1711 son of Henry and Mary (Blunt) Gray; Samuel d. probably in New Hampshire.

77) ii EPHRAIM ABBOT, b. 22 Jul 1718; d. about 1775 at Amherst, NH; m. 1st, 3 Nov 1740 his 2nd cousin (and George Abbott descendant) MARY ABBOTT, b. 7 Jan 1723/4 daughter of Timothy and Mary (Foster) Abbott; Mary d. 9 Mar 1744. Ephraim m. 2nd 1 Feb 1745/6, MARY KNEELAND,[59] b. about 1720 of

---

[58] *Essex County, MA: Probate File Papers, 1638-1881.* Probate of Ephraim Abbot, 4 Jul 1748, Case number 41.
[59] The Abiel Abbot and Ephraim Abbot Genealogy gives her name as Hannah Kneeland, but the marriage record says Mary Kneeland and the birth records for each of her children with Ephraim Abbot give the mother's name as Mary. She is possibly Mary Neeland (Kneeland) baptized in Topsfield 21 May 1721 daughter of

Ipswich; death is not known but likely at Amherst, NH.

78) iii MARY ABBOTT, b. Jul 1720; date of death unknown but likely in Amherst, NH; m. 11 May 1743, ROBERT READ, b. 25 Dec 1720 at Chelmsford son of William and Hannah (Bates) Read; Robert d. at Amherst, NH 11 Sep 1803.[60]

79) iv JOSHUA ABBOTT, b. 25 Sep 1722; d. at Amherst, NH after 2 Mar 1772 (the date of his will); m. 7 Jul 1749, PHEBE INGALLS, b. 7 Jul 1725 daughter of Joseph and Phebe (Farnum) Ingalls; Phebe d. after 2 Mar 1772.

v DANIEL ABBOTT, b. 3 Sep 1724; d.10 Aug 1761; m. 21 May 1752, Lydia Henfield widow. Daniel and Lydia had no children. In his will probated 31 Aug 1761, Daniel Abbott has bequests to the following persons: beloved wife Lydia, beloved brother Ebenezer Abbott, beloved brother Peter Abbott, beloved cousin Daniel Abbott, and his brethren and sisters: Ephraim Abbott, Joshua Abbott, Josiah Abbott, Ebenezer Abbott, Peter Abbott, Sarah Gray, Mary Reed, Elizabeth Abbott, and Martha Towne.[61] The will addresses the reports in published genealogies that Archelaus Towne first married Mary Abbott and then her younger sister Martha. Archelaus Towne and Martha Abbott were married by at least 1761. Martha's sister Mary was at that

---

Philip. Philip died in 1742 and his son Philip relocated to Ipswich which would make it possible that Mary accompanied her brother to Ipswich.

[60] His grave site has been located at the Amherst Town Hall Burying Ground and bears this inscription: Erected to the Memory of Col. Robert Read who died Sept. 11, 1803 in the 83 Year of his age. (findagrave.com)

[61] *Essex County, MA: Probate File Papers, 1638-1881.* Probate of Daniel Abbot, 31 Aug 1761, Case number 27.

Generation Three

same time married to Robert Reed. There does not seem to be any evidence that Archelaus Towne was married to anyone other than Martha Abbott.

80) vi ELIZABETH ABBOTT, b. 29 Jun 1726; d. 18 Dec 1819; m. 20 Sep 1744, her 2nd cousin ASA ABBOT, b. 17 Oct 1721 son of Timothy and Mary (Foster) Abbot; Asa d. 22 Dec 1796.

81) vii JOSIAH ABBOTT, b. 26 Sep 1728; d. at Lyndeborough, NH, Dec 1777 at Lyndeborough, NH; m. by 1755 HANNAH HOBBS, b. at Middleton, 28 Aug 1729 daughter of William and Amme (Towne) Hobbs.

82) viii EBENEZER ABBOTT, b. 20 Feb 1731; d. 19 Dec 1771; m. 1 Jan 1752, LYDIA FARRINGTON, b. 24 Oct 1735 daughter of John and Sarah (Houghton) Farrington. It is possible that Lydia married Abraham Sheldon of Reading in 1774, but that is not certain.

ix MARTHA ABBOTT, b. 30 Mar 1733; d. 5 May 1733.

83) x PETER ABBOTT, b. 8 May 1734; d. 19 Apr 1774 at Kingston, NH; m. 22 Sep 1757, the widow ELIZABETH (-) DAMON.

84) xi MARTHA ABBOTT, b. 13 Jul 1737; d. 13 Aug 1773 at Amherst, NH; m. about 1757 ARCHELAUS TOWNE,[62] b. 1734 at Topsfield son of Israel and

---

[62] Several marriages are reported for Archelaus Towne in various published sources, but he seems to have married only Martha and they were married by 1761 when her brother Daniel leaves a bequest to his sister Martha Town in his will.

Grace (Gardner) Towne; Archelaus d. Nov 1779 at Fishkill, NY during the Revolution.

17) JOSHUA ABBOTT (*John², George¹*), b. 17 Jun 1685 son of John and Sarah (Barker) Abbott; d. at Billerica 11 Feb 1769; m. 1st, 10 Jun 1710 REBECKAH SHED, b. at Billerica, 21 May 1685 daughter of John and Sarah (Chamberlain) Shed; Rebeckah d. 7 Apr 1720. Joshua m. 2nd, 2 Mar 1720/1, DORCAS WHITING, b. at Billerica 21 Mar 1692 daughter of Oliver and Anna (Danforth) Whiting; Dorcas d. 23 Dec 1765.

In his will, Joshua Abbott makes bequests to the following persons: "Tis my will and pleasure and I do give to Dorcas my beloved wife" one third part of the personal estate and other bequests to son John Abbott, daughter Sarah Goodwin, daughter Mary Jefts, daughter Elizabeth Walker, daughter Dorcas Abbott, granddaughter Hannah Osgood got forty shillings in full for the remainder of her mother's portion, son Joshua Abbott, son Oliver Abbott, and son David Abbott.[63]

Six children of Joshua Abbott and Rebeckah Shed were born at Billerica.

	i	REBECKAH ABBOTT, b. 27 Mar 1711; d. 9 May 1761; she did not marry.
85)	ii	JOHN ABBOTT, b. 5 May 1713; d. 22 Oct 1791 at Westford; m. 30 Dec 1735, HANNAH RICHARDSON, b. 2 Apr 1714 at Billerica daughter of Jonathan and Hannah (French) Richardson; Hannah d. 29 Nov 1795.
86)	iii	SARAH ABBOTT, b. 24 Feb 1714/5; d. about 1798; m. 1 Jan 1736, CHRISTOPHER OSGOOD, b. 21 Jul 1712

---

[63] *Middlesex County, MA: Probate File Papers, 1648-1871.* Probate of Joshua Abbott, 1769, Case number 36.

at Billerica son of Christopher and Mary (Keyes) Osgood; Christopher d. 26 Aug 1748. Sarah m. 2nd, about 1750, JAMES GOODWIN, b. at Reading, 1 Nov 1714 son of John and Tabitha (Pearson) Goodwin; James d. at Worcester, 2 Jun 1776. James was first married to Mary Mansfield who died in 1749.

87) iv MARY ABBOTT, b. 28 Aug 1717; d. about 1800; m. 29 Nov 1743, HENRY JEFTS, b. at Billerica, 24 Apr 1717 son of Henry and Elizabeth (Hayward) Jefts; Henry d. at Billerica 19 Aug 1772.

88) v HANNAH ABBOTT, twin of MARY, b. 28 Aug 1717; d. 11 Jan 1753; m. 6 Feb 1739, PHINEAS OSGOOD, b. at Billerica 20 Jun 1714 son of Christopher and Mary (Keyes) Osgood; Phineas d. 3 Jun 1756.

89) vi ELIZABETH ABBOTT, b. 7 Dec 1719; d. about 1803; m. 7 Dec 1743, ROBERT WALKER whose origin is unknown to me; he is *perhaps* the son of John and Abigail (Wesson) Walker of Chelmsford; Robert d. 26 Jan 1757.

Five children of Joshua Abbott and Dorcas Whiting were born at Billerica.

90) i JOSHUA ABBOTT, b. 28 Oct 1722; 7 Aug 1807; m. 6 Mar 1746, SARAH STEARNS, b, at Billerica, 10 Dec 1726 daughter of Isaac and Alice (-) Stearns; Sarah d. 7 Sep 1803.

ii DORCAS ABBOT, b. 6 Nov 1724; d. 7 Jan 1810; Dorcas did not marry. Dorcas did leave a will which

Children of John Abbott and Sarah Barker

includes bequests to niece Dorcas Bowers, niece Abigail Kidder, niece Elizabeth Abbot, grandniece Abigail E. A. Kidder, nephew Blaney Abbot, and niece Joanna Winship. Blaney Abbot is named executor.[64]

91)   iii   OLIVER ABBOTT, b. 26 Mar 1727; d. 10 Apr 1796; m. 13 Feb 1752, JOANNA FRENCH, b. at Billerica 27 Nov 1729 daughter of William and Joanna (Hill) French; Joanna d. 20 Aug 1768. OLIVER m. 2nd at Westford, 1 Aug 1769, ABIGAIL HALL, b. 19 Jul 1734 daughter of Willard and Abigail (Cotton) Hall; Abigail d. 4 Aug 1804.

92)   iv   DAVID ABBOTT, b. 27 Apr 1729; d. 15 Nov 1801; m. 25 Aug 1752, HANNAH ELLIS, b. about 1727 but origin is unknown; Hannah d. 17 Dec 1767. DAVID m. 2nd 28 Jun 1768 HULDAH PAINE of Malden who d. 8 Sep 1797.

     v   LYDIA ABBOTT, b. 26 Jun 1732; d. 13 Oct 1748.

18)   EBENEZER ABBOT ($John^2$, $George^1$), b. 27 Sep 1689 son of John and Sarah (Barker) Abbott; d. 14 Jan 1761; m. 5 Apr 1720, HANNAH TURNER, widow of Francis Dane; Hannah was b. at Charlestown about 1694 daughter of James and Hannah (Lazell) Turner; Hannah d. 1788.

In his will, Ebenezer Abbot had bequests to the following persons: beloved wife Hannah, son Isaac, son James, daughter Hannah, daughter Mary, daughter Phebe, and grandson Joseph Chandler.[65]

---

[64] *Middlesex County, MA: Probate File Papers, 1648-1871. Probate of* Dorcas Abbot, *1810, Case number* 15.
[65] *Essex County, MA: Probate File Papers, 1638-1881.* Probate of Ebenezer Abbot, 2 Feb 1761, Case number 32.

Generation Three

The original gravestone of Ebenezer Abbot in the Old South Burying Ground bore the inscription HERE LIES BURIED THE BODY ON ENs EBENEZER ABBOT WHO DEPARTED THIS LIFE JAN^{RY} 14 1761 IN Y^E 72 YEAR OF HIS AGE.[66]

Ebenezer Abbot and Hannah Turner had eight children whose births are recorded at Andover.

	i	EBENEZER ABBOTT, b. 1 Jan 1720/1; d. 18 Jul 1721.
65)	ii	HANNAH ABBOTT, b. 29 Dec 1721; d. 2 Jun 1805 at Chester, MA; m. 12 Nov 1741, her first cousin JOSEPH ABBOTT, b. 24 Apr 1719 son of John and Elizabeth (Harnden) Abbott; Joseph d. 30 Jan 1790.
	iii	EBENEZER ABBOTT, b. 23 Nov 1723; d. 28 Apr 1725.
93)	iv	MARY ABBOTT, b. 2 Apr 1725; d. 20 Apr 1760; m. 1st 4 Oct 1742, JOSEPH CHANDLER, b. 20 Nov 1720 son of Thomas and Mary (Stevens) Chandler (confirmed by the will of Thomas Chandler); Joseph d. 31 Mar 1745. MARY m. 2nd 8 Apr 1746, ISAAC BLUNT, b. 5 Nov 1712 son of William and Sarah (Foster) Blunt; Isaac d. 6 Jan 1798.
	v	NEHEMIAH ABBOTT, b. 5 Feb 1726/7; d. 25 Mar 1727.
94)	vi	ISAAC ABBOTT, b. 30 Jan 1728; d. after 1790 at Fryeburg, ME; m. 29 May 1753, SUSANNA FARNUM, whose origins are not firmly known but

---

[66] The Essex Antiquarian, volume 2, number 8, Salem, Mass., August 1898, Andover Inscriptions Old South Burying Ground

most likely the daughter of Ebenezer and Priscilla (Ingalls) Farnum.

95) vii PHEBE ABBOTT, b. 3 Jan 1731/2; d. Feb 1805; m. 30 May 1751, JAMES GRIFFIN whose origins are unknown; James d. 9 Oct 1815.

96) viii JAMES ABBOTT, b. 14 Apr 1736; d. unknown; m. at Dracut, 25 Feb 1758, LYDIA COBURN whose origins are not known definitively, although she is probably the daughter of Joseph and Hannah (Jones) Coburn of Dracut. The family seems to have relocated to New Hampshire.

Section II: The Children of Hannah Abbott and John Chandler

19) JOHN CHANDLER (*Hannah Abbott Chandler², George¹*), b. 14 Mar 1679/80 son of John and Hannah (Abbott) Chandler; d. 3 May 1741; m. 4 Jun 1701, HANNAH FRYE, b. 12 Apr 1683 daughter of Samuel and Mary (Aslett) Frye; Hannah d. 1 Aug 1727.

In his will, John Chandler has bequests to the following persons: well-beloved sons John, Nathan, and Abiel; well-beloved daughters Hannah Ballard, Phebe Lovejoy, and Lydia Chandler; and well-beloved grandsons Zebadiah and Joshua Chandler who are the sons of Joshua deceased. Nathan is named executor of the estate.[67]

John Chandler and Hannah Frye had twelve children all born at Andover.

54) i JOHN CHANDLER, b. May 1702; d. 26 Jul 1775 at Concord, NH; m. 5 Jan 1726/7, his first cousin, once removed TABITHA ABBOTT, b. about 1707 daughter of Nathaniel and Dorcas (Hibbert) Abbott; Tabitha d. probably at Concord, NH, date unknown.

71) ii JOSHUA CHANDLER, b. 1705; d. 24 Mar 1734; m. 18 Feb 1728/8 his first cousin SARAH CHANDLER, b. 1707 daughter of Zebadiah and Sarah (Abbott) Chandler; Sarah d. 28 Mar 1768.

97) iii NATHAN CHANDLER, b. 31 Jan 1708; d. 31 Jul 1784; m. 14 May 1729, PRISCILLA HOLT, b. Apr 1709 daughter of Oliver and Hannah (Russell) Holt; Priscilla d. 25 Nov 1803.

---

[67] *Essex County, MA: Probate File Papers, 1638-1881.* Probate of John Chandler, 1 Jun 1741, Case number 4940.

Children of Hannah Abbott and John Chandler

98) iv HANNAH CHANDLER, b. 1710; d. 29 May 1784; m. 4 Jun 1729, TIMOTHY BALLARD, b. 1702 son of Joseph and Rebecca (Johnson) Ballard; Timothy d. 30 Oct 1773.

v MARY CHANDLER; b. 7 May 1712; d. 28 Dec 1728

99) vi PHEBE CHANDLER, b. 2 Jan 1714/5; d. Jan 1805? at Concord, NH; m. 1 Jan 1735, HENRY LOVEJOY, b. 14 Aug 1714 son of Henry and Sarah (Farnum) Lovejoy; Henry d. 15 Mar 1793 at Concord.[68]

57) vii ABIEL CHANDLER, b. 14 Nov 1717; d. about 1752 at Concord, NH; m. 18 Mar 1741/2, his first cousin, once removed REBECCA ABBOTT, b. 24 Apr 1717 daughter of Nathaniel and Dorcas (Hibbert) Abbott. REBECCA m. 2nd by 1754, her first cousin, once removed AMOS ABBOTT,[69] b. 18 Feb 1725/6 son of James and Abigail (Farnum) Abbott; Rebecca d. 13 Feb 1803 at Concord;[70] Amos d. 3 Dec 1821 at Concord.

viii SAMUEL CHANDLER, b. 14 Nov 1717; d. 9 Dec 1717.

100) ix LYDIA CHANDLER, b. 10 Aug 1720; d. 9 Nov 1803; m. 30 Nov 1741, HEZEKIAH BALLARD, b. Jun 1720 son of Hezekiah and Rebecca (Davis) Ballard; Hezekiah d. 31 Dec 1801.

x SAMUEL CHANDLER, b. 2 Aug 1723; d. 29 Sep 1723.

xi ISAAC CHANDLER, b. 22 Feb 1725; d. 10 Mar 1725.

---

[68] New Hampshire, Death and Burial Records Index, 1654-1949, ancestry.com
[69] Ezra R. Stearns, William F. Witcher, and Edward E. Parker. *Genealogical and Family History of the State of New Hampshire*. (Lewis Publishing Company, 1908).
[70] New Hampshire Death and Disinterment Records, 1754-1947, ancestry.com

xii DORCAS CHANDLER, b. 18 Jul 1727; d. 2 Aug 1727.

15) ZEBADIAH CHANDLER (*Hannah Abbott Chandler², George¹*) and SARAH ABBOTT (*John², George¹*) Please see Family #15 covered above.

20) ABIEL CHANDLER (*Hannah Abbott Chandler², George¹*), b. 9 Jan 1686/7 son of John and Hannah (Abbott) Chandler; d. 1 Sep 1711; m. 22 Mar 1711 HEPHZIBAH HARNDEN, b. at Reading 19 Sep 1688, daughter of Richard and Mary (-) Harnden. Hephzibah m. 2nd Timothy Chandler; Hephzibah d. 17 Mar 1783.

Abiel Chandler and Hephzibah Harnden had one child born at Andover. Hephzibah's second husband, Timothy Chandler, wrote his will December 1770 and in that will he includes a bequest to Abial Chandler his wife's daughter by her first husband.[71]

101) i ABIAL (f) CHANDLER, b. 11 Dec 1711; d. 29 Jun 1780; m. 13 May 1731, DAVID CHANDLER, b. 11 Jan 1697/8 son of Thomas and Mary (Peters) Chandler; David d. before 1774 probably at Pembroke, NH.[72]

21) HANNAH CHANDLER (*Hannah Abbott Chandler², George¹*), b. 12 May 1690 daughter of John and Hannah (Abbott) Chandler; d. at Woodstock, CT 3 Mar 1755; m. 1st DANIEL ABBOTT (*George²,*

---

[71] *Essex County, MA: Probate File Papers, 1638-1881. Probate of* Timothy Chandler, 2 Dec 1771, *Case number* 4978.
[72] Chandler, *The Descendants of William and Annis Chandler*. The Chandler Genealogy notes that the widow Abial Chandler was received at the church in Andover September 1774 from the church in Pembroke. The family had been dismissed from the church at Andover to Pembroke 21 May 1738.

George¹), b. 10 Jan 1687/8 son of George and Dorcas (Graves) Abbott; Hannah and Daniel were first cousins; Daniel d. about Jul 1731 at Woodstock. Hannah m. 2nd John Bartholomew.

Hannah Chandler and Daniel Abbott were married in Andover and the births of their first eight children were recorded there. The family then relocated to Woodstock, Connecticut which was an area to which several members of this kinship network migrated in the early to mid-18th century.

Daniel Abbott wrote his will 3 November 1729 and it was presented at court for probate 19 July 1731. "I Daniel Abbott of Woodstock in the County of Suffolk in his majesty's Province of the Massachusetts Bay in New England. . . give and bequeath to Hannah my dearly beloved wife all my household goods whatsoever."[73] Other bequests are to son Daniel Abbott, £30 when he reaches the age of 21 and a gun; son Joseph Abbott, £15 when he reaches the age of 21 and a gun; to his daughters Hannah, Dorcas, Elizabeth, Phebe, and Sarah who will divide the household goods after their mother's death or remarriage; and all the rest to be divided among his nine children: Daniel, Joseph, Nathan, John, Hannah, Dorcas, Elizabeth, Phebe, and Sarah. (The youngest son of Daniel and Hannah, George, was born 21 January 1730 after the will was written.)

The births of the first eight children are recorded at Andover and the youngest two children at Woodstock.[74]

        i   HANNAH ABBOTT, b. 12 Sep 1712; d. 3 Mar 1734.

102)   ii   DORCAS ABBOTT, b. 16 Dec 1713; d. 22 Aug 1798 at Woodstock; m. 11 17 1740, THOMAS CHAFFEE, b. at Swansea 18 Oct 1716 son of Joseph and Jemima

---

[73] *Probate Records (Worcester County, Massachusetts); Index 1731-1881*, Case number 17, accessed through ancestry.com

[74] Barbour and Newton, *Vital Records of Woodstock 1686-1854.*

(Chadwick) Chaffee; Thomas d. at Woodstock 3 May 1753.

iii DANIEL ABBOTT, b. 18 Feb 1715; d. Feb 1741; Daniel did not marry. His will includes a bequest to his honored mother Hannah Bartholomew.

103) iv JOSEPH ABBOTT, b. 19 Sep 1716; m. at Woodstock, 22 Apr 1738, ABIGAIL CUTLER, b. 28 Aug 1711 at Colchester, CT, daughter of Jonathan and Abigail (Bigelow) Cutler; published genealogies (Bigelow and Abbot genealogies) give the dates of death for both Joseph and Abigail as 22 Sep 1776, but I have located no records for the deaths of either of them.

104) v ELIZABETH ABBOTT, b. 9 Jul 1719; d. at Woodstock, 1 Jan 1785; m. at Woodstock, 27 May 1737, MATTHEW MURRAY, perhaps of Scotland; d. at Pomfret about 1788 when his estate was probated.

105) vi PHEBE ABBOTT, b. 7 Apr 1721; d. at Woodstock after 10 Jul 1756 (the birth of her last child);[75] m. at Woodstock 20 Aug 1742, EBENEZER HOLMES, b. at Woodstock 27 Feb 1720/1 son of Ebenezer and Joanna (Ainsworth) Holmes. Ebenezer m. 2nd Martha Howlet, 12 Apr 1759; Ebenezer d. at Woodstock, 28 Jun 1794.[76]

106) vii NATHAN ABBOTT, b. 16 Oct 1723; d. likely at Brimfield after 1790 (listed as head of household in

---

[75] Published sources give her death as 30 May 1756, but the birth date of her youngest child in the Woodstock records in 10 Jul 1756.
[76] Barbour and Newton, *Vital Records of Woodstock 1686-1854*.

1790 Census); m. at Woodstock 2 Jun 1746, ANNA LEACH.

107) viii JOHN ABBOTT, b. 11 Jan 1726; d. at Woodstock 7 Mar 1806; m. at Ashford, 28 Nov 1750, MARY WRIGHT, b. at Ashford, 29 Sep 1730 daughter of John and Judith (Wyman) Wright; Mary d. 30 May 1811.

108) ix SARAH ABBOTT, b. 5 May 1728; d. 7 Oct 1802; m. 1st, 1758, JABEZ CORBIN, b. at Woodstock, 21 Mar 1724 son of Jabez and Hannah (Peake) Corbin; Jabez d. 1774 (probate 7 Jun 1774). Sarah m. 2nd 31 May 1780, as his second wife, William Chapman; William d. 1792.

109) x GEORGE ABBOTT, b. 21 Jan 1730; d. before 18 Dec 1772; m. 16 Jan 1754, MARY WHITNEY, b. at Uxbridge, 27 Oct 1732 daughter of Joshua and Hannah (Rockett) Whitney.

22) SARAH CHANDLER (*Hannah Abbott Chandler², George¹*), b. 8 Oct 1693 daughter of John and Hannah (Abbott) Chandler; d. at Woodstock, CT 15 Mar 1737;[77] m. 12 Jan 1712/3 as his 1st wife, JOSEPH WRIGHT, b. 29 Oct 1693 son of Walter and Elizabeth (Peters) Wright. Joseph m. 2nd Elizabeth Chamberlain and m. 3rd Hannah Ashley.[78] Joseph d.? (A Joseph Wright of Norwich with a wife Hannah has a will probated in 1753; the will requests the division of his estate equally "among all my children" but they are not named).

The family of Sarah Chandler and Joseph Wright was beset by tragedy when Sarah, 11-year old son Abiel, and a servant John Page died in a house fire. "Mrs. Sarah Wright the wife of Leut.

---

[77] Barbour and Newton, *Vital Records of Woodstock 1686-1854*.
[78] Barbour and Newton, *Vital Records of Woodstock 1686-1854*.

Joseph Wright Aged about 44 years and Abial Wright Son of the Said Joseph wright by Sarah his wife having Jest Completed the Eleventh year of his age and John Page, a Servent to Said Wright aged about 30 years ware all burnt to Death the following night after the fifteenth Day of March 1736/7 in the Dissolation of his house by fire."[79]

Sarah Chandler and Joseph Wright had twelve children. The births of the oldest five children are recorded at Andover, the remainder at Woodstock.

110) i JOSEPH WRIGHT, b. Mar 1712/3; d. at Winchester, NH, 27 May 1785; m. 1st at Woodstock, ABIGAIL CHAFFEE, b. at Swansea, 5 Mar 1715 daughter of Joseph and Jemima (Chadwick) Chaffee;[80] it is not known when Abigail died. Joseph had a second wife named Mary about whom nothing else is known.

111) ii SARAH WRIGHT, b. 7 Aug 1715; d. not known; m. 17 Jan 1733/4, EDMUND CHAMBERLAIN, b. 6 Mar 1701/2 son of Edmund and Elizabeth (Bartholomew) Chamberlain; Edmund d. 9 Dec 1779; it is possible that Sarah remarried but that is not verified.

112) iii HANNAH WRIGHT, b. 20 Jun 1717; no death record found (the Peters genealogy reports her death as 1796); m. 6 Jan 1734/5, BEAMSLEY PETERS, b. at Andover 1710 son of Samuel and Phebe (Frye) Peters.

---

[79] Barbour and Newton, *Vital Records of Woodstock, 1686-1854*.
[80] William Henry Chaffee, *The Chaffee Genealogy*. (Grafton Press, 1909), 78.

113) iv   ELIZABETH WRIGHT, b. 13 Feb 1718/9; death unknown; m. 23 Nov 1738, JOHN CARPENTER, b. at Woodstock, 17 Jul 1713 son of Eliphalet and Rebecca (Gardner) Carpenter.

114) v   HEPHZIBAH WRIGHT, b. 14 Oct 1720; d, at Woodstock, 1797; m. 16 Dec 1736, ENOS BARTHOLOMEW, b. about 1714 possibly the son of John and Mary (Harrington) Bartholomew. John Bartholomew and his family relocated from Branford to Woodstock 7 Feb 1732/3.[81]

vi   MARY WRIGHT, b. 3 Aug 1722; no further record found.

vii   JOHN WRIGHT, b. 20 Apr 1724; d. 13 Jan 1733/4.

viii ABIEL WRIGHT, 11 Mar 1725/6; d. 15 Mar 1737.

115) ix   ABIGAIL WRIGHT, b. 15 Feb 1727/8; m. 22 Mar 1748/9, ABIJAH CORBIN, b. 8 Feb 1722 son of Jabez and Hannah (Peake) Corbin; d. at Woodstock, 16 Oct 1808.

116) x   DOROTHY WRIGHT, b. 3 Apr 1730; death not known; m. 3 Aug 1747, PENUEL BACON, b. at Woodstock, 8 Jan 1725/6 son of Joseph and Rebeckah (Carpenter) Bacon.

xi   DORCAS WRIGHT, b. 12 Mar 1731/2; death not known; m. 26 Apr 1750, THOMAS JEWELL.; Thomas d. 1753 at Mansfield, estate inventoried 28 Nov 1753; widow Dorcas is administrator; no births for this couple were located. It is possible that she is the Dorcas Jewell who married Ezekiel Corbin in Woodstock, 27 Dec 1758. On that same date (27 Dec

---

[81] Connecticut Church Record Abstracts 1630-1920, volume 010, Brandford

1758), Ezekiel's brother Jabez married Dorcas's first cousin Sarah Abbott. In any event, no further records were located for Dorcas either as Dorcas Jewell or Dorcas Corbin. No birth records for children were located.

xii JOHN WRIGHT, b. 29 Jun 1734; d. 22 Oct 1734.

Section III: The Children of George Abbott and Dorcas Graves

23) HANNAH ABBOTT (*George²*, *George¹*), b. 27 Feb 1684 daughter of George and Dorcas (Graves) Abbott; d. 25 Dec 1774; m. 16 Sep 1708 JOHN OSGOOD, b. 28 Jun 1683 son of John and Hannah (Eires) Osgood; John d. at Andover, 22 Nov 1765.

In the probate record for John Osgood (he did not leave a will), widow Hannah (Annah) requests that her son John be the administrator. In the division of the estate in April 1768, the first division is assigned to John Osgood, the second to John Osgood as eldest son, third division to Mary Allen, the fourth to the heirs of Elizabeth Frye who is deceased, the fifth to Joseph Osgood, and the sixth to the heirs of Hannah Chickering deceased. Co-signers are William Allen and Dudley Woodbridge.[82]

In another document, widow Hannah Osgood signs over her parts of the inheritance in the following manner: 2/7 to John Osgood, 1/7 to Joseph, 1/7 to the children of daughter Hannah Chickering who is deceased (was married to Samuel Chickering); nine children of daughter Hannah are named Samuel, John, Zachariah, Hannah, Sarah, Susanna, Dorcas, Mary, and Phebe, and each is given 1/10 of the seventh; the final 1/10 of the seventh goes to the children of her granddaughter Elizabeth [this is the 10th child of daughter Hannah] (wife of Moses Sargent) who are Elizabeth, Susanna, Christopher, Hannah, and Moses; to the children of her daughter Elizabeth (wife of James Frye) who is deceased namely James, Jonathan, Elizabeth, Sarah, Hannah, Dorcas, and Molly (each gets 1/8 of the seventh); and 1/8 of the seventh to the children of her granddaughter Joanna (wife of Thomas Farrington) who is deceased namely Elizabeth, Thomas, Mareh, Frederick, and Daniel; daughter Mary the wife of William Allen gets 1/7; granddaughter Dorcas the wife of Dudley Woodbridge 1/7.

---

[82] *Essex County, MA: Probate File Papers, 1638-1881.* Probate of John Osgood, 7 Apr 1766, Case number 20218.

Generation Three 55

Hannah Abbott and John Chandler had seven children born at Andover.

117) i HANNAH OSGOOD, b. 22 Aug 1710; d. 16 Mar 1761; m. 24 Jun 1728, SAMUEL CHICKERING, b. at Charlestown, 10 Jul 1704 son of John and Susanna (Symmes) Chickering. Samuel m. 2nd the widow Mehitable Stevens; Samuel died about 1787 the year his estate was probated.

118) ii JOHN OSGOOD, b. 22 Aug 1711; d. 10 Jul 1775; m. 1st 20 Feb 1746, MARTHA CARLETON, b. 12 Jun 1722 daughter of Christopher and Martha (Barker) Carleton; Martha d. about 1755. JOHN m. 2nd 1760, HULDAH FRYE, b. 13 May 1737 daughter of Isaac and Naamah (Haskell) Frye. Huldah Osgood was listed in the 1800 Census as a head of household in Andover, but no record of her after that time.

iii CHILD OSGOOD, unnamed; 17 Jul 1712.

119) iv ELIZABETH OSGOOD, b. 15 Aug 1714; d. 8 Dec 1756; m. 28 Nov 1734, JAMES FRYE, b. at Bradford 24 Jun 1710 son of James and Joanna (Sprague) Frye. James married 2nd Sarah Robey; James d. 8 Jan 1776.

120) v JOSEPH OSGOOD, b. 5 Sep 1718; d. 11 Jan 1797; m. at Boston 1 Dec 1743, MARGARET BINNEY, b. at Hull 12 Apr 1719 daughter of Thomas and Margaret (Miller) Binney; Margaret d. 16 Feb 1797.

121) vi DORCAS OSGOOD, b. Sep 1721; d. at Boston about 1749 (Thomas remarried in 1750); m. at Boston 5 Jan 1743/4, THOMAS MARCH whose origins are

unknown to me; Thomas d. at Boston about 1752 (when his will was probated). Thomas married 2nd Mary Hill on 7 Aug 1750.

122) vii MARY OSGOOD, b. 10 Jun 1726; d. 1806 at New Gloucester, ME; m. 11 Apr 1745, WILLIAM ALLEN, b. at Gloucester Jun 1717 son of Joseph and Mary (Coit) Allen; a death record for William was not located.

21) DANIEL ABBOTT (*George², George¹*) and HANNAH CHANDLER (*Hannah Abbott Chandler², George¹*) (Please see Family #21 above.)

24) ELIZABETH ABBOTT (*George², George¹*), b. 25 Jul 1690 daughter of George and Dorcas (Graves) Abbott; d. 3 Sep 1718; m. 24 Dec 1716, BENJAMIN ABBOTT (*Benjamin², George¹*), b. 11 Jul 1686 son of Benjamin and Sarah (Farnum) Abbott; Elizabeth and Benjamin were first cousins. Benjamin m. 2nd Mary Carleton and 3rd Abigail Abbott (his second cousin and great granddaughter of the immigrant George Abbott of Rowley); Benjamin died before 5 Dec 1748 the date of probate of his estate.

Elizabeth and Benjamin Abbott had one child born at Andover. Benjamin's families with his two other wives are covered in Family #39.

123) i SARAH ABBOTT, b. 2 Aug 1718; d. 5 Mar 1778; m. 10 Apr 1746, her second cousin and George Abbott descendant JAMES HOLT, b. 13 Jan 1722/3 son of Nicholas and Dorcas (Abbott) Holt. James m. 2nd Phebe Ballard who was the widow of Abiel Abbott son of Benjamin and Abigail (Abbott) Abbott; James Holt d. 22 Aug 1812.

25) GEORGE ABBOTT (*George²*, *George¹*), b. 22 Dec 1692 son of George and Dorcas (Graves) Abbott; d. 19 Mar 1768; m. 29 Nov 1721, MARY PHILLIPS, b. at Salem 5 Aug 1694, daughter of Samuel and Mary (Emerson) Phillips; Mary d. 4 Oct 1785.

In his will George Abbott made bequests to the following persons: beloved wife Mary, eldest and beloved son George Abbott, beloved son Samuel Abbott, beloved daughter Mary Abbott (who married an Abbott), beloved daughter Elizabeth Abbott (who married an Abbott), beloved daughter Sarah Holt, and beloved daughter Hannah Foster. Son George is named executor.[83]

George Abbott and Mary Phillips had seven children all born at Andover.

69)   i   MARY ABBOTT, b. 12 Mar 1722/3; d. 8 Aug 1792; m. 24 May 1743, her second cousin STEPHEN ABBOTT, b. 2 Mar 1717/8 son of Stephen and Sarah (Stevens) Abbott; Stephen d. 8 Nov 1768. Mary m. 2nd JONATHAN ABBOTT, also a second cousin, who was the widower of Martha Lovejoy.

124) ii   GEORGE ABBOTT, b. 14 Dec 1724; d. 26 Dec 1775; m. 1 Jan 1746/7, HANNAH LOVEJOY, b. 27 Dec 1724 daughter of John and Hannah (Foster) Lovejoy; Hannah d. 8 Sep 1813.

      iii ELIZABETH ABBOTT, b. 10 Sep 1726; d. 7 Jan 1727.

125) iv   ELIZABETH ABBOTT, b. 5 Nov 1727; d. at Westford, about 1802 (date of will 10 Aug 1802); m. 2 Apr 1747, her second cousin BENJAMIN ABBOTT, b. 21 Oct 1723 son of Benjamin and Mary (Carleton) Abbott;

---

[83] *Essex County, MA: Probate File Papers, 1638-1881.* Probate of George Abbott, 5 Apr 1768, Case number 47.

Children of George Abbott and Dorcas Graves

Benjamin d. at Hollis, 1771.[84] Elizabeth m. 2nd, James Pollard and 3rd, Josiah Bowers.

126) v SARAH ABBOTT, b. 14 Jan 1729/30; d. 29 Dec 1797; m. 4 Aug 1757, her second cousin and George Abbott descendant NATHAN HOLT, b. 28 Feb 1725 son of Nicholas and Dorcas (Abbott) Holt; Nathan d. at Danvers, 2 Aug 1792.

vi SAMUEL ABBOTT, b. 25 Feb 1731/2; d. 12 Apr 1812; m. 21 Feb 1760, SARAH MULBERRY, b. 31 Dec 1727 daughter of Benjamin and Ann (Everton) Mulberry; Sarah was the widow of John Kneeland; Sarah d. about 1815. Samuel and Sarah did not have any children. He was a merchant in Boston but maintained a residence in Andover. Samuel reared Sarah's three children from her first marriage. One of Sarah's sons from her first marriage, John Kneeland, named one of his children Samuel Abbott Kneeland after his step-father. In his will, Samuel makes generous allowance for his wife, but provides a bequest to the trustees of Phillips Academy in Andover. He also created a trust for Samuel Abbott Kneeland.

127) vii HANNAH ABBOTT, b. 14 Dec 1733; d. 26 Mar 1820; m. 9 Jan 1755, WILLIAM FOSTER, b. 4 Mar 1729/30 son of John and Mary (Osgood) Foster; William d. 1 Sep 1803.

26) HENRY ABBOT (*George²*, *George¹*), b. 12 Jun 1696 son of George and Dorcas (Graves) Abbott; d. Feb 1776; m. 27 Oct 1721,

---

[84] There is a 1771 probate record at Middlesex County, MA for Benjamin Abbot of Hollis with widow Elizabeth Abbot of Hollis.

Generation Three

MARY PLATTS, b. at Rowley 5 Sep 1700, daughter of James and Lydia (Hale) Platts; Mary d. Aug 1784.

The will of Henry Abbot includes bequests to the following persons: dear and well-beloved wife Mary, beloved son Henry, eldest and beloved daughter Lydia, beloved daughter Dorcas, and beloved daughter Mary.[85]

Henry Abbot and Mary Platts had five children born at Andover.

128) i   LYDEA ABBOTT, b. 10 Feb 1722/3; d. 11 Sep 1807; m. 24 Mar 1742/3, JOSHUA LOVEJOY, b. 2 Dec 1719 son of Henry and Sarah (Farnum) Lovejoy; Joshua d. 2 Feb 1812.

129) ii   HENRY ABBOTT, b. 31 Jan 1724; d. 21 Feb 1805; m. 1st 2 Oct 1750, ELIZABETH SIBSON (I think the daughter of Joseph); Elizabeth d. about 1764. Henry m. 2nd his first cousin PHEBE ABBOTT, b. 14 Nov 1746 daughter of Isaac and Phebe (Lovejoy) Abbott; Phebe d. 29 Jun 1833.

iii   MARY ABBOTT, b. 28 Mar 1727; d. 27 Jan 1734.

130) iv   DORCAS ABBOTT, b. 11 May 1729; d. at Nottingham, NH 10 Apr 1789; m. 17 Apr 1754, BENJAMIN BUTLER, b. at Edgartown, 9 Apr 1729 son of Malachi and Jemima (Dagget) Butler; Benjamin d. at Nottingham 26 Oct 1804.

131) v   MARY ABBOTT, b. 13 Aug 1737; d. 26 Nov 1813; m. 22 Mar 1759, THOMAS HOVEY, b. at Ipswich 1 Oct

---

[85] *Essex County, MA: Probate File Papers, 1638-1881.* Probate of Henry Abbot, 4 Mar 1776, Case number 56.

1736 son of Thomas and Sarah (Rust) Hovey; Thomas d. 29 Jul 1826.

27) ISAAC ABBOT (*George²*, *George¹*), b. 4 Apr 1699 son of George and Dorcas (Graves) Abbott; d. 9 Aug 1784; m. 1st 29 Nov 1739, PHEBE LOVEJOY, b. 20 Jan 1715, daughter of William and Sarah (Frye) Lovejoy; Phebe d. 17 Dec 1751. Isaac m. 2nd Lydia Stimson.

Isaac Abbot attended Harvard graduating in 1723. He was deacon of South Church of Andover for 44 years.[86]

In his will, Isaac Abbott made bequests to the following persons: Lydia my dearly beloved wife, beloved son Isaac, beloved daughter Phebe wife of Capt. Henry Abbot, and beloved daughter Sarah wife of Timothy Abbott. Isaac is the executor of the estate.[87]

Isaac Abbot and Phebe Lovejoy had six children all born at Andover.

	i	SON ABBOTT, b. 21 Jul 1741; d. 21 Jul 1741.
	ii	WILLIAM ABBOTT, b. 21 Jul 1741; d. 29 Dec 1768.
132)	iii	ISAAC ABBOTT, b. 3 Feb 1745; d. 21 May 1836; m. 22 Apr 1766, his second cousin, once removed and George Abbott descendant PHEBE CHANDLER, b. 2 Jun 1742 daughter of Nathan and Priscilla (Holt) Chandler; Phebe d. 1 Jul 1800.
129)	iv	PHEBE ABBOTT, b. 14 Nov 1746; d. 29 Jun 1833; m. 21 Mar 1765 her first cousin, HENRY ABBOTT, b. 31 Dec 1724 son of Henry and Mary (Platts) Abbott; Henry d. 21 Feb 1805.

---

[86] Chandler, *The Descendants of William and Annis Chandler*, p. 7
[87] *Essex County, MA: Probate File Papers, 1638-1881.* Probate of Isaac Abbot, 5 Oct 1784, Case number 58.

	v	SON ABBOTT; b. 12 Nov 1747; d. 14 Nov 1747.
133)	vi	SARAH ABBOTT, b. 2 Jan 1749/50; d. 2 Apr 1835; m. 2 Jan 1770, her second cousin once removed, TIMOTHY ABBOTT, b. 2 Jun 1745 son of Asa and Elizabeth (Abbott) Abbott; Timothy d. 22 Mar 1826.

Section IV: The Children of William Abbott and Elizabeth Geary

28) ELIZABETH ABBOTT (*William²*, *George¹*), b. 29 Apr 1683 daughter of William and Elizabeth (Geary) Abbott; d. 18 Jul 1762 at Pomfret, CT;[88] m. 13 Mar 1710/1 JOSEPH PHELPS, b. 8 Feb 1688/9 son of Samuel and Sarah (Chandler) Phelps; Joseph d. about 1773 at Pomfret when his will was probated.

Elizabeth and Joseph married and had their children in Andover. They then relocated to Pomfret, Connecticut. In the first two decades of the 18th century, more than 20 Andover men and their families had relocated to Windham County in Connecticut. This included seven Abbott family units.[89]

Joseph Phelps wrote his will 29 July 1762. He added a codicil to the will 19 March 1770. The will was probated 5 March 1773. In his will, Joseph made bequests to the following persons: beloved daughter Elizabeth Barrett; grandson Joseph Lawrence son of daughter Hannah who is deceased; youngest and well-beloved daughter Sarah Phelps; and grandson Joseph Barrett. Grandson Joseph Barrett was named executor. The codicil seems to relate to a conflict with his grandson Joseph Lawrence. Joseph Phelps had bequeathed several household items to his grandson in the 1762 will. But as he lived longer than he thought he might, Joseph had gone ahead and delivered these items to his grandson. But Joseph Lawrence refused to sign a statement that he had received his inheritance, so Joseph Phelps added the codicil to make it clear that his grandson had already received his whole inheritance.[90]

---

[88] Connecticut Town Death Records, pre-1870 (Barbour Collection). The vital records for Connecticut are from the Barbour Collections unless otherwise noted.
[89] Greven, *Four Generations*
[90] *Connecticut Wills and Probate, 1609-1999*, Probate of Joseph Phelps, Hartford, 1773, Case number 3237.

Generation Three

Elizabeth Abbott and Joseph Phelps had three children born at Andover.

134) i ELIZABETH PHELPS, b. 29 Oct 1712; d. at Brooklyn, CT 19 Jul 1787; m. at Pomfret 14 May 1741, BENONI BARRETT, b. 17 Aug 1718 son of Moses and Sarah (-) Barrett; Benoni d. 20 Jun 1755 at Brooklyn, CT.

135) ii HANNAH PHELPS, b. 20 May 1715; d. at Pomfret 13 Jan 1746/7; m. at Pomfret 15 Nov 1744, SAMUEL LAWRENCE; no definite information about Samuel has been obtained. He may have been a member of a Lawrence family in Killingly, CT.

iii SARAH PHELPS, b. Jun 1717; she was living at the time of her father's will in 1762 and there is no adjustment in the 1770 codicil so likely still living then; she was unmarried at the time of her father's will.

29) JAMES ABBOTT (*William², George¹*), b. 12 Feb 1694/5 son of William and Elizabeth (Geary) Abbott; d. 27 at Concord, NH possibly in 1778;[91] m. 6 Jan 1713/4, ABIGAIL FARNUM, b. 3 May 1692, daughter of Ralph and Sarah (Sterling) Farnum; Abigail's date of death is not known.

James was a farmer. He and Abigail married and had all their fifteen children in Andover. The family then relocated to New

---

[91] The death date for James Abbott is not certain. Published genealogies, including the Abbott genealogy by Abiel Abbot and Ephraim Abbot, list a date of 27 Dec 1787, but I cannot locate a record that supports this. There is a transcription of a death record for a James Abbott in Concord, NH for 1778 that lists the age at death as 83 which would be the right age for this James Abbott.

Hampshire about 1735. He lived for a time in one of the garrison houses of early Concord.[92]

136)   i   ABIGAIL ABBOTT, b. 1 Jan 1714/5; d. at Charlestown about 1737; m. 13 May 1734, JOHN KIDDER, b. at Charlestown 13 Feb 1709 son of Stephen and Mary (Johnson) Kidder. John married second Anna Walker and third Mary Snow.

137)   ii   JAMES ABBOTT, b. 12 Jan 1716/7; d. at Newbury, VT, 27 Dec 1803; m. about 1742, SARAH BANCROFT, b. 19 Feb 1722 daughter of Samuel and Sarah (Lampson) Bancroft; Sarah d. 1765.[93]

     iii   ELIZABETH ABBOTT, b. 24 Jun 1718.

     iv   WILLIAM ABBOTT, b. 8 Sep 1719; d. 29 Oct 1741.

     v   RACHEL ABBOTT, b. 17 Nov 1720; (little other information yet). The Abbot genealogy states she had husbands named Manning and Russell and a daughter named Phebe. She was also reported to have gone to Londonderry, but no information has been found for her.

     vi   EZRA ABBOTT, b. 11 Mar 1721/2; d. 5 Dec 1741.

138)   vii   REUBEN ABBOTT, b. 4 Apr 1723; d. at Concord, NH, 13 May 1822; m. 1st RHODA WHITTEMORE, b. at Malden, 18 Aug 1729 daughter of Elias and Rhoda (Holt) Whittemore; d. 29 Jan 1785. Reuben m. 2nd widow Diana Blanchard; Diana d. 11 Mar 1826.

     viii   SIMEON ABBOTT, b. 18 Sep 1724; d. 15 Nov 1741.

---

[92] Bouton, *History of Concord*, p 627
[93] A gravestone engraved with the names James Abbott and Sarah Bancroft is in Oxbow Cemetery in Newbury, VT.

Generation Three

57) ix AMOS ABBOTT, b. 18 Feb 1725/6; d. at Concord 3 Dec 1821; m. by 1754, as her 2nd husband, REBECCA ABBOTT (widow of ABIEL CHANDLER), b. 24 Apr 1717 daughter of Nathaniel and Dorcas (Hibbert) Abbott; Rebecca d. 13 Feb 1803. These families are considered together in Family #57.

139) x PHEBE ABBOTT, b. 22 Nov 1727; d. at Conway NH, 29 Sep 1754; m. 5 Nov 1747, as his 1st wife, THOMAS MERRILL, b. 5 Feb 1723/4 at Haverhill son of John and Lydia (Haynes) Merrill. Thomas had a total of four marriages, his 2nd to Mehitable Harriman, 3rd to Abigail Goodhue, and 4th to Elizabeth Abbott daughter of Benjamin and Abigail (Abbott) Abbott. Thomas Merrill d. at Conway 21 Jun 1788.

xi SON ABBOTT, b. and d. 1729.

140) xii REBECCA ABBOTT, b. 13 Aug 1730; d. at NH date unknown; m. 1750, ENOCH EASTMAN, b. at Salisbury, 1 Jun 1725 son of Joseph and Abigail (Merrill) Eastman.

141) xiii SARAH ABBOTT, twin of Rebecca, b. 13 Aug 1730; m. about 1751, as her 1st husband, her second cousin, JOB ABBOTT, b. 3 Oct 724 son of Jonathan and Zerviah (Holt) Abbott. Sarah m. 2nd about 1765, RICHARD EASTMAN, b. at Haverhill, 9 Aug 1712 son of Jonathan and Hannah (Green) Eastman; Richard d. at Lovell, ME, 29 Dec 1807.

142) xiv MARY ABBOTT, b. 12 Oct 1732; d, about 1780; m. by 1760 ADONIJAH TYLER, b. 26 Nov 1738[94] son of Moses and Miriam (Bailey) Tyler; Adonijah d. 12 Oct 1812 at Hopkinton, NH.

xv HANNAH ABBOTT, b. 12 Jan 1734/5; d. 10 Sep 1736.

30) PAUL ABBOTT (*William²*, *George¹*), b. 28 Mar 1697 son of William and Elizabeth (Geary) Abbott; d. at Hampton, CT 8 May 1752; m. 8 Feb 1719/20, ELIZABETH GRAY, b. 28 Mar 1700 daughter of Henry and Mary (Blunt) Gray; Elizabeth d. at Pomfret, CT 9 Jul 1765.[95]

In his will dated 20 February 1752, Paul Abbott has bequests to the following persons: beloved wife Elizabeth who receives the whole of the house in which they live plus many provisions for grain, beef, etc. to be provided by the executor; dearly beloved sons William, Nathan, Benjamin, Isaac, Asa, and Darius; and dearly beloved daughters Mary Holt, Sarah Ingalls, Elizabeth Abbott, and Hannah Abbott.[96]

Paul and Elizabeth had twelve children. The birth of the oldest child was recorded at Andover and those of the other eleven were recorded at Pomfret, Connecticut.

143) i NATHAN ABBOTT, b. 10 Apr 1721; d. unknown but he might have gone to Pennsylvania; m. 1st at Pomfret, 24 Nov 1742, EUNICE MARSH, b. at Plainfield, CT 17 Feb 1724 daughter of Thomas and Eunice (Parkhouse) Marsh; Eunice d. at Ashford 27 Oct 1760. Nathan m. 2nd HEPHZIBAH BROWN, b.

---

[94] New Hampshire: Births, Deaths and Marriages, 1654-1969 (accessed through americanancestors.org)
[95] Connecticut Town Death Records, pre-1870 (Barbour Collection).
[96] Probate Records, 1747-1918; Author: Connecticut. Probate Court (Plainfield District); Probate Place: Windham, Connecticut

about 1727; Hepzibah d. 26 May 1790 at Hampton, CT.

144) ii WILLIAM ABBOTT, b. 18 Feb 1723; d. at Pomfret 1 Nov 1805; m. 1st 9 May 1745, JERUSHA STOWELL, b. 22 Sep 1721 at Newton, MA daughter of David and Mary (Dillaway) Stowell; Jerusha d. 29 Feb 1768. William m. 2nd 4 Jun 1778, HANNAH EDMUND; Hannah d. 5 Feb 1808; nothing else is known of her at this time.

145) iii BENJAMIN ABBOTT, b. 25 Jul 1724; d. at Brookfield, VT, 21 Jun 1807;[97] m. 1st at Ashford, 16 Jan 1745/6, MARY ANN ANDREWS, b. at Windham 25 Jul 1727 daughter of John and Hannah (-) Andrews; Mary Ann d. 8 Dec 1788. Benjamin m. 2nd 30 Jun 1793 the widow HANNAH BROWN about whom nothing else is known.

iv ELIZABETH ABBOTT, b. 5 Feb 1726; d. 10 Sep 1736.

146) v MARY ABBOTT, b. 3 Mar 1728/9; d. at Windham 10 Aug 1769; m. 28 Jun 1749, JOSHUA HOLT, b. 19 Mar 1728/9 son of Joshua and Keturah (Holt) Holt. Joshua m. 2nd Susanna Goodell; Joshua d. 5 Jul 1791.

147) vi SARAH ABBOTT, b. 15 Oct 1730; d. 17 Dec 1811; m. 24 May 1749, JOSEPH INGALLS, b. at Andover, 9 Aug 1723 son of Joseph and Phebe (Farnum) Ingalls; Joseph d. 26 Oct 1790.

---

[97] His grave site is in the Brookfield, VT cemetery. (findagrave.com)

148) vii   ISAAC ABBOTT, b. 29 Aug 1732; d. at Milford, NH about 1800;[98] m. 29 Apr 1756, MARY BARKER about whom nothing else concrete is known.[99]

149) viii   DARIUS ABBOTT, b. 16 Oct 1734; d. about 1817 at Hillsborough, NH;[100] m. at Andover 1 Nov 1757, MARY HOLT, b. 30 Apr 1739 daughter of Henry and Rebecca (Gray) Holt; Mary d. about 1787.

150) ix   ELIZABETH ABBOTT, b. 20 Jul 1737; d. possibly 1828;[101] m. 28 Sep 1761 as his 2nd wife, JOSEPH PHELPS, b. 27 Feb 1723/4 son of Samuel and Hannah (Dane) Phelps; Joseph d. at Andover 27 Jan 1802.

x   HARRIET ABBOTT, b. 18 Sep 1740; d. 18 Sep 1740.

xi   HANNAH ABBOTT, b. 24 Jun 1741; d. 18 Nov 1763.

xii   ASA ABBOTT, b. 7 Jan 1743; d. 5 Sep 1754.

31)   PHILIP ABBOTT (*William², George¹*), b. 3 Apr 1699 son of William and Elizabeth (Geary) Abbott; d. 4 Nov 1748 at Hampton;[102] m. 8 Oct 1723 at Windham ABIGAIL BIGFORD whose origins are not known; Abigail's date of death is not known although it is after 1748 as she was living at the time of the codicil to Philip's will that was written 1 Nov 1748.[103]

---

[98] 1800 is the year of death used by the Daughters of the American Revolution.
[99] Abbot and Abbot, *Genealogical Record of Descendants* gives her name as Sarah Barker, but the marriage record and all the birth records for the children give her name as Mary.
[100] Abbot and Abbot, *Genealogical Record of Descendants*
[101] Abbot and Abbot, *Genealogical Record of Descendants* gives a death date of June 1828, but I have not located a record.
[102] Connecticut, Hale Collection of Cemetery Inscriptions and Newspaper Notices, 1629-1934
[103] Connecticut, Wills and Probate Records, 1609-1999 (accessed through ancestry.com)

Generation Three

Philip Abbott was a farmer. He relocated to Windham with his family as a young man in 1722. He acquired property in Windham, Pomfret, and Willington.

Philip Abbott wrote his will 1 November 1748. One-third of the estate in both Windham and Pomfret is set off for the support of well-beloved wife Abigail. Son Abiel receives all the estate in Pomfret and Windham. Son Stephen receives all the land in Willington when he reaches age 21. Daughter Hannah Abbott is to receive the equivalent of 183 ounces of silver to be paid when she reaches age 21 or at marriage. Son Joseph Abbott is to receive 316 ounces of silver and there is also a second payment of 100 ounces after his mother's decease. Daughter Mary Abbott receives the same bequest as Hannah. Son John receives the same bequest as Joseph.

Phillip Abbott and Abigail Bigford had eight children all born at Windham.

	i	JOHN ABBOTT, b. 12 Jul 1724; d. 18 Jul 1740.
151)	ii	ABIEL ABBOTT, b. 3 Mar 1726; d. 21 May 1772; m. 5 Jun 1750, ABIGAIL FENTON, b. at Willington, 27 Aug 1730 daughter of Francis and Ann (Berry) Fenton. Abigail m. 2nd John Chamberlain; Abigail d. 14 Aug 1776.
152)	iii	STEPHEN ABBOT, b. 21 Apr 1728; d. at Ashford, 29 Sep 1801; m. 3 Jan 1750, FREELOVE BURGESS, b. at Windham 14 Jul 1731 daughter of Benjamin and Susannah (Sabin) Burgess. The date of death for Freelove is not known, but after 1801 as she was living at the time of the probate of Stephen's estate.
153)	iv	HANNAH ABBOTT, b. 16 Mar 1730; d. 18 Dec 1801; m. Aug 1748, SAMUEL UTLEY, b. at Windham 28

Children of William Abbott and Elizabeth Geary

May 1723 son of James and Annah (-) Utley; Samuel d. 15 Nov 1782.

 v ZEBADIAH ABBOTT; d. 2 Dec 1731.

154) vi MARY ABBOTT, b. 6 Jul 1732; d. at Sheshequin, PA, 5 May 1803; m. 17 Oct 1751, STEPHEN FULLER, b. at Windham 3 Nov 1730 son of Stephen and Hannah (Moulton) Fuller; Stephen d. at Sheshequin 24 May 1813.

155) vii JOSEPH ABBOTT, b. 14 Feb 1735; d. at Ellington, CT 5 Jan 1815; m. 1st 20 Apr 1758, ELIZABETH STEDMAN, b. at Windham 30 Apr 1739 daughter of Thomas and Anna (-) Stedman; Elizabeth d. 2 Mar 1766. Joseph m. 2nd OLIVE PEARCE, b. at Brooklyn, CT, Mar 1738 daughter of Benjamin and Naomi (Richards) Pearce; Olive d. at Vernon, CT 9 Sep 1822.

156) viii JOHN ABBOTT, b. 27 Sep 1741; d. at Jacobs Plains, PA, 18 Jul 1778; m. 4 Nov 1762, ALICE FULLER, b. 1741 daughter of Stephen and Hannah (Moulton) Fuller. Alice m. 2nd Stephen Gardner; Alice d. at Plains, PA 1 Jun 1816.[104]

32) HANNAH ABBOTT (*William², George¹*), b. 5 Apr 1701 daughter of William and Elizabeth (Geary) Abbott; d. 11 Feb 1751/2 at Windham; m. 21 Feb 1721 ABIEL HOLT, b. 28 Jun 1698 son of Nicholas and Mary (Russell) Holt. Abiel m. 2nd Sarah Downer; Abiel d. 11 Nov 1772 at Willington.

Hannah and Abiel were part of the migration of several Andover families to Windham. There are records for ten children,

---

[104] William Blair, *The Michael Shoemaker Book (Schumacher).* (Scranton PA: International Textbook Press, 1924), 66.

Generation Three

all born at Windham, Connecticut. Most of the children in this family relocated to Willington.

157)   i   HANNAH HOLT, b. 17 Apr 1723; d. 25 Jan 1750/1; m. 14 Jul 1742, her first cousin WILLIAM HOLT, b. at Andover 10 Dec 1720 son of Thomas and Alice (Peabody) Holt. William m. 2nd Sybel Durkee; William d. at Hampton 2 Aug 1793.

158)   ii   ELIZABETH HOLT, b. 16 Feb 1724/5; d. about 1753; m. 10 Jun 1746, FRANCIS FENTON, b. at Willington, b. 16 Mar 1718 son of Francis and Ann (Berry) Fenton.[105] Francis m. 2nd Ann Newcomb.

159)   iii   ABIEL HOLT, b. 1 Feb 1726/7; d. 2 Oct 1785; m. 1st 22 Apr 1755, MARY DOWNER whose origins are unknown; Mary d. 28 Jan 1766. Abiel m. 2nd 2 Apr 1767, EUNICE KINGSBURY (widow of John Marshall), b. about 1733; Eunice d. 2 Jun 1784.

160)   iv   CALEB HOLT, b. 6 Mar 1729; d. 18 Aug 1810; m. 29 Jan 1755, MARY MERRICK, b. 6 Dec 1726 daughter of John and Sarah (Parsons) Merrick; Mary d. 4 Jun 1790. Caleb m. 2nd Chloe Hatch.

161)   v   NATHAN HOLT, b. 18 Apr 1733; d. 31 May 1800; m. 1st 19 Jan 1758, ABIGAIL MERRICK, b. 17 Jun 1737 daughter of John and Sarah (Parsons) Merrick; Abigail d. 1 Dec 1765. Nathan m. 2nd 26 Nov 1766, BATHSHEBA WILLIAMS, b. at Lebanon, 22 Mar 1737 daughter of Samuel and Deborah (Throope) Williams; Bathsheba d. 1 Aug 1769. Nathan m. 3rd 6

---

[105] William Weaver, *Genealogy of the Fenton Family*. (Willimantic, CT, 1867).

Children of William Abbott and Elizabeth Geary

Jun 1770, LYDIA KINGSBURY, b. at Bolton, 1737 daughter of John and Deborah (Spaulding) Kingsbury; Lydia d. 22 Mar 1776.

162) vi   ANNA HOLT, b. 14 Jan 1735; d. 10 Oct 1806; m. 29 Jan 1755, JOSEPH MERRICK, b. 17 Oct 1733 son of John and Sarah (Parsons) Merrick; Joseph d. 9 Apr 1787.

163) vii   ISAAC HOLT, b. 2 Mar 1737/8; d. 14 Oct 1822; m. 26 May 1762, SARAH ORCUTT, b. at Stafford, 7 Nov 1740 daughter of William and Sarah (Leonard) Orcutt; Sarah d. 30 Mar 1816.

164) viii TIMOTHY HOLT, b. 2 Dec 1739; d. 7 May 1807; m. 7 May 1761 as her 2nd husband, REBECCA CHAMBERLAIN (widow of Nathaniel Fenton);[106] Rebecca was b. about 1730 probably the daughter of Edmund and Sarah (Furbush) Chamberlain; Rebecca d. 11 Apr 1809.

165) ix   MARY HOLT, b. 4 May 1742; d. 13 Jan 1823; m. 27 Nov 1760, JOSEPH PERSONS, birth record not found but son of Joseph and Hannah (-) Persons; Joseph d. at Willington, 4 Nov 1812.

166) x   JAMES HOLT, b. 27 Aug 1746; d. 30 Sep 1818; m. 1st 20 Apr 1769, ESTHER OWENS, b. 20 Feb 1747 son of Eleazer and Jerusha (Russ) Owens; Esther d. 5 Dec 1774. JAMES m. 2nd LUCE SAWINS, b. 28 Sep 1740 daughter of George and Anne (Farrar) Sawins; Luce d. 25 Dec 1824.

---

[106] This information is confirmed by the 1809 probate record of Rebecca Holt which includes heirs from her first marriage to Nathaniel Fenton.

33)   CALEB ABBOTT (*William², George¹*), b. 8 Oct 1704 son of William and Elizabeth (Geary) Abbott; died at Union, CT 31 Jan 1778; m. at Pomfret 3 Dec 1730[107] ELIZABETH PAINE, b. 9 Aug 1710 at Pomfret daughter of Samuel and Ruth (Perrin) Paine; Elizabeth d. 1 Apr 1772 at Union, CT.

Caleb was one of the first Abbotts to leave the Andover area. He purchased a farm in Pomfret Connecticut in 1726.[108] He married Elizabeth Paine there in 1730. He relocated again from Pomfret to Union Connecticut in 1749. Caleb and Elizabeth had seven children all born at Pomfret. Their oldest child, Caleb, Jr., died in the Revolutionary War.

    i   CALEB ABBOTT, b. 9 Sep 1731; d. by Mar 1776 when his estate entered probate; m. at unknown date, MARGARET PAUL, b. about 1727; d. 11 Jan 1806 at Union, CT; there are no known children. Caleb died during the Revolutionary War.[109] He was in the service of General Putnam. The inventory of Caleb Abbott's estate had a value of about £39. His widow, Margaret Abbott, requested that Abner Sepians be named administrator of the estate.

    ii   ELIZABETH ABBOTT, b. 12 Mar 1733; d. 31 Aug 1742.

---

[107] New England Historical and Genealogical Register, 1913, volume LXVII, Marriages at Pomfret, Conn., p. 372

[108] Margaret T. Abbott, Ten Generations of Abbotts in America, 1952, unpublished, Retrieved from https://www.mhl.org/sites/default/files/files/Abbott/Abbott%20Family.pdf

[109] The death date for Caleb, Jr. is often confused with the death date of his father Caleb who died 31 Jan 1778. Caleb, Jr.'s estate was probated in 1776 with his widow Margaret declining administration of the estate.

167) iii HANNAH ABBOTT, b. 27 Oct 1734; d. 19 Apr 1813 at Hartland, VT; m. at Union, CT, 24 Mar 1761, JOHN HENDRICK, b. at Norwich, 3 Oct 1722 son of Israel and Ann (Babson) Hendrick; John d. at Hartland 8 Nov 1810.[110]

168) iv SARAH ABBOTT, b. 6 Jul 1736; d. 12 Nov 1761 at Brimfield, MA; m. 11 Nov 1754, JONATHAN BURK, b. 26 Feb 1733 son of Jonathan and Thankful (Waite) Burk. Jonathan m. 2nd Sarah Gould; Jonathan d. 18 May 1775 at Hartland, VT.

v MARY ABBOTT, b. 21 Mar 1739; she m. JOHN CAPEN of Hartland, VT; they moved to Scipio, NY and they did not have children.[111]

169) vi SAMUEL ABBOTT, b. 4 Mar 1743; d. 25 Sep 1825 at Hartland, VT; m. 1st at Union, CT, RACHEL WARD, b. about 1748 (based on age at death); Rachel d. at Hartland, VT 15 Oct 1774. Samuel m. 2nd 3 Dec 1778 the widow LYDIA STONE; Lydia d. 25 Sep 1825.

170) vii WILLIAM ABBOTT, b. 17 Oct 1745; d. 25 Jul 1832 at Clinton, NY; m. 1st at Union, CT, 15 Nov 1770, MARY COY; Mary d. 10 Dec 1776. William m. 2nd 24 Sep 1778, ESTHER GREEN, b. at Thompson, CT, 31 Dec 1753 daughter of Amos and Lydia (Johnson) Green;[112] Esther d. at Clinton, NY 23 Dec 1839.

---

[110] Vermont, Vital Records, 1720-1908. (ancestry.com)
[111] Abbot and Abbot, *Genealogical Record of Descendants*
[112] Esther's birthdate and name of her father are engraved on her gravestone. (findagrave.com)

Section V: The Children of Sarah Abbott and Ephraim Stevens

14) SARAH STEVENS (*Sarah Abbott Stevens², George¹*) and STEPHEN ABBOTT (*John², George¹*) (Please see Family #14 above.)

34) ELIZABETH STEVENS (*Sarah Abbott Stevens², George¹*), b. 7 Aug 1683 daughter of Ephraim and Sarah (Abbott) Stevens; d. 28 Apr 1763; m. 20 Mar 1706/7 JOSEPH ROBINSON, b. about 1678 son of Joseph and Phebe (Dane) Robinson; Joseph d. at Andover, 9 Apr 1761.

The will of Joseph Robinson was dated 1 May 1758 and has bequests to the following persons: well beloved wife Elizabeth, son Joseph Robinson, son Isaac Robinson, son Ephraim Robinson, daughter Sarah wife of Samuel Barker, and daughter Elizabeth wife of James Seaton. Isaac is named the executor.[113]

There are records for eight children, all born at Andover.

	i	ELIZABETH ROBINSON, b. 1707; d. 19 Jan 1723/4.
171)	ii	JOSEPH ROBINSON, b. 22 Dec 1710; d. at Boxford, 29 Nov 1777; m. 25 Jul 1733, MEHITABLE EAMS, of Boxford, b. 1713 (based on age at time of death); her parentage is not clear; Mehitable d. 11 Aug 1782.
	iii	UNKNOWN CHILD, likely b. and d. 1 Jun 1713.
172)	iv	ISAAC ROBINSON, b. Sep 1715; d. at Boxford, 15 Apr 1804; m. 19 Jun 1740, DOROTHY POOR, b. at Andover 1716 daughter of Daniel and Dorothy (Kimball) Poor; Dorothy d. 13 Jul 1801.

---

[113] *Essex County, MA: Probate File Papers, 1638-1881. Probate of* Joseph Robinson, 6 Jul 1761, *Case number* 23905.

173) v SARAH ROBINSON, b. about 1716;[114] d.?; m. 10 Apr 1746, as his second wife, SAMUEL BARKER, b. 13 Feb 1691/2 son of William and Mary (Dix) Barker; Samuel d. 13 May 1770.

vi PHEBE ROBINSON, b. 25 Nov 1717; d. 2 Sep 1738.

174) vii EPHRAIM ROBINSON, b. 11 Aug 1723; death date not located; m. 2 Aug 1750, HANNAH KIMBALL, b. at Bradford 19 Mar 1730/1 daughter of Joseph and Abial (Peabody) Kimball; no death record was located for Hannah.

viii ELIZABETH ROBINSON, b. 7 Aug 1727; d. likely at Amherst, NH, date unknown; m. 5 May 1748, JAMES SEATON of unknown birth or origin, but seems to have been the brother of Deacon John Seaton thought to have come from Ireland (of Scottish origin); no death record or probate record was found for James. There is one birth record for a child born in Andover, but no further record for that child, and there is no record of Elizabeth and James having children while they lived in Amherst, NH.[115]

35) HANNAH STEVENS (*Sarah Abbott Stevens², George¹*), b. 18 Nov 1685 daughter of Ephraim and Sarah (Abbott) Stevens; d. before 28 Sep 1773 when her will was probated; m. 17 Mar 1708/9 ROBERT SWAN, b. at Haverhill 28 May 1686 son of Robert and Elizabeth (Storie) Swan; Robert died before 4 Sep 1770 when his estate was probated.

---

[114] Sarah is mentioned in her father's will, but no birth record was located for her.
[115] Daniel F. Secomb, *History of the Town of Amherst, Hillsborough County, New Hampshire.* (Concord, NH: Evans, Sleeper, and Woodbury, 1883).

Robert Swan was from Haverhill and Hannah joined him there where they lived and raised their four children. They did relocate to Andover, apparently, as their deaths are recorded there.

The will of Robert Swan has bequests to the following persons: well beloved wife Hannah, daughter Elizabeth wife of Nathan(iel) Lovejoy, daughter Hannah wife of Peter Parker, to six grandsons, sons of son Robert of Methuen who is deceased (Jonathan, Joseph, Benjamin, Richard, Robert, and Phineas), and son Ephraim. Son Ephraim is the executor.[116]

In her will (probate 28 September 1773), Hannah Stevens Swan made the following bequests: four granddaughters who are Sarah Swan the daughter of Ephraim, Mary Isley, Hannah Parker, and Lydia Parker who are the daughters of Hannah the wife of Peter Parker; son Ephraim Swan; grandsons Jonathan, Robert, Richard, and Phineas Swan sons of Robert who is deceased; Joseph Swan who is the son of grandson Benjamin Swan of Methuen who is deceased; grandson Nathaniel Lovejoy who is son of daughter Elizabeth who is deceased; and grandsons Nathan, Peter, Robert, Isaac, Simeon Parker who are the sons of daughter Hannah who is deceased. Her grandson Ephraim Swan is named executor. She also makes mention of property she received as inheritance from her father Ephraim Stevens.[117]

There are records for four children, all born at Haverhill.

175) i ELIZABETH SWAN, b. 14 Feb 1709/10; d. at Andover 21 Jun 1770; m. 4 Jul 1743, NATHANIEL LOVEJOY, b. 16 Feb 1698/9 son of Nathaniel and Dorothy (Hoyt) Lovejoy; Nathaniel d. 25 Aug 1768.

---

[116] *Essex County, MA: Probate File Papers, 1638-1881. Probate of* Robert Swan, 4 Sep 1770, *Case number* 26899.
[117] *Essex County, MA: Probate File Papers, 1638-1881. Probate of* Hannah Swan, 28 Sep 1773, *Case number* 26887.

Children of Sarah Abbott and Ephraim Stevens

176) ii ROBERT SWAN, b. 2 Mar 1711/2; d. at Methuen, 31 Oct 1752; m. 1731, ELIZABETH FARNUM, b. at Andover, 9 Nov 1711. Elizabeth m. 2nd James Howe; Elizabeth d. 5 Dec 1780.

177) iii EPHRAIM SWAN, b. 3 Sep 1713; d. at Andover before Oct 1777 (when his will was probated); m. 23 May 1738, SARAH POOLE, b. at Lynn, 11 Sep 1713 daughter of John and Mary (Gooding) Poole; Sarah d. likely after 1790 (she seems to be listed as the head of household with her daughter living with her in the 1790 Census).

178) iv HANNAH SWAN, b. 28 Dec 1716; d. at Andover, 7 Jul 1761; m. 14 Aug 1734, PETER PARKER, b. Jul 1714 son of Joseph and Lydia (Frye) Parker; Peter d. 9 Jan 1795.

36) MARY STEVENS (*Sarah Abbott Stevens², George¹*), b. 10 Feb 1693/4 daughter of Ephraim and Sarah (Abbott) Stevens; d. at Pomfret, 9 Mar 1773; m. 5 Nov 1719, JAMES INGALLS, b. 9 Aug 1695 son of James and Hannah (Abbott) Ingalls. Hannah Abbott Ingalls is from the Rowley Abbott line; James d. at Pomfret 6 Mar 1767.

This family was part of the migration from Andover to Pomfret in the mid-1730's.

In his will, James Ingalls has bequests for the following persons: beloved wife Mary, beloved son James of Methuen, beloved son Ephraim, beloved son Zebadiah, and beloved daughter Abiah Rogers.[118]

James and Mary had eight children all born at Andover.

---

[118] *Connecticut Wills and Probate, 1609-1999*, Probate of James Ingalls, Hartford, 1767, Case number 2276.

Generation Three

179) i JAMES INGALLS, b. 20 Aug 1720; d. at Methuen 8 May 1804; m. 6 Dec 1744, MARY FRYE, b. about 1725 whose parentage is not yet proved; Mary d. 6 Apr 1797.

ii DEBORAH INGALLS, b. 22 Apr 1722; d. at Pomfret, 5 Dec 1752; m. 19 Dec 1751, BENJAMIN SHARPE, b. about 1714 with parents unproved at this point. Benjamin m. 2nd MARY CRAFT. Benjamin d. about 1782 when his will was proved. Deborah and Benjamin had an infant daughter, Deborah, b. 27 Nov 1752 and d. 17 Apr 1753; mother Deborah died one week after her daughter's birth.

iii EPHRAIM INGALLS, b. 26 Nov 1723; d. 19 Jan 1724/5.

180) iv EPHRAIM INGALLS, b. 6 Nov 1725; d. at Pomfret 16 May 1805; m. 19 Dec 1751, MARY SHARP, b. at Pomfret, b. 10 Jul 1733 daughter of John and Dorcas (Davis) Sharp; Mary d. 16 Feb 1809.

v MARY INGALLS, b. 7 Sep 1727; d. 13 Mar 1750/1. Mary did not marry.

181) vi ZEBADIAH INGALLS, b. 3 Nov 1729; 11 Jun 1800; m. 20 Feb 1755, ESTHER GOODELL, b. at Pomfret, 19 May 1735 daughter of Zachariah and Hannah (Cheney) Goodell; Esther d. 30 Sep 1778.

182) vii ABIAH INGALLS, b. 19 Oct 1731; d. likely at Palmer or Monson, MA; m. 16 Mar 1753, NATHANIEL

ROGERS, b. about 1730 of not yet proved origins; d. probably about 1786, but no records were located.[119]

viii SIMEON INGALLS, b. 12 Jan 1735/6; d. 4 Apr 1753.

37) MEHITABLE STEVENS (*Sarah Abbott Stevens²*, *George¹*), b. 31 Aug 1700 daughter of Ephraim and Sarah (Abbott) Stevens; d. probably in NH; m. 4 Dec 1729, EBENEZER HOLT, b. 8 Apr 1705 son of Samuel and Sarah (Farnum) Holt; Ephraim probably died in NH. There is some record conflict about Mehitable Stevens. Published genealogies give a death date of May 1805 at the age of 97 which would make her born about 1708 which conflicts with the available birth transcription.

This family is believed to have relocated to New Hampshire and records related to the latter part of their lives have not been located.[120]

Both Secomb's History of Amherst, New Hampshire[121] and Durrie's Holt genealogy give a daughter Mary in this family and list her as marrying Darius Abbott. However, the probate record of Henry Holt, husband of Rebecca Gray, support that Mary who married Darius Abbott was their daughter. Although Henry Holt died in 1754, the final settlement of his estate in 1762 includes the settlement of one lot on Mary wife of Darius Abbot.[122] The birth records for the family of Ebenezer Holt and Mehitable Stevens do not include a daughter Mary.

---

[119] This is the date used by the SAR and the DAR as his approximated death, although it is not clear why this date was chosen. There is a marriage record for Abijah Rogers marrying Gideon Graves in Palmer in October 1786, but I do not think this is the widow Abijah marrying. The Gideon Graves in question seems to be about 30 years younger than Abijah. Perhaps this record is for a daughter Abijah.
[120] Durrie, *A Genealogical History of the Holt Family*
[121] Secomb, *History of the Town of Amherst*
[122] *Essex County, MA: Probate File Papers, 1638-1881. Probate of* Henry Holt, 14 Oct 1754, *Case number* 13640.

183)	i	EBENEZER HOLT, b. 7 Sep 1730; d. at Mount Vernon, NH, Apr 1805;[123] m. 15 Feb 1753, LYDIA PEABODY, b. 5 Jul 1731 daughter of Moses and Sarah (Holt) Peabody; Lydia's date of death is not known.
184)	ii	MEHITABLE HOLT, b. 3 Sep 1733; d. 4 Mar 1767; m. 2 Jan 1755, her first cousin JAMES HOLT, b. 18 Feb 1732/3 son of Obadiah and Rebecca (Farnum) Holt. James m. 2nd the widow Mary McEntire whose identity has not been found.
	iii	RACHEL HOLT (twin), b. 15 Jun 1737; d. 14 Jul 1737.
	iv	PRISCILLA HOLT (twin), b. 15 Jun 1737; no further record.
185)	v	EZEKIEL HOLT (twin), b. 7 Jul 1741; d. at Amherst, NH date unknown; m. by 1772, MARY STEWART, b. 2 Sep 1749.
	vi	RACHEL HOLT (twin), b. 7 Jul 1741; no further record.
186)	vii	REUBEN HOLT, b. 27 Jun 1744; d. at Landgrove, VT 2 Mar 1836;[124] m. at Amherst, NH, 6 Feb 1772, LYDIA SMALL, b. Mar 1745[125] daughter of William and Sarah (Clark) Small daughter of William and Sarah (Clark) Small; Lydia d. at Amherst, NH, 9 Mar 1795.

---

[123] Secomb, *History of the Town of Amherst*
[124] *Vermont, Vital Records, 1720-1908* (Provo, UT, USA: Ancestry.com Operations, Inc., 2013).
[125] Lydia was baptized at Salem but may have been born at Andover.

    viii   HEPHZIBAH HOLT, b. 13 Jun 1748; d. at Amherst, NH, 11 Jan 1851;[126] m. at Amherst, 27 Apr 1790, WILLIAM HARTSHORN, b. at Reading, 1753 son of Benjamin and Mary (Swain) Hartshorn; William d. 22 Jun 1831 at Amherst.[127] Hephzibah and William do not seem to have had children.

    ix   HANNAH HOLT, b. 27 Oct 1749; no further record.

38)   DEBORAH STEVENS (*Sarah Abbott Stevens²*, *George¹*), b. 4 Oct 1704 daughter of Ephraim and Sarah (Abbott) Stevens; d. 17 Jun 1748 at Salem; m. 20 Jun 1726, SAMUEL CARLETON, b. 3 Jun 1696 son of John and Hannah (Osgood) Carleton; Samuel d. at Salem 9 Mar 1767.

Several of the children of Deborah and Samuel were either mariners or married to mariners. One of their sons, William, died while on a return voyage from Barbados. Two sons-in-law, Jacob Crowninshield and John Bowditch, also died at sea: Jacob in 1774 on a voyage from Jamaica and John in 1793.

In his will, Samuel Carleton has bequests for the following persons: son Ephraim, son Samuel, son William, daughter Hannah Crowninshield, and daughter Mary Bowditch. He specifies that he has five children.[128]

There are eight children recorded for Deborah and Samuel. The oldest child was born at Andover and the others at Salem.

    i   DEBORAH CARLETON, b. 17 Mar 1728/9; a death record was not found, but she died prior to the time of her father's will in 1767.

---

[126] Hephzibah's longevity is confirmed by her listing in the 1850 US Census as being at age 103 on the census report.
[127] William Hartshorn is listed in the 1810 US Census of Amherst but is not in the 1820 census.
[128] *Essex County, MA: Probate File Papers, 1638-1881. Probate of* Samuel Carleton, 7 Apr 1767, *Case number* 4689.

Generation Three

187) ii SAMUEL CARLETON, b. 11 Aug 1731; d. 25 Mar 1804; m. 27 Oct 1754, EUNICE HUNT, b. 25 Oct 1730 daughter of William and Eunice (Bowditch)Hunt; Eunice d. 12 Aug 1827.

188) iii HANNAH CARLETON, b. 26 Jul 1734; d. 14 May 1824; m. 30 Mar 1756, JACOB CROWNINSHIELD, b. 9 Jan 1732/3 son of John and Anstus (Williams) Crowninshield; Jacob was a mariner who died on a passage from Jamaica in Nov 1774.

iv BENJAMIN CARLETON, b. 5 Apr 1736; no death record found but not living at the time of his father's will in 1767.

189) v MARY CARLETON, b. about 1738; d. 24 Dec 1805; m. 12 Jul 1759, JOHN BOWDITCH, b. 3 Apr 1732 son of Ebenezer and Mary (Turner) Bowditch; John was a mariner and died at sea around April 1793.

vi EPHRAIM CARLETON, b. 20 Jan 1739; no further record found although he was living at the time of his father's will in 1767.

vii JOHN CARLETON, b. 24 May 1741; no death record found but before the time of his father's will in 1767.

190) viii WILLIAM CARLETON, b. 8 Apr 1744 son of Samuel and Deborah (Stevens) Carleton; d. Jun 1791 while on a trip to Barbados; m. 1st, (-) Palfrey who died before 1777. William m. 2nd, at Boston, 1 May 1777, MARY FARMER whose origins are uncertain but perhaps the daughter of Paul and Thankful (Sprague) Farmer of Boston.

Section VI: The Children of Benjamin Abbott and Sarah Farnum

24) BENJAMIN ABBOTT (*Benjamin², George¹*) and ELIZABETH ABBOTT (*George², George¹*) (Please see the family of Benjamin Abbott with his first wife Elizabeth Abbott at Family #24.)

39) BENJAMIN ABBOTT, b. 11 Jul 1686 son of Benjamin and Sarah (Abbott) Farnum; d. before 5 Dec 1748; m. 1st 24 Dec 1716 ELIZABETH ABBOTT, b. 25 Jul 1690 daughter of George and Dorcas (Graves) Abbott. BENJAMIN m. 2nd 23 Oct 1722 MARY CARLETON, b. 7 Apr 1700 daughter of John and Hannah (Osgood) Carleton; Mary died 19 Jan 1725/6. BENJAMIN m. 3rd 1729, ABIGAIL ABBOTT, b. 7 Oct 1699 daughter of Nehemiah and Abigail (Lovejoy) Abbott. Abigail Abbott is from the George Abbott of Rowley line; Abigail d. 8 Dec 1753.

As the oldest son, Benjamin assumed ownership of his father's farm. His father died when Benjamin was about 17. Benjamin married three times, first to his cousin Elizabeth Abbott who died after the birth of their only child. Next, he married Mary Carleton by whom he had two children. His third marriage was to Abigail Abbott, a descendant from the George Abbott of Rowley line.

Benjamin did not leave a will. His estate entered probate 5 December 1748 and includes an 81-page probate document. The probate settlement dated 18 February 1754 includes the following heirs: eldest son Benjamin, second son Daniel, daughter Mary, daughter Sarah the wife of James Holt, daughter Abigail, son Abiel, son Jacob, daughter Elizabeth, daughter Anna, and daughter Dorcas. Jacob, Elizabeth, Anna, and Dorcas have guardians who represent their interests, so these youngest four children are under age. Sarah the wife of James Holt is the daughter of Benjamin with his first wife Elizabeth Abbott.[129]

Children of Benjamin Abbott and his second wife, Mary Carleton, born at Andover:

125)   i   BENJAMIN ABBOTT, b. 21 Oct 1723; d. at Hollis, NH, 1771;[130] m. 2 Apr 1747, his second cousin, ELIZABETH ABBOTT, b. 5 Nov 1727 daughter of George and Mary (Phillips) Abbott. Elizabeth m. 2nd, 22 Mar 1775, James Pollard.[131] Elizabeth m. 3rd, Josiah Bowers of Billerica who died in 1794. Elizabeth died about 1802 at Westford (date of will 10 Aug 1802). There is a 1790 deed from Josiah Bowers of Billerica to his son Benjamin and named in the deed record is Josiah's wife Elizabeth.[132] Benjamin Abbott and Elizabeth Abbott are Family #125.

191)   ii   DANIEL ABBOTT, b. 29 Dec 1725; d. Apr 1793;[133] m. 3 Apr 1756, LUCY PARKER, b. 5 Jun 1732 daughter

---

[129] *Essex County, MA: Probate File Papers, 1638-1881. Probate of* Benjamin Abbott, 5 Dec 1748, *Case number* 23.

[130] There is a probate record in Middlesex County, MA in 1771 related to Benjamin's estate and includes information about Benjamin being a mortgagee of Samuel Abbott. Twenty-three acres were set off to widow Elizabeth Abbott. Perley's article in the Essex Antiquarian gives a date of 5 Jan 1770.

[131] This marriage may not be accurate. There is a record for a marriage in Hollis 22 Mar 1775 for "Captain Jonas Pollard" of Westford and Mrs. Elizabeth Abbott. There is a Captain James Pollard of Westford who died in 1781 with a widow Elizabeth named in the will. James Pollard was born about 1708 and he was widowed in 1774. I believe the marriage transcription in the Hollis records is an error and the spouse is James Pollard.

[132] Middlesex County Deeds, 1792-1827, volumes 110-112, Images 85-86, Familysearch.org.

[133] Abbot and Abbot, *Genealogical Record of Descendants*

of Thomas and Lydia (Richardson) Parker; the date of death of Lucy is not known.

Benjamin Abbott and third wife, Abigail Abbott, had nine children born at Andover.

	i	ABIGAIL ABBOTT, b. 28 Mar 1731; d. 21 Oct 1733.
192)	ii	MARY ABBOTT, b. 21 Jul 1732; d. at Milford, NH, 9 Aug 1798; m. 13 Nov 1759, NEHEMIAH BARKER, b. at Methuen, 11 Feb 1734 son of Ebenezer and Abigail (Morse) Barker; Nehemiah d. 20 Jan 1810.
193)	iii	ABIGAIL ABBOTT, b. 13 Jan 1733/4; d. 1 Feb 1807; m. 1 Jun 1758, her second cousin, once removed, JOHN ABBOTT, b. 12 Sep 1735 son of John and Phebe (Fiske) Abbott; John d. 24 Apr 1818.
194)	iv	ABIEL ABBOT, b. 24 Jul 1735; d. 24 Jun 1764; m. 5 Feb 1761, his third cousin PHEBE BALLARD, b. 25 Jul 1738 daughter of Josiah and Mary (Chandler) Ballard. Phebe m. 2nd as his second wife, her third cousin (and great grandson of George Abbott), JAMES HOLT son of Nicholas and Dorcas (Abbott) Holt; Phebe d. 9 Jun 1815.
	v	JACOB ABBOTT, b. 2 Feb 1736/7; d. at Albany while in the army "of cold and fatigue" Feb 1760.[134]
195)	vi	ELIZABETH ABBOTT, b. 27 Oct 1738; d. at Conway, NH, 12 Oct 1789;[135] m. 1st 1 Jun 1758, EBENEZER CUMMINGS, b. at Groton, 17 Apr 1735 son of William and Lucy (Colburn) Cummings; Ebenezer d. 1 Jun 1778. Elizabeth m. 2nd as his fourth wife,

---

[134] Abbot and Abbot, *Genealogical Record of Descendants*
[135] *New Hampshire, Death and Disinterment Records, 1754-1947*

THOMAS MERRILL, b. at Haverhill, 5 Feb 1723/4 son of John and Lydia (Haynes) Merrill. Thomas had married as his first wife, Phebe Abbott (Family #139); Thomas Merrill d. at Conway, NH, 21 Jul 1788.

196) vii ANNA ABBOTT, b. 13 Oct 1740; d. at Hollis, NH, 15 Jan 1810; m. Jan 1762, EPHRAIM BURGE, b. at Westford, 1 May 1738 son of Josiah and Susannah (Jaquith) Burge; Ephraim d. 20 Jul 1784.

viii JOEL ABBOTT, b. 20 Oct 1742; d. 23 Mar 1742/3.

197) ix DORCAS ABBOT, b. 1 Aug 1744; d. at Wilton, NH, 23 Feb 1829;[136] m. 20 Nov 1764, her second cousin, once removed, ABIEL ABBOT, b. 19 Apr 1741 son of John and Phebe (Fiske) Abbott; Abiel d. 19 Aug 1809.

40) JONATHAN ABBOTT (*Benjamin²*, *George¹*), b. Sep 1687 son of Benjamin and Sarah (Abbott) Farnum; d. reported as 21 Mar 1770 although record was not located;[137] m. 6 May 1713, ZERVIAH HOLT, b. 24 Mar 1688/9 daughter of Henry and Sarah (Ballard) Holt; Zerviah d. 26 Mar 1768 (recorded at Andover).

The births of eight children of Jonathan Abbott and Zerviah Holt are recorded at Andover. Published genealogies include a daughter Mary in this family, but I can find no record of her.

198) i JONATHAN ABBOTT, b. Dec 1714; d. 31 May 1794; m. 1st 8 Oct 1739, MARTHA LOVEJOY, b. 2 Nov 1720

---

[136] *New Hampshire: Births, Deaths and Marriages, 1654-1969.* (From microfilmed records. Online database: *AmericanAncestors.org*, New England Historic Genealogical Society, 2014.)
[137] Holt Association of America. *First Three Generations of Holts in America*, Newburgh, NY, p. 316

daughter of Henry and Sarah (Farnum) Lovejoy; Martha d. about 1768. Jonathan m. 2nd as her second husband, his second cousin MARY ABBOTT daughter of George and Mary (Phillips) Abbott.

199) ii DAVID ABBOTT, b. Dec 1716; d. 1777 at Rockingham, NH (probate 31 Dec 1777); m. 10 Aug 1741, his second cousin, once removed, HANNAH CHANDLER, b. 1724 daughter of Joseph and Mehitable (Russell) Chandler; Hannah's death not known but she was living at the time of her husband's will.

iii NATHAN ABBOTT, b. Apr 1719; d. 28 Jun 1798; m. 12 Mar 1744/5, his second cousin and George Abbott descendant, ABIGAIL AMES, b. about 1722 daughter of Samuel and Hannah (Stevens) Ames; Abigail d. 27 Aug 1812. Nathan Abbott and Abigail Ames did not have any children. Nathan Abbott wrote his will 21 March 1776 and the estate entered probate 3 September 1798. Dearly beloved wife Abigail receives "all my household stuff proper for woman's use." She receives other provisions for her support and the use and improvements of one-third of the real property. He makes a bequest to his "cousin" Nathan Abbott who is the son of his brother Job who is deceased. The nephew Nathan is named executor and has the remainder of the estate bequeathed to him.

200) iv ZERVIAH ABBOTT, b. Aug 1722; d. likely at Pembroke, NH; m. 17 Sep 1745, EPHRAIM BLUNT, b. 5 Feb 1720/1 son of William and Sarah (Foster) Blunt.

141) v   JOB ABBOTT, b. 3 Oct 1724; d. likely at Pembroke, NH; m. about 1751, his second cousin, SARAH ABBOTT, b. 13 Aug 1730 daughter of James and Abigail (Farnum) Abbott.

201) vi SAMUEL ABBOTT, b. 20 Sep 1727; m. 12 Jul 1749, MIRIAM STEVENS whose origins are undetermined but may be the Miriam baptized in 1730 at Newbury.

      vii JEREMIAH ABBOTT, b. 30 Sep 1733; d. 1755 in the French and Indian War.

41)   DAVID ABBOT (*Benjamin², George¹*), b. 18 Jan 1688/9 son of Benjamin and Sarah (Abbott) Farnum; d. 14 Nov 1753; m. 20 Mar 1717/8, HANNAH DANFORTH, b. at Billerica 20 Aug 1698 daughter of Samuel and Hannah (Crosby) Danforth; Hannah d. 8 Jan 1788.

David had a farm at Merrimack Corner in Andover. He and his wife Hannah had nine children all born at Andover.

The will of David Abbot, written 7 November 1753, has the following bequests: beloved wife Hannah receives the widow's third; beloved son Solomon receives land and meadows above the brook, and "all the rest" of the children receive the rest of the estate. These children are David, Josiah, Jonathan, Benjamin, Hannah, and Sarah. The four boys share equally while the two daughters get half as much as each of the boys. The bequests to the younger children do include bequests of land. David calls on his "trusty friends" Ebenezer Abbot, Samuel Abbot, and Thomas Abbot to divide the land. David goes into detail about how the division of the land should proceed. The sons are to buy out the value of the portion of the daughters.[138]

---

[138] *Essex County, MA: Probate File Papers, 1638-1881. Probate of* David Abbot, 26 Nov 1753, *Case number* 28.

Two of the sons, Josiah and Benjamin, died within a week after the death of their father. A third child, daughter Elizabeth, died two months before her father. The family might have been a victim of one of the several epidemics that came through the colonies. In 1753, some areas of Massachusetts had an outbreak of "putrid fever"[139] and there was also a smallpox outbreak. The causes of death are not given on the death records for these four family members.

        i   HANNAH ABBOT, b. 21 Oct 1721; d. 25 Feb 1721/2.

        ii   HANNAH ABBOT, b. 23 Dec 1723; d. 12 Mar 1813; Hannah did not marry.

202)   iii   SARAH ABBOT, b. 7 Apr 1726; d. at Bedford, 5 Mar 1814; m. 1st 30 Jan 1753, ROBERT HILDRETH, b. at Dracut, 18 May 1713 son of Ephraim and Mercy (Richardson) Hildreth; Robert d. 1760. Sarah m. 2nd 28 May 1761, JOHN LANE, b. at Bedford, 2 Oct 1720 son of Job and Martha (Ruggles) Lane; John d. 7 Dec 1789. Sarah m. 3rd 14 Jul 1791, Benjamin Parker.

203)   iv   DAVID ABBOT, b. 28 Mar 1728; d. at Billerica 1 Nov 1798; m. 28 Dec 1752, PRUDENCE SHELDON, b. at Billerica 31 Aug 1732 daughter of Samuel and Sarah[140] (Hutchinson) Richardson. A death record for Prudence was not located, although she was living at the time of her husband's death and she was on the tax rolls in Billerica for 1798.

---

[139] Ernest Caulfield (1950, January). The Pursuit of a Pestilence. In *Proceedings of the American Antiquarian Society* (Vol. 60, No. 1, p. 21). American Antiquarian Society.

[140] The marriage record lists her name as Mary Hutchinson, but all the births of the children, including a daughter Sarah born in 1719, list the mother's name as Sarah.

Generation Three

204) v SOLOMON ABBOT, b. 14 Feb 1730/1; d. probably at Dracut 17 Dec 1797;[141] m. 3 May 1756, HANNAH COLBE, b. 22 Oct 1735 daughter of Daniel and Hannah (Gray) Colbe; Hannah's date of death is not known.

vi ELIZABETH ABBOT, b. 2 Aug 1733; d. 31 Aug 1753.

vii JOSIAH ABBOT, b. 1735; d. 26 Nov 1753.

205) viii JONATHAN ABBOT, b. 24 Oct 1739; d. 10 Apr 1817; m. 13 Nov 1759, his second cousin, once removed and George Abbott descendant, MARY CHANDLER, b. 15 Jun 1740 daughter of Nathaniel and Priscilla (Holt) Chandler; Mary d. 1 Apr 1824.

ix BENJAMIN ABBOT, b. 16 Jan 1743; d. 20 Nov 1753.

---

[141] Abbot and Abbot, *Genealogical Record of Descendants* gives this date of death; a death record or probate record was not located.

Section VII: The Children of Timothy Abbott and Hannah Graves

42) TIMOTHY ABBOT (*Timothy², George¹*), b. 20 Jun 1693 son of Timothy and Hannah (Graves) Abbott; d. 10 Jul 1766; m. Dec 1717, MARY FOSTER, b. at Boxford 2 Aug 1698 daughter of William and Sarah (Kimball) Foster; Mary d. 31 Aug 1784.

As the only son of his father Timothy, Timothy the younger took over his father's homes and lands. He and his wife Mary had eleven children all born at Andover.

In his will, Timothy Abbot has bequests to the following persons: son Asa gets all his lands; well beloved wife Mary receives mourning apparel, but also receives all the money in hand and a regular supply of apples; other bequests go to son Nathan, daughter Hannah Parker, daughter Sarah Farmer, daughter Lydia Farnam, daughter Dorcas Abbot, daughter Phebe Abbot, and grandchildren who are the children of daughter Mary who is deceased namely Mary, Ephraim, and Hannah. Son Asa is the sole executor.[142]

	i	MARY ABBOT, b. 5 Oct 1718; d. 28 Oct 1718.
	ii	TIMOTHY ABBOT, b. 26 Oct 1719; 26 Mar 1745.
80)	iii	ASA ABBOT, b. 17 Oct 1721; d. 22 Dec 1796; m. 20 Sep 1744, his second cousin, ELIZABETH ABBOTT, b. 29 Jun 1726 daughter of Ephraim and Sarah (Crosby) Abbott; Elizabeth d. 18 Dec 1819.
77)	iv	MARY ABBOT, b. 7 Jan 1723/4; d. 9 Mar 1744; m. her second cousin, EPHRAIM ABBOTT, b. 22 Jul 1718 son of Ephraim and Sarah (Crosby) Abbott. Ephraim m. 2nd Mary Kneeland; Ephraim d. at Amherst, NH about 1775.

---

[142] *Essex County, MA: Probate File Papers, 1638-1881. Probate of* Timothy Abbot, 7 Oct 1766, *Case number* 144.

206) v HANNAH ABBOTT, b. 21 Jun 1726; d. likely at Pembroke, NH but unknown; m. 25 Apr 1754, JOSEPH PARKER, b. 15 Jul 1726 son of Joseph and Mary (Emery) Parker.

207) vi NATHAN ABBOTT, b. 7 Jan 1728/9; d. likely at Wilton, NH; m. 11 Jan 1759, JANE PAUL, described as "resident of Andover," but whose origins are unknown; Jane d. at Wilton, 28 May 1772.

208) vii SARAH ABBOTT, b. 5 May 1731; m. 1 Mar 1757, EDWARD FARMER.

209) viii LYDIA ABBOTT, b. 28 Mar 1733; d. at Andover, 13 Mar 1816; m. 13 Jan 1756, THOMAS FARNUM, b. 6 Sep 1734 son of Thomas and Phebe (Towns) Farnum; Thomas's death is not known but was perhaps in NH.

ix DORCAS ABBOTT, b. 2 Oct 1735; d. after 1798 (when she is on the Andover tax list); m. 3 Jan 1775 as his second wife, SAMUEL BAILEY, b. at Bradford, 20 Feb 1705 son of James and Hannah (Wood) Bailey; Samuel d. 5 Jan 1784. Dorcas married later in life and did not have any children with her husband Samuel Bailey.

210) x PHEBE ABBOTT, b. 16 Feb 1736/7; d. not certain but perhaps before 1799; m. 22 Jul 1766 as his second wife, WILLIAM DANE, b. 15 Mar 1727/8 son of John and Sarah (Chandler) Dane. William is likely the William Dane that died at Brookfield in 1825 at age 99.

xi CALEB ABBOT, b. 9 Aug 1738; d. 7 Sep 1738.

43) HANNAH ABBOTT (*Timothy², George¹*), b. 8 Oct 1695 daughter of Timothy and Hannah (Graves) Abbott; d. 22 Apr 1769; m. 16 Mar 1732 as his 2nd wife JOHN LANE, b. 20 Oct 1691 son of John and Susannah (Whipple) Lane; John d. at Bedford, 23 Sep 1763.

There are discrepancies in published genealogies as to which Hannah Abbott married Abiel Holt and went to Connecticut and which Hannah Abbott married John Lane. This issue seems to be settled by probate records for Timothy Abbott, father of Hannah. Timothy died in 1730. During the probate, Hannah files a document as Hannah Abbott, spinster of Andover, acknowledging the settlement from her brother Timothy related to the estate of their father Timothy. This would eliminate Hannah the daughter of Timothy as the wife of Abiel Holt as Abiel Holt and Hannah Abbott were married in 1721. So, it seems that Abiel Holt married Hannah the daughter of William Abbott, and Hannah the daughter of Timothy married John Lane.

Hannah married late at age 36 and had just two children with her husband John Lane. One of those children died in childhood. The will of John Lane, written 1 April 1761 and proved in 1763, includes bequests for his four children from his first marriage and his son Samuel, his son with Hannah.[143]

        i   HANNAH LANE, b. 16 May 1734; d. 22 Apr 1769.

211)   ii   SAMUEL LANE, b. 21 Oct 1737; d. 1822 (year of probate); m. 8 Dec 1763, ELIZABETH FITCH, b. 6 Jan 1738/9 daughter of Zachariah and Elizabeth (Grimes) Fitch; Elizabeth d. 19 Sep 1807.[144]

---

[143] *Middlesex County, MA: Probate File Papers, 1648-1871. Probate of John Lane, 1766, Case number* 13578.

[144] The death record states just __, w. Samuel, complicated complaint, Sept. 19, 1807, a. 69. C.R. There was another Samuel Lane in town with a wife also born in 1738. However, that woman, Frances Hutchins Blood Lane, died in 1811 in Carlisle and has the following death listing: Lane, Frances, wid. "first wid. Stephen Blood, jr.," Apr. 17, 1811, a. 73 y. G. R. 1.

Generation Three

44) DORCAS ABBOTT (*Timothy², George¹*), b. 25 Apr 1698 daughter of Timothy and Hannah (Graves) Abbott; d. 25 Oct 1758; m. 12 Apr 1717 as his 2nd wife NICHOLAS HOLT, b. 21 Dec 1683 son of Nicholas and Mary (Russell) Holt; Nicholas d. 1 Dec 1756.

In his will, Nicholas Holt makes bequests to the following persons: dearly beloved wife Dorcas, eldest and well-beloved son Benjamin, well-beloved son Stephen, well-beloved son Nicholas, well-beloved son Timothy, well-beloved son James, well-beloved son Nathan, well-beloved son Joshua, well-beloved son Daniel, eldest and well-beloved daughter Mary, and well-beloved daughter Dorcas. Benjamin, Mary, Stephen, and Nicholas are Nicholas's children from his first marriage to Mary Manning.[145]

Nicholas and Dorcas had six children all born at Andover.

212) i TIMOTHY HOLT, b. 17 Jan 1720/1; d. at Wilton, NH, Nov 1801; m. 18 Sep 1744, his second cousin, ELIZABETH HOLT, b. Jun 1718 daughter of John and Mehitable (Wilson) Holt; Elizabeth d. at Wilton 21 Mar 1776.

123) ii JAMES HOLT, b. 13 Jan 1722/3; d. 22 Aug 1812; m. 1st, SARAH ABBOTT, b. 2 Aug 1718 daughter of Benjamin and Elizabeth (Abbott) Abbott; Sarah d. 5 Mar 1778. James m. 2nd, 22 Jun 1779, PHEBE BALLARD daughter of Josiah and Mary (Chandler) Ballard and widow of Abiel Abbot (Family #194); Phebe d. 9 Jun 1815.

126) iii NATHAN HOLT, b. 28 Feb 1725; d. at Danvers, 2 Aug 1792; m. 4 Aug 1757, SARAH ABBOTT, b. 14 Jan

---

[145] *Essex County, MA: Probate File Papers, 1638-1881. Probate of* Nicholas Holt, 27 Dec 1756, *Case number* 13680.

1729/30 daughter of George and Mary (Phillips) Abbott; Sarah d. 29 Dec 1797.

213) iv DORCAS HOLT, b. 4 Sep 1727; death unknown but may have been at Wilton, NH; m. 26 Jan 1749, as his second wife, her first cousin, THOMAS HOLT, b. Mar 1711/2 son of Thomas and Alice (Peabody) Holt; Thomas d. at Andover, 21 Nov 1776.

214) v JOSHUA HOLT, b. 30 Jun 1730; d. 24 Jul 1810; m. 2 Dec 1755, PHEBE FARNUM, b. 10 Oct 1731 daughter of Timothy and Dinah (Ingalls) Farnum; Phebe d. 26 Jan 1806.

215) vi DANIEL HOLT, b. 10 Feb 1732/3; d. at Andover, 15 Feb 1796; m. 29 Nov 1759, his first cousin once removed, HANNAH HOLT, b. 11 Feb 1738/9 daughter of Thomas and Hannah (Kimball) Holt; Hannah d. at Andover, 2 Aug 1831.

Section VIII: The Children of Thomas Abbott and Hannah Gray

45) THOMAS ABBOTT (*Thomas², George¹*), b. 3 Jan 1698/9 son of Thomas and Hannah (Gray) Abbott; d. 11 Jul 1774; m. 28 Jan 1724/5, ELIZABETH BALLARD, b. 14 Jan 1700/1 daughter of Joseph and Rebecca (Johnson) Ballard; Elizabeth d. 31 Jul 1782.

Thomas Abbott and Elizabeth Ballard lived their lives in Andover where all their children were born. However, four sons of this family relocated to Concord, New Hampshire near the time of the first settlement of Concord. Of those four, Jabez, Aaron, and Nathan, seem to have stayed in New Hampshire. Jesse seems to have returned to Massachusetts prior to his death.

No probate record was located for Thomas Abbott. Thomas Abbott and Elizabeth Ballard had ten children whose births are recorded at Andover.

    i SAMUEL ABBOTT, b. 1 Nov 1725; d. 19 Nov 1725.

216) ii ELIZABETH ABBOTT, b. 10 Jan 1726/7; d. at Andover 27 Sep 1792; m. 4 Jan 1753, as his 2nd wife, SAMUEL OSGOOD, b. 29 May 1714 son of Ezekiel and Rebecca (Wardwell) Osgood; Samuel d. 16 Mar 1774.

217) iii THOMAS ABBOTT, b. 4 Apr 1729; d. at Andover 29 Mar 1775; m. 12 Feb 1756, LYDIA BLUNT, b. 6 Apr 1731 daughter of David and Lydia (Foster) Blunt; Lydia d. 16 Nov 1798.

218) iv JABEZ ABBOTT, b. 18 Apr 1731; d. 7 Jan 1804 at Concord; m. 1st by 1756, his first cousin, PHEBE ABBOTT, b. 13 Feb 1732 daughter of Edward and

Dorcas (Chandler) Abbott; Phebe d. 6 Jan 1770. Jabez m. 2nd 8 Aug 1772, HEPHZIBAH STEVENS, b. 28 Feb 1739/40 daughter of Samuel and Hephzibah (Ingalls) Stevens.

219) v AARON ABBOTT, b. 17 Feb 1732/3; d. at Concord 31 Dec 1812; m. his first cousin, LYDIA ABBOTT, b. 15 Jun 1737 daughter of Edward and Dorcas (Chandler) Abbott; Lydia d. 15 Dec 1811.

vi JOSEPH ABBOTT, b. 27 Dec 1734; d. at Quebec in prison Jun 1758; Joseph was taken captive by the Indians at Lake George 19 Sep 1756 and was carried to Canada and died in prison at Quebec sometime in Jan 1758. This information is recorded in the death records.[146]

220) vii NATHAN ABBOTT, b. 7 Feb 1736/7; d. at Concord, 18 Jan 1805; m. 1766, BETTY FARNUM, b. 1743 daughter of Joseph and Zerviah (Hoit) Farnum; Betty d. 11 Nov 1821.

viii JESSE ABBOTT, b. 3 May 1740; d. 15 Jul 1740.

ix JESSE ABBOTT, b. 4 Oct 1741; d. 12 May 1808 recorded at Haverhill; m. at Andover, 27 Sep 1765, SARAH SCALES, b. 11 Sep 1743 daughter of Moses and Rebecca (Barnard) Scales; Sarah's date of death is not known. Jesse and Sarah did not have any children.

x LYDIA ABBOTT, b. 5 Oct 1743; d. 2 Jun 1749.

---

[146] Joseph, s. Thomas and Elizabeth, "taken Captive by the Indians at Lake George, Sept. 19, 1756, and carry'd to Canada and dyed in prison at Quebeck sometime in Jan. 1758," in his 24th y. Massachusetts: Vital Records, 1620-1850

Generation Three

46) EDWARD ABBOTT (*Thomas², George¹*), b. 9 Jun 1702 son of Thomas and Hannah (Gray) Abbott; died at Concord, NH 14 Apr 1759; m. 15 Jul 1728, DORCAS CHANDLER, b. about 1705 daughter of Thomas and Mary (Peters) Chandler; Dorcas d. 16 May 1748. Edward married 2nd 23 Jan 1748/9, MEHITABLE EASTMAN, b. at Haverhill 17 Nov 1707.

Edward Abbott was a first proprietor at Concord.[147] The births of all ten children of Edward and Dorcas are recorded at Rumford or Concord, New Hampshire.[148] No probate record was located for Edward.

221) i DORCAS ABBOTT, b. at Rumford 15 Feb 1728/9; d. 28 Sep 1797; m. 17 Jun 1746, EBENEZER HALL, b. at Bradford, 19 Sep 1721 son of Joseph and Sarah (Kimball) Hall; Ebenezer d. 24 Apr 1801. Ebenezer was the brother of Joseph Hall who married Deborah Abbott [daughter of Thomas and Hannah (Gray) Abbott].

222) ii EDWARD ABBOTT, b. 27 Dec 1730; d. 15 Sep 1801; m. about 1760 DEBORAH STEVENS, origins not certain but likely the Deborah born 1738 in Rumford, NH daughter of Aaron and Deborah (Stevens) Stevens; Aaron Stevens was an early settler at Concord; Deborah d. Nov 1817.

218) iii PHEBE ABBOTT, b. 13 Feb 1732; d. 6 Jan 1770; m. by 1756, her first cousin, JABEZ ABBOTT, b. 18 Apr

---

[147] Bouton, *The History of Concord*
[148] *New Hampshire, Births and Christenings Index, 1714-1904 (accessed through ancentry.com)*

	iv	1731 son of Thomas and Elizabeth (Ballard) Abbott. Jabez m. 2nd Hephzibah Stevens; Jabez d. 7 Jan 1804.

          iv   LYDIA ABBOTT, b. 7 May 1735; d. 18 Jun 1736.

219)   v   LYDIA ABBOTT, b. 15 Jun 1737; d. 15 Dec 1811; m. her first cousin, AARON ABBOTT, b. 17 Feb 1732/3 son of Thomas and Elizabeth (Ballard) Abbott; Aaron d. 31 Dec 1812.

          vi   TIMOTHY ABBOTT, b. 21 Jul 1739; d. at Concord, 1814; no marriages or children are known for him; his probate from 1814 specifies he left no widow or children.

          vii   RACHEL ABBOTT, b. 31 Mar 1742; d. 26 Jul 1742.

223)   viii   BETSEY ABBOTT, b. 25 Aug 1743; d. 2 Oct 1827 at Goffstown, NH; m. 1759, THOMAS SALTMARSH, b. at Watertown, 2 Mar 1736 son of Thomas and Mary (Hazen) Saltmarsh; Thomas d. at Goffstown, NH 8 May 1826.[149]

          ix   JEMIMA ABBOTT, b. 23 Jun 1746; d. 13 Jul 1746.

          x   JEMIMA ABBOTT, b. 29 Apr 1748; d. 31 Jul 1748.

47)   DEBORAH ABBOTT (*Thomas²*, *George¹*), b. 1 Dec 1704 daughter of Thomas and Hannah (Gray) Abbott; d. at Concord, NH 25 Oct 1801; m. 5 Jul 1736, JOSEPH HALL, b. at Bradford 15 Dec 1707 son of Joseph and Sarah (Kimball) Hall; Joseph d. 8 Apr 1784 at Concord.[150]

---

[149] The graves of Elizabeth Abbott and Thomas Saltmarsh are in the Westlawn Cemetery at Goffstown with a gravestone that lists their names as Thomas Saltmarsh and Elisabeth Abbott, his wife. (accessed through findagrave.com)

[150] New Hampshire Death and Disinterment Records, 1754-1947, accessed through ancestry.com

Deacon Joseph Hall was from Bradford. He was deacon of the church at Concord for 40 years. Deborah is reported to have died after she lost her way while walking to pick berries, and then fell causing injuries that led to her death at the age of 97.[151]

Deborah Abbott and Joseph Hall had five children born at Concord.

    i   JOSEPH HALL, b. 17 Jul 1737; d. 10 Jun 1807; Joseph was a deacon and does not seem to have married or had children. His will leaves several bequests to what seem to be nieces and nephews (Wilkins and Thorndike who may be his sister Mary's children or grandchildren), a bequest to a local doctor, and he left his plot of land to the town of Concord.

    ii   SARAH HALL, b. 20 Sep 1738; d. 21 Oct 1746.

    iii   HANNAH HALL, b. 24 Nov 1740; d. 21 Oct 1746.

224)   iv   MARY HALL, b. 17 Mar 1743; d. 12 Dec 1773; m. THOMAS WILSON who d. at Concord 23 May 1818. After Mary's death, Thomas married Mary Hopkins Bancroft.

    v   JEREMIAH HALL, b. 6 Jan 1746; d. 6 Oct 1770; m., 1769, ESTHER WHITTEMORE, b. 2 Aug 1752 daughter of Aaron and Abigail (Coffin) Whittemore; Esther d. 12 Jul 1803. Esther m. 2nd, Joseph Woodman.

---

[151] Bouton, *The History of Concord*

48) GEORGE ABBOTT (*Thomas²*, *George¹*), b. 7 Nov 1706 son of Thomas and Hannah (Gray) Abbott; d. at Concord, NH 6 Oct 1785; m. 1 Feb 1737, SARAH ABBOTT (*Samuel³*, *John²*, *George¹*) (who was his first cousin, once removed), b. Oct 1711 daughter of Samuel and Sarah (Stevens) Abbott and granddaughter of John and Sarah (Barker) Abbott; Sarah d. at Concord 14 Jun 1769.

George Abbott settled in Concord around 1732. He served as deacon of the church for 41 years.

In his will dated 28 February 1774, George made the following bequests: beloved son Daniel has already received his inheritance; to beloved son George, he orders that the executor provide him with a comfortable maintenance as long as he is single; beloved son Stephen receives 20 acres of land; beloved son Ezra receives a land bequest; and beloved son Joseph is named executor and also receives a parcel of land. The wording of the will suggests that son George may have had some type of disability. The inventory of his estate included real estate in Concord and Warner.[152]

George and Sarah had nine children born at Concord.

225) i DANIEL ABBOTT, b. 7 Aug 1738; d. 11 Jun 1804; m. 1st by 1761, his second cousin RACHEL ABBOTT, b. 7 Apr 1743 daughter of Nathaniel and Penelope (Ballard) Abbott; Rachel d. 13 Jun 1788. Daniel m. 2nd 1 Jan 1789 at Boscawen, MERCY KILBURN whose origins are not fully verified; she was born about 1760 based on the birth of her last child in 1799; she was living in 1830 when she was listed as a head of household in the 1830 US Census of Concord (between age 60-70).

---

[152] *New Hampshire Wills and Probate Records 1643-1982,* Probate of George Abbott, Rockingham, 16 Oct 1785, Case number 5147.

Generation Three 103

        ii   GEORGE ABBOTT, b. 9 Apr 1740; d. 17 Sep 1791; George did not marry.

226) iii   JOSEPH ABBOTT, b. 23 Oct 1741; d. at Concord, NH, 19 Jan 1832; m. 25 Apr 1765, PHEBE LOVEJOY, b. 20 Sep 1735 daughter of Henry and Phebe (Chandler) Lovejoy; Phebe d. 4 Jan 1789.

        iv   SAMUEL ABBOTT, b. 30 Mar 1743; d. 5 Nov 1761 at Crown Point during the French and Indian War.

        v   STEPHEN ABBOTT, b. 10 Dec 1744; d. 10 Oct 1746.

227) vi   STEPHEN ABBOTT, 28 Oct 1746; d. 12 May 1811; m. 11 Apr 1778, MARY GILE, b. about 1755 (parentage not verified at this point); Mary d. Jan 1822.

        vii   NATHAN ABBOTT, b. 16 Nov 1748; d. 7 Mar 1749

        viii NATHAN ABBOTT; b. 3 Jul 1752; d. 15 Nov 1758.

228) ix   EZRA ABBOTT, b. 22 Aug 1756; d. 21 Feb 1837; m. 1st 21 Nov 1782, BETTY ANDREWS, b. 12 May 1762 daughter of Thomas and Mary (Burnham) Andrews; Betty d. 25 Aug 1794. Ezra m. 2nd 10 May 1795, ANNER CHOATE, b. at Ipswich 12 Jan 1758 daughter of Thomas and Dorothy (Proctor) Choate; Anner d. 21 Mar 1798. Ezra m. 3rd 15 Nov 1798, JANE JACKMAN, b. at Boscawen, 20 Dec 1767 daughter of Benjamin and Jane (-) Jackman; Jane d. 2 May 1847.

49)   BENJAMIN ABBOTT (*Thomas², George¹*), b. 31 Mar 1710 son of Thomas and Hannah (Gray) Abbott; d. at Concord, NH 8 Mar 1794; m. 23 Jun 1742, HANNAH ABBOTT (*Samuel³, John², George¹*) (who was his first cousin once removed), b. 30 Jul 1716 daughter of

Samuel and Sarah (Stevens) Abbott and granddaughter of John and Sarah (Barker) Abbott; Hannah d. at Concord 27 Jul 1786.

Benjamin was also an early settler of Concord. He was renowned for his physical prowess, including a report that he hoed four acres of corn in one day when he was over the age of 80.[153]

The will of Benjamin Abbott has bequests for the following persons (although one whole page of the will appears to be missing): son Benjamin, son Isaac, and daughter Hannah. Son Isaac is named executor.[154]

Benjamin and Hannah had eight children, all born at Concord.

229)   i   HANNAH ABBOTT, b. 22 Jan 1743; d. 22 Oct 1820; m. at Hopkinton, 25 Sep 1783, JEREMIAH STORY, JR. (origins not fully verified, but perhaps the Jeremiah Story of Ipswich); d. about 1806 based on the date of probate of his estate May 1806 with widow Hannah Story as administrator.

        ii   ISAAC ABBOTT, b. 7 Feb 1745; d. 24 Nov 1746.

        iii   ISAAC ABBOTT, b. 30 Aug 1747; d. 4 Mar 1799; m. at Ipswich, 28 Feb 1771, LUCY BURNHAM of Ipswich, b. about 1738 (as reported on death record); d. 3 Sep 1826. Isaac and Lucy do not seem to have had any children. The estate of Isaac Abbott entered probate 12 March 1799 in Rockingham County, New Hampshire. Isaac did not leave a will. Lucy Abbott declined administration of the estate and requested that Isaac's brother Benjamin take on that duty. The estate had a value of $745.

---

[153] Bouton, *The History of Concord*
[154] *New Hampshire Wills and Probate Records 1643-1982,* Probate of Benjamin Abbott, Rockingham, 1 Apr 1794, Case number 5986.

Generation Three

230) iv BENJAMIN ABBOTT, b. 10 Feb 1750; d. 11 Dec 1815; m. 29 Jan 1778, SARAH BROWN, b. 1758 at Brunswick, ME; Sarah d. 27 Sep 1801. Benjamin m. 2nd, 17 Jun 1805, HANNAH GREENLEAF who was still living at the time of Benjamin's death.

v EPHRAIM ABBOTT, b. 15 Jun 1752; d. 30 Oct 1778; Ephraim did not marry. He was wounded at the Battle of Bennington.

vi THOMAS ABBOTT, b. 7 Oct 1754; d. 2 Sep 1773.

vii THEODORE ABBOTT; b. 7 Mar 1759; d. 22 Sep 1778.

viii SARAH ABBOTT; b. 20 Feb 1761; d. 4 Jul 1761.

Section IX: The Children of Nathaniel Abbott and Dorcas Hibbert

50) MARY ABBOTT (*Nathaniel²*, *George¹*), b. 28 Jan 1697/8 daughter of Nathaniel and Dorcas (Hibbert) Abbott; d.?; m. 29 Dec 1718, BENJAMIN BLANCHARD, b. 14 Feb 1693 son of Jonathan and Anne (Lovejoy) Blanchard; Benjamin d. likely in NH.

Benjamin and Mary had twelve children whose births are recorded at Andover. Their family fell victim to an epidemic of throat distemper in 1739. The family relocated to Hollis, New Hampshire where Benjamin was elected "fence viewer" at the first town meeting in 1746.[155] The family lived in West Parish of the District of Dunstable.

- 231) i MARY BLANCHARD, b. 6 Dec 1719; m. at Andover, 11 Jan 1742/3, EDWARD TAYLOR. The family resided in Hollis, NH.

- 232) ii BENJAMIN BLANCHARD, b. 19 Mar 1720/1; d. 7 Mar 1791 at Canterbury, NH; m. at Hollis, 27 Dec 1744, KEZIAH HASTINGS, b. at Lexington, 7 Jul 1723 daughter of Thomas and Sarah (White) Hastings.

- 233) iii ANNE BLANCHARD, b. 22 Nov 1722; d. at Hollis, before 1758 (when her second husband remarried); m. 26 Feb 1743, JONATHAN DANFORTH, b. at Billerica, 1 Nov 1714 son of Jonathan and Elizabeth (Manning) Danforth; Jonathan d. 1747 at Hollis, NH. Anne m. 2nd, STEPHEN MARTIN. After Anne's death, Stephen m. 21 Mar 1759, Patience Pope.

---

[155] Worcester, *History of the Town of Hollis*

234) iv   JACOB BLANCHARD, b. 11 May 1724; d. at Groton, 26 Apr 1770; m 1745, REBECCA LAWRENCE, b. at Groton, 17 Apr 1724 daughter of Nathaniel and Anne (Scripture) Lawrence. Rebecca m. 2nd, 1772 John Sheple who died in 1785; it is not known what became of Rebecca after that. She was living in 1786 at the time of the settlement of John Sheple's estate.

235) v   JOSHUA BLANCHARD, b. 29 Mar 1726; d. 10 Oct 1818 at Wilton, NH; m. 23 Dec 1747, SARAH BURGE, b. 30 May 1728 daughter of John and Sarah (Taylor) Burge.

vi   JONATHAN BLANCHARD, b. 7 Feb 1727/8; d. 16 Oct 1739.

vii   DORCAS BLANCHARD, b. 28 Mar 1730; d. 13 Oct 1739.

viii   DAVID BLANCHARD. B. 14 Feb 1731/2; d. 19 Oct 1739.

ix   ELIZABETH BLANCHARD, b. 17 May 1734; no further record.

x   ABIEL BLANCHARD, b. 25 Sep 1737; d. 15 Oct 1739.

xi   DAVID BLANCHARD, b. 19 Feb 1739/40; d. 10 Apr 1740.

xii   ABIEL BLANCHARD, b. 20 Oct 1741; d. 28 Jan 1742/3.

51)   NATHANIEL ABBOTT (*Nathaniel²*, *George¹*), b. 9 Jun 1700 son of Nathaniel and Dorcas (Hibbert) Abbott; d. at Concord, NH

1770;[156] m. 23 Nov 1726, PENELOPE BALLARD, b. 1705 daughter of Joseph and Rebecca (Johnson) Ballard; Penelope d. at Concord, date unknown (there is a death record transcription that gives the place of death, but not the date).

Nathaniel and Penelope married in Andover and had their first two children there. The family then headed up to Concord, New Hampshire as first settlers in that new development. Nathaniel Abbott was prominent in the early history of Concord serving multiple official functions.[157]

No will or probate record was located for Nathaniel. The births of the oldest two children are recorded in Andover and the youngest ten children are recorded in Concord.

236) i NATHANIEL ABBOTT, b. 10 Mar 1726/7; d. at Concord 4 Feb 1806; m. by 1749, MIRIAM CHANDLER, b. at Amesbury 24 Nov 1728 daughter of Nathaniel and Susannah (Rowel) Chandler; Miriam d. at Concord Jan 1811.

237) ii DORCAS ABBOTT, b. 11 Nov 1728; d. probably at Concord date unknown; m. by 1749, MOSES MERRILL, b. at Haverhill 27 Sep 1727 son of John and Lydia (Haynes) Merrill; Moses d. 1767.

238) iii REBECCA ABBOTT, b. 27 May 1731; d. after 1799 at Thetford, VT date unknown; m. 1st by 1750 JOHN MERRILL, b. at Haverhill 25 Nov 1725 son of John and Lydia (Haynes) Merrill; John d. at Bow, NH 1760. Rebecca m. 2nd JACOB DOYNE, b. about 1729;

---

[156] New Hampshire Death and Disinterment Records, 1754-1947
[157] Bouton's *History of Concord* is relied on heavily for information about this family. When records have been located, they coincide exactly with the information provided in the Bouton text.

Generation Three 109

d. 1799 at Pembroke where his will was probated May 1799 with his widow Rebecca as administrator.

239) iv ELIZABETH ABBOTT, b. 1 Jul 1733; d. at Concord 25 Jan 1834; m. by 1755, JOSEPH HAZELTINE, b. at Rumford 27 Dec 1731 son of Richard and Sarah (Barnes) Hazeltine; Richard d. 30 May 1798.

240) v MARY ABBOTT, b. 7 Mar 1735; d. Mar 1795; m. JOSEPH WALKER,[158] b. at Concord, 24 Apr 1732 son of Isaac and Sarah (Breed) Walker; Joseph d. about 1800 at Fryeburg, ME.

241) vi HANNAH ABBOTT, b. 7 Mar 1736; d. after 1792 when dower rights were set off to her; m. EPHRAIM MOAR whose origin is not yet established. Ephraim d. at Bow, NH about 1791 when his estate was probated. This record includes documents related to the dower of Hannah Moor.

242) vii RUTH ABBOTT, b. 28 Jan 1738; d. 27 Feb 1817; m. by 1759, JAMES A. WALKER, b. at Concord 2 Sep 1739 son of Isaac and Sarah (Breed) Walker; James d. 9 Feb 1821.

243) viii JOSHUA ABBOTT, b. 24 Feb 1740; d. Mar 1815; m. at Bradford 23 Oct 1766, ELIZA CHANDLER, b. at Bradford 20 Jul 1739 daughter of Josiah and Sara (Parker widow) Chandler; Eliza d. 27 May 1812.

225) ix RACHEL ABBOTT, b. 7 Apr 1743; d. 13 Jun 1788; m. by 1761 as his 1st wife, her second cousin DANIEL ABBOTT, b. 7 Aug 1738 son of George and Sarah

---

[158] E. W. Foster and Philip Walker, "The Walkers of Woburn," *Massachusetts, Historical Bulletin, volumes 6-9*, pp 64-65

(Abbott) Abbott. Daniel m. 2nd MERCY KILBURN; Daniel d. 11 Jun 1804.

244) x JEREMIAH ABBOTT, b. 17 Mar 1744; d. at Conway, NH 8 Nov 1823; m. ELIZABETH STICKNEY, b. at Rumford 7 Dec 1753 daughter of Thomas and Anna (Osgood) Stickney; Elizabeth d. about 1836.

245) xi DOROTHY ABBOTT, b. 28 Dec 1746; d. 27 Sep 1776; m. 29 May 1766, DAVID GEORGE, b. at Haverhill, 27 Oct 1745 son of David and Anne (Cottle) George; David d. about 1816 (date of probate) at Littleton, NH. David m. 2nd, Hannah Colby.

246) xii SARAH ABBOTT, b. 3 Dec 1748 daughter of Nathaniel and Penelope (Ballard) Abbott; d. Jun 1842; m. 1 Dec 1764, SAMUEL FARNUM, b. at Concord, 10 Feb 1743 son of Zebadiah and Mary (Walker) Farnum.

52) SARAH ABBOTT (*Nathaniel², George¹*), b. about 1702 daughter of Nathaniel and Dorcas (Hibbert) Abbott; d. 11 Nov 1757; m. 4 Apr 1722, JOSEPH BLANCHARD, b. 19 Feb 1701 son of Thomas and Rose (Holmes) Blanchard. Joseph m. 2nd, 17 May 1758, the widow Mary Frost.

Sarah Abbott and Joseph Blanchard had eight children whose births are recorded at Andover. After the death of Sarah, Joseph married the widow Mary Frost and left Andover. He was for a time in Tewksbury and in 1772 he was in Wilmington.[159]

    i   SARAH BLANCHARD, b. 25 Jul 1723; d. 15 Apr 1729.

---

[159] Charlotte Helen Abbott, Early Records of the Blanchard Family of Andover

Generation Three 111

	ii	ELIZABETH BLANCHARD, b. 17 Jul 1726; d. 29 Mar 1728.
247)	iii	HANNAH BLANCHARD, b. 8 Oct 1728; d. likely at Hillsborough, NH; m. 19 May 1748, her third cousin, STEPHEN BLANCHARD, b. 9 Aug 1726 son of Stephen and Deborah (Phelps) Blanchard. Stephen had a second marriage to Elizabeth whose identity is not known; Stephen d. at Hillsborough about 1802 (will written 4 Mar 1796 and probate 1802).
248)	iv	JOSEPH BLANCHARD, b. 9 Feb 1730/1; d. 22 Mar 1776; m. 27 Feb 1753, his third cousin, DINAH BLANCHARD, b. 28 Dec 1731 daughter of Stephen and Deborah (Phelps) Blanchard. Dinah m. 2nd, as his second wife, REUBEN ABBOTT son of James and Abigail (Farnum) Abbott; Dinah d. 11 Mar 1826.
249)	v	JEREMIAH BLANCHARD, b. Jun 1733; d. at Weston, VT, 29 Jan 1826; m. 1st, 17 May 1759, DOROTHY SMITH who d. about 1770. Jeremiah m. 2nd, Aug 1772, SUSANNA MARTIN, b. 6 Apr 1743 daughter of John and Hannah (-) Martin.
250)	vi	DANIEL BLANCHARD, b. 15 Jul 1735; d. 19 Mar 1776; m. 29 Sep 1757, JERUSHA EATON, b. 19 Sep 1737 daughter of Silas and Jerusha (Gould) Eaton.
251)	vii	JOHN BLANCHARD, b. 19 Jul 1737; d. at Concord, NH, 10 Feb 1823; m. 5 Feb 1761, ELEANOR STEVENS, b. 1739 daughter of Samuel and Phebe (Bodwell) Stevens.
	viii	PHEBE BLANCHARD, b. 3 Nov 1741; d. 29 Sep 1749.

Children of Nathaniel Abbott and Dorcas Hibbert

53) JOSEPH ABBOTT (*Nathaniel²*, *George¹*), b. 22 Jan 1704/5 son of Nathaniel and Dorcas (Hibbert) Abbott; d. 23 Aug 1787 at Wilton, NH[160]; m. 12 Aug 1731, DEBORAH BLANCHARD, b. 18 Apr 1712 daughter of Thomas and Rose (Holmes) Blanchard; Deborah d. at Andover 21 Jul 1773.

Joseph Abbott was a farmer and lived on his father's homestead.[161] Joseph and his wife Deborah Blanchard had fourteen children born in Andover. Of their fourteen children, eight of them died in early childhood. A few years after Deborah's death in 1773, Joseph relocated to Wilton, New Hampshire. He served as a deacon. A probate record was not located.

   i DEBORAH ABBOTT, b. 17 Sep 1732; d. 9 Jul 1736.

   ii JOSHUA ABBOTT, b. 21 Jan 1733/4; d. 31 Dec 1736.

252) iii BATHSHEBA ABBOTT, b. 16 Sep 1735; d. 8 Dec 1784; m. 2 Jul 1752, NATHAN BLANCHARD, b. 30 Mar 1730 son of Stephen and Deborah (Phelps) Blanchard; Nathan d. before 1784 probably at Wilton, NH (Bathsheba was listed as a widow on her death record.

   iv NATHANIEL ABBOTT, b. 12 Aug 1737; d. 5 Apr 1740.

   v JOSHUA ABBOTT, b. 27 Apr 1739; d. 15 Oct 1739.

   vi DEBORAH ABBOTT, b. 15 Jul 1740; d. 22 Nov 1745.

   vii JOSEPH ABBOTT, b. 16 Jul 1740; d. 14 Sep 1741.

253) viii HANNAH ABBOTT, b. 15 Jun 1742; d. about 1770 at Wilton, NH (about this time her husband remarried);

---

[160] Grave is in the Vale End Cemetery, Wilton, NH and bears the following inscription: "Erected in memory of Deacon Joseph Abbot who Departed this life August ye 23erd 1787 in the 83rd year of his age." Findagrave.com

[161] Abbot Genealogy, p 128

m. 15 Jan 1761, TIMOTHY DALE, b. at Danvers, 9 May 1733 son of John and Abigail (Putnam) Dale. Timothy m. 2nd Rebeckah (-); date of death of Timothy is not known.

254) ix JOSEPH ABBOTT, b. 2 Apr 1744; d. at Wilton, NH about 1792; m. about 1763 MARY BARKER whose parentage is uncertain.

255) x JACOB ABBOTT, b. 9 Feb 1745/6; d. 5 Mar 1820 at Brunswick, ME; m. 1 Dec 1767, LYDIA STEVENS, b. 3 May 1745 daughter of John and Lydia (Gray) Stevens; Lydia d. Jun 1821.

xi DORCAS ABBOTT, b. 19 Jan 1747/8; d. 17 Oct 1749.

xii ODEDIAH ABBOTT, b. 23 Nov 1749; d. 8 Feb 1750.

256) xiii NATHANIEL ABBOTT, b. 27 Oct 1751; d. Mar 1791 at Wilton, NH; m. 31 Aug 1773, SARAH STEVENS.

257) xiv REBECCA ABBOTT, b. 19 Jun 1754; d. 19 Apr 1795 at Wilton, NH; m. 6 Apr 1775, DANIEL BATCHELDER, b. 2 Oct 1751 son of Joseph and Judith (Rea) Batchelder. Daniel m. 2nd Mrs. Sarah Kidder; Daniel d. 17 May 1832.

54) TABITHA ABBOTT (*Nathaniel^2, George^1*), b. abt. 1707 daughter of Nathaniel and Dorcas (Hibbert) Abbott; d. at Concord, NH date unknown but before her husband's will in 1775; m. 5 Jan 1726/6, her first cousin once removed, JOHN CHANDLER (*John Chandler^3, Hannah Abbott Chandler^2, George^1*), b. May 1702 son of John and Hannah (Frye) Chandler; John d. at Concord 26 Jul 1775.

The will of John Chandler has the following bequests: grandsons Timothy and Abiel who are the sons of his son Timothy, his two granddaughters Tabitha and Elizabeth who are the daughters of son Timothy, son Daniel Chandler, son Joshua Chandler, and son John Chandler.

There are six children recorded to this couple, the eldest two born in Andover and the youngest four in Rumford, New Hampshire.

	i	HANNAH CHANDLER, b. 10 Jul 1728; d. 4 Aug 1728.
258)	ii	JOHN CHANDLER, b. 15 Aug 1730; d. at Concord, 1 Mar 1807; m. Oct 1751, MARY CARTER, b. 1729 (based on age at time of death) whose parents are unknown; Mary d. 9 Jun 1793.
259)	iii	TIMOTHY CHANDLER, b. 15 Aug 1733; d. 24 Mar 1770; m. by 1760, ELIZABETH COPP, b. at Amesbury, 5 Apr 1740 daughter of Solomon and Elizabeth (Davis) Copp; Elizabeth d. at Concord, 20 Mar 1830. Elizabeth m. 2nd, Feb 1774, STEPHEN WARD.
260)	iv	DANIEL CHANDLER, b. 15 Feb 1735; d. at Concord, 25 Oct 1795; m. 1st, about 1755, SARAH EASTMAN, b. 14 Jul 1737 daughter of Ebenezer and Eleanor (-) Eastman; Sarah died by 1757 (after the birth of her only child). Daniel m. 2nd, by 1759, SARAH MERRILL, b. 24 Apr 1741 daughter of John and Lydia (Haynes) Merrill; Sarah d. at Chatham, NH, 1810.
261)	v	JOSHUA CHANDLER, b. 9 Jun 1740; d. 3 Dec 1816; m. 1768, IRENE COPP, b. at Amesbury, 17 May 1745 daughter of Solomon and Elizabeth (Davis) Copp; Irene d. 7 Dec 1810.

vi HANNAH CHANDLER, b. 3 Sep 1744; d. before 1775 (father's will); m. JACOB? WORTHEN and AUSTIN? There is no confirmed information on Hannah other than the birth record which lists John Chandler and Tabitha Abbott as her parents. Both the Chandler genealogy book and the Abbot genealogy book suggest these spouses (Worthen and Austin), but no record has been located. As Hannah is not mentioned in her father's will, and no heirs of hers are mentioned, it seems she died before 1775 and likely had no children that lived until 1775.

55) JEREMIAH ABBOTT (*Nathaniel², George¹*), b. 4 Nov 1709 son of Nathaniel and Dorcas (Hibbert) Abbott; d. at Billerica 28 Aug 1748; m. 2 Jan 1734/5, HANNAH BALLARD, b. 27 Jun 1714 daughter of Hezekiah and Rebecca (Davis) Ballard. Hannah m. 2nd WILLIAM STICKNEY; Hannah d. 11 Feb 1789 at Billerica.

William Stickney who married the widow Hannah Abbott is one of the persons assigned to take the inventory of Jeremiah Abbott's estate. Hannah is the administrator. Jeremiah did not leave a will. There is a guardianship case for the children in 1749 at the time of Hannah's remarriage. Daughter Hannah at age 15 selected Joshua Davis of Billerica as her guardian. Rebecca, William, and Jeremiah also have Joshua Davis as guardian.

Jeremiah and Hannah had six children, all born at Billerica.

262) i   HANNAH ABBOTT, b. 10 Oct 1735; d. 13 Sep 1819; m. 3 Jul 1766, OLIVER FARMER, b. 31 Jul 1728 son of Oliver and Abigail (Johnson) Farmer; Oliver d. 24 Sep 1814.

       ii JEREMIAH ABBOTT, b. 24 Aug 1738; d. 12 Apr 1740.

263) iii REBECCA ABBOTT, b. 13 Jul 1741, m. 29 Oct 1761, RICHARD BOYNTON, b. at Tewksbury, 22 Mar 1741 son of Richard and Jerusha (Hutchins) Boynton.

iv JEREMIAH ABBOTT, b. 20 Jul 1745; d. 7 Aug 1745.

264) v WILLIAM ABBOTT, b. 21 Jul 1746; d. after 1800 at Wheelock, VT; m. 28 Dec 1769, BRIDGET SPAULDING, b. 11 Mar 1748/9 daughter of David and Phebe (-) Spaulding; Bridget's death is not known but likely in Vermont about 1795. William married second, Mehitable Scott (according to the Abbot genealogy book).[162]

265) vi JEREMIAH ABBOTT, b. 11 Aug 1748; d. ; m. 19 Jan 1769, SUSANNAH BALDWIN, b. 1746 (probably the daughter of Josiah Baldwin of Tewksbury); Susanna d. 9 Apr 1825.

56) ELIZABETH ABBOTT (*Nathaniel²*, *George¹*), b. 1 Feb 1713 daughter of Nathaniel and Dorcas (Hibbert) Abbott; d. 25 Jul 1799; m. 26 May 1741, TIMOTHY MOOAR, b. 16 Jun 1713 son of Timothy and Anne (Blanchard) Mooar; Timothy d. 20 Jan 1787.

Timothy Mooar did not leave a will. His widow Elizabeth requested that Nehemiah Abbot be named administrator. The debts of the estate exceeded the value of the estate.[163]

There are birth records for five children, all born at Andover.

i TIMOTHY MOOAR, b. 14 Feb 1742; d. 9 Sep 1817; Timothy did not marry.

---

[162] Abbot and Abbot, *Genealogical Record of Descendants*
[163] *Essex County, MA: Probate File Papers, 1638-1881. Probate of* Timothy Mooar, 8 May 1787, *Case number 18696.*

Generation Three

266) ii JOHN MOOAR, b. Jun 1745; d. 1777 at Saratoga, NY during the Revolution; m. 28 Jul 1774, MARY BALLARD, b. 1754 daughter of William and Hannah (Howe) Ballard. Mary m. 2nd 13 Dec 1781, JONATHAN BOYNTON; Mary d. by 1795 when probate petition filed related to John Mooar's estate requesting administration of her widow's portion which reverted to creditors as she is deceased.

267) iii ELIZABETH MOOAR, b. 8 Mar 1747/8; d. 16 Mar 1818; m. 29 Jul 1766, MOSES BAILEY, b. at Bradford, 16 Jan 1743/4 son of Nathan and Mary (Palmer) Bailey; Moses d. 14 Mar 1842. Moses Bailey was the proprietor of what is now known as the Moses Bailey Abbott homestead at 72 Brundrett Avenue in Andover.[164]

268) iv JOSHUA MOOAR, b. 3 Jun 1751; d. at Milford, NH, 10 Sep 1824; m. 17 Sep 1776, DEBORAH CHANDLER, b. 26 Apr 1757 daughter of Zebadiah and Deborah (Blanchard) Chandler; Deborah was still living in 1822 when Joshua wrote his will.

269) v MARY MOOAR, b. 26 May 1760; b. 2 Aug 1820; m. 30 Jul 1778, WILLIAM HARRIS whose origins are not pinned down; his death is unknown but was before Mary died in 1820.

57) REBECCA ABBOTT (*Nathaniel²*, *George¹*), b. 24 Apr 1717 daughter of Nathaniel and Dorcas (Hibbert) Abbott; d. 13 Feb 1803 at Concord, NH; m. 18 Mar 1741/2, ABIEL CHANDLER *(John*

---

[164] Andover Historic Preservation, retrieved from https://preservation.mhl.org/72-brundrett-avenue

Chandler³, Hannah Abbott Chandler², George¹), b. 14 Mar 1717 son of John and Hannah (Frye) Chandler; Abiel d. abt. 1752 at Concord. Rebecca m. 2nd by 1754, AMOS ABBOTT *(James³, William², George¹)*, b. 18 Feb 1725/6 son of James and Abigail (Farnum) Abbott; Amos d. at Concord 3 Dec 1821.

Abiel Chandler and Rebecca Abbott had four children, the first recorded at Andover and the youngest three in Rumford/Concord, New Hampshire.

	i	ABIEL CHANDLER, b. 27 Jun 1742; died young.
270)	ii	ABIEL CHANDLER, b. 11 May 1744; d. 27 Aug 1776 at Long Island, NY during the Revolutionary War; m. about 1766, JUDITH WALKER, b. at Rumford, 21 Dec 1744 daughter of Timothy and Sarah (Burbeen) Walker. Judith m. 2nd Nathaniel Rolfe; Judith d. at Concord 1806.
	iii	PETER CHANDLER, b. 9 Oct 1747; d. 25 Jun 1776 while serving in the Army.
	iv	SARAH CHANDLER, b. about 1749; Sarah is included as a child in published genealogies, but there seem to be no records related to her.

Rebecca Abbott and Amos Abbott had three children.

271)	i	AMOS ABBOTT, b. 15 Jul 1754; d. at Concord 11 Oct 1834; m. JUDITH MORSE, b. at Newburyport, 1 Mar 1766 daughter of Moses and Sarah (Hale) Morse.
	ii	JOHN ABBOTT, b. 23 Jun 1756; d. 31 Aug 1779. John served in the Revolutionary War.
272)	iii	REBECCA ABBOTT, b. 26 Sep 1760; d. at Loudon, NH, 24 Dec 1846; m. 9 Oct 1781, MOSES

CHAMBERLAIN, b. at Hopkinton, 5 Oct 1757 son of Samuel and Martha (Mellen) Chamberlain; Moses d. 21 Oct 1811.

Section X: The Children of Elizabeth Abbott and Nathan Stevens

58) NATHAN STEVENS (*Elizabeth Abbott Stevens², George¹*), b. 22 Sep 1693 son of Nathan and Elizabeth (Abbott) Stevens; d. at Andover, 20 Sep 1741; m. 3 Nov 1715 HANNAH ROBINSON, b. 29 Jan 1694/5 daughter of Dane and Mary (Chadwick) Robinson; Hannah d.? (possible death is 1753 in Boxford).

The will of Nathan Stevens has bequests for the following persons: well-beloved wife Hannah, eldest son Nathan, he makes a provision for early payment of the portions of daughters Hannah and Elizabeth in case either of them marries before son Nathan is 21, eldest daughter Mary Stevens, son Benjamin, son Phineas, and youngest daughter Sarah Stevens.[165]

The births of ten children are recorded at Andover. There are no clear records for any of these children beyond their births. A marriage for one of the children has been reasonably established. There are also marriages for two other children suggested by Charlotte Helen Abbott and these are also noted. But all marriages for these children should be considered preliminary. It is likely that other children married, but that cannot be firmly established at this time.

Charlotte Helen Abbott thinks it is possible that Mary married Samuel Parker. She states that Elizabeth married Samuel Ames. I think it is reasonable that Hannah married Abner Tyler of Boxford. There are two reasons to propose this marriage for Hannah. There is a death record in Boxford for the widow Hannah Stevens in Boxford in 1753 at age 58 and this would be the right age for Hannah Robinson Stevens. If her daughter Hannah married a man in Boxford, that would explain the mother Hannah's presence there. Also, Abner Tyler is a signer of one of the receipts in the

---

[165] *Essex County, MA: Probate File Papers, 1638-1881. Probate of* Nathan Stevens, 26 Oct 1741, *Case number* 26409.

probate record of Nathan Stevens attesting that he has received the settlement from the estate. It is possible that Abner Tyler was simply a creditor of the estate, but I have concluded for the time being that he is the husband of Hannah Stevens. In addition, the oldest child of Hannah and Abner was named Nathan, the name of Hannah's father who died just the prior year. Some sources suggest that the Hannah who married Abner Tyler was the daughter of Benjamin Stevens and Hannah Farnum, but their daughter seems to have married Aaron Gage, as indicated by Hannah Stevens alias Gage receiving a disbursement from the estate of her father Benjamin Stevens.

273) i MARY STEVENS, b. Apr 1716; d.?; m. 3 May 1742, SAMUEL PARKER, b. at Bradford, 6 Oct 1716 son of Daniel and Anne (Morse) Parker; Samuel d. 4 Oct 1796.

ii RACHEL STEVENS, b. 6 Feb 1719/20; d. 1 May 1738.

274) iii HANNAH STEVENS, b. about 1721; d. at Brookfield, 17 Nov 1789; m. 11 Feb 1741/2, ABNER TYLER of Boxford, b. 15 Feb 1708/9 son of John and Anna (Messenger) Tyler; Abner d. 8 Dec 1777.

275) iv ELIZABETH STEVENS, b. 2 Jul 1722; d.?; m. 11 Jul 1744, SAMUEL AMES, b. 1719 son of Samuel and Abigail (Spofford) Ames.

v NATHAN STEVENS, b. 16 Mar 1723/4.

vi ABIGAIL STEVENS, b. 18 May 1726; d. 27 Oct 1736.

vii BENJAMIN STEVENS, b. 1 Apr 1729.

> viii PHINEAS STEVENS, b. 7 Mar 1730/1; there are no further records for Phineas beyond his mention in his father's will.
>
> ix SARAH STEVENS, b. 17 Jan 1733/4; d. 5 May 1738.
>
> x SARAH STEVENS, b. 1 Feb 1740/1.

59) ELIZABETH STEVENS (*Elizabeth Abbott Stevens², George¹*), b. 14 Oct 1697 daughter of Nathan and Elizabeth (Abbott) Stevens; d. at Windham, CT 28 Aug 1736; m. 24 Aug 1722, TIMOTHY PEARL, b. at Bradford 23 Feb 1695 son of John and Elizabeth (Holmes) Pearl. Timothy m. 2nd Mary Leach; Timothy d. at Windham 9 Oct 1773.

The will of Timothy Pearl has bequests to the following persons: "faithful well-beloved wife Mary," eldest son Timothy, son John, son Nathan, eldest daughter Elizabeth Hibbard, daughter Phebe Durkee, daughter Lydia Denison, son James Pearl, son Richard, daughter Mary Towbridge, son David, daughter Ruth Pearl, daughter Hannah Pearl, son Phineas, and son Philip.[166] Some of these heirs are Timothy's children from his second marriage to Mary Leach.

Elizabeth Stevens and Timothy Pearl had six children, all born at Windham.[167]

> 276) i TIMOTHY PEARL, b. 24 Oct 1723; d. at Willington, 19 Oct 1789; m. 6 Nov 1746, DINAH HOLT, b. at Windham, 17 Mar 1725/6 daughter of Joshua and Keturah (Holt) Holt; Dinah d. at Willington, 25 Sep 1806.

---

[166] *Connecticut Wills and Probate, 1609-1999*, Probate of Timothy Pearl, Hartford, 1773, Case number 2980.
[167] Lorraine Cook White, ed., *The Barbour Collection of Connecticut Town Vital Records. Vol. 1-55*. Baltimore, MD, USA: Genealogical Publishing Co., 1994-2002. (accessed through ancestry.com)

Generation Three 123

  ii JOHN PEARL, b. 20 Jan 1725/6; d.?; m. 17 Jun 1750, KETURAH HOLT, b. 22 Nov 1729 daughter of John and Keturah (Holt) Holt; Keturah d. at Willington, 1805. There do not seem to be any children for this couple. There is a probate record for Keturah from 1805. The distributions of the estate of Keturah Holt Pearl are to the following persons: sister Dinah Pearl; sister Phebe Goodale; and heirs of brother Joshua Holt who is deceased.

277) iii NATHAN PEARL, b. 22 Nov 1727; d.?; m. 7 Mar 1748, ELIZABETH UTLEY, b. 22 Apr 1729 daughter of James and Annah (-) Utley.

278) iv ELIZABETH PEARL, b. Jan 1729/30; d. ?; m. 24 May 1749, JOHN HIBBARD, b. 9 Dec 1727 son of John and Martha (Durkee) Hibbard; John d. at Royalton, VT, 31 Dec 1804.

279) v PHEBE PEARL, b. 12 May 1732; d. at Yarmouth, Nova Scotia, date unknown; m. 29 Nov 1750, PHINEAS DURKEE, b. 16 Sep 1730 son of Stephen and Lois (Moulton) Durkee; Phineas d. at Yarmouth, Nova Scotia, 5 Nov 1801.[168]

280) vi LYDIA PEARL, b. 31 Jul 1734; d. Sep 1819; m. 27 Nov 1753, DANIEL DENISON, b. 5 Sep 1730 son of Daniel and Hannah (Crocker) Denison; Daniel d. at Hampton, 4 Aug 1823.

60) HANNAH STEVENS (*Elizabeth Abbott Stevens², George¹*), b. 1701 daughter of Nathan and Elizabeth (Abbott) Stevens; d. after

---

[168] *Yarmouth, Nova Scotia, Genealogies* [database on-line]. (ancestry.com)

1782; m. 13 Jan 1720/1 as his 2nd wife, SAMUEL AMES, b. 6 Feb 1695/6 son of Robert and Bethia (Gatchell) Ames; Samuel d. at Groton 1784.

Samuel and Hannah moved several times during their marriage. They lived first in Andover, spent some time in Natick where son Nathan was born in 1729, were then in Andover again for the birth of the rest of their children, and finally settled in Groton. Samuel had one child, a son Samuel, from his first marriage to Abigail Spofford.

Samuel wrote his will 13 February 1782 and the estate went to probate 29 March 1784. The will is in poor condition, but it is possible to make out the names of the heirs. His wife is mentioned. The children named in the will are oldest son Samuel; "youngest son" Robert who receives the husbandry tools; the remaining sons Benjamin, Nathan, and Amos; and daughter Abigail Abbott. Abigail Abbott is clearly the only daughter.[169]

Samuel Ames and Hannah Stevens had seven children, all of them born or baptized in Andover except Nathan whose baptism is recorded at Natick.

    i   ABIGAIL AMES, b. about 1722; d. 27 Aug 1812; m. 12 Mar 1744/5, NATHAN ABBOTT, b. Apr 1719 son of Jonathan and Zerviah (Holt) Abbott; Nathan d. 28 Jun 1798. Nathan Abbott and Abigail Ames did not have any children. Nathan Abbott wrote his will 21 March 1776 and the estate entered probate 3 September 1798. Dearly beloved wife Abigail receives "all my household stuff proper for woman's use." She receives other provisions for her support and the use and improvements of one-third of the real property. He makes a bequest to his "cousin"

---

[169] *Middlesex County, MA: Probate File Papers, 1648-1871. Probate of* Samuel Ames, *1784, Case number* 400.

Nathan Abbott who is the son of his brother Job who is deceased. The nephew Nathan is named executor and has the remainder of the estate bequeathed to him.

ii HANNAH AMES, b. about 1722; death unknown but she is not in her father's will and there is not a marriage record.

281) iii BENJAMIN AMES, b. 6 Jun 1724; d. 10 Jan 1809; m. 1st 4 Dec 1746, his second cousin, HEPHZIBAH CHANDLER, b. 7 Apr 1726 daughter of Timothy and Hephzibah (Harnden) Chandler; Hephzibah d. 19 Jan 1768. Benjamin m. 2nd about 1770, his second cousin, once removed and George Abbott descendant, DORCAS LOVEJOY, b. 18 Aug 1749 daughter of Joshua and Lydea (Abbott) Lovejoy; Dorcas d. 25 Jun 1843.

282) iv NATHAN AMES, b. Apr 1729; d. at Groton 7 Mar 1791; m. 19 Apr 1763, DEBORAH BOWERS, b. at Groton, 2 Sep 1746 daughter of Samuel and Deborah (Farnsworth) Bowers; Deborah d. 8 Apr 1782.

283) v AMOS AMES, baptized 20 Jan 1733/4; d. 4 Aug 1817; m. 27 Oct 1757, ABIGAIL BUCKLEY, b. at Concord, 28 Oct 1733 daughter of John and Abigail (-) Buckley; Abigail d. 20 Aug 1809.[170]

284) vi ROBERT AMES, baptized 1737; d. ?; m. 1st 2 Dec 1762, SARAH WOODS, b. 19 Aug 1742 daughter of Isaac and Abigail (Stevens) Woods; Sarah d. 23 Nov

---

[170] Green, *Groton Historical Series*, volume 3, p 159. Abigail Ames the wife of Amos Ames departed this life August ye 20th day, age 77 years.

1774. Robert m. 2nd 29 Apr 1777, SUSANNA GREEN (widow of Abijah Warren), b. 20 Mar 1746 daughter of Isaac and Martha (Boyden) Green.

vii SIMEON AMES, b. 23 Jun 1741; d. 10 Dec 1760 of smallpox.

61) PHEBE STEVENS (*Elizabeth Abbott Stevens[2], George[1]*), b. 1704 daughter of Nathan and Elizabeth (Abbott) Stevens; date of death is unknown, although she is perhaps the Phebe Steel who is the head of household in the 1790 US Census for Andover; m. 7 Nov 1734, NICHOLAS STEEL whose origins are unknown.

The births of six children are recorded at Andover, but there are no death records in Massachusetts for either Phebe or Nicholas. Phebe Steel is listed in the 1790 US Census for Andover as the head of household which consists of two females[171], so it is assumed that Nicholas died before that time.

In her father's will, there is a bequest to the oldest daughter of Phebe who is named as "Eunos Ginnins" (or perhaps Germin, but it is not clear) in the will. Phebe's daughter is to receive ten pounds when she reaches age 21. This child is not from Phebe's marriage to Nicholas Steel and Phebe does not have a marriage prior to her marriage to her marriage to Nicholas as the marriage transcription lists her name as Phebe Stevens. One possibility is the Eunice is a child born out-of-wedlock. Phebe was about 30 years old when she married Nicholas, so it is certainly possible she had a child prior to this marriage. No other records associated with this daughter have been located. Search based on the last name as written in the will is difficult as the spelling of the last name is so uncertain. For the time being, the child mentioned in the will remains an interesting puzzle. One possibility is that "Eunos Ginnins" is the Eunice Jennings who

---

[171] Year: 1790; Census Place: Andover, Essex, Massachusetts; Series: M637; Roll: 4; Page: 20; Image: 35; Family History Library Film: 0568144. (ancestry.com)

married Francis Ingalls, Jr. who was the step-son of Phebe's sister Lydia. In her will, Lydia Stevens Ingalls leaves her entire estate to the family of Eunice and Francis Ingalls and three of their children. This will includes a bequest to "daughter Eunes" all the estate that is not otherwise disposed of. Although Lydia Stevens Ingalls had other living step-grandchildren, the only bequests are to Eunice and Francis and their children. Published genealogies give the parents of Eunice Jennings who married Francis Ingalls, Jr. as Joseph Jennings and Elizabeth Rolfe, but there is no birth record for Eunice (although there are records for all the other children of Joseph and Elizabeth).

285) i PHEBE STEEL, b. 27 Sep 1735; d. unknown but still living in 1783; m. 22 Nov 1776, as his second wife, JOHN ABBOTT (of the George Abbott of Rowley line), b. 10 Mar 1724/5 son of Uriah and Sarah (Mitchell) Abbott; John d. of smallpox 3 Jan 1779.

286) ii ELIZABETH STEEL, b. 21 Feb 1737; date of death not known but she appears to be the Elizabeth Ingalls in Andover in the 1810 US Census; m. 9 Sep 1760, JOSHUA INGALLS, b. 13 Aug 1732 son of Joseph and Phebe (Farnum) Ingalls; Joshua d. 1785, his will probated 5 Jul 1785.

287) iii RACHEL STEEL, b. 1 Jul 1739; death unknown; m. 11 Dec 1767, DUDLEY FOSTER, b. at Boxford, 21 Feb 1737/8 son of Zebadiah and Margaret (Tyler) Foster.

288) iv BENJAMIN STEEL, b. 25 Jan 1741; d. at Wilton, NH 14 Nov 1817; m. 16 Jun 1768, HANNAH LOVEJOY, b. 1748 (parentage uncertain); Hannah d. at Wilton, 31 Aug 1812.

Children of Elizabeth Abbott and Nathan Stevens

v   HANNAH STEEL, b. 17 Sep 1743; d. at Andover 23 Mar 1827; Hannah did not marry.

vi   LYDIA STEEL, b. 20 Nov 1745; d. 14 Feb 1747/8.

Generation Four

Section I: The Grandchildren of John Abbott and Sarah Barker

John³, John², George¹

62) JOHN ABBOT (*John³, John², George¹*), b. 3 Aug 1704 son of John and Elizabeth (Harnden) Abbot; d. 10 Nov 1793; m. 28 Sep 1732, PHEBE FISKE, b. at Boxford 4 Aug 1712 daughter of John and Abigail (Poore) Fiske; Phebe d. 7 Dec 1802.

In his will, Captain John Abbot has bequests to his loving wife Phebe who receives improvements of half the dwelling house and half the cellar plus other bequests of a money payment and other provisions needed for her maintenance (a lengthy and specific list), eldest and beloved son John receives all of the lands and buildings in Andover, beloved son Abiel receives a tract of land in Wilton, beloved son Jeremiah also receives land in Wilton, beloved son William receives land in Wilton, and beloved daughter Phebe receives one-half of the household goods and a token of £1 which supplements the £57 she received at the time of her marriage. The land bequests in Wilton total in the hundreds of acres.[172]

There are birth records for seven children, all born at Andover. Of the four children in this family that married, three of them married fellow George Abbott descendants.

   289)   i   PHEBE ABBOTT, b. 14 Apr 1733; d. 26 Jul 1812; m. 18 Apr 1754, her third cousin and George Abbott

---

[172] *Essex County, MA: Probate File Papers, 1638-1881. Probate of* John Abbot, 2 Jun 1794, *Case number* 73.

descendant, NATHAN CHANDLER, b. 19 Feb 1729/30 son of Nathan and Phebe (Holt) Chandler; Nathan d. 30 Apr 1786.

193) ii JOHN ABBOTT, b. 12 Sep 1735; d. 24 Apr 1818; m. 1 Jun 1758, his second cousin once removed, ABIGAIL ABBOTT, b. 13 Jan 1733/4 daughter of Benjamin and Abigail (Abbott) Abbott; Abigail d. 1 Feb 1807.

iii EZRA ABBOTT, b. 27 Sep 1737; d. 15 Sep 1760.

197) iv ABIEL ABBOT, b. 19 Apr 1741; d. at Wilton, NH, 19 Aug 1809; m. 20 Nov 1764, his second cousin once removed, DORCAS ABBOT, b. 1 Aug 1744 daughter of Benjamin and Abigail (Abbott) Abbott; Dorcas d. 23 Feb 1829.

290) v JEREMIAH ABBOTT, b. 14 May 1743; d. 2 Nov 1825 at Wilton, NH; m. 16 Sep 1766, CLOE ABBOTT (from the George Abbott of Rowley line), b. 5 Nov 1737 daughter of Zebadiah and Anne (Lovejoy) Abbott; Cloe d. at Wilton 21 Aug 1809.

291) vi WILLIAM ABBOTT, b. 3 Jan 1747/8; d. at Wilton, NH 30 Nov 1793; m. 12 Nov 1772, his third cousin and George Abbott descendant, PHEBE BALLARD, b. 5 Nov 1752 daughter of Timothy and Hannah (Chandler) Ballard; Phebe d. at Wilton, Jan 1846.

vii BENJAMIN ABBOTT, b. 29 May 1751; d. 1 Aug 1751.

63) BARACHIAS ABBOT (*John³, John², George¹*), b. 14 May 1707 son of John and Elizabeth (Harnden) Abbot; d. 2 Oct 1784; m. 22 Mar 1733, HANNAH HOLT, b. 18 Dec 1709 daughter of Timothy and Rhoda (Chandler) Holt; Hannah d. 2 Aug 1775.

Barachias Abbot married Hannah Holt, his second cousin once removed. Hannah was the great-granddaughter of William Chandler and Annis Bayford.

The death record for Barachias lists his cause of death as cancer. A probate record has not been located for Barachias. There are birth records for eleven children all born at Andover.

        i   BARACHIAS ABBOTT, b. 16 Jan 1733/4; d. 24 Jun 1738.

292)   ii   MOSES ABBOTT, b. 9 Aug 1735; d. 23 Feb 1826; m. 31 Dec 1761, his third cousin, ELIZABETH HOLT, b. 8 Jun 1743 daughter of Henry and Rebecca (Gray) Holt; Elizabeth d. 23 Sep 1838.

293)   iii   HANNAH ABBOTT, b. 18 May 1737; d. Nov 1812 at Wilton, NH; m. 21 Apr 1756, her third cousin, JEREMIAH HOLT, b. 31 Mar 1734 son of John and Mary (Lewis) Holt; Jeremiah's death record not located, but after the 1790 US Census.

294)   iv   BARACHIAS ABBOT, b. 22 May 1739; d. 29 Jan 1812; m. 6 Dec 1770, his third cousin and George Abbott descendant, SARAH HOLT, b. 7 Mar 1746/7 daughter of James and Sarah (Abbott) Holt; Sarah d. 11 Feb 1808.

295)   v   ELIZABETH ABBOTT, b. 2 Nov 1740; d. 9 Sep 1780; m. 30 Aug 1759, her second cousin and George Abbott descendant, ZEBADIAH SHATTUCK, b. 26 Oct 1736 son of Joseph and Joanna (Chandler) Shattuck. Zebadiah m. 2nd 25 Dec 1781, Sarah Chandler (widow of Ralph Holbrook) and George Abbott descendant, b. 8 May 1751 daughter of

Zebadiah and Deborah (Blanchard) Chandler; Zebadiah d. 10 Mar 1826.

296) vi PRISCILLA ABBOTT, b. 13 Feb 1742/3; d. likely at Bethel, ME; m. 16 Nov 1762, ZELA HOLT, b. 29 Dec 1738 son of James and Mary (Chandler) Holt.

297) vii LYDIA ABBOTT, b. 7 Mar 1744/5; d. 11 Jul 1829; m. 15 Aug 1771, URIAH RUSSELL, b. 1743 son of Thomas and Abigail (Ballard) Russell; Uriah d. 9 Nov 1822.

viii RHODA ABBOTT, b. 23 Apr 1747; d. 11 Aug 1775; Rhoda did not marry.

ix TIMOTHY ABBOTT, b. 23 Apr 1747; d. 30 Mar 1772.

298) x PHEBE ABBOTT, b. 29 Aug 1749; d. 17 Apr 1809; m. 1 Feb 1774, JOHN RUSSELL, b. 1 Jul 1746 son of John and Hannah (Foster) Russell. John m. 2nd Mary Wilkins; John d. 12 Aug 1830.

299) xi ABIGAIL ABBOTT, b. 25 Jul 1751; d. at Greenfield, NH, 1841; m. 10 Oct 1786, as his second wife, JOHN JOHNSON, b. at Andover, 1748 *perhaps* the son of John and Lydia (Osgood) Johnson (gravestone gives his age as 85); d. at Greenfield, NH 3 Oct 1833. He was first married to Hannah Abbott daughter of John and Hannah (Farnum) Abbott who died in 1785 and then married Abigail.

64) ELIZABETH ABBOT (*John³, John², George¹*), b. 28 Oct 1711 daughter of John and Elizabeth (Harnden) Abbot; d. 4 Jul 1758; m. 26 Oct 1732, ASA FOSTER, b. 16 Jun 1710 son of William and Sarah (Kimball) Foster; Asa d. 17 Jul 1787. Asa m. 2nd, Lucy Wise the widow of Richard Rogers. Lucy Wise was born at Ipswich, Mar 1723.

There are records for nine children for Elizabeth and Asa, all born at Andover. Five sons and one daughter relocated to New Hampshire and most remained in Canterbury. One son, Benjamin, could not be reliably traced; the only record for him is a baptism in Andover. One child died in early infancy. A second daughter, Elizabeth, married and stayed in Andover where she died at age 31.

Captain Asa Foster served in the Revolutionary War. Asa Foster did not leave a will. His estate entered probate 7 August 1787. His widow Lucy Foster declined administration of the estate due to her ill health. Abiel Foster was named administrator.[173]

300) i ASA FOSTER, b. 29 Aug 1733; d. at Canterbury, NH 23 Sep 1814; m. 1st HANNAH SYMONDS, b. at Boxford, 5 Nov 1733 daughter of Joseph and Mary (-) Symonds; Hannah d. 29 Jun 1775. Asa m. 2nd 1776, HANNAH PETERS, b. at Andover 11 Dec 1730 daughter of Samuel and Mary (Robinson) Peters; Hannah Peters d. 11 Jan 1815.

301) ii ABIEL FOSTER, b. 8 Aug 1735; d. at Canterbury, NH 6 Feb 1806; m. 1st 15 May 1761, HANNAH BADGER, b. at Haverhill, 16 Nov 1742 daughter of Joseph and Hannah (Pearson) Badger; Hannah d. 10 Jan 1768. Abiel m. 2nd 11 Oct 1769, MARY ROGERS, b. 11 Nov 1745 daughter of Samuel and Hannah (Wise) Rogers; Mary d. 12 Mar 1813.

302) iii DANIEL FOSTER, b. 25 Sep 1737; d. at Canterbury 25 Jan 1833; m. 16 Dec 1760, HANNAH KITTREDGE,

---

[173] *Essex County, MA: Probate File Papers, 1638-1881. Probate of* Asa Foster, 7 Aug 1787, *Case number* 9812.

b. Aug 1742 daughter of Jacob and Hannah (French) Kittredge.

iv DAVID FOSTER, b. 7 May 1740; died in infancy.

303) v DAVID FOSTER, b. 24 Sep 1741; d. at Canterbury, 9 Dec 1810; m. 24 Nov 1768, SARAH FOSTER, b. about 1750 who parents are not yet determined; Sarah d. about 1830.[174]

304) vi ELIZABETH FOSTER, b. 14 Apr 1744; d. at Andover 24 Apr 1775; m. 3 Nov 1768, her third cousin and George Abbott descendant, (General) NATHANIEL LOVEJOY, b. 29 Apr 1744 son of Nathaniel and Elizabeth (Swan) Lovejoy; Nathaniel d. 5 Jul 1812.

vii BENJAMIN FOSTER; baptized 1747; no further certain record.

305) viii JONATHAN FOSTER, b. 28 Jul 1747; d. about 1818 at Canterbury, NH (will dated 5 Sep 1818); m. Nov 1770, LUCY ROGERS, b. 19 Oct 1748 daughter of Samuel and Hannah (Wise) Rogers; Lucy d. about 1830.

306) ix SARAH FOSTER, b. 15 Feb 1749/50; d. at Concord, NH, 7 Feb 1825; m. at Andover, 23 Dec 1773, TIMOTHY BRADLEY b. at Rumford, 30 Oct 1743 son of Timothy and Abijah (Stevens) Bradley; Timothy d. 31 Jul 1811 at Concord (will 27 May 1811).

65) JOSEPH ABBOT *(John³, John², George¹)*, b. 24 Apr 1719 son of John and Elizabeth (Harnden) Abbot; d. 30 Jan 1790 at Chester, MA; m. 12 Nov 1741 his first cousin, HANNAH ABBOTT *(Ebenezer³,*

---

[174] Lyford, *History of Canterbury*, p. 135

John², George¹), b. 29 Dec 1721 daughter of Ebenezer and Hannah (Turner) Abbott; Hannah d. 2 Jun 1805 at Chester.

After their marriage and the birth of their first child, Joseph and Hannah relocated to the western part of Massachusetts, first in Lancaster and finally in Chester. Their children all married spouses from that general area of the state, and most of the children settled in Chester.

Joseph and Hannah had nine children, the birth of the oldest child recorded at Andover and the remainder recorded at Lancaster.

307) i JOSEPH ABBOTT, b. 29 Mar 1742; d.?; m. at Lancaster, 22 Aug 1774,[175] HANNAH PITSON, b. at Boston, 28 Feb 1740 daughter of James and Rachel (Danforth) Pitson.

308) ii HANNAH ABBOTT, b. 23 Sep 1743; d. at Chester, 2 Mar 1802; m. 27 Sep 1774, as his second wife, JOHN NEWTON PARMENTER, b. at Boston, Sep 1742 son of Benjamin and Elizabeth (Bigelow) Parmenter; John d. 6 Dec 1828. John married Mrs. Dolly Blair 19 Feb 1806. John was first married to Lydia Baldwin.

309) iii ELIZABETH ABBOTT, b. 6 Jul 1746; d.?; m. 31 Jan 1779, JACOB FOWLE, b. at Lancaster, 14 Sep 1749 son of Jacob and Phebe (Osgood) Fowle. Elizabeth Abbott's first cousin once removed, Priscilla Abbott, was the second wife of Jacob Fowle the elder, father of Jacob.

310) iv ABIEL ABBOTT, b. about 1749; d. at Chester, 7 Dec 1831; m. 23 Jan 1783, SARAH MANN, b. 12 Nov 1764

---

[175] Nourse, *Register of Lancaster, Massachusetts*, p 135

311) v JOHN ABBOTT, b. 8 Oct 1751; d. 1798; m. 4 Feb 1775, LOIS BENNET, b. at Lancaster, 2 Sep 1757 daughter of Elisha and Lois (Wilder) Bennet. Lois seems to have remarried Aaron Bell 31 Jan 1811.

312) vi EBENEZER ABBOTT, b. 14 Oct 1753; d. ; m. 13 Dec 1781, ANNA WRIGHT, b. at Spencer, 23 Feb 1758 daughter of Edward and Tryphena (Hinds) Wright.

vii PHEBE ABBOTT, b. about 1756; there is no further record.

313) viii RELIEF ABBOTT, b. 11 May 1759; d. at Chester, 9 Feb 1817; m. 29 May 1784, JOHN WILLIAMS, b. at Middleborough, 23 Jan 1761 son of Larkin and Anna (Warren) Williams; John d. 28 Mar 1813.

314) ix DOROTHY ABBOTT, b. Dec 1762; d. 8 Mar 1848; m. 28 Dec 1784, ROBERT MOOR, *possibly* the Robert b. at Palmer, 1 May 1760 son of James and Elizabeth (Little) Moor, although there is also a Robert Moor born in Bolton son of John and Rhosanna who has been suggested; the family seems to have relocated to New York; Robert perhaps d. 26 Oct 1810 at Ulster County, New York.[176] It is possible that this family moved on from New York to perhaps Kentucky but that is not yet fully verified.

Joseph³, John², George¹

66) JOSEPH ABBOT *(Joseph³, John², George¹)*, b. 31 May 1724 son of Joseph and Hannah (Allen) Abbot; d. 10 Dec 1766; m. 9 Feb 1748/9

---

[176] Some of the vital records information is that used by the DAR.

Generation Four

ANNA PEABODY, b. at Boxford 21 Jul 1723 daughter of Jonathan and Alice (Pearl) Peabody; Anna d. 20 May 1766. Joseph married 2nd 1 Nov 1766, EDNA PLATTS, b. 15 Nov 1737 at Bradford; Joseph died just one month after his second marriage.

Joseph Abbott did not leave a will. The estate entered probate 3 February 1767. Edna Abbott, widow, requests that George Abbott be administrator. There are four minor children under the age of 14 and Henry Abbott, Jr. and John Abbott are suggested as guardians. Guardians are named for six children altogether including Anna and Sarah who are over 14. The guardianships are for daughter "Anner", Sarah, Dorcas, Lydia, Huldah, and Joseph.[177]

315) i ANNA ABBOTT, b. 15 Nov 1749; d. at NH perhaps in 1788 (when the estate of widow Anna Stevens was probated); m. 18 Aug 1774, her third cousin, THEODORE STEVENS, b. 20 May 1750 son of John and Mary (Phelps) Stevens.

316) ii SARAH ABBOTT, b. 14 Sep 1751; d. at Salem 19 Apr 1820; m. 1st 23 Mar 1775, BENJAMIN HERRICK, b. 6 Dec 1752 son of Edward and Mary (Kimball) Herrick; Edward d. by 1782 when his estate was probated. Sarah m. 2nd WILLIAM WHITTIER in 1789.

317) iii LYDIA ABBOTT, b. 23 Oct 1753; d. at Wilton, NH 20 Sep 1826; m. by 1775, SAMUEL LOVEJOY, b. 1750 son of William and Hannah (Evans) Lovejoy; Samuel d. 6 Oct 1801.

---

[177] *Essex County, MA: Probate File Papers, 1638-1881. Probate of* Joseph Abbot, 3 Feb 1767, *Case number* 87 and Case number 126 for the guardianships.

318) iv DORCAS ABBOTT, b. 26 Oct 1755; d. at Salem 19 Aug 1821; m. 12 Nov 1780, her fourth cousin, JOSEPH CHANDLER, b. 30 Jan 1753 son of John and Hannah (Phelps) Chandler; Joseph d. 27 Nov 1827.

319) v JOSEPH ABBOTT, b. 16 Feb 1758; d. at Andover, VT 3 May 1835;[178] m. 30 Dec 1784, LUCY KING, b. 18 May 1760 daughter of Richard and Lucy (Butterfield) King; Lucy d. at Andover, VT 2 Nov 1842.

320) vi HULDAH ABBOTT, b. 21 Oct 1760; d. 6 Apr 1830 at Roxbury, NH; m. by 1785, her third cousin and George Abbott descendant, JOSHUA ABBOTT, b. at Wilton, NH, 5 Nov 1765 son of Joseph and Mary (Barker) Abbott; Joshua d. 30 Nov 1798. Huldah m. 2nd Gideon Phillips.

Stephen³, John², George¹

67) EPHRAIM ABBOTT *(Stephen³, John², George¹)*, b. 1710 son of Stephen and Sarah (Stevens) Abbott; d. 14 Apr 1745; m. 14 Feb 1733/4 HANNAH PHELPS, b. 1709 (est. based on age at death) daughter of Samuel and Hannah (Dane) Phelps. Hannah m. 2nd John Chandler; Hannah d. 5 Aug 1781.

Ephraim Abbott did not leave a will. His estate entered probate 10 June 1745. Hannah Abbott and Stephen Abbott, Jr. serve as administrators. The available probate records include an inventory and then multiple receipts for payments made to creditors of the estate.[179]

Ephraim Abbott and Hannah Phelps had seven children born at Andover.

---

[178] Vermont, Vital Records, 1720-1908 (ancestry.com).
[179] *Essex County, MA: Probate File Papers, 1638-1881. Probate of* Ephraim Abbott, 10 Jun 1745, *Case number* 40.

Generation Four 139

      i   HANNAH ABBOTT, b. 26 Dec 1734; d. 17 Nov 1798; Hannah did not marry. Her grave has the following inscription: In memory of Miss HANNAH ABBOT, who died 17 Nov. 1798. Aged 64 years. *Death thou hast concord me, I by thy dart are slain, But Christ has concord thee, And I shall rise again.*[180]

321) ii   MEHITABLE ABBOTT, b. 11 Aug 1736; d. 1 Jan 1777; m. about 1762, her third cousin and George Abbott descendant, JONATHAN ABBOTT, b. at Lunenburg, 29 Aug 1740 son of Jonathan and Martha (Lovejoy) Abbott. Jonathan m. 2nd, another cousin, DORCAS ABBOTT, b. 23 Sep 1758 daughter of Stephen and Mary (Abbott) Abbott; Jonathan d. 26 Dec 1821.

      iii   SARAH ABBOTT, b. Nov 1737, d. 20 Mar 1831; Sarah did not marry. As reported in the Abbott genealogy, she lived with Judge Phillips and after his death took care of his farm and orchards.[181] She did leave a will in which she has bequests for her numerous nieces and nephews.

      iv   EPHRAIM ABBOTT, b. 22 Jun 1739; d. 3 Nov 1739.

322) v   RHODA ABBOTT, b. 22 Jun 1741; d. 12 Jan 1821 at Albany, ME; m. 22 Mar 1764, JACOB HOLT, b. 29 Mar 1739 son of Jacob and Mary (Osgood) Holt; Jacob d. 12 May 1816.

      vi   EPHRAIM ABBOTT, b. 8 May 1743; d. 23 Apr 1809; m. 1st 27 Aug 1774, LYDIA POOR, b. 18 Jul 1751

---

[180] The Essex Antiquarian, 1898, Andover Inscriptions, Old South Burying Ground.
[181] Abbot and Abbot, *Genealogical Record of Descendants*.

daughter of Timothy and Mary (Stevens) Poor; Lydia d. 3 Jul 1788. Ephraim m. 2nd 26 Aug 1789, SARAH who was the widow of Thomas Safford, and she was the widow Sarah Lasser when she married Thomas Safford. It is possible, but not yet determined, that her maiden name was Herrick and that her first husband was John Lacer. Ephraim does not seem to have had children. In his will, he left his entire estate to his wife Sarah.

323) vii ABIEL ABBOTT (f), b. 14 Apr 1745; d. May 1795; m. 1st, 4 Apr 1763, BENJAMIN WALKER, b. at Billerica 6 Aug 1741 son of Benjamin and Hannah (Frost) Walker. Benjamin was wounded at the Battle of Bunker Hill, taken prisoner, and died in prison at Boston Aug 1775. Abiel m. 2nd 23 Apr 1778, as his second wife, SAMUEL FITCH, b. 9 Nov 1736 son of Jeremiah and Elizabeth (-) Fitch; Samuel Fitch d. 21 Jul 1809.

48) SARAH ABBOTT *(Stephen^3, John^2, George^1)* and GEORGE ABBOTT *(Thomas^2, George^1)* (This is Family #48 in Generation Three.)

68) MARY ABBOTT *(Stephen^3, John^2, George^1)*, b. 4 Aug 1713 daughter of Stephen and Sarah (Stevens) Abbott; d. at Lunenburg 5 Aug 1748; m. 14 Aug 1742, JOSEPH HOLT, b. 28 Feb 1715/6 son of Thomas and Alice (Peabody) Holt. Joseph m. 2nd Dorcas Boynton (widow of Thomas Frost); Joseph d. at Lunenburg 1754 (based on date of probate 26 Sep 1754).

Joseph Holt wrote his will 16 February 1754. Dearly beloved wife Dorcas receives the improvements on the farm, house, and barn. This full use of the family homestead is just until the youngest son, Joseph Holt, is 7 years 4 months old, and that is with the provision that she keeps the house, barn, and fence in good repair and keeps the brush cut down. After Joseph reaches seven years old, she will have improvements on one-third of the property. Dorcas does receive all the livestock, husbandry tools, smith tools, smith shop, and household items for her use forever except what is bequeathed to the daughters Mary Holt and Sarah Holt. Because of this bequest, Dorcas is obliged to pay all his debts. Dorcas is also to pay her daughter Dorcas Frost three pounds six shillings for services she has provided to the family and a small payment to Joseph's brother Daniel Holt. Dorcas also needs to care for the sons Abiel and Joseph until the age of seven years. Sons Abiel and Joseph receive two-thirds of the real estate after Joseph reaches the age of seven. His two daughters, Mary and Sarah, receive household items and some clothing items that belonged to their mother which are currently in the care of Stephen Abbott in Andover. His books are to be equally divided among his four children. Dorcas and Joseph's brother Thomas Holt are named executors.[182] Of the children mentioned in the will, Mary, Sarah, and Abiel are from the marriage of Joseph Holt and Mary Abbott. Joseph Holt is the son of Joseph Holt and Dorcas Boynton. Dorcas Frost is the daughter of Thomas Frost and Dorcas Boynton.

Mary Abbott and Joseph Holt had four children all born at Lunenburg.

        i   JOSEPH HOLT, b. 4 Apr 1744; d. in infancy.

324) ii   MARY HOLT, b. 17 Aug 1745; d. at Worcester. County, MA about 1814 (date of probate 24 May 1814); m. 26 Jun 1766, BENJAMIN DARLING, b. 28 Apr 1728 son of John and Lois (Gowing) Darling;

---

[182] *Worcester County, MA: Probate File Papers, 1731-1881*, Probate of Joseph Holt, 26 Sep 1754, Case number 30653.

Benjamin d. at Lunenburg, about 1783 based on date of probate.

iii   SARAH HOLT, b. about 1746; no further record beyond her mention in her father's will.

325)   iv   ABIEL HOLT, b. 14 Jul 1748; d. at Temple, NH, 7 Jan 1811; m. 25 Nov 1773, his third cousin once removed and George Abbott descendant, SARAH ABBOTT, b. at Suncook, 1751 daughter of Job and Sarah (Abbott) Abbott; Sarah d. 9 Oct 1854 (age at death inscribed as 103 years, 2 months, 25 days on her gravestone).[183]

49)   HANNAH ABBOTT *(Stephen³, John², George¹)* and BENJAMIN ABBOTT *(Thomas², George¹)* (This is Family #49 in Generation Three.)

69)   STEPHEN ABBOT *(Stephen³, John², George¹)*, b. 2 Mar 1717/8 son of Stephen and Sarah (Stevens) Abbott; d. 8 Nov 1768; m. 24 May 1743, MARY ABBOTT *(George³, George², George¹)*, his second cousin, b. 12 Mar 1722/3 daughter of George and Mary (Phillips) Abbott. Mary m. 2nd as his second wife, her second cousin JONATHAN ABBOTT *(Jonathan³, Benjamin², George¹)* son of Jonathan and Zerviah (Holt) Abbott; Mary d. 8 Aug 1792.

Stephen lived on his father's homestead in Andover. He died at the young age of 51 leaving his wife with 10 children ranging in age from 2 years to 24 years. Stephen Abbott did not leave a will. His estate entered probate 6 February 1769. Widow Mary declined being administrator of the estate and asked that George Abbott, Esq. be appointed. One-third of the estate was set aside for support of the widow. As part of the settlement of the estate, £100 was received by Jonathan Fisk the husband of Deborah. In an agreement dated 3 March 1772, Jonathan Fisk is to disburse payments of £20 to

---

[183] Findagrave.com

each of the following heirs: Jonathan Fisk as the right of his wife Deborah, Sarah Abbot, George Abbot, Abner Abbot, and Elizabeth Abbot. On 3 March 1772, a similar agreement included Stephen Abbot as receiving a £100 settlement and his is to make payments of £20 payments to Mary Abbot, Hannah Abbot, and Dorcas Abbot.

In an undated document with the probate file, Mary Abbot, now the wife of Jonathan Abbot, petitions that her one-third dower portion be released for sale with the remainder of the estate so that debts can be paid and there can be a settlement for the children. More than one-third of Stephen Abbot's estate was needed to pay his debts. "The remainder of the real estate is thrown into such an unhappy situation, it will not sell for what it is judged to be worth except the said dower might be sold with the same, and as her said Mary's other children by her said deceased husband stand in need of their respective parts of the remainder of said estate above mentioned. . . you petitioners viz. the said Mary and her son Stephen pray your Honor would empower them to make sale of said thirds."[184] It is likely that this petition is just prior to the settlement payments to the children in 1772.

In 1770, Mary remarried to Jonathan Abbott who was also widowed in 1768. Stephen and Mary had eleven children all born at Andover. Two children died in early childhood.

      i   MARY ABBOTT, b. 8 Mar 1743/4; d. 15 Sep 1820. Mary did not marry. She was called "Aunt Molly" and cared for the sick in Andover.

326) ii   DEBORAH ABBOTT, b. 13 Oct 1745; d. after 1804 (husband's probate); m. 19 Sep 1766, JONATHAN

---

[184] *Essex County, MA: Probate File Papers, 1638-1881. Probate of* Stephen Abbott, 6 Feb 1769, *Case number* 133.

FISKE; Jonathan d. at Groton about 1804 (date of probate). Births of two children are recorded at Andover and one at Groton.

327) iii SARAH ABBOTT, b. 1 Aug 1747; d. 8 Jul 1824; m. 7 Jul 1772, JOSEPH STEVENS, baptized at Boston, Oct 1750 son of Joseph and Hephzibah (Baker) Stevens; Joseph d. 20 Feb 1803.

328) iv STEPHEN ABBOTT, b. 1 Aug 1749; d. at Salem, 9 Aug 1813; m. 1st SARAH CROWELL, b. at Salem, Dec 1750 daughter of William and Sarah (Stone) Crowell; Sarah d. 14 Apr 1805. Stephen m. 2nd 5 Nov 1805, MARY BADGER of Dunstable, NH; Mary still living at the time of Stephen's probate in 1813.

v ABNER ABBOTT, b. 26 Aug 1751; d. 11 Mar 1758.

vi HANNAH ABBOTT, b. 10 Aug 1753; was living in 1769 when guardian appointed (over 14 years of age) and is still mentioned in the probate records in 1772 as Hannah Abbot. She might have married, but there is not an obvious marriage for her and no death record as Hannah Abbot that would fit.

329) vii GEORGE ABBOTT, b. 13 Jun 1756; d. likely in NH; m. 1 Apr 1779, REBECCA BLANCHARD, b. at Billerica, 1754 daughter of Simon and Rebeckah (Sheldon) Blanchard.

321) viii DORCAS ABBOTT, b. 23 Sep 1758; d. 3 Mar 1844; m. 17 Dec 1778 as his second wife, her third cousin, JONATHAN ABBOTT, b. 29 Aug 1740 son of Jonathan and Martha (Lovejoy) Abbott. Jonathan's first wife was another cousin, Mehitable Abbott. Jonathan d. 26 Dec 1821.

330) ix ABNER ABBOTT, b. 29 Jan 1761; d. at Albany, ME, Sep 1833; m. 29 Jan 1784, RUTH HOLT, b. 25 Feb 1765 daughter of Joseph and Ruth (Johnson) Holt; Ruth d. 17 Nov 1806. Abner m. 2nd, DORCAS NASON, b. 1773 and d. 19 Jul 1862.

x SAMUEL ABBOTT, b. Apr 1763; d. 10 Aug 1769. Samuel was killed by a cart. The following inscription is on his gravestone: *Tho' sudden was the stroke, Which stopt his vital breath, He must obey, twas God who spoke, and yield to cruel death.*[185]

331) xi ELIZABETH ABBOTT, b. 22 Oct 1766; d. at Salem 19 Sep 1833; m. 27 Sep 1788, ABRAHAM VALPY, b. 1766 (based on age at time of death) son of Richard and Hannah (Ives) Valpy; Benjamin d. at Ipswich 26 Feb 1848.

70) SAMUEL ABBOT *(Stephen³, John², George¹)*, b. 23 Jun 1726 son of Stephen and Sarah (Stevens) Abbott; d. 1758 at Ft. George, NY during the French and Indian War; m. 14 Dec 1754, ELIZABETH WYMAN probably born about 1730, described as "of Pelham" but no further information has been located on her origins. Elizabeth m. 2nd Joseph Dane; Elizabeth d. 26 Sep 1778.

Samuel Abbot died at age 31 in 1758 near Lake George during the French and Indian Wars. Elizabeth was left with two young children. Elizabeth married Joseph Dane as the second of his three wives. She and Joseph had three children. Elizabeth died at age 57.

Samuel Abbot did not leave a will and his estate entered probate 4 December 1758. Widow Elizabeth was administrator of

---

[185] Essex Antiquarian, 1898, Andover Inscriptions, Old South Burying Yard

the estate. There is an accounting as administrator 27 April 1767 which she signs as Elizabeth Dane along with Joseph Dane.[186]

Samuel Abbot and Elizabeth Wyman had two children whose births are recorded at Andover.

332) i ELIZABETH ABBOTT, b. 2 Nov 1755; d. 28 Oct 1815; m. 15 Feb 1780, EBENEZER JONES, b. 1757 son of Jacob and Mary (Winn) Jones; Ebenezer m. 2nd 2 Dec 1819, Dorcas Dane, b. 1769 daughter of Joseph and Elizabeth (Wyman) Dane; Ebenezer d. 24 Aug 1832. Ebenezer's two wives, Dorcas Dane and Elizabeth Abbott, were half-sisters.

333) ii HANNAH ABBOTT, b. 24 Apr 1757; d. 31 Dec 1837; m. 24 Apr 1777, BENJAMIN GOLDSMITH, b. at Ipswich, 1755 son of William and Hannah (Burnham) Goldsmith; Benjamin d. 5 Apr 1817.

Sarah Abbott Chandler³, John², George¹ *and* Zebadiah Chandler³, Hannah Abbott Chandler², George¹

[The families in this next section are descendants of George and Hannah (Chandler) Abbott by the two paths above.]

71) SARAH CHANDLER *(Sarah Abbott Chandler³, John², George¹ and Zebadiah Chandler³, Hannah Abbott Chandler², George¹)*, b. 1707 (based on age at time of death) daughter of Zebadiah and Sarah (Abbott) Chandler; d. 28 Mar 1768; m. 18 Feb 1728/9, JOSHUA CHANDLER *(John Chandler³, Hannah Abbott Chandler², George¹)*, her first cousin, b. 1705 son of John and Hannah (Frye) Chandler; Joshua d. 24 Mar 1734; Sarah did not remarry.

---

[186] *Essex County, MA: Probate File Papers, 1638-1881. Probate of* Samuel Abbot, 4 Dec 1758, *Case number* 122.

Generation Four

Joshua did not leave a will. His estate entered probate 26 April 1734. The total value of the estate available for disbursement to the heirs was £85. One-third, £28 was paid to the widow, £38 as the double portion to the older son Zebadiah Chandler, and £19 to son Joshua Chandler.[187]

334) i ZEBADIAH CHANDLER, b. 23 May 1729; d. 30 Jun 1775; m. 19 Jun 1750, DEBORAH BLANCHARD, baptized Nov 1727 daughter of Stephen and Deborah (Phelps) Blanchard; Deborah d. May 1799.

335) ii JOSHUA CHANDLER, b. 23 Jul 1732; d. 15 Mar 1807; m. 31 Mar 1757, his first cousin and George Abbott descendant, HANNAH CHANDLER, b. 20 May 1735 daughter of Nathan and Priscilla (Holt) Chandler; Hannah d. 14 Feb 1791. Joshua m. 2nd 7 Jun 1792, his first cousin (and George Abbott descendant), HANNAH BALLARD (the widow of Obadiah Foster); Hannah Ballard b. 6 Dec 1748 daughter of Hezekiah and Lydia (Chandler) Ballard; Hannah Ballard d. 22 Dec 1838.

72) JOANNA CHANDLER *(Sarah Abbott Chandler³, John², George¹ and Zebadiah Chandler³, Hannah Abbott Chandler², George¹)*, b. 1710 (based on age at time of death) daughter of Zebadiah and Sarah (Abbott) Chandler; d. 12 Sep 1791; m. 3 Jun 1728, JOSEPH SHATTUCK, b. 1707 (based on age at time of death); Joseph d. 21 Mar 1772.

---

[187] *Essex County, MA: Probate File Papers, 1638-1881. Probate of* Joshua Chandler, 26 Apr 1734, *Case number* 4953.

Joseph and Joanna Shattuck lived in West Parrish of Andover. Joseph had a farm, part of which he had purchased from his father-in-law Zebadiah Chandler.[188][189] There is some uncertainty about his parentage and a couple of different families have been suggested but without confirming information.

In his will written 6 Jun 1761, Joseph has bequests for the following persons: well beloved wife Joanna, son Joseph, son Isaac, son Zebadiah, daughter Hannah the wife of Samuel Stevens, daughter Sarah the wife of John Barnard, daughter Mary who is single and not yet 21, and grandson Joseph Shattuck. His estate was valued at £232.[190]

Joanna and Joseph had nine children born at Andover.

336) i HANNAH SHATTUCK, b. 14 Jul 1729; death record not found; m. 18 Oct 1753, SAMUEL STEVENS, b. at Methuen, 27 Aug 1730 son of Samuel and Phebe (Bodwell) Stevens; Samuel d. 10 Aug 1810.

337) ii JOSEPH SHATTUCK, b. 27 Nov 1731; d. 9 Apr 1778; m. 13 Apr 1765, ANNA JOHNSON, b. at Haverhill, 6 Apr 1737 daughter of Cornelius and Lydia (Clement) Johnson; Anna reported to have died at Hillsborough.[191]

338) iii ISAAC SHATTUCK, b. 24 Mar 1733/4; d. 27 Apr 1822; m. 24 Mar 1757, MARY BARNARD, b. 4 Dec 1739 daughter of Nathaniel and Ruth (Preston) Barnard; Mary d. 2 Jun 1804.

295) iv ZEBADIAH SHATTUCK, b. 26 Oct 1736; d. 10 Mar 1826; m. 1st 30 Aug 1759, his second cousin (and

---

[188] Chandler, *Descendants of William and Annis Chandler*, p 159
[189] Shattuck, *Memorials of the Descendants of William Shattuck*, pp 104-105
[190] *Essex County, MA: Probate File Papers, 1638-1881.* Probate of Joseph Shattuck, 7 Apr 1772, *Case number* 25124.
[191] Chandler, *The Descendants of William and Annis Chandler*

George Abbott descendant) ELIZABETH ABBOTT, b. 2 Nov 1740 daughter of Barachias and Hannah (Holt) Abbott; Elizabeth d. 9 Sep 1780. Zebadiah m. 2nd 25 Jul 1781, his first cousin once removed (and George Abbott descendant), SARAH CHANDLER, b. 8 May 1751 daughter of Zebadiah and Deborah (Blanchard) Chandler.

339)   v   SARAH SHATTUCK, b. 9 Apr 1739; d. 9 Jan 1832; m. 6 Jan 1757, JOHN BARNARD, b. 8 May 1728 son of John and Sarah (Osgood) Barnard; John d. 27 Feb 1802.

        vi   ABIEL SHATTUCK, b. 25 Nov 1741; d. 12 Nov 1742.

340)   vii MARY SHATTUCK, b. 13 Jul 1743; d. at Andover about 1815 (probate Feb 1816); m. 17 Oct 1765, THOMAS PHELPS, b. 1 Jun 1739 son of Thomas and Prudence (Wyman) Phelps; Thomas d. 28 May 1795.

        viii ELIZABETH SHATTUCK, birth not found; d. 16 Dec 1747.

        ix   ELIZABETH SHATTUCK, b. 9 Oct 1749; d. 11 Mar 1753.

73)   PRISCILLA CHANDLER *(Sarah Abbott Chandler³, John², George¹ **and** Zebadiah Chandler³, Hannah Abbott Chandler², George¹)*, b. 26 Apr 1713 daughter of Zebadiah and Sarah (Abbott) Chandler; d. 4 Jan 1778; m. 29 Jan 1735/6, SAMUEL PHELPS, b. 5 Feb 1712/3 son of Samuel and Hannah (Dane) Phelps; Samuel d. 17 Apr 1795.

Samuel wrote his will 9 August 1775, 20 years before his death. In his will, he made bequests to the following persons: Prisilla dearly beloved wife (who died in 1778), beloved son Joshua, beloved son Henry, beloved daughter Hannah Moar wife of

Benjamin Moar, and beloved daughter Prisilla Dane wife of Philemon Dane. His books are to be divided among his four children.[192]

Samuel and Priscilla had five children all born at Andover.

   i SAMUEL PHELPS, b. 21 Oct 1736; d. 18 Oct 1756 at Lake George during the French and Indian War.

341) ii JOSHUA PHELPS, b. 25 Jun 1738; d. 22 Dec 1798; m. 17 Feb 1767, his second cousin (and George Abbott descendant), LOIS BALLARD, b. 19 Jul 1746 daughter of Hezekiah and Lydia (Chandler) Ballard; Lois d. 21 Dec 1836.

342) iii HENRY PHELPS, b. 5 Sep 1740; d. 31 Oct 1807; m. 31 Oct 1780, MARY BALLARD (also a George Abbott descendant), b. 27 Feb 1750/1 daughter of Hezekiah and Lydia (Chandler) Ballard; Mary d. 11 Aug 1835.

343) iv HANNAH PHELPS, b. 5 May 1745; d. 1826 at Lewiston, ME; m. 29 Sep 1767, BENJAMIN MOOAR, b. 28 Oct 1743 son of Benjamin and Abijah (Hill) Mooar; Benjamin d. 15 Aug 1828 at Lewiston.

344) v PRISCILLA PHELPS, b. 10 May 1748; d. 9 Sep 1799; m. 11 Jul 1769, her second cousin, PHILEMON DANE, b. 2 Feb 1741/2 son of John and Elizabeth (Chandler) Dane. Philemon m. 2nd 29 Jan 1801, widow Sarah Foster of Tewksbury; Philemon d. 13 May 1816.

74) MEHITABLE CHANDLER *(Sarah Abbott Chandler³, John², George¹ and Zebadiah Chandler³, Hannah Abbott Chandler², George¹)*, b. 1717 daughter of Zebadiah and Sarah (Abbott) Chandler; d. 26 Jan

---

[192] *Essex County, MA: Probate File Papers, 1638-1881. Probate of* Samuel Phelps, 23 Jul 1795, *Case number* 21658.

1786 (reported, but no record found); m. 26 Jan 1738, CALEB LOVEJOY, b. 28 Dec 1716 son of Henry and Sarah (Farnum) Lovejoy; the family relocated to Suncook, NH. Caleb reported to have died there 1781 (this is the date used by the Daughters of the American Revolution).

Six children have been located for this family. The primary information comes from the History of Pembroke, New Hampshire.[193]

345) i ELIZABETH LOVEJOY, b. 1738; d. after 1810 at Bow, NH;[194] m. about 1766, JOHN ROBERTSON, b. at Londonderry, 9 Jun 1732 son of Samuel and Margaret (Woodend) Robertson; John d. at Bow, NH 11 Oct 1816.

346) ii MEHITABLE LOVEJOY, b. 1745; d. 2 Mar 1835 at Allenstown, NH; m. JONATHAN HUTCHINSON, b. 20 Mar 1747 son of Jonathan and Theodate (Morrill) Hutchinson; Jonathan d. at Pembroke, 3 May 1830.

347) iii CALEB LOVEJOY, b. 1749; d. 1821 (estate probate 7 Sep 1821);[195] m. ELIZA KIMBALL. Caleb m. 2nd JEMIMA JUDKINS; Jemima d. 15 Sep 1853.

348) iv JERUSHA LOVEJOY, b. 5 Oct 1753; d. at Pembroke, 11 Oct 1841; m. 6 Jun 1775, JOHN LADD, b. at Kingston, 6 Jan 1755 son of Trueworthy and Lydia (Harriman) Ladd; John d. 8 Jun 1835.

---

[193] Carter and Fowler, *History of Pembroke, NH*
[194] She appears to still be living at the 1810 Census as a woman in her age category is in the household headed by John Robertson.
[195] Caleb's brothers-in-law Jonathan Hutchinson and John Ladd participate in the administration of the estate in addition to widow Jemima.

349) v MARTHA LOVEJOY, b. about 1760 at Pembroke, NH; death record not found; m. at Pembroke, 21 May 1781, her third cousin (and George Abbott descendant) JOHN PARKER, b. 15 Aug 1760 son of Joseph and Hannah (Abbott) Parker; John d. at Pembroke 27 May 1825.

350) vi OBADIAH LOVEJOY, b. 1756; he is reported to have been in the Battle of Bunker Hill and is believed to have died while serving in the Army.[196] But the Lovejoy book says he married Tryphena Waugh.[197] More research needs to be done.

vii Daughter, name not known who married John Moor of Pembroke the son of James and Agnes (Colbreath) Moor. This is a daughter listed in the Lovejoy Genealogy (p 74) and the History of Pembroke but her name is not yet found. However, the children that the History of Pembroke assigned to John Moor and the unknown daughter Lovejoy have birth records that list a mother's name as Martha. As Martha Lovejoy from this family married John Parker, it is nor clear how all this disparate information fits together. This is most likely just a misidentification of the wife of John Moor.

75) ELIZABETH CHANDLER *(Sarah Abbott Chandler³, John², George¹* **and** *Zebadiah Chandler³, Hannah Abbott Chandler², George¹)*, b. 5 Feb 1721 daughter of Zebadiah and Sarah (Abbott) Chandler; d. probably in NH, date unknown; m. 26 Mar 1741, DAVID LOVEJOY, b. 10 Oct 1715 son of Henry and Sarah (Farnum) Lovejoy; the family relocated to Suncook, NH; the DAR gives the death date of David as

---

[196] Carter and Fowler, *The History of Pembroke, NH*
[197] Lovejoy, *The Lovejoy Genealogy*, p 105

18 Feb 1819, although I believe this to be the death date of a different David Lovejoy.

According to the History of Pembroke, NH, David Lovejoy came to Pembroke between 1738 and 1740.[198] The births of eleven children were reported at Pembroke.

351) i ELIZABETH LOVEJOY, b. 10 Jan 1742; d. at Pembroke, 11 Apr 1815; m. 12 Jan 1764, JEREMIAH MORGAN, b. at Pembroke, 18 Aug 1741 son of Luther and Abigail (-) Morgan; Jeremiah d. 21 Jul 1819.

ii CHANDLER LOVEJOY, b. 9 Apr 1744; d. 15 Jul 1810; m. 9 Mar 1809, ABIGAIL DAVIS, Abigail d. 23 Mar 1831; there are no known children.

iii PRISCILLA LOVEJOY; b. 12 Mar 1746; d. 14 Apr 1832; Priscilla does not seem to have married.

352) iv MOLLY LOVEJOY, b. 29 Apr 1748; d. at Salisbury, NH, 23 Feb 1813; m. 21 Nov 1769, JEREMIAH WARDWELL, b. at Andover 6 Dec 1748 son of Thomas and Abigail (Gray) Wardwell; Jeremiah d. 9 Jan 1817. Jeremiah remarried to Betsy after the death of Molly.

353) v ABIGAIL LOVEJOY, b. 12 Sep 1750; d. 18 Mar 1833; m. about 1770, her third cousin once removed, DANIEL HOLT, b. at Pembroke 14 Sep 1744 son of Benjamin and Sarah (Frye) Holt; Daniel d. 5 Dec 1813.

---

[198] Carter and Fowler, *History of Pembroke*, p 243

	vi	MARTHA LOVEJOY, b. 16 Aug 1752; no further record was found for Martha.
354)	vii	PHEBE LOVEJOY, b. 28 Sep 1754; d. at Pembroke, Jun 1804; m. Feb 1779, NATHANIEL AMBROSE,[199] b. about 1752 (based on age at time of death). Nathaniel m. 2nd Elizabeth (-); Nathaniel d. 24 Mar 1835 at Deerfield, NH.[200]
355)	viii	OLIVE LOVEJOY, b. 13 Nov 1756; d. Feb 1843; m. 6 Mar 1781, THOMAS KIMBALL, b. at Andover, 17 Jul 1753 son of Thomas and Penelope (Johnson) Kimball; Thomas d. 20 Oct 1825.
356)	ix	DORCAS LOVEJOY, b. 1 Oct 1758; d. 1828 in Ohio; m. 28 Jan 1783, BENJAMIN MILLS, b. at Plaistow, NH, 30 Dec 1755 son of Reuben and Mary (Howard) Mills; Benjamin d. at Scioto County, OH, 15 Jul 1829.
357)	x	ESTHER LOVEJOY, b. 8 Mar 1764; d. likely in Vermont; m. 25 Aug 1792, AMOS LAKEMAN, b. at Bradford, 7 Jan 1762 son of Samuel ad Margaret (Kimball) Lakeman; Amos d. at Woodbury, VT 20 Dec 1850.
	xi	DAVID LOVEJOY, b. 16 Sep 1767; d. perhaps 1819; m. 16 Sep 1790, JANE COCHRAN, b, 1766 daughter of William and Betsy (Gile) Cochran;[201] Jane d. 28 Oct 1844. David and Jane did not have children.

Ephraim[3], John[2], George[1]

---

[199] Goodhue, *History and Genealogy of the Goodhue Family*. The Goodhue Family genealogy suggests parents as Jonathan and Abigail (Goodhue) Ambrose. The Pembroke, NH history suggests parent is Robert Ambrose.

[200] Nathaniel Ambrose's will was written 17 Mar 1835 and entered probate April 1835.

[201] Carter and Fowler, *History of Pembroke*, p. 36

76) SARAH ABBOTT *(Ephraim³, John², George¹)*, b. 25 Jan 1715/6 daughter of Ephraim and Sarah (Crosby) Abbott; d. at NH; m. 8 Sep 1736, SAMUEL GRAY, b. Jul 1711 son of Henry and Mary (Blunt) Gray; Samuel d. 3 Oct 1769 at Amherst, NH.[202]

Sarah and Samuel married in Andover and their first child was born there. They then moved on to New Hampshire, and the births of three children are recorded at Rumford. Samuel had some property in Pembroke that he sold to Moses Foster in 1742.[203] They settled in Amherst, New Hampshire.

No probate record was located for Samuel. Of the four children for whom there are birth records, three died in early childhood.

    i   SAMUEL GRAY, b. 11 Jan 1736/7; d. 15 Dec 1737.

    ii   SARAH GRAY, b. 25 Jan 1739; d. 10 May 1740.

    iii   SARAH GRAY, b. 16 Mar 1741; d. 4 Sep 1746.

358)   iv   MARY GRAY, b. 29 Dec 1743; d. at Amherst, NH 19 Oct 1775; m. at Amherst, 3 Dec 1762, MOSES TOWNE, b. at Topsfield, May 1739 son of Israel and Grace (Gardner) Towne; Moses d. at Milford, NH 9 Feb 1824.

77) EPHRAIM ABBOT *(Ephraim³, John², George¹)*, b. 22 Jul 1718 son of Ephraim and Sarah (Crosby) Abbott; d. abt. 1775 at Amherst, NH; m. 1st, 3 Nov 1740 his second cousin MARY ABBOTT *(Timothy³, Timothy², George¹)*, b. 7 Jan 1723/4 daughter of Timothy and Mary (Foster) Abbott; Mary d. 9 Mar 1744. Ephraim m. 2nd at Ipswich, 1

---

[202] Secomb, *History of the Town of Amherst*, p. 667.
[203] Carter and Fowler, *History of Pembroke*, p. 98.

Feb 1745/6, MARY KNEELAND,[204] *possibly* b. at Topsfield, May 1721 daughter of Philip and Martha (Graves) Kneeland; death is not known but likely at Amherst, NH.

   Ephraim Abbot and Mary Abbott had three children all born at Andover.

- 359) i MARY ABBOTT, b. 11 Mar 1741; d.?; m. 9 Dec 1762, PETER GOSS, b. at Bradford, 17 Jun 1737 son of John and Mehitable (Bailey) Goss.

- 360) ii EPHRAIM ABBOTT, b. 5 Dec 1742; d. 1827 at Bedford, NH; m. by 1765, DOROTHY STILES, b. 2 Sep 1740 daughter of Caleb and Sarah (Walton) Stiles.

- 361) iii HANNAH ABBOTT, b. 1 Mar 1744; d. unknown; m. NATHANIEL SHATTUCK; the information I have so far is a guess. Nathaniel Shattuck and a wife Hannah had two children in Hollis. There is a Nathaniel Shattuck married to Catherine Andrews and they have children in Temple starting in 1774, but I think that is a different Nathaniel. There is another Nathaniel Shattuck born in Hollis and later in Groton who married Eunice Hazen. The Abbot genealogy gives the name of Hannah's husband as _____ Shattuck and I cannot locate a record.

---

[204] The Abiel Abbot and Ephraim Abbot Genealogy gives her name as Hannah Kneeland, but the marriage record says Mary Kneeland and the birth records for each of her children with Ephraim Abbot give the mother's name as Mary. She is possibly Mary Neeland (Kneeland) baptized in Topsfield 21 May 1721 daughter of Philip. Philip died in 1742 and his son Philip relocated to Ipswich which would make it possible that Mary accompanied her brother to Ipswich. Ipswich was the location for the marriage of Ephraim Abbot and Mary Kneeland. This is the identity made in Kneeland's *Seven Centuries in the Kneeland Family*, p. 153

Generation Four 157

The children of Ephraim Abbott and Mary Kneeland were all born at Amherst, NH.

362) i KNEELAND ABBOTT, b. 17 May 1748; m. BETSEY STANLEY; relocated to Vermont.

363) ii SARAH ABBOTT, b. 14 Jun 1751; d. at Hillsborough, 22 Jan 1811; m. by 1775, WILLIAM CODMAN, b. 1748 son of William and Sarah (Wilkins) Codman; William d. 9 Nov 1813.

364) iii DORCAS ABBOTT, b. 7 Aug 1752; she is perhaps the Dorcas Wiley who died at Landgrove, VT in 1823; m. JOHN WILLEY.

365) iv ESTHER ABBOTT, b. 6 Mar 1755; d. likely at Montpelier, VT; m. 13 Dec 1781, BENJAMIN PIKE.

366) v ABIGAIL ABBOTT, b. 30 Jul 1756; d. 1852 at New Boston, NH; m. 25 Apr 1781, SAMUEL TWISS, b. at Tewksbury, 31 Jan 1755 son of John and Sarah (Patten) Twiss; Samuel d. at New Boston, NH, Oct 1799.

367) vi DANIEL ABBOTT, b. 1 Apr 1762; d. likely at Cavendish, VT; m. 28 Jul 1786, SARAH STEVENS possibly the daughter of Samuel and Rebecca (Stiles) Stevens.

78) MARY ABBOTT *(Ephraim³, John², George¹)*, b. Jul 1720 daughter of Ephraim and Sarah (Crosby) Abbott; date of death unknown but likely in Amherst, NH before 1792;[205] m. 11 May 1743,

---

[205] Secomb, *The History of Amherst*, p. 741 reports that Robert Read had a second marriage 11 January 1792 and this is confirmed by record.

ROBERT READ, b. 25 Dec 1720 at Chelmsford son of William and Hannah (Bates) Read; Robert. Robert m. 2nd 11 Jan 1792, Joanna Danforth;[206] Robert d. at Amherst, NH 11 Sep 1803.[207]

The information for this family has been pieced together in a sketchy fashion from published genealogies and the History of Amherst, New Hampshire. There is consistency among sources in that five children are proposed, and records were located for three of these children. Marriages were located for three of the children. I did not locate a probate record for Robert Read. He relocated his family at least twice, starting in Massachusetts, being for a time in Litchfield, New Hampshire before settling in Amherst, New Hampshire. The information for this family should be considered, for the most part, preliminary.

   i LEMUEL READ, b. about 1746; no records found.

   ii ROBERT READ, b. at Litchfield 31 May 1748; no record found beyond birth record.

368) iii MARY READ,[208] b. at Litchfield 31 May 1748; d. by 1792 (date of husband's second marriage); m. by about 1775, BENJAMIN BRADFORD of Hillsborough. Benjamin m. 2nd 21 Dec 1792, Mary "Molly" Mc Adams.

369) iv WILLIAM READ, b. 14 Aug 1754; d. at Amherst, NH, 10 Sep 1834;[209] m. 1st BRIDGET GREELEY, b. at

---

[206] "New Hampshire Marriages, 1720-1920," database, *FamilySearch* (https://familysearch.org/ark:/61903/1:1:FDK1-FPD: 31 December 2014), Col. Robert Read and Joana Danforth, 11 Jan 1792; citing reference; FHL microfilm 1,001,296.

[207] His grave site has been located at the Amherst Town Hall Burying Ground and bears this inscription: Erected to the Memory of Col. Robert Read who died Sept. 11, 1803 in the 83 Year of his age. (findagrave.com)

[208] Browne, *The History of Hillsborough, 1735-1921*, Volume 2, p 82

[209] Date of death is found in his Revolutionary War pension payment index

Hudson, NH, 3 Feb 1764 daughter of Ezekiel and Eunice (Lovewell) Greeley;[210] Bridget d. at Amherst, 2 Feb 1789. William m. 2nd 26 Jun 1791, ABIGAIL HOWARD, b. 1771 and d. 15 Jun 1852.

370)   v   OLIVE READ, b. at Hudson, NH, 23 Jul 1757; d. at Wilton, NH, 23 Feb 1811; m. at Nottingham, 8 Nov 1779,[211] SAMUEL GREELEY, b. at Nottingham, 29 Sep 1752 son of Samuel of Abigail (Blodgett) Greeley; Samuel d. 29 Sep 1798.

79)   JOSHUA ABBOTT *(Ephraim³, John², George¹)*, b. 25 Sep 1722 son of Ephraim and Sarah (Crosby) Abbott; d. at Amherst, NH after 2 Mar 1772 (the date of his will); m. 7 Jul 1749, PHEBE INGALLS, b. 7 Jul 1725 daughter of Joseph and Phebe (Farnum) Ingalls; Phebe d. after 2 Mar 1772.

    In his will dated 2 March 1772, Joshua Abbott orders that all his property (except his household furniture) be sold following his death. One-third of the proceeds is to be set aside for his wife Phebe. His wife is to also have her choice of one of his cows. The remainder of the proceeds are to be divided among his children: oldest son Joshua and other sons Stephen and Peter, with the sons to have £4 more than any of the daughters; daughter Phebe the wife of John Everden; daughters Elizabeth and Sarah are to have equal portions; and the youngest son Joseph to be provided for by the executor from the estate proceeds until he arrives at an age to be

---

[210] Bridget's parents are confirmed by the 1793 will of Ezekiel Greeley that includes a bequest to Robert Read, Jr. son of William and his late wife Bridget. Robert Read, Jr. received one-third part of Ezekiel's estate.

[211] New Hampshire, Marriage Records Index, 1637-1947 (ancestry.com)

bound out as an apprentice. At the age of 21, Joseph will receive a cash payment for his portion.[212]

The birth of oldest daughter, Phebe, is recorded at Andover and the births of ten children are recorded at Amherst, New Hampshire.[213]

371) i PHEBE ABBOTT, b. 31 Aug 1750; m. about 1770, JOHN EVERDEN; the birth of one child for this couple is recorded at Amherst. John Everden seems to have seen service during the Revolution in Colonel Moses Nichols Regiment that marched from New Hampshire to Rhode Island in August 1778.[214] There is a John Everden that died 21 Aug 1837 at Winchester, NH but that may not be him.

ii SARAH ABBOTT, b. 27 Jan 1752; d. 4 Jan 1754.

iii JOSHUA ABBOTT, b. 10 May 1754. The Amherst, NH book[215] has Joshua Abbott marrying a Deborah Chandler, but I cannot find that anywhere else and there is no record of the marriage and I could not locate any possible children.

iv ELIZABETH ABBOTT, b. 12 Nov 1756.

v STEPHEN ABBOTT, b. 29 Sep 1759; m. 8 Aug 1782, SARAH LOVEJOY, b. 7 Nov 1765 daughter of

---

[212] *New Hampshire Wills and Probate Records 1643-1982,* Will of Joshua Abbot, Hillsborough, 2 Mar 1772.

[213] Ancestry.com, *New Hampshire, Births and Christenings Index, 1714-1904* (Provo, UT, USA: Ancestry.com Operations, Inc., 2011).

[214] "New Hampshire Revolutionary War Records, 1675-1835," database with images, *FamilySearch* (https://familysearch.org/ark:/61903/1:1:Q242-NWWR: accessed 6 February 2018), John Everden, 05 Aug 1778; citing New Hampshire, United States, Archives and Records Management, Concord.

[215] Secomb, *History of the Town of Amherst,* p 478

Hezekiah and Hannah (Phelps) Lovejoy.[216] No children have yet been located for this couple and it is not clear where they might have settled.

372) vi SARAH ABBOTT, b. 19 Feb 1761; d. about 1848, Crown Point, NY; m. 29 Jan 1782, AARON NICHOLS, born about 1757; d. 13 Oct 1821 at Crown Point, NY.[217]

373) vii PETER ABBOTT, b. 28 Jul 1762; d. unknown but perhaps in NY; m. 23 Oct 1788, ABIGAIL FARNUM, b. at Amherst, 27 Dec 1767 daughter of Joseph and Mary (Lyon) Farnum. The children for this family are recorded in Windham, VT.

viii INFANT ABBOTT, b. and d. 16 Apr 1764.

ix INFANT ABBOTT, b. 3 Apr 1765; infant death.

x INFANT ABBOTT, b. 16 Feb 1767; infant death.

xi JOSEPH ABBOTT, b. 23 Jan 1772.

80) ELIZABETH ABBOTT *(Ephraim³, John², George¹)*, b. 29 Jun 1726 daughter of Ephraim and Sarah (Crosby) Abbott; d. 18 Dec 1819; m. 20 Sep 1744, her second cousin ASA ABBOT *(Timothy³, Timothy², George¹)*, b. 17 Oct 1721 son of Timothy and Mary (Foster) Abbot; Asa d. 22 Dec 1796.

The death record for Asa Abbot relates that he was injured by a blow from an ox's horn in 1791. This injury caused the loss of

---

[216] The will of Hezekiah Lovejoy includes a bequest to daughter Sarah wife of Stephen Abbott.

[217] Ancestry.com. *New York Pensioners, 1835* [database on-line]. Provo, UT, USA: Ancestry.com Operations Inc, 1998. Aaron Nichols who served in the Revolution in New Hampshire received a pension beginning 30 Apr 1818 in New York. Aaron Nichols is also head of household in the 1820 Census at Crown Point, Essex, NY.

Asa's eye which brought about "a languishment" from which he ultimately died in 1796. No probate record for Asa Abbot was located.

Elizabeth and Asa had six children whose births are recorded at Andover.

133) i TIMOTHY ABBOTT, b. 4 Jun 1745; d. 22 Mar 1826; m. 2 Jan 1770, his second cousin once removed, SARAH ABBOTT, b. 2 Jan 1749/50 daughter of Isaac and Phebe (Lovejoy) Abbott; Sarah d. 2 Apr 1835. This is family #133 which is more fully covered further down in Generation Four.

374) ii ELIZABETH ABBOTT, b. 21 May 1747; d. by 1802 (when husband married his third wife); m. 30 May 1779 as his 2nd wife, JESSE MANNING, b. at Billerica, 18 Aug 1745 son of Jacob and Martha (Beard) Manning. Jesse m. 3rd Abigail Baldwin; Jesse's first wife was Anne Carleton. Jesse d. at Billerica about 1825 (will probated 1825). There are no children recorded for Elizabeth and Jesse, and the only two children mentioned in his will are from Jesse's first marriage to Anne Carleton.

iii ASA ABBOTT, b. 14 Jun 1749; d. 5 Jun 1763.

375) iv CALEB ABBOTT, b. 28 Oct 1751; d. 12 Apr 1837; m. 21 Jan 1779, LUCY LOVEJOY, b. 3 Aug 1757 daughter of Isaac and Mary (Peavey) Lovejoy; Lucy d. 21 Feb 1802. Caleb m 2nd 18 Nov 1802, his third cousin (and George Abbott descendant), DEBORAH AMES, b. 6 Apr 1768 daughter of Nathan and Deborah (Bowers) Ames. Deborah died 7 Dec 1819. He married for a third time to Hannah Shattuck Clark.

v   DANIEL ABBOTT, b. 15 Jun 1754; d. 1776 while serving in the Army. "Daniel, s. Asa, in the Army, __, 1776."

376)   vi   NATHAN ABBOTT, b. 18 Nov 1756; d. at Billerica 10 Jan 1840; m. at Danvers, 22 May 1785, MARGARET "Peggy" WILSON, b. at Danvers, 25 Sep 1760 daughter of Benjamin and Lydia (Bancroft) Wilson; Margaret d. 21 Dec 1841.

81)   JOSIAH ABBOTT *(Ephraim³, John², George¹)*, b. 26 Sep 1728 son of Ephraim and Sarah (Crosby) Abbott; d. Dec 1777 at Lyndeborough, NH; m. by 1755 HANNAH HOBBS, b. at Middleton, 28 Aug 1729 daughter of William and Amme (Towne) Hobbs.[218]

There are eight children in this family for whom there is some evidence.[219] The births of the first seven children are recorded at Amherst, NH; the youngest daughter was likely born at Lyndeborough.

---

[218] This identification of the parents of Hannah Hobbs is not proved, but there is circumstantial evidence. There were brothers William and Humphrey Hobbs both living in Middleton. It is known that Humphrey Hobbs relocated to Amherst, NH. It is not known what became of William as there is no death or probate record for him, but it seems reasonable that there could be a relationship established between the Hobbs and Abbott families in Amherst. In addition, two of the children of Josiah and Hannah Abbott were named William and Amy.

[219] Birth records through Ancestry.com. *New Hampshire, Births and Christenings Index, 1714-1904* [database on-line]. Provo, UT, USA: Ancestry.com Operations, Inc., 2011. The birth information for Sarah was obtained through the DAR Ancestor page of Josiah Abbott as no birth record was located for her.

377)	i	HANNAH ABBOTT, b. 18 Sep 1755; d. at Lyndeborough, NH 25 Sep 1784;[220] m. by 1775, SAMUEL CHAMBERLAIN, b. at Chelmsford, 4 Apr 1745 son of Jonathan and Elizabeth (Cram) Chamberlain. Samuel m. 2nd 8 Nov 1785, Naomi Richardson; Samuel d. about 1812 at Lyndeborough.[221]
	ii	AMY ABBOTT, b. 5 Jun 1757; d. about 1777.
	iii	JOSIAH ABBOTT, b. 18 Dec 1759; no further record.
	iv	WILLIAM ABBOTT, b. 21 Dec 1761; d. 23 Dec 1764.
378)	v	LEMUEL ABBOTT, b. 13 May 1764; d. at Windham, VT 19 Jan 1841;[222] m. by 1799, DEBORAH BALCH, b. at Keene, NH, 13 Nov 1780 daughter of Hart and Dorcas (Somers) Balch; Deborah d. 15 Sep 1862.
	vi	WILLIAM ABBOTT, b. 28 Apr 1766; d. 10 May 1766.
379)	vii	DANIEL ABBOTT, b. 31 Jul 1769; d. at Westford, MA, 27 Jan 1854; m. 5 Jul 1798, SARAH ALLISON, b. at Londonderry, 12 Dec 1770 daughter of Samuel and Janet (McFarland) Allison; Sarah d. in New York, 22 Nov 1837.[223]
380)	viii	SARAH ABBOTT, b. 24 Apr 1773; d. at Cameron, NY 12 Jun 1870;[224] m. 19 Feb 1794, ENOCH ORDWAY, b. at Lyndeborough, 4 Aug 1762 son of John and

---

[220] *New Hampshire: Births, Deaths and Marriages, 1654-1969.* (From microfilmed records. Online database: *AmericanAncestors.org*, New England Historic Genealogical Society, 2014.)
[221] Donovan, *The History of the Town of Lyndeborough, NH*, p. 180
[222] Ancestry.com. Vermont, Vital Records, 1720-1908
[223] Morrison, *A History of the Alison Family*, p 63
[224] In the 1870 U.S. Census, 97-year-old Sarah Ordway was living with her son Daniel and his wife Hannah. Year: 1870; Census Place: Cameron, Steuben, New York; Roll: M593_1094; Page: 506A; Family History Library Film: 552593

Frances (Chase) Ordway; Enoch d. at Greenwood, NY 8 Jan 1843.

82) EBENEZER ABBOTT *(Ephraim³, John², George¹)*, b. 20 Feb 1731 son of Ephraim and Sarah (Crosby) Abbott; d. 19 Dec 1771; m. 1 Jan 1752, LYDIA FARRINGTON, b. 24 Oct 1735 daughter of John and Sarah (Houghton) Farrington; it is possible that Lydia married Abraham Sheldon of Reading in 1774, but that is not certain.

Ebenezer did not leave a will. His widow Lydia was administrator of the estate. There are records for seven children all born at Andover.

381)	i	HANNAH ABBOTT, b. 27 Jun 1752; d. 24 Jul 1816; m. 18 Sep 1777, ABIJAH CLARK, b. 1742 (based on age at time of death); Abijah d. 25 May 1818.
	ii	LYDIA ABBOTT, b. 18 Jun 1754; d. 10 Jan 1775; m. 26 Dec 1773, PETER TOWNE, b. 10 Aug 1749 son of Nathan and Eunice (-) Towne. Peter m. 2nd Rebecca Sheldon; Peter d. 20 May 1830. Lydia and Peter had one son, Peter, who lived about 10 days and died the day before his mother died.
382)	iii	EBENEZER ABBOTT, b. 15 Jan 1757; d. at Reading 1803; m. 21 Oct 1783, SARAH GRAVES, b. at Reading, Mar 1765 daughter of Daniel and Sarah (-) Graves; Sarah was living at the time of Ebenezer's will in 1803. Sarah remarried to Lieutenant William Flint in 1804 and died in 1809.
383)	iv	EPHRAIM ABBOTT, b. 18 Mar 1759; d. 1 Jan 1834 at Sherbrooke, Quebec; m. 26 Oct 1781, ESTHER EASTMAN of Conway, ME, b. 6 May 1761 daughter

		of Richard and Mary (Lovejoy) Eastman; Esther d. at Sherbrooke, Quebec 30 Dec 1846.[225]
	v	JETHRO ABBOTT, b. 18 Apr 1761; d. 2 May 1764.
	vi	THEODORE ABBOTT, b. 10 Sep 1763; d. 14 May 1764.
384)	vii	SARAH ABBOTT, b. 7 Dec 1765; d. after 1834 and likely in 1856 in Ohio;[226] m. 28 Dec 1784, her third cousin, DAVID STEVENS, b. 3 Feb 1761 son of Thomas and Sarah (Gray) Stevens; David d. 29 Jan 1834.

83)   PETER ABBOTT *(Ephraim³, John², George¹)*, b. 8 May 1734 son of Ephraim and Sarah (Crosby) Abbott; d. 19 Apr 1774 at Kingston, NH; m. 22 Sep 1757 ELIZABETH DAMON widow.[227]

This was a family beset by tragedy. Four children ranging in age from three years to seven years old died between 2 March and 6 March 1765.

Peter Abbott did not leave a will, but his estate entered probate 25 May 1774 at Kingston, New Hampshire. Widow Elizabeth declined administration of the estate. David Clifford assumed the bond for the probate. There was an inventory in 1774 and an additional inventory 29 March 1777. The debts against the estate were £150 and the value of the personal estate was £106. There is nothing in the probate papers to suggest there are heirs

---

[225] Quebec, Canada, Vital and Church Records (Drouin Collection), 1621-1968 (ancestry.com)

[226] Sarah was still living at the time of the probate of her husband's estate. She seems to have traveled to Ohio to live with her son Ebenezer and his wife Lucy Herrick. There is a Sarah Stevens age 85 living with Ebenezer and Lucy Stevens in Springfield, Ohio in the 1850 US. Census. If this is indeed our Sarah (and it seems to be), Sarah died in Ohio in 1856.

[227] The death record of one of the children gives the mother's maiden name as Elizabeth Kent, but I cannot locate an Elizabeth Kent that married a Damon and was then widowed.

other than the mention of the widow. There is no settlement to heirs included; there is just a list of creditors against the estate.[228]

There are seven births recorded for this family. The two oldest, twins Peter and Edmund, were recorded at Andover. The third child is recorded at Concord, and the youngest four are recorded at Kingston, New Hampshire.

385)   i   PETER ABBOTT, b. 22 Jun 1758; d. at Chester, NH Feb 1825; m. 7 Mar 1782, PHEBE SPRATT[229] who was "of Deerfield" but parents not located; Phebe d. at Chester 16 Feb 1846.

   ii   EDMUND ABBOTT, b. 22 Jun 1758; d. 2 Mar 1765.

   iii   BENJAMIN ABBOTT, b. Sep 1760; d. 4 Mar 1765.

   iv   DANIEL ABBOTT, b. 7 Jun 1762; d. 6 Mar 1765.

   v   BETTY ABBOTT, b. 7 Jun 1762; d. 4 Mar 1765.

   vi   EPHRAIM ABBOTT, b. 16 Dec 1764; no further record located.

   vii   BETTY ABBOTT, b. 15 Dec 1766; no further record located.

84)   MARTHA ABBOTT *(Ephraim³, John², George¹)*, b. 13 Jul 1737 daughter of Ephraim and Sarah (Crosby) Abbott; d. 13 Aug 1773 at Amherst, NH; m. about 1757 ARCHELAUS TOWNE, b. 1734 at Topsfield son of Israel and Grace (Gardner) Towne; Archelaus d. Nov 1779 at Fishkill, NY during the Revolution.

---

[228] *New Hampshire Wills and Probate Records 1643-1982,* Probate of Peter Abbott, Rockingham, 25 May 1774, Case number 4103.

[229] Some sources give her name as Pratt, but the marriage record and the birth records for the children give her name as Phebe Spratt.

Archelaus Towne was a tavern owner in Monson, New Hampshire. He was a militia Captain in the Revolutionary War and raised a company in the Amherst area and joined the continental army. He was reported to have seen service at Bunker Hill and Bennington. He remained in the service until his death. He was also a selectman in Monson.[230]

Six children are reported in published genealogies, although a record was located for just one child.[231] The children were likely born at Monson or Amherst, New Hampshire.

        i   SARAH TOWNE, b. 23 May 1758; no further record.

386) ii   ARCHELAUS TOWNE, b. 13 Jul 1760; d. at Hillsborough 8 Jul 1818; m. 22 Sep 1787, ESTHER WESTON, b. at Amherst 7 Jul 1763 daughter of Ebenezer and Esther (Kendall) Weston; Esther d. 6 Apr 1850 at Amherst.

387) iii   SUSANNAH TOWNE, b. 29 Dec 1762; d. at Norwich, VT 2 Dec 1840; m. 21 Oct 1779, TIMOTHY NICHOLS, b. at Reading, 16 Feb 1756 son of Timothy and Mehitable (Weston) Nichols; Timothy d. at Norwich, VT 22 Aug 1846.

388) iv   ABIGAIL TOWNE, b. 18 Feb 1765; d. at Merrimack, NH 11 Apr 1832; m. 12 Jan 1790, Dr. PETER ALLEN, b. at Surry, NH, 13 Feb 1764 son of Abel and Elizabeth (Chapin) Allen; d. 18 Mar 1809.[232]

389) v   MARTHA TOWNE, b. 12 Nov 1771; d. about 1845 at Wells River, VT; m. 1792, DANIEL HOLT, b. 5 Feb

---

[230] Spaulding, An Account of Some Early Settlers of West Dunstable, p 108
[231] Information on births obtained from Spaulding's, *An Account of Some of the Early Settlers of West Dunstable, Monson and Hollis, N.H.*, p 108
[232] Littlefield and Pfister, *Genealogies of the Early Settlers of Weston, Vermont*

1767 son of Isaac and Mary (Marble) Holt; Daniel d. at Wells River, VT 18 Jun 1854.

vi MARY TOWNE, b. 12 Nov 1771; m. AMOS DODGE, b. 18 Jun 1769 son of Bartholomew and Martha (Hartshorne) Dodge; Mary and Amos do not seem to have had any children.[233]

Joshua³, John², George¹

85) JOHN ABBOTT *(Joshua³, John², George¹)*, b. 5 May 1713 son of Joshua and Rebeckah (Shed) Abbott; d. 22 Oct 1791 at Westford, MA; m. 30 Dec 1735, HANNAH RICHARDSON, b. 2 Apr 1714 at Billerica daughter of Jonathan and Hannah (French) Richardson; Hannah d. 29 Nov 1795.

John Abbott was born in Billerica but relocated with his family to Westford where he served as deacon from 1762 through at least 1777. He was active in town functions and served on various building and other civic committees.[234]

In his will written 3 November 1785, John Abbott made bequests to the following persons: well beloved wife Hannah, daughter Martha Prescott, son John, and five grandchildren, the children of daughter Rebeckah Jewett who is deceased (Jonathan, John, Patty, Leonard, and Joshua).[235]

There are births of six children record for this family, all at Westford.

i HANNAH ABBOTT, b. 4 Jan 1736/7; d. 5 Oct 1738.

---

[233] Dodge. *Genealogy of the Dodge Family of Essex County, Mass.*, p 106
[234] Hodgman, *History of the Town of Westford*
[235] *Middlesex County, MA: Probate File Papers, 1648-1871.* Probate of John Abbott, 1791, Case number 30.

390) ii REBECCA ABBOTT, b. 17 Feb 1738/9; d. 19 Feb 1785; m. 3 Nov 1763, JOSEPH JEWETT, b. at Littleton, 15 Jun 1740 son of Ezra and Mary (Herrick) Jewett. Joseph m. 2nd 20 Dec 1785, Esther Symons; Joseph d. 25 Aug 1814.

iii HANNAH ABBOTT, b. 11 Mar 1740/1; d. 5 Dec 1783; Hannah did not marry.

391) iv JOHN ABBOTT, b. 2 Dec 1743; d. 8 May 1804; m. 1st Jul 1769, LUCY PROCTOR, b. at Chelmsford, 28 Nov 1746 daughter of Daniel and Susanna (Hill) Proctor; Lucy d. 27 Apr 1779. John m. 2nd 22 Jun 1780, MARY FARRAR, b. at Concord, 4 Jul 1747 daughter of Jacob and Mary (Merriam) Farrar; Mary d. 26 Feb 1815.

v JOSHUA ABBOTT, b. 25 Oct 1750; d. 8 Oct 1752.

392) vi MARTHA ABBOTT, b. 17 Sep 1755; d. at Reading, 20 Oct 1842; m. 16 Nov 1776, JOHN PRESCOTT, b. 25 Apr 1752 son of Jonas and Rebecca (Jones) Prescott; John d. 30 Oct 1842.

86) SARAH ABBOTT (*Joshua³, John², George¹*), b. 24 Feb 1714/5 daughter of Joshua and Rebeckah (Shed) Abbott; d. about 1798;[236] m. 1 Jan 1736, CHRISTOPHER OSGOOD, b. 21 Jul 1712 at Billerica son of Christopher and Mary (Keyes) Osgood; Christopher d. 26 Aug 1748. Sarah m. 2nd, about 1750, JAMES GOODWIN, b. at Reading, 1 Nov 1714 son of John and Tabitha (Pearson) Goodwin; James d. at Worcester, 2 Jun 1776. James was first married to Mary Mansfield who died in 1749.

Christopher Osgood wrote his will 25 August 1748 just one day before his death. He wills that his real estate be sold and after

---

[236] It is possible that she is the widow Sarah Goodwin who died in Wakefield 24 July 1798 at age 86.

the payment of debts that the proceeds be divided among his children. He orders that the timber at the mill be sawed and applied toward his debts. All his personal estate is at the disposal of his well-beloved wife Sarah. William Stickney and Thomas Kidder are appointed executors.[237]

At the time of Christopher Osgood's death in 1748, guardians were appointed for five minor children: Sarah, Mary, Christopher, Rebecca, and John. Sarah remarried about 1750 to James Goodwin of Worcester and the family relocated there. It is known that Sarah Abbott Osgood marries a Goodwin as the will of Joshua Abbott includes a bequest to his daughter Sarah Goodwin. James Goodwin of Worcester is one of the signers on the 1757 guardianship request for Christopher Osgood when he selects David Bancroft of Worcester as his guardian.

Children of Sarah Abbott and Christopher Osgood, born at Billerica:

393) i SARAH OSGOOD, b. 28 May 1738; d. at Lancaster 24 May 1805; m. at Worcester, 10 May 1756, TIMOTHY WHITING, b. 13 Feb 1731/2 son of Samuel and Deborah (Hill) Whiting; Timothy d. 12 Jul 1799.

394) ii MARY OSGOOD, b. 31 Aug 1740; d. at Worcester, 5 Sep 1761; m. 14 May 1757, JOHN GREEN, b. at Leicester, 14 Aug 1736 son of Thomas and Martha (Lynde) Green. John m. 2nd MARY RUGGLES; John d. 29 Oct 1799.

395) iii CHRISTOPHER OSGOOD, b. 12 Apr 1743; death uncertain; m. by 1765, HANNAH BROWN, b. 21 Sep

---

[237] *Middlesex County, MA: Probate File Papers, 1648-1871. Probate* of Christopher Osgood, *1748, Case number* 16268.

1742 daughter of Luke and Elizabeth (-) Brown; Hannah d. at Newfane, VT 1779.

    iv   REBECKAH OSGOOD, b. 11 Jun 1746; d. 22 Oct 1749.

    v   JOHN OSGOOD, b. 24 Apr 1748; d. 17 Oct 1749.

Sarah Abbott and James Goodwin had three children born at Worcester.

396) i REBECCA GOODWIN, b. 21 Oct 1751; m. at Worcester, 1 May 1781, AMOS JOHNSON, *possibly* b. at Worcester, 13 Jan 1756 son of John and Susannah (-) Johnson.

397) ii JOHN GOODWIN, b. 6 Aug 1753; d. at Putney, VT, 2 Sep 1801; m. at Leicester, 11 Feb 1773, MARTHA MOORE, b. at Worcester, 14 Jul 1752 daughter of Asa and Sarah (Hayward) Moore.[238]

398) iii TABITHA GOODWIN, b. 4 May 1756; d. at Shoreham, VT, 31 Jul 1825; m. 12 Jul 1776, JOEL DOOLITTLE, b. at Worcester, 8 Dec 1752 son of Ephraim and Sarah (Morton) Doolittle; Joel d. 19 Dec 1829.

87)   MARY ABBOTT *(Joshua³, John², George¹)*, b. 28 Aug 1717 daughter of Joshua and Rebeckah (Shed) Abbott; d. about 1800; m. 29 Nov 1743, HENRY JEFTS b. at Billerica 24 Apr 1717 son of Henry and Elizabeth (Hayward) Jefts; Henry d. 19 Aug 1772.

---

[238] The will of Asa Moore written in 1798 includes a bequest to his daughter Patty Goodwin.

Henry Jefts did not leave a will. An inventory of his estate was filed 5 November 1772. The probate record does not include a distribution of the estate.

The births of five children are recorded at Billerica.

    i   JOHN JEFTS, b. 9 Nov 1744; d. 20 Apr 1750.

    ii   ELIZABETH JEFTS, b. 3 Oct 1746; no further record.

399) iii   HENRY JEFTS, b. 7 Oct 1748; d. unknown but he appears on the 1810 Census in Billerica; m. 24 Feb 1774, ELIZABETH STEARNS, b. 20 Jun 1751 daughter of Samuel and Hannah (Trask) Stearns; Elizabeth was still living when her father wrote his will 1 May 1801.

    iv   MARY JEFTS, b. 24 Aug 1750; d.?; m. 15 May 1771, SAMUEL HAZELTINE, b. at Tewksbury, 24 Mar 1745, son of Samuel and Sarah (Bixby) Hazeltine. It is not clear what happened to this family. There are no records for them in either Massachusetts or New Hampshire after their marriage.

    v   ALICE JEFTS, b. 8 Sep 1756; no further record.

88)   HANNAH ABBOTT *(Joshua³, John², George¹)*, twin of MARY, b. 28 Aug 1717 daughter of Joshua and Rebeckah (Shed) Abbott; d. 11 Jan 1753; m. 6 Feb 1739, PHINEAS OSGOOD, b. at Billerica 20 Jun 1714 son of Christopher and Mary (Keyes) Osgood; Phineas d. 3 Jun 1756.

There are just two children recorded for this family. Phineas Osgood did not leave a will. David Osgood was named administrator of the estate. As part of the probate, Oliver Abbot was appointed guardian of daughter Hannah Osgood under 14 years of age. There are no other children mentioned.[239]

    i   PHINEAS OSGOOD, b. at Holliston 3 Sep 1739; d. at Billerica 25 Nov 1752.

    ii   HANNAH OSGOOD, b. at Billerica 24 Sep 1743; in Billerica records, there is this marriage record for Hannah: Hannah [d. Phinehas and Hannah] and —— —— Williams, —— ——, ——, in Boston.* There is a marriage for Hannah Osgood and John Williams at Boston 3 Jun 1809, but I have no idea if this is her.

89)   ELIZABETH ABBOTT *(Joshua[3], John[2], George[1])*, b. 7 Dec 1719 daughter of Joshua and Rebeckah (Shed) Abbott; d. about 1803;[240] m. 7 Dec 1743, ROBERT WALKER whose origin is unknown to me; he is perhaps the son of John and Abigail (Wesson) Walker of Chelmsford; Robert d. 26 Jan 1757.

Very little in terms of records have been located for Robert Walker. Hazen's *History of Billerica, Massachusetts* (p. 180) lists his seat in the meeting house as a second seat in the side gallery very near the seat of Henry Jefts, Jr. who was married to Elizabeth Abbott's sister Mary. There is no probate record for Robert Walker. There is no record that Elizabeth remarried. The births of eight children are recorded at Billerica.

    i   ELIZABETH WALKER, b. 9 Apr 1745; no further record.

---

[239] *Middlesex County, MA: Probate File Papers, 1648-1871. Probate* of Phineas Osgood, *1756, Case number* 16280.
[240] This is the death date given in published genealogies (for example, Hazen's *The History of Billerica*, p. 154) but no source for this information is given and I could locate no records associated with it.

400)	ii	ABIGAIL WALKER, b. 6 Oct 1746; d. at Grafton, VT, 7 Apr 1818; m. 10 Mar 1768, WILLIAM STICKNEY, b. 3 Apr 1743 son of William and Anna (Whiting) Stickney.
	iii	SAMUEL WALKER, b. 12 Apr 1748; no further record.
	iv	JOEL WALKER, b. 17 Feb 1749/50; no further record.
401)	v	LYDIA WALKER, b. 22 Mar 1752; d.?; m. 20 Oct 1770, JOSIAH RICHARDSON, b. 19 Jun 1751 son of Josiah and Judith (Kendall) Richardson.
402)	vi	REBECKAH WALKER, b. 12 Jun 1754; d. 17 May 1782; m. 25 Apr 1776, EBENEZER RICHARDSON, b. 25 Feb 1754 son of Ebenezer and Elizabeth (Shed) Richardson.
	vii	SARAH WALKER, b. 6 Jun 1756; no further record.
403)	viii	HANNAH WALKER, b. 6 Jun 1756; m. 4 Sep 1775, JOHN WRIGHT,[241] b. at Wilmington, 29 Jun 1756 son of Josiah Wright and Abigail (Graves) Wright. The births of the children in this family are recorded at Billerica, but then there is no more record of them.

90) JOSHUA ABBOTT (*Joshua³, John², George¹*), b. 28 Oct 1722 son of Joshua and Dorcas (Whiting) Abbott; d. at Billerica, 7 Aug 1807;

---

[241] Hazen's *The History of Billerica* gives the wife of John Wright as Hannah the daughter of Joseph Walker. But Hannah the daughter of Joseph was born in 1744 making her seemingly too old for this John. In addition, the 1807 will of Joshua Abbott (the brother of Elizabeth Abbott Walker) includes a bequest for his niece Hannah Wright. Also, John and Hannah Wright's last child was born in 1796 which would rule out Hannah born in 1744 as the mother in this family.

m. 6 Mar 1746, SARAH STEARNS, b, at Billerica 10 Dec 1726 daughter of Isaac and Alice (Wilson) Stearns; Sarah d. 7 Sep 1803.

Just one child was located for this family. In his will, Joshua Abbott made bequests to his siblings, nieces, and nephews. There are bequests for the following persons: sister Dorcas Abbott who receives one-half of the homestead, Joshua Kidder who receives the other half of the homestead, Blaney Abbot gets his pew in the Billerica meeting house, Joanna Winship (niece) of Lexington, the widow Dorcas Bowers (niece) of Billerica, Abigail Kidder (niece), and Elizabeth Abbot of Billerica each receive $150; and to Henry Jefts (nephew), Elizabeth Jefts (nephew), Alice Jefts (niece), Lydia Richardson, and Hannah Wright (niece) all of Billerica; to Sarah Spaulding, Alice Trull, and Abigail Shattuck daughters of Oliver Stearns (children of Oliver Stearns and Susanna Winch?) late of Billerica each to receive $25; and to Polly Wilson who lives with him he gives some household items and $40; Samuel Stearns and Abbot Stearns sons of Oliver Stearns, and to James Abbot of Billerica who is also named executor.[242]

Child of Joshua Abbott and Sarah Stearns:
    i   JOSHUA ABBOTT, b. 2 Nov 1747; d. 7 Jun 1752.

91)   OLIVER ABBOTT *(Joshua³, John², George¹)*, b. 26 Mar 1727 son of Joshua and Dorcas (Whiting) Abbott; d. 10 Apr 1796; m. 13 Feb 1752, JOANNA FRENCH, b. at Billerica 27 Nov 1729 daughter of William and Joanna (Hill) French; Joanna d. 20 Aug 1768. OLIVER m. 2nd at Westford 1 Aug 1769, ABIGAIL HALL, b. 19 Jul 1734 daughter of Willard and Abigail (Cotton) Hall; Abigail d. 4 Aug 1804.

The following heirs to the estate of Oliver Abbott signed approving of Simon Winship of Lexington as administrator of the

---

[242] *Middlesex County, MA: Probate File Papers, 1648-1871. Probate* of Joshua Abbott, *1807, Case number* 37.

estate: Abigail Abbott, Joanna Winship, Dorcas Bowers, Abigail Abbott (jr.), and Elizabeth Abbott.

Oliver and Joanna had nine children, but six of those children died in early childhood. Children of Oliver Abbott and Joanna French all born at Billerica:

	i	JOANNA ABBOTT, b. 15 Apr 1753; d. 19 Apr 1753.
	ii	LYDIA ABBOTT, b. 11 Jul 1754; d. 22 Jul 1788. Lydia did not marry.
404)	iii	JOANNA ABBOTT, b. 24 Jul 1775; d. after 1813 (alive at time of husband's probate); m. 21 May 1776, SIMON WINSHIP, b. at Lexington, Nov 1749 son of Samuel and Abigail (Crosby) Winship; Simon d. at Lexington 24 Jan 1813.
	iv	OLIVER ABBOTT, b. 1 Dec 1756; d. 9 Feb 1757.
	v	OLIVER WHITING ABBOTT, b. 5 Dec 1757; d. 1 May 1758.
	vi	BERIAH ABBOTT, b. and d. 1 Apr 1759.
	vii	SILENCE ABBOTT, b. and d. 21 Jul 1760.
	viii	SILENT ABBOTT, b. likely 1761; d. 13 May 1761.
405)	ix	DORCAS ABBOTT, b. 19 Dec 1764; d. after 1850 likely in Williamsburg, NY;[243] m. 21 Apr 1783, JONATHAN BOWERS, b. at Chelmsford, 18 Feb

---

[243] In the 1850 U.S. Census, Dorcas Bowers age 85 was in the household of Mary and Alfred Curtis in Williamsburg, NY. Mary Bowers Curtis was Dorcas's granddaughter. Also in the home was Dorcas's son (and Mary Curtis's father) Alexander Bowers. Year: 1850; Census Place: Williamsburg, Kings, New York; Roll: M432_522; Page: 400A; Image: 530

1761 son of William and Hannah (Kidder) Bowers; Jonathan d. 21 Feb 1804.

Oliver Abbott had three children with his second wife Abigail Hall. The children were all born at Billerica.

        i   JOSHUA ABBOTT, b. 29 Jul 1772; d. 7 Jun 1795 at the Island of Hispaniola.[244]

406)   ii   ABIGAIL ABBOTT, b. 14 Dec 1774; d. at Boston 12 Sep 1816; m. 25 Dec 1796, EPHRAIM KIDDER, b. 10 Apr 1766 son of Ephraim and Lucy (Pollard) Kidder; Ephraim d. 22 Dec 1807.

       iii   ELIZABETH ABBOTT, b. 4 Dec 1779; d. at Boston 23 Feb 1852. Elizabeth did not marry. At the time of the 1850 US Census, she was living with her niece, Abigail Kidder, in Chelmsford.[245]

92)   DAVID ABBOTT *(Joshua³, John², George¹)*, b. 27 Apr 1729 son of Joshua and Dorcas (Whiting) Abbott; d. 15 Nov 1801; m. 25 Aug 1752, HANNAH ELLIS, b. about 1727 but origin is unknown; Hannah d. 17 Dec 1767. DAVID m. 2nd 28 Jun 1768 HULDAH PAINE of Malden, who d. 8 Sep 1797.

There is just one child recorded for David Abbott and Hannah Ellis.

       i   DAVID ABBOTT, b. 5 Jun 1760; d. 19 Dec 1761.

---

[244] Ancestry.com, U.S., Newspaper Extractions from the Northeast, 1704-1930. Joshua Abbot son of Oliver Abbot d. at Island of Hispaniola, 7th June, age 23.
[245] 1850 U.S. Census, Chelmsford, enumerated 17 Oct 1850. Household consists of E. Abbott female age 71 and A. Kidder female age 50.

Births of two children are recorded for David Abbott and Huldah Paine.

    i   DAVID ABBOTT, b. 18 Dec 1770; d. 9 Apr 1804; David does not seem to have married.

    ii   BLANEY ABBOTT, b. 25 Oct 1772; d. 17 Jul 1855. Blaney did not marry; his death record lists him as single. He did leave a will in which he leaves his estate to two nieces, Lydia Wilson and Betsy Wilson of Marblehead. The parents of Lydia and Betsy seem to be George Wilson and Polly Hooper (uncertain of that), but I have not worked out how these young women are his nieces.

Ebenezer^3, John^2, George^1

65)   HANNAH ABBOT *(Ebenezer^3, John^2, George^1)* and JOSEPH ABBOTT *(John^3, John^2, George^1)* This is the same as Family #65 that was covered earlier.

93)   MARY ABBOTT *(Ebenezer^3, John^2, George^1)*, b. 2 Apr 1725 daughter of Ebenezer and Hannah (Turner) Abbot; d. 20 Apr 1760; m. 1st 4 Oct 1742, her second cousin once removed, JOSEPH CHANDLER, b. 20 Nov 1720 son of Thomas and Mary (Stevens) Chandler (confirmed by the will of Thomas Chandler[246]); Joseph d. 31 Mar 1745. MARY m. 2nd 8 Apr 1746, ISAAC BLUNT, b. 5 Nov

---

[246] The will of Thomas Chandler in 1751 includes a bequest to his grandson Joseph Chandler the only son of his son Joseph who is deceased.

1712 son of William and Sarah (Foster) Blunt. Isaac m. 2nd Mary Kimball; Isaac d. at Andover, 6 Jan 1798.

Mary Abbott and Joseph Chandler had one child before Joseph's early death. Mary then remarried Isaac Blunt and they had six children.

The will of Isaac Blunt has bequests to the following persons: beloved wife Mary (who is Mary Kimball that he married after Mary Abbott died); daughter Anna; daughter Elizabeth (from his marriage to Mary Abbott) who is single and is allowed to live with her brother Isaac who gets the house; daughters get household goods (Elizabeth, Abigail, Anna, Tabitha, and Mehitable, the latter four being daughters form his marriage to Mary Kimball); and then three other daughters (Mary, Hannah, and Sarah who are daughters from his marriage to Mary Abbott) get a small amount of money; son John Blunt (land in Amherst, New Hampshire); and son Isaac the remainder of the estate.[247]

There is one child recorded at Andover for Mary Abbott and Joseph Chandler.

407)   i   JOSEPH CHANDLER, b. 8 Jun 1743; d. 8 Jun 1834 at Atkinson, NH; m. at Newbury, 7 Jan 1768, ELIZABETH COOK, b. at Newbury, 22 May 1747 daughter of Samuel and Elizabeth (-) Cook.

Mary Abbott and Isaac Blunt had six children whose births are recorded at Andover.

408)   i   MARY BLUNT, b. 14 Feb 1746/7; d. before 1818[248] likely at Exeter, NH; m. 2 May 1771; JEREMIAH

---

[247] *Essex County, MA: Probate File Papers, 1638-1881. Probate of* Isaac Blunt, 6 Mar 1798, *Case number* 2654.

[248] She was not living at the time of the probate of her husband's estate 14 September 1818.

LEAVITT, b. about 1749 and likely the son of Jeremiah and Mary (-) Leavitt; Jeremiah d. at Exeter, NH, 3 Aug 1818.

409) ii HANNAH BLUNT, b. 25 Sep 1758; d. likely at Wilmington, MA; m. 10 Aug 1773, EZRA CARTER, b. at Wilmington, 26 Feb 1745/6 son of Ezra and Lydia (Jenkins) Carter; Ezra d. at Wilmington, 11 Feb 1827.

iii SARAH BLUNT, b. 12 Dec 1750; d. at Haverhill, 2 Aug 1841; m. 13 Aug 1774, DAVID WEBSTER, b. at Haverhill, 13 Jul 1749 son of Jonathan and Abigail (Duston) Webster; David d. 9 Oct 1828. David and Sarah do not seem to have had any children. In his will, David Webster had bequests to his wife Sarah and to several nephews.

iv ELIZABETH BLUNT, b. 27 Jul 1752; d. 24 Mar 1801; Elizabeth did not marry.

410) v JOHN BLUNT, b. 31 Jan 1756; d. at Amherst, NH, 27 Nov 1836;[249] m. at Wilmington, 26 Oct 1780, SARAH EAMES daughter of Caleb and Mary (Harvey) Eames; Sarah d. at Milford, 25 Jan 1858.

vi ISAAC BLUNT, b. 12 Sep and d. 13 Sep 1757.

94) ISAAC ABBOTT *(Ebenezer³, John², George¹)*, b. 30 Jan 1728 son of Ebenezer and Hannah (Turner) Abbot; d. after 1790 at Fryeburg,

---

[249] The gravestone for this family has the following inscription: JOHN BLUNT DIED Nov. 27, 1836, AEt. 80; SARAH EAMES his wife Died Jan. 25, 1858, AEt. 93; Isaac 14 m's, Alva L. 3d's; Twin sons 1 d., Alva L. 17 d's & Rebecca K. 4 1/2 y's. Children of John & Sarah Blunt rest here. Blessed are the dead that die in the Lord. (findagrave.com, ID 61561179)

ME; m. 29 May 1753, SUSANNA FARNUM, whose origins are not known to me. Susanna is either the daughter of Ebenezer Farnum and Priscilla Ingalls or Barachias and Hephzibah Farnum, but I have not located any records that confirm which.[250]

The births of seven children are recorded at Andover. Three other children born in Maine can be reasonably placed in this family. Each of them has a record for a marriage in Fryeburg.

411) i SUSANNA ABBOTT, b. 29 Aug 1754;[251] d. at Oxford County, ME, 21 Sep 1827; m. SAMUEL CHARLES, b. 28 Aug 1754 son of John and Abigail (Bliss) Charles; Samuel d. 14 Dec 1843.

412) ii OLIVE ABBOTT, b. 17 Feb 1756; d. in Oxford County, ME, 27 Aug 1828; m. about 1782, as his second wife, JOHN CHARLES, b. 28 Feb 1744 son of John and Abigail (Bliss) Charles; John d. 6 Jun 1831. John was first married to Phebe Russell.

413) iii LUCY ABBOTT, b. 20 Mar 1759; d. at Maine about 1790; m. WILLIAM KIMBALL. William m. 2nd, BETHIAH GORDON; William d. about 1813 (date of probate).

iv EBENEZER ABBOTT, b. 7 Dec 1760.

414) v ISAAC ABBOTT, b. 16 Jun 1762; d. at Fryeburg, ME, 23 Jun 1861; m. SUSANNA NOYES KNIGHT, b. about 1770 daughter of Stephen and Susanna (Noyes) Knight; Susanna d. 3 Sep 1851. Isaac is likely also the father of Enoch Eaton Abbott, an out-of-wedlock child born to Sarah Eaton in 1785.

---

[250] Farnham's *The New England Descendants of the Immigrant Ralph Farnum* states Ebenezer and Priscilla are her parents and that seems more likely.
[251] The transcription of this record indicates the record was torn and only the last letter "a" is present.

Generation Four 183

415) vi SIMEON ABBOTT, b. 20 May 1764; d. at Stow, ME, 7 May 1851; m. 3 Jul 1791, MARY DAY, b. Feb 1768 daughter of Moses and Hannah (-) Day; Mary d. 14 Sep 1840.

vii MICAH ABBOTT, b. 15 May 1766; d. 16 Aug 1767.

416) viii JAMES ABBOTT, b. 1770 (based on age 89 at death); d. at Stow, ME, Dec 1859; m. at Fryeburg, 16 Aug 1795, ELIZABETH DAY, b. 18 Jun 1773 daughter of Moses and Hannah (-) Day; Elizabeth d. 6 Nov 1857.

417) ix MICAH ABBOTT, b. at Fryeburg, 1 Nov 1774; d. at Stow, ME, 2 Jul 1825; m. about 1795, ALICE WILLEY, b. at Stow, 20 May 1778 daughter of Benjamin and Alice (Kilgore) Willey; Alice d. 14 Sep 1858. After Micah's death, Alice married Samuel Huntress.

418) x DOROTHY "DOLLY" ABBOTT, b. 16 Aug 1778; d. at Richland, MI, 11 Nov 1858; m. at Fryeburg, 26 Oct 1795, JOSEPH CHARLES, b. 7 Apr 1773 son of Abner and Sarah (Walker) Charles; Joseph d. at Wyoming County, NY, 26 Jan 1846.

95) PHEBE ABBOTT *(Ebenezer³, John², George¹)*, b. 3 Jan 1731/2 daughter of Ebenezer and Hannah (Turner) Abbot; d. Feb 1805; m. 30 May 1751, JAMES GRIFFIN whose origins are unknown; James d. at Andover, 9 Oct 1815.

The births of seven children of Phebe Abbott and James Griffin are recorded at Andover.

i PHEBE GRIFFIN, b. 1 Oct 1751; d. likely at Nottingham, NH; m. 29 Sep 1791, as his second wife,

BENJAMIN BUTLER, b. at Edgartown, 9 Apr 1729 son of Malachi and Jemima (Dagget) Butler; Benjamin d. at Nottingham 26 Dec 1804. Benjamin was first married to Dorcas Abbott (Family #130).

ii HANNAH GRIFFIN, b. 5 Mar 1754; no further clear record.

iii ELIZABETH GRIFFIN, b. 7 Jul 1758.

iv SARAH GRIFFIN, b. 7 Oct 1764.

419) v ABIGAIL GRIFFIN, b. 7 Oct 1764; d. at Middleton, 26 Jan 1860;[252] m. 1st at Wilmington, 9 Jan 1790, SAMUEL FROST; Samuel d. by 1796. Abigail m. 2nd, 9 Oct 1796, ASA HOLT, b. 26 Mar 1768 son of Asa and Dinah (Holt) Holt.

420) vi MARY "POLLY" GRIFFIN, b. 7 Aug 1768; d. before 1847 (not living when husband wrote his will); m. 9 May 1796, BENJAMIN CLEMENT, b. at Haverhill, about 1760 son of Benjamin and Mary (Bartlett) Clement; Benjamin d. at Haverhill about 1853 (probate 6 Apr 1853).

421) vii EBENEZER GRIFFIN, b. 5 Jun 1771; d. 1848 at Litchfield, NH; m. at Leominster, 20 Sep 1792, BETSY CARTER, b. 23 Nov 1774 daughter of Josiah and Elizabeth (Graves) Carter; Betsy d. at Litchfield, 1 Oct 1854.

96) JAMES ABBOTT *(Ebenezer³, John², George¹)*, b. 14 Apr 1736 son of Ebenezer and Hannah (Turner) Abbot; d. unknown, but his duties as town physician were taken over by Dr. Amos Bradley in

---

[252] New England Historic Genealogical Society; Boston, Massachusetts; Massachusetts Vital Records, 1840–1911 (accessed through ancestry.com)

1785; m. at Dracut 25 Feb 1758, LYDIA COBURN, b. at Dracut, 18 Jan 1739 daughter of Joseph and Hannah (Jones) Coburn.

Dr. James Abbott was a physician in Dracut. His father-in-law, Dr. Joseph Coburn was the first town physician in Dracut. Dr. Abbott served in the Revolutionary War as a surgeon's mate. He and his family lived on a farm at Collinsville.[253]

The births of twelve children are recorded at Dracut. Five of the children relocated to New Hampshire. It is possible that the parents accompanied the children to New Hampshire, but that is not known.

422)	i	NEHEMIAH ABBOTT, b. 22 Nov 1759; d. likely at Glover, VT; m. 16 Oct 1788, ANNA VARNUM, b. at Dracut, 23 Apr 1767 daughter of Jonathan and Anna (East) Varnum.
423)	ii	RACHEL ABBOTT, b. 22 Mar 1761; d. at Lowell, 15 Mar 1844; m. 13 Dec 1783, JONATHAN COBURN, b. 19 Aug 1757 son of Jonathan and Marcy (Hildreth) Coburn; death record not located for Jonathan but may have been at Bethel, VT.
	iii	LYDIA ABBOTT, b. 20 May 1762; d. 29 Jun 1767.
	iv	MOLLY ABBOTT, b. 14 Jan 1764; d. 13 Oct 1765.
424)	v	NATHANIEL ABBOTT, b. 19 Jan 1766; d. 28 Feb 1815 in NH; m. 3 Jan 1788, PHEBE CUMMINGS, b. at Westford, 2 Jun 1770 daughter of Thomas and Lucy (Laurence) Cummings; Phebe d. 14 Mar 1843.
	vi	JOSEPH ABBOTT, b. 17 Oct 1767; d. 7 Sep 1778.

---

[253] Coburn, *History of Dracut*, p 155 and p 281

425)	vii	HANNAH ABBOTT, b. 14 Jul 1769; d. at Glover, VT, 15 Jan 1857; m. 17 Dec 1795, JAMES VANCE, b. at Londonderry, 15 Apr 1769; James d. 26 Nov 1864.
	viii	EBENEZER ABBOTT, b. 25 Jan 1771; no further record.
	ix	RONE ABBOTT, b. 13 Jan 1773; d. 3 Sep 1778.
426)	x	SIBYL ABBOTT, b. 21 Dec 1774; d. after 1850 in NH; m. 21 Dec 1797, DAVID WILSON, b. about 1770; David d. after 1850.[254]
427)	xi	RELIEF ABBOTT, b. 8 Sep 1778; d. likely in NH;[255] m. 13 Aug 1796, EBENEZER BROWN, b. at Dunstable, 12 Sep 1773 son of Samuel and Bridget (Bryant) Brown; Ebenezer d. at Dracut 3 Aug 1860.
428)	xii	MERCY ABBOTT, b. 24 Aug 1780; d. 1 Nov 1863 at Hancock; m. Feb 1808, EBENEZER BARTLETT, b. 10 Aug 1779 son of Thomas and Sarah (Rider) Bartlett; Ebenezer d. at Hancock, NH, 8 Nov 1854.

---

[254] Both Sibyl and David were living at the 1850 US Census living in the home of John and Sophia Ellenwood. They are listed as Sibyl A. Wilson age 75 and David Wilson age 79. John Ellenwood married Sophia Wilson at Pelham in 1844. Unsure how they are related. It certainly is possible that these are a different David and Sibyl Wilson, but they are the right ages.

[255] The births of their children are recorded at Londonderry. The family did return to Dracut but unsure whether this was before or after the death of Relief.

Section II: The Grandchildren of Hannah Abbott and John Chandler

John Chandler³, Hannah Abbott Chandler², George¹

54) JOHN CHANDLER *(John Chandler³, Hannah Abbott Chandler², George¹)* and TABITHA ABBOTT *(Nathaniel², George¹)* This is Family #54 covered in Generation Three.

71) JOSHUA CHANDLER *(John Chandler³, Hannah Abbott Chandler², George¹)* and SARAH CHANDLER *(Sarah Abbott Chandler³, John², George¹)* This is Family #71 covered earlier in Generation Four.

97) NATHAN CHANDLER *(John Chandler³, Hannah Abbott Chandler², George¹)*, b. 31 Jan 1708 son of John and Hannah (Frye) Chandler; d. at Andover, 31 Jul 1784; m. 14 May 1729, PRISCILLA HOLT, b. Apr 1709 daughter of Oliver and Hannah (Russell) Holt; Priscilla d. 25 Nov 1803.

Nathan was the lieutenant of a company that marched August 15, 1757 for the relief of Fort William Henry which had come under siege from the French.[256]

In his will (probate 5 October 1784), Nathan Chandler makes bequests to the following persons: dearly beloved wife Priscilla receives use of the house from the bottom of the cellar to the top of the house and the kitchen also and the liberty of using the well; Priscilla also receives several specific provisions for her continued maintenance and the "time and improvement" of his Negro woman Flora. Other bequests are to beloved son Nathan Chandler, beloved

---

[256] Chandler, *The Descendants of William and Annis Chandler*, p 139

son Isaac Chandler, daughter Hannah wife of Joshua Chandler, Mary wife of Jonathan Abbott, and Phebe wife of Isaac Abbott.[257]

There are five births recorded at Andover for Nathan Chandler and Priscilla Holt. Four of the five children married other George Abbott of Andover descendants. The fifth child married a second cousin who was not a George Abbott descendant.

289) i NATHAN CHANDLER, b. 19 Feb 1729/30; d. 30 Apr 1786; m. 18 Apr 1754, his third cousin, PHEBE ABBOTT, b. 14 Apr 1733 daughter of John and Phebe (Fiske) Abbott; Phebe d. 26 Jul 1812. (This is the same couple as Family #62, child i.)

429) ii ISAAC CHANDLER, b. 8 Apr 1732; d. 6 Mar 1817; m. 14 Apr 1757, his second cousin once removed, HANNAH BALLARD, b. 3 Jan 1732/3 daughter of Josiah and Mary (Chandler) Ballard;[258] Hannah d. 2 Oct 1824.[259]

335) iii HANNAH CHANDLER, b. 20 May 1735; d. 14 Feb 1791; m. 31 Mar 1757, as his 1st wife, her first cousin (and George Abbott descendant), JOSHUA CHANDLER, b. 23 Jul 1732 son of Joshua and Sarah (Chandler) Chandler. Joshua m. 2nd 7 Jun 1792, Hannah Ballard the daughter of Hezekiah and Lydia (Chandler) Ballard who was the widow of Obadiah Foster; Joshua Chandler d. 15 Mar 1807. (This couple is the same as Family #71, child ii.)

---

[257] *Essex County, MA: Probate File Papers, 1638-1881. Probate of* Nathan Chandler, 5 Oct 1784, *Case number* 4962.
[258] The 1780 will of Josiah Chandler includes a bequest to his daughter Hannah the wife of Mr. Isaac Chandler.
[259] This is the date of death used in *The Descendants of William and Annis Chandler*, p. 330. The deaths of both Isaac and Hannah are reported by the Chandler book as occurring in Concord, NH, but the record of Isaac's death is in the Andover records with the same specific date as the Chandler book.

205) iv MARY CHANDLER, b. 15 Jun 1740; d. 1 Apr 1824; m. 13 Nov 1759, her second cousin once removed, JONATHAN ABBOTT, b. 24 Oct 1739 son of David and Hannah (Danforth) Abbott; Jonathan d. 10 Apr 1817.

132) v PHEBE CHANDLER, b. 2 Jun 1742; d. 1 Jul 1800; m. 22 Apr 1766, her second cousin once removed, ISAAC ABBOTT, b. 3 Feb 1745 son of Isaac and Phebe (Lovejoy) Abbott; Isaac d. 21 May 1836.

98) HANNAH CHANDLER *(John Chandler³, Hannah Abbott Chandler², George¹)*, b. 1710 daughter of John and Hannah (Frye) Chandler; d. 29 May 1784; m. 4 Jun 1729, her second cousin, TIMOTHY BALLARD, b. 1702 son of Joseph and Rebecca (Johnson) Ballard; Timothy d. at Andover, 30 Oct 1773.

Timothy was a yeoman and owned a share of the Ballardvale saw and grist mill.[260] The inventory of his estate includes a share in the grist mill and one-fourth part of the saw mill. He also had several land parcels and the total value of the estate was £1057.

In his will (written 14 May 1770; probate 6 Dec 1773), Timothy Ballard made bequests to the following persons: Hannah his well-beloved wife, the male heirs of his son Timothy who is deceased, well-beloved son Joseph, well-beloved son Nathan, eldest and beloved daughter Mary Chandler, beloved daughter Hannah Abbott, beloved daughter Elizabeth, beloved daughter Phebe, and beloved daughter Dorothy. Joseph is named executor.[261]

---

[260] Charlotte Helen Abbott, Ballard Family
[261] *Essex County, MA: Probate File Papers, 1638-1881.* Probate of Timothy Ballard, 6 Dec 1773, *Case number* 1602.

The births of eleven children are recorded at Andover. Of the seven children known to have married, five married fellow George Abbott descendants.

430) i TIMOTHY BALLARD, b. 1 Mar 1729/30; d. 12 Jul 1768; m. 21 Jan 1755, his third cousin, SARAH ABBOTT, b. 3 Aug 1733 daughter of Zebadiah and Anne (Lovejoy) Abbott. Sarah did not remarry after Timothy's death and she died 2 Aug 1809.

431) ii MARY BALLARD, b. 1 May 1732; d. at Reading 15 Dec 1803; m. 30 Aug 1750, her third cousin once removed, DAVID CHANDLER, b. 15 Dec 1724 son of Josiah and Sarah (Ingalls) Chandler; David d. at Cambridge 1 Feb 1776. Mary m. 2nd 10 Nov 1779, Daniel Parker.

iii JOHN BALLARD, b. 9 Jun 1734; d. 11 Dec 1736.

432) iv HANNAH BALLARD, b. 8 Jun 1736; d. 27 Sep 1778; m. 11 Mar 1756, as his first wife, her third cousin, NEHEMIAH ABBOTT, b. 24 Aug 1731 son of Zebadiah and Anne (Lovejoy) Abbott. Nehemiah m. 2nd, LYDIA CLARK; Nehemiah d. 13 Oct 1808.

v JOHN BALLARD, b. 9 Apr 1739; no further record and he is not mentioned in his father's will.

vi JOSEPH BALLARD, b. 19 Jul 1741; d. 17 Jan 1746/7.

433) vii NATHAN BALLARD, b. 1 Nov 1744; d. at Concord, NH 14 Jan 1835; m. 1763, his third cousin, HANNAH HOLT, b. 19 Dec 1745 daughter of Jonathan and Lydia (Blanchard) Holt; Hannah d. 1 Dec 1818.

viii ELIZABETH BALLARD, b. 29 Nov 1746; Elizabeth was living at the time of her father's will (1770); it is not known what became of her.

434)	ix	JOSEPH BALLARD, b. Oct 1749; d. 15 Feb 1819; m. 1st 10 Sep 1771, MOLLY SMITH of Shrewsbury; Molly d. by 1773 when Joseph m. 2nd, 16 Dec 1773, his third cousin, HANNAH ABBOTT, b. 10 Oct 1749 daughter of George and Hannah (Lovejoy) Abbott; Hannah d. 29 May 1784.
291)	x	PHEBE BALLARD, b. 5 Nov 1752; d. at Wilton, NH Jan 1846; m. 12 Nov 1772, her third cousin, WILLIAM ABBOTT, b. 3 Jan 1747/8 son of John and Phebe (Fiske) Abbott; William d. at Wilton 13 Nov 1793.
435)	xi	DOROTHY BALLARD, b. 12 Dec 1757; d. at likely Bow, NH after 1820 (alive at the time of her husband's probate January 1820); m. 17 Apr 1783, her first cousin once removed (and George Abbott descendant), JOHN CHANDLER, b. 21 Nov 1759 son of Isaac and Hannah (Ballard) Chandler; John d. at Bow, NH Sep 1819.

99) PHEBE CHANDLER *(John Chandler³, Hannah Abbott Chandler², George¹)*, b. 2 Jan 1714/5 daughter of John and Hannah (Frye) Chandler; d. Jan 1805? at Concord, NH; m. 1 Jan 1735, HENRY LOVEJOY, b. 14 Aug 1714 son of Henry and Sarah (Farnum) Lovejoy; Henry d. 15 Mar 1793 at Concord.[262]

Phebe and Henry married in Andover and most of their children were born there. They left for Rumford, NH by 1745. Henry Lovejoy was a selectman in Concord in 1749.[263] There are

---

[262] New Hampshire, Death and Burial Records Index, 1654-1949, ancestry.com
[263] Lyford, *History of Concord*, p 1339

records for seven children in this family, the oldest five recorded at Andover and the two youngest at Rumford, NH.

Although published genealogies report seven children in this family and there are records for the births of these seven children, it is likely there was an eighth child, Sarah, in this family. According to Bouton's *History of Concord* (p 660), Theodore Farnum of Concord married a Sarah Lovejoy and that couple had four children. Theodore Farnum was born in 1749 son of Josiah and Mary (Frye) Farnum. It is not known that Sarah Lovejoy belongs in this family, but there is no other obvious family for her in Concord at the time. The estate of Theodore Farnum entered probate in 1789 with widow Sarah as administrator and with Chandler Lovejoy and Phineas Virgin assuming the obligation of the bond. Chandler Lovejoy is a son in this family and Phineas Virgin is likely a brother-in-law to Chandler Lovejoy.

226) i PHEBE LOVEJOY, b. 20 Sep 1735; d. at Concord, 4 Jan 1789; m. 25 Apr 1765, her third cousin, JOSEPH ABBOTT, b. at Concord 23 Oct 1741 son of George and Sarah (Abbott) Abbott. Joseph married 2nd Abigail Tyler; Joseph d. at Concord 19 Jan 1832.

436) ii ABIEL LOVEJOY, b. 25 Jul 1737; d. at Conway, NH 27 May 1817; m. 1764, ANNA STICKNEY, b. at Rumford, 3 Sep 1741 daughter of Jeremiah and Elizabeth (Carleton) Stickney, Anna d. 15 Jan 1815.

437) iii DORCAS LOVEJOY, b. 10 Sep 1739; d. likely at Rumford, ME; m. EBENEZER VIRGIN, b. at Rumford, NH 28 May 1735 son of Ebenezer and Hannah (Foster) Virgin. This family relocated to Rumford, ME where they were first settlers.[264]

---

[264] Lapham, *History of Rumford, Oxford County, Maine*

438)	iv	CHANDLER LOVEJOY, b. 23 Jan 1741/2; d. at Concord 20 Nov 1827; m. MIRIAM VIRGIN, b. at Rumford 23 May 1744 daughter of Ebenezer and Hannah (Foster) Virgin. Chandler m. 2nd 28 Sep 1814, AZUBAH GRAHAM.
	v	HENRY LOVEJOY, b. 19 Oct 1744; died in infancy.
	vi	HENRY LOVEJOY, b. 27 Sep 1746; d. 18 Aug 1747.
439)	vii	HANNAH LOVEJOY, b. 26 Jan 1749; d. at Thetford, VT 29 May 1809; m. JONATHAN WEST, b. at Rumford, 20 Oct 1749 son of Nathaniel and Sarah (Burbank) West; Jonathan d. 30 Aug 1826.
440)	viii	SARAH LOVEJOY, b. 8 Jun 1752; d. at Concord, 1815; m. about 1772, her second cousin, THEODORE FARNUM, b. at Andover, 24 Jan 1749 son of Josiah and Mary (Frye) Farnum; Theodore d. about 1789 (probate of estate). After Theodore's death, Sarah married Jedediah Hoit.

57) ABIEL CHANDLER *(John Chandler^3, Hannah Abbott Chandler^2, George^1)* and REBECCA ABBOTT *(Nathaniel^2, George^1)*
REBECCA ABBOTT and AMOS ABBOTT *(James^3, William^2, George^1)* This is the same family group as Family #57 covered in Generation Three.

100) LYDIA CHANDLER *(John Chandler^3, Hannah Abbott Chandler^2, George^1)*, b. 10 Aug 1720 daughter of John and Hannah (Frye) Chandler; d. 9 Nov 1803; m. 30 Nov 1741, HEZEKIAH BALLARD, b. Jun 1720 son of Hezekiah and Rebecca (Davis) Ballard; Hezekiah d. at Andover, 31 Dec 1801.

Deacon Hezekiah Ballard wrote his will 12 April 1801. In the will, he bequeaths to Lydia "my beloved wife, all my household stuff and furniture, proper for woman's use, to be entirely at her own disposal." She also has use of the easterly half of the dwelling house. Beloved son Hezekiah Ballard receives the westerly half of the dwelling house. Hezekiah also receives the remainder of the personal estate. He makes a token bequest of one dollar to each of his daughters as they have already received their portions of the estate. The daughters are Lydia, Rebecca, Lowis, Hannah, Mary, Sarah, and Lucy. He also grants to his grandson, Joshua Ballard the son of Hezekiah, all his lands on the easterly side of Boston road. Beloved grandson Zebadiah Abbot is named executor of the estate.[265]

The births of ten children were recorded at Andover. Of the eight children who married, seven of them married fellow George Abbott of Andover descendants.

441) i LYDIA BALLARD, b. 30 Jul 1742; d. 28 Nov 1813; m. 13 Dec 1763, her third cousin once removed, DANE HOLT, b. 1 Apr 1740 son of Timothy and Hannah (Dane) Holt; Dane d. 15 Dec 1818.

442) ii REBECCA BALLARD, b. 15 May 1744; d. 15 Sep 1821; m. 1 Oct 1765, her third cousin, ZEBADIAH ABBOTT, b. 27 Sep 1739 son of Zebadiah and Anne (Lovejoy) Abbott; Zebadiah d. 24 Nov 1793.

341) iii LOIS BALLARD, b. 19 Jul 1746; d. 21 Dec 1836; m. 17 Feb 1767, her second cousin (and George Abbott descendant) JOSHUA PHELPS, b. 25 Jun 1738 son of Samuel and Priscilla (Chandler) Phelps; Joshua d. 22

---

[265] *Essex County, MA: Probate File Papers, 1638-1881. Probate of* Hezekiah *Ballard,* 1 Feb 1802, *Case number 1587.*

Dec 1798. This is the same couple as Family #73, child ii.

335) iv HANNAH BALLARD, b. 6 Dec 1748; d. 22 Dec 1838; m. 1st 30 May 1769, OBADIAH FOSTER, b. 25 May 1741 son of John and Mary (Osgood) Foster; Obadiah d. at Andover, 25 Jul 1780. Hannah m. 2nd as his second wife JOSHUA CHANDLER, b. 23 Jul 1732 son of Joshua and Sarah (Chandler) Chandler. Joshua's first wife was HANNAH CHANDLER daughter of Nathan and Priscilla (Holt) Chandler. This is the same as Family #71, child ii.

342) v MARY BALLARD, b. 27 Feb 1750/1; d. 11 Aug 1835; m. 31 Oct 1780, her second cousin (and George Abbott descendant) HENRY PHELPS, b. 5 Sep 1740 son of Samuel and Priscilla (Chandler) Phelps; Henry d. 31 Oct 1807.

vi JOSHUA BALLARD, b. 28 Jun 1753; d. 31 Jan 1755

443) vii SARAH BALLARD, b. 28 Dec 1755; d. 20 Aug 1825; m. 8 May 1777, her third cousin, NATHAN ABBOTT, b. at Pembroke, 4 Sep 1753 son of Job and Sarah (Abbott) Abbott; Nathan d. 1801.

viii DORCAS BALLARD, b. 16 Oct 1757; d. 25 Aug 1775.

444) ix LUCY BALLARD, b. 4 Apr 1760; d. 29 Jun 1827; m. 27 Nov 1782, her first cousin once removed (and George Abbott descendant) NATHAN CHANDLER, b. 16 Jun 1756 son of Nathan and Phebe (Abbott) Chandler; Nathan d. 27 Jun 1837.

445) x HEZEKIAH BALLARD, b. 18 Jul 1762; d. 4 Oct 1848; m. 10 Dec 1783, his first cousin once removed (and

George Abbott descendant), MARY "Molly" CHANDLER, b. 4 Apr 1764 daughter of Zebadiah and Deborah (Blanchard) Chandler; Molly d. 30 Mar 1834.

Abiel Chandler³, Hannah Abbott Chandler², George¹

101) ABIAL (f) CHANDLER *(Abiel Chandler³, Hannah Abbott Chandler², George¹)*, b. 11 Dec 1711 daughter of Abiel and Hephzibah (Harnden) Chandler; d. 29 Jun 1780; m. 13 May 1731, her first cousin once removed, DAVID CHANDLER, b. 11 Jan 1697/8 son of Thomas and Mary (Peters) Chandler; David d. before 1774 probably at Pembroke, NH.[266]

Seven children for this couple were found in the birth records. The births of the two oldest and the two youngest children are recorded at Andover; the three middle children were born at Suncook/Rumford. Chandler's *The Descendants of William and Annis Chandler* (p. 75) lists a son Samuel born 4 November 1757 with this family, but Samuel with that birthdate is recorded as the child of David and Mary (Ballard) Chandler.[267]

	i	INFANT CHANDLER, b. and d. 1731/2.
446a	ii	MARY CHANDLER, b. 8 Aug 1734; likely d. at Blue Hill, ME, 21 Mar 1830. *Likely* the wife of ISAAC

---

[266] Chandler, *The Descendants of William and Annis Chandler* notes that the widow Abial Chandler was received at the church in Andover September 1774 from the church in Pembroke. The family had been dismissed from the church at Andover to Pembroke 21 May 1738.

[267] Massachusetts: Vital Records, 1621-1850 (Online Database: *AmericanAncestors.org*, New England Historic Genealogical Society, 2001-2016).

INGALLS b. at Andover, 13 Sep 1733 son of Henry and Hannah (Martin) Ingalls.[268]

446) iii TIMOTHY CHANDLER, b. 5 Apr 1738 at Suncook; m. at Townsend, 26 Aug 1762, MARY WALKER whose identity is not certain, but born about 1742 (based on age at time of death); Mary d. at Shelburne, NH, 5 Sep 1777.

447) iv HULDAH CHANDLER, b. at Suncook, 16 Aug 1740; d. likely at Hillsborough; m. 1st, 27 Dec 1763, NATHAN WARDWELL, b. 20 Jan 1740/1 son of William and Margery (Gray) Wardwell; Nathan d. 14 Aug 1769. Huldah m. 2nd at Andover, 9 Jan 1772, STEPHEN STILES, b. at Andover, 27 Mar 1741 son of Hezekiah and Hannah (Barnard) Stiles.

448) v HEPHZIBAH CHANDLER, b. 16 Oct 1743; d. 25 Oct 1810; m. 12 Apr 1762, WILLIAM FARNSWORTH, b. at Pepperell, 27 Dec 1737 son of William and Ruth (Hobart) Farnsworth. William m. 2nd, 20 May 1813, Sarah Green; William d. about 1837 in New York.

449) vi LYDIA CHANDLER, b. 28 May 1746; d. after 1816 at Langdon, NH (received a distribution from her husband's estate in 1816); m. 1st, as his second wife, JOSEPH PARKER, b. 15 Jul 1726 son of Joseph and Mary (Emery) Parker; Joseph d. 1777. Joseph's first wife was Hannah Abbott and that family is considered elsewhere (Family #206). Lydia m. 2nd,

---

[268] Porter, Bangor Historical Magazine, volume 4, p 156 gives Issac's wife as Mary Chandler. The Ingalls genealogy, p56, suggests she may be Mary Osgood or Mary Chandler, but the birth date they give is the birth date of Mary Chandler.

THOMAS KENNEY, b. unknown but does not seem to be the son of Thomas Kenney who died in New Hampshire in 1762 (as he is not mentioned in that will); Thomas d. about 1814 at Langdon, NH (probate of will).

vii HANNAH CHANDLER, b. 21 Jun 1755; no further record. There is a Hannah Chandler that married Phineas Parker, but that is Hannah Chandler born in 1756 the daughter of William (as evidenced by the 1800 will of William Chandler that includes a bequest to his daughter Hannah Parker).

Hannah Chandler³, Hannah Abbott Chandler², George¹ *and* Daniel³, George², George¹

[The families in this next section are descended from George Abbott by the two paths listed above.]

102) DORCAS ABBOTT *(Hannah Chandler Abbott³, Hannah Abbott Chandler², George¹* **and** *Daniel³, George², George¹)*, b. 16 Dec 1713 daughter of Daniel and Hannah (Chandler) Abbott; d. 22 Aug 1798 at Woodstock; m. 17 Nov 1740, THOMAS CHAFFEE, b. at Swansea 18 Oct 1716 son of Joseph and Jemima (Chadwick) Chaffee; Thomas d. at Woodstock 3 May 1753.[269]

The family of Dorcas Abbott and Thomas Chaffee was part of the secondary migration in which families from the Massachusetts colony relocated to Connecticut, primarily settlements within Windham County. The couple had four daughters, three of whom lived to adulthood. Thomas died at 36 years old, but Dorcas did not remarry. She remained in Woodstock where she died in 1798.

---

[269] Vital statistics for Woodstock are from Barbour and Brainard's Woodstock Vital Records unless otherwise noted.

Thomas did not leave a will, but there is a 1753 probate record which includes disbursements for the widow Dorcas and her three daughters Jemima, Dorcas, and Rhoda.[270]

One interesting element for this family is that two of the daughters, Jemima and Rhoda, seem to have children out-of-wedlock. The Woodstock Vital Records book has the following entry: "Asenath Hodges Daughter of Jemime Chaffe Born July 22nd 1760." The Connecticut Church Record Abstracts contain the following entries that may be related to this. On 2 August 1761, Jemima Chaffee "confessed and was pardoned." She had her daughter "Asenah" baptized on 21 February 1762.[271] Woodstock Vital Records have the following entry for Rhoda: "Anice Corbin Daughter of Rhoda Chaffe born May 18 - 177[1]." Rhoda confessed 17 March 1771 and had her daughter "Anise" baptized 20 October 1771. There were not corresponding confessions for either Mr. Hodge or Mr. Corbin, so it is not determined who those fathers might be. Both Rhoda and Jemima went on to marry other men.

450) i JEMIMA CHAFFEE, b. 12 May 1741; d. 28 Aug 1818; out-of-wedlock relationship with Mr. Hodges 1759-1760; m. 5 Jun 1766, as his second wife, AMOS PERRIN son of Peter and Abigail (Carpenter) Perrin; Amos d. 11 Jan 1811.

ii DORCAS CHAFFEE, b. 17 May 1744; d. 31 Aug 1746.

451) iii DORCAS CHAFFEE, b. 12 Jun 1747; d. unknown (living at time of husband's death); m. at Ashford 6

---

[270] *Connecticut Wills and Probate, 1609-1999*, Probate of Thomas Chaffee, Hartford, 1753, Case number 873.
[271] Ancestry.com, *Connecticut, Church Record Abstracts, 1630-1920*. Original data: Connecticut Church Records Index. Connecticut State Library, Hartford, Connecticut.

Oct 1767, FRANCIS GREEN CHAFFEE,²⁷² b. 6 Apr 1745 son of Benjamin and Priscilla (Green) Chaffee; Francis d. 3 Jul 1786.

452) iv RHODA CHAFFEE, b. 10 May 1751; d. 19 Nov 1834; out-of-wedlock relationship with Mr. Corbin 1770-1771; m. by 1772, DARIUS TRUESDELL, b. at Pomfret 16 Jan 1752 son of Joseph and Mary (Holt) Truesdell; Darius d. at Woodstock 6 May 1808.

103) JOSEPH ABBOTT *(Hannah Chandler Abbott³, Hannah Abbott Chandler², George¹* **and** *Daniel³, George², George¹)*, b. 19 Sep 1716 son of Daniel and Hannah (Chandler) Abbott; m. at Woodstock, 22 Apr 1738, ABIGAIL CUTLER, b. 28 Aug 1711 at Colchester, CT, daughter of Jonathan and Abigail (Bigelow) Cutler; published genealogies (Bigelow²⁷³ and Abbot genealogies) give the dates of death for both Joseph and Abigail as 22 Sep 1776, but I have located no records for the deaths of either of them.

The Abbot genealogy book²⁷⁴ adds children Olive and Zebadiah to this family. However, the Woodstock Vital Records attributes those two children to Nathan and Ann Abbott. There are only four births recorded for Joseph and Abigail at Woodstock.

i HANNAH ABBOTT, b. 12 Jul 1739.

453) ii DANIEL ABBOTT, b. 18 Oct 1740; d. likely at Lebanon, NH; he did marry and had several children, but the name of his wife has not yet been located.

454) iii JOSEPH ABBOTT, b. 17 Feb 1742/3; d. at Pittstown, NY, 26 Jan 1813; m. 11 Dec 1764, PERSIS PERRIN, b.

---

²⁷² Connecticut, Town Marriage Records, pre-1870 (Barbour Collection)
²⁷³ Howe, *Genealogy of the Bigelow Family*
²⁷⁴ Abbot and Abbot, *Genealogical Record of Descendants*

4 Jun 1742 daughter of Nathaniel and Abigail (-) Perrin; Persis d. 23 Jan 1817.

455) iv SARAH ABBOTT, b. 8 Jul 1748; m. at Union, CT, 24 Nov 1768, JONAS HOUGHTON son of Edward and Abigail (-) Houghton; Jonas d. at Woodstock 13 Nov 1791.

104) ELIZABETH ABBOTT *(Hannah ChandlerAbbott ^{3}, Hannah Abbott Chandler^2, George^1* **and** *Daniel^3, George^2, George^1)*, b. 9 Jul 1719 daughter of Daniel and Hannah (Chandler) Abbott; d. at Woodstock, 1 Jan 1785; m. at Woodstock, 27 May 1737, MATTHEW MURRAY, perhaps of Scotland; d. at Pomfret about 1788 when his estate was probated.

Matthew Murray relocated to Pomfret after the death of Elizabeth. At the time of the probate of his estate in 1788, there were three heirs living and they signed quit claim deeds related to a property in Pomfret to settle the estate. These heirs were James Murray, Asa and Elizabeth Childs, and Jeremiah and Phebe Jackson.[275]

There are six children recorded at Woodstock for Matthew and Elizabeth.

 i JAMES MURRAY, b. 29 Aug 1737; d. 1739.
456) ii PHEBE MURRAY, b. 2 Aug 1739; m. 16 Mar 1758, JEREMIAH JACKSON, b. 22 Aug 1739[276] son of

---

[275] *Connecticut Wills and Probate, 1609-1999*, Probate of Matthew Murry, Hartford, 1788, Case number 2983.
[276] Ancestry.com, *Mayflower Births and Deaths, Vol. 1 and 2* (Provo, UT, USA: Ancestry.com Operations, Inc., 2013).

Joseph and Zipporah (-) Jackson; Jeremiah d. at Lafayette, NY, 10 Mar 1802.[277]

457) iii ELIZABETH MURRAY, b. 10 Sep 1741; d. 28 Apr 1790; m. 17 Nov 1763, ASA CHILDS, b. at Woodstock, 6 Apr 1743 son of Ephraim and Mary (-) Childs; Asa d. 20 Oct 1826.

458) iv JAMES MURRAY, b. 8 Dec 1743; m. 26 Jan 1769, SARAH REYNOLDS who is not yet identified.

v SARAH MURRAY, b. 24 Jan 1745/6; no further record.

vi JOHN MURRAY, b. 1 Apr 1753; no further record.

105) PHEBE ABBOTT *(Hannah Chandler Abbott³, Hannah Abbott Chandler², George¹* **and** *Daniel³, George², George¹)*, b. 7 Apr 1721 daughter of Daniel and Hannah (Chandler) Abbott; d. at Woodstock after 10 Jul 1756 (the birth of her last child);[278] m. at Woodstock 20 Aug 1742, EBENEZER HOLMES, b. at Woodstock 27 Feb 1720/1 son of Ebenezer and Joanna (Ainsworth) Holmes. Ebenezer m. 2nd Martha Howlet, 12 Apr 1759 and 3rd 16 Nov 1775 Elizabeth Barrett. Ebenezer d. at Woodstock, 28 Jun 1794.[279]

Ebenezer Holmes did not leave a will, but the probate record does contain the disbursements to the heirs, four of whom are from his marriage to Phebe Abbott: eldest son Ebenezer, Ralph Vinton on behalf of his wife Phebe, John Vinton on behalf of his wife Dorothy, and Zephaniah Tucker on behalf of his wife Huldah.[280]

---

[277] The grave of Jeremiah Jackson is in Lafayette Cemetery and includes an inscription with date of birth as 13 Aug 1739 and death as 10 Mar 1802. Findagrave.com memorial I.D. 44074277
[278] Published sources give her death as 30 May 1756, but the birth date of her youngest child in the Woodstock records is 10 Jul 1756.
[279] Barbour and Newton, *Vital Records of Woodstock 1686-1854*
[280] *Connecticut Wills and Probate, 1609-1999*, Probate of Ebenezer Holmes, Hartford, 1794, Case number 2118.

Phebe Abbott and Ebenezer Holmes had five children whose births are recorded at Woodstock.

459) i PHEBE HOLMES, b. 22 Jun 1743; d. at Dudley, MA 6 Feb 1828; m. at Dudley, 15 Jun 1766, RALPH VINTON, b. 17 Oct 1740 son of Joseph and Hannah (Baldwin) Vinton; Ralph d. 14 Apr 1832.

460) ii DOROTHY HOLMES, b. 13 Apr 1745; d. likely after 1830 when she seems to be the Dorothy Vinton as head of household in the 1830 Census; m. at Dudley, 11 Jan 1770, JOHN VINTON, b. 14 Feb 1742 son of Joseph and Hannah (Baldwin) Vinton; John d. at Charlton, MA Jul 1814.[281]

461) iii EBENEZER HOLMES, b. 1 Nov 1748; d. at Boston 29 Jan 1810; m. 7 Apr 1778, MARCELLA COLBURN, b. at Stafford, 11 May 1760 daughter of Jonathan and Hannah (Royce) Colburn; Marcella d. at Boston 28 Apr 1815, age at death given as 55 years.

 iv CHANDLER HOLMES, b. 27 Dec 1750; d. 4 May 1755.

462) v HULDAH HOLMES, b. 10 Jul 1756; d. at Woodstock, 2 Feb 1853; m. 4 Feb 1779, ZEPHANIAH TUCKER, b. at Leicester, 15 Nov 1756 son of Stephen and Mary (Pike) Tucker; Zephaniah d. 25 Apr 1817.

106) NATHAN ABBOTT (*Hannah Chandler Abbott³, Hannah Abbott Chandler², George¹* **and** *Daniel³, George², George¹*), b. 16 Oct 1723 son of Daniel and Hannah (Chandler) Abbott; d. after 1790 perhaps at

---

[281] The date of death is that used by the DAR Ancestor listing.

Brimfield; m. at Woodstock 2 Jun 1746, ANNA LEACH who origins are unknown to me; a death record has not been located for Anna. There was a Leach family in Woodstock, but it is uncertain how she might be related to this family.

Nathan and Anna married at Woodstock and had three children there. The family then seems to have gone to Brimfield where at least two more children were born. The two oldest children in this family, who were born at Woodstock, married at Brimfield.

Nathan Abbott is listed in the History of Brimfield including his pew assignment in the meeting house in 1757. His name is listed as a signer of a 1774 covenant in support of the colonies and suspension of commerce with Great Britain.[282] It is possible that he is the Nathan Abbott listed in the 1790 U.S. Census at Brimfield with a household of seven persons.

There is disagreement in published genealogies related to Nathan Abbott which I believe results from the confusion of two different Nathan Abbotts (who were second cousins once removed) who were both in Woodstock near the same time. The second Nathan married Judith Stoddard and had several children with her in Woodstock. That Nathan died at Woodstock 19 January 1794 and his probate record includes administration by his widow Judith. According to the Abbot genealogy, it is Nathan born in 1744 son of Nathan and Eunice (Marsh) Abbott who married Judith Stoddard and remained in Woodstock and died there 14 January 1794 (or some state 14 January 1793). The Chandler genealogy, on the other hand, states it is Nathan the son of Daniel and Hannah (Chandler) Abbott that died in Woodstock in 1793 or 1794. But the probate record for that Nathan establishes that was the husband of Judith. That is also supported by records from the Connecticut cemetery inscriptions and newspaper notices that give the age at death in 1794

---

[282] Hyde, *Historical Celebration of the Town of Brimfield, Hampden, Massachusetts*, p 305, p 311

of 49 for Nathan Abbott. This fits for the age of Nathan son of Nathan born in 1744, but not for Nathan the son of Daniel born in 1723.[283] I have concluded that Nathan the son of Daniel and Hannah (Chandler) Abbott married Anna Leach in Woodstock and then relocated to Brimfield. Nathan the son of Nathan and Eunice (Marsh) Abbott married Judith Stoddard and remained in Woodstock where he died January 1794.

There are records of births of three children for Nathan and Anna at Woodstock and two at Brimfield. It is possible there were two other daughters in this family, Hannah and Mary. There are marriage records in Brimfield for Hannah and Mary about the time for them to be the right ages to be in this family, but that has not been established.

463) i ELLINOR ABBOTT, b. at Woodstock, 5 May 1747; m. at Brimfield, 28 May 1772, EPHRAIM BOND, b. at Leicester, 3 Dec 1746 son of John and Lydia (Gray) Bond.

464) ii OLIVE ABBOTT, b. at Woodstock, 27 May 1749; d. at Lebanon, CT, 7 Oct 1784; m. at Brimfield, 25 Oct 1770, ELEAZER HUTCHINSON, b. at Windham, 12 Feb 1744/5 son of Joseph and Ruth (Read) Hutchinson; Eleazer d. Apt 1824.[284] Olive and Eleazer do not seem to have had children. They were admitted to the church in Lebanon in 1772 and their deaths are entered in the church records, but there

---

[283] *Connecticut, Hale Collection of Cemetery Inscriptions and Newspaper Notices, 1629-1934*. Newspaper notice gives age at death as 49, and states he was in the Revolutionary War.

[284] *Connecticut, Church Record Abstracts, 1630-1920*.

465) iii ZEBADIAH ABBOTT, b. at Woodstock, 1750; m. at Sturbridge, 25 Mar 1780, MOLLY CHUBB, b. at Needham, 14 Nov 1754 daughter of Samuel and Prudence (Fisher) Chubb.

466) iv HENRY ABBOTT, b. at Brimfield, 30 May 1754;[285] d. at Brimfield, 31 Jul 1797; m. TABITHA RUSSELL, b. at Brimfield, 22 Aug 1749 the daughter of Ruth Blodget and unknown father Russell (apparently a child born out of wedlock);[286] Tabitha d. at Brimfield, 9 Mar 1832.

v NATHAN ABBOTT, b. at Brimfield, 2 Jan 1757; d. 15 Sep 1758.

107) JOHN ABBOTT *(Hannah Chandler Abbott³, Hannah Abbott Chandler², George¹* **and** *Daniel³, George², George¹)*, b. 11 Jan 1726 son of Daniel and Hannah (Chandler) Abbott; d. at Woodstock 7 Mar 1806; m. at Ashford, 28 Nov 1750, MARY WRIGHT, b. at Ashford, 29 Sep 1730 daughter of John and Judith (Wyman) Wright; Mary d. 30 May 1811.

The births of eleven children of John Abbott and wife Mary were located. The births of ten of these children were recorded at Ashford and the birth of one child, Mary, is recorded at Woodstock. There may be a question whether daughter Mary goes in this family, but she fits in terms of birthdate. I did not locate another John Abbott married to a Mary in Windham County around that time, so I am leaving her in this family. There is not a probate record for either John Abbott or his wife Mary Wright Abbott.

---

[285] Henery, s. Nathan and Annah, May 30, 1754, Brimfield births
[286] Tabitha, d. Ruth Blodget, Aug. 22, 1749. [Tabitha Blogget, C.R.]

Generation Four

	i	JOHN ABBOTT, b. 18 Oct 1751; d. 22 Nov 1782.
467)	ii	MARY ABBOTT, b. 31 Aug 1753; d. at Ashford, 16 Nov 1790; m. at Ashford, 21 Oct 1784, EBENEZER WRIGHT.
468)	iii	ABIEL ABBOTT, b. 22 Mar 1756; d. 5 Apr 1812; m. 8 Jun 1786, JEAN BARTLET, b. about 1766; Jean d. after 1850 at Northampton, NY (living with son Daniel at the 1850 U. S. Census).
469)	iv	DAVID ABBOTT, b. 19 Apr 1758; d. 27 Feb 1827; m. POLLY PAINE.
	v	JUDAH ABBOTT, b. 20 Nov 1760; d. 27 Feb 1845.
470)	vi	NATHAN ABBOTT, b. 31 Jul 1763; d. at Cardiff, NY, 21 Mar 1836; m. 1st, 31 Aug 1785, ELIZABETH BOWEN, b. at Ashford, 13 Feb 1765 daughter of Joseph and Thankful (Chandler) Bowen; Elizabeth d. before 1808. Nathan m. 2nd, 16 Oct 1808 HULDAH SKINNER, b. at Stafford, 2 Feb 1777 daughter of Joseph and Mehitable (-) Skinner; Huldah d. at Cardiff, 15 Apr 1848.[287]
	vii	ABIGAIL ABBOTT, b. 26 Mar 1766; d. 7 Sep 1823.
	viii	DANIEL ABBOTT, b. 3 Sep 1768; d. at Woodstock?, 29 Mar 1812; m. IRENA CHAMBERLAIN, b. at Woodstock, 15 Nov 1765 daughter of Samuel and Anna (Kingsley) Chamberlain. Daniel and Irena did not have children.

---

[287] The graves of Nathan and Huldah Abbott are in Cardiff Cemetery with Nathan's age on gravestone as 72 and Huldah his wife, age 70. It is not a certainty that these are the graves of this same couple.

471) ix JOSEPH ABBOTT, b. 13 Feb 1771; d. 24 Jun 1829; m. 6 Mar 1794, ANNA SKINNER, b. at Stafford, daughter of Joseph and Mehitable (-) Skinner. There are two sisters, Anna and Huldah Skinner, born at Woodstock in 1770 and 1771, but this is about six years too old for Huldah Skinner who married Nathan Abbott (based on her age at time of death). I did not locate probate records that would confirm one way of the other, so I am leaving Anna and Huldah as the sisters from Stafford for the time being.

472) x AMOS ABBOTT, b. 15 Nov 1772; d. at Otisco, NY, 21 Sep 1852; m. 9 Apr 1800, SARAH GRIGGS, b. at Ashford, 17 Sep 1776 daughter of Joseph and Rebecca (Chaffee) Griggs.

xi HANNAH ABBOTT, b. 1 Aug 1776; d. 24 Nov 1844; m. at Ashford, 16 Aug 1814, NATHANIEL ROUND of Bristol, RI. Hannah does not seem to have had children.

108) SARAH ABBOTT *(Hannah Chandler Abbott³, Hannah Abbott Chandler², George¹* **and** *Daniel³, George², George¹)*, b. 5 May 1728 daughter of Daniel and Hannah (Chandler) Abbott; d. 7 Oct 1802; m. 1st, JABEZ CORBIN, b. at Woodstock, 21 Mar 1724 son of Jabez and Hannah (Peake) Corbin; Jabez d. 1774 (probate 7 Jun 1774). Sarah m. 2nd, 31 May 1780, as his second wife, WILLIAM CHAPMAN; William d. 1792.

The estate of Jabez Corbin entered probate on 7 June 1774. Widow Sarah is administrator of the estate. There is an inventory of the estate, but no documents related to heirs. The value of the estate was just over £62.[288]

William Chapman wrote his will 5 April 1783. He makes mention of a settlement agreement with Sarah prior to their marriage executed 31 May 1780. In addition to this, she receives a list of specific household items including an iron trammel and a pewter chamber pot. If Sarah relinquishes her title and interest in his dwelling house which was part of the marital agreement, she will receive, on January 1 of each year, one-bushel wheat, one-bushel rye, and two bushels Indian corn as long as she remains his widow. He also makes bequests to his children from his first marriage.[289]

There are just two births recorded for Sarah Abbott and Jabez Corbin.

473) i JONATHAN CORBIN, b. 22 Aug 1760; d. at Dudley, MA; m. at Oxford, 24 Dec 1781, ABIGAIL WIGHT, b. at Thompson, CT, 30 Jan 1757 daughter of Levi and Susannah (Barstow) Wight; Abigail d. at Dudley 31 Jul 1825.

474) ii SARAH CORBIN, b. 11 Jan 1764; d. at Centerville, NY 15 Apr 1852; m. at Oxford, 24 Oct 1782, LEVI WIGHT, b. at Thompson, CT, 3 Jul 1761 son of Levi and Susannah (Barstow) Wight;[290] Levi d. at Centerville 2 Jan 1831.[291]

---

[288] *Connecticut Wills and Probate, 1609-1999*, Probate of Jabez Corbin, Hartford, 1774, Case number 1264
[289] *Connecticut Wills and Probate, 1609-1999*, Probate of William Chapman, Hartford, 1792, Case number 735.
[290] Wight, *The Wights*, p 71
[291] The graves of Levi Wight and his wife Sarah are located at Bates Cemetery in Centerville, NY. Findagrave.com

109) GEORGE ABBOTT *(Hannah Chandler Abbott³, Hannah Abbott Chandler², George¹* and *Daniel³, George², George¹)*, b. 21 Jan 1730 son of Daniel and Hannah (Chandler) Abbott; d. before 18 Dec 1772²⁹²; m. 16 Jan 1754, MARY WHITNEY, b. at Uxbridge, 27 Oct 1732 daughter of Joshua and Hannah (Rockwood or Rockett) Whitney.

George and Mary married at Woodstock and their first child was born there. The young family then relocated to Palmer, Massachusetts where the births of six other children were recorded. No marriage or death records were located for the children. It is not known what became of Mary Whitney Abbott after her husband's death.

    i   GEORGE ABBOTT, b. 1755; died young
    ii   HANNAH ABBOTT, b. 22 Jun 1758
    iii   NATHAN ABBOTT, b. 26 Jun 1760
    iv   MOLLY ABBOTT, b. 20 Sep 1762
    v   SARAH ABBOTT, b. 25 Oct 1765
    vi   BETHIAH ABBOTT, b. 13 May 1768
    vii   GEORGE ABBOTT, b. 4 Sep 1770

Sarah Chandler Wright³, Hannah Abbott Chandler², George¹

110) JOSEPH WRIGHT *(Sarah Chandler Wright³, Hannah Abbott Chandler², George¹)*, b. Mar 1712/3 son of Joseph and Sarah (Chandler) Wright; d. at Winchester, NH, 27 May 1785; m. 1ˢᵗ at Woodstock, ABIGAIL CHAFFEE, b. at Swansea, 5 Mar 1715 daughter of Joseph

---

²⁹² Ward, "The Footloose Joshua Whitney", *American Genealogist* (1999, volume 74, p 200) states Mary Whitney Abbott was a widow in a deed of 18 Dec 1772. The Footloose Joshua Whitney

and Jemima (Chadwick) Chaffee.²⁹³ It is not known when Abigail died but likely by 1746 as Joseph and second wife Mary started having children in 1747. Joseph had a second wife named MARY about whom nothing else is known.

The 1786 New Hampshire probate of the son Samuel Wright makes a reference to the inventory of the possessions of the widow Mary Wright who is his step-mother. "An inventory of the household furniture of the Widow Wright mother to Samuel Wright late of Winchester, deceased."²⁹⁴

Births of five children of Joseph Wright and Abigail Chaffee are recorded at Woodstock.

475) i SARAH WRIGHT, b. 24 Sep 1737; d. likely at Winchester, NH; m. 23 Apr 1761, JOSEPH NARRIMORE, b. at Thompson, CT, 11 May 1735 son of Samuel and Lydia (Davis) Narrimore; Joseph d. at Winchester, 20 Feb 1808.

ii ABIEL WRIGHT, b. 9 Oct 1739; no further record.

iii ABIGAIL WRIGHT, b. 8 Sep 1741; died young.

476) iv SAMUEL WRIGHT, b. 28 Jan 1744/5; d. Jul 1786 at Winchester, NH; m. 27 Oct 1768, MARY COBURN, b. at Woodstock, 25 Oct 1745 daughter of John and Deborah (Goddard) Coburn.

v INFANT WRIGHT, abt. 1746.

---

²⁹³ Chaffee, *The Chaffee Genealogy*, p. 78

²⁹⁴ *New Hampshire Wills and Probate Records 1643-1982,* Probate of Samuel Wright, Cheshire, 1786, Case number 47.

Joseph Wright and Mary had four children whose births are recorded at Woodstock.

477) i HANNAH WRIGHT, b. 11 Dec 1747; d. at Winchester, 31 Mar 1812; m. 5 Nov 1767, ASAHEL JEWELL, b. 2 Aug 1744 son of Archibald and Rebecca (Leonard) Jewell; Asahel d. at Winchester, 30 Apr 1790.[295]

ii ABIGAIL WRIGHT, b. 8 Apr 1750; no further record.

478) iii BENJAMIN WRIGHT, b. 25 Feb 1753; d. in Caledonia County, VT 1839; m. 24 Jul 1776, SYBIL BRETT (Burt), b. at Bridgewater, 16 May 1756 daughter of Seth and Patience (Curtis) Brett.

479) iv LEMUEL WRIGHT, b. 15 May 1757; d. at Quebec, Canada, 13 Feb 1846; m. 21 Dec 1779, DEBORAH ERSKINE, b. about 1755 daughter of John and Deborah (Studley) Erskine; Deborah buried at Shefford, Québec in 1843.[296]

111) SARAH WRIGHT *(Sarah Chandler Wright³, Hannah Abbott Chandler², George¹)*, b. 7 Aug 1715 daughter of Joseph and Sarah (Chandler) Wright; d. 22 Dec 1783;[297] m. 17 Jan 1733/4, EDMUND CHAMBERLAIN, b. 6 Mar 1701/2 son of Edmund and Elizabeth (Bartholomew) Chamberlain; Edmund d.at Woodstock, 9 Dec 1779.

Sarah and Edmund Chamberlain had six children whose births are recorded at Woodstock.

---

[295] New Hampshire, Death and Disinterment Records, 1754-1947
[296] Ancestry.com, database, The New England Historical & Genealogical Register, 1847-2011
[297] This is according to Cutter's *New England Families and Genealogy*.

	i	WILLIAM CHAMBERLAIN, b. 23 Oct 1734; d. 30 Oct 1739.
	ii	ZERVIAH CHAMBERLAIN, b. 29 Aug 1736; d. 2 Mar 1737.
480)	iii	ABIEL CHAMBERLAIN, b. 20 Dec 1737; d. at Woodstock, 12 Jan 1818; m. 1760, GRACE AINSWORTH, b. at Woodstock, 1 Jun 1743 daughter of Nathan and Huldah (Peake) Ainsworth; Grace d. 10 Jan 1788.
	iv	WILLIAM CHAMBERLAIN, b. 14 Mar 1740/1; no further record.
481)	v	EDMUND CHAMBERLAIN, b. 7 Mar 1742/3; d. 24 Oct 1824; m. 20 Nov 1766, ELIZABETH KINGSLEY possibly the daughter of Jonathan and Experience (Sabin) Kingsley b. at Pomfret 23 Jun 1747. Elizabeth d. perhaps at Sturbridge, MA, 12 Jul 1835
	vi	DAUGHTER CHAMBERLAIN, b. 14 Sep and d. 15 Sep 1745.

112) HANNAH WRIGHT *(Sarah Chandler Wright³, Hannah Abbott Chandler², George¹)*, b. 20 Jun 1717 daughter of Joseph and Sarah (Chandler) Wright; no death record found (the Peters genealogy reports her death as 1796);[298] m. 6 Jan 1734/5, BEAMSLEY PETERS, b. at Andover 1710 son of Samuel and Phebe (Frye) Peters; Beamsley d. unknown but was between 1757 and 1762. Beamsley is listed in his mother's 1757 will but he is not listed in the final estate settlement.

The birth of one child of Hannah and Beamsley Peters is recorded at Woodstock.

---

[298] Peters, *Peters of New England*, p 111

      i   HANNAH PETERS, b. at Woodstock, 28 Feb 1734/5; nothing else is known.

113) ELIZABETH WRIGHT *(Sarah Chandler Wright³, Hannah Abbott Chandler², George¹)*, b. 13 Feb 1718/9 daughter of Joseph and Sarah (Chandler) Wright; death unknown; m. 23 Nov 1738, JOHN CARPENTER, b. at Woodstock, 17 Jul 1713 son of Eliphalet and Rebecca (Gardner) Carpenter

    The births of only three children were recorded at Woodstock. No probate record was found in Connecticut, Massachusetts, New Hampshire or Vermont. It is possible that the son Beamsley Carpenter went to Vermont as there is a marriage record there for a Beamsley Carpenter in 1827 who could be a son of Beamsley. The son John relocated to New York.

- 482) i   JOHN CARPENTER, b. 22 Feb 1739/40; d. at Whitestown, NY, 12 Jan 1809; m. 9 Feb 1757, MERCY MORGAN. John served in the Revolutionary War along with his sons William and Abiel.
- 483) ii BEAMSLEY CARPENTER, b. 3 Jul 1743; m. MARTHA.
- iii JOSEPH CARPENTER, b. 10 Jul 1752

114) HEPHZIBAH WRIGHT *(Sarah Chandler Wright³, Hannah Abbott Chandler², George¹)*, b. 14 Oct 1720 daughter of Joseph and Sarah (Chandler) Wright; d. 1797 at Woodstock; m. 16 Dec 1736, ENOS BARTHOLOMEW, b. about 1714 and perhaps the son of John and Mary (Harrington) Bartholomew; d. before 1797 (Hephzibah was a widow at the time of her death).

    There are the births of five children recorded at Woodstock. No probate record was located. Daughter Mercy did have a son out-of-wedlock (Lemuel Dunham 1769-1779). That son died at about 10 years old and there is a marriage record for Marcy Bartholomew after her son died.

   i SARAH BARTHOLOMEW, b. 4 Apr 1737; d. 31 Mar 1797. Sarah does not seem to have married.

484) ii HANNAH BARTHOLOMEW, b. 7 Jun 1739; *possibly* m. 13 Jul 1758, ELKANAH STEPHENS, b. at Dighton, 18 Mar 1736 son of Nicholas and Rachel (Andrews) Stephens.

485) iii JOHN BARTHOLOMEW, b. 20 Feb 1741/2; d. at Woodstock 8 Jul 1798; m. CANDACE AINSWORTH, b. at Woodstock, 31 Aug 1748 daughter of Daniel and Sarah (Bugbee) Ainsworth.

   iv MERCY BARTHOLOMEW, b. 10 Apr 1744; out-of-wedlock relationship with Mr. Dunham 1769; *possibly* m. 23 Dec 1783, GEORGE COTENEY perhaps the son of George and Sarah (-) Coteney. Mercy had one son, Lemuel Dunham, who died about 10 years old. There are no known children for Mercy and George Coteney.

486) v MARY BARTHOLOMEW, b. 28 Jun 1746; perhaps the widow Mary Leach who d. at Woodstock, 7 Mar 1811; likely m. 25 Jul 1765, ROBERT LEACH, perhaps from Bridgewater b. 4 May 1740 the son of Nehemiah and Mercy (Staples) Leach. Robert d. at Tolland about 1800 (probate of estate). The children in this family do include a son named Enos.

115) ABIGAIL WRIGHT *(Sarah Chandler Wright³, Hannah Abbott Chandler², George¹)*, b. 15 Feb 1727/8 daughter of Joseph and Sarah (Chandler) Wright; death unknown; m. 22 Mar 1748/9, ABIJAH CORBIN, b. 8 Feb 1722 son of Jabez and Hannah (Peake) Corbin; d. at Woodstock, 16 Oct 1808.[299]

There are births of six children recorded for this family that were located. Only one possible marriage was identified from the Woodstock records. No probate record was located for Abijah Corbin.

    i   HANNAH CORBIN, b. 26 Apr 1750

    ii   ESTHER CORBIN, b. 24 Oct 1755

    iii   ABIGAIL CORBIN, b. 17 Jun 1759

    iv   ALICE CORBIN, b. 22 Mar 1766; d. unknown; *possibly* m. 9 Jan 1803, as his second wife, WILLIAM PAUL.

    v   DANIEL CORBIN, b. 6 Oct 1768

    vi   DAUGHTER CORBIN, b. 24 Oct 1775

116) DOROTHY WRIGHT *(Sarah Chandler Wright³, Hannah Abbott Chandler², George¹)*, b. 3 Apr 1730 daughter of Joseph and Sarah (Chandler) Wright; death not known; m. 3 Aug 1747, PENUEL BACON, b. at Woodstock, 8 Jan 1725/6 son of Joseph and Rebeckah (Carpenter) Bacon.

There is the birth of one son recorded for this family at Woodstock, and then no further records. There is a Penuel Bacon who served in the French and Indian War from Connecticut, and

---

[299] Lawson, *History and Genealogy of the Descendants of Clement Corbin of Muddy River*, p. 51

that is probably this Penuel as he seems to have been the only one in Connecticut at the time. There is a Penuel Bacon who shows up in upstate New York in 1776 tax rolls and that might be him. However, there are no birth, death, or probate records for this family that could be located.

      i   PINIAS BACON, b. 15 Nov 1747; no further record. There is a Deacon Phineas Bacon in Middleton, Connecticut of about the right age, but that seems to be a different Phineas Bacon.

Section III: The Grandchildren of George Abbott and Dorcas Graves

Hannah Abbott Osgood³, George², George¹

117) HANNAH OSGOOD *(Hannah Abbott Osgood³, George², George¹)*, b. 22 Aug 1710 daughter of John and Hannah (Abbott) Osgood; d. 16 Mar 1761; m. 24 Jun 1728, SAMUEL CHICKERING, b. at Charlestown 10 Jul 1704 son of John and Susanna (Symmes) Chickering. Samuel m. 2nd the widow Mehitable Stevens; Samuel died about 1787 the year his estate was probated.

The estate of Samuel Chickering entered probate 5 November 1787. He did not leave a will. His widow Mehitable is administrator of the estate. Henry Ingalls and Stephen Holt assume responsibility for the bond. There is an inventory, but no disbursement to heirs in the available probate papers.

The births of ten children to Samuel and Hannah are recorded at Andover.

487) i HANNAH CHICKERING, b. 13 Jul 1730; d. at Wakefield, 10 Aug 1791; m. 22 Mar 1753, BENJAMIN PETERS, b. 25 Aug 1728 son of Samuel and Mary (Robinson) Peters; Benjamin d. at Wakefield, 17 Apr 1812.

488) ii SAMUEL CHICKERING, b. 28 Sep 1732; d. 16 Mar 1814; m. 17 Apr 1755, his third cousin once removed, MARY DANE, b. 27 Sep 1733 daughter of John and Sarah (Chandler) Dane; Mary d. 24 Jun 1824.

489) iii SARAH CHICKERING, b. 5 Mar 1734/5; d.?; m. 13 Dec 1753, JAMES FRYE, b. 13 Sep 1731 son of Samuel and Sarah (Osgood) Frye; James d. 17 Dec 1804.

Generation Four 219

490) iv ELIZABETH CHICKERING, b. 25 Jan 1736/7; d. at Methuen, 20 Sep 1767; m. 24 May 1757, MOSES SARGENT, b. 23 May 1738 son of Christopher and Sara (Peaslee) Sargent. Moses m. 2nd 29 Nov 1767, Esther Runnells.

      v SUSANNA CHICKERING, b. 25 Jan 1738/9; there is no further record and perhaps died young.

      vi DORCAS CHICKERING, b. 14 Jul 1742; d. about 1807 when the estate of Dorcas Chickering, single woman of Andover, was probated.

491) vii JOHN CHICKERING, b. 15 Aug 1744; d.; m. 13 Nov 1770, SARAH WEBSTER, b. 3 Oct 1748 daughter of Ebenezer and Sarah (Gage) Webster.[300]

492) viii ZACHARIAH CHICKERING, b. 29 Mar 1747; d. at Hartford, ME; m. 20 Nov 1771, SARAH POOR, b. 22 May 1750 daughter of John and Rebecca (Stevens) Poor.

493) ix MARY CHICKERING, b. 17 Jan 1749/50; d. at Danville, VT, 20 Aug 1820;[301] m. 24 Oct 1770, JOHN SHORT, b. at Newbury, 16 Aug 1741 son of Joseph and Hannah (Prowse) Short.

494) x PHEBE CHICKERING, b. 9 Nov 1751; d. likely in NH; m. 28 Jul 1778, THOMAS HUTCHINSON whose identity is uncertain, although he could be Thomas Hutchinson born in Lynn in 1750. Cutter

---

[300] Sarah's parentage is confirmed by the probate settlement of the estate of Ebenezer Webster which includes a disbursement to Sarah Chickering.
[301] Vermont, Vital Records, 1720-1908. Ancestry.com

reports he is the son of Jonathan and Elizabeth (Ganson) Hutchinson.[302]

118) JOHN OSGOOD *(Hannah Abbott Osgood³, George², George¹)*, b. 22 Aug 1711 son of John and Hannah (Abbott) Osgood; d. 10 Jul 1775; m. 1st 20 Feb 1746, MARTHA CARLETON, b. 12 Jun 1722 daughter of Christopher and Martha (Barker) Carleton; Martha d. about 1755. JOHN m. 2nd 20 Feb 1756, HULDAH FRYE, b. 13 May 1737 daughter of Isaac and Naamah (Haskell) Frye; Huldah was listed in the 1800 Census as a head of household in Andover, but no record of her after that time.

John Osgood wrote a will 14 Jun 1775. He has a bequest to his wife Huldah and "each of my children," but he does not name them.

John Osgood and Martha Carleton had five children born at Andover.

495) i MARTHA OSGOOD, b. 3 May 1747; d. at Exeter, NH 15 Jun 1830;[303] m. ENOCH POOR, b. 21 Jun 1736 son of Thomas and Mary (Adams) Poor. Brigadier General Enoch Poor d. at Hackensack, NJ while serving in the military, 8 Sep 1780. The cause of death of Enoch Poor is a mystery.[304] The National Archives have on file a letter written by George Washington to Brigadier General Enoch Poor 22 Feb 1779.[305]

---

[302] Cutter, *New England Families*, volume 3, p 1441
[303] Ancestry.com. *New Hampshire, Death and Burial Records Index, 1654-1949* [database on-line]. Provo, UT, USA: Ancestry.com Operations, Inc., 2011.
[304] A biography of Enoch Poor can be found at the site of the New Hampshire Division of Historical Resources at this link: http://rkc.org/poor/poorofnh.html
[305] National Archives, letter from George Washington to Brigadier General Enoch Poor, retrieved from https://founders.archives.gov/documents/Washington/03-19-02-0260

Generation Four 221

           ii   HANNAH OSGOOD, b. 27 Dec 1748; d. 16 Feb 1754.

           iii   JOHN OSGOOD, b. 12 Nov 1750; d. 5 Apr 1754.

496) iv   DORCAS OSGOOD, b. 24 Mar 1752; d. at Roxbury 17 Oct 1810;[306] m. 1st ISAAC MARBLE, b. 9 Jun 1740 son of Noah and Mary (Ingalls) Marble; Isaac d. by 1780. Dorcas m. 2nd as his second wife, HENRY DEARBORN; Henry d. 1829. General Henry Dearborn was the Secretary of War under President Jefferson.

497) v   MARY OSGOOD, b. 30 Jun 1753; d. 22 May 1820;[307] m. by 1771, ISAAC FARNUM, b. 19 Dec 1742 son of John and Sarah (Frye) Farnum; Isaac d. 8 Sep 1823.[308]

John Osgood and Huldah Frye had four children born at Andover.

           i   CHARLOTTE OSGOOD, b. 27 Nov 1767; d. 25 Apr 1783.

498) ii   JOHN OSGOOD, b. 2 Jun 1770; d. at Haverhill, NH, 29 Jul 1840; m. SARAH PORTER, b. at Boxford, 22 Apr 1777 daughter of William and Mary (Adams) Porter; Sarah d. at Haverhill, NH 5 Feb 1858.[309]

499) iii   ALFRED OSGOOD, b. 7 Mar 1773; d. at Newburyport 25 May 1847; m. 18 Jun 1800, MARY

---

[306] Ancestry.com, *U.S., Newspaper Extractions from the Northeast, 1704-1930* (Provo, UT, USA: Ancestry.com Operations, Inc., 2014).
[307] Massachusetts Vital Records Project: Mary, w. Isaac, May 22, 1820, a. 66 y.
[308] Massachusetts Vital Records Project: Isaac [h. Mary (Osgood). PR61], Sept. 8, 1823, a. 80 y. 8 m.
[309] Ancestry.com. New Hampshire, Death and Burial Records Index, 1654-1949

SMITH, b. 4 Apr 1778 daughter of John and Mary (-) Smith; Mary d. at Newburyport 23 Sep 1855 at age 77. Mary's parents' names are given as John and Mary Smith on her death record.

500)   iv   ENOCH OSGOOD, b. 7 Nov 1775; d. at Newburyport 20 May 1848; m. 15 Feb 1807 MARY BROWN of not yet known origins; Mary d. Dec 1863.[310] She was known to be living in 1859 when her daughter's estate was probated.

119)   ELIZABETH OSGOOD *(Hannah Abbott Osgood³, George², George¹)*, b. 15 Aug 1714 daughter of John and Hannah (Abbott) Osgood; d. 8 Dec 1756; m. 28 Nov 1734, JAMES FRYE, b. at Bradford 24 Jun 1710 son of James and Joanna (Sprague) Frye. James married 2nd Sarah Robey. Colonel James Frye died 8 Jan 1776 "while in the Continental Service." His death is recorded at Andover.

James Frye had much military experience and was a Lieutenant Colonel in the French and Indian War. In 1775, he was a Colonel in charge of a regiment of Minutemen that fought at the Battle of Bunker Hill. He was wounded during the battle, although he continued to fight on after being wounded. He died of his wounds about six months later.[311]

The will of James Frye has bequests to the following persons: well beloved wife Sarah, son Frederick, son James, son Jonathan, daughter Elizabeth wife of Samuel Frye, his grandchildren who are the children of his daughter Joanna Farrington (Thomas, March, Elizabeth), daughter Sarah the wife of John Boyden, grandsons John and James Boyden, daughter Hannah the wife of Daniel Poor, daughter Dorcas the wife of Ezekiel

---

[310] Osgood, *Genealogy of Descendants. . . Osgood*, p 69
[311] National History Society, "Colonel James Frye," http://www.nahistoricalsocietyexhibits.org/veterans/revolutionary-war/

Carleton, daughter Molly Frye (who is unmarried), and daughter Pamela Frye (who is under 18).[312] [Frederick is a son and Pamela is a daughter from James's second marriage to Sarah Robey. The other children are from his marriage to Elizabeth Osgood.]

Elizabeth Osgood and James Frye had eight children whose births are recorded at Andover.

501) i ELIZABETH FRYE, b. 7 Dec 1735; d. 14 May 1807; m. 24 May 1753, her second cousin once removed, SAMUEL FRYE, b. 22 Dec 1729 son of Samuel and Sarah (Osgood) Frye; Samuel d. 1819.

502) ii JOHANNA FRYE, b. 19 Feb 1736/7; d. at Groton 24 Jun 1767; m. by 1758, THOMAS FARRINGTON, b. 8 Mar 1735/6 son of Daniel and Elizabeth (Putnam) Farrington. Thomas m. 2nd Betty Woods and he relocated to Kennebec, ME for a time. Thomas m. 3rd Jerusha Hammond. Thomas d. 9 Apr 1808 at Delhi, NY.

503) iii SARAH FRYE, b. 8 Mar 1738/9; d. at Conway, MA 29 Jul 1785; m. about 1764, JOHN BOYDEN, b. at Groton, 12 Jan 1736 son of Josiah and Eunice (Parker) Boyden. John m. 2nd Esther Gilmore; John d. 10 Oct 1819.

504) iv JAMES FRYE, b. 9 Jan 1740/1; d. 28 Jan 1826; m. 1st 21 Feb 1765, his third cousin (and George Abbott descendant), MEHITABLE ROBINSON, b. at Boxford, Oct 1742 daughter of Joseph and Mehitable

---

[312] *Essex County, MA: Probate File Papers, 1638-1881. Probate of* James Frye, 5 Feb 1776, *Case number* 10297.

(Eams) Robinson;[313] Mehitable d. 6 Jun 1787. James m. 2nd Phebe Campbell.

505) v JONATHAN FRYE, b. 4 Dec 1742; d. at Bucksport, ME 12 Jul 1793; m. by 1766 to unidentified wife;[314] no marriage record has been located.

506) vi HANNAH FRYE, b. 12 Sep 1744; d. 16 Jan 1824; m. 31 Mar 1763, DANIEL POOR, b. 21 Sep 1740 son of Thomas and Mary (Adams) Poor; Daniel d. 20 Jun 1814.

507) vii DORCAS FRYE, b. 3 Jun 1750; d. 1 Dec 1821; m. 10 Nov 1768, EZEKIEL CARLETON, b. 22 Nov 1742 son of Ezekiel and Marcy (Kimball) Carleton; Ezekiel d. 1 Jan 1831.

508) viii MOLLY FRYE, b. 9 Mar 1752; d. at East Andover, ME, 13 Jun 1796; m. 9 May 1776, INGALLS BRAGG, b. 24 Jun 1753 son of Thomas and Dorothy (Ingalls) Bragg; Thomas d. at East Andover, ME about 1808 the year of the probate of his estate.

120) JOSEPH OSGOOD *(Hannah Abbott Osgood³, George², George¹)*, b. 5 Sep 1718 son of John and Hannah (Abbott) Osgood; d. at Andover, 11 Jan 1797; m. at Boston 1 Dec 1743, MARGARET

---

[313] The 1777 will of Joseph Robinson includes a bequest to his daughter Mehitable wife of James Frye.

[314] The "internet", the DAR, and even Barker's Frye genealogy identify his wife as Sarah Peabody (who was born 1729) daughter of Moses, but that is not correct. The marriage of Sarah Peabody and a different Jonathan Frye (born 1717) occurred in 1753 when this Jonathan was 11 years old. There are baptismal records for three children of Jonathan at Methuen but those records list only the father's name. Those three children can be supported as being this Jonathan's as one of the grandsons (Phineas Barnes) later placed a monument in the Wardwell Cemetery for this Jonathan. There are several other possible children born at Methuen for whom there are not available records.

BINNEY, b. at Hull 12 Apr 1719 daughter of Thomas and Margaret (Miller) Binney; Margaret d. 16 Feb 1797.

Joseph Osgood graduated Harvard in 1737[315] and was a physician in Andover.

The will of Joseph Osgood has bequests for the following persons: beloved wife Margaret, son Joseph, son John, son George, and grandson John Cushing is to be boarded for two years by George who is the executor.[316] John Cushing was the son of his daughter Mehitable from her marriage to John Cushing.

Joseph and Margaret had eight children, the oldest three born at Boston and the younger five children at Andover.

509) i JOSEPH OSGOOD, b. 25 Nov 1746; d. at Salem, Jun 1812; m. 14 Jun 1770, LUCRETIA WARD, b. at Salem, Sep 1748 daughter of Miles and Hannah (Hathorne) Ward; Lucretia d. Sep 1809. Lucretia's name is given as Mehitable in the Osgood genealogy, but the birth, marriage, and death record say Lucretia.

ii JOHN OSGOOD, b. 22 Oct 1748; d. Jun 1749.

510) iii MEHITABLE OSGOOD,[317] b. at Boston, 11 Dec 1749; d. 6 Oct 1788 (according to the Cushing Genealogy, but no record found); m. by 1770, JOHN CUSHING, b. at Haverhill, 11 Dec 1749 son of James and Anna (Wainwright) Cushing. John m. 2nd Mary Marsh; John d. at Goffstown, NH 1833.

---

[315] Harvard University, *Quinquennial Catalogue of the Officers and Graduates of Harvard University*
[316] *Essex County, MA: Probate File Papers, 1638-1881*. Probate of Joseph Osgood, 6 Feb 1797, *Case number* 20231.
[317] Cushing, *The Genealogy of the Cushing Family*, p. 61

      iv   JOHN GEORGE OSGOOD, b. 20 Aug 1742; d. 17 May 1754.

511)   v   JOHN OSGOOD, b. 14 Nov 1754; d. at Newbury, 5 Apr 1820; m. at Newbury, 3 Dec 1778, LYDIA NEWELL, b. at Brookline, 20 Apr 1754 daughter of Moses and Sarah (Gerrish) Newell; Lydia d. at West Newbury, 1 Feb 1836.

      vi   THOMAS OSGOOD, b. 29 Oct 1756; d. 12 Sep 1771.

512)   vii   GEORGE OSGOOD, b. 1 Dec 1758; d. 24 Oct 1823; m. 7 Jan 1782, ELIZABETH OTIS, b. at Barnstable, 12 Jan 1760 daughter of Joseph and Rebecca (Sturgis) Otis; Elizabeth d. 22 May 1802. George m. 2nd 8 Mar 1803, SARAH VOSE, b. at Milton, 29 Jul 1762 daughter of Joseph and Sarah (How) Vose; Sarah d. 17 Mar 1812. After Sarah's death, George married Mary Messer, 2 Oct 1815.

      viii   MARGARET OSGOOD, b. 4 Nov 1760; d. 25 Oct 1762. "Margaret, d. Joseph and Margaret, Oct. 25, 1762, a. 1 y. 11 m. 21 d. GR1"

121)   DORCAS OSGOOD *(Hannah Abbott Osgood³, George², George¹)*, b. Sep 1721 daughter of John and Hannah (Abbott) Osgood; d. at Boston about 1749 (Thomas remarried in 1750); m. at Boston 5 Jan 1743/4, THOMAS MARCH whose origins are unknown to me; Thomas d. at Boston about 1752 (when his will was probated). Thomas married 2nd Mary Hill on 7 Aug 1750.

    The will of Thomas March includes a bequest to his daughter Dorcas of a dozen of the gilt pictured plates and all the linen that was given to "me or my late wife by my father-in-law Mr. Osgood." He makes a general bequest to "all my children" but does not specify them. The guardianship of Dorcas was assumed by Joseph Osgood and John Osgood.[318]

There are birth records for two children of Dorcas and Thomas both born at Boston. However, the son, Thomas, died as an infant suggested by the fact that Thomas March named his first child with his second wife, Thomas.

	i	THOMAS MARCH, b. 26 May 1745; died young.
513)	ii	DORCAS MARCH, b. 11 Jun 1746; d. at Salem, Mar 1820; m. at Andover, 19 Jan 1763, DUDLEY WOODBRIDGE, b. at Salem, 3 Mar 1732/3 son of Benjamin and Mary (Osgood) Woodbridge; Dudley d. 21 Oct 1799.

122)   MARY OSGOOD *(Hannah Abbott Osgood[3], George[2], George[1])*, b. 10 Jun 1726 daughter of John and Hannah (Abbott) Osgood; d. 1806 at New Gloucester, ME; m. 11 Apr 1745, WILLIAM ALLEN, b. at Gloucester Jun 1717 son of Joseph and Mary (Coit) Allen; a death record for William was not located.

Mary Osgood and William Allen were early settlers in New Gloucester, Maine which was incorporated in 1774. The first land grants in that area were in the mid-1730's. The settlement was first called New Gloucester in 1738, likely named after the settlement in Massachusetts where most of the settlers were born. William and Mary Allen made their move to New Gloucester after the births of all their children at Gloucester. In 1770, the lot for the town meeting house was purchased from William Allen. He also served

---

[318] *Suffolk County, MA: Probate File Papers,* Probate of Thomas March, 1742, Case number 9976.

on a committee in 1774 related to the proposed boycott of British goods in the period prior to the Revolutionary War.[319]

There are births for thirteen children in this family recorded at Gloucester and two other births at New Gloucester, Maine.

        i   MARY ALLEN, b. 29 Mar 1746; d. 5 Apr 1746.

514)   ii   JOSEPH ALLEN, b. 24 Feb 1746/7; m. 30 Dec 1782, MARY BAKER. Joseph m. 2nd, DORCAS EMERY.

514a iii   MARY ALLEN, b. 3 Nov 1748; m. 8 Jul 1775, as his second wife, PETER GRAFFAM[320] son of Caleb and Lois (Bennett) Graffam.

        iv   WILLIAM ALLEN, b. 30 Jul 1750; d. at Gloucester, MA, Mar 1826. He married and had children, but those details are not yet worked out.

515)   v   ELIZABETH ALLEN, b. 27 Oct 1752; d. at Portland, ME, Apr 1850; m. 12 Oct 1773, SAMUEL STEVENS, b. at Gloucester, 12 Mar 1748 son of William and Elizabeth (Allen) Stevens; Samuel d. at Gloucester, 9 Dec 1795.

516)   vi   DORCAS ALLEN, b. 11 Aug 1754; d. at Cumberland County, ME, 27 Dec 1785; m. 24 Jun 1779, DAVID HAYS, b. 12 Oct 1755 son of John and Judith (Moulton) Hays; David d. in Cumberland County, ME, 30 Aug 1793.

517)   vii   JOHN ALLEN, b. 25 Mar 1756; d. at Minot, ME, 6 Mar 1834; m. 9 Apr 1791, RACHEL WORTHLEY, b. at Yarmouth, ME, 24 Mar 1764 daughter of John and Martha (Bailey) Worthley.

---

[319] Haskell, *The New Gloucester Centennial*
[320] The codicil of her brother Samuel's will incudes a mention of his sister Graffam.

	viii	BENJAMIN ALLEN, b. 4 Jan 1758
	ix	NATHANIEL COIT ALLEN, b. 29 Aug 1759. Served as paymaster in the 10th Massachusetts Regiment. He may not have married.
	x	AARON ALLEN, b. 12 Jan 1761; d. 16 Feb 1766.
	xi	CHRISTOPHER ALLEN, b. 29 Aug 1763; d. 17 Nov 1763.
518)	xii	CHRISTOPHER ALLEN, b. 16 Apr 1765; d. at Hebron, ME, 20 Jul 1819; m. 25 Jun 1808, DOLLY POOR, b. at Andover, 12 Oct 1772 daughter of Ebenezer and Susanna (Varnum) Poor; Dolly d. 26 Jul 1819.[321]
519)	xiii	AARON ALLEN, b. 17 Dec 1766; m. at New Gloucester, ME, 27 Aug 1797, MARTHA PRINCE, b. at New Gloucester, 7 Jul 1773 daughter of John and Mary (-) Prince.
	xiv	JEREMIAH ALLEN, b. 13 May 1769; he is perhaps the Jeremiah Allen who died at New Gloucester, June 1843 at age 75. There is no record of a marriage.
	xv	SAMUEL ALLEN, b. 14 Apr 1771; d. at Oxford, ME about 1846 (date of codicil of will). Samuel did not marry. In his will, he left his estate to the four children of his brother Chrsitopher.

Elizabeth[3], George[2], George[1] *and* Benjamin[3], Benjamin[2], George[1]

---

[321] King, *Annals of Oxford*, Maine, p 128

[The families in the next section are descendants of George Abbott by the two paths noted above. These are the families from the marriage Elizabeth Abbott to Benjamin Abbott, which is just one family of Benjamin's three families. The families that descend from Benjamin and his two other wives begin at family #191.]

123) SARAH ABBOTT *(Elizabeth³, George², George¹* **and** *Benjamin³, Benjamin², George¹)*, b. 2 Aug 1718 daughter of Benjamin and Elizabeth (Abbott) Abbott; d. 5 Mar 1778; m. 10 Apr 1746, her second cousin, JAMES HOLT *(Dorcas Abbott Holt³, Timothy², George¹)*, b. 13 Jan 1722/3 son of Nicholas and Dorcas (Abbott) Holt. James m. 2nd, Phebe Ballard who was the widow of Abiel Abbott son of Benjamin and Abigail (Abbott) Abbott; James Holt d. at Andover, 22 Aug 1812

In his will written 24 March 1804, James Holt has bequests to the following persons: well beloved wife Phebe (second wife), grandson James Abbot (who has lived with him for 10 years), beloved daughter Sarah wife of Barachias Abbott, beloved daughter Abigail wife of Isaac Chandler, and his two sons-in-law Barachias Abbott and Isaac Chandler. Grandson James Abbot is named executor.[322]

In the will, James Holt elaborates on his bequest to his grandson: "For special and weighty reasons in my mind, I give to my beloved grandson, James Abbot, who has lived with me about ten years, and to his heirs and assigns, all my estate, both real and personal, not herein disposed of." He goes on to list several household items that are to go to him stating these were mostly items that had belonged to James Abbot's uncle. We can only imagine the nature of these "special and weighty reasons."

Sarah and James had seven children, all born at Andover.

---

[322] *Essex County, MA: Probate File Papers, 1638-1881. Probate of* James Holt, 5 Nov 1812, *Case number* 13653.

| | i | JAMES HOLT, b. 16 Apr 1749; d. 26 Nov 1800; m. 5 Jun 1778, HANNAH FOSTER, b. 23 Jul 1754 daughter of Jacob and Abigail (Frost) Foster; Hannah died from consumption 24 Oct 1794. They do not seem to have had any children that lived to adulthood. There is a daughter Hannah baptized in 1777 who is perhaps their child, but there is no further record for her and since she is not mentioned in the wills of either of her grandfathers, she likely died young. James is not mentioned in his father's will. Likewise, Hannah Foster is not mentioned in the will of her father Jacob who died in 1806. |

| | ii | ELIZABETH HOLT, b. 10 Mar 1750/1; d. 12 Nov 1777; Elizabeth did not marry. |

| | iii | JOEL HOLT, b. 7 Aug 1753; d. 20 Mar 1755. |

| | iv | DORCAS HOLT, b. 6 May 1756; d. 16 May 1778; Dorcas did not marry. |

520) v   ABIGAIL HOLT, b. 18 Jun 1758; d. 2 Oct 1824; m. 7 Dec 1780, her fourth cousin, ISAAC CHANDLER, b. 4 Oct 1754 son of William and Rebecca (Lovejoy) Chandler; Isaac d. 12 Jan 1832. After Abigail's death, Isaac married Elizabeth Upton.

294) vi SARAH HOLT, b. 7 Mar 1746/7; d. 11 Feb 1808; m. 6 Dec 1770, her third cousin (by two paths), BARACHIAS ABBOTT, b. 22 May 1739 son of Barachias and Hannah (Holt) Abbott; Barachias d. 29 Jan 1812.

| | vii | SUSANNA HOLT, b. 27 Oct 1760; d. 26 Nov 1760. |

George³, George², George¹

69) MARY ABBOTT *(George³, George², George¹)*, b. 12 Mar 1722/3 daughter of George and Mary (Phillips) Abbott; d. 8 Aug 1792; m. 24 May 1743, her second cousin STEPHEN ABBOTT *(Stephen³, John², George¹)*, b. 2 Mar 1717/8 son of Stephen and Sarah (Stevens) Abbott; Stephen d. 8 Nov 1768; Mary m. 2nd JONATHAN ABBOTT *(Jonathan³, Benjamin², George¹)*, also a second cousin, who was the widower of Martha Lovejoy. This is the same as Family #69 covered above.

124) GEORGE ABBOT *(George³, George², George¹)*, b. 14 Dec 1724 son of George and Mary (Phillips) Abbott; d. at Andover, 26 Dec 1775; m. 1 Jan 1746/7, HANNAH LOVEJOY, b. 27 Dec 1724 daughter of John and Hannah (Foster) Lovejoy; Hannah d. 8 Sep 1813.

George Abbot's estate entered probate November 1776. In his will he has bequests for the following persons: dearly beloved wife Hannah, son George Abbot, beloved son John Lovejoy, beloved son Samuel Abbot, beloved daughter Hannah Ballard wife of Joseph Ballard, beloved daughter Mary Poor wife of Joseph Poor, beloved daughter Elizabeth Lummus wife of Samuel Lummus, beloved daughter Sarah, beloved daughter Martha, beloved daughter Dorcas, and beloved daughter Tammerson (Tamison).[323]

George and Hannah had 12 children whose births are recorded at Andover.

    i   GEORGE ABBOTT, b. 9 Feb 1747/8; d. at Salem 5 Oct 1784; m. 12 Mar 1772, PRISCILLA MANNING, b. at Ipswich, 17 Oct 1733 daughter of Joseph and

---

[323] *Essex County, MA: Probate File Papers, 1638-1881. Probate of* George Abbot, 5 Nov 1776, *Case number* 49.

Elizabeth (Boardman) Manning;[324] Priscilla d. 17 Mar 1804.[325] George and Priscilla had one daughter Priscilla who died at age 15. George Abbott did not leave a will; his widow Priscilla requested that William Gray be named administrator. In her will, Priscilla Abbott made bequests to her nieces and nephew.

434) ii HANNAH ABBOTT, b. 15 Oct 1749; d. 29 May 1784; m. 16 Dec 1773, as his second wife, her third cousin (and George Abbott descendant), JOSEPH BALLARD, b. Oct 1749 son of Timothy and Hannah (Chandler) Ballard. Joseph m. 1st in 1771, Molly Smith; Joseph d. 15 Feb 1819. This is the same as Family #98, child ix.

iii MARY ABBOTT, b. 4 Sep 1751; d. 12 Sep 1752.

521) iv MARY ABBOTT, b. 29 Jun 1753; d. 17 Aug 1820; m. 26 Dec 1768, JOSEPH POOR, b. 7 Nov 1748 son of Thomas and Mary (Adams) Poor; Joseph d. at Danvers 2 Mar 1815.

522) v ELIZABETH ABBOTT, b. 10 Jul 1755; d. 18 Aug 1821; m. 26 Jan 1775, SAMUEL LUMMUS, b. 31 Jul 1751 son of John and Hannah (Porter) Lummus; Samuel d. 10 Apr 1810.

---

[324] Parents are confirmed by the 1784 probate record of Joseph Manning in which Priscilla Abbot signs that she has received her portion of the estate from her brother who is the administrator.

[325] Massachusetts Vital Records Project: Abbott, Priscilla, Mrs., Mar. 17, 1804, a. 71 y. NR9

523) vi JOHN LOVEJOY ABBOTT, b. 12 Apr 1757; d. 1 Nov 1837; m. 29 Oct 1782, his third cousin once removed, PHEBE ABBOTT, b. Apr 1763 daughter of Nehemiah and Hannah (Ballard) Abbot; Phebe d. about 1826.

vii SAMUEL ABBOTT, b. 12 Jun 1759; d. before 1760.

524) viii SAMUEL ABBOTT, b. 19 Sep 1760; d. at Saco, ME, 8 May 1792; m. 24 Jun 1788, MARY CUTTS, b. at Saco, 19 Jul 1763 daughter of Thomas and Elizabeth (Scammon) Cutts; Mary d. 27 Mar 1796.[326]

ix SARAH ABBOT, b. 3 Oct 1762; d. 2 Mar 1848; m. 3 Mar 1785, her third cousin once removed, NEHEMIAH ABBOT, b. 10 Mar 1757 son of Nehemiah and Hannah (Ballard) Abbot; Nehemiah d. 30 Dec 1823. Sarah and Nehemiah did not have children. Sarah Abbot used her wealth to help fund the Abbot Academy of Andover, an academy for females. The Abbot Academy is named for Sarah.[327]

525) x MARTHA ABBOTT, b. 17 Oct 1764; d. at Salem, 15 Sep 1798; m. 31 Aug 1788 as his second wife, JOHN JENKS, b. at Medford, 6 Dec 1751 son of John and Rebecca (Newhall) Jenks. John married first Hannah Andrew and third Annis Pauling. John d. 14 Oct 1817.

526) xi DORCAS ABBOTT, b. Dec 1766; d. 15 Mar 1841; m. 6 Jan 1792, her third cousin (and George Abbott descendant), JOHN HOLT, b. 12 Jan 1765 son of Joshua and Phebe (Farnum) Holt; John d. 11 Feb 1835. This couple is the same as Family #214, child vi.

---

[326] Howard, *Genealogy of the Cutts Family in America*, p. 85
[327] McKeen, *Annals of Fifty Years: A History of Abbot Academy*

xii TAMISON ABBOTT (some records spelled Tammerson), b. 14 Jan 1769; d. at Salem, 27 Jun 1850; m. 23 Jul 1797, as his second wife, WILLIAM APPLETON, b. at Ipswich, 30 Jun 1765 son of William and Sarah (Kinsman) Appleton. William had first married Anna Bowditch. William d. 23 Sep 1822 of "intemperance." Tamison does not seem to have had children.

125) ELIZABETH ABBOTT *(George³, George², George¹)*, b. 5 Nov 1727 daughter of George and Mary (Phillips) Abbott; d. about 1802 at Westford, MA; m. 2 Apr 1747, her second cousin BENJAMIN ABBOTT *(Benjamin³, Benjamin², George¹)*, b. 21 Oct 1723 son of Benjamin and Mary (Carleton) Abbott; Benjamin d. at Hollis 1771.[328] Elizabeth married 2nd, James Pollard of Westford 22 Mar 1775 and third married Josiah Bowers of Billerica.

There are records for nine children in this family, the oldest two recorded at Andover and the remainder at Hollis, New Hampshire.

Benjamin Abbot was active in the community of Hollis serving as selectman six times between 1752 and 1761. He also served on several committees and as the moderator of the town meeting in 1759. In 1757, he served in a regiment that participated in the French and Indian War.[329]

Elizabeth Bowers wrote her will at Westford 10 August 1802. Her will has bequests to the following persons: daughter Elizabeth Powers; daughter-in-law Lydia Abbott; granddaughter Betty Wright; Susan daughter of son Samuel Abbott; Abigail Read;

---

[328] There is a probate record from 1771 in Middlesex County, MA for Benjamin Abbot of Hollis with widow Elizabeth Abbot of Hollis.
[329] Worcester, *History of the Town of Hollis*

and the remainder of the estate divided among "all my children" Benjamin Abbott, George Abbott, Joel Abbott, Jacob Abbott, Elizabeth Powers, and the children of daughter Polly Boynton.[330]

        i   BENJAMIN ABBOTT, b. 13 Apr 1748; d. 11 Jun 1748

527) ii   BENJAMIN ABBOTT, b. 11 Apr 1749; d. at Hollis about 1838; m. by 1778, SARAH "SALLY" WRIGHT, b. 16 May 1763[331] daughter of Joshua and Abigail (Richardson) Wright.

528) iii ELIZABETH ABBOTT, b. 22 Feb 1751; d. at Hollis, 19 Feb 1836; m. 1st about 1770, EBENEZER NUTTING; he died at Hollis, 1773 (probate 24 Nov 1773). Elizabeth m. 2nd 4 Aug 1774, SAMPSON POWERS, b. at Hollis, 2 Apr 1748 son of Peter and Anna (Keyes) Powers; Sampson d. 2 Jan 1822 at Hollis (will written 10 Oct 1821).

529) iv SAMUEL ABBOTT, b. 13 Apr 1753; d. Feb 1794; m. SUSAN HUBBARD.

        v   MARY ABBOTT, b. 31 Dec 1754; d. 23 Jan 1755.

530) vi GEORGE ABBOTT, b. 29 Dec 1755; d. 15 Sep 1818; m. 29 Dec 1784, NAOMI TUTTLE, b. at Littleton, 28 Sep 1764 daughter of Samuel and Mary (Russell) Tuttle; Naomi d. about 1833.

531) vii JOEL ABBOTT, b. 4 Dec 1757; d. at Westford, 12 Apr 1806; m. 4 Sep 1786, LYDIA CUMMINGS, b. at Westford, 26 Nov 1769 daughter of Isaac and

---

[330] *Middlesex County, MA: Probate File Papers, 1648-1924*. Will of Elizabeth Bowers, 10 Aug 1802. Case number 2269.

[331] This identification involves a young marriage for Sarah at age 15. However, her last child was born in 1807 so she would have to be very young at the time of the birth of the first child in 1778.

Elizabeth (Trowbridge) Cummings; Lydia d. at Littleton, 5 Mar 1813.

532) viii JACOB ABBOTT, b. 12 Apr 1760; d. at Westford, 11 Apr 1815; m. 14 Sep 1787, POLLY CUMMINGS, b. 12 Jul 1767 daughter of Thomas and Lucy (Laurence) Cummings.

533) ix MARY ABBOTT, b. about 1762; d. at Westford, 7 Jul 1797; m. 28 Jul 1782, ABEL BOYNTON, b. at Westford, 9 Aug 1755 son of Nathaniel and Rebeckah (Barrett) Boynton. Abel m. 2nd Polly Pierce.

126) SARAH ABBOTT *(George³, George², George¹)*, b. 14 Jan 1729/30 daughter of George and Mary (Phillips) Abbott; d. 29 Dec 1797; m. 4 Aug 1757, her second cousin, NATHAN HOLT *(Dorcas Abbott Holt³, Timothy², George¹)*, b. 28 Feb 1725 son of Nicholas and Dorcas (Abbott) Holt; Nathan d. at Danvers 2 Aug 1792.

Sarah and Nathan had four children. The births of the three daughters are recorded at Danvers. The son James is attributed to this family in Durrie's Holt genealogy.[332] Nathan did not leave a will. The administrator of the estate was his son-in-law William Frost.

534) i SARAH HOLT, b. 29 Oct 1758; d. 17 Sep 1841; m. at Danvers, 2 Dec 1777, WILLIAM FROST, b. at New Castle, NH, 15 Nov 1754 son of William and Elizabeth (Prescott) Frost; William d. at Andover 28 Sep 1836. Sarah and William are second great grandparents of Robert Frost.

---

[332] Durrie, *Genealogical History of the Holt Family*, p 44

535) ii MARY HOLT, b. 3 Oct 1761; d. at Beverly, 7 Jan 1850; m. 1 Nov 1781, ROBERT ENDICOTT, b. 29 Oct 1756 son of John and Elizabeth (Jacobs) Endicott; Robert d. at Beverly, 6 Mar 1819.

536) iii HANNAH HOLT, b. 11 May 1769; d. at Beverly 26 Jul 1857; m. 23 Jan 1793, her first cousin and George Abbott descendant, PETER HOLT, b. at Andover 12 Jun 1763 son of Joshua and Phebe (Farnum) Holt; Peter d. at Greenfield, NH 25 Apr 1851. Two of the daughters of Hannah and Peter married Samuel Endicott son of Mary Holt and Robert Endicott (Hannah's sister Mary just above).

537) iv JAMES HOLT, b. 1772; d. in India, Aug 1807;[333] m. 30 Aug 1796, LUCY WHIPPLE, b. 8 Mar 1778; Lucy d. at Danvers, 6 Mar 1839. Although James's death is reported as August 1807, the probate of his estate was April 1807.

127) HANNAH ABBOTT *(George³, George², George¹)*, b. 14 Dec 1733 of George and Mary (Phillips) Abbott; d. 26 Mar 1820; m. 9 Jan 1755, WILLIAM FOSTER, b. 4 Mar 1729/30 son of John and Mary (Osgood) Foster; William d. at Andover, 1 Sep 1803.

The will of William Foster has bequests for the following persons: beloved wife Hannah and his four children, son William, daughter Hannah the wife of Timothy Rogers, daughter Mary the wife of Timothy Ballard, and daughter Sarah the wife of Joseph Brown.[334]

The births of four children are recorded at Andover.

---

[333] James, h. Lucy (Whipple), at India, Aug. —, 1807.
[334] *Essex County, MA: Probate File Papers, 1638-1881. Probate of* William Foster, 4 Oct 1803, *Case number* 10013.

Generation Four 239

538) i HANNAH FOSTER, b. 20 Jun 1756; d. at Tewksbury 7 Nov 1830; m. 27 Feb 1777, TIMOTHY ROGERS, b. at Tewksbury 16 Jun 1745 son of Timothy and Rebecca (French) Rogers; Timothy d. 27 Feb 1814.

539) ii WILLIAM FOSTER, b. 1 Jun 1758; d. 20 Aug 1843; m. late in life, 18 Nov 1826, SALLY WELCH KIMBALL, b. at Plaistow, NH, 20 Dec 1786 daughter of Joseph and Anna (Welch) Kimball. Despite their late marriage, William and Sally did have one son. Sally d. 29 Jan 1850.

iii MARY FOSTER, b. 21 Jul 1763; d. 30 Mar 1834; m. 30 Oct 1783, her third cousin once removed (and George Abbott descendant), TIMOTHY BALLARD, b. 28 Jul 1757 son of Timothy and Sarah (Abbott) Ballard; Timothy d. 29 Feb 1828 when he committed suicide by cutting his throat.[335] Mary and Timothy did not have any children. Mary Foster Ballard wrote her will 3 March 1831. The will includes bequests to her brother William Foster and to her nieces and nephews who are named as follows: nephew Thadeus Brown, nephew George Brown, niece Sarah B. Gray, nephew Rev. Timothy Rogers, and niece Hannah Kidder wife of Samuel Kidder. These nieces and nephews receive money bequests of $20 except Thadeus who receives $100. The remainder of the estate is given to her two nieces who are the daughters of her late sister Sarah Brown:

---

[335] Massachusetts Vital Records Project: Timothy, "who cut his own throat," Feb. 29, 1828, a. 70 y. 7 m.

Mary Ballard Gould wife of Abraham Gould and Hannah Brown.

540) iv SARAH "SALLY" FOSTER, b. 9 Sep 1765; d. at Tewksbury 30 Nov 1807; m. 8 Jun 1794, JOSEPH BROWN, b. at Tewksbury, 19 Jun 1762 son of William and Mary (Osgood) Brown; Joseph d. 21 Nov 1829.

Henry³, George², George¹

128) LYDEA ABBOTT (*Henry³, George², George¹*), b. 10 Feb 1722/3 daughter of Henry and Mary (Platts) Abbott; d. 11 Sep 1807; m. 24 Mar 1742/3, JOSHUA LOVEJOY, b. 2 Dec 1719 son of Henry and Sarah (Farnum) Lovejoy; Joshua d. 2 Feb 1812.

Joshua and Lydea had six children whose births are recorded at Andover.

541) i JOSHUA LOVEJOY, b. 8 Jan 1743/4; d. at Sanbornton, NH 28 Jan 1832; m. 30 Apr 1769, SARAH PERKINS, b. at Middleton, 10 Mar 1744 daughter of Timothy and Phebe (Peters) Perkins; Sarah d. 3 May 1828.

ii MARY LOVEJOY, b. 13 Aug 1745; d. 15 Apr 1826; m. 24 Sep 1765, JAMES PARKER whose parentage is not entirely clear;[336] James d. 23 Oct 1801. Mary m. 2nd Jonathan Cummings. There are not any records of children for Mary and James.

---

[336] His death record from 1801 gives his age as 66 years which would mean he was born in 1735. That conflicts with most published genealogies which have him born in 1745 son of James. The death record may be wrong.

542) iii   LYDIA LOVEJOY, b. 21 Jul 1747; death unknown; m. 23 Jun 1767, third cousin once removed, ABIEL HOLT, b. 3 Apr 1746 son of Thomas and Hannah (Kimball) Holt; Abiel d. 17 Nov 1824

281) iv   DORCAS LOVEJOY, b. 18 Aug 1749; d. 25 Jun 1843; m. about 1770, as his second wife, her second cousin once removed (and George Abbott descendant), BENJAMIN AMES, b. 6 Jun 1724 son of Samuel and Hannah (Stevens) Ames; Benjamin d. 10 Jan 1809. This is the same as Family #281 which also includes Benjamin's first wife Hephzibah Chandler.

543) v   CHLOE LOVEJOY, b. 26 Mar 1753; d. 21 Nov 1843; m. 26 Dec 1776, her fourth cousin, JOHN POOR, b. 16 Apr 1754 son of John and Rebecca (Stevens) Poor; John d. 7 Jul 1823. John Poor is a descendant of George Abbott of Rowley.

544) vi   LUCY LOVEJOY, b. 4 Aug 1755; d. at Andover, 2 Apr 1844; m. 11 Apr 1776, THEOPHILUS FRYE, b. at Andover, 12 Oct 1753 son of Samuel and Elizabeth (Frye) Frye; Theophilus d. 2 Apr 1830.

129)   HENRY ABBOT *(Henry³, George², George¹)*, b. 31 Jan 1724 son of Henry and Mary (Platts) Abbot; d. 21 Feb 1805; m. 1st 2 Oct 1750, ELIZABETH SIBSON (I think the daughter of Joseph); Elizabeth d. about 1764. Henry m. 2nd his first cousin PHEBE ABBOT *(Isaac³, George², George¹)*, b. 14 Nov 1746 daughter of Isaac and Phebe (Lovejoy) Abbot; Phebe d. 29 Jun 1833.

Henry and Betsy Sibson did not have any children. The births of seven children of Henry and Phebe Abbot are recorded at Andover.

The will of Henry Abbot was written 2 February 1805 and includes the following bequests: well beloved wife Phebe Abbot receives one-third of the real estate in Andover for her use during her life; after she is "done with it," two sons Henry and Isaac will divide that property. Isaac is the son charged with taking care of his mother. Son Henry Abbot receives a tract of land known as the Lovejoy lot and Peavy meadow. There are other land bequests and Henry also receives the silver tankard marked H.A.P. Daughter Phebe Porter wife of Jonathan Porter receives $50. Daughter Elizabeth Kneeland Abbot receives $600 in cash and a State Note of the Commonwealth of Massachusetts valued at $186.84. Elizabeth also is to receive cords of wood delivered to her door as long as she remains unmarried. Henry's wife Phebe further is allowed use of his clock and she can place it anywhere in the house she wants. She also receives use of the silver tankard marker I.A.P. as long as she remains a widow. Phebe is also to have one-half of the dwelling house for her use. Son Isaac receives the remainder of the real estate and buildings not otherwise disposed of in the will. Henry then goes on the describe the disposition of the estate if either of the sons dies before returning from sea. He also notes that if Isaac should die before his return from sea and if he shall not have made provision for "his particular friend Miss Charlotte Houghton," then Charlotte will receive $200 from the estate. His sons Henry and Isaac are named executors of the estate.[337] Isaac did return from the sea and went on the marry Miss Charlotte Houghton.

545) i PHEBE ABBOT, b. 25 Jan 1766; d. at Medford 10 Oct 1852; m. 7 Nov 1790, as his second wife, JONATHAN PORTER, b. at Braintree, 12 Mar 1745 son of Jonathan and Hannah (Hayden) Porter; Jonathan d. 4 Nov 1817.

ii MARY ABBOT, b. 4 Apr 1768; d. 17 Aug 1769.

---

[337] *Essex County, MA: Probate File Papers, 1638-1881. Probate of* Henry Abbot, 6 Nov 1805, *Case number* 57.

        iii   HENRY ABBOT, b. Jul 1770; d. 10 Aug 1770.

        iv   HENRY ABBOT, b. 6 Sep 1771; d. 19 May 1776.

546)   v   HENRY ABBOT, b. 8 Apr 1777; d. 13 Jan 1862; m. 20 May 1807, JUDITH FOLANSBEE, b. 15 Dec 1782likely the daughter of Moody and Judith (-) Folansbee of Newbury; Judith d. at Andover, 10 Feb 1864.

        vi   ISAAC ABBOT, b. 9 Jun 1779; d. 1838;[338] m. 22 Feb 1808, CHARLOTTE HOUGHTON, b. about 1780; Charlotte d. 21 Aug 1821. Isaac and Charlotte did not have children.

        vii   ELIZABETH KNEELAND ABBOT; b. 10 Jan 1783; d. 20 Aug 1812. Elizabeth did not marry.

130)   DORCAS ABBOTT *(Henry³, George², George¹)*, b. 11 May 1729 daughter of Henry and Mary (Platts) Abbott; d. at Nottingham, NH 10 Apr 1789; m. 17 Apr 1754, BENJAMIN BUTLER, b. at Edgartown 9 Apr 1729 son of Malachi and Jemima (Dagget) Butler. Benjamin m. 2nd, 29 Sep 1791, Phebe Griffin daughter of James and Phebe (Abbott) Griffin; Benjamin d. at Nottingham 26 Oct 1804.

     Benjamin studied at Harvard, was an ordained minister, and was the minister in Nottingham, New Hampshire. Dorcas and Benjamin's oldest child was born at Andover. Following that, the family relocated to Nottingham where seven other children were born including a set of triplets. Five of the children died in early

---

[338] Abbot and Abbot, *Genealogical Record of Descendants* report a death year as 1838, but I could not locate a death or a probate record.

childhood.[339] Only three children, Henry, Mary, and Dorcas, are mentioned in the will of Benjamin Butler.[340] After the death of his first wife Dorcas, Benjamin married Phebe Griffin who was the second cousin, once removed of Dorcas.

In his will, Benjamin Butler bequeaths to his beloved wife Phebe the full use of the dwelling house and the garden as long as she remains a widow. She also receives all the household furnishings she brought to the marriage and any that were procured after their marriage. Phebe also receives ten Spanish milled dollars annually. His son Henry is to provide for the ongoing maintenance (firewood, etc.) of Phebe. Daughters Dorcas and Mary receive the remainder of the household goods. Son Henry receives all the remainder of the estate, both real and personal, not otherwise disposed of in the will. The value of the estate was $1,923 not counting a one-third part of the dwelling.

547)   i   HENRY BUTLER, b. 27 Nov 1754; d. 17 Jan 1808; m. 11 Apr 1776, ISABELLA FISKE, b. at Epping, 2 Aug 1757 (or 2 Aug 1759)[341] daughter of Ebenezer and Elizabeth (Cotton) Fiske; Isabella d. 17 Jan 1808. After Isabella's death, Henry married Ruth Parsons.

       ii   BENJAMIN BUTLER, b. 23 Feb 1757; d. 30 Apr 1757.

       iii   BENJAMIN BUTLER, b. 14 Jun 1758; d. 29 Aug 1759.

548)   iv   MARY BUTLER, b. 30 Mar 1760; d. 1846; m. 1776, ABRAHAM BROWN, b. at Epping, 8 May 1753 son of Abraham and Hannah (Osgood) Brown; Abraham d. at Northfield 8 Mar 1824.

---

[339] Most of the information on children in this family obtained from Cogswell's *History of Nottingham, Deerfield, and Northwood*, p. 172
[340] *New Hampshire Wills and Probate Records 1643-1982*, Probate of Benjamin Butler, Rockingham, 10 Jan 1805, Case number 7333.
[341] Ancestry.com. New Hampshire, Births and Christenings Index, 1714-1904

	v	ELIZABETH BUTLER, b. 30 Aug 1762; d. 3 Oct 1762.
549)	vi	DORCAS BUTLER, b. 9 Oct 1766; d. at Colerian Township, OH, 9 Oct 1857;[342] m. 5 Jun 1786, JONATHAN CILLEY, b. 8 Mar 1762 son of Joseph and Sarah (Longfellow) Cilley; Jonathan d. 21 Mar 1807.
	vii	JEMIMA BUTLER, b. 9 Oct 1766; d. 14 Oct 1766.
	viii	JAMES PLATT BUTLER, b. 9 Oct 1766; d. 19 Oct 1766.

131) MARY ABBOTT *(Henry³, George², George¹)*, b. 13 Aug 1737 daughter of Henry and Mary (Platts) Abbott; d. 26 Nov 1813; m. 22 Mar 1759, THOMAS HOVEY, b. at Ipswich 1 Oct 1736 son of Thomas and Sarah (Rust) Hovey; Thomas d. at Dracut, 29 Jul 1826.

Thomas Hovey wrote his will 13 December 1815 and his estate entered probate in 1826. His will includes bequests for the following persons: son Henry Abbot Hovey receives a token amount of $10 as he has already receive the full portion of his inheritance; son Samuel Hovey receives $100 to supplement what he has already been given; son Benjamin Hovey also receives $100; son Joseph Hovey receives $100 and a feather bed; daughter Mary Whiting wife of Moses Whiting receives a feather bed, a bedstead, and some pillows, in addition to what she received at the time of her marriage; daughter Elizabeth Hovey receives her mother's wearing apparel, silver teaspoons, and other household items, use of one room in the house as long as she remains unmarried, some sheep, and $100; and son James Platts Hovey receives land and

---

[342] Year: 1850; Census Place: Colerain, Hamilton, Ohio; Roll: M432_686; Page: 367B; Image: 256. In the 1850 U.S. Census, 83-year-old Dorcas Cilley, born in NH, was living in the household of Samuel and Mary Hardin who is Dorcas's daughter.

buildings, and farming tools and utensils. James Platts Hovey is named executor.[343]

Mary and Thomas had ten children whose births were recorded at Dracut.

        i   THOMAS HOVEY, b. 15 Jan 1762; d. at Dracut, 7 Sep 1812; Thomas does not seem to have married.

550) ii   HENRY ABBOTT HOVEY, b. 15 Jan 1764; d. at Milford about 1830;[344] m. 29 May 1791, HANNAH BRADLEY, b. at Dracut, 1 May 1768 daughter of Amos and Elizabeth (Page) Bradley; Hannah d. at Boston 14 May 1851.[345]

        iii   JOHN HOVEY, b. 14 Mar 1765; no further record; he is not mentioned in his father's will.

551) iv   JAMES PLATTS HOVEY, b. 21 Jul 1767; d. at Dracut, 30 Nov 1831; m. 20 Feb 1801, REBECKAH HOVEY, b. at Boxford, about 1777 daughter of Ivory and Lucy (Peabody) Hovey; Rebeckah d. at Lowell, 1 Feb 1853.

        v   MARY HOVEY, b. 13 Feb 1769; d. at Pelham, NH, 1837;[346] m. 10 May 1794, MOSES WHITING perhaps the son of Oliver and Ruth (Proctor) Whiting; Moses d. at Pelham about 1823. The date of Moses's will is 27 Jan 1823. Mary and Moses do not seem to have had children. No records for children were located and Moses's will leaves his entire estate to his wife.

---

[343] *Middlesex County, MA: Probate File Papers, 1648-1871. Probate of* Thomas Hovey, *1826, Case number* 11965.

[344] U.S., Newspaper Extractions from the Northeast, 1704-1930; Columbian Centinel; Henry A. Hovey died at Milford in edition 31 Jul 1830.

[345] *Massachusetts: Vital Records, 1841-1910.* (From original records held by the Massachusetts Archives. Online database: *AmericanAncestors.org*, New England Historic Genealogical Society, 2004.)

[346] Daniel Hovey Association, *The Hovey Book*, p 153

	vi	ELIZABETH HOVEY, b. 26 Jul 1771; d. at Dracut, 6 Dec 1845. Elizabeth did not marry. In 1838, there was a probate case to appoint a guardian for her as she was found *non compos mentis*.[347]
552)	vii	SAMUEL HOVEY, b. 26 Oct 1773; d. after 1850;[348] m. 12 Sep 1795, MARTHA "PATTY" BRADLEY, b. at Dracut, 31 Jan 1774 daughter of Amos and Elizabeth (Page) Bradley; Martha d. 5 Jul 1825 at Dracut.
553)	viii	BENJAMIN HOVEY, b. 9 May 1775; d. at Dracut, 30 Mar 1866; m. at Medford, 2 Aug 1797, LOIS (Louisa) JENKINS, b. at Malden, 2 Aug 1767 daughter of Ezekiel and Margaret (Floyd) Jenkins;[349] Lois d. at Dracut, 8 Aug 1846.
	ix	JOSHUA HOVEY, b. 23 Sep 1778; d. at Dracut, 26 Jul 1804; Joshua does not seem to have married.
554)	x	JOSEPH HOVEY, b. 25 May 1784; d. 29 Aug 1860; m. 4 Jul 1812, MARY HOVEY, b. at Boxford, 9 Aug 1781 daughter of Joseph and Mary (Porter) Hovey.

Isaac³, George², George¹

132)   ISAAC ABBOT (*Isaac³, George², George¹*), b. 3 Feb 1745 son of Isaac and Phebe (Lovejoy) Abbott; d. at Andover, 21 May 1836; m. 22 Apr 1766, his second cousin once removed, PHEBE CHANDLER

---

[347] *Middlesex County, MA: Probate File Papers, 1648-1871*. Probate (non compos mentis) of Elizabeth Hovey, *1838*, Case number 11954.
[348] Year: 1850; Census Place: Cambridge, Middlesex, Massachusetts; Roll: M432_325; Page: 46B; Image: 98. Samuel Hovey living in Cambridge at the 1850 U.S. Census, age 76.
[349] Floyd, "Descendants of Joel Jenkins," NEHGR, p 319

(*Nathan Chandler⁴, John Chandler³, Hannah Abbott Chandler², George¹*), b. 2 Jun 1742 daughter of Nathan and Priscilla (Holt) Chandler; Phebe d. 1 Jul 1800.

Isaac Abbot served in the Revolutionary War and was wounded at Bunker Hill.[350] He served as a deacon and was also the first postmaster of Andover. He lost his eyesight several years prior to his death.

Isaac Abbot made the following bequests in his will which was written 14 September 1833. His granddaughter Mrs. Mary Shattuck of Andover received one silver tablespoon, six silver teaspoons and $10. Daughter-in-law Mrs. Mary Abbot widow of his son Isaac received a clock and $10. Grandchildren Josiah F., Samuel, and Isaac Abbot children of son Isaac received $10 each. His wearing apparel was divided among William, Issac, and Moses Abbot who are the children of his son William Abbot of Concord. Granddaughter Phebe Abbot daughter of son William received the dictionary, the bible, and the umbrella. Granddaughter Rebeckah Abbot daughter of William received the looking glass. All the named grandchildren received $10 each. His dwelling house and all the remainder of the estate is bequeathed to son William Abbot of Concord.[351]

Isaac and Phebe had four children whose births are recorded at Andover.

        i   PHEBE ABBOT, b. 27 May 1767; d. 8 Nov 1772.

555) ii   ISAAC ABBOT, b. 9 Dec 1768; d. 27 Dec 1806; m. 1st, 5 Jul 1798, HEPHZIBAH FISKE, b. 21 Apr 1773 daughter of John and Hephzibah (-) Fiske; Hephzibah d. 22 Mar 1800. Isaac m. 2nd, 7 Oct 1801,

---

[350] The Essex Antiquarian, volume 1, Abbot Genealogy, p 80
[351] *Essex County, MA: Probate File Papers, 1638-1881. Probate of* Isaac Abbot, 7 Jun 1836, *Case number* 60.

Generation Four 249

> MARY MOULTON, b. at Danvers, 16 Mar 1775 daughter of Ebenezer and Elizabeth (Curtis) Moulton; Mary d. 19 Aug 1851.
>
> iii   PRISCILLA ABBOT, b. 1 Jun 1770; d. 10 Feb 1830; m. 6 Jun 1820, as his third wife, JOHN KNEELAND, b. at Boston, 14 Oct 1748 son of John and Sarah (Mulberry) Kneeland. John married a fourth time after Priscilla's death; John d. 4 Sep 1831. John Kneeland was the stepson of Samuel Abbot who was Priscilla's first cousin once removed. Priscilla married late in life and did not have children.

556) iv   WILLIAM ABBOT, b. 30 Oct 1772; d. at Concord, NH about 1856 (probate date 24 Jun 1856); m. 14 May 1801, his third cousin once removed (and George Abbott descendant) REBECCA BAILEY, b. 10 Apr 1781 daughter of Moses and Elizabeth (Mooar) Bailey; Rebecca was still living in 1860 when she was living in Concord with her son Moses.[352] This is the same as Family #267, child viii.

129)   PHEBE ABBOTT *(Isaac³, George², George¹)* and HENRY ABBOTT. This is Family #129 covered above.

133)   SARAH ABBOTT *(Isaac³, George², George¹)*, b. 2 Jan 1749/50 daughter of Isaac and Phebe (Lovejoy) Abbott; d. at Andover, 2 Apr 1835; m. 2 Jan 1770, her second cousin, once removed TIMOTHY ABBOTT *(Elizabeth Abbott Abbott⁴, Timothy³, Timothy², George¹)*, b. 2

---

[352] Year: *1860*; Census Place: *Concord Ward 7, Merrimack, New Hampshire*; Roll: *M653_675*; Page: *945*; Family History Library Film: *803675*

Jun 1745 son of Asa and Elizabeth (Abbott) Abbott; Timothy d. 22 Mar 1826.

No probate record was located for Timothy. Sarah and Timothy had four children whose births are recorded at Andover.

557) i ASA ABBOTT, b. 15 Nov 1770; d. at Andover, 6 Jul 1850; m. at Billerica, 29 May 1798, JUDITH JAQUITH, b. 2 Feb 1777 daughter of Joseph and Elizabeth (Needham) Jaquith; Judith d. 15 Jul 1843.

ii TIMOTHY ABBOTT, b. 28 Sep 1774; d. by drowning, 17 Aug 1777.

558) iii DANIEL ABBOTT, b. 25 Feb 1777; d. at Nashua, NH, 3 Dec 1853; m. at Salem, 11 Aug 1805, ELIZABETH PICKMAN, b. at Salem, 11 Feb 1782 daughter of William and Elizabeth (Leavitt) Pickman; Elizabeth d. 29 Mar 1850.

559) iv SARAH ABBOTT, b. 22 May 1783; d. at Andover, 11 Sep 1858; m. 27 Nov 1803, NATHANIEL SWIFT, b. at Dorchester, 15 Jul 1778 son of Nathaniel and Mary (Baker) Swift; Nathaniel d. 7 Dec 1840.

Section IV: The Grandchildren of William Abbott and Elizabeth Geary

Elizabeth Abbott Phelps³, William², George¹

134)   ELIZABETH PHELPS *(Elizabeth Abbott Phelps³, William², George¹)*, b. 29 Oct 1712 daughter of Joseph and Elizabeth (Abbott) Phelps; d. at Brooklyn, CT 19 Jul 1787; m. at Pomfret 14 May 1741, BENONI BARRETT, b. 17 Aug 1718[353] son of Moses and Sarah (-) Barrett; Benoni d. 20 Jun 1755 at Brooklyn, CT.

The final distribution of the estate of Benoni Barret was in January 1773 at the time the children had all reached age 18 years. Heirs receiving distributions were widow Elizabeth Barret, eldest son Joseph Barret who receives two-fifths, the heirs of daughter Elizabeth Barret who is deceased who receive one-fifth, son William Barret, and son James Barret who each also receive one-fifth.[354]

Elizabeth and Benoni had four children, the births of the sons recorded at Pomfret[355] and the birth of Elizabeth recorded at Woodstock.

560)   i   JOSEPH BARRETT, b. 12 Jul 1742; date of death uncertain; m. at Pomfret, 20 Feb 1765, JEMIMA CARPENTER, b. 9 Jan 1742/3 daughter of Samuel and Keziah (Carpenter) Carpenter.

---

[353] Ancestry.com, *Connecticut, Church Record Abstracts, 1630-1920* (Provo, UT, USA: n.p., 2013).
[354] *Connecticut Wills and Probate, 1609-1999*, Probate of Benoni, Hartford, 1755, Case number 307.
[355] Barbour Collection, Pomfret

ii   ELIZABETH BARRETT, b. 6 Mar 1743/4;[356] d. before Jan 1773; likely the Elizabeth Barrett who had an out-of-wedlock child born at Pomfret 1765. That child was named Elizabeth Lawrence. There is not a record of the father, but it is *possible* that the father was her first cousin Joseph Lawrence. The daughter seems to be still living at the time of the final distribution of Benoni Barrett's estate in 1773 as it includes the "heirs of Elizabeth Barret deceased daughter to said Benoni Barret deceased," but no record was found of Elizabeth Lawrence after that time.

561)   iii   WILLIAM BARRETT, b. 12 Apr 1751; d. at Brooklyn, CT, 7 Mar 1838; m. 26 Feb 1778, LUCY ADAMS, b. at Pomfret, 25 May 1753 daughter of Paul and Mary (Hubbard) Adams; Lucy d. 4 Apr 1834.

iv   JAMES BARRETT, b. 28 Feb 1754; d. 25 Jun 1776.

135)   HANNAH PHELPS *(Elizabeth Abbott Phelps[3], William[2], George[1])*, b. 20 May 1715 daughter of Joseph and Elizabeth (Abbott) Phelps; d. at Pomfret 13 Jan 1746/7; m. at Pomfret 15 Nov 1744, SAMUEL LAWRENCE; no definite information about Samuel has been obtained. He may have been a member of a Lawrence family in Killingly, CT, most likely the son of Daniel Lawrence.[357]

Hannah and Samuel had just one child born at Pomfret. Following the death of his first wife, Samuel Lawrence married Hannah Tatman and relocated to Worcester where he had several children. He then seems to have left Worcester. It is possible he is the Samuel Lawrence who died in 1773 in Montague, MA with wife Hannah.

---

[356] Barbour and Newton, *Vital Records of Woodstock*
[357] Collections of the Worcester Society of Antiquity, Volume 13, pp 57-58

562) i JOSEPH LAWRENCE, b. 9 Aug 1745; d. at Pomfret 14 Oct 1775. There are births of three children at Pomfret for Joseph and wife Betty. There is no information on the identity of Betty.

James³, William², George¹

136) ABIGAIL ABBOTT *(James³, William², George¹)*, b. 1 Jan 1714/5 daughter of James and Abigail (Farnum) Abbott; d. at Charlestown about 1737; m. 13 May 1734, JOHN KIDDER, b. at Charlestown 13 Feb 1709 son of Stephen and Mary (Johnson) Kidder; John married second Anna Walker and third Mary Snow.

The Abbot genealogy[358] lists Abigail as marrying Jacob Waldron, having children Sarah, Ezra, and Elizabeth and then marrying (-) Hibbard of Charlestown. However, available records give Jacob Waldron (who was born 1743) as marrying Abigail's niece Sarah [daughter of James and Sarah (Bancroft) Abbott]. There are also three birth records for children of Jacob and Sarah named Sarah, Ezra, and Elizabeth. The only marriage of Abigail seems to be to John Kidder of Charlestown and she seems to have died soon after the birth of her only child.

There is just one child and he likely died young as John Kidder named another son John that he had with his third wife.

    i   JOHN KIDDER, b. 12 Sep 1735; likely died young

137) JAMES ABBOTT *(James³, William², George¹)*, b. 12 Jan 1716/7 son of James and Abigail (Farnum) Abbott; d. at Newbury, VT, 27

---

[358] Abbot and Abbot, *Genealogical Record of Descendants*, p 28

Dec 1803; m. about 1742, SARAH BANCROFT, b. 19 Feb 1722 daughter of Samuel and Sarah (Lampson) Bancroft; Sarah d. 1765.

James Abbott and Sarah Bancroft had ten children. The oldest child's birth is recorded at Andover, and there are records of the births of some of the other children in New Hampshire. Information on other children was obtained from the Abbot genealogy, pp 28-29.[359]

563) i SARAH ABBOTT, b. 1 Mar 1743; death unknown; m. by 1765, JACOB WALDRON, b. at Rumford, 2 Mar 1743 son of Isaac and Susannah (Chandler) Waldron; the date or place of death is not known.

564) ii ABIGAIL ABBOT, b. 22 Jan 1745/6; d. at Bath, NH, 11 Feb 1815; m. 15 Apr 1767, ASA BAILEY, b. at Salem, NH, 13 May 1745 son of Edward and Elizabeth (Burbank) Bailey. Abigail divorced Asa in 1793 following years of abuse, the last straw being the sexual abuse of one of their daughters. What happened to Asa is not clear. *The Memoirs of Mrs. Abigail Bailey* recounting the events of her marriage was published in 1815 just after her death.[360]

565) iii MARY ABBOTT, b. 6 Feb 1748; m. 1st, 22 Oct 1773, RICHARD MINCHEN; Richard d. 1776. Mary m. 2nd, at Haverhill, NH, 22 Mar 1777, URIAH CROSS.[361]

566) iv JAMES ABBOTT, b. 10 Oct 1750; d. in Ohio 1814; m. at Groton, VT, 29 Mar 1781, ZILPHA SMITH. James

---

[359] Abbot and Abbot, *Genealogical Record of Descendants*
[360] Bailey, *Memoirs of Mrs. Abigail Bailey*
[361] New Hampshire Marriage Record Index 1637-1947 (ancestry.com)

Generation Four 255

m. 2nd, at Groton, VT, 25 Jul 1785, MEHITABLE HIDDEN.[362,363]

567) v JUDITH ABBOTT, b. 19 Feb 1753; d. at Newbury, VT, 30 Dec 1806; m. 27 Oct 1772, THOMAS BROCK, b. about 1745; Thomas d. at Newbury, 10 Jun 1811. Thomas Brock's origins are not clear at this point; he was perhaps born in Scotland.

568) vi WILLIAM ABBOTT, b. 24 Apr 1755; d. at Bath, NH, 14 Jun 1807; m. 9 Dec 1777, MABEL WHITTLESEY, b. at Guilford, CT, 25 Jun 1757 daughter of Josiah and Elizabeth (Jackson) Whittlesey; Mabel d. at Haverhill, NH, 2 Nov 1836.

569) vii BANCROFT ABBOTT, b. 4 Jun 1757; d. at Newbury, VT, 29 Oct 1829;[364] m. 1787, LYDIA WHITE, b. at Plaistow, NH, 1 Jan 1763 daughter of Ebenezer and Hannah (Merrill) White; Lydia d. 25 Jun 1853.

viii EZRA ABBOTT, b. 8 Oct 1759; died young.

ix SUSANNAH ABBOTT, b. 3 Mar 1763; no further record.

570) x EZRA ABBOTT, b. 2 Jun 1765; d. in Vermont, 5 Jul 1842; m. at Newbury, VT, 8 Aug 1788, his first cousin, HANNAH ABBOTT, b. 29 Mar 1762 daughter of Reuben and Rhoda (Whittemore) Abbott; Hannah d. 2 Sep 1832.

---

[362] Abbott Family, Groton Families in 1790, Groton Vermont Historical Society.
[363] Vermont Vital Records 1720-1908 (ancestry.com)
[364] *Vermont, Vital Records, 1720-1908* (Provo, UT, USA: Ancestry.com Operations, Inc., 2013).

138) REUBEN ABBOTT *(James³, William², George¹)*, b. 4 Apr 1723 son of James and Abigail (Farnum) Abbott; d. at Concord, NH, 13 May 1822; m. 1st, by 1752, RHODA WHITTEMORE, b. at Malden, 18 Aug 1729 daughter of Elias and Rhoda (Holt) Whittemore; d. 29 Jan 1785. Reuben m. 2nd DINAH BLANCHARD the widow of Joseph Blanchard; Dinah was b. 28 Dec 1731 daughter of Stephen and Deborah (Phelps) Blanchard; Dinah d. 11 Mar 1826.

Reuben and Rhoda had ten children whose births are recorded at Concord, New Hampshire. Of the six children who married, three married other George Abbott descendants.

    i REUBEN ABBOTT, b. 18 May 1752; d. 11 Dec 1752.

571) ii REUBEN ABBOTT, b. 5 Feb 1754; d. 12 Dec 1834; m. 24 Sep 1776, his second cousin once removed, ZERVIAH FARNUM, b. at Concord, about 1752 daughter of Joseph and Zerviah (Hoit) Farnum; Zerviah d. at Concord, Dec 1818.[365]

572) iii RHODA ABBOTT, b. 31 Dec 1755; d. at Boscawen, 31 Aug 1839; m. at Concord, 8 Jan 1778, JONATHAN JOHNSON, b. at Boscawen, 29 Dec 1753 son of John and Eleanor (Eastman) Johnson; Jonathan d. 16 Sep 1820.

573) iv ELIAS ABBOTT, b. 24 Oct 1757; d. at Northfield, NH, 19 Mar 1847; m. Sep 1782, ELIZABETH BUSWELL, b. at Kingston, 4 Sep 1761 daughter of James and Elizabeth (Clough) Buswell; Elizabeth d. 25 Jan 1832.[366]

    v PHEBE ABBOTT, b. 14 Apr 1759; d. 4 Jul 1760.

    vi PHEBE ABBOTT, b. 6 Dev 1760; d. Nov 1777.

---

[365] New Hampshire, Death and Disinterment Records, 1754-1947
[366] History of the Town of Canterbury, p 1

Generation Four 257

570) vii HANNAH ABBOTT, b. 29 Mar 1762; d. at Vermont, 2 Sep 1832; m. at Newbury, VT, 8 Aug 1788, her first cousin, EZRA ABBOTT, b. at Haverhill, 2 Jun 1765 son of James and Sarah (Bancroft) Abbott; Ezra d. 5 Jul 1842. This is the same couple as Family #137, child x.

viii RUTH ABBOTT, b. 14 Feb 1764; d. 2 Sep 1764

574) ix EZRA ABBOTT, b. 8 Aug 1765; d. 24 Apr 1839; m. his third cousin, MARY WALKER, b, about 1763 daughter of Joseph and Mary (Abbott) Walker; Mary d. at Concord, 22 Sep 1852. This is the same as Family #240, child v.

575) x NATHAN ABBOTT, b. 8 Aug 1765; d. at Concord, 13 May 1849; m. his third cousin, PHEBE ABBOTT, b. 8 Aug 1764 daughter of Nathaniel and Miriam (Chandler) Abbott; Phebe d. 11 Aug 1854. This is the same as Family #236, child vii.

57) AMOS ABBOTT *(James³, William², George¹)* and REBECCA ABBOTT; REBECCA ABBOTT and ABIEL CHANDLER. This family group is Family #57 in Generation Three.

139) PHEBE ABBOTT *(James³, William², George¹)*, b. 22 Nov 1727 daughter of James and Abigail (Farnum) Abbott; d. at Conway NH, 29 Sep 1754; m. 5 Nov 1747, as his 1st wife, THOMAS MERRILL, b. 5 Feb 1723/4 at Haverhill son of John and Lydia (Haynes) Merrill. Thomas had a total of four marriages, his 2nd to Mehitable Harriman, 3rd to Abigail Goodhue, and 4th to Elizabeth Abbott daughter of Benjamin and Abigail (Abbott) Abbott. Thomas Merrill d. at Conway 21 Jun 1788.

Phebe Abbott and Thomas Merrill had five children born at Conway, New Hampshire. Three of the sons, William, Thomas, and Amos, bought adjoining farms on the Saco River in Conway.[367] Two of the sons married two Ambrose sisters who were the daughters of Jonathan and Abigail (Goodhue) Ambrose. Abigail Goodhue Ambrose was one of the wives of Thomas Merrill making these couples, step-siblings.

576) i THOMAS MERRILL, b. 31 Aug 1748; d. May 1821;[368] m. 7 Dec 1775, HANNAH AMBROSE, b, about 1750 daughter of Jonathan and Abigail (Goodhue) Ambrose.

ii WILLIAM MERRILL, b. about 1749. William did not marry.

577) iii ENOCH MERRILL, b. 10 Nov 1750; d. 1838; m. about 1772, MARY AMBROSE, b. at Exeter, 11 Nov 1755 daughter of Jonathan and Abigail (Goodhue) Ambrose; Mary d. at Conway, 27 Mar 1815.

578) iv AMOS MERRILL, b. Jul 1752; d, at Conway, 13 Mar 1840; m. 30 Dec 1779, LOIS WILLEY, b. Jan 1760; Lois d. 28 Mar 1855.

579) v PHEBE MERRILL, b. Dec 1753; d. at North Conway, 9 Oct 1839; m. 3 Dec 1775, her second cousin, ABIATHER EASTMAN, b. 29 Apr 1745 son of Richard and Mary (Lovejoy) Eastman; Abiather d. 10 Jan 1815.

Thomas Merrill and Elizabeth Abbott had two children born at Conway. (See Family #195)

---

[367] Merrill, *A Merrill Memorial*, p 294
[368] Merrill, *A Merrill Memorial*, p 294

140) REBECCA ABBOTT *(James³, William², George¹)*, b. 13 Aug 1730 daughter of James and Abigail (Farnum) Abbott; d. at NH date unknown; m. 13 Aug 1750, ENOCH EASTMAN, b. at Salisbury, 1 Jun 1725 son of Joseph and Abigail (Merrill) Eastman.[369]

Rebecca ad Enoch were early settlers in Hopkinton. Enoch held the position of town clerk and fulfilled other civic responsibilities.[370]

Rebecca and Enoch were the parents of 12 children all born in Rumford[371] and Hopkinton.[372]

   i ENOCH EASTMAN, b. 22 Feb 1752; d. 14 Mar 1756 by drowning.

   ii EZRA EASTMAN, b. 25 Mar 1754; died young.

580) iii SIMEON EASTMAN, b. 23 Oct 1755; m. about 1780, MEHITABLE PIPER.

   iv ENOCH EASTMAN, b. 2 Mar 1757; no further record.

581) v ABIGAIL EASTMAN, b. 25 Feb 1759; d. at Hopkinton, 19 Dec 1836; m. 14 Sep 1780, MOSES COLBY, b. at Newton, NH, 7 Jun 1751 son of Moses and Mary (Sargent) Colby; Moses d. at Hopkinton, 16 Mar 1790.

---

[369] Rix, *History and Genealogy of the Eastman Family of America*
[370] Lord, *Life and Times in Hopkinton, N.H.*
[371] Ancestry.com. *New Hampshire, Births and Christenings Index, 1714-1904*
[372] Ancestry.com. *New Hampshire, Births and Christenings Index, 1714-1904*

582) vi SAMUEL EASTMAN, b. 13 Nov 1760; d. at Hopkinton, NH after 1840;[373] m. SARAH HARRIS.

583) vii REBECKAH EASTMAN, b. 10 Apr 1762; m. JAMES PUTNEY, b. at Hopkinton, 8 Feb 1761 son of John and Mary (-) Putney.

584) viii LUCY EASTMAN, b. 1 Dec 1763; d. 5 Jan 1816 at Tunbridge, VT; m. at Dunbarton, 16 Jan 1794, BENJAMIN ORDWAY, b. 1763 (based on age at time of death) perhaps the son of Moses and Susannah (Bly) Ordway; Benjamin d. 1 Dec 1849. After Lucy's death, Benjamin married Betsey Gilman.

585) ix EZRA EASTMAN, b. 15 Aug 1764; d. 14 Jun 1816; m. 28 Jun 1787, MOLLY EATON, b. 10 Aug 1769 daughter of Thomas and Molly (-) Eaton; Molly d. 11 Jan 1825.

586) x TAMISON EASTMAN, b. 19 Oct 1766; d. after 1850; m. SAMUEL FRENCH, b. at South Hampton, 3 Apr 1762 son of Offen and Abigail (French) French;[374] d. at Bradford, 7 Feb 1799.[375]

587) xi JOSEPH EASTMAN, b. 18 Sep 1768; d. at Contoocook, NH, 16 Feb 1823; m. 26 Oct 1790, BETSEY CLOUGH, b. 30 Jun 1770 daughter of James and Ruth (Webster) Clough; Betsey d. at Contoocook, NH, 1 Sep 1861.

---

[373] Ancestry.com, New Hampshire, Compiled Census and Census Substitutes Index, 1790-1890. Samuel Eastman, age 79, is recorded living at Hopkinton in 1840.

[374] South Hampton Congregational Church, 1743-1801, marriages and baptisms, p 22

[375] Gould & Beals, *Early Families of Bradford*, p 168

588) xii SARAH EASTMAN, b. 27 Aug 1771; m. 5 Oct 1790, THOMAS EATON, b. 21 Jul 1771 son of Thomas and Molly (-) Eaton.

141) SARAH ABBOTT *(James³, William², George¹)*, twin of Rebecca, b. 13 Aug 1730 daughter of James and Abigail (Farnum) Abbott; m. about 1751, as her 1st husband, her second cousin, JOB ABBOTT *(Jonathan³, Benjamin², George¹)*, b. 3 Oct 724 son of Jonathan and Zerviah (Holt) Abbott; Job died before 1765. Sarah m. 2nd about 1765, as his second wife, RICHARD EASTMAN, b. 9 Aug 1712 son of Jonathan and Hannah (Green) Eastman; Richard d. at Lovell, ME, 29 Dec 1807.

Sarah Abbott and Job Abbott had four children. Three of these four children married fellow George Abbott descendants. In addition, three of the children of the second child, Nathan, married three of the children of the third child, Job.

325) i SARAH ABBOTT, b. 1751 at Suncook; d. at Temple, NH, 9 Oct 1854;[376] m. 25 Nov 1773, her third cousin (and George Abbott descendant), ABIEL HOLT, b. at Lunenburg, 14 Jul 1748 son of Joseph and Mary (Abbott) Holt; Abiel d. 7 Jan 1811.

443) ii NATHAN ABBOTT, b. at Pembroke 4 Sep 1753; d. at Andover 1801 (probate of will 31 Mar 1801); m. 8 May 1777, his third cousin (and George Abbott descendant), SARAH BALLARD, b. 28 Dec 1755 daughter of Hezekiah and Lydia (Chandler) Ballard; Sarah d. 20 Aug 1825.

---

[376] Gravestone inscription: Aged 103 yrs. 2 ms. & 25 ds.

589) iii JOB ABBOTT, b. about 1755 at Pembroke; d. at Wilton 12 Jul 1805; m. at Andover, 12 Dec 1780, his third cousin once removed (and George Abbott descendant), ANNA BALLARD, b. 15 Nov 1762 daughter of Timothy and Sarah (Abbott) Ballard; Anna d. at Wilton, 7 Apr 1805.[377]

590) iv ABIGAIL ABBOTT, b. about 1757; d. 1 May 1845 at Lovell, ME;[378] m. by 1778, STEPHEN DRESSER, b. at Andover, 25 Oct 1754 son of Jonathan and Sarah (Foster) Dresser; Stephen d. at Frye, ME, 28 Sep 1829.

Richard Eastman was first married to Molly Lovejoy and had 12 children from his first marriage. He settled in Pembroke but relocated to Conway about 1768. Very soon after, the family made one more move to Lovell, Maine. Richard established a ferry across the Saco River in Maine.[379]

Sarah Abbott and Richard Eastman had five children, the oldest two born at Pembroke, and the three youngest born at Fryeburg, Maine.

591) i DANIEL EASTMAN, b. 21 Apr 1766; d. at Lovell, ME, 16 Jan 1844; m. at Dracut, 1 Mar 1787, SARAH WHITING, b. about 1762 (based on age of 44 at time of death) of parents not yet determined; Sarah d. at Lovell, 19 Jan 1806.

---

[377] Date of death obtained from her gravestone which has the following inscription: Erected to the memory of Mrs. Anne Abbott, consort of Mr. Job Abbott, who died April 7, 1805, in the 43 year of her age. Findagrave Memorial ID: 34218725

[378] Ancestry.com, *U.S., Find A Grave Index, 1600s-Current* (Provo, UT, USA: Ancestry.com Operations, Inc., 2012).

[379] Rix, *History and Genealogy of the Eastman Family of America* ..., Volumes 1-5, pp 82-83

592)	ii	CYRUS EASTMAN, b. 10 Jul 1767; m. BETSEY WEBSTER. Betsey's origins are unknown, but the births for the two sons of this marriage, according to Rix's Eastman genealogy, are 1821 and 1827, so she would be born not much earlier than 1785-1790. However, there is a marriage record for Cyrus "Easton" and Betsey Webster in 1799.[380] There are questions yet to be resolved about this family. It may be that the two sons attributed to this couple are from a Cyrus from the following generation. There are other Cyrus Eastmans in the New Suncook area about 20 years younger than this Cyrus.
	iii	SUSANNAH EASTMAN, b. 29 Apr 1769; d. 1770.
593)	iv	JEREMY EASTMAN, b. 25 Apr 1771; d. at Stow, ME, 8 Oct 1846; m. by 1794, BETSEY KILGORE, b. 2 Apr 1776 daughter of Joseph and Abigail (Page) Kilgore; Betsey d. 16 Feb 1873.
	v	JAMES EASTMAN, b. 30 Jan 1775; d. 1778.

142) MARY ABBOTT (*James³, William², George¹*), b. 12 Oct 1732 daughter of James and Abigail (Farnum) Abbott; d, about 1780; m. by 1760 ADONIJAH TYLER, b. 26 Nov 1738[381] son of Moses and Miriam (Bailey) Tyler; Adonijah d. 12 Oct 1812 at Hopkinton, NH.

Mary Abbott and Adonijah Tyler had eight children. The births of the first six children are recorded at Henniker, New

---

[380] "Maine Marriages, 1771-1907," database, *FamilySearch* (https://familysearch.org/ark:/61903/1:1:F4FZ-NXX: 4 December 2014), Cyrus Easton and Betsy Webster, 1799; citing Fryeburg, Oxford, Maine, reference; FHL microfilm 10,915.

[381] New Hampshire: Births, Deaths and Marriages, 1654-1969 (accessed through americanancestors.org)

Hampshire[382] and the youngest two at Chester, New Hampshire. A probate record was not located. The family settled in Hopkinton, New Hampshire where Adonijah was a signer of the declaration of fidelity in 1776.[383]

594) i JAMES TYLER, b. 2 Apr 1760; d. at Thetford, VT, 20 Aug 1855;[384] m. by 1779, SARAH GOULD, b. at Hampton, 24 Jul 1760 daughter of Christopher and Abigail (Shepherd) Gould; Sarah's death record was not located.

595) ii RACHEL TYLER, b. 2 Mar 1762; d. in New York, Feb 1843; m. about 1782, JACOB STANLEY, b. at Hopkinton, 9 Sep 1761 son of Matthew and Mary (Putney) Stanley.

596) iii MIRIAM TYLER, b. 22 Mar 1764; d. Jun 1840; m. 11 May 1790, MOSES HASTINGS son of James and Mary (Foster) Hastings; Moses d. 25 Jan 1815.

597) iv JEREMIAH TYLER, b. 6 Apr 1766; d. at Thetford, VT, 19 Jan 1844; m. 31 Oct 1802, IRENE HEATON, b. 17 Apr 1774 daughter of William and Irene (King) Heaton; Irene died at Thetford, VT, 4 May 1840.[385]

598) v SIMEON TYLER, b. 22 Mar 1768; d. at Hopkinton, 24 Dec 1855; m. 14 Mar 1799, HANNAH ROWELL, b. 1766, parents unknown; Hannah d. 28 Jun 1831. Simeon m. 2nd, SUSAN PAIGE who was born about 1786 and d. 21 Mar 1865.

---

[382] Ancestry.com, *New Hampshire, Births and Christenings Index, 1714-1904* (Provo, UT, USA: Ancestry.com Operations, Inc., 2011).
[383] Lord, *Life and Times in Hopkinton*, p 59
[384] Ancestry.com, *Vermont, Vital Records, 1720-1908* (Provo, UT, USA: Ancestry.com Operations, Inc., 2013).
[385] Her grave is in Post Mills Cemetery, Vermont. Findagrave Memorial ID 121161310

599) vi MOSES TYLER, b. 9 Apr 1770; d. at Tyler's Bridge, NH, 21 Dec 1857; m. 21 Jun 1798, BETSY MCCONNELL, b. at Pembroke, 30 Jan 1774 daughter of Samuel and Ann (Cunningham) McConnell; Betsy d. 9 Sep 1866.

600) vii MARY TYLER, b. 4 Jun 1773; d. 1839 at Cap Grove, IL; m. 16 Nov 1797, JACOB MARTIN, b. about 1770; Jacob likely died about 1830 in New Hampshire.

601) viii SARAH TYLER, b. Mar 1775; d. at Ogle County, IL, 7 Feb 1839; m. at Hopkinton, 14 Jun 1796, ROBERT CROWELL *possibly* the son of Aaron and Elizabeth(-) Crowell; Robert d. 22 Sep 1862.[386]

Paul³, William², George¹

143) NATHAN ABBOTT *(Paul³, William², George¹)*, b. 10 Apr 1721 son of Paul and Elizabeth (Gray) Abbott; d. unknown but he might have gone to Pennsylvania; m. 1st at Pomfret, 24 Nov 1742, EUNICE MARSH, b. at Plainfield, CT 17 Feb 1724 daughter of Thomas and Eunice (Parkhouse) Marsh; Eunice d. at Ashford 27 Oct 1760. Nathan m. 2nd HEPHZIBAH BROWN, b. about 1727; Hepzibah d. 26 May 1790 at Hampton, CT.

Nathan Abbott and Eunice Marsh had eight children whose births are recorded in Windham County, the oldest two children at Ashford and the remining six children at Pomfret. Five of the children are known to have died in early childhood, four of the children dying in a two-week period in 1754. In 1754, there were

---

[386] Brigham, *The Tyler Genealogy* p 237

outbreaks of "throat distemper" and "malignant fever" in various locations in the New England colonies.[387]

602) i NATHAN ABBOTT, b. 18 May 1744; d. at Woodstock, 19 Jan 1794;[388] m. JUDITH STODDARD, b. 24 Sep 1749 daughter of Ebenezer and Anna (Stowell) Stoddard. There is a probate record for Nathan Abbott from 1794 that names wife Judith as administrator of the estate with Ebenezer Stoddard as co-signer on the surety bond.[389]

ii EUNICE ABBOTT, b. 20 Nov 1746; no further record. There is a Eunice Abbott as head of household in the 1790 US Census in Fairfield, but there is no reason to believe that is this Eunice.

iii GIDEON ABBOTT, b. 3 Jun 1748; d. 5 Sep 1754.

iv HANNAH ABBOTT, b. 25 Mar 1750; d. 27 Aug 1754.

v PAUL ABBOTT, b. 11 Feb 1753; d. 30 Aug 1754.

vi ELIZABETH ABBOTT, b. 12 Feb 1754; d. 11 Sep 1754.

603) vii STEPHEN ABBOTT, b. 20 Oct 1757; d. at North Providence, RI, 24 Jul 1813;[390][391] m. 28 Jun 1781, ESTHER INGALLS, b. 26 Nov 1762 daughter of

---

[387] Caulfield, Ernest. "The Pursuit of a Pestilence." In *Proceedings of the American Antiquarian Society*, vol. 60, no. 1, p. 21. American Antiquarian Society., 1950.
[388] *Connecticut, Hale Collection of Cemetery Inscriptions and Newspaper Notices, 1629-1934*. Newspaper notice gives age at death as 49, and states he was in the Revolutionary War.
[389] *Connecticut Wills and Probate, 1609-1999*, Probate of Nathan Abbott, Hartford, 1794, Case number 4.
[390] Ancestry.com, Rhode Island, Vital Extracts, 1636-1899
[391] There is a Rhode Island probate record for Col. Stephen Abbott from August 1813 that contains an inventory and provides for widow Esther to administer the estate. Probate Files, Early to 1885 (Pawtucket, R.I.); Author: Pawtucket (Rhode Island). Court of Probate; Probate Place: Providence, Rhode Island

Zebadiah and Esther (Goodell) Ingalls; Esther d. 4 Feb 1851. This is the same as Family #181, child v.

viii RUFUS ABBOTT, b. 18 Sep 1759; d. 1 Mar 1760.

144) WILLIAM ABBOTT *(Paul³, William², George¹)*, b. 18 Feb 1723 son of Paul and Elizabeth (Gray) Abbott; d. at Pomfret 1 Nov 1805; m. 1st 9 May 1745, JERUSHA STOWELL, b. 22 Sep 1721 at Newton, MA daughter of David and Mary (Dillaway) Stowell; Jerusha d. 29 Feb 1768. William m. 2nd 4 Jun 1778, HANNAH EDMUND; Hannah d. 5 Feb 1808; nothing else is known of her at this time.

There are four births records at Pomfret for William Abbott and his first wife Jerusha Stowell.

      i   ANNA ABBOTT, b. 29 Jun 1748; d. at Pomfret, 5 Nov 1791. Anna does not seem to have married.

604) ii   WILLIAM ABBOTT, b. 27 May 1752; d. at Lisle, NY, 1806 (probate 15 Jul 1806); m. 8 Jul 1776, HANNAH SNOW, b. at Ashford, 2 Jul 1754 daughter of Samuel and Hannah (Mason) Snow.

      iii   ELIZABETH ABBOTT, b. 3 Mar 1758; d. 31 Dec 1769.

      iv   RHODA ABBOTT, b. 27 Jul 1761; d. likely in New York. The Abbot genealogy states she married and went to New York with her brother, but a spouse was not suggested. There was a Rhoda Abbott who married DAVID HEACOCK the son of David and Sarah (DeWulf) Heacock. Some sources suggest it was a daughter Rhoda of Jesse and Johannah (Kellogg) Abbott of the Rowley Abbott line, and that family was in Putnam County, NY where David

Heacock also shows up. Remains an area for further research.

145) BENJAMIN ABBOTT *(Paul³, William², George¹)*, b. 25 Jul 1724 son of Paul and Elizabeth (Gray) Abbott; d. at Brookfield, VT, 21 Jun 1807;[392] m. 1st at Ashford, 16 Jan 1745/6, MARY ANN ANDREWS, b. at Windham 25 Jul 1727 daughter of John and Hannah (-) Andrews; Mary Ann d. 8 Dec 1788. Benjamin m. 2nd 30 Jun 1793 the widow HANNAH BROWN about whom nothing else is known.

Benjamin Abbott and Mary Ann Andrews had ten children whose births are recorded at several towns in Windham County including Ashford, Pomfret, and Windham. The Abbot genealogy[393] lists a daughter named Isabel in this family but omits the daughter Louisa; there are records for Louisa but not for Isabel, so she is not included here. This may just be a matter of the name being confused.

      i   HENRY ABBOTT, b. 12 Nov 1746; d. 27 Jan 1749.

605) ii   HENRY ABBOTT, b. 3 Jun 1749; d. at Vermont, 31 Mar 1807; m. at Hampton, 7 Apr 1772, a fourth cousin, SARAH BURNHAM, b. 21 Aug 1750 daughter of Isaac and Eunice (Holt) Burnham. Sarah had married first John Greenslit with whom she had two children.

      iii   STEPHEN ABBOTT, b. 23 May 1751; d. 21 Aug 1754.

      iv   BENJAMIN ABBOTT, b. 21 Jan 1753; d, 21 Aug 1754.

606) v   MARY ABBOTT, b. 4 Aug 1754; d. at Brookfield, VT, 28 Feb 1811; m. 17 May 1781, THOMAS ADAMS, b. at Canterbury, CT, 24 Apr 1757 son of Eliphalet and

---

[392] His grave site is in the Brookfield, VT cemetery. (findagrave.com)
[393] Abbot and Abbot, *Genealogical Record of Descendants*

Generation Four 269

Mary (Frost) Adams; Thomas d. at Brookfield, 1803 (distribution of estate 5 Aug 1803).

607) vi ASA ABBOTT, b. 25 May 1756; d. at Hampton, 1834 (will dated 10 Apr 1834); m. by 1783, SARAH BIDLACK, b. at Hampton, 30 Sep 1756 daughter of James and Mehitable (Durkee) Bidlack. Sarah was first married to STEPHEN FULLER son of Stephen and Mary (Abbott) Fuller. Stephen died at the Battle of Wyoming. These families are considered together.

608) vii HANNAH ABBOTT, b. 10 Feb 1759; m. at Hampton, 24 May 1775, JOSIAH COLLINS, b. about 1749 (based on age 63 at time of death); Josiah d. at Hampton, 24 Feb 1812. There is a Josiah Collins who was born at Wethersfield in 1750 and died in 1826 but that is not this Josiah.

609) viii TRYPHENA ABBOTT, b. 22 Sep 1760; d. at Stafford, 21 Nov 1835; m. May 1781, ABNER ASHLEY, b. at Hampton, 19 Jan 1754 son of Abner and Mary (Crossley) Ashley; Abner d. at Tolland 1837 (will proved 2 January 1838).

610) ix LOUISA ABBOTT, b. 24 Dec 1762; d. at New York, 16 Mar 1806; m. at Canterbury, 1 Sep 1785, SAMUEL PRESTON, b. 19 Feb 1763 son of Jacob and Mary (Butts) Preston.

611) x BENJAMIN ABBOTT, b. 2 Oct 1764; d. at Brookfield, VT, 12 Sep 1829;[394] m. about 1786, LUCY FLINT, b. 10 Jun 1767 daughter of Nathaniel and Lucy (Martin) Flint; Lucy d. 24 Sep 1839.

---

[394] Benjamin's estate entered probate in Orange County, VT in 1830.

146) MARY ABBOTT *(Paul³, William², George¹)*, b. 3 Mar 1728/9 daughter of Paul and Elizabeth (Gray) Abbott; d. at Windham 10 Aug 1769; m. 28 Jun 1749, JOSHUA HOLT, b. 19 Mar 1728/9 son of Joshua and Keturah (Holt) Holt. Joshua m. 2nd Susanna Goodell; Joshua d. 5 Jul 1791.

In his will written 13 April 1791,[395] Joshua Holt has bequests for the following persons: dear and loving wife Susannah, daughter Dinah Stoel, daughter Mary Fuller, son Uriah, son Lemuel, daughter Keturah Amidown, daughter Sarah Durkee (although there are other last names for Sarah crossed out, one of them Holt), daughter Hannah Carpenter, daughter Dorcas Fuller, daughter Zilphia, and sons Samuel and Oliver who divide equally everything not given to the other children. Zilphia, Samuel, and Oliver are children from his second marriage to Susannah Goodell.

Mary Abbott and Joshua Holt had eight children whose births are recorded at Windham.

612) i DINAH HOLT, b. 22 Mar 1750; d. 21 Feb 1826; m. 30 Jun 1778, SETH STOWELL, b. 29 May 1742 son of Nathaniel and Margaret (Trowbridge) Stowell; Seth d. about 1798 (when estate went to probate). Dinah m. 2nd, 27 Nov 1800, PAUL HOLT, b. 1743 and d. 1827. Dinah was Paul Holt's third wife. Paul Holt and his first wife Sarah Welch were the parents of Sarah Holt who married Stephen Utley who is considered below in Family #153, child viii.

613) ii MARY HOLT, b. 11 Jul 1752; d. at Hampton, 23 Oct 1824; m. 7 Nov 1771, JOSEPH FULLER, b. at Ipswich, 1738 son of John and Hannah (Lord) Fuller; Joseph d. 29 Jan 1805.

---

[395] *Connecticut Wills and Probate, 1609-1999*, Probate of Joshua Holt, Hartford, 1791, Case number 1945.

614)	iii	URIAH HOLT, b. 23 Mar 1754; d. at West Springfield, MA, 22 Sep 1828; m. at Ashford, 11 Nov 1779, MARGARET MASON, b. at Ashford, 13 Aug 1754 daughter of Ebenezer and Mehitable (Holmes) Mason; Margaret d. 1817.
615)	iv	LEMUEL HOLT, b. 28 Feb 1756; d. at Lyme, NH, 1 Aug 1836; m. 1778, his first cousin, MARY ABBOTT, b. 20 Jan 1757 daughter of Isaac and Mary (Barker) Abbott; Mary d. 8 Sep 1849. This is the same as Family #148, child i.
616)	v	KETURAH HOLT, b. 21 Aug 1758; d. at Randolph, VT, 25 Jul 1839;[396] m. 29 Jan 1784, JONATHAN AMIDON, b. 7 Feb 1759 son of Henry and Sarah (Doubleday) Amidon; Jonathan d. at Randolph, 15 Apr 1838.
617)	vi	SARAH HOLT, b. 26 Oct 1761; d. at Stockbridge, VT, 19 Feb 1813; m. 1783, JOHN DURKEE, b. at Windham, 2 Jul 1762 son of Joseph and Elizabeth (Fiske) Durkee; John d. at Stockbridge, 2 May 1838.
618)	vii	HANNAH HOLT, b. 24 May 1764; d. in Vermont, 7 Aug 1855; m. at Clarendon, VT, 21 Jan 1788, AARON CARPENTER, b. at Rehoboth, 9 May 1763 son of Jabez and Abigail (Dyer) Carpenter; Aaron d. 26 Feb 1836.[397]
619)	viii	DORCAS HOLT, b. 30 Mar 1767; d. at Middlebury, VT, 1 Jul 1800; m. JOSIAH FULLER, b. 30 Oct 1764

---

[396] Ancestry.com, *Vermont, Vital Records, 1720-1908* (Provo, UT, USA: Ancestry.com Operations, Inc., 2013).
[397] Ancestry.com, Vermont, Vital Records, 1720-1908

son of David and Hannah (Fuller) Fuller; Josiah d. Potsdam, NY, 4 Dec 1835.

147) SARAH ABBOTT *(Paul³, William², George¹)*, b. 15 Oct 1730 daughter of Paul and Elizabeth (Gray) Abbott; d. at Pomfret, 17 Dec 1811; m. 24 May 1749, JOSEPH INGALLS, b. at Andover, 9 Aug 1723 son of Joseph and Phebe (Farnum) Ingalls; Joseph d. 26 Oct 1790.

There is a 1791 probate record for Joseph Ingalls. There is no will. Part of the probate includes Sarah being named as the guardian of the youngest child Harvey. The estate was deemed to be insolvent. The whole of the real and personal estate was ordered to be sold, with most of the benefit of the sale to go to the creditors.[398]

There are records for twelve children of Joseph and Sarah all born at Pomfret.

      i   PHEBE INGALLS, b. 22 Aug 1750; d. 22 Sep 1759.

620) ii   PETER INGALLS, b. 12 Feb 1752; d. at Pomfret, 11 Jun 1808; m. 20 Apr 1775, SARAH ASHLEY, b. at Windham, 2 Nov 1752 daughter of Joseph and Sarah (Cressy) Ashley, Sarah d. at Pomfret, 18 Nov 1811.

     iii   DORCUS INGALLS, b. 27 Jun 1754; no further record was located for Dorcus.

621) iv DARIUS INGALLS, b. 27 Jun 1754; d. likely in Vermont, 1824; m. Mar 1796, LODEMA LEE, b. at Killingly, 3 Nov 1757 daughter of Seth and Molly (Conant) Lee.

     v   ASA INGALLS, b. 29 Feb 1756; d. 25 Dec 1775.

---

[398] *Connecticut Wills and Probate, 1609-1999*, Probate of Joseph Ingalls, Hartford, 1791, Case number 2280.

Generation Four 273

622) vi LUTHER INGALLS, b. 24 Aug 1758; d. at Hanover, NH, 4 Jul 1855; m. 23 Jun 1781, LUCY UTLEY, born about 1760; Lucy d. 7 Jan 1831.

623) vii CALVIN INGALLS, b. 22 Nov 1760; d. at Stafford, Oct 1830; m. 1st, 28 Nov 1782, CATHERINE TERRINGTON; Catherine d. 31 Dec 1783. Calvin m. 2nd, 28 May 1795, MARY HORTON, b. at Union, 1 Oct 1759 daughter of Ezra and Mary (Hempstead) Horton; Mary d. 12 May 1833.

624) viii CHESTER INGALLS, b. 7 Aug 1762; d. at Hanover, NH, 27 May 1842; m. 4 Apr 1784, SYLVIA STEVENS, b. 25 Mar 1763 daughter of Robert and Mary (Hathaway) Stevens.

ix JOSEPH ROYAL INGALLS, b. 24 Aug 1764; d. 5 Sep 1783.[399]

625) x SARAH INGALLS, b. 18 Dec 1766; d. at Jericho, VT, 24 Apr 1833;[400] m. 22 Jan 1788, ABRAHAM FORD, b. 15 May 1764 son of Abraham and Abigail (Woodward) Ford; Abraham d. 9 Apr 1813 while on a trip to Lebanon, CT. The family settled in Vermont in 1803.

626) xi HANNAH INGALLS, b. 22 Aug 1769; m. 25 Jan 1791, JOSIAH INGERSOLL, *possibly* the son of Richard and Zipporah (-) Ingersoll; this family relocated to Westford, VT.

---

[399] Connecticut, Church Record Abstracts, 1630-1920
[400] *Vermont, Vital Records, 1720-1908.*

627)　xii　HARVEY INGALLS, b. 7 Jul 1775; d. 20 Dec 1833[401] at Brookfield, VT; m. ELLA FORD, b. at Windham, 6 Apr 1775 daughter of Abraham and Abigail (Woodward) Ford; Ella d. at Brookfield, 1857.

148)　ISAAC ABBOTT *(Paul³, William², George¹)*, b. 29 Aug 1732 son of Paul and Elizabeth (Gray) Abbott; d. at Milford, NH about 1800;[402] m. 29 Apr 1756, MARY BARKER about whom nothing else concrete is known.[403]

Isaac Abbott was a farmer. He was born in Pomfret and there married Mary (although some sources say Sarah) Barker who was also from Pomfret, but her parentage is not known. The births of their first seven children are recorded at Pomfret, but there is also a recording of these births at Princeton, Massachusetts. The young family left Pomfret by 1769, were for a time in Princeton where they were early settlers recorded there in 1769,[404] and finally settled in Milford, New Hampshire where they were about 1778.[405] Isaac Abbott served as a private in the company of Colonel Stickney during the Revolutionary War.

Isaac Abbott and Mary Barker had twelve children, the oldest seven recorded at Pomfret, the births of four children recorded at Princeton, and the youngest child whose birthplace is unknown. This youngest child died in Milford.

---

[401] The inscription on the gravestone gives exact age of 58 yrs. 5 mo. & 12 dys; Find a Grave Memorial # 92380131

[402] 1800 is the year of death used by the Daughters of the American Revolution and in Ramsdell's *History of Milford, volume 1*.

[403] Abbot and Abbot, *Genealogical Record of Descendants* gives her name as Sarah Barker, but the marriage record and all the birth records for the children give her name as Mary.

[404] Blake, *The History of Princeton*, p 81

[405] Ramsdell, *The History of Milford, volume 1*, p 560

Generation Four 275

615) i MARY ABBOTT, b. at Pomfret, 20 Jan 1757; d. at Lyme, NH, 8 Sep 1849; m. 9 Dec 1778, her first cousin, LEMUEL HOLT, b. at Windham, 28 Feb 1756 son of Joshua and Mary (Abbott) Holt; Lemuel d. 1 Aug 1836. This is the same as Family #146, child iv.

628) ii HANNAH ABBOTT, b. at Pomfret, 2 Aug 1758; d. at Stoddard, NH, 9 Mar 1847; m. at Amherst, NH, 25 May 1781, ISRAEL TOWNE, b. at Stoddard, NH, 17 Jun 1761 son of Israel and Lydia (Hopkins) Towne; Israel d. 2 May 1848.

iii CHLOE ABBOTT, b. at Pomfret, 7 Aug 1760; d. at Lyme, 1835. Chloe is reported to have married twice, but the name of her first husband has not been found. She m. 2nd, about 1801, WILLIAM PORTER, b. 1761 son of William and Esther (Carpenter) Porter. William was a widower with several children, his wife Phebe Kingsbury having died in 1800. William d. 3 Mar 1847. Chloe did not have children.

629) iv SARAH "SALLY" ABBOTT, b. at Pomfret, 14 Oct 1762; d. at Mason, NH, 1846; m. at Amherst, 25 Oct 1795, JAMES BROWN.

v METYLDA ABBOTT, b. at Pomfret, 29 Aug 1764.

630) vi ISAAC ABBOTT, b. at Pomfret, 17 Jul 1766; d. at Milford, NH, 1 Sep 1831; m. 15 Oct 1793, RUTH AMES, b. at Wilmington, MA, 31 Jul 1776 daughter of Caleb and Mary (Harvey) Ames/Eams; Ruth d. at Milford, 29 Jul 1844.

vii ESTHER ABBOTT, b. at Pomfret, 28 Jun 1768.

viii FIDELIA ABBOTT, b. at Princeton, 29 May 1770.

631) ix OLIVE ABBOTT, b. at Princeton, 28 Oct 1772. It is possible that she married Isaac Parker 6 Feb 1794 at Amherst. The Olive Abbott that married Isaac was of Milford and she died 2 Jan 1862 at age 89 which fits for this Olive. Isaac Parker was b. at Monson, NH, 2 Mar 1769 son of Josiah and Sarah (Parkis) Parker.

x DOROTHY ABBOTT, b. at Princeton, 10 Sep 1774; d. at Milford, 16 Aug 1802.

xi DEBORAH ABBOTT, b. at Princeton, 10 Sep 1774; d. at Milford, 22 May 1806.

xii STEPHEN ABBOTT, b. 1778; d. at Milford, 9 Jul 1792.

149) DARIUS ABBOTT *(Paul³, William², George¹)*, b. 16 Oct 1734 son of Paul and Elizabeth (Gray) Abbott; d. about 1817 at Hillsborough, NH;[406] m. at Andover 1 Nov 1757, MARY HOLT, b. 30 Apr 1739 daughter of Henry and Rebecca (Gray) Holt; Mary d. about 1787.

Darius Abbott was born at Pomfret and married Mary Holt of Andover. Darius was a housewright and likely the builder of the historic Andover home at 142 Hidden Road. The property on which this home was built was purchased from the Holt family in 1760 and 1763 by Darius Abbott and Samuel Holt. Darius Abbott sold the homestead land with the dwelling to Jacob Jones 16 April 1776 with the deed recorded 17 March 1778.[407]

The births of the first nine children of this family are recorded at Andover. The four youngest children were likely born

---

[406] Abbot and Abbot, *Genealogical Record of Descendants*
[407] Andover Preservation Commission, 142 Hidden Road, https://preservation.mhl.org/142-hidden-road

at either Amherst or Hillsborough. The family went first to Amherst before finally settling at Hillsborough.[408]

  i ANNA ABBOTT, b. 31 Aug 1758; d. 14 Oct 1775.

  ii HENRY ABBOTT, b. 1 Jun 1761; no further record.

  iii ELIZABETH ABBOTT, b. 23 Mar 1763; according to the Holt genealogy, Elizabeth married but not known to whom; she lived in Holderness, NH.[409]

  iv HANNAH ABBOTT, b. Mar 1765; d. 11 Sep 1775.

632) v PAUL ABBOTT, b. 18 Mar 1767; death date not known but in NH; m. about 1795, NAOMI CARR whose origins are unknown.

633) vi TRYPHENA ABBOTT, b. 23 Feb 1769; d. at Putney, VT, Jun 1836; m. 2 Jun 1790, JOHN WALLACE, b. at Bedford, NH, 12 May 1764 son of John and Sarah (Woodburn) Wallace; John d. 1834 (probate 25 Nov 1834).

634) vii CALVIN HOLT ABBOTT, b. 15 Apr 1771; d. at Barre, VT, 14 Aug 1841; m. 10 Apr 1800, LUCY DUTTON, b. 16 May 1781 daughter of John and Elizabeth (Spaulding) Dutton; Lucy d. 15 Apr 1851.

  viii LUTHER ABBOTT, b. May 1773; d. 14 Sep 1773.

  ix ASA ABBOTT, b. Sep 1774; d. 12 Sep 1775.

  x LUTHER ABBOTT, twin of Hannah, b. about 1778; no further record.

---

[408] Stearns, *Genealogical and Family History of the State of New Hampshire, volume 1*, p 360
[409] Durrie, *Genealogical History of the Holt Family*

	xi	MARY ABBOTT, b. about 1780; no further record.
635)	xii	NANCY ABBOTT, b. about 1780; m. 23 Apr 1804, JOEL JONES (see Hannah below).
635)	xiii	HANNAH ABBOTT, b. 1783 (baptized 4 May 1783);[410] d. about 1803; m. about 1800, JOEL JONES, *possibly* the son of Joel and Mary (Bishop) Jones b. at Hillsborough, 7 Aug 1783. Joel m. 2nd, Hannah's sister Nancy (see above).

150) ELIZABETH ABBOTT *(Paul³, William², George¹)*, b. 20 Jul 1737 daughter of Paul and Elizabeth (Gray) Abbott; d. possibly 1828;[411] m. 28 Sep 1761 as his 2nd wife, JOSEPH PHELPS, b. 27 Feb 1723/4 son of Samuel and Hannah (Dane) Phelps; Joseph d. at Andover 27 Jan 1802.

Elizabeth Abbott married Joseph Phelps after he was widowed and with two small children. His first wife was Lydia Osgood who died at Pomfret 20 July 1761. Just two months later, Elizabeth and Joseph married. Elizabeth and Joseph had six children, the oldest two born at Pomfret. The family then returned to Massachusetts settling in Princeton in Worcester County where their youngest four children were born. In later life, the couple returned to their roots in Andover.

The will of Joseph Phelps includes bequests to the following persons: beloved wife Elisabeth, beloved son Joseph gets some oxen and a yoke to make up the rest of his part, beloved son Elisha gets carpenter tools to make up the rest of his part, and beloved daughters Hannah, Elisabeth, Lydia, and Tryphenea get one dollar each (which is in addition to what he has already given them).

---

[410] Historical Society of Amherst, Transcriptions of Baptisms of Children from Volume I of the Congregational Church of Amherst, New Hampshire, http://www.hsanh.org/Baptisms%202.htm

[411] Abbot and Abbot, *Genealogical Record of Descendants* gives a death date of June 1828, but I have not located a record.

Legacies at the final settlement are to Hannah Adams, Elizabeth Harrington, Lydia Whittemore, Tryphena Russell, Elisha Phelps, and Joseph Phelps. Elizabeth Phelps also receives a payment.[412] Joseph Phelps and Hannah Adams are Joseph's children from his marriage to Lydia Osgood.

636) i ELIZABETH PHELPS, b. 1 Mar 1765; d. at Lexington, 26 Jun 1835; m. about 1787, NATHAN HARRINGTON, b. at Lexington, 29 Apr 1762 son of Daniel and Anna (Munroe) Harrington; Nathan d. 27 Sep 1818.

637) ii LYDIA PHELPS, b. 5 Feb 1767; d. at Cambridge, 10 Nov 1834; m. PHILIP CARTERET WHITTEMORE, b. at Arlington, 1 Sep 1766 son of William and Abigail (De Carteret) Whittemore; Philip d. 30 Jun 1855.

638) iii TRYPHENA PHELPS, b. 28 Sep 1769; d. at Woburn, 8 Oct 1818; m. at Woburn, 19 Jun 1791, WILLIAM "BILL" RUSSELL, b. 4 May 1763 son of Jesse and Elizabeth (Whipple) Russell. After Tryphena's death, Bill Russell married Mrs. Phebe Dorman. Bill Russell d. at Billerica, 4 Jul 1842.

iv ELISHA PHELPS, b. 10 Oct 1771; d. at Andover, 27 Jan 1823; m. at Woburn, 28 Oct 1795, RHODA TAY, b. at Wilmington, 19 Nov 1770 daughter of Benjamin and Sybil (Marion) Tay; Rhoda d. 16 Oct 1841. Elisha and Rhoda do not seem to have had any children. Elisha died at the almshouse in Andover.[413]

---

[412] *Essex County, MA: Probate File Papers, 1638-1881. Probate of* Joseph Phelps, 10 Mar 1802, *Case number* 21650.
[413] *Massachusetts, Town and Vital Records, 1620-1988.*

v   SAMUEL PHELPS, b. 5 Aug 1773; d. 19 Aug 1778.

vi POLLY PHELPS, b. 8 Oct 1775; d. 11 Aug 1778.

Philip³, William², George¹

151)   ABIEL ABBOTT *(Philip³, William², George¹)*, b. at Windham, 3 Mar 1726 son of Philip and Abigail (Bigford) Abbott; d. at Windham, 21 May 1772; m. 5 Jun 1750, ABIGAIL FENTON, b. at Willington, 27 Aug 1730 daughter of Francis and Ann (Berry) Fenton. Abigail m. 2nd John Chamberlain of Amenia Precinct in New York;[414] Abigail d. 14 Aug 1776.

Abiel Abbott was a farmer in Windham, Connecticut. He and Abigail had five children whose births are recorded at Windham. Their children seem to have had the wanderlust as all the children relocated to other states including one son settling in Quebec.

Abiel Abbott's estate entered probate in 1772 and the distributions of the estate property were made 18 Apr 1777, after the decease of the widow Abigail, in the following manner: eldest son Philip Abbott allotted two-sixths of the estate; second son James Abbott; son Abiel Abbott; daughter Abigail; and daughter Anne. Each of the younger children received one-sixth part of the estate.[415]

639) i   PHILIP ABBOTT, b. 23 Mar 1751; d. at Kingston, PA, Mar 1834;[416] m. 6 Jul 1775, ANNA HEWETT, b. at Canterbury, 1 Jul 1754 daughter of Henry and Joanna (Denison) Hewett; Anna d. at Windham 29 Dec 1796.

---

[414] Abbot and Abbot, *Genealogical Record of Descendants*, p 51

[415] *Connecticut Wills and Probate, 1609-1999*, Probate of Abial Abbott, Hartford, 1772, Case number 34.

[416] Philip Abbott, age 70-79, is head of household in the 1830 U.S. Census; 1830; Census Place: *Plymouth, Luzerne, Pennsylvania*; Series: *M19*; Roll: *145*; Page: *431*; Family History Library Film: *0020619*

Generation Four 281

Philip m. 2nd, 17 Mar 1815 at Wilkes-Barre, MABEL MERRITT.

640) ii JAMES ABBOTT, b. 9 Mar 1753; d. at Cornell, NY, 2 May 1830; m. 1st, 1 Jan 1778, his third cousin, HANNAH DENISON, b. 18 Mar 1757 daughter of Daniel and Lydia (Pearl) Denison; Hannah d. 17 Jan 1784. James m. 2nd, as her second husband, PHEBE HOWE (widow of John Coray), married at Kingston, PA 17 Jan 1798; James and Phebe may have divorced after 1813. Phebe died at Naples, IL, 9 Sep 1842. Phebe Howe was born at Luzerne 21 Feb 1763 daughter of John and Mary (Stephens) Howe. This is the same as Family #280, child ii.

641) iii ABIEL ABBOTT, b. 28 Nov 1754; d. at Hatley, Quebec, 1838; m. 13 Nov 1777, RUTH HOVEY, b. 28 Aug 1754 daughter of Nathaniel and Ruth (Parker) Hovey; Ruth d. at Hatley 1832.

642) iv ABIGAIL ABBOTT, b. 21 Feb 1763; d. about 1843 perhaps in Ohio where she went to stay with her children; m. about 1784, JOSEPH UTLEY who was "of Hartford" but whose parents have not been fully verified, although *perhaps* the son of Joseph and Jerusha (Martin) Utley.

643) v ANNA ABBOTT, b. 18 Sep 1765; d. at Armada, MI, 13 Sep 1846; m. 29 Aug 1787, SETH LATHROP, b. at Springfield, 11 Apr 1762 son of Joseph and Elizabeth (Dwight) Lathrop; Seth d. 26 Feb 1831.

152) STEPHEN ABBOTT *(Philip³, William², George¹)*, b. 21 Apr 1728 son of Philip and Abigail (Bigford) Abbott; d. at Ashford 29 Sep

1801; m. 3 Jan 1750, FREELOVE BURGESS, b. at Ashford, 14 Jul 1731 daughter of Benjamin and Susannah (Sabin) Burgess; the date of death for Freelove is not known, but she was living at the time of probate of her husband's estate.

The estate of Captain Stephen Abbott entered probate 1 December 1801. There was not a will. Widow Freelove Abbot was administrator. The estate was valued at $719.99. The personal estate was used to pay debts and the real property was divided for distribution among the heirs. Distribution was to the widow Freelove Abbott, daughter Susannah, and son Reuben.[417]

Stephen Abbott and Freelove Burgess had four children. The births of the two oldest children are recorded at Windham. The youngest son, Reuben, was born at Ashford. There is not a record for daughter Lucy; she is just in published genealogies and perhaps she is mis-assigned to this family. In any event, there are just two children as heirs to the estate, Susannah and Reuben. The youngest child, Reuben, was born about 20 years after his next oldest sibling, but there is a son Reuben in this family as evidenced by the probate distribution; Reuben married in 1798 which fits with a birth year of 1774.

644) i SUSANNAH ABBOTT, b. 23 Cot 1752; d. at Fort Ann, NY, Oct 1815;[418] m. 15 Sep 1773, STEPHEN BURGESS, b. at Ashford, 12 Jan 1751 son of Benjamin.

ii PHILIP ABBOTT, b. 1753; d. 1776. Philip served in the Revolutionary War. He was taken prison and died aboard a prison ship in the harbor of New York.[419]

---

[417] *Connecticut Wills and Probate, 1609-1999*, Probate of Stephen Abbott, Hartford, 1772, Case number 5.
[418] Abbot and Abbot, *Genealogical Record of Descendants*, p 54
[419] Abbot and Abbot, *Genealogical Record of Descendants*, p 54

	iii	LUCY ABBOTT, b. about 1755; she may not go in this family; no further record.
645)	iv	REUBEN ABBOTT, b. 15 Apr 1774; d. at Mansfield, CT, 1 Jan 1863; m. 8 Nov 1798, MARY "POLLY" SNOW, b. about 1773 (based on age at time of death; Abbot genealogy gives birth as 12 May 1773) whose parents are not verified; Polly d. 15 Apr 1857.

153)   HANNAH ABBOTT *(Philip³, William², George¹)*, b. 16 Mar 1730 daughter of Philip and Abigail (Bigford) Abbott; d. 18 Dec 1801; m. Aug 1748, SAMUEL UTLEY, b. at Windham 28 May 1723 son of James and Annah (-) Utley; Samuel d. 15 Nov 1782.

Samuel Utley did not leave a will, but his probate record includes a list of heirs who are to receive distributions. Those listed are the heirs of Abigail Butts (who is deceased), Ann Hare, Elizabeth Utley, Samuel, Phillip, Stephen, Timothy, Cyrus, Antipas, Rufus, and Elijah.[420]

Son Philip Utley did not marry, and he did leave a will dated 24 January 1832. He made bequests to his siblings and their heirs. Those named in the will are as follows: heirs of his brother Samuel who is deceased; heirs of his brother Cyrus who is deceased; heirs of his sister Anna Hare who is deceased; Betsy Utley daughter of his brother Stephen; brother Timothy; Lewis Utley son of his brother Antipas; to Orren Utley who is the brother of Lewis (and thus also a son of Antipas); and to Philip Utley who is the son of Rufus who is deceased, and to the other remaining heirs of brother Rufus. Mr. Royal Copeland is named executor.[421] Stephen, Timothy, and Antipas are not described as deceased. Elizabeth is not mentioned,

---

[420] *Connecticut Wills and Probate, 1609-1999*, Probate of Samuel Utley, Hartford, 1782, Case number 3893.
[421] *Connecticut Wills and Probate, 1609-1999*, Will of Philip Utley, Windham, 24 Jun 1832.

so she is assumed to be deceased and without heirs. Elijah also is not mentioned. His oldest sister Abigail Butts is not mentioned. Abigail died in 1774 and had one daughter living at the time of her death. It is possible that Abigail's daughter was deceased by 1832.

Hannah Abbott and Samuel Utley had 13 children whose births are recorded at Windham.

646) i ABIGAIL UTLEY, b. 19 Nov 1749; d. at Canterbury, 4 Jul 1774; m. 15 Feb 1770, JAMES BUTTS, b. 14 Jun 1748 son of Samuel and Mary (Cleveland) Butts. James m. 2nd, Elizabeth Hibbard.

ii PHILIP UTLEY, b. 26 Jul 1751; d. 18 May 1754.

iii HANNAH UTLEY, b. 5 Jan 1753; d. 25 Feb 1778.

647) iv ANNA UTLEY, b. 6 Jan 1755; m. about 1780, STEPHEN HARE, b. at Ellington, 12 Sep 1755.[422]

v ELIZABETH UTLEY, b. 18 Jan 1757; d. at Hampton, 14 Nov 1825. Elizabeth did not marry.

648) vi SAMUEL UTLEY, b. 2 Feb 1759; d. at Ashford, CT, 13 Sep 1801; m. at Hampton, 7 Jan 1790, SARAH EASTMAN, b. at Ashford, 7 Aug 1761 daughter of Ebenezer and Mary (Fletcher) Eastman; Sarah d. 4 Jan 1828.

vii PHILIP UTLEY, b. 26 Feb 1760; d. about 1832. Philip did not marry.

649) viii STEPHEN UTLEY, b. 21 Nov 1762; d. 1 Mar 1841; m. 1797, SARAH HOLT, b. 3 Mar 1775 daughter of Paul and Sarah (Welch) Holt; Sarah d. 10 Feb 1833.

ix TIMOTHY UTLEY, b. 22 Mar 1765; d. after 1832

---

[422] The birth record in the Barbour Collection lists his date of birth but not the names of parents.

650)	x	CYRUS UTLEY, b. 11 Mar 1767; d. at Homer, NY between 1820 and 1832;[423] m. at Hampton, 4 Apr 1797, POLLY BENNET, b. at New Milford, 6 Jun 1771 daughter of Edward and Rhoda (Canfield) Bennett.
651)	xi	ANTIPAS UTLEY, b. 16 Feb 1770; d. after 1830; m. at Hampton, 29 May 1795, POLLY LUCE daughter of Nathan and Elizabeth (Lasel) Luce.[424] Polly seems to have died between 1810 and 1820.[425]
652)	xii	RUFUS UTLEY, b. 25 May 1773; m. MARY "POLLY" SILL probably the daughter of Ezra and Charity (Pratt) Sill.
	xiii	ELIJAH UTLEY, b. 15 Feb 1778; d. at Hampton, 15 Feb 1825. Elijah did not marry.

154) MARY ABBOTT (*Philip³, William², George¹*), b. 6 Jul 1732 daughter of Philip and Abigail (Bigford) Abbott; d. at Sheshequin, PA, 5 May 1803; m. 17 Oct 1751, STEPHEN FULLER, b. at Windham

---

[423] He is listed in the 1820 U.S. Census at Homer, New York, but he is listed as deceased in his brother Philip's 1832 will. *1820 United States Federal Census*, 1820 U S Census; Census Place: Homer, Cortland, New York; Page: 555; NARA Roll: M33_66; Image: 308.

[424] Her parents are verified by the 1816 will of Nathan Luce which includes a bequest to his daughter Polly wife of Antipas Utley. Ancestry.com. *New York, Wills and Probate Records, 1659-1999* [database on-line]. Provo, UT, USA: Ancestry.com Operations, Inc., 2015. Original data: New York County, District and Probate Courts.

[425] Antipas is a head of household in 1800, 1810, 1820, and 1830 Census in Windham County, CT and there is a female of the right age for Polly through 1810, but not in 1820 or 1830.

3 Nov 1730 son of Stephen and Hannah (Moulton) Fuller; Stephen d. at Sheshequin 24 May 1813.[426]

Several members of the Fuller and Abbott families relocated from Connecticut to the Wyoming Valley of Pennsylvania and became casualties in the Battle of Wyoming also known as the Wyoming Valley massacre. As a back-drop to the massacre, which occurred as part of the Revolutionary War, was a longer standing land dispute between earlier settlers in the Wyoming Valley and the newer settlers from Connecticut. This land dispute dated to the mid-17th century originating with competing claims between Dutch and English settlers, that followed by overlapping land grants from King Charles II to both William Penn and to the province of Connecticut. Thrown into the mix was conflict/resentment with Native American peoples in the area. The conflicts between the earlier settlers (Pennamites) and the Connecticut settlers (Yankees) were carried out from 1768 through 1784 and were finally settled by the young United States Congress after the end of the Revolutionary War.[427]

The Battle of Wyoming was part of a campaign by the British to wage a guerilla war against colonial frontier settlers. The British recruited colonial Loyalists who were under the command of Colonel John Butler; this militia was known as Butler's Rangers. Other British commanders recruited native warriors such as Seneca. These bands conducted raids on frontier settlements. In the summer of 1778, they decided on raids of the Wyoming Valley in Pennsylvania. The Loyalist troops with Seneca warriors engaged the little trained Patriot militia men on 3 July 1778. The Loyalist forces numbered about 1,000 compared to 350 Patriots. It is reported that the Loyalist forces had three killed while all but 60 of the Patriots were killed. This included the taking of 227 scalps. Raiding in the area in the aftermath included burning 1,000 homes of the settlers. There were reported follow-up raids by Iroquois with more killing

---

[426] Information on this family derived from Fuller, *Genealogy of Some Descendants of Thomas Fuller*, p 92 and Bradsby, *History of Luzerne County*, p 718
[427] Boyer, "A Dangerous Combination of Villains"

of settlers. The aftermath also included regrouped Patriot militias conducting raids on Indian villages in the area.[428]

Two of the children of Mary Abbott and Stephen Fuller, Thomas and Stephen, died at the Battle of Wyoming.

Mary Abbott and Stephen Fuller had seven children whose births are recorded in Windham County, Connecticut. There is some disagreement in published genealogies about the marriages of daughters Abigail and Mary, but what I have provided matches the available records.

653) i ABIGAIL FULLER, b. at Windham, 3 Jan 1752; d. at Athens, PA, 31 Jan 1834; m. about 1772, JAMES BIDLACK, b. 26 Nov 1750 son of James and Mehitable (Durkee) Bidlack; James d. at Wyoming, PA, 3 Jul 1778. Abigail married 2nd, as his second wife, JOHN FRANKLIN, b. at Canaan, CT, 12 Sep 1749 son of John and Keziah (Pierce) Franklin. John Franklin d. at Athens, PA, 1 Mar 1831.

607) ii STEPHEN FULLER, b. 22 Jan 1755; d. at the Battle of Wyoming, 3 Jul 1778; m. SARAH BIDLACK, b. at Hampton, 30 Sep 1756 daughter of James and Mehitable (Durkee) Bidlack. Sarah m. 2nd, about 1783, ASA ABBOTT, b. at Pomfret, 25 May 1756 son of Benjamin and Mary Ann (Andrews) Abbott; Asa d. at Hampton, 1834.

iii THOMAS FULLER, b. 7 May 1757; d. at the Battle of Wyoming, 3 Jul 1778.

654) iv MARY FULLER, b. 28 May 1759; d. in New York after 1810 (living at the time of husband's probate);

---

[428] Trussell, "The Battle of Wyoming and Hartley's Expedition"

m. at Wilkes-Barre, 2 Jan 1782, THOMAS BALDWIN, b. 23 Feb 1755 son of Isaac and Patience (Rathburn) Baldwin; Thomas d. in New York about 1810.

655) v JOHN FULLER, b. at Windham, 26 Jan 1762; d. at Carleton, NY, 11 Mar 1817; m. about 1788, AMY SHAW, b. 1766 (based on age at time of death) whose parents are unknown to me; Amy d. 13 Nov 1834.

656) vi REUBEN FULLER, b. 19 Feb 1769; d. at Carleton, NY, 7 Jul 1837; m. 23 May 1793, MARY P. CASH, b. 10 Dec 1775 daughter of Daniel and Mary "Polly" (Tracy) Cash; Mary d. Sep 1849.

657) vii HANNAH FULLER, b. 17 Aug 1772; d. 1 Sep 1817; m. 18 Oct 1792, WILKES DURKEE, b. at Windham, 25 Jul 1768 son of Andrew and Mary (Benjamin) Durkee; Wilkes d. in Michigan, 23 Dec 1844.[429] Wilkes remarried Mariah after the death of Hannah.

155) JOSEPH ABBOT *(Philip³, William², George¹)*, b. 14 Feb 1735 son of Philip and Abigail (Bigford) Abbott; d. at Ellington, CT 5 Jan 1814; m. 1st 20 Apr 1758, ELIZABETH STEDMAN, b. at Windham 30 Apr 1739 daughter of Thomas and Anna (Seaver) Stedman; Elizabeth d. 2 Mar 1766.[430] JOSEPH m. 2nd OLIVE PEARCE, b. at Brooklyn, CT, Mar 1738 daughter of Benjamin and Naomi (Richards) Pearce; Olive d. at Vernon, CT 9 Sep 1822.

---

[429] Wilkes Durkee was in New York for a time but received a homestead patent 22 Apr 1824 in the Michigan-Toledo strip. United States, Bureau of Land Management. *Michigan Pre-1908 Homestead & Cash Entry Patent and Cadastral Survey Plat Index*. General Land Office Automated Records Project, 1994. (accessed through ancestry.com)
[430] Ancestry.com. *Connecticut Town Death Records, pre-1870 (Barbour Collection)*

Joseph served in the militia during the Revolutionary War and held the rank of Lieutenant Colonel. He was a wealthy farmer in Ellington.

There is a probate record which has a first inventory 9 March 1814 and a second inventory in February 1815. Joseph, Delano, and Lemuel Abbot agree to complete the second inventory. The value of the estate given at the first inventory was $30,790. The disbursement of the estate includes distributions to the following persons: sons Joseph, Lemuel, Delano, and John, daughters Mary Scarborough and Abigail Whitman. There is also a distribution to widow Olive Abbot.[431]

Births of four children of Joseph Abbott and Elizabeth Stedman are recorded at Pomfret and Ellington.

658) i MARY ABBOTT, b. 6 Apr 1759; d. at Windsor, 25 Dec 1835; m. 1st, about 1785, DANIEL ELLSWORTH, b. 3 Dec 1758 son of Daniel and Mary (-) Ellsworth; Daniel d. at Presque Isle, 3 Mar 1798.[432] Mary m. 2nd, EBENEZER SCARBOROUGH, b. 1 Mar 1743 and d. 2 Oct 1813.

ii ELIZABETH ABBOTT, b. 11 Apr 1761; d. 1 Nov 1784.

659) iii ABIGAIL ABBOTT, b. at Ellington, 17 Dec 1762; d. at West Hartford, 11 Sep 1844; m. about 1784, SAMUEL WHITMAN, b. 26 Jul 1753 son of John and Abigail (Pantry) Whitman; Samuel d. 7 Feb 1810 when he was kicked by a horse.

---

[431] *Connecticut Wills and Probate, 1609-1999*, Probate of Joseph Abbot, Hartford, 1814, Case number 38.
[432] Connecticut, Hale Collection of Cemetery Inscriptions and Newspaper Notices, 1629-1934

iv JOSEPH ABBOT, b. 31 Jan 1766; d. 5 Feb 1834; m. around 1800 (the marriage record lists only 12 Mar with no year), LAURA WEST, b. 30 Dec 1781 daughter of Jeremiah and Amelia (Ely) West; Laura d. 26 Aug 1853. Joseph and Lucy did not have any children. Joseph did leave an extensive will that disposes of his large amount of property to siblings and nieces and nephews.

The births of four children of Joseph Abbot and Olive Pearce are recorded at Pomfret.

660) i LEMUEL ABBOT, b. 9 Mar 1768; d. at Vernon, 9 Jun 1846; m. 8 May 1792, LUCRETIA BINGHAM, b. 22 Jul 1766 daughter of Ithamar and Sarah (Kellogg) Bingham; Lucretia d. 17 Mar 1835.

ii OLIVE ABBOTT, b. 1772; d. 18 Dec 1776.

661) iii DELANO ABBOT, b. 16 Apr 1774; d. at Ira, NY, 11 Mar 1852; m. 1 Jan 1801, MARY "POLLY" BINGHAM, b. 1778 daughter of Ithamar and Sarah (Kellogg) Bingham; Polly d. at Ira, 11 Mar 1852.

662) iv JOHN ABBOT, b. 6 Jul 1784; d. at Vernon, 13 Mar 1859; m. 31 Mar 1813, ACHSAH CONE, b. at East Haddam, 17 Jul 1789 daughter of Daniel and Keziah (Chapman) Cone; Achsah d. 4 Aug 1882.

156) JOHN ABBOTT *(Philip³, William², George¹)*, b. 27 Sep 1741 son of Philip and Abigail (Bigford) Abbott; d. at Jacobs Plains, PA, 4 Aug 1778; m. 4 Nov 1762, ALICE FULLER, b. 1741 daughter of Stephen

and Hannah (Moulton) Fuller. Alice m. 2nd Stephen Gardner; Alice d. at Plains, PA 1 Jun 1816.[433]

John Abbott fought during the Battle of Wyoming 3 July 1778 and survived the initial battle. He was killed at his home in August 1778 as part of the ongoing raids and skirmishes related to the guerilla campaign conducted against the Wyoming Valley, Pennsylvania settlers by Butler's Rangers and Indian allies.[434]

John Abbott and Alice Fuller had eleven children. Published genealogies give two daughters named Abigail, the first Abigail born 12 Dec 1764 dying early and then a second daughter Abigail with unknown birth date. However, there is a death record for Abigail, daughter of John and Alice, born about 1765 with a death date of 5 February 1790.[435] John and Alice married in November 1762 and had daughter Alice in April 1763. This would make it very unlikely that there is a second daughter Abigail as the Abigail born about 1765 lived until 1790.

663) i ALICE ABBOTT, b. at Windham 17 Apr 1763; d. at Hampton, 16 Jan 1809; m. 27 Apr 1790, AMOS UTLEY, b. at Windham, 22 Aug 1764 son of Amos and Grace (Martin) Utley; Amos d. at Hampton, 24 Apr 1810.

ii ABIGAIL ABBOTT, b. 12 Dec 1764; d. at Hampton, 5 Feb 1790.

664) iii CELINDA "LINDA" ABBOTT, b. 20 May 1766; d. at Scott, PA, 8 Apr 1854; m. about 1786, REUBEN

---

[433] Blair and Shoemaker, *The Shoemaker Book (Schumacher)*, p 66
[434] Blair and Shoemaker, *The Shoemaker Book*, p 65
[435] Connecticut, Deaths and Burials Index, 1650-1934; Connecticut State Library; Hartford, Connecticut; The Charles R. Hale Collection of Connecticut Cemetery Inscriptions

		TAYLOR, b. 28 Nov 1759 son of Reuben and Rebecca (Weeks) Taylor; Reuben d. at Greenfield, PA, 1849.
	iv	STEPHEN ABBOTT, b. 6 Dec 1767; d. 19 Jun 1770.
665)	v	CHARLES ABBOTT, b. 3 Jun 1769; d. at Delaware County, OH, after 1853; m. URANIA (also named Lorena in some sources) MANVILLE, b. 24 Mar 1775 son of Nicholas Manville; Urania d. at Sunbury, OH, 21 Dec 1848.[436]
666)	vi	STEPHEN ABBOTT, b. 19 Apr 1771; d. at Plains, PA, 22 Jul 1853;[437] m. 14 Jul 1799, ABIGAIL SEARLE, b. 25 Jun 1779 daughter of William and Philena (Frink) Searle; Abigail d. 2 Jun 1842. Stephen m. 2nd, 1 Jun 1843, SARAH DENISON the widow of Thomas Ferrier and daughter of Nathan and Elizabeth (Sill) Denison.
	vii	REUBEN ABBOTT, b. about 1774. Reuben is a son in published genealogies, but without any other information. There seem to be no records related to him.
667)	viii	LYDIA ABBOTT, b. about 1775; d. at Know County, OH after 1853; m. ARTEMAS SWETLAND, b. in Connecticut about 1769 son of Luke and Hannah (Tiffany) Swetland; Artemas d. 1855.
668)	ix	MARY ABBOTT, b. about 1776; m. JOHN CORTWRIGHT, b. 7 Apr 1774 son of Benjamin and Catherine (Hoover) Cortwright; John d. 4 Dec 1822. [Cortwright is also spelled Courtright.]

---

[436] Ancestry.com, *Web: Delaware County, Ohio, Burial Index, 1784-2011* (Provo, UT, USA: Ancestry.com Operations, Inc., 2013).
[437] Ancestry.com, *Pennsylvania, Deaths, 1852-1854* (Provo, UT, USA: Ancestry.com Operations, Inc., 2011), Pennsylvania State Archives; Reel Number: 671.

         x   HANNAH ABBOTT, b. about 1776, twin of Mary; no further information known.

669)   xi   SARAH ABBOTT, b. 28 Feb 1778; d. Tunkhannock, PA; m. 16 Apr 1800, JAMES KENNEDY, b. at Deer Park, NY, 13 Jul 1775 son of John and Mary (Van Fleet) Kennedy; James d. 19 Oct 1864.

Hannah Abbott Holt³, William², George¹

157)   HANNAH HOLT *(Hannah Abbott Holt³, William², George¹)*, b. 17 Apr 1723 daughter of Abiel and Hannah (Abbott) Holt; d. 25 Jan 1750/1; m. 14 Jul 1742, her first cousin WILLIAM HOLT, b. at Andover 10 Dec 1720 son of Thomas and Alice (Peabody) Holt. William m. 2nd SYBEL DURKEE daughter of Stephen and Lois (Moulton) Durkee; William d. at Hampton 2 Aug 1793.

Hannah Holt and William Holt had four children whose births are recorded at Windham.

670)   i   WILLIAM HOLT, b. 15 Jul 1743; d. at Hampton, 6 Aug 1815;[438] m. 8 Sep 1763, his third cousin, MERCY HOLT, b. 14 Feb 1740/1 daughter of Zebadiah and Sarah (Flint) Holt; Mercy d. 15 Sep 1799.

        ii   HANNAH HOLT, b. 26 Jan 1744/5; d. 30 Aug 1754.

671)   iii ALICE HOLT, b. 26 Apr 1747; d. at Stockbridge, VT, 28 Nov 1814;[439] m. 13 Nov 1764, ROBERT LYON, b. at Pomfret, 30 Sep 1743 son of Peletiah and Sarah (Holt) Lyon; Robert d. 12 Feb 1809.

---

[438] *Connecticut, Deaths and Burials Index, 1650-1934.*
[439] *Vermont, Vital Records, 1720-1908.*

672) iv SARAH HOLT, b. 21 Jun 1748; d. at Hampton, 7 Apr 1777; m. 16 Nov 1769, HENRY DURKEE, b. 29 Sep 1749 son of Henry and Relief (Adams) Durkee. Henry m. 2nd, Sarah Loomis; Henry d. 22 Apr 1820.

158) ELIZABETH HOLT *(Hannah Abbott Holt³, William², George¹)*, b. 16 Feb 1724/5 daughter of Abiel and Hannah (Abbott) Holt; d. about 1753; m. 10 Jun 1746, FRANCIS FENTON, b. at Willington, b. 16 Mar 1718 son of Francis and Ann (Berry) Fenton.[440] Francis m. 2nd Ann Newcomb, 31 Oct 1754. Francis Fenton d. at Willington, 1781 (date of probate).

Elizabeth Holt and Francis Fenton had two children whose births are recorded at Willington.

673) i MARY FENTON, b. 13 Apr 1749; d. at Willington, 14 Apr 1822; m. 1st, 21 May 1770, ISAAC SAWIN, b. 23 Sep 1748 son of George and Anna (Farrar) Sawin; Isaac d. 29 Oct 1776. Mary m. 2nd, 2 Jul 1778, as his second wife, JAMES NILES, b. at Braintree, 2 Apr 1747 son of John and Dorothy (Reynolds) Niles; James d. 18 Jan 1822.

674) ii FRANCIS FENTON, b. 13 Feb 1750/1; m. 25 May 1775, CHLOE GOODALE, b. at Pomfret, 28 Dec 1755 daughter of Ebenezer and Phebe (Holt) Goodale; Chloe d. at New Haven, Oct 1833.[441]

159) ABIEL HOLT *(Hannah Abbott Holt³, William², George¹)*, b. 1 Feb 1726/7 son of Abiel and Hannah (Abbott) Holt; d. at Willington, 2 Oct 1785; m. 1st 22 Apr 1755, MARY DOWNER whose origins are unknown, although perhaps the daughter of Andrew Downer and

---

[440] Weaver, *Genealogy of the Fenton Family*
[441] Connecticut, Deaths and Burials Index, 1650-1934

Sarah Lazell; Mary d. 28 Jan 1766. Abiel m. 2nd 2 Apr 1767, EUNICE KINGSBURY (widow of John Marshall), b. about 1733; Eunice d. 2 Jun 1784.

The distributions from the estate of Abiel Holt were made 19 December 1785 to the following heirs: Hannah Pearl, eldest daughter; Sarah Crocker, second daughter; Mary Needham, third daughter; Abial Holt, eldest son; Bethiah Holt, fourth daughter; Andrew Holt, second son; Abel Holt, third son; and Eunice Holt, youngest daughter. The first five children are from Abiel's marriage to Mary Downer; Eunice Kingsbury is the mother of the three youngest children.[442]

Abiel Holt and Mary Downer had six children born at Willington.

675) i HANNAH HOLT, b. 14 Mar 1756; d. 20 Nov 1832; m. 24 Apr 1782, as his second wife, her second cousin (and George Abbott descendant), OLIVER PEARL, b. 9 Oct 1749 son of Timothy and Dinah (Holt) Pearl. Oliver was married first to Mercy Hinkley. This is the same of Family #276, child iii.

676) ii SARAH HOLT, b. 8 Dec 1757; d. at Willington, 1856;[443] m. 24 Oct 1782, ZEBULON CROCKER, b. at Willington, 5 Mar 1757 son of Ebenezer and Hannah (Hatch) Crocker; Zebulon d. at Willington, 17 Jan 1826.

iii MARY HOLT, b. 13 Jul 1759; d. 4 Feb 1760.

---

[442] *Connecticut Wills and Probate, 1609-1999*, Probate of Abial Holt, Hartford, 1785, Case number 1057.
[443] In the 1850 U.S. Census, 92-year old widow Sarah Crocker was living at the home of her daughter Bethiah Hull. Probate of estate was 1856 with Joseph Hull as administrator.

677) iv MARY HOLT, b. 8 Dec 1760; m. at Charlton, MA, 17 Feb 1783,[444] DANIEL NEEDHAM possibly the son of Daniel and Hannah (Allen) Needham; Daniel d. at Paxton, MA 1801 (date of probate 6 Oct 1801; will written 4 Mar 1801).

678) v ABIEL HOLT, b. 12 Jul 1762; d. at Fairfax, VT, 6 Jun 1829; m. by 1787, MARY MOSHER, b. 21 Jul 1762 daughter of Nathaniel and Elizabeth (Crandall) Mosher; Mary d. 6 Sep 1827.

vi BETHIAH HOLT, b. 26 Mar 1764; d. 1833. Bethiah did not marry.

Abiel Holt and Eunice Kingsbury had three children born at Willington.

i ANDREW HOLT, b. 3 May 1768; d. at Hadley, MA, 21 Sep 1853;[445] m. HANNAH SMITH, b. at Hadley, 28 Aug 1775, daughter of Joseph and Nancy (Day) Smith; Hannah d. 28 Jul 1855. Andrew and Hannah did not have children.

679) ii ABEL HOLT, b. 1770; m. 1st, about 1796, ANNA whose identity is not clear (the Holt genealogy suggests Kercheval); Anna d. at Vermont 13 Apr 1797. Abel m. 2nd, by 1798, RUTH KING, b. at Wilbraham, MA, 13 Feb 1779 daughter of Oliver and Ruth (Cooley) King. This family had nine children

---

[444] *Massachusetts, Compiled Marriages, 1633-1850*. Daniel and Mary Holt of Willington, int. Feb. 17, 1783.

[445] *Massachusetts, Death Records, 1841-1915*, New England Historic Genealogical Society; Boston, Massachusetts; Massachusetts Vital Records, 1840–1911. Parents are listed on the death record as Abiel and Eunice Holt.

born in Vermont and then seem to have relocated to Oneida, New York.

iii EUNICE HOLT, b. 5 Mar 1772. She was living at the time of her father's will, but no record found following that.

160) CALEB HOLT *(Hannah Abbott Holt³, William², George¹)*, b. 6 Mar 1729 son of Abiel and Hannah (Abbott) Holt; d. at Willington, 18 Aug 1810; m. 29 Jan 1755, MARY MERRICK, b. 6 Dec 1726 daughter of John and Sarah (Parsons) Merrick; Mary d. 4 Jun 1790. Caleb m. 2nd Chloe Hatch.

Caleb wrote a will 11 Apr 1793.[446] There are bequests for wife Chloe, sons Elijah and Caleb, and daughter Elizabeth Howe(?). He wrote a codicil 4 April 1798, it which he bequeathed to his wife Chloe the whole of a farm that he purchased from Samuel Dunham so long as she gives up rights to property she brought with her into the marriage. There are no other changes to heirs. The estate entered probate 29 August 1810. The distribution documents include the division set off to widow Chloe and an acknowledgment from Elijah and Caleb that they have received their portions. There is not a distribution document related to Elizabeth. The will is difficult to decipher in terms of Elizabeth's married name (it might be Howe or Hovey or something else altogether or maybe it is a poorly written Holt). In any event, no marriage record was located for her and no death record.

Caleb Holt and Mary Merrick had five children whose births are recorded at Willington.

---

[446] *Connecticut Wills and Probate, 1609-1999,* Probate of Caleb Holt, Hartford, 1810, Case number 1059.

	i	ELIZABETH HOLT, b. 29 Apr 1756. From her father's will, it seems that Elizabeth married, but the last name is unclear. It could be Howe or Hovey or some other name. No marriage record was located that would fit with the name in the will. Durrie's Holt genealogy gives her spouse as Abiel Stevens. But Abiel Stevens and Elizabeth Holt married at Andover so that does not seem right, and other sources suggest it was Elizabeth the daughter of Nathaniel Holt that married Abiel Stevens.
680)	ii	ELIJAH HOLT, b. 24 Oct 1757; d. 4 Jul 1817; m. 5 Nov 1783,[447] MOLLY SIMMONS, b. 1754 possibly the daughter of Paul and Mary (Isham) Simmons, but this is not confirmed; Molly d. 6 May 1814. Elijah m. 2nd, Lovina *Marcy* Dunton 17 Aug 1815. Lovina Marcy was first married to Samuel Dunton.
681)	iii	CALEB HOLT, b. 23 Apr 1759; d. at Willington, 8 Sep 1826; m. 8 Jan 1783, SALLY GOODALE likely the daughter of Ebenezer and Phebe (Holt) Goodale; Sally d. 4 Oct 1831.
	iv	JOSHUA HOLT, b. 31 Mar 1763; d. 12 Aug 1790.
	v	JAMES HOLT, 24 Oct 1764; d. 25 Jan 1766.

161) NATHAN HOLT *(Hannah Abbott Holt[3], William[2], George[1])*, b. 18 Apr 1733 son of Abiel and Hannah (Abbott) Holt; d. at Willington, 31 May 1800; m. 1st 19 Jan 1758, ABIGAIL MERRICK, b. 17 Jun 1737 daughter of John and Sarah (Parsons) Merrick; Abigail d. 1 Dec 1765. Nathan m. 2nd 26 Nov 1766, BATHSHEBA

---

[447] "Connecticut Marriages, 1640-1939," database with images, *FamilySearch* (https://familysearch.org/ark:/61903/1:1:F7PB-68K: 11 February 2018), Elijah Holt and Molley Simons, Marriage 05 Nov 1783, Willington Tolland, Connecticut, United States; Connecticut State Library, Hartford; FHL microfilm 1,376,042.

WILLIAMS, b. 22 May 1737 daughter of Samuel and Deborah (Throope) Williams; Bathsheba d. 1 Aug 1769. Nathan m. 3rd 6 Jun 1770, LYDIA KINGSBURY, b. 1737 daughter of John and Deborah (Spaulding) Kingsbury; Lydia d. 22 Mar 1776.

In his will written March 1790, Nathan leaves his estate to his two children, Nathan and Abigail. In the will, Nathan is allowed used of one-half of the homestead including use of half the well (as long as he maintains it), a chamber in the house, and privilege to use of part of the cellar. The remainder of the estate is left to his daughter Abigail, both real and personal, and she is to pay her brother Nathan 50 pounds over a three-year period. Nathan and Abigail are the sole executors of the estate.[448] The will is unusual in that the daughter is bequeathed the whole estate and the son receives just use of part of the house.

Nathan Holt and Abigail Merrick had one child.

682) i NATHAN HOLT, b. 29 Aug 1761; d. at Willington, 5 Sep 1820; m. his second cousin, LOIS GOODALE, b. at Pomfret, 31 Jul 1764 daughter of Ebenezer and Phebe (Holt) Goodale; Lois d. 20 May 1842.

Nathan Holt and Bathsheba Williams had one child born at Willington.

i ABIGAIL HOLT, b. 4 Sep 1767; she was living at the time of probate of her father's estate in 1800 as Abigail Holt.

Nathan Holt and Lydia Kingsbury had two children born at Willington.

---

[448] *Connecticut Wills and Probate, 1609-1999*, Probate of Nathan Holt, Hartford, 1800, Case number 1066.

i BATHSHEBA HOLT, b. 11 Jan 1772; d. 20 Jan 1790.

ii JOHN HOLT, b. 11 Apr 1774; d. 11 Mar 1776.

162) ANNA HOLT *(Hannah Abbott Holt[3], William[2], George[1])*, b. 14 Jan 1735 daughter of Abiel and Hannah (Abbott) Holt; d. at Willington, 10 Oct 1806; m. 29 Jan 1755, JOSEPH MERRICK, b. 17 Oct 1733 son of John and Sarah (Parsons) Merrick; Joseph d. 9 Apr 1787.

Captain Joseph Merrick commanded a militia company during the Revolutionary War.

Anna Merrick's estate entered probate in 1806.[449] She did not leave a will. The value of the personal property resulted in a value of personal items of $56.67 to each of the heirs. There are distributions to the following heirs: Timothy Merrick, Thomas Merrick, Joseph Merrick, Caleb Merrick, Constant Merrick, Anna Hinkley, Hannah Merrick, and Elizabeth Nye.

Anna Holt and Joseph Merrick had eight children whose births are recorded at Willington.

683) i ANNE MERRICK, b. 19 Sep 1756; d. 2 May 1809; m. 10 Jan 1782, DAVID HINCKLEY, b. 24 Feb 1754 son of John and Susannah (Harris) Hinckley; David d. 24 Jan 1835.

684) ii TIMOTHY MERRICK, b. 31 Aug 1760; d. 4 Jan 1810; m. 29 Nov 1787, MEHITABLE ATWOOD, b. 1765 daughter of Thomas and Sarah (Fenton) Atwood; Mehitable d. 14 May 1855.

685) iii THOMAS MERRICK, b. 6 Jan 1763; d. at Willington, 8 Sep 1840; m. 10 Jan 1790, JOANNA NOBLE, b. 8

---

[449] *Connecticut Wills and Probate, 1609-1999*, Probate of Anna Merrick, Hartford, 1806, Case number 1476.

Generation Four

Oct 1769 daughter of Gideon and Christian (Cadwell) Noble; Joanna d. 28 Apr 1860.

686) iv JOSEPH MERRICK, b. 22 Feb 1765; death uncertain but about 1814 possibly by drowning; m. 21 Oct 1796, IRENA ALDEN, b. at Bellingham, MA, 24 Feb 1772 daughter of Elisha and Irene (Markham) Alden. Irena m. 2nd, Samuel Churchill; Irena d. at Pleasantville, PA, 13 Nov 1858.

687) v CALEB MERRICK, b. 17 May 1767; d. at Vernon, CT, Jun 1822; m. 15 Sep 1791, CHARLOTTE NOBLE, b. at Willington, 19 Aug 1771 daughter of Gideon and Christian (Cadwell) Noble; Charlotte d. at Franklin, CT, 21 Nov 1805.

vi HANNAH MERRICK, b. 23 Jul 1769; d. 31 May 1842. Hannah did not marry.

688) vii CONSTANT MERRICK, b. 14 Jan 1772; d. at Lebanon, NY, 29 Jul 1828; m. at Longmeadow, MA, 22 Sep 1796, EXPERIENCE BURT, b. 8 Aug 1776 daughter of Nathaniel and Experience (Chapin) Burt; Experience d. 1833 at Lebanon, NY, 24 Jul 1833.

689) viii ELIZABETH MERRICK, b. 13 Jul 1774; d. at Tolland, 29 Jun 1824; m. 24 Apr 1800, as his second wife, SAMUEL NYE, b. 25 Dec 1773 son of Samuel and Abigail (Benton) Nye. Samuel m. 3rd, Anna Hatch; Samuel's first wife was Elizabeth Brewster; Samuel d. at Tolland 25 Nov 1837.

163) ISAAC HOLT (*Hannah Abbott Holt[3], William[2], George[1]*), b. 2 Mar 1737/8 son of Abiel and Hannah (Abbott) Holt; d. at Willington,

14 Oct 1822; m. 26 May 1762, SARAH ORCUTT, b. at Stafford, 7 Nov 1740 daughter of William and Sarah (Leonard) Orcutt; Sarah d. 30 Mar 1816.

Isaac and Sarah Holt made their home in Willington where they were admitted to full communion of the Church of Willington 12 July 1767.[450]

Isaac Holt wrote his will 8 May 1798. In the will, he makes special provision for his son Moses "being sensible that he is unable to provide for himself." The will has bequests for well beloved wife Sarah Holt, son Isaac, daughter Sarah, daughter Hannah, daughter Mary, daughter Elizabeth, son Leonard, daughter Anne, son Oliver, and son Moses. The estate entered probate 18 November 1822. Son Oliver Holt served as administrator.[451]

Isaac Holt and Sarah Orcutt had nine children whose births are recorded at Willington.

690) i ISAAC HOLT, b. 3 Nov 1763; d. at Sharon, VT, 7 Aug 1813; m. at Sharon, 1 Jan 1789,[452] MEHITABLE ORCUTT, b. at Stafford, CT, 17 Jan 1769 daughter of Caleb and Chloe (Parker) Orcutt; Mehitable d. 12 Nov 1851.

ii MOSES HOLT, b. 28 Oct 1765; d. 7 Mar 1819.

iii SARAH HOLT, b. 22 Feb 1769; d. 13 May 1836. Sarah did not marry.

691) iv HANNAH HOLT, b. 19 May 1771; d. likely at Clarksfield, OH before 1850;[453] m. 9 Apr 1795,

---

[450] Talcott, Mary, "Records of the Church at Willington, Conn.", *New England Historical and Genealogical Register*, volume 67, 1913, p 217
[451] *Connecticut Wills and Probate, 1609-1999*, Probate of Isaac Holt, Hartford, 1822, Case number 1063.
[452] *Vermont, Vital Records, 1720-1908.*
[453] In the 1850 U.S. Census, Eleazer Fellows, age 78, was living in Clarksfield OH; also in the home are Betsey Haskins age 43 and five children named Haskins.

ELEAZER FELLOWS, b. at Tolland, 2 Apr 1772 son of Verney and Hannah (Lathrop) Fellows; Eleazer d. after 1850 in Ohio.

692) v MARY HOLT, b. 1 May 1773; d. at Willington, 6 Jun 1861; m. 27 Nov 1799, WILLIAM CURTIS, b. about 1774; William d. 3 Nov 1860.

693) vi OLIVER HOLT, b. 16 Jul 1775; d. 6 Mar 1869; m. 16 May 1799, MARTHA "PATTY" SIBLEY,[454] b. 9 Feb 1776 daughter of Jonathan and Patty (Brooks) Sibley; Martha "Patty" d. 16 Dec 1846.

694) vii ELIZABETH HOLT, b. 6 Aug 1777; m. 11 Apr 1799, DANIEL GLAZIER, b. 2 Jun 1776 son of Silas and Suze (Johnson) Glazier; Daniel d. 28 Dec 1852.

695) viii LEONARD HOLT, b. 15 Feb 1782; d. 12 Mar 1857; m. 1st, 29 Dec 1809, his first cousin once removed (and George Abbott descendant), ASENATH HOLT, b. 26 Jan 1786 daughter of Nathan and Lois (Goodell) Holt; Asenath d. 13 Feb 1813. Leonard m. 2nd, about 1813, JOANNA ALDEN, b. 14 Jul 1782 daughter of Elisha and Irene (Markham) Alden; Joanna d. 30 Sep 1849.

696) ix ANNE HOLT, b. 21 Oct 1784; d. 27 Jun 1855; m. SIMEON CARPENTER, b. 13 Dec 1783 son of Elijah and Sarah (Younglove) Carpenter; Simeon d. 24 Aug 1862.

Betsey is the daughter of Eleazer and Hannah. Eleazer and Hannah's son Leonard also relocated to Huron County, Ohio.

[454] Connecticut, Marriage Index, 1620-1926; the handwritten marriage record confirms that the marriage is to Patty and not to her younger sister Polly.

164) TIMOTHY HOLT *(Hannah Abbott Holt³, William², George¹)*, b. 2 Dec 1739 son of Abiel and Hannah (Abbott) Holt; d. 7 May 1807; m. 7 May 1761 as her 2nd husband, REBECCA CHAMBERLAIN (widow of Nathaniel Fenton).[455] Rebecca was b. about 1730 probably the daughter of Edmund and Sarah (Furbush) Chamberlain; Rebecca d. 11 Apr 1809.

The settlement of the estate of Timothy Holt in 1807 included distributions to the following persons: widow Mrs. Rebeckah Holt, son Timothy Holt, and daughter Anna Crocker. The probate of the estate of Rebeckah Chamberlain Fenton Holt in 1809 included distributions to the following persons: Timothy Holt, Nathaniel Fenton, Anna Crocker, Eleazer Fenton, and Rebecca Knowlton.[456] Nathaniel Fenton, Eleazer Fenton, and Rebecca Knowlton were children of Rebecca and her first husband Nathaniel Fenton.

Timothy Holt and Rebecca Chamberlain had two children whose births are recorded at Willington.

697) i ANNA HOLT, b. 12 Feb 1762; m. 17 Nov 1785, STEPHEN CROCKER, b. 14 Dec 1760 son of Ebenezer and Hannah (Hatch) Crocker. It is not firmly established where this family located, but they perhaps went to Schoharie County, New York. On the other hand, they may have stayed in Willington as a Stephen Crocker is of appropriate age there in the 1820 census.

698) ii TIMOTHY HOLT, b. 19 May 1765; d. 17 Apr 1850; m. 10 Dec 1789, ESTHER SCRIPTURE, b. 26 Aug 1765

---

[455] This information is confirmed by the 1809 probate record of Rebecca Holt which includes heirs from her first marriage to Nathaniel Fenton.
[456] *Connecticut Wills and Probate, 1609-1999*, Probate of Rebekah Holt, Hartford, 1809, Case number 1069.

son of John and Esther (Lee) Scripture; Esther d. 1 Aug 1841.

165) MARY HOLT *(Hannah Abbott Holt³, William², George¹)*, b. 4 May 1742 daughter of Abiel and Hannah (Abbott) Holt; d. 13 Jan 1823; m. 27 Nov 1760, JOSEPH PERSONS, birth record not found but son of Joseph and Hannah (-) Persons of Willington; Joseph d. at Willington, 4 Nov 1812.

Joseph and Mary do not seem to have had children. Joseph's will included bequests to his wife Mary and to his siblings and their heirs. In her will, written 10 June 1819 and proved 1 Feb 1823, Mary Parsons left her entire estate to the children of Joseph and Betsy Holt. Joseph and Betsy Holt were deceased at that time; their children who were heirs were Hannah Whitaker, Esther Heath, Alva Holt, Lucy Holt, Joseph P. Holt, and Mary Holt.[457] This is the family of Joseph and Betsy (Parker) Holt. Joseph Holt was a nephew of Mary Holt Persons, the son of Mary's brother James.

This Joseph Persons is often confused (at least in "internet" trees) with Joseph Parsons of Springfield, Massachusetts who married Naomi Hitchcock and had several children in Springfield. Joseph Persons, Jr. and Mary Holt lived in Willington. They were members of the church in Willington, Joseph, Jr. and Mary admitted as members February 1777. They were also listed as members in 1806 and Joseph's death is noted in the church records in 1813.[458] It is during this same time frame that Joseph Parsons and Naomi Hitchcock were married and having children in Springfield. Adding to the confusion is that each of these Josephs had fathers named

---

[457] *Connecticut Wills and Probate, 1609-1999*, Probate of Mary Parsons, Hartford, 1823, Case number 1617.
[458] Ancestry.com, Connecticut, Church Record Abstracts, 1630-1920

Joseph and mothers named Hannah, but they are two different people.

166) JAMES HOLT *(Hannah Abbott Holt³, William², George¹)*, b. 27 Aug 1746 son of Abiel and Hannah (Abbott) Holt; d. at Willington, 30 Sep 1818; m. 1st 20 Apr 1769, ESTHER OWENS, b. 20 Feb 1747 son of Eleazer and Jerusha (Russ) Owens; Esther d. 5 Dec 1774. JAMES m. 2nd LUCE SAWINS, b. 28 Sep 1740 daughter of George and Anne (Farrar) Sawins; Luce d. 25 Dec 1824.

James Holt wrote his will 7 February 1814 (proved 19 October 1818) and includes bequests to the following persons: well beloved wife Lucy Holt who receives one half of the personal estate which is to be at her disposal forever; sons James, Joseph, and Solomon each receive $25; daughter Esther Parker, $1; son Abiel Holt, $25; and daughter Lucy Walker, $1. These are token money bequests as the children have previously received their full portions from the estate. The entire remainder of the estate is bequeathed to son John Holt who is also named the executor.[459]

James Holt and Esther Owens had four children whose birth are recorded at Willington, Connecticut.

699) i JAMES HOLT, b. 12 Apr 1770; d. at Willington, 16 Jan 1856; m. 4 Dec 1794, MARY POOL, b. at Willington, 14 Aug 1770 daughter of Timothy and Deborah (Presson) Pool; Mary d. 18 Jan 1853.

700) ii JOSEPH HOLT (twin of James), b. 12 Apr 1770; d. at Willington, 29 Jan 1816; m. 6 Mar 1794, BETSY PARKER, b. at Willington, 23 Feb 1775 daughter of Jonathan and Betsy (Johnson) Parker; Betsy d. 7 May 1814.

---

[459] *Connecticut Wills and Probate, 1609-1999*, Probate of James Holt, Hartford, 1818, Case number 1064.

Generation Four

701) iii SOLOMON HOLT, b. 14 Apr 1772; d. in Iowa, 4 Jun 1838; m. at Franklin, CT, 7 Apr 1799, ZERVIAH ABELL, b. at Norwich, 26 Aug 1780 daughter of Thomas and Zerviah (Hyde) Abell; Zerviah d. 1845.

702) iv ESTHER HOLT, b. 20 Nov 1774; m. 9 Jan 1800, DANIEL PARKER, b. at Willington, 5 Mar 1777 son of Jonathan and Betsy (Johnson) Parker.

James Holt and Luce Sawins had three children whose births are recorded at Willington.

703) i JOHN HOLT, b. 11 Apr 1776; d. at Willington, 22 Apr 1841; m. 6 Sep 1804, CLARISSA HOLT, b. 1775 (based on age at time of death); Clarissa d. 25 Feb 1840. I have no idea who Clarissa Holt is and suspect she may be the widow of a Holt but have not been able to track her down.

704) ii LUCE HOLT, b. 11 Jun 1778; d. 22 Feb 1847;[460] m. at Ashford, 26 Jan 1809, AARON WALKER, b. 21 Jan 1776 son of Samuel and Alice (Case) Walker; Aaron d. at Ashford, 1 Nov 1815.

705) iii ABIEL HOLT, b. 14 Jan 1780; d. at Mansfield, about 1826 (probate of estate in 1826); m. 30 Apr 1805, SALLY CONVERSE, b. at Stafford, 9 Mar 1781 daughter of Stephen and Zerviah (Sanger) Converse;[461] Sally's date of death is uncertain. She was alive in 1823 when her father wrote his will but

---

[460] Durrie, *A Genealogy of the Holt Family*, p 50
[461] The 1823 will of Stephen Converse includes a bequest to his daughter Sally Holt.

there is no mention of her in the probate of Abiel's estate. The probate includes some provisions of the support of the two younger sons (Sanford and Arnold) who were underage at the time.

Caleb³, William², George¹

167) HANNAH ABBOTT *(Caleb³, William², George¹)*, b. 27 Oct 1734 daughter of Caleb and Elizabeth (Paine) Abbott; d. 19 Apr 1813 at Hartland, VT; m. at Union, CT, 24 Mar 1761, JOHN HENDRICK, b. at Norwich, 3 Oct 1722 son of Israel and Ann (Babson) Hendrick; John d. at Hartland, 8 Nov 1810.[462]

Hannah and John married in Connecticut and started their family there. They relocated to Vermont with several other members of this family network. John was a farmer. John and Hannah were members of the congregational church in Hartland.[463]

Hannah and John had seven children; the births of the three oldest children are recorded in Union, Connecticut. The other children may have been born in Vermont, but records have not yet been located. The birth dates for the younger children are from published genealogies.[464]

    i   EZRA HENDRICK, b. 21 Feb 1762; d. Jun 1770.

    ii   JOHN HENDRICK, b. 4 Apr 1764; d. about 1826 in Chautauqua County, NY. John does not seem to have married and did not have any children.

706)   iii   MARY HENDRICK, b. 5 Dec 1765; d. after 1845 at Putney, VT; m. 14 Sep 1786, JOHN STODDARD, b. 19 Nov 1761 son of Joshua and Sarah (Humphrey)

---

[462] Vermont, Vital Records, 1720-1908. (ancestry.com)
[463] Darling, *History and Anniversary of Hartland, Vermont*
[464] Abbot and Abbot, *Genealogical Record of Descendants*

Stoddard; John d. at Westminster, VT, 13 Aug 1831.[465]

707) iv CALEB HENDRICK, b. 17 Sep 1767; d. at Hartland, VT, 26 Aug 1837; m. by 1796, his first cousin, SARAH ABBOTT, b. 15 Apr 1773 daughter of Samuel and Rachel (Ward) Abbott; Sarah d. 11 Feb 1849.

708) v HANNAH HENDRICK, b. 22 Mar 1770; d. at Waterford, VT, 12 Apr 1843; m. about 1800, ZEDEKIAH GOODELL, b. at Pomfret, 31 Aug 1769 son of Jacob and Mehitable (Goodell) Goodell; Zedekiah d. 11 Sep 1863.

709) vi EZRA HENDRICK, b. 13 Mar 1772; d. 28 Dec 1799; m. about 1797, ESTHER GOODELL, b. at Pomfret, 1 Jul 1776 son of Jacob and Mehitable (Goodell) Goodell.

vii ELIZABETH HENDRICK, b. 11 Jun 1775; d. at Fowlerville, NY, 7 May 1857; m. 12 Mar 1818, as his second wife, LOT JENNE, b. at Dartmouth, MA, 5 Jun 1760 son of Samuel and Bethiah (Rider) Jenne. Elizabeth did not have any children.

168) SARAH ABBOTT *(Caleb³, William², George¹)*, b. 6 Jul 1736 daughter of Caleb and Elizabeth (Paine) Abbott; d. 12 Nov 1761 at Brimfield, MA; m. 11 Nov 1754, JONATHAN BURK, b. 26 Feb 1733 son of Jonathan and Thankful (Waite) Burk. Jonathan m. 2nd Sarah Gould; Jonathan d. 18 May 1775 at Hartland, VT.

The births of four children of Sarah Abbott and Jonathan Burk are recorded at Brimfield, Massachusetts. The Abbot genealogy

---

[465] *Vermont, Vital Records, 1720-1908.*

also lists a daughter Betsy, but she is the child of Jonathan and his second wife.[466]

710) i   SARAH BURK, b. 18 Jan 1755; d. at Windsor, VT about 1783; m. at Windsor, 17 May 1774, LAZARUS BANNISTER, b. at Brookfield, 7 Feb 1748 son of Thomas and Mary (Wheeler) Bannister. Lazarus m. 2nd, about 1784, Anne Worcester. Lazarus d. at Windsor about 1813 (probate of estate).

ii JONATHAN BURK, b. 7 Jun 1756; died in the Army.

711) iii JOSEPH BURK, b. 27 Apr 1758; d. at Warner, NH, 7 May 1829; m. at Hartland, VT, 25 Apr 1784, JUDITH BARRELL, b. at Bridgewater, 1 May 1763 daughter of John and Judith (Snow) Barrell.

712) iv ABIGAIL BURK, b. 12 Nov 1761; d. at Westminster, VT, 18 Oct 1801;[467] m. 26 Aug 1779, REUBEN ROBINSON, b. at Cumberland, RI, 4 Aug 1753 son of Nathaniel and Kezia (Robbins) Robinson; Reuben d. 16 Dec 1839.

169) SAMUEL ABBOTT *(Caleb[3], William[2], George[1])*, b. 4 Mar 1743 son of Caleb and Elizabeth (Paine) Abbott; d. 25 Sep 1825 at Hartland, VT; m. 1st at Union, CT, RACHEL WARD, b. about 1748 (based on age at death); Rachel d. at Hartland, VT 15 Oct 1774. Samuel m. 2nd 3 Dec 1778 the widow LYDIA STONE; Lydia d. 25 Sep 1825.

---

[466] Abbot and Abbot, *Genealogical Record of Descendants*, p 59
[467] Vermont Births, Marriages and Deaths to 2008. (From microfilmed records. Online database: AmericanAncestors.org, New England Historic Genealogical Society, 2013.)

Samuel saw service during the Revolutionary War in the militia guarding frontier regions in Vermont. He had two children with his first wife, Rachel Ward; one of those children died as an infant. Samuel did not have children in his second marriage.

        i   SARAH ABBOTT, b. 12 Apr 1771; d. 3 Jul 1772.

707)   ii   SARAH ABBOTT, b. 15 Apr 1773; d. at Hartland, 11 Feb 1849; m. by 1796, her first cousin (and George Abbott descendant), CALEB HENDRICK, b. 17 Sep 1767 son of John and Hannah (Abbott) Hendrick; Caleb d. 26 Aug 1837. This is the same as Family #167, child iv.

170)   WILLIAM ABBOTT *(Caleb³, William², George¹)*, b. 17 Oct 1745 son of Caleb and Elizabeth (Paine) Abbott; d. 25 Jul 1832 at Clinton, NY; m. 1st at Union, CT, 15 Nov 1770, MARY COY; Mary d. 10 Dec 1776. William m. 2nd 24 Sep 1778, ESTHER GREEN, b. at Thompson, CT, 31 Dec 1753 daughter of Amos and Lydia (Johnson) Green;[468] Esther d. at Clinton, NY 23 Dec 1839.

William Abbott and Mary Coy had two children born at Union County, Connecticut.

713)   i   CALEB ABBOTT, b. 2 Feb 1774; d. at Colden, NY, 25 Jan 1851; m. by 1794, HANNAH WHEET, b. at Bernardston, MA, 6 Jan 1772 daughter of Samuel and Jerusha (Allen) Wheet; Hannah d. 4 Sep 1842.

        ii   NEHEMIAH ABBOTT, b. 2 May 1776; d. 25 Sep 1776.

---

[468] Esther's birthdate and name of her father are engraved on her gravestone. (findagrave.com)

William Abbott and Esther Green had seven children born at Union County, Connecticut.

  i MARY ABBOTT, b. 3 Aug 1779; d. after 1860 at Kirkland, NY.[469] Mary did not marry.

714) ii NEHEMIAH ABBOTT, b. 4 Jun 1781; d. 11 Jan 1869, Kirkland, NY; m. 4 Oct 1803, ESTHER BARKER, b. at Watertown, CT, 29 Oct 1776 daughter of Eliasaph and Mabel (Sanford) Barker; Esther d. 2 Jan 1857, Oneida County, NY.

715) iii PAUL ABBOTT, b. 7 May 1783; d. at Lowville, NY, 18 Mar 1831; m. 1st, 6 Mar 1807, MARY GAYLORD; Mary d. 2 Sep 1809. Paul m. 2nd, 7 Mar 1811, PATTY EELS, b. 26 Oct 1787 daughter of Daniel and Martha (Hamlin) Eels.

716) iv ESTHER ABBOTT, b. 4 Oct 1784; d. after 1860 at Kirkland, NY (living with her daughter at 1860 Census); m. 30 Jan 1810, ELIHU WAKELEE, b. 27 Dec 1789 son of Platt and Mary (Minor) Wakelee; Elihu d. 1 Aug 1833.

717) v ORINDA ABBOTT, b. 1 May 1786; d. at Panama, NY, 11 May 1850; m. 17 Oct 1805, JOEL HUBBARD, b. 15 Mar 1784; Joel d. 1 Apr 1862.

  vi SAMUEL ABBOTT, b. 18 Jul 1789. Samuel was a mechanic. He did not marry.

  vii WILLIAM ABBOTT, b. 2 Dec 1792; d. at Clinton, NY, 21 Oct 1819. William was a tailor. He did not marry.

---

[469] In the 1860 U.S. Census, she was living with her brother Nehemiah in Kirkland, NY. Year: 1860; Census Place: Kirkland, Oneida, New York; Roll: M653_824; Page: 104; Family History Library Film: 803824

Section V: The Grandchildren of Sarah Abbott and Ephraim Stevens

Elizabeth Stevens Robinson³, Sarah Abbott Stevens², George¹

171) JOSEPH ROBINSON (*Elizabeth Stevens Robinson³, Sarah Abbott Stevens², George¹*), b. 22 Dec 1710 son of Joseph and Elizabeth (Stevens) Robinson; d. at Boxford, 29 Nov 1777; m. 25 Jul 1733, MEHITABLE EAMS, of Boxford, b. 1713 (based on age at time of death); her parentage is not clear; Mehitable d. 11 Aug 1782.

Joseph and Mehitable resided in Boxford where their six children were born. He owned a farm of about 100 acres in Boxford that he listed for sale in 1770, although he perhaps did not sell the property as he continued to live there until his death.[470]

Joseph wrote his will 17 November 1777. His widow Mehitable receives the use of all the household goods, one-half of the cow currently being fattened, and as much pork and other provisions that she requires for her support. Mehitable also receives the improvements from one-third part of the real estate. Son Joseph receives £260 which will be paid to him from the estate by son John. Jeremy is also bequeathed Joseph's best gun. Daughter Mary wife of Henry Bodwell receives £12. Daughter Mehitable wife of James Frye receives £12. His two daughter will also receive the household goods after the decease of their mother. Son John receives all the remainder of the estate and is named sole executor.[471] [Son Jeremy is called Jeremiah in the available vital records.]

---

[470] "The Dwellings of Boxford," *Essex Institute Historical Collections*, volumes 27-29, p 87

[471] *Essex County, MA: Probate File Papers, 1638-1881*. Probate of Joseph Robinson, 2 Feb 1778, Case number 23906.

Birth records were located for six children, the oldest three at Andover and the births of the youngest three children recorded at Boxford.

        i   NATHAN ROBINSON, b. 1 Sep 1734; d. 13 Jul 1736.

718)   ii   MARY ROBINSON, b. 3 Aug 1737; d. at Methuen, 16 Nov 1811; m. 20 Sep 1759, HENRY BODWELL, b. at Methuen, 26 Jul 1729 son of Henry and Anne (Pottelle) Bodwell; Henry d. 9 Apr 1816.

719)   iii   JOHN ROBINSON, b. 2 Sep 1739; d. at Boxford, 22 Jan 1810; m. 30 Jun 1763, REBECCA "BECKY" WOOD, b. Feb 1743/4 (baptized 12 Feb) daughter of Daniel and Sarah (Peabody) Wood; Becky d. 30 Mar 1810.

504)   iv   MEHITABLE ROBINSON, b. Oct 1742 (baptized 17 Oct); d. at Methuen, 6 Jun 1787; m. 21 Feb 1765, her third cousin (and George Abbott descendant), JAMES FRYE, b. at Andover, 9 Jan 1740/1 son of James and Elizabeth (Osgood) Frye; James d. 28 Jan 1826.

        v   ELIZABETH ROBINSON, b. Sep 1746 (baptized 7 Sep); d. 22 Oct 1777. Elizabeth did not marry.

        vi   JEREMIAH ROBINSON, b. 1754; d. 27 May 1780. Jeremiah did not marry.

172)   ISAAC ROBINSON *(Elizabeth Stevens Robinson³, Sarah Abbott Stevens², George¹)*, b. Sep 1715 son of Joseph and Elizabeth (Stevens) Robinson; d. at Boxford, 15 Apr 1804; m. 19 Jun 1740, DOROTHY POOR, b. at Andover 1716 daughter of Daniel and Dorothy (Kimball) Poor; Dorothy d. 13 Jul 1801.

Isaac Robinson wrote his will 20 March 1788.[472] His well-beloved wife Dorothy is to receive the improvement on one-third of the real estate. She is to have other considerations if needed to maintain her comfort. Son Isaac receives £5. Son Jonathan receives £50. Daughter Phebe the wife of Nathan Eams receives £5 as does daughter Hannah the wife of Jonathan Parker. His two daughters receive the household goods after the decease of their mother. Son John receives all the real estate in Andover and elsewhere. The three sons Isaac, Jonathan, and John receive wearing apparel. Wife Dorothy is mentioned in this 1788 will, but she died in 1801 prior to the probate of the estate.

Isaac Robinson and Dorothy Poor had eight children whose births are recorded at Andover.

  i ISAAC ROBINSON, b. 24 Apr 1741; he was living in 1788 when his father wrote his will; it is not clear what became of him.

 ii PHEBE ROBINSON, b. 3 Aug 1742; m. 27 Feb 1765, NATHAN EAMS, b. at Boxford, 16 Sep 1738 son of Jeremiah and Sarah (Kimball) Eams. It is unknown what became of this couple. Charlotte Helen Abbott attributes several children to them, but those are children of Nathan Ames and Deborah Bowers (that Nathan being the son of Samuel Ames and Hannah Stevens). There is no record of children for Nathan and Phebe in Massachusetts or New Hampshire and no probate record.

---

[472] *Essex County, MA: Probate File Papers, 1638-1881.* Probate of Isaac Robinson, 7 May 1804, Case number 23887.

720)   iii   HANNAH ROBINSON, b. 27 Sep 1744; m. 17 Feb 1767, JONATHAN PARKER, b. 26 Mar 1738 son of Jonathan and Hannah (Frye) Parker.

iv   DOLLY ROBINSON, b. 6 Feb 1746/7; d. at Boxford, Jun 1767.

v   DANIEL ROBINSON, b. 8 Aug 1750; d. at St. Croix, Jul 1771; *Daniel, s. Isaac, at St. Croix, July —, 1771, a. 21 y. GR1.*

721)   vi   JONATHAN ROBINSON, b. 25 Jun 1753; d. at Surry, NH, 17 Mar 1838;[473] m. at Boxford, 24 Apr 1783, BETTY CHADWICK, b. at Boxford, 22 Aug 1756 daughter of John and Susannah (Peabody) Chadwick; Betty d. 23 Oct 1818.

vii   NATHAN ROBINSON, b. 20 Apr 1756; d. 19 Sep 1762.

722)   viii   JOHN ROBINSON, b. 11 Apr 1758; d. at Boxford, 17 May 1807; m. at Boxford, 3 Apr 1781, SARAH TYLER, b. at Boxford, 8 Feb 1758 daughter of Gideon and Mehitable (Kimball) Tyler;[474] Sarah d. 3 May 1840 (*Sarah, wid. John, d. Gideon Tyler, May 3, 1840, a. 82 y. GR1*).

173)   SARAH ROBINSON (*Elizabeth Stevens Robinson[3], Sarah Abbott Stevens[2], George[1]*), b. about 1716[475] daughter of Joseph and Elizabeth (Stevens) Robinson; d.?; m. 10 Apr 1746, as his second wife, SAMUEL BARKER, b. 13 Feb 1691/2 son of William and Mary (Dix) Barker; Samuel d. at Andover, 13 May 1770.

---

[473] Kingsbury, *The History of Surry, NH*
[474] The 1800 will of Gideon Tyler includes a bequest to daughter Sarah the wife of John Robinson. *Essex County, MA: Probate File Papers, 1638-1881.*
[475] Sarah is mentioned in her father's will, but no birth record was located for her.

Samuel Barker wrote his will 21 November 1767. Wife Sarah receives one-third of the personal and real estate for use and improvement. Son-in-law Jedediah Holt and his wife Phebe receive all the estate real and personal. Jedediah Holt was named sole executor.[476]

Samuel's two children with his first wife died in infancy. Sarah Robinson and Samuel Barker had two children born at Andover.

    i   SARAH BARKER, b. 4 Oct 1747; d. 29 Sep 1763.

723)   ii   PHEBE BARKER, b. 2 Jan 1749/50; m. 19 Jun 1766, her second cousin once removed, JEDEDIAH HOLT, b. at Suncook, 23 Feb 1743/4 son of Stephen and Mary (Farnum) Holt; Jedediah d. at Andover, 12 Feb 1790.

174)   EPHRAIM ROBINSON *(Elizabeth Stevens Robinson³, Sarah Abbott Stevens², George¹)*, b. 11 Aug 1723 son of Joseph and Elizabeth (Stevens) Robinson; death date not located; m. 2 Aug 1750, HANNAH KIMBALL, b. at Bradford 19 Mar 1730/1 daughter of Joseph and Abial (Peabody) Kimball; no death record was located for Hannah.

Little information has yet been located for this family. Some marriages for the children are suggested here, but these are preliminary. There are records for eight children, the oldest six and Andover and the youngest two at Haverhill.

---

[476] *Essex County, MA: Probate File Papers, 1638-1881.* Probate of Samuel Barker, 4 Jun 1770, Case number 1712.

i   JOSEPH ROBINSON, b. 23 Aug 1751; m. at Haverhill, 8 Jun 1788, SUSANNA NOYES. No information has been found for this couple following their marriage.

ii   SARAH ROBINSON, b. 21 May 1753; died young.

iii HANNAH ROBINSON, b. 28 Jun 1755

iv   NAOMY ROBINSON, b. 1758; d. 20 Oct 1762.

v   ELIZABETH ROBINSON, b. 17 Oct 1760; d. 9 Oct 1762.

vi   NAOMY ROBINSON, b. 18 Mar 1763; d. unknown but living in 1828; m. at Haverhill, 8 Jul 1798, as his second wife, REUBEN CURRIER, b. at Haverhill, 21 Jul 1738 son of Reuben and Elizabeth (Robinson) Currier; Reuben d. at Haverhill, 15 Apr 1827. Reuben did not leave a will; Naomy Currier was administrator of the estate. Reuben and Naomy did not have children. Reuben's first wife was Lydia Atwood with whom he had several children.

vii SARAH ROBINSON, b. 31 Jan 1766.

viii ELIZABETH ROBINSON, b. 24 Nov 1768.

Hannah Stevens Swan³, Sarah Abbott Stevens², George¹

175)   ELIZABETH SWAN *(Hannah Stevens Swan³, Sarah Abbott Stevens², George¹)*, b. 14 Feb 1709/10 daughter of Robert and Hannah (Stevens) Swan; d. at Andover 21 Jun 1770; m. 4 Jul 1743, NATHANIEL LOVEJOY, b. 16 Feb 1698/9 son of Nathaniel and Dorothy (Hoyt) Lovejoy; Nathaniel d. 25 Aug 1769.[477]

---

[477] 1769 is the date on the transcription of the death record. The gravestone has a date of 1768.

There are only two births recorded at Andover for Elizabeth Swan and Nathaniel Lovejoy. One son died in infancy. The second son was General Nathaniel Lovejoy, educated at Harvard and served in the Revolutionary War.

304) i NATHANIEL LOVEJOY, b. 29 Apr 1744; d. 5 Jul 1812; m. 3 Nov 1768, his third cousin (and George Abbott descendant), ELIZABETH FOSTER, b. 14 Apr 1744 daughter of Asa and Elizabeth (Abbott) Foster (same as Family #64, child vi). Elizabeth d. 24 Apr 1775. Nathaniel m. 2nd, by 1776, ELIZABETH BRANDON, b. at Cambridge, 18 Nov 1750 daughter of Benjamin and Elizabeth (Foxcroft) Brandon; Elizabeth Brandon d. 19 Nov 1788. Nathaniel m. 3rd, 1 Dec 1803, his third cousin once removed (and George Abbott descendant), BENJAMINA WOODBRIDGE, b. at Salem, Mar 1772 daughter of Dudley and Dorcas (March) Woodbridge. Benjamina d. at Worcester, 6 May 1851. Prior to her death, a guardian was appointed for her due to "insanity."

ii JONATHAN LOVEJOY, b. 22 Apr 1748; d. 5 Jan 1749/50.

176) ROBERT SWAN *(Hannah Stevens Swan³, Sarah Abbott Stevens², George¹)*, b. 2 Mar 1711/2 son of Robert and Hannah (Stevens) Swan; d. at Methuen, 31 Oct 1752; m. 1731, ELIZABETH FARNUM, b. at Andover, 9 Nov 1711 daughter of Jonathan and Elizabeth (Barker) Farnum. Elizabeth m. 2nd James Howe; Elizabeth d. 5 Dec 1780.

Robert Swan did not leave a will. The probate record contains a 1762 document which refers to his widow as Elizabeth Swan now Howe.

The births of eight children are recorded for Robert and Elizabeth. The oldest four and youngest two children have births recorded at Andover and the births of the other two children are recorded at Methuen.

724) i JONATHAN SWAN, b. 1 Sep 1732; d. at Methuen, 15 Aug 1783; m. 13 Dec 1759, as the second of her three husbands, ABIGAIL GREEN, b. at Haverhill, 7 Nov 1728 daughter of Peter and Martha (Singletary) Green.

ii JOSEPH SWAN, b. 17 May 1734; d. 29 Sep 1760 at Crown Point during the French and Indian War. *Joseph, s. Robert and Elezebeth, at Crown Point, Sept. 29, 1760, in his 26th y.*

iii BENJAMIN SWAN, b. 5 Jan 1737/8; d. 28 Jan 1738/9.

iv ELIZABETH SWAN, b. 1 Dec 1739; d. 14 May 1742.

v BENJAMIN SWAN, b. 27 Apr 1743

vi RICHARD SWAN, b. 8 Mar 1745/6

725) vii ROBERT SWAN, b. 19 Jan 1748/9; d. at Andover, 25 Dec 1832; m. 1st, 29 Apr 1773, AFFA FARRINGTON, b. 8 Mar 1756 daughter of John and Sarah (Holton) Farrington; Affa d. 11 Feb 1788. Robert m. 2nd, 21 May 1789, SUSANNAH EMERY, b. about 1759; Susannah d. 6 Apr 1842. Susannah's first husband was Nehemiah Abbott a descendant of George Abbott of Rowley.

726) viii PHINEAS SWAN, b. 14 Jun 1752; d. at Haverhill, NH, 16 Jan 1829; m. 21 Oct 1773, TRYPHENA WEBSTER, b. at Haverhill, 11 Sep 1754 daughter of Stephen and Susannah (Ladd) Webster; Tryphena d. 23 Mar 1843.

177)   EPHRAIM SWAN *(Hannah Stevens Swan³, Sarah Abbott Stevens², George¹)*, b. 3 Sep 1713 son of Robert and Hannah (Stevens) Swan; d. at Andover before Oct 1777 (when his will was probated); m. 23 May 1738, SARAH POOLE, b. at Lynn, 11 Sep 1713 daughter of John and Mary (Gooding) Poole; Sarah d. likely after 1790 (she seems to be listed as the head of household with her daughter living with her in the 1790 Census).

In his will, Ephraim has bequests to the following persons: well-beloved wife Sarah receives one-half of the household; daughter Sarah Swan receives the improvements on the other half of the house sharing equal with her mother; granddaughter Martha Swan; daughter-in-law Martha Swan widow of son Ephraim receives the use of a room in his house; and grandson Ephraim receives the real property at the age of 21. Wife Sarah is named executor.[478]

Ephraim Swan and Sarah Poole had two children whose births are recorded at Andover. Daughter Sarah did not marry. Ephraim's son Ephraim also died in 1777, the younger Ephraim dying a few months before his father.

727)   i   EPHRAIM SWAN, b. 12 Oct 1739; d. likely early 1777 (probate 3 Apr 1777); m. 24 Oct 1765, MARTHA FARRINGTON, b. 5 Oct 1741 daughter of John and Sarah (Holton) Farrington. Martha m. 2nd, 30 Dec 1777, Thomas Clark.

        ii   SARAH SWAN, b. 13 Jun 1742; d. 7 Jun 1812.

---

[478] *Essex County, MA: Probate File Papers, 1638-1881*. Probate of Ephraim Swan, 6 Oct 1777, Case number 26885.

178) HANNAH SWAN *(Hannah Stevens Swan³, Sarah Abbott Stevens², George¹)*, b. 28 Dec 1716 daughter of Robert and Hannah (Stevens) Swan; d. at Andover, 7 Jul 1761; m. 14 Aug 1734, PETER PARKER, b. Jul 1714 son of Joseph and Lydia (Frye) Parker; Peter d. at Andover, 9 Jan 1795.

The will of Peter Parker has bequests to the following persons: son Nathan Parker, son Peter Parker, son Robart Parker, son Isaac Parker, son Simeon Parker, grandson Parker Elsly son of daughter Mary Elsly who is deceased (who gets 100 acres in the newly incorporated Bluehill), and grandson Parker Elwell son of daughter Hannah Elwell who is deceased (also 100 acres in Bluehill), daughter Lydia wife of Hezekiah Coburn, and grandson Joseph Parker son of Nathan gets the house and barn. Son Isaac is named executor. Bluehill refers to Blue Hill, Maine first settled in 1762 by people from Andover.[479]

Hannah Swan and Peter Parker had eleven children whose births are recorded at Andover.

728) i MARY PARKER, b. 28 Nov 1734; died before 1795; m. ENOCH ILSLEY, b. at Newbury, 16 Dec 1730 son of Isaac and Abigail Moody Ilsley; Enoch d. at Falmouth/Portland, ME, 10 Nov 1811.

ii HANNAH PARKER, b. 20 Dec 1736; d. 15 Mar 1741/2.

729) iii NATHAN PARKER, b. 3 Jun 1739; d. at Blue Hill, ME, about 1819; m. at Blue Hill, 20 Dec 1764, MARY WOOD, b. at Beverly, 15 Nov 1748 daughter of Joseph and Mary (Haskell) Wood.

730) iv PETER PARKER, b. 28 May 1741; d. at Blue Hill, 24 Oct 1822; m. 5 Jun 1766, PHEBE MARBLE, b. at

---

[479] *Essex County, MA: Probate File Papers, 1638-1881.* Probate of Peter Parker, 8 Apr 1795, Case number 20543.

Generation Four

Andover, 29 Jul 1744 daughter of Job and Phebe (Barker) Marble; Phebe d. 1 Oct 1805.

 v HANNAH PARKER, b. 2 Apr 1743; d. 26 Jan 1745/6.

731) vi ROBERT PARKER, b. 2 Mar 1744/5; d. at Blue Hill, 12 Feb 1818; m. 29 Nov 1773, RUTH WOOD, b. at Beverly, 18 Dec 1753 daughter of Joseph and Mary (Haskell) Wood; Ruth d. 20 Jan 1825.

732) vii HANNAH PARKER, b. 4 Apr 1747; d. about 1782; m. at Pelham, NH, 23 May 1775,[480] HENRY BUTLER ELWELL, b. at Gloucester, 27 Mar 1746 son of William and Elizabeth (Butler) Elwell.

733) viii ISAAC PARKER, b. 29 Aug 1749; d. 9 Oct 1814; m. a cousin, MARY "POLLY" PARKER, b. about 1761 (based on age at time of death) whose parents have not been fully verified; Mary d. at Andover 19 Nov 1834. It is also possible that Polly's maiden name is not Parker.

734) ix LYDEA PARKER, b. 24 Apr 1752; d. at Lowell, MA, 29 Mar 1849; m. at Dracut, 29 Oct 1774, HEZEKIAH COBURN, b. 29 Mar 1748 son of Samuel and Mary (Bradstreet) Coburn; Hezekiah d. at Dracut, 13 Mar 1816.

 x SIMEON PARKER, b. 3 May 1754; Simeon likely married, but there are several Simeon Parkers of similar age in Massachusetts at this time and it is not clear yet where he settled. He does not seem to have gone to Blue Hill with his brothers. There is a Simeon

---

[480] Ancestry.com, New Hampshire, Marriage Records Index, 1637-1947

Parker that married Mary Pratt, but that does not seem to be this Simeon.

xi   PHEBE PARKER, b. 14 Nov 1757; d. 11 Jan 1759.

Mary Stevens Ingalls[3], Sarah Abbott Stevens[2], George[1]

179)   JAMES INGALLS *(Mary Stevens Ingalls[3], Sarah Abbott Stevens[2], George[1])*, b. 20 Aug 1720 son of James and Mary (Stevens) Ingalls; d. at Methuen 8 May 1804; m. 6 Dec 1744, MARY FRYE, b. about 1725 whose parentage is not yet proved; Mary d. 6 Apr 1797

James Ingalls's will, written 5 April 1797, is of some interest as it omits the standard "In the name of god, amen" and the associated commending of his soul to god to start the will. He begins his will "... being advanced in years, have no means to flatter myself with long life, therefore think it my duty to discharge my mind of all temporal concerns, as far as the domestic and social duties of life which I owe my family and which the public will admit... I may with as little interruption as possible spend the remainder of my days in preparation for that further state to which I am hastening." He makes bequests to the following persons: daughter Mary Swan wife of Lieutenant Joshua Swan; daughter Hannah Hall the wife of Lieutenant Benjamin Hall; daughter Dorcas Swan the wife of Captain Caleb Swan; daughter Sarah Foster the wife of John Foster; daughter Lydia Ingalls who receives use of one room in the house for as long as she remains unmarried; to the children and heirs of his daughter Deborah Hibbard who is deceased namely Daniel Hibbard, Jr., Joshua Ingalls Hibbard, and Deborah Hibbard; son Charles Ingalls; and son Alfred receives the bulk of the estate including all the lands in Andover. Alfred is also executor of the estate.[481]

---

[481] *Essex County, MA: Probate File Papers, 1638-1881.* Probate of James Ingalls, 5 Jun 1804, Case number 14514.

Generation Four

James Ingalls and Mary Frye had twelve children. The first six children were born at Andover and the youngest six children were born at Methuen.

735) i MARY INGALLS, b. 1 Dec 1745; d. in NH, 3 Jul 1811; m. 10 Oct 1765, her third cousin once removed, JOSHUA SWAN, b. at Methuen, 6 Aug 1745 son of Timothy and Mary (Abbott) Swan. Joshua Swan's mother Mary Abbott is from the Rowley Abbott line.

ii JAMES INGALLS, b. Aug 1747; d. 28 May 1748.

736) iii HANNAH INGALLS, b. 27 Dec 1748; d. 10 Jul 1811; m. 18 Nov 1765, BENJAMIN HALL; Benjamin d. at Gloversville, NY, 24 Dec 1830.

737) iv DORCAS INGALLS, b. 18 Feb 1750/1; d. at Methuen, 16 Jul 1821; m. 30 Sep 1777, her third cousin once removed, CALEB SWAN, b. 4 Oct 1749 son of Timothy and Mary (Abbott) Swan.

738) v DEBORAH INGALLS, b. 28 May 1753; d. 20 Sep 1779; m. 24 Mar 1773, DANIEL HIBBARD, b. at Methuen, 15 Sep 1748 son of Ebenezer and Abigail (Whittier) Hibbard. Daniel m. 2nd, Sarah Lovejoy.

vi JAMES INGALLS, b. 19 Jun 1755; d. 8 Jul 1775. James was wounded at the Battle of Bunker Hill and died from his wounds.

vii JOSHUA INGALLS, b. 30 Jul 1757; d. 12 May 1759.

viii JOSHUA INGALLS, b. 10 Aug 1759; d. 5 Apr 1761.

739) ix SARAH INGALLS, b. 5 Oct 1761; d. at Boxford, 25 Jul 1849; m. 25 Nov 1788, JOHN FOSTER, b. at

740) x CHARLES INGALLS, b. 12 Oct 1763; d. at Greenwich, NY, 2 Sep 1812; m. CYNTHIA RUSSELL, b. 14 Mar 1769 daughter of Thomas and Mary (Patterson) Russell; d. 17 Mar 1801.

741) xi ALFRED INGALLS, b. 16 Oct 1765; d. at Methuen, 15 Sep 1843; m. 1st, 9 Nov 1790, ABIGAIL "NABBY" PAGE, b. 1768 *possibly* daughter of Daniel Page; Nabby d. 29 Nov 1795. Alfred m. 2nd, 24 Jul 1797, MARY CARLETON who was "of Bradford."

742) xii LYDIA INGALLS, b. 7 Dec 1767; d. at Corinth, VT, 7 Nov 1810; m. at Corinth, 28 Jan 1806, as his second wife, DAVID MCKEEN, b. at Londonderry, NH, 12 Jun 1750 son of James and Elizabeth (Dinsmore) McKeen; David d. 2 Dec 1824. David's first marriage was to Margaret McPherson.

180) EPHRAIM INGALLS *(Mary Stevens Ingalls³, Sarah Abbott Stevens², George¹)*, b. 6 Nov 1725 son of James and Mary (Stevens) Ingalls; d. at Pomfret 16 May 1805; m. 19 Dec 1751, MARY SHARP, b. at Pomfret, b. 10 Jul 1733 daughter of John and Dorcas (Davis) Sharp; Mary d. 16 Feb 1809.

Ephraim Ingalls owned a tavern on the common in Pomfret and kept a public house.[482]

Ephraim Ingalls wrote his will 13 January 1795 and it was presented to the probate court 10 June 1805. In his will, Ephraim provides his well-beloved wife Mary improvements on one-third of the real estate during her natural life and one-third of the personal estate to be at her disposal. There are also other provisions for her

---

[482] Griggs, *Early Homesteads of Pomfret and Hampton*

care and support. Son Simeon receives £5 which together with the part of the estate he has already received constitutes his full portion. Daughter Deborah Allyn receives £25 with what she has already received constitutes her full portion. Daughter Sarah Grosvenor receives £15 to complete her portion. Daughter Mary Osgood receives £5 to complete her portion. Son Edmund receives £70 which is his full portion of the estate. Son Ephraim receives the remaining two-thirds of the real estate and stock animals as well as the carpentry and farming tools. It is Ephraim's responsibility to make the payments to his brothers and sisters per the schedule set out in the will. His wearing apparel is divided among sons Simeon, Edmund, and Ephraim. Ephraim is named sole executor. The inventory of the estate had a total value of $2,641.19 with $2,400 of that being the value of 80 acres of property with buildings.[483]

Ephraim Ingalls and Mary Sharp had eleven children whose births are recorded at Pomfret. Five of the children died in childhood, three of them in a two-week period in October 1764.

      i   MARY INGALLS, b. 5 Dec 1752; d. 29 Oct 1764

743) ii   SIMEON INGALLS, b. 28 May 1754; d. at Hartwick, NY, 23 May 1827; m. 1st, OLIVE GROSVENOR, b. 17 May 1760 daughter of Joshua and Esther (Payson) Grosvenor; Olive d. 17 Apr 1782. Simeon m. 2nd, EUNICE WHEELER, b. 1 Nov 1756 daughter of Benjamin and Prudence (Huet) Wheeler; Eunice d. 5 Oct 1807. Simeon m. 3rd, 8 Mar 1808, RACHEL HARRIS.

     iii   DORCAS INGALLS, b. 9 Nov 1755; d. 25 Oct 1764.

---

[483] *Connecticut Wills and Probate, 1609-1999*, Will of Ephraim Ingalls, Windham, 13 Jan 1795.

	iv	DEBORAH INGALLS, b. 28 Aug 1757; d. at Walpole, NH, 7 Nov 1811;[484] m. 14 Dec 1780, General AMASA ALLEN, b. at Pomfret, 7 Apr 1752[485] son of Peter and Elizabeth (Craft) Allen; Amasa d. at Walpole, NH, 12 Jul 1821. Deborah and Amasa did not have children.
	v	RHODA INGALLS, b. 28 Nov 1759; d. 15 Oct 1764.
744)	vi	SARAH INGALLS, b. 17 Feb 1762; d. 10 Mar 1807; m. 10 Feb 1784, JOSHUA GROSVENOR, b. 24 Apr 1758 son of Joshua and Esther (Payson) Grosvenor; Joshua d. 2 Apr 1838.
745)	vii	EPHRAIM INGALLS, b. 6 Sep 1764; d. at Pomfret, 12 Feb 1831; m. 26 Apr 1801, LUCY GOODELL, b. at Pomfret, 22 Apr 1779 daughter of Amasa and Lucy(-) Goodell;[486] Lucy d. 22 Apr 1859. Several sources give the name of Lucy's mother as Lydia Chandler, and that may be correct, but the birth transcription for Lucy gives her mother's name as Lucy.
746)	viii	MOLLY INGALLS, b. 27 Jan 1766; m. 1st, MOSES OSGOOD, b. 28 Nov 1766 son of Zachariah and Rachel (Kenne) Osgood; Moses d. about 1801. Molly m. 2nd, Mr. Wilson.
	ix	CHARLES INGALLS, b. 16 Sep 1768; d. 21 Nov 1772
747)	x	EDMUND INGALLS, b. 7 Sep 1770; d. at Cavendish, VT, 23 Dec 1850; m. 16 Apr 1801,[487] DOROTHY WHITE, b. about 1774 in Massachusetts, parents not yet determined; Dorothy d. after 1850 (she was living

---

[484] New Hampshire, Death and Disinterment Records, 1754-1947
[485] The transcription in the Barbour Collection has a mistyping of the birth date as 7 Apr 1852.
[486] The 1814 will of Amasa Goodell includes a bequest to his daughters Lucy Ingalls.
[487] *Vermont, Vital Records, 1720-1908.*

xi   DORCAS INGALLS, b. 3 Apr 1772; d. 6 Dec 1774.

181)   ZEBADIAH INGALLS *(Mary Stevens Ingalls³, Sarah Abbott Stevens², George¹)*, b. 3 Nov 1729 son of James and Mary (Stevens) Ingalls; d. at Pomfret, 11 Jun 1800; m. 20 Feb 1755, ESTHER GOODELL, b. at Pomfret, 19 May 1735 daughter of Zachariah and Hannah (Cheney) Goodell; Esther d. 30 Sep 1778.

Zebadiah Ingalls lived on his father's homestead and after 1750 he built the FitzHenry Paine House in Pomfret. The family lived in this home until after the Revolution. Zebadiah then sold this property to his son Lemuel and Zebadiah returned to the family homestead. Zebadiah also had a blacksmith shop.[488]

Captain Zebadiah Ingalls was the leader of a militia company and on 22 April 1775 led his company in the march to Lexington.

Zebadiah Ingalls wrote his will 11 May 1799. He includes bequests to his beloved wife (who is not named), son Lemuel receives all the real estate, son James has already received his portion, son Oliver receives $200, daughter Esther Abbott receives $17, daughter Aly Holbrook receives $17, daughter Mary Williams receives $35, and daughter Allethiah Ingalls receives $117.[489]

There are birth records for 13 children of Zebadiah and Esther at Pomfret.

---

[488] Griggs, *Early Homesteads of Pomfret and Hampton*
[489] *Connecticut Wills and Probate, 1609-1999*, Probate of Zebadiah Ingalls, Hartford, 1800, Case number 2295.

748) i LEMUEL INGALLS, b. 6 Dec 1755; d. at Pomfret, 17 Nov 1839; m. 24 Aug 1780, DOROTHY SUMMER, b. 20 Aug 1759 daughter of Samuel and Dorothy (Williams) Summer; Dorothy d. 10 Mar 1851.

ii ZEBADIAH INGALLS, b. 19 Apr 1757; d. 17 Sep 1779. Zebadiah served in the Revolutionary War.

iii SILVANIUS INGALLS, b. 27 Jan 1759; d. 25 Sep 1776.

749) iv JAMES INGALLS, b. 31 Dec 1760; d. at Middlefield, NY, 19 Mar 1813; m. at Brooklyn, CT, 2 Feb 1786, SARAH WILLIAMS, b. at Pomfret, 12 May 1760 daughter of Thomas and Meriam (Wolcott) Williams; Sarah d. 27 Jan 1831.

603) v ESTHER INGALLS, b. 26 Nov 1762; d. at Providence, RI, 4 Feb 1851; m. 28 Jun 1781, her third cousin, STEPHEN ABBOTT, b. at Pomfret, 20 Oct 1757 son of Nathan and Eunice (Marsh) Abbott; Stephen d. at North Providence, RI, 24 Jul 1813. This is the same as Family #143, child vii.

vi ALICE INGALLS, b. 28 Oct 1764; d. at Woodstock, 8 Dec 1838; m. 13 Feb 1783, CALVIN HOLBROOK, b. at Pomfret, 10 Aug 1758 son of Ebenezer and Mary (Osgood) Holbrook; Calvin d. 4 Aug 1845. Alice and Calvin did not have children, at least not children for whom there is a record or who lived to adulthood. Calvin's will makes bequests to his brothers and sisters and their heirs.

vii OLIVE INGALLS, b. 20 Oct 1766; d. 13 Feb (year not given).

750) viii MARY "MOLLY" INGALLS, b. 31 Jul 1768; d. at Danielson, CT, 21 Apr 1839; m. 2 Dec 1790, ELEAZER WILLIAMS, b. at Pomfret, 29 Nov 1764

Generation Four 331

751) ix OLIVER INGALLS, b. 7 Apr 1770; d. at Pomfret, 10 Apr 1815; m. Dec 1803, his niece,[490] BETSEY ABBOTT, b. likely at Providence, 4 May 1786 daughter of Stephen and Esther (Ingalls) Abbott; Betsey d. 17 Feb 1839 (will written at Providence, RI, 7 Feb 1839).

x OLIVE INGALLS, b. 16 May 1772; no further record and she is not living at the time of her father's will. See the note for Chloe below.

xi ALLETHIAH INGALLS, b. 15 Mar 1774; unmarried at the time of her father's will in 1799.

xii JOHN INGALLS, b. 26 Aug 1776; d. 23 Jan 1777.

xiii CHLOE INGALLS; there is not a birth record, just a death record that has just 26 Apr 17__. The transcription for this record suggests that the name is also torn, and Chloe seems to be a best guess for the name. It is possible that this is the death record for the daughter Olive for whom there is no further record after her birth.

son of Samuel and Susannah (Danielson) Williams; Eleazer d. 16 Sep 1841.

182) ABIAH INGALLS *(Mary Stevens Ingalls³, Sarah Abbott Stevens², George¹)*, b. 19 Oct 1731 daughter of James and Mary

---

[490] Although the relationship between Betsey and her husband is unusual, it seems to be true. Betsey Abbott Ingalls's gravestone (buried in Swan Point Cemetery in Providence) includes an inscription that she is the wife of Oliver and the daughter of Colonel Stephen Abbott and this makes Betsey the niece of her husband Oliver Ingalls. Oliver Ingalls was the brother of Esther Ingalls who married Colonel Stephen Abbott.

(Stevens) Ingalls; d. likely at Palmer or Monson, MA; m. 16 Mar 1753, NATHANIEL ROGERS, b. about 1730 of not yet established origins but *possibly* the son of Nathaniel and Mary (Haggit) Rogers and born at Billerica; d. probably about 1786, but no records were located.[491]

The children of this family should be considered preliminary at least the youngest four children. There are records for the oldest three children born at Pomfret and for the next three children born at Monson. There is some at least circumstantial evidence for placing the remaining four children in this family.

752) i NATHANIEL ROGERS, b. at Pomfret, 18 Nov 1755; d. at Salem, CT, 12 Feb 1799; m. 23 Sep 1792, SARAH TUBBS. There is another Nathaniel Rogers in Connecticut who was born in 1753 (son of Joseph) and he is also suggested as the husband of Sarah Tubbs. However, the records for Nathaniel Rogers's marriage, death, etc. specify that he is Nathaniel Rogers, Jr. And although it is possible that the "Jr." does not designate a father-son, I believe that it does in this case.

ii MOLLY ROGERS, b. at Pomfret, 6 Oct 1757.

iii ELIAS ROGERS, b. at Pomfret, 11 Aug 1759.

753) iv ABISHAI ROGERS, b. at Monson, 1 Feb 1762; d. at Sheldon, NY, 18 Jul 1831; m. 1st, Feb 1786, SARAH HAWKS who d. at Hawley, 1790; m. 2nd, 15 Mar 1792, ELIZABETH RUDD, b. 28 Jun 1765 daughter of Nathaniel and Alice (Kingsley) Rudd; Elizabeth d. 18 Jun 1848.

---

[491] This is the date used by the SAR and the DAR as his approximated death, although it is not clear why this date was chosen.

Generation Four

754) v SIMEON ROGERS, b. at Monson, 1 Feb 1762; d. at Whitestown, NY, 18 Jun 1848; m. ANNA (-), b. 1765 and d. 1849.[492]

755) vi JAMES AUGUSTUS ROGERS, b. at Monson, 2 May 1765; d. at Rockport, OH, 5 Aug 1837; m. 17 Nov 1790, DOROTHY LEONARD, b. at Rutland, MA, 6 Apr 1759 daughter of Andrew and Hannah (Pierce) Leonard; Dorothy d. at Pownal, VT, 5 Jun 1796. James m. 2nd, JEMIMA ROOT.

vii ABIAH ROGERS who perhaps married GIDEON GRAVES 3 Oct 1786 at Palmer. Gideon was b. at Palmer, 25 Aug 1758 son of Daniel and Joanna (-) Graves. Abiah the wife of Gideon died about 1787 and no children are known from this marriage. Gideon then married Hannah Dake.

756) viii DEBORAH ROGERS; m. about 1790, her third cousin once removed (and George Abbott descendant), WILLIAM FARNSWORTH, b. 15 Nov 1766 son of William and Hephzibah (Chandler) Farnsworth. The children of this couple include Oren Rogers Farnsworth and James Ingalls Farnsworth.

757) ix OREN ROGERS, b. at Monson about 1770; d. at Charlemont, MA, 15 Oct 1853; m. 23 Mar 1797, ABY BIRGE, b. at Deerfield, 22 Aug 1774 daughter of John and Esther (Pierce) Birge.

758) x MOSES ROGERS is also a possibility of a child in this family; he died 1 Feb 1808 with a child named Abishai. His wife was Mehitable Sears who was

---

[492] Information from SAR

born 21 Dec 1778 daughter of Rowland Sears. Moses Rogers was a mill keeper in Hawley, MA and died when he was crushed by the wheel when trying to remove ice from the wheel.

Mehitable Stevens Holt[3], Sarah Abbott Stevens[2], George[1]

183) EBENEZER HOLT *(Mehitable Stevens Holt[3], Sarah Abbott Stevens[2], George[1])*, b. 7 Sep 1730 son of Ebenezer and Mehitable (Stevens) Holt; d. at Mont Vernon, NH, Apr 1805;[493] m. 23 Sep 1752, LYDIA PEABODY, b. 5 Jul 1731 daughter of Moses and Sarah (Holt) Peabody; Lydia's date of death is not known.

Ebenezer Holt was a farmer in Mont Vernon. The History of the Town of Amherst, New Hampshire lists just two children for this family (p. 636). Only a birth record for daughter Rebecca was located. There is perhaps some mis-transcription with either the marriage or the birth record, as the records give the date of birth of the oldest child as three weeks after the marriage. But perhaps they are correct.

759) i REBECCA HOLT, b. at Amherst, NH, 7 Sep 1752; m. 14 Mar 1782, JONATHAN LAMSON, b. at Amherst, 10 Aug 1756 son of Jonathan and Mehitable (Holt) Lamson. Jonathan d. 4 Feb 1842.[494] I have not been able to locate the origins of Mehitable Holt which is needed to know how Rebecca and Jonathan might be related.

ii SARAH HOLT, b. at Amherst, 1757; m. 25 May 1786, MOSES PEABODY, b. about 1755; Moses d. about 1842 at Mont Vernon (probate of estate 1842). Sarah

---

[493] Secomb, *History of the Town of Amherst*
[494] Index to Selected Final Payment Vouchers, 1818-1864 4 Feb 1842, fold3.com

and Moses do not seem to have any children, at least not any children that survived childhood. In his will, Moses mentions only wife Sarah.[495]

184) MEHITABLE HOLT *(Mehitable Stevens Holt[3], Sarah Abbott Stevens[2], George[1])*, b. 3 Sep 1733 daughter of Ebenezer and Mehitable (Stevens) Holt; d. 4 Mar 1767; m. 2 Jan 1755, her first cousin JAMES HOLT, b. 18 Feb 1732/3 son of Obadiah and Rebecca (Farnum) Holt. James m. 2nd the widow Mary McEntire whose identity has not been found.

There is just one child recorded at Andover for Mehitable and James. The Holt genealogy[496] lists two other children for James, but those children are the children of James Holt (listed as James 3rd in the records) and Dorothy Lovejoy. As that James Holt and Dorothy Lovejoy married seven years before the death of Mehitable, that cannot be the same James. The Holt genealogy also states that the son Jesse married Molly and relocated to Tewksbury. However, that Jesse (who married Mary *Clark* Gray widow of Moses Gray[497] in 1781 at Tewksbury) has a birth year of about 1738 based on age at time of death (age 79 in 1817), so that does not seem to be this Jesse. Of course, the death transcription could be incorrect. Also, Mary Clark Gray who is recorded as marrying Jesse Holt was baptized in 1745 so perhaps a little old for the Jesse who is the son of Mehitable and James. Alternatively, there is a completely different Molly who married Jesse but there are no records to support that.

    i   JESSE HOLT, b. at Andover, 8 Oct 1755. Nothing further is known by me.

---

[495] *New Hampshire, Wills and Probate Records, 1643-1982*, Probate Records, 1771-1921.
[496] Durrie, *Genealogical History of the Holt Family*, p 58
[497] Essex Institute Historical Collections, 1913, p 59

185) **EZEKIEL HOLT** *(Mehitable Stevens Holt³, Sarah Abbott Stevens², George¹)* (twin), b. 7 Jul 1741 son of Ebenezer and Mehitable (Stevens) Holt; d. at Mont Vernon, NH date unknown;[498] m. by 1772, MARY STEWART, b. at Amherst, NH, 2 Sep 1749 daughter of Samuel and Sarah (Tarbell) Stewart.

Five children have been located for this family all born at Amherst, New Hampshire. The family was then in Mont Vernon. No probate record was located. A marriage was found for just one of the children.

	i	ELIZABETH HOLT, b. 8 Jul 1773
	ii	MARY HOLT, b. 11 Dec 1775
	iii	SARAH HOLT, b. 10 Sep 1780
760)	iv	EZEKIEL HOLT, b. 19 Aug 1782; d. at Marshfield, VT, 4 Aug 1845; m. 13 Dec 1810, ABIGAIL PIKE, b. at East Montpelier, VT, 17 Sep 1791; Abigail d. 24 Dec 1873.
	v	DAVID HOLT, b. 27 Feb 1792

186) **REUBEN HOLT** *(Mehitable Stevens Holt³, Sarah Abbott Stevens², George¹)*, b. 27 Jun 1744 son of Ebenezer and Mehitable (Stevens) Holt; d. at Landgrove, VT 2 Mar 1836;[499] m. at Amherst, NH, 6 Feb 1772, LYDIA SMALL, b. Mar 1745[500] daughter of William and Sarah (Clark) Small; Lydia d. at Amherst, 9 Mar 1795.

Reuben Holt and Lydia Small had six children born at Amherst, New Hampshire. Following the death of Lydia, Reuben

---

[498] Smith, *History of Mont Vernon*, p 78. Ezekiel Holt was a resident of Mont Vernon in 1804.
[499] *Vermont, Vital Records, 1720-1908* (Provo, UT, USA: Ancestry.com Operations, Inc., 2013).
[500] Lydia was baptized at Salem but may have been born at Andover.

relocated to Landgrove, Vermont where he was an early settler. His son Reuben accompanied him and served as the town clerk in Landgrove for many years.[501]

761) i SARAH HOLT, b. 10 Nov 1772; d. 20 Oct 1851; m. 16 Nov 1797, STEPHEN TUTTLE, b. 10 Mar 1772 son of Jotham and Molly (Worthley) Tuttle; Stephen d. 1854.

762) ii REUBEN HOLT, b. 11 Feb 1775; d. at Landgrove, VT, 25 Nov 1836; m. 1st, 27 Dec 1798, JUDITH HILL, b. at Amherst, 31 Jan 1779; Judith d. at Landgrove, 2 Nov 1813. Reuben m. 2nd, 3 Aug 1817, SIBYL PIPER, b. at Sharon, NH, 28 Jun 1793 daughter of Thomas and Judith (Powers) Piper.

763) iii RACHEL HOLT, b. 2 Sep 1776; d. at Weston, VT, 4 Mar 1860; m. 30 Aug 1797, TIMOTHY HILL, b. about 1776 in Vermont;[502] Timothy d. at Weston after 1850.

iv EBENEZER HOLT, b. 2 Jul 1778

v LYDIA HOLT, b. 19 Apr 1781

vi WILLIAM HOLT, b. 15 May 1783; d. at Landgrove, VT, 29 Mar 1811.

Deborah Stevens Carleton[3], Sarah Abbott Stevens[2], George[1]

187) SAMUEL CARLETON (*Deborah Stevens Carleton[3], Sarah Abbott Stevens[2], George[1]*), b. 11 Aug 1731 son of Samuel and Deborah

---

[501] American Series of Popular Biographies, *Biographical Sketches Massachusetts*, p 683

[502] Based on information from the 1850 U.S. Census

(Stevens) Carleton; d. at Salem, 25 Mar 1804; m. 27 Oct 1754, EUNICE HUNT, b. 25 Oct 1730 daughter of William and Eunice (Bowditch) Hunt; Eunice d. at Salem, 12 Aug 1827.

Samuel Carleton was an officer in the continental army during the Revolutionary War including service at Valley Forge. He was also a member of the Massachusetts General Court. He was a master mariner and member of the Masons.[503]

The 1827 probate record for Eunice Hunt Carleton includes the following heirs-at-law who sign approving James Barr (husband of daughter Eunice) as administrator of the estate: John Carleton, Deborah Helme, Hannah Carleton, Elizabeth Carleton, and Elisabeth Carleton, Jr. The value of the estate was $800 in real estate and $32.49 for her personal estate.[504] Elizabeth Carleton, Jr. in the probate documents in the daughter of Eunice's son Benjamin who died in 1820.

Samuel Carleton and Eunice Hunt had eight children whose births are recorded at Salem.

764) i EUNICE CARLETON, b. 22 Dec 1754; d. at Salem, Mar 1838; m. 23 Dec 1779, JAMES BARR, b. at Salem, 1755 son of James and Mary (Ropes) Barr; James d. 19 Jan 1848.

ii SAMUEL CARLETON, b. 6 May 1757; no further clear record. It is possible that he married, but if so he did not have children as none are listed as heirs in either the estate of his mother or the will of his brother John who left his estate to siblings, nieces,

---

[503] *Massachusetts: Grand Lodge of Masons Membership Cards, 1733-1990.* Online database. *AmericanAncestors.org.* New England Historic Genealogical Society, 2010. (From records held by the Grand Lodge of Ancient Free and Accepted Masons of Massachusetts.)

[504] *Essex County, MA: Probate File Papers, 1638-1881.* Probate of Eunice Carleton, 2 Oct 1827, Case number 4642.

and nephews. It is possible that Samuel died before adulthood.

765) iii DEBORAH CARLETON, b. 17 Dec 1759; d. at Salem, Apr 1831; m. 5 Oct 1783, HUGH HELME whose origins are unknown; Hugh d. 1792 (probate of estate 14 July 1792).

iv HANNAH CARLETON, b. 5 Sep 1762; d. 7 Sep 1842. Hannah did not marry.

766) v BENJAMIN CARLETON, b. 5 Jun 1765; d. 8 Sep 1820; m. 25 Mar 1787, his first cousin, ELIZABETH HOLMAN, b. 1762 daughter of Samuel and Ruth (Hunt) Holman; Elizabeth d. 25 Dec 1801.

vi MARY CARLETON, b. 29 Aug 1767; d. 18 Dec 1814. Mary did not marry.

vii JOHN CARLETON, b. 6 Nov 1770; d. at Philadelphia, 12 Aug 1847. He was a U.S. naval officer and sailing master. His will has bequests to his sisters, nieces, and nephew.

viii ELIZABETH CARLETON, b. 6 May 1773; d. after 1855 (still living at the 1855 Massachusetts Census when her niece Elizabeth, the daughter of Benjamin, was living with her).

188) HANNAH CARLETON *(Deborah Stevens Carleton³, Sarah Abbott Stevens², George¹)*, b. 26 Jul 1734 daughter of Samuel and Deborah (Stevens) Carleton; d. 14 May 1824; m. 30 Mar 1756, JACOB CROWNINSHIELD, b. 9 Jan 1732/3 son of John and Anstus (Williams) Crowninshield; Jacob was a mariner who died on a passage from Jamaica in Nov 1774.

Captain Jacob Crowninshield was a member of the renowned Crowninshield mariner family. Jacob was lost at sea. He did not leave a will and his estate entered probate 4 January 1775. Hannah Crowninshield was administrator of the estate. The estate was declared insolvent and it was ordered to be sold 17 February 1790. The widow's dower had been set out to Hannah but was returned to the estate for sale in 1790, although she retained her right to live in a portion of the house. The estate included two Negros who claimed and took their freedom.[505]

Hannah Carleton Crowninshield's will was written 12 June 1810 and it was recorded 6 July 1824. Hannah's daughter Hannah and son Benjamin were executors of the estate. "Whereas the providence of God has blessed with prosperity my beloved son Benjamin Crowninshield, and he has no need of my assistance, I do will and bequeath to my only daughter, Hanna Crowninshield, the companion and friend of my widowhood, in reward for her faithful duty, all the property of every name..." Hannah did add a codicil in which "being disposed to express my fondest regards to my son Benjamin, I do will and bequeath to my said son Benjamin, the family tankard, as the best testimony of my affection."[506]

Hannah Carleton and Jacob Crowninshield lived in half of what is now known as the Crowninshield-Bentley house in Salem. This house was built about 1727 most likely by Jacob's grandfather. After Jacob's death, Hannah and her daughter lived in the East half of the house and supported themselves by taking in boarders. The Reverend William Bentley was one of the boarders from 1791 to 1819, and he kept a diary of the daily goings on in Salem. Hannah's son Benjamin inherited the West half of the house. Benjamin was quite successful and made substantial improvements to his half. In

---

[505] *Essex County, MA: Probate File Papers, 1638-1881.* Probate of Jacob Crowninshield, 4 Jan 1775, Case number 6677.
[506] *Essex County, MA: Probate File Papers, 1638-1881.* Probate of Hannah Crowninshield, 6 Jul 1824, Case number 6675.

1795, Benjamin's half was valued at $1,350 while his mother's half had a value of $250.[507]

There is record evidence for three children of Hannah Carleton and Jacob Crowninshield.

767) i BENJAMIN CROWNINSHIELD, b. 15 Feb 1758; d. at Salem, 1836; m. 9 Nov 1780, MARY LAMBERT, b. at Salem, Nov 1760 daughter of Joseph and Mary (Foote) Lambert;[508] Mary d. at Charlestown, 21 Jun 1851.

ii JOHN CROWNINSHIELD, b. 1762; d. at Salem, 19 Feb 1786; m. SARAH HATHORNE, b. about 1761 daughter of Daniel and Rachel (Phelps) Hathorne; Sarah d. 18 Jan 1829. John and Sarah do not seem to have had children. In her 1829 will, Sarah left her estate to her sister Ruth Hathorne. *John, m., mate with Capt. Lambert, s. wid. Hannah [s. Jacob and Hannah, h. Sarah (Hathorne)], dysentery, Feb. 19, 1786, a. 24 y. CR4.*

iii HANNAH CROWNINSHIELD, b. 1764; d. at Salem, Apr 1832. Hannah did not marry.

189) MARY CARLETON *(Deborah Stevens Carleton³, Sarah Abbott Stevens², George¹)*, b. about 1738 daughter of Samuel and Deborah (Stevens) Carleton; d. 24 Dec 1805; m. 12 Jul 1759, JOHN BOWDITCH, b. 3 Apr 1732 son of Ebenezer and Mary (Turner)

---

[507] Crowninshield-Bentley House, Peabody Essex Museum, 2006. http://teh.salemstate.edu/educatorsguide/pages/Federal/CBHouse.pdf

[508] Belknap, *The Lambert Family of Salem, Massachusetts*, p 30

Bowditch; John was a mariner and died at sea before 1797 and perhaps in 1793.

A son in this family, John Bowditch, died in April 1793 and there is an associated probate record for the son. There is not a death record or probate record for the father. It is certainly possible that father and son died in the same marine disaster and the elder John is deceased before 1797 when his widow wrote her will.

Mary Carleton Bowditch wrote her will 22 November 1797. She divided her wearing apparel equally among her three daughters namely Mary Hunt, Hannah Ingersoll, and Deborah Moriarty. The remainder of her personal estate is to be sold. She also orders that as soon as convenient that the one-fourth part of her pew in the East Meeting House and one-fourth of a plot of land on Cromwell Street (that she owns with other heirs) be sold. She bequeaths to her daughter Deborah Moriarty the southern part of her real estate where her house now stands which is on the west side of Union Street in Salem. The northern half of her real estate where her own house stands is to be let out along with the house; the rents are to be accumulated and draw interest and the interest reinvested until her two grandchildren, Nancy Bowditch and Polly Bowditch, are at lawful age or the age of marriage. Nancy and Polly will each receive one-fifth part of the accumulation of the value of the estate. Her three daughters also each receive one-fifth of that amount. Her daughters Mary Hunt and Deborah Moriarty are named executors.[509] Granddaughter Nancy Bowditch is the daughter of son Samuel who died in 1791 and Polly Bowditch is the daughter of son John who died in 1793.

There are records for seven children born at Salem.

768) i MARY BOWDITCH, b. Jun 1760; d. at Salem, 18 Mar 1829; m. 7 Apr 1782, as his second wife, LEWIS

---

[509] *Massachusetts Wills and Probate Records 1635-1991,* Essex, Probate Record, Mary Bowditch; will and probate (15 Jan 1806), Case 2889.

HUNT, b. 23 Mar 1746 son of William and Eunice Bowditch Hunt; Lewis d. 22 Oct 1797.

769) ii HANNAH BOWDITCH, b. Dec 1761; d. at Salem, 14 Dec 1825; m. 21 Jul 1792, as his second wife, JOHN INGERSOLL, b. Jun 1756 son of Nathaniel and Bethiah (Gardner) Ingersoll; John d. 12 Feb 1840.

770) iii JOHN BOWDITCH, b. Mar 1764; d. at sea, Apr 1793; m. 11 Mar 1791, POLLY COOK, b. about 1760 whose identity is uncertain; Polly d. at Salem 28 Apr 1844.

771) iv DEBORAH BOWDITCH, b. Oct 1767; d. at Salem, 4 Jul 1823; m. 31 Oct 1782, THOMAS MORIARTY who is of uncertain origin; Thomas likely d. in early 1790 (Deborah Moriarty is a head of family in Salem in the 1790 U.S. Census) although other sources give his death as 1797. The estate of Thomas Moriarty was probated 8 Aug 1790. Deborah Moriarty was administrator of the estate.

772) v SAMUEL BOWDITCH, b. May 1769; d. at sea, 21 Mar 1791; m. 15 Aug 1790; ANNA "NANCY" WELMAN, baptized 2 Sep 1770 daughter of Samuel and Mary (Kempton) Welman. Nancy m. 2nd, William Richardson (or Richardson Russell, both names are given on the transcription of the marriage record).

vi SARAH BOWDITCH, b. May 1770; no further record; not living at the time of her mother's will.

vii EBENEZER BOWDITCH, b. Oct 1771; no further record and not living at the time of his mother's will.

190) WILLIAM CARLETON *(Deborah Stevens Carleton³, Sarah Abbott Stevens², George¹)*, b. 8 Apr 1744 son of Samuel and Deborah (Stevens) Carleton; d. Jun 1791 while on a trip to Barbados; m. 1st, (-) Palfrey who died before 1777. m. 2nd, at Boston, 1 May 1777, MARY FARMER whose origins are uncertain but perhaps the daughter of Paul and Thankful (Sprague) Farmer of Boston.

There is little information available about this family. There is record evidence for one son of William, who seems to be from a first marriage to a woman with the last name of Palfrey. That son was the editor of the Salem Register and this information is given for the transcription of his death recorded at Salem: William [editor of the Salem Register. NR9], printer, s. William and —— (Palfry), h. —— —— (Cooke), fever, July 24, 1805, a. 34 y. CR4

773) i WILLIAM CARLETON, b. 1771 (based on age at time of death); d. at Salem, 24 Jul 1805; m. at Salem, 22 May 1796, ELIZABETH COOKE, b. about 1771 daughter of Charles and (Stone) Cooke; Elizabeth d. at Salem, 22 Aug 1805. Salem vital records: *Elizabeth, d. Charles and ____ (Stone) Cooke [proprietress of the Salem Register, G. R. 9.], wid. William, consumption. Aug. 25, 1805, a. 34 y.* William was the publisher of the *Salem Register* and his wife continued as publisher after his death until her death a few months later.

Section VI: The Grandchildren of Benjamin Abbott and Sarah Farnum

Benjamin³, Benjamin², George¹

125)   BENJAMIN ABBOTT *(Benjamin³, Benjamin², George¹)*, b. 21 Oct 1723 son of Benjamin and Mary (Carleton) Abbott; d. at Hollis, NH, 1771[510]; m. 2 Apr 1747, his second cousin, ELIZABETH ABBOTT *(George³, George², George¹)*, b. 5 Nov 1727 daughter of George and Mary (Phillips) Abbott; Elizabeth d. at Westford, about 1802. Same as Family #125 previously covered.

191)   DANIEL ABBOTT *(Benjamin³, Benjamin², George¹)*, b. 29 Dec 1725 son of Benjamin and Mary (Carleton) Abbott; d. Apr 1793;[511] m. 3 Apr 1756, LUCY PARKER, b. 5 Jun 1732 daughter of Thomas and Lydia (Richardson) Parker; the date of death of Lucy is not known.

The births of four children of Daniel Abbott and Lucy Parker are recorded at Dracut.

      i   DANIEL ABBOTT, b. 8 Sep 1757; d. at Claremont, NH, 10 Aug 1827. Daniel did not marry.

774)   ii   WILLIAM ABBOTT, b. 22 Feb 1760; d. likely at Bedford, NH; m. at Dracut, 13 Nov 1784, MARTHA "PATTY" COBURN, b. at Dracut about 1765.[512]

---

[510] New Hampshire, Death and Burials Record Index, 1654-1949, ancestry.com
[511] Abbot and Abbot, *Genealogical Record of Descendants*
[512] *The History of Dracut*, p 130, gives Patty's parents as Jacob and Lydia, but their daughter Patty died unmarried in 1802 (at least the death record gives her name as Patty Caburn).

775) iii SAMUEL ABBOTT, b. 16 Feb 1765; d. at Claremont, NH, 13 Apr 1840; m. by 1794, his first cousin, ELIZABETH COTTON, b. about 1768 daughter of Rev. Samuel and Elizabeth (Parker) Cotton of Claremont; Elizabeth d. at Claremont, NH, 7 Jun 1837.[513] The mothers of Samuel Abbott and Elizabeth Cotton were sisters.

776) iv JONATHAN ABBOTT, b. 20 Jan 1772; d. at Litchfield, NH, 4 Jul 1855; m. 1st, 21 Feb 1795, REBECCA MASSEY, b. 24 Mar 1772 daughter of Bartholomew and Mary (Fox) Massey; Rebecca d. 19 Dec 1795. Jonathan m. 2nd, 31 Dec 1800, DOLLY PARKER, b. 12 Sep 1779.[514] Dolly died at Litchfield, 19 Sep 1824.[515] After Dolly's death, Jonathan married a widow named Miranda who d. at Claremont 23 Feb 1854.

192) MARY ABBOTT (*Benjamin³, Benjamin², George¹*), b. 21 Jul 1732 daughter of Benjamin and Abigail (Abbott) Abbott; d. at Milford, NH, 9 Aug 1798; m. 13 Nov 1759, NEHEMIAH BARKER, b. at Methuen, 11 Feb 1734 son of Ebenezer and Abigail (Morse) Barker; Nehemiah d. 20 Jan 1810.

Nehemiah Barker was an inn owner in Methuen from 1777 to 1785. He also owned one-half of an iron works. This family

---

[513] Spofford, *Gravestone Records: From the Ancient Cemeteries in the Town of Claremont*, p 6, Elizabeth (Cotton) Abbott wife of Samuel, June 7, 1837, 69y; Samuel Abbott, April 13, 1840, 76y

[514] Family Tree Samplers, 1759-1894. Online database. AmericanAncestors.org. New England Historic Genealogical Society, 2013. (From the collection of Dan and Marty Campanelli.) Vital records for this family are contained in a sampler stitched by Dolly Parker.

[515] Findagrave.com memorial ID 167676976

relocated to Milford, New Hampshire about 1785.[516] Nehemiah Barker was listed as a taxpayer in Milford in 1794.[517]

Mary Abbott and Nehemiah Barker had five children, the oldest daughter's birth recorded at Andover and the youngest four at Methuen.

  i ABIGAIL BARKER, b. 24 Jan 1762; d. Jul 1793.[518]

777) ii JOEL BARKER, b. 11 Aug 1764; d. at Milford, 5 Dec 1832; m. at Milford, 24 Dec 1793, SARAH "SALLY" FOSTER, b. at Milford, 1774 daughter of Edward and Phebe (Pierce) Foster; Sarah d. 5 Sep 1820. Joel m. 2nd, 27 Nov 1821, CATHERINE LOVEJOY of Bow.[519]

  iii MARY BARKER, b. 19 Sep 1766; d. 23 Oct 1766.

778) iv MARY BARKER, b. 18 Dec 1767; d. at Hollis, 3 Sep 1824; m. at Hollis, 6 Jan 1791, JACOB SPAULDING, b. at Chelmsford, 13 Dec 1767 son of Benjamin and Mary (Spaulding) Spaulding. Jacob m. 2nd, Susanna Robertson. Jacob d. at Hollis, 14 May 1838.

779) v DORCAS BARKER, b. 4 Sep 1770; d. at Peterborough, NH, 25 Jul 1840; m. About 1792, MERRILL PIERCE, b. at Chelmsford, 29 Jan 1764 son of Benjamin and Elizabeth (Merrill) Pierce. Merrill Pierce was the brother of Phebe Pierce (born 1748) the mother of Sarah Foster who married Dorcas's older brother Joel.

---

[516] Charlotte Helen Abbott, Early Records of the Barker Family of Andover. https://www.mhl.org/sites/default/files/files/Abbott/Barker%20Family.pdf
[517] History of Hillsborough County, New Hampshire, published 1885
[518] Abbot and Abbot, *Genealogical Record of Descendants*, p 68
[519] Ramsdell, *History of Milford, Volume 1*, p 576

193) ABIGAIL ABBOTT *(Benjamin³, Benjamin², George¹)*, b. 13 Jan 1733/4 daughter of Benjamin and Abigail (Abbott) Abbott; d. 1 Feb 1807; m. 1 Jun 1758, her second cousin, once removed, JOHN ABBOT *(John⁴, John³, John², George¹)*, b. 12 Sep 1735 son of John and Phebe (Fiske) Abbot; John d. at Andover, 24 Apr 1818.

John Abbot lived on the farm that he inherited from his father. He was apparently successful as he was able to pay for the college educations of three of his sons.

The estate of John Abbot entered probate 20 October 1818. His will, written 8 March 1805, has bequests for the following persons: dear and beloved wife Abigail (her yearly maintenance includes 50 pounds of good pork and 100 pounds of good beef plus all the other things she needs), eldest and well beloved son John, second and well beloved son Ezra (gets all the land in the town of Wilton), third and well beloved son Benjamin, eldest and well beloved daughter Abigail, well beloved daughter Elizabeth, third and well beloved daughter Phebe, youngest, and well beloved son Abiel. He notes having paid for the educations of John, Benjamin, and Abiel and that is considered part of their portion. The books are divided among the seven children. Abigail is mentioned in the will; however, she died between the time of the will and her husband's death.[520]

The births of eight children of Abigail and John Abbott are recorded at Andover.

    i   JOHN ABBOT, b. 8 Apr 1759; d. at Andover, 2 Jul 1843. John Abbot attended Harvard and graduated in 1784. Ill health prevented his entering the ministry which was his original plan. He was a tutor at Harvard for five years and later was a cashier at a Portland bank. He then found a position at Bowdoin

---

[520] *Essex County, MA: Probate File Papers, 1638-1881.* Probate of John Abbot, 20 Oct 1818, Case number 74.

College. His tenure as a professor of classical languages was rather lackluster. He was described as awkward and absentminded and fell victim to practical jokes.[521] He was criticized for his lack of scholarship. He later assumed the position of librarian which better suited him. He continued in this position at Bowdoin until 1828. He resided in Waterford, Maine. He was living with his brother in Andover at the time of his death. John did not marry.

780) ii EZRA ABBOTT, b. 3 Dec 1760; d. at Andover, 22 Jan 1844; m. 24 Apr 1798, his third cousin once removed (and George Abbott descendant), HANNAH POOR, b. 15 Jan 1770 daughter of Daniel and Hannah (Frye) Poor; Hannah d. 11 Sep 1861.

781) iii BENJAMIN ABBOTT, b. 17 Sep 1762; d. at Exeter, NH, 25 Oct 1849; m. 1st, HANNAH TRACY EMERY, b. at Exeter, 7 Mar 1771 daughter of John and Margaret (Gookin) Emery; Hannah d. 6 Dec 1793. Benjamin m. 2nd, at Boston, 1 May 1798, MARY PERKINS, b. at Boston, 24 May 1769 daughter of James and Elizabeth (Peck) Perkins; Mary d. at Exeter, 13 Mar 1863. Hannah Tracy Emery was mentioned in the diary of John Quincy Adams having met her on a visit to a Mr. Carter. "Miss H. Emery was there, a young lady with a beautiful

---

[521] Hatch, *History of Bowdoin College*, pp 16-17

countenance, an elegant person, and (I am told) an amiable mind."[522]

782) iv ABIGAIL ABBOTT, b. 15 Sep 1764; d. at Portland, ME, 22 Apr 1841; m. at Andover, 21 Apr 1791, WILLIAM DOUGLAS, baptized at Rutland, MA, 29 Mar 1761 son of Robert and Elinor (Fales) Douglas; William d. at Portland, 4 Dec 1827.

783) v ELIZABETH ABBOTT, b. 2 Aug 1766; d. at Peterborough, NH, 6 Apr 1853; m. 19 May 1796, her first cousin, ABIEL ABBOT, b. at Wilton, 14 Dec 1765 son of Abiel and Dorcas (Abbott) Abbot; Abiel d. at Cambridge, MA, 31 Jan 1859. This is a quadruple Abbott marriage; all four of the parents of this couple are Abbotts. Dr. Abiel Abbot was a distinguished minister and scholar. This is the same as Family #197, child i.

784) vi PHEBE ABBOTT, b. 18 Nov 1768; d. at Portland, ME, 30 Apr 1852; m. 9 Apr 1789, EDWARD CARLETON, b. at Bradford, 2 Jul 1762 son of Dudley and Abigail (Wilson) Carleton; Edward d. 12 Jun 1825.

785) vii ABIEL ABBOT, b. 17 Aug 1770; d. at New York in transit from Cuba, 7 Jun 1828; m. at Haverhill, 19 Jul 1796, EUNICE WALES, b. at Roxbury, 21 Sep 1772 daughter of Ebenezer and Eunice (Davis) Wales; Eunice d. at Dorchester, 29 Dec 1831.

viii JACOB ABBOTT, b. 25 Jul 1771; d. Jul 1772.

---

[522] John Quincy Adams, Charles Francis Adams, 1903, Life in a New England Town 1787, 1788: Diary of John Quincy Adams While a Student in the Office of Theophilus Parsons at Newburyport, p 45

194) ABIEL ABBOT *(Benjamin³, Benjamin², George¹)*, b. 24 Jul 1735 son of Benjamin and Abigail (Abbott) Abbott; d. 24 Jun 1764; m. 5 Feb 1761, his third cousin PHEBE BALLARD, b. 25 Jul 1738 daughter of Josiah and Mary (Chandler) Ballard. Phebe m. 2nd as his second wife, her third cousin (and great grandson of George Abbott), JAMES HOLT son of Nicholas and Dorcas (Abbott) Holt; Phebe d. 9 Jun 1815.

Abiel Abbot, called Dr. Abiel Abbot, attended Harvard for a time. He did study medicine and served as a physician during the French and Indian War.

Abiel Abbot did not leave a will. Joshua Holt, Jr. was administrator of the estate. There were many creditors to the estate and it was declared insolvent.[523]

Abiel Abbot and Phebe Ballard had two children born at Andover.

      i   ABIEL ABBOTT, b. 6 Nov 1761; d. 18 Aug 1828. Abiel did not marry. He did not leave a will but had many creditors and his property was sold at auction to settle the estate.

786) ii   BENJAMIN ABBOTT, b. 28 May 1763; d. at Newburyport, 18 Aug 1821; m. 21 Nov 1786, JOANNA HOLMES, b. at Newburyport, 1765 daughter of Francis and Mary (Smith) Holmes; Joanna d. 11 Aug 1828.

195) ELIZABETH ABBOTT *(Benjamin³, Benjamin², George¹)*, b. 27 Oct 1738 daughter of Benjamin and Abigail (Abbott) Abbott; d. at

---

[523] *Essex County, MA: Probate File Papers, 1638-1881. Probate of* Abiel Abbot, 12 Jul 1764, *Case number* 6.

Conway, NH, 12 Oct 1789;[524] m. 1st, 1 Jun 1758, EBENEZER CUMMINGS, b. at Groton, 17 Apr 1735 son of William and Lucy (Colburn) Cummings; Ebenezer d. of smallpox, 1 Jun 1778. Elizabeth m. 2nd as his fourth wife, THOMAS MERRILL, b. at Haverhill, 5 Feb 1723/4 son of John and Lydia (Haynes) Merrill; Thomas had married as his first wife, Phebe Abbott (Family #139).

Ebenezer Cummings enlisted in the army for service in the Revolutionary War. After his death from smallpox in 1778, the town agreed to care for the widows of the Continental soldiers including Mrs. Cummings.[525]

Elizabeth Abbott and Ebenezer Cummings had eight children born at Hollis, New Hampshire.

787) i ELIZABETH CUMMINGS, b. 23 Nov 1759; d. 3 Oct 1812; m. 13 Jun 1780, her third cousin, HENRY LOVEJOY, b. at Andover, 23 Nov 1753 son of William and Hannah (Evans) Lovejoy.

788) ii EBENEZER CUMMINGS, b. 15 Sep 1761; d, about 1842;[526] m. at Surry, NH, 29 May 1787, HANNAH WASHER, b. at Amherst, about 1767 daughter of Stephen and Sarah (Wilkins) Washer; Hannah d. at Andover, VT, 6 Aug 1837.

---

[524] *New Hampshire, Death and Disinterment Records, 1754-1947*

[525] Mooar, *The Cummings Memorial*, p 100

[526] His death is reported by several sources as occurring in Wisconsin. However, he seems to have still been in Vermont in 1839 when his son Stephen made an appeal related to his father not having received his military service pension which he first applied for in 1832. It is possible that he relocated to Wisconsin in his very last years, perhaps to be with one of his children, but that needs further investigation. There is a death record for Ebenezer's wife 6 Aug 1837 in Vermont, so Ebenezer was still in Vermont in 1837. Some of his children did relocate to Wisconsin.

789) iii ABIGAIL CUMMINGS, b. 1 Jul 1763; d. Nov 1801; m. at Conway, 8 Apr 1788, JOSEPH SEAVEY, b. 1762 son of Jonathan and Comfort (Cates) Seavey; Joseph d. about 1812.

iv BRIDGET CUMMINGS, b. 15 Jul 1765; d. 24 Jan 1786.

790) v LUCY CUMMINGS, b. 9 Jul 1767; d. 15 Oct 1854; m. 8 Apr 1788, PETER PEAVEY, b. at Andover, 14 Apr 1762 son of Thomas and Dorcas (Holt) Peavey; Peter d. at Greenfield, NH, 28 Jul 1836.

791) vi MARY CUMMINGS, b. 22 Oct 1770; d. at Francestown, NH, 6 Apr 1856; m. 8 Dec 1810, WILLIAM BIXBY, b. 4 Nov 1779 son of Edward and Lucy (Barnes) Bixby; William d. 30 Oct 1862. Mary and William had one adopted child.[527]

792) vii JACOB ABBOT CUMMINGS, b. 2 Nov 1772; d. at Boston, 24 Feb 1820; m. 9 Aug 1807, ELIZABETH MERRILL, b. at Haverhill, 10 Mar 1781 daughter of Gyles and Lucy (Cushing) Merrill; Elizabeth d. at Portland, ME, 24 Dec 1867.

viii SARAH CUMMINGS, b. 28 Jan 1775; d. after 1850 likely at Francestown. Sarah did not marry. At the 1850 U.S. Census, she was living with her sister Mary Bixby in Francestown.[528]

Elizabeth Abbott and her second husband Thomas Merrill had two children born at Conway, New Hampshire.

---

[527] Cochrane and Wood, *History of Francestown*, p 518
[528] *1850 United States Federal Census*, Year: 1850; Census Place: Francestown, Hillsborough, New Hampshire; Roll: M432_434; Page: 37A; Image: 75.

793) i JOHN MERRILL, b. 2 Mar 1782; d. at Portland, ME, 7 Jun 1855; m. at Portland, 26 Sep 1820, MARY SOUTHGATE BOYD, b. at Portland, 20 Jan 1797 daughter of Joseph Coffin and Isabella (Southgate) Boyd; Mary d. Apr 1861.[529]

ii BENJAMIN MERRILL, b. 15 Mar 1784; d. at Salem, MA, 30 Jul 1847.[530] Benjamin did not marry. He did graduate from Harvard in 1804 and was awarded an LLD in 1845. He worked as an attorney, practicing first in Lynn, but for most of his career practiced in Salem. In his will, he makes bequests to his siblings Jonathan A. Merrill, Sally Cummings, and John Merrill.[531] Jonathan and Sally are half-siblings.

196) ANNA ABBOTT *(Benjamin³, Benjamin², George¹)*, b. 13 Oct 1740 daughter of Benjamin and Abigail (Abbott) Abbott; d. at Hollis, NH, 15 Jan 1810; m. Jan 1762, EPHRAIM BURGE, b. at Westford, 1 May 1738 son of Josiah and Susannah (Jaquith) Burge; Ephraim d. 20 Jul 1784.

Ephraim Burge was active in the civic life of Hollis, New Hampshire. For example, during the Revolutionary War, he was part of a 1781 committee to "class the town" which seems to have been a method of sectioning the town to answer call-ups for more soldiers for the war. He was also part of a committee charged with caring for the families of soldiers.[532]

---

[529] Chapman, *Monograph of the Southgate Family*, p 27
[530] Benja[min], b. Conway, N. H., councillor-at-law, s. Thomas [and ____ (Abbot), N. R. 9.], apoplexy, July 30, 1847, a. 73 y. Massachusetts: Vital Records, 1620-1850
[531] *Essex County, MA: Probate File Papers, 1638-1881. Probate of* Benjamin Merrill, 3 Aug 1847, *Case number* 46886.
[532] Worcester, *History of the Town of Hollis*

Generation Four

There are records for the births of nine children at Hollis, New Hampshire.

794) i   ANNA BURGE, b. 20 Nov 1762; d. at Dunstable, 31 Oct 1794; m. 17 Nov 1783, PHINEAS FLETCHER, b. 28 Nov 1757 son of Joseph and Elizabeth (Underwood) Fletcher. Phineas m. 2nd, Alice Ames; Phineas d. 31 Jul 1833.

795) ii EPHRAIM BURGE, b. 7 Jun 1764; d. at Hollis, 2 Mar 1853; m. 28 Jan 1793, PATTY BALDWIN, b. at Amherst, NH, 2 Mar 1764 daughter of Nahum and Mary (Lowe) Baldwin; Patty d. 2 Aug 1822.

      iii JOSIAH BURGE, b. 15 Apr 1766; d. 25 Mar 1790. Josiah graduated from Harvard in 1787[533] and was a preacher.

      iv JACOB BURGE, b. 7 Jan 1768; d. at Hollis, 10 Jun 1809. Jacob does not seem to have married.

796) v   SUSANNAH "SUKEY" BURGE, b. 21 Jul 1773; d. at Hollis, 6 Sep 1816; m. 16 Apr 1799, THOMAS FARLEY, b. 28 Dec 1769 son of Caleb and Elizabeth (Farley) Farley; Thomas d. 17 Mar 1832.

      vi ABIAL BURGE, b. 27 May and d. 30 May 1775.

      vii SARAH "SALLY" BURGE, b. 2 May 1777; d. at Bedford, NH, Oct 1825; m. at Hollis, 14 Apr 1821, as his second wife, Deacon STEPHEN THURSTON, b. at Rowley, 2 Jan 1770 son of Daniel and Judith (Chute) Thurston. Stephen married a third time after

---

[533] Harvard University, *Quinquennial Catalogue*, p 140

Sally's death; Stephen died 13 Sep 1833. Sally did not have any children.

797) viii SAMUEL BURGE, b. 28 Mar 1779; d. at Francestown, NH, 5 Sep 1824; m. by 1805, ANNA MAY,[534] b. 1787 (age 30 at time of death); d. 30 Oct 1817. Samuel m. 2nd, 5 Feb 1822, DEBORAH STARETT, b. 26 Dec 1782 daughter of William and Abigail (Fisher) Starett.

ix BENJAMIN BURGE, b. 5 Aug 1782; d. at Hollis, 15 Jun 1815. Benjamin attended Harvard graduating in 1805 earning a medical degree.[535] Benjamin does not seem to have married.

197) DORCAS ABBOT *(Benjamin³, Benjamin², George¹)*, b. 1 Aug 1744 daughter of Benjamin and Abigail (Abbott) Abbott; d. at Wilton, NH, 23 Feb 1829;[536] m. 20 Nov 1764, her second cousin once removed, ABIEL ABBOT *(John⁴, John³, John², George¹)*, b. 19 Apr 1741 son of John and Phebe (Fiske) Abbott; Abiel d. 19 Aug 1809.

Dorcas Abbot and Abiel Abbot were born in Andover but had their children and raised their family in Wilton, New Hampshire. Abiel served in the Revolutionary War as paymaster in Baldwin's Regiment. He was a deacon in the church at Wilton. Three of their sons attended Harvard. The total number of children in the family is not certain. There are records for the births of 12

---

[534] Cochrane's *History of Francestown, NH* suggests her name might be Charlotte Morrill. However, her grave stone gives her name as Anna wife of Samuel. In addition, the son of Samuel and Anna, Benjamin, was a graduate of Dartmouth College. Benjamin's biographical sketch for the alumni of Dartmouth College gives his mother's name as Anna May. Chapman, *Sketches of the Alumni of Dartmouth College*, p 275

[535] Harvard University, *Quinquennial Catalogue*, p 151

[536] *New Hampshire: Births, Deaths and Marriages, 1654-1969*. (From microfilmed records. Online database: *AmericanAncestors.org*, New England Historic Genealogical Society, 2014.)

children, and some sources report there were 16 children. In any event, ten children lived to adulthood.

Abiel Abbot wrote his will 4 August 1809. Beloved wife Dorcas Abbott receives the use of the dwelling house, $200, and a lengthy list of provisions to be provided for her support. She also receives one-third part of the pew on the lower floor of the Wilton meeting house for as long as she remains his widow. Beloved son Abiel Abbot receives a one-tenth portion of his books and clothing in addition to the expense of his education which he has already received. Beloved son Jacob receives $100 in addition to the expense of his education. Son Benjamin receives the largest bored gun in addition to the lands and utensils he has received. Son Samuel receives a portion of books plus the expense of education. Daughter Dorcas Putnam receives one-tenth of the books in addition to what she has received. Daughters Abigail Livermore, Persis Lovejoy, Rhoda Peabody receive the same bequest of one-tenth portion of the books in addition to what they have already received. Daughter Phebe Abbot receives her portion of the books and $333, one-half on interest when she reaches the age of 18 and one-half when she reaches age 21. Son Ezra receives all the lands in Wilton, Mason, and Greenfield that have not otherwise been conveyed. Ezra also receives the tools of all kinds including the husbandry and cooper tools. Ezra is named executor.[537]

There are records for the following children born at Wilton, New Hampshire. Of the nine children who married, four of them married cousins who were George Abbott descendants.

783) i ABIEL ABBOT, b. 14 Dec 1765; d. at Cambridge, 31 Jan 1859; m. 19 May 1796, his first cousin,

---

[537] *New Hampshire Wills and Probate Records 1643-1982*, will of Abiel Abbot, Hillsborough, 4 Aug 1809.

		ELIZABETH ABBOTT, b. 2 Aug 1766 daughter of John and Abigail (Abbott) Abbott.
798)	ii	JACOB ABBOTT, b. 7 Jan 1768; d. 2 Nov 1834; m. 11 Feb 1802, CATHERINE THAYER, b. at Hampton, 28 Sep 1779 daughter of Ebenezer and Martha (Cotton) Thayer; Catherine d. 27 Jan 1843.
799)	iii	BENJAMIN ABBOTT, b. 17 Mar 1770; d. at Temple, ME, 10 Sep 1823; m. at Andover, 17 Jan 1793, his third cousin, PHEBE ABBOTT, b. at Wilton, 25 Jun 1774 daughter of Jacob and Lydia (Stevens) Abbott; Phebe d. 18 Apr 1857.
800)	iv	EZRA ABBOT, b. 8 Feb 1772; d. at Wilton, 3 Apr 1847; m. at Coventry, CT, 6 Oct 1799, REBEKAH HALE, b. at Coventry, 9 Jan 1781 daughter of Joseph and Rebecca (Harris) Hale; Rebekah d. 5 May 1860.[538]
801)	v	DORCAS ABBOTT, b. 30 Jan 1774; died after 2 Oct 1846, the date of her will;[539] m. 3 Jan 1795, ELIPHALET PUTNAM, b. at Wilton, 23 Jan 1766 son of Nathaniel and Mary (Eastman) Putnam; Eliphalet d. 25 Feb 1826.
	vi	CHILD ABBOTT, b. and d. 20 Apr 1776.
	vii	SAMUEL ABBOTT, b. 11 Jun 1777; d. 10 Jan 1782.
802)	viii	ABIGAIL ABBOTT, b. 13 Jul 1779; d. 5 Jun 1812; m. 19 May 1808, JONATHAN LIVERMORE, b. at Wilton, 10 Jul 1770 son of Jonathan and Elizabeth (Kidder) Livermore; Jonathan d. 24 Dec 1845.

---

[538] Abbott, *Family Tree of Ezra Abbot*. See this source of additional information.
[539] *Probate Records, 1771-1921; Indexes to Probate Records, 1771-1859, 1885-1961*; Author: New Hampshire. Probate Court (Hillsborough County); *Probate Place: Hillsborough, New Hampshire*

803) ix   PERSIS ABBOTT, b. 25 Dec 1781; d. at Milford, NH, 13 Nov 1859; m. 12 Jan 1804, her third cousin (and George Abbott descendant of the 6th generation), HENRY LOVEJOY, b. 16 Aug 1781 son of Samuel and Lydia (Abbott) Lovejoy; Henry d. 23 Sep 1863.

804) x   RHODA ABBOTT, b. 17 Mar 1784; d. at Peterborough, 19 Mar 1853; m. 14 Nov 1805, EPHRAIM PEABODY, b. at Wilton, 17 Jun 1776 son of Ephraim and Sarah (Hutchinson) Peabody; Ephraim d. 5 Jul 1816.

xi   SAMUEL ABBOTT, b. 30 Mar 1786; d. 2 Jan 1839. Samuel did not marry. He attended Harvard, was admitted to the bar, but later developed an interest in chemistry.

805) xii   PHEBE ABBOTT, b. 25 Jun 1788; d. at Jackson, ME, 25 Nov 1825, m. 25 Jun 1818, her first cousin, EZRA ABBOTT, b. at Wilton, 3 Jul 1785 son of William and Phebe (Ballard) Abbott; Ezra d. 7 Jun 1871. Ezra is a 6th generation descendant of George Abbott.

Jonathan³, Benjamin², George¹

198)   JONATHAN ABBOT *(Jonathan³, Benjamin², George¹)*, b. Dec 1714 son of Jonathan and Zerviah (Holt) Abbott; d. at Andover, 31 May 1794; m. 1st 8 Oct 1739, his second cousin, MARTHA LOVEJOY, b. 2 Nov 1720 daughter of Henry and Sarah (Farnum) Lovejoy; Martha d. about 1768. Jonathan m. 2nd as her second husband, his second cousin MARY ABBOTT daughter of George and Mary (Phillips) Abbott.

In his will written 13 November 1787 (probate 9 July 1794), Jonathan Abbot has bequests to the following persons: well beloved wife Mary, son William Abbot, daughter Martha Whiting, and son Jonathan Abbot who is named executor.[540]

Jonathan Abbot and Martha Lovejoy had four children. The births of the three oldest children are recorded at Lunenburg. The birth of the youngest child was recorded at Andover.

321)   i   JONATHAN ABBOT, b. 20 Aug 1740; d. at Andover, 26 Dec 1821; m. 1st, about 1762, his third cousin, MEHITABLE ABBOTT, b. at Andover 11 Aug 1736 daughter of Ephraim and Hannah (Phelps) Abbott; Mehitable d. 1 Jan 1777. Jonathan m. 2nd, 17 Dec 1778, his third cousin, DORCAS ABBOTT, b. 23 Sep 1758 daughter of Stephen and Mary (Abbott) Abbott; Dorcas d. 3 Mar 1844.

       ii   NATHAN ABBOT, b. Jan 1743/4; died young.

806)   iii   WILLIAM ABBOT, b. 24 Nov 1745; d. likely at Temple, NH; m. 26 Aug 1766, his third cousin, SARA HOLT, b. 11 Aug 1746 daughter of Timothy and Hannah (Dane) Holt.

807)   iv   MARTHA ABBOT, b. 23 Jan 1749/50; d. at Temple, NH, 10 Jan 1842; m. 3 May 1774; OLIVER WHITING, b. at Pelham, NH, 6 Apr 1750 son of Eleazer and Dorothy (Crosby) Whiting; Oliver d. 28 Sep 1829.

199)   DAVID ABBOT *(Jonathan³, Benjamin², George¹)*, b. Dec 1716 son of Jonathan and Zerviah (Holt) Abbot; d. 1777 at Rockingham, NH (probate 31 Dec 1777); m. 10 Aug 1741, his second cousin, once removed, HANNAH CHANDLER, b. 1724 daughter of Joseph and

---

[540] *Essex County, MA: Probate File Papers, 1638-1881. Probate of* Jonathan Abbot, 9 Jul 1794, *Case number* 81.

Mehitable (Russell) Chandler; Hannah's death not known but she was living at the time of her husband's will.

The will of David Abbot, written 11 June 1771, includes bequests to the following persons: son John Abbot receives a pair of three year old steers, one cow and all his wearing apparel; daughter Hannah Holt receives 5 shillings; daughter Bridget Abbot receives 15 pounds and a yearling heifer; daughter Mehitable also get 15 pounds and a heifer at marriage or the age of 21; son Job Abbot is to be the sole executor; beloved wife Hannah has use of all the household during her widowhood; son Job receives remainder of real and personal estate, although noting that certain tracts of land have been granted to son John by warrantee deed.[541]

The five children listed in the will are given here. The History of Pembroke and other sources list a son Benjamin with this family. However, I believe that Benjamin is the son of David Abbott and Hannah Danforth, and as he is not mentioned/living at the time of the will, he is not included here. Five children were born at Pembroke.

808)	i	JOB ABBOT, b. about 1742; d. at West Barnet, VT, 15 Dec 1815; m. PHEBE FARNUM whose parentage is unknown at this time.
809)	ii	HANNAH ABBOT, b. 7 Sep 1743; d. at Pembroke, 17 Mar 1813; m. her third cousin, BENJAMIN HOLT, b. 28 Feb 1741 son of Benjamin and Sarah (Frye) Holt.
	iii	JOHN ABBOT, b. about 1752 (although he may be the oldest child in this family born in the early 1740's); still living in 1771. There are no records located yet for him. As he was an adult at the time of

---

[541] *New Hampshire Wills and Probate Records 1643-1982,* Probate of David Abbott, Rockingham, 31 Dec 1777, Case number 4406.

his father's will having already received land through deed, it is possible that he married although clear evidence not found yet.

810)   iv   BRIDGET ABBOT, b. about 1761; m. 24 Dec 1787, her third cousin (and George Abbott descendant), PHINEAS AMES, b. 7 Sep 1764 son of Samuel and Elizabeth (Stevens) Ames. This is the same as Family #275, child viii.

       v   MEHITABLE ABBOT, b. about 1762; still living in 1771.

200) ZERVIAH ABBOTT (*Jonathan³, Benjamin², George¹*), b. Aug 1722 daughter of Jonathan and Zerviah (Holt) Abbott; d. likely at Pembroke, NH; m. 17 Sep 1745, EPHRAIM BLUNT, b. 5 Feb 1720/1 son of William and Sarah (Foster) Blunt.

There is record evidence for three children of Zerviah Abbott and Ephraim Holt. This family seems to have moved several times and were at various times in Massachusetts, New Hampshire, and Vermont.

       i   EPHRAIM BLUNT, b. at Andover, 9 Aug 1747; died young.

811)   ii   EPHRAIM BLUNT, b. at Danville, VT, 20 Jun 1754; d. at Danville, 15 Feb 1829; m. 21 Nov 1776, MARTHA ORDWAY, b. at Amesbury, 28 Mar 1753 daughter of Moses and Anna (-) Ordway.

812)   iii   ZERVIAH BLUNT, b. at Suncook, NH, 1759;[542] d. at Calais, VT, 18 Jan 1860; m. at Canterbury, NH, 26 Feb

---

[542] Zerviah Hartshorn's death record lists her parents as Zerviah Blunt and Ephraim "Hartshorn" although this seems just to be a confusion of the name of

1778, AARON HARTSHORN, b. at Reading, 1754 son of Thomas and Abia (-) Hartshorn; Aaron d. at Danville, VT, 19 Jun 1799.

141)   JOB ABBOTT *(Jonathan³, Benjamin², George¹)* and SARAH ABBOTT *(James³, William², George¹)* This is the same as Family #141 covered above.

201)   SAMUEL ABBOTT *(Jonathan³, Benjamin², George¹)*, b. 20 Sep 1727 son of Jonathan and Zerviah (Holt) Abbott; m. 12 Jul 1749, MIRIAM STEVENS whose origins are undetermined but may be the Miriam baptized in 1730 at Newbury.

Samuel Abbott and Miriam Stevens had eleven children whose births are recorded at Pembroke, New Hampshire.

813)   i   SAMUEL ABBOTT, b. 16 Apr 1750; d. at North Pembroke, 11 Mar 1836; m. 22 Mar 1781, LYDIA PERRIN, b. about 1752 (based on age at time of death) parents not yet certain; Lydia d. 1 Apr 1829.

       ii   EBENEZER ABBOTT, b. 18 Oct 1751; no further record.

814)   iii ABIGAIL ABBOTT, b. 6 Sep 1753; d. likely at Salisbury, NH; m. 23 Nov 1773, BENJAMIN WHITTEMORE, b. 4 Dec 1750 son of Aaron and Abigail (Coffin) Whittemore.

       iv   JUDITH ABBOTT, b. 28 Jul 1755; m. 18 Apr 1791, perhaps as his third wife, HEZEKIAH YOUNG.

---

her spouse and the name of her father. Her age on the death record is 100 years, 11 months, 21 days. *Vermont Vital Records 1720-1908*

Published genealogies report that Judith was Hezekiah's first wife, but the available records are that Judith married Hezekiah in 1791 as his second, or perhaps even his third, wife. He married Mary Kimball in 1783 and Judith Abbott in 1791 at Pembroke. There is another marriage for Hezekiah Young and Mary Young in 1777 at Canterbury, but that may be a different Hezekiah. There are no records for any children for Judith and Hezekiah.[543]

815) v JEREMIAH ABBOTT, b. 9 May 1757; d. at Montville, ME, 27 Jan 1816; m. 29 Nov 1787, ELIZABETH "BETSEY" FRYE, b. 18 Feb 1767 daughter of Ebenezer and Hannah (Baker) Frye; Betsey d. 27 Aug 1841.

816) vi SARAH ABBOTT, b. 21 Jul 1759; m. 4 Nov 1790, as his second wife, JEREMIAH WHEELER, b. at Concord, MA, Feb 1745 son of Jeremiah and Esther (Russell) Wheeler; Jeremiah d. at Concord, NH, 17 Oct 1827.

817) vii LYDIA ABBOTT, b. 14 Jul 1761; d. at Bethel, VT, 9 Dec 1840; m. 29 Mar 1787, NATHANIEL MORRILL, b. at South Hampton, NH, 10 Jun 1761 son of Paul and Martha (Worthen) Morrill; Nathaniel d. 17 Nov 1832.

818) viii EZRA ABBOTT, b. 4 Aug 1763; d. at Sanbornton, NH, 16 Nov 1824; m. 30 Nov 1794, MOLLY BROWN daughter of William and Ruth (McDuffee) Brown;[544] Molly d. at Cabot, VT, 1836.

---

[543] Ancestry.com, New Hampshire, Marriage Records Index, 1637-1947
[544] Chase, *History of Old Chester*, p 478

819) ix WILLIAM ABBOTT, b. 10 Sep 1765; d. at Pembroke, 22 Jul 1838; m. his third cousin (and George Abbott descendant), DORCAS PARKER, b. at Andover, 17 Feb 1769 daughter of Joseph and Hannah (Abbott) Parker; Dorcas d. 9 Nov 1853. This is the same as Family #206, child v.

820) x RACHEL ABBOTT, b. 15 Jun 1768; d. at Pembroke, 28 Dec 1854; m. 30 Dec 1789, JOHN KELLEY, b. 22 Jul 1764 son of Samuel and Sarah (Barker) Kelley.

821) xi MARIAM ABBOTT, b. 5 Sep 1771; d. at Randolph, VT, 21 Jun 1820; m. JOHN MORRILL, b. 17 Jan 1759 son of Paul and Martha (Worthen) Morrill; John d. 21 Sep 1849.

David³, Benjamin², George¹

202) SARAH ABBOT (*David³, Benjamin², George¹*), b. 7 Apr 1726 daughter of David and Hannah (Danforth) Abbott; d. at Bedford, 5 Mar 1814[545]; m. 1st 30 Jan 1753, ROBERT HILDRETH, b. at Dracut, 18 May 1713 son of Ephraim and Mercy (Richardson) Hildreth; Robert d. at Chelmsford, 1760. Sarah m. 2nd 28 May 1761, JOHN LANE, b. at Bedford, 2 Oct 1720 son of Job and Martha (Ruggles) Lane; John d. 7 Dec 1789. Sarah m. 3rd 14 Jul 1791, BENJAMIN PARKER; Benjamin d. Feb 1801.

Robert Hildreth died in 1760 at Chelmsford. His estate entered probate in October 1760; his widow Sarah requested that David Abbott of Andover be named administrator of the estate.

---

[545] Sarah's death record at Bedford is reported as Parker, Sarah, wid., "formerly the wife of Mr. John Lane," Mar. 5, 1814, a. 88. G.R.

Robert did not leave a will. Only one child was located for Sarah and Robert.

After the death of her first husband, Sarah married John Lane of Bedford. John's first wife, Ruth Bowman, had died in 1759. The births of three children were recorded for Sarah and John Lane at Bedford. A probate record was not located for John Lane. After John Lane's death in 1789, Sarah married Benjamin Parker in 1791.

Child of Sarah Abbott and Robert Hildreth:

    i   BENJAMIN HILDRETH, b. at Dracut, 23 Jan 1754; d. 13 Feb 1754

Children of Sarah Abbott and John Lane all born at Bedford:

    i   JOSIAH LANE, b. 25 Feb 1762; d. 15 Mar 1762.

822) ii   JONATHAN LANE, b. 15 Oct 1763; d. at Bedford, 4 Mar 1808; m. 1 Feb 1787, his second cousin (and George Abbott descendant), HANNAH LANE, b. 26 Feb 1765 daughter of Samuel and Elizabeth (Fitch) Lane; Hannah d. at Lowell, 1848 (date of probate). This is the same as Family #211, child i.

823) iii SARAH LANE, b. 1 Oct 1765; d. at Billerica, 11 Jun 1849; m. 1 Nov 1787, TIMOTHY STEARNS, b. at Billerica, 25 Sep 1763 son of Isaac and Sarah (Abbott) Stearns; Timothy d. 8 Aug 1816. Sarah's mother and Timothy's mother were both named Sarah Abbott. Timothy's mother Sarah Abbott was from the Rowley Abbott lane.

203)   DAVID ABBOT ($David^3$, $Benjamin^2$, $George^1$), b. 28 Mar 1728 son of David and Hannah (Danforth) Abbott; d. at Billerica 1 Nov 1798; m. 28 Dec 1752, PRUDENCE SHELDON, b. at Billerica 31 Aug

1732 daughter of Samuel and Sarah[546] (Hutchinson) Richardson; a death record for Prudence was not located, although she was living at the time of her husband's death and she was on the tax rolls in Billerica for 1798.

David and Prudence had eleven children, the first ten births recorded at Andover and the youngest son born at Billerica. David owned property in Andover, Billerica, and New Suncook (now Lovell), Maine. The children in this family scattered to the four winds ending up in New Hampshire, Vermont, Maine, Ohio, and Quebec.

David Abbot wrote his will 7 December 1797. Beloved wife Prudence receives the use and improvements on one-half of the dwelling house and a horse to convey her to meetings and other occasions. There are also provisions made for her support in terms of annual allotments of grains, beef, firewood, etc. Sons Josiah and Samuel receive token bequests of six shillings in addition to their portions they have already received. Son David receives all his land in New Suncook in the county of York. Son Benjamin receives all the lands in Billerica and Andover. Son Jeremiah receives $167 to make up his full portion. Daughter Elizabeth Dugles (sic) receives one pound, six shillings, and six dollars to make up the rest of her portion. Daughter Prudence Sawyer receives six shillings, daughter Parker (this is Hannah who married Aaron Parker) receives $5, daughter Olive McDole receives $30, and daughter Dorcas Abbot receives $100. Son Benjamin is named executor.[547]

---

[546] The marriage record lists her name as Mary Hutchinson, but all the births of the children, including a daughter Sarah born in 1719, list the mother's name as Sarah.
[547] *Middlesex County, MA: Probate File Papers, 1648-1871. Probate of* David Abbot, *1798, Case number 13.*

824) i ELIZABETH ABBOTT, b. 26 Feb 1754; m. at Cavendish, VT, 19 Aug 1792, WILLIAM DOUGLASS.

ii Son, b. 7 Feb 1756; d. 2 Mar 1756.

825) iii PRUDENCE ABBOTT, b. 3 Oct 1757; d. at Wilton, 15 Dec 1839; m. 13 Oct 1778, NATHANIEL SAWYER, b. at Methuen, 16 Jun 1750 son of Josiah and Hannah (Gowing) Sawyer; Nathaniel d. 15 Oct 1807.

826) iv JOSIAH ABBOTT, b. 29 Dec 1759; d. Feb 1837; m. 1st, 15 May 1784, RUTH BODWELL; Ruth d. by 1790. Josiah m. 2nd, 30 Mar 1790, ANNA FURBUSH, b. Oct 1768 daughter of Charles and Sarah (Corey) Furbush.

827) v HANNAH ABBOTT, b. 5 Jan 1762; d. at Compton, Quebec, 1856; m. at Billerica, 21 Jan 1787, AARON PARKER, b. at Methuen, 22 Feb 1759 son of Timothy and Priscilla (Carleton) Parker; Aaron d. 1857; living in Compton in 1851 listed as 93 years old.[548]

828) vi SAMUEL ABBOTT, b. 27 Mar 1764; d. at Bennington, NH, 29 Mar 1833; m. 1st, at Billerica, 26 Jan 1786, his second cousin once removed, RHODA BLANCHARD, b. 17 Nov 1762 daughter of Samuel and Mary (Brown) Blanchard; Rhoda d. about 1800. Samuel m. 2nd at Hancock, NH, 22 Dec 1801, ANNA WALLACE.

---

[548] 1851 Census of Canada East, Canada West, New Brunswick, and Nova Scotia; Year: 1851; Census Place: Compton, Sherbrooke County, Canada East (Quebec); Schedule: A; Roll: C_1142; Page: 89; Line: 41

829) vii DAVID ABBOTT, b. 4 Mar 1766; d. at Barton, VT, 11 Mar 1847; m. about 1786, SARAH "SALLY" PARKER;[549] Sally d. May 1816.

830) viii BENJAMIN ABBOTT, b. 26 Jun 1768; d. at Ashtabula, OH, 22 May 1856; m. in Vermont about 1800, BETSEY NOONING whose origins are unknown; Betsey d. 4 Sep 1854.

831) ix OLIVE ABBOTT, b. 24 Jul 1770; d. at Thurso, Quebec, 27 Jun 1834; m. 1st, ALEXANDER MCDOLE, b. 15 Jun 1760 son of William McDowell and Rosannah (McLaughlin) McDole; Alexander d. at Grand Isle, VT, 26 Jan 1814. Olive m. 2nd 31 Mar 1816, as his second wife, DAVID TOWN, b. 25 Jun 1762; David d. at Waterbury, VT, 4 Sep 1828.

832) x DORCAS ABBOTT, b. 5 Dec 1773; d. likely at Chelmsford after 1850 (still living at the 1850 U.S. Census); m. 4 Feb 1798, JOHN SNOW, b. 5 Jul 1774 son of Richard and Lydia (Wright) Snow.

833) xi JEREMIAH ABBOTT, b. 18 May 1776; d. in New York, 28 Mar 1835;[550] Jeremiah lived in Portland, Maine much of his adulthood. He did marry and had some children. One child has been identified, but the identity of his wife has not been found. The most likely candidate for a wife is Susanna Centre

---

[549] Published genealogies give her name as Sarah Keyser, but every birth record for this couple lists her name as Sarah Parker and Parker is included as the middle name of one of their children.

[550] Ancestry.com, *U.S., Newspaper Extractions from the Northeast, 1704-1930* (Provo, UT, USA: Ancestry.com Operations, Inc., 2014). This notice gives place of death as New York but notes that he was until recently in Portland, Maine.

who married Jeremiah Abbott at Boston in 1797. There is a Maine death record for her for 1844 with age of 74 at time of death. There are gravestones in Portland for Jeremiah and his wife Susanna with the appropriate death years so perhaps that is this Jeremiah and Susannah.

204) SOLOMON ABBOT (*David³, Benjamin², George¹*), b. 14 Feb 1730/1 son of David and Hannah (Danforth) Abbott; d. probably at Dracut 17 Dec 1797;[551] m. 3 May 1756, HANNAH COLBE, b. 22 Oct 1735 daughter of Daniel and Hannah (Gray) Colbe; Hannah's date of death is not known.

Solomon and Hannah settled in Dracut soon after the birth of their first child. In 1758, Solomon Abbott bought property and rights to a ferry in Dracut from John White. Solomon then sold half of this property to Daniel Colby in 1759 and the other half to Amos Bradley in 1761. Solomon received a deed for 100 acres from John White in 1768. Solomon Abbott is also listed on the Roll of Honor for Dracut as serving in the Revolutionary War.[552]

Seven births are recorded for Solomon Abbott and Hannah Colbe, the oldest at Andover and the remainder in Dracut.

834) i HANNAH ABBOTT, b. 1 May 1757; d. after 1827 (living at the probate of her second husband's estate); m. 1st, 27 Feb 1776, PARKER BODWELL, b. at Methuen, 29 Oct 1750 son of Daniel and Abigail (Ladd) Bodwell; Parker d. 7 Aug 1795. Hannah m. 2nd, as his third wife, DAVID JONES, b. 12 Feb 1740/1 son of David and Hannah (Fox) Jones.

---

[551] The date of death is given in Abbot and Abbot, *Genealogical Record of Descendants*; a death record or probate record was not located.
[552] Coburn, *History of Dracut*

835)	ii	SOLOMON ABBOTT, b. 7 May 1759; d. at Dracut, 5 Jan 1842; m. about 1785, RACHEL BOWERS, b. 16 Jul 1763 daughter of John and Rachel (Varnum) Bowers; Rachel d. 7 Jan 1845.
836)	iii	SARAH ABBOTT, b. 22 Mar 1761; m. at Methuen, 16 Mar 1786, SAMUEL MORSE, b. at Methuen, 28 Mar 1759 son of Joseph and Lydia (Huse) Morse.
837)	iv	DANIEL COLBY ABBOTT, b. 26 Oct 1766; d. at Dracut, 18 Sep 1842; m. about 1792, PATIENCE COBURN, b. at Methuen, 1768 daughter of Aaron and Phebe (Harris) Coburn; Patience d. 15 Apr 1830.
838)	v	ELIZABETH DANFORTH ABBOTT, b. 11 Oct 1768; d. at Walpole, NH, 5 Jul 1856; m. 18 Sep 1793, EPHRAIM LANE, b. at Bedford, 11 Mar 1767 son of Samuel and Ruth (Davis) Lane; Ephraim d. 15 Aug 1837.
839)	vi	LYDIA ABBOTT, b. 22 May 1771; m. JOSHUA MARTIN.[553]
840)	vii	DAVID ABBOTT, b. 18 May 1775; d. at Windham, NH, 1855 (probate 8 Aug 1855); m. 1st, 13 May 1797, HANNAH CROSBY, b. 20 Sep 1773 daughter of Jonathan and Hannah (Goodhue) Crosby; Hannah d. before 1816. David m. 2nd, 21 Feb 1816, DOLLY ABBOTT, b. at Amherst, 1775 daughter of Ephraim and Dorothy (Stiles) Abbott; Dolly d. 1822. David m. 3rd, about 1827, SARAH MCKINLEY, b. 1789

---

[553] This is a marriage reported in Abbot and Abbot, *Genealogical Record of Descendants* but have yet to find records associated with the family.

daughter of Robert and Sarah (Harriman) McKinley; Sarah d. 30 Jan 1869.

205) JONATHAN ABBOT *(David³, Benjamin², George¹)*, b. 24 Oct 1739 son of David and Hannah (Danforth) Abbott; d. at Andover, 10 Apr 1817; m. 13 Nov 1759, his second cousin once removed, MARY CHANDLER *(Nathan Chandler⁴, John Chandler³, Hannah Abbott Chandler², George¹)*, b. 15 Jun 1740 daughter of Nathaniel and Priscilla (Holt) Chandler; Mary d. 1 Apr 1824.

Captain Jonathan Abbot was part of Johnson's Regiment of Militia. This regiment was part of the first alarm that marched in response to the Lexington alarm. This regiment participated at Bunker Hill.[554]

Jonathan Abbot did not leave a will. Nathan Abbott was administrator of the estate. The widow's third is set out to widow Mary. The personal estate was sold at public auction to pay debts. Mary petitioned to the Court asking for allowances from the estate as Jonathan left ten children, two of whom are dependent on her for support. The value of the personal estate was $3,160 and the real estate value was $4,442. There was a deduction for the widow's dower of $1,480, and the debts were $7,500. The heirs-at-law signing that they agree to the administration of the estate by Nathan Abbott are as follows: Mary Abbott, Jonathan Abbott, Jr., David Abbott, Solomon Abbott, Joseph Shattuck, Benjamin Abbott, Hannah Abbott, Sarah Abbott, and Joshua Chandler signing on behalf of Abiel Chandler and Gilbert Barker.[555]

Jonathan Abbott and Mary Chandler had twelve children whose births are recorded at Andover. Two of the children died as infants. Two children did not marry. Of the eight children who

---

[554] Patrakis, Joan, "Andover in the Revolutionary War," Andover Historical Society, retrieved from http://andoverhistorical.org/explore-andover-stories-blog/andover-in-the-revolutionary-war

[555] *Essex County, MA: Probate File Papers, 1638-1881.* Probate of Jonathan Abbot, 6 May 1817, Case number 82.

married, six married George Abbott descendants; three of the marriages were to first cousins.

The oldest son, Jonathan Abbott, did not marry but he did leave a will that created dissension in the family. One of the heirs-at-law of the will, Benjamin Abbott, questioned its validity claiming that Jonathan was not of sound mind and memory at the time the will was made. There was a suit involving Benjamin and Jonathan Abbott, Jr. (Jonathan's nephew), and some other parties. The witnesses to the will attested that Jonathan was of sound mind. The will that Jonathan did make has bequests to the following persons: sister Mary Chandler wife of Abiel Chandler receives $100; brother Nathan, $15; brother Benjamin, $50; sister Phebe Shattuck the wife of Joseph Shattuck, $100; brother Solomon, $30; sister Hannah Barker wife of Richard Barker, $100; sister Sarah Abbott, $30; sister Priscilla Barker wife of Gilbert Barker, $30; Rebecca Shattuck, $50; nephew David Abbott receives his pasture land that adjoins his land; nephew Ezra Abbott, $200; nephew Herman Abbott, $50; niece Phebe Abbott, $20; niece Hannah Shattuck, $5; niece Phebe Abbott, $5; niece Priscilla Abbott, $20; niece Mary Abbott, $10; niece Lucinna/Susanna? Abbott, $10; nephew Nathan the son of brother David who is deceased and Joseph Shattuck receive the homestead farm in Andover; Nathan, Jr. son of Nathan, $15; nephew Gilbert Abbott, $15; nephew Jonathan Abbott receives all the residue of the estate and Jonathan is to quit-claim about three acres of property to nephew David. Nephew Jonathan is named executor.[556]

    i   JONATHAN ABBOT, b. 3 Mar 1760; d. 21 May 1830. Jonathan did not marry.

---

[556] *Essex County, MA: Probate File Papers, 1638-1881.* Probate of Jonathan Abbot, 1 Jun 1830, Case number 84.

841) ii MARY ABBOTT, b. 10 Jan 1762; d. 1 May 1845; m. 17 Oct 1782, her first cousin (and 6th generation George Abbott descendant), ABIEL CHANDLER, b. 28 Aug 1760 son of Joshua and Hannah (Chandler) Chandler; Abiel d. at Boston, 2 Nov 1833.

842) iii DAVID ABBOT, b. 11 Mar 1764; d. 1 Jun 1823; m. 26 May 1789, his first cousin, PRISCILLA CHANDLER, b. 30 Jun 1768 daughter of Nathan and Phebe (Abbott) Chandler; Priscilla d. 19 Feb 1831. Priscilla is a 6th generation descendant of George Abbott.

843) iv PHEBE ABBOTT, b. 26 Feb 1766; d 1 Dec 1848; m. 30 Mar 1790, her third cousin once removed (and George Abbott descendent), JOSEPH SHATTUCK, b. 8 Nov 1757 son of Joseph and Anna (Johnson) Shattuck; Joseph d. 8 Jul 1847. Joseph had first married Hannah Chandler (a 6th generation descendant) who died in the first year of the marriage.

844) v NATHAN ABBOT, b. 17 May 1768; d. at Andover, 7 Apr 1850; m. 11 Dec 1792, his second cousin (and George Abbott descendent), HANNAH PHELPS, b. 10 Sep 1769 daughter of Joshua and Lois (Ballard) Phelps; Hannah d. 17 Dec 1853.

845) vi BENJAMIN ABBOTT, b. 7 Jun 1770; d. at Andover, 20 Oct 1835; m. 26 Nov 1793, his first cousin (and a 6th generation George Abbott descendant), RHODA CHANDLER, b. 2 Mar 1774/5 daughter of Nathan and Phebe (Abbott) Chandler; Rhoda d. 19 Mar 1853.

846) vii SOLOMON ABBOTT, b. 1 Nov 1772; d. 1 Sep 1840; m. 8 Jul 1794, his third cousin once removed (and George Abbott descendent), LUCY FRYE, b. 4 Jul

Generation Four

1778 daughter of Theophilus and Lucy (Lovejoy) Frye.

viii JOSHUA ABBOTT, b. 14 Nov 1774; d. 26 Mar 1775.

ix HANNAH ABBOTT, b. 14 Oct 1776; d. at Andover, 11 Jul 1840; m. 22 Dec 1818, RICHARD BARKER, b. at Methuen, 10 Dec 1775 son of John and Hannah (Dow) Barker. Hannah and Richard did not have children.

x SARAH ABBOTT, b. 9 Jul 1778; d. at Andover, 1 Jul 1860. Sarah did not marry. Sarah Abbott, age 81, single, died at the almshouse of chronic rheumatism.[557]

xi PRISCILLA ABBOTT, b. 29 Jul 1780; d. at Saugus, 23 Mar 1862; m. 30 May 1816, GILBERT BARKER, b. at Methuen, 25 Jan 1774 son of John and Hannah (Dow) Barker; Gilbert d. at Saugus, 21 Sep 1853. Priscilla and Gilbert did not have children.

xii JOSHUA ABBOTT, b. 9 Jun 1784; d. 9 Jul 1784.

---

[557] *Massachusetts: Vital Records, 1841-1910.* (From original records held by the Massachusetts Archives. Online database: *AmericanAncestors.org*, New England Historic Genealogical Society, 2004.)

Section VII: The Grandchildren of Timothy Abbott and Hannah Graves

Timothy³, Timothy², George¹

80) ASA ABBOT *(Timothy³, Timothy², George¹)* and ELIZABETH ABBOTT *(Ephraim³, John², George¹)* This is Family #80 covered above.

77) MARY ABBOT *(Timothy³, Timothy², George¹)* and EPHRAIM ABBOTT *(Ephraim³, John², George¹)* Please see Family #77 covered above.

206) HANNAH ABBOTT *(Timothy³, Timothy², George¹)*, b. 21 Jun 1726 daughter of Timothy and Mary (Foster) Abbott; d. likely at Pembroke, NH; m. 25 Apr 1754, JOSEPH PARKER, b. 15 Jul 1726 son of Joseph and Mary (Emery) Parker.

Joseph and Hannah relocated to Pembroke after the births of their children. Joseph signed the association test at Pembroke in 1776. He also belonged in a militia company that was part of Colonel Daniel Moor's regiment.[558]

The births of five children of Hannah Abbott and Joseph Parker are recorded at Andover.

        i   JOSEPH PARKER, b. 10 May 1756; d. 14 Aug 1762

        ii   HANNAH PARKER, b. 30 Apr 1758; d. 23 Aug 1762

349) iii JOHN PARKER, b. 15 Aug 1760; d. at Pembroke, NH, 27 May 1825; m. at Pembroke, 21 May 1781, his third cousin (and George Abbott descendant), MARTHA LOVEJOY, b. about 1755 daughter of

---

[558] Cutter, *New England Families*, volume 3, p 1246

Caleb and Mehitable (Chandler) Lovejoy. Same as Family #74, child vi.

  iv MOLLY PARKER, b. 7 Sep 1766

819) v DORCAS PARKER, b. 17 Feb 1769; d. at Pembroke, 9 Nov 1853; m. 24 May 1792, WILLIAM ABBOTT, b. at Pembroke, 10 Sep 1765 son of Samuel and Miriam (Stevens) Abbott; William d. at Pembroke, 22 Jul 1838. This is the same as Family #201, child ix.

207) NATHAN ABBOTT *(Timothy³, Timothy², George¹)*, b. 7 Jan 1728/9 son of Timothy and Mary (Foster) Abbott; d. likely at Wilton, NH; m. 11 Jan 1759, JANE PAUL, described as "resident of Andover," but whose origins are unknown; Jane d. at Wilton, 28 May 1772. He is perhaps the Nathan Abbott listed as head of household in Wilton, NH in the 1790 U.S. Census with a total household of eight.

  Some published sources (including the Abbot genealogy and the Granite State Monthly, volume 9) place a son Caleb in this family who marries Lucy Lovejoy and Deborah Ames. However, Caleb was born, had both marriages, and died in Andover and Nathan and Jane lived in New Hampshire. Caleb died in 1837 at the age of 86 making his birth in 1751 eight years before Nathan Abbott and Jane Paul married. There is no room for Caleb in the family of Nathan and Jane until 1764. I have concluded that Caleb that married Lucy Lovejoy is Caleb born in 1751 the son of Asa and Elizabeth (Abbott) Abbott. Asa and Nathan were brothers.

  There are records for seven children of Nathan and Jane, the oldest two at Methuen and the youngest five at Wilton. Marriages for these children are uncertain. Asa married Miriam Smith and settled in Bradford, New Hampshire[559] and it is likely that Timothy married Miriam's sister Sarah Smith. Miriam and Sarah Smith were the daughters of Ezekiel and Ruth (Child) Smith of Henniker.[560] Timothy and Sarah (Smith) Abbott had children named Nathan and Jane and that would fit with this family.

      i   PAUL ABBOTT, b. 2 Dec 1759

      ii   NATHAN ABBOTT, b. 9 Mar 1761; died young

847) iii TIMOTHY ABBOTT, b. 15 Oct 1762; d. at Thetford, 8 Sep 1831; m. by 1788, SARAH SMITH, b. 1765 daughter of Ezekiel and Ruth (Childs) Smith.

848) iv ASA ABBOTT, b. 24 Jan 1765; d. at Bradford, NH, 5 Nov 1852; m. MIRIAM SMITH, b. 1770 daughter of Ezekiel and Ruth (Childs) Smith; Miriam d. 12 Feb 1819.

      v   NATHAN ABBOTT, b. 13 Feb 1767. Cutter suggests that Nathan married Mary Wilson and settled in Billerica but records that support that were not located.[561]

      vi   MARY "POLLY" ABBOTT, b. 14 May 1769

      vii MARTHA "PATTY" ABBOTT, b. 12 Apr 1771

208)   SARAH ABBOTT *(Timothy³, Timothy², George¹)*, b. 5 May 1731 daughter of Timothy and Mary (Foster) Abbott; m. at Andover, 1 Mar 1757, as his second wife, EDWARD FARMER. Edward Farmer was first married to Mary Winn the daughter of Samuel and Sara (-) Winn.

---

[559] Gould and Beals, *Early Families of Bradford, New Hampshire*
[560] Cogswell, *History of Town of Henniker*, p 736
[561] Cutter, *New England Families*, volume I, p 452

Birth records for six children were located for this couple, but a marriage was identified for just one of the children. The family lived in Hillsborough County, New Hampshire and Edward signed the association test at Hudson in 1776.[562] All the births are recorded in New Hampshire.

   i SARAH FARMER, b. 6 Sep 1758

   ii MOLLY FARMER, b. 29 Mar 1760

849) iii PHEBE FARMER, b. 21 Sep 1761; d. at Pelham, 23 Apr 1839; m. ENOS HADLEY, b. at Amesbury, 24 Oct 1755 son of Eliphalet and Elizabeth (Davis) Hadley; Enos d. about 1838.

   iv LYDIA FARMER, b. 21 Jul 1763

   v TIMOTHY FARMER, b. 23 Apr 1765

   vi CALEB FARMER, b. 30 Jun 1767

209) LYDIA ABBOTT (*Timothy³, Timothy², George¹*), b. 28 Mar 1733 daughter of Timothy and Mary (Foster) Abbott; d. at Andover, 13 Mar 1816; m. 13 Jan 1756, THOMAS FARNUM, b. 6 Sep 1734 son of Thomas and Phebe (Towns) Farnum; Thomas death is not known but was perhaps in NH living with his grandchildren.

Lydia Abbott and Thomas Farnum had seven children whose births are recorded at Andover.

   i LYDIA FARNUM, b. 10 Nov 1756; m. 27 Oct 1774, her second cousin (and George Abbott descendant), THOMAS HOLT, b. 15 Jun 1750 son of Thomas and

---

[562] Webster and Browne, *History of Hudson, NH*, p 237

Dorcas (Holt) Holt. This is the same as Family #213, child i. No children have been located for this couple.

850) ii ISRAEL FARNUM, b. 14 Jun 1758; d. at Mont Vernon, NH, 1842; m. 3 Aug 1786, PHEBE SHELDON; Phebe d. 2 Feb 1824. Israel m. 2nd, 17 May 1825, SUSANNAH FARNUM, b. 22 Mar 1772 daughter of Asa and Susannah (Town) Farnum.[563]

851) iii TIMOTHY FARNUM, b. 13 May 1759; m. 23 Sep 1786, SUSANNA BERRY, b. 27 Apr 1767 daughter of Nathaniel and Susanna (-) Berry; Susanna d. 16 Jul 1854.

852) iv PHEBE FARNUM, b. 25 Jul 1762; m. SAVAGE (according to Charlotte Helen Abbott). No records for this marriage were located, but it may be that this is the Phebe that married Aaron Putnam, but that has not been verified.

853) v SARAH FARNUM, b. 21 Sep 1764; m. ENOS ABBOTT of Andover, ME, b. 7 Feb 1769 son of Jonathan and Ruth (Bragg) Abbott of The Rowley Abbott line.

854) vi DORCAS FARNUM, b. 27 Dec 1766; m. 25 Dec 1789, NATHAN JONES, b. 1767; Nathan d. at Andover, 14 Aug 1804.

vii MARY FARNUM, b. 1770; d. at Andover, 25 Jan 1809. Mary did not marry.

210) PHEBE ABBOTT *(Timothy³, Timothy², George¹)*, b. 16 Feb 1736/7 daughter of Timothy and Mary (Foster) Abbott; d. not certain but perhaps before 1799; m. 22 Jul 1766 as his second wife, WILLIAM DANE, b. 15 Mar 1727/8 son of John and Sarah

---

[563] Smith, *History of Mont Vernon*, p 63

(Chandler) Dane. William is likely the William Dane who died at Brookfield in 1825 at age 99. William's first wife was Mary Osgood.

There are births for six children of Phebe Abbott and William Dane recorded at Andover.

855) i PHEBE DANE, b. 18 Dec 1767; d. at Greenfield, NH, 12 Sep 1854; m. 10 Nov 1794, BENJAMIN HARDY, b. at Tewksbury, 10 Aug 1768 son of James and Jemima (Palmer) Hardy; Benjamin d. 16 Apr 1834.

ii LYDIA DANE, b. 13 Jul 1769

856) iii DORCAS DANE, b. 22 Apr 1771; m. 9 Oct 1794, her first cousin, EZRA HOLT, b. 20 Mar 1762 son of Timothy and Hannah (Dane) Holt.

857) iv TIMOTHY DANE, b. 9 May 1773; d. at Hillsborough, Aug 1856; m. 2 Apr 1806, ESTHER WHEELER, b. at Hillsborough, 24 Mar 1778 daughter of Oliver and Hephzibah (Munroe) Wheeler.

v HANNAH DANE, b. 14 Nov 1776

vi JOHN DANE, b. 16 Nov 1779

Hannah Abbott Lane[3], Timothy[2], George[1]

211) SAMUEL LANE *(Hannah Abbott Lane[3], Timothy[2], George[1])*, b. 21 Oct 1737 son of John and Hannah (Abbott) Lane; d. at Bedford, 1822 (year of probate); m. 8 Dec 1763, ELIZABETH FITCH, b. 6 Jan 1738/9 daughter of Zachariah and Elizabeth (Grimes) Fitch; Elizabeth d. 19 Sep 1807.[564]

---

[564] The death record states just __, w. Samuel, complicated complaint, Sept. 19, 1807, a. 69. C.R. There was another Samuel Lane in Bedford with a wife also born

Samuel Lane wrote his will 10 April 1818 and it was presented to probate 3 September 1822. He directs that his entire estate, real and personal, be sold at auction. Daughter Phebe is to receive $500 from the estate. Following that, the estate is to be divided equally among his four daughters (or their heirs). Those daughters are Hannah Lane, Dorcas White, Phebe Lane, and the children of his daughter Polly Stearns who is deceased. John Stearns, the father of Polly's children, is to hold their portion in trust. Moses Fitch, yeoman of Bedford, and his son-in-law John Stearns are name executors of the estate. The sale of the estate yielded just over $3,600. Phebe received her separate $500 legacy, although she did marry between the time of the will and the settlement of the estate. Phebe married in 1822, David Lane who was widowed in 1820. David Lane signs the final settlement agreement along with his wife Phebe. The signers on the final settlement are John Stearns signing as guardian for Polly's seven children (Franklin, Mary, John O., Eliza Ann, Onslow, Lorenzo, and Barnard), David Lane, Phebe Lane, Hannah Lane, and Dorcas White.[565]

Samuel Lane and Elizabeth Fitch had four children born at Bedford.

822) i HANNAH LANE, b. 26 Feb 1765; d. at Lowell, 1848 (date of probate); m. 1 Feb 1787, her second cousin (and George Abbott descendant), JONATHAN LANE, b. 15 Oct 1763 son of John and Sarah (Abbott) Lane; Jonathan d. 4 Mar 1808. This is the same as Family #202, child ii.

---

in 1738. However, that woman, Frances Hutchins Blood Lane, died in 1811 in Carlisle and has the following death listing: Lane, Frances, wid. "first wid. Stephen Blood, jr.," Apr. 17, 1811, a. 73 y. G. R. 1.

[565] *Middlesex County, MA: Probate File Papers, 1648-1871. Probate of* Samuel Lane, *1822, Case number 13590.*

858) ii DORCAS LANE, b. 8 Feb 1771; d. 11 Feb 1849; m. 3 Jan 1788, NATHAN WHITE.

iii PHEBE LANE, b. 12 Feb 1773; d. 8 Aug 1838; m. 30 Apr 1822, as his second wife, DAVID LANE, b. 11 Mar 1759 son of James and Mary (Wellington) Lane; David d. 10 Sep 1842. Phebe did not have children.

859) iv MARY "POLLY" LANE, b. 15 Aug 1776; d. at Billerica, 30 Nov 1815; m. 10 Feb 1801, JOHN STEARNS, b. 18 Sep 1765 son of Isaac and Sarah (Abbott of the Rowley Abbott line) Stearns; John d. at Woburn, 4 Nov 1836. After Mary's death, John married Susanna Winn.

Dorcas Abbott Holt^3, Timothy^2, George^1

212) TIMOTHY HOLT *(Dorcas Abbott Holt^3, Timothy^2, George^1)*, b. 17 Jan 1720/1 son of Nicholas and Dorcas (Abbott) Holt; d. at Wilton, NH, Nov 1801; m. 18 Sep 1744, his second cousin, ELIZABETH HOLT, b. Jun 1718 daughter of John and Mehitable (Wilson) Holt; Elizabeth d. at Wilton 21 Mar 1776.

Timothy Holt and Elizabeth Holt had four children whose births are recorded at Andover. The family relocated to Wilton.

i TIMOTHY HOLT, b. 19 May 1746

860) ii ELIZABETH HOLT, b. 25 Nov 1748; m. 1 Jun 1769, ISAAC FRYE, b. at Andover, 6 Feb 1748 son of Abiel and Abigail (Emery) Frye; Isaac d. at Wilton, NH, 3 Nov 1791.

861) iii HANNAH HOLT, b. 18 Jan 1754; m. about 1774, as his second wife, RICHARD WHITNEY, b. at Oxford, MA, 22 Apr 1743 son of Israel and Hannah (Blodgett) Whitney. Richard was first married to Sarah Butterfield who died in 1773. This family lived in Wilton until 1795 but may have relocated to Vermont after all the children were born.

iv SARAH HOLT, b. 31 May 1757; m. WILLIAM PIERCE, b. about 1757 likely the son of William and Hannah (-) Pierce of Wilton, NH.[566] No firm information has been located for this couple.

123) JAMES HOLT *(Dorcas Abbott Holt³, Timothy², George¹)* and SARAH ABBOTT (Benjamin³, Benjamin², George¹) This is Family #123 covered above.

126) NATHAN HOLT *(Dorcas Abbott Holt³, Timothy², George¹)* and SARAH ABBOTT *(George³, George², George¹)* This is Family #126 covered above.

213) DORCAS HOLT *(Dorcas Abbott Holt³, Timothy², George¹)*, b. 4 Sep 1727 daughter of Nicholas and Dorcas (Abbott) Holt; death unknown but may have been at Wilton, NH; m. 26 Jan 1749, as his second wife, her first cousin, THOMAS HOLT, b. Mar 1711/2 son of Thomas and Alice (Peabody) Holt; Thomas d. at Andover, 21 Nov 1776.

Thomas's first marriage was to Hannah Kimball with whom he had six children. Following her death, Thomas married his cousin Dorcas and they had six children. The story is that Thomas Holt was the largest landholder in Andover at that time. Dorcas was also a horse lover and is supposed to have had the first horse

---

[566] Livermore, *History of Wilton*, p 470

gig in town.⁵⁶⁷ After the death of her husband, Dorcas went with one, or perhaps more, of her children to Wilton and she is believed to have died there.

Thomas wrote his will 8 Oct 1774. Dorcas was named executor of the estate in Thomas's will, but she requested that this duty be assumed by her brother Joshua Holt. In his will, Thomas Holt has bequests for the following persons: dearly beloved wife Dorcas who receives use of the West end of the dwelling house as well as other provisions for her support and son William is charged with seeing to her support and care; well-beloved son Nathan receives a token bequest of six shillings to make up his total portion; well-beloved son Daniel receives £13; well-beloved son Asa, six shillings; well-beloved son Thomas, a tract of land that was purchased from Samuel Ames; well-beloved son William, real and personal estate not otherwise disposed of; well-beloved son Joseph, a tract of land lying south of the land of the widow Rebecca Gray; beloved daughters Hannah and Mehitable receive six shillings each; beloved daughter Dorcas receives a piece of pasture land; beloved daughter Mary, £53; beloved daughter Lois, £53; daughters Lois and Mary also allowed use of a bed and chest in the house where they might stay in times of sickness as long as they are unmarried.⁵⁶⁸ Hannah, Mehitable, Nathan, Daniel, and Asa are children from Thomas's first marriage.

There are birth records for six children of Dorcas Holt and Thomas Holt recorded at Andover.

i THOMAS HOLT, b. 15 Jun 1750; m. 27 Oct 1774, his second cousin, LYDIA FARNUM, b. 10 Nov 1756

---

[567] Livermore, *History of the Town of Wilton*, p 404
[568] *Essex County, MA: Probate File Papers, 1638-1881. Probate of* Thomas Holt, 3 Feb 1777, *Case number* 13699.

daughter of Thomas and Lydia (Abbott) Farnum
This is the same as Family #209, child i. No children have been located for this couple.

862) ii DORCAS HOLT, b. 19 Mar 1753; m. 25 Nov 1773, her third cousin, MOSES LOVEJOY, b. 9 Sep 1751 son of Daniel and Mary (Holt) Lovejoy.

iii MARY HOLT, b. 11 Mar 1758. Durrie's Holt genealogy lists Mary as the Mary Holt that married John Adams in 1776 (his third marriage). However, John Adams's Mary died in 1829 at age 89, meaning she was born about 1740 so that is not this Mary. There are several marriages for Mary Holts about the time this Mary would have married, but all those other options are not yet explored.

863) iv LOIS HOLT, b. 29 Oct 1760; d. at Andover, 17 Apr 1852; m. 4 Jan 1785, MOSES PEARSON, b. at Wilmington, about 1752 son of Nathan and Mary (Wilson) Pearson; Moses d. at Andover 11 Aug 1835.

864) v WILLIAM HOLT, b. 7 Sep 1763; m. 29 Jul 1784, ELIZABETH JONES daughter of Jacob Jones; Elizabeth d. at Weld, ME, 1829.

865) vi JOSEPH HOLT, b. 29 Sep 1766; d. at Andover, 8 Jun 1791; m. 27 Nov 1788, his third cousin once removed, ABIGAIL HOLT, b. 19 May 1767 daughter of Samuel and Abigail (Blanchard) Holt; Abigail d. 13 May 1821.

214) JOSHUA HOLT *(Dorcas Abbott Holt³, Timothy², George¹)*, b. 30 Jun 1730 son of Nicholas and Dorcas (Abbott) Holt; d. 24 Jul 1810; m. 2 Dec 1755, his second cousin once removed, PHEBE FARNUM, b.

10 Oct 1731 daughter of Timothy and Dinah (Ingalls) Farnum; Phebe d. 26 Jan 1806.

Joshua Holt and Phebe Farnum had as their homestead what is now 111 Reservation Road in Andover, known as the Solomon Holt farm. Joshua is believed to have built this homestead in 1790. His son Solomon, as noted in the will, received the homestead from his father.[569]

Joshua was deacon of the South Parish church in Andover for 34 years. He also served in the Revolutionary War as a member of the 4th Essex County militia.[570]

Joshua Holt revised his will 24 May 1807 in response to "great alterations" that had taken place in his family. Perhaps these "great alterations" related to the death of his wife Phebe in 1806. Four sons, John, Joshua, Timothy, and Stephen, each receive $40. Son Peter receives $110. Each of his daughters receive $33.34. These daughters are Phebe the wife of Joseph Batchelder, Mary the wife of Isaac Foster, Abiah the wife of Deacon Daniel Kimbal, Hannah the wife of Ephraim Holt, and Chloe the wife of Francis Bowers. The daughters also receive all the household goods and furniture. Son Samuel receives all the lands and buildings that Joshua still holds at the time as his death as well as his pew in the meeting house. His six sons will divide his wearing apparel, although Solomon is free to select what items he wants. Solomon is named sole executor.[571]

Solomon was the only child in this family that remained in Andover. All the other children moved to New Hampshire and settled in towns in Hillsborough County.

---

[569] Andover Historic Preservation. https://preservation.mhl.org/111-reservation-road

[570] Massachusetts Soldiers and Sailors, volume 8, p 193

[571] *Essex County, MA: Probate File Papers, 1638-1881. Probate of* Joshua Holt, 9 Aug 1810, *Case number* 13666.

Joshua Holt and Phebe Farnum had eleven children whose births are recorded at Andover. Some sources (e. g., Durrie's *A Genealogical History of the Holt Family*) also list a child Ruth in this family, but there was another Joshua Holt married to Ruth Burnap who was in Andover at the same time and rearing a family. There were records for two girls named Ruth in Andover, one baptized in January 1756 and the other born 11 May 1758; both these dates conflict with births of other children of Joshua and Phebe, so perhaps Ruth was the daughter of Joshua and Ruth.

866) i PHEBE HOLT, b. 28 Nov 1756; d. at Greenfield, 1849; m. 11 Dec 1778, JOSEPH BATCHELDER, b. 6 Mar 1748 son of Joseph and Judith (Rea) Batchelder; Joseph d. 1826.

867) ii JOSHUA HOLT, b. 17 Jan 1758; d at Greenfield, 14 Mar 1835; m. 1787, HANNAH INGALLS, b. 20 Feb 1759 daughter of David and Priscilla (Howe) Ingalls; Hannah d. 1 Dec 1838.

868) iii MARY HOLT, b. 5 Dec 1759; d. at Greenfield, 9 Jul 1819; m. 26 Aug 1784, ISAAC FOSTER, b. 23 Dec 1751 son of Jacob and Abigail (Frost) Foster.

869) iv ABIAH HOLT, b. 16 Apr 1761; d. at Hancock, NH, 4 May 1841; m. 21 Jun 1791, as his second wife, DANIEL KIMBALL, b. at Ipswich, 20 Oct 1755 son of Daniel and Hephzibah (Howe) Kimball; d. 24 May 1843. Daniel's first wife was Elizabeth Osgood.

536) v PETER HOLT, b. 12 Jun 1763; d. at Greenfield, 25 Apr 1851; m. 23 Jan 1793, his first cousin (and George Abbott descendant), HANNAH HOLT, b. at Danvers, 11 May 1769 daughter of Nathan and Sarah (Abbott) Holt; Hannah d. at Beverly, 26 Jul 1857.

Generation Four 389

526) vi JOHN HOLT, b. 12 Jan 1765; d, at Greenfield, 11 Feb 1835; m. 6 Jan 1792, his third cousin, DORCAS ABBOTT, b. Dec 1766 daughter of George and Hannah (Lovejoy) Abbott; Dorcas d. 15 Mar 1841. This is the same as Family #124, child xi.

870) vii TIMOTHY HOLT, b. Apr 1767; d. at Peterborough, 1856; m. 7 Nov 1793, his second cousin once removed, LYDIA HOLT, b. 18 Apr 1767 daughter of Joseph and Ruth (Johnson) Holt; Lydia d. 22 Nov 1825.

871) viii SOLOMON HOLT, b. Dec 1768; d. 15 Apr 1830; m. 22 May 1798, MARY CUMMINGS, b. about 1775 daughter of Justin and Mary (-) Cummings;[572] Mary d. 8 Oct 1852.

872) ix HANNAH HOLT, b. Jun 1771; d. at Greenfield, 21 Apr 1842; m. 27 Nov 1794, her third cousin once removed (and George Abbott descendant of the 6th generation), EPHRAIM HOLT, b. 19 Mar 1769 son of Jacob and Rhoda (Abbott) Holt; Ephraim d. 24 Oct 1836.

873) x STEPHEN HOLT, b. May 1773; d. at Greenfield, 26 Mar 1868; m. 1799, FANNY BOWERS, b. at Chelmsford, Jun 1773 daughter of Francis and Elizabeth (Holt) Bowers; Fanny d. 18 Apr 1828. Stephen married in 1831, MARGARET BATCHELDER, b. 1784 and d. 1867.

---

[572] These are the parents given by Durrie's Holt family genealogy. There are no records that support this.

874) xi CHLOE HOLT, b. Jun 1775; d. at Peterborough, 6 Nov 1849; m. 23 Oct 1798, FRANCIS BOWERS, b. at Chelmsford, 20 May 1775 son of Francis and Elizabeth (Holt) Bowers; Francis d. 15 Oct 1835.

215) DANIEL HOLT *(Dorcas Abbott Holt³, Timothy², George¹)*, b. 10 Feb 1732/3 son of Nicholas and Dorcas (Abbott) Holt; d. at Andover, 15 Feb 1796; m. 29 Nov 1759, his first cousin once removed, HANNAH HOLT, b. 11 Feb 1738/9 daughter of Thomas and Hannah (Kimball) Holt; Hannah d. at Andover, 2 Aug 1831.

There are births for three children in this family that are recorded at Andover. A probate record was not located, and no other specific information about this couple.

875) i DANIEL HOLT, b. Dec 1761; d. at Fitchburg, 27 Nov 1830; m. 5 Jan 1790, MARY JONES, b. at Andover, about 1769 daughter of Jacob and Mary (Winn) Jones.[573]

876) ii ABIEL HOLT, b. 8 Jun 1765; d. at Fitchburg; m. 26 Jul 1791, PHEBE PUTNAM, b. at Fitchburg, 20 Sep 1770 daughter of Daniel and Rachel (-) Putnam; Phebe d. at Fitchburg, 12 Nov 1827.

iii NATHAN HOLT, b. 13 Jul 1767; d. 1 Sep 1778.

---

[573] The will of Jacob Jones includes a bequest to his granddaughter Mary Holt the child of his daughter Mary who is deceased.

Section VIII: The Grandchildren of Thomas Abbott and Hannah Gray

Thomas³, Thomas², George¹

216) ELIZABETH ABBOTT *(Thomas³, Thomas², George¹)*, b. 10 Jan 1726/7 daughter of Thomas and Elizabeth (Ballard) Abbott; d. at Andover 27 Sep 1792; m. 4 Jan 1753, as his 2nd wife, SAMUEL OSGOOD, b. 29 May 1714 son of Ezekiel and Rebecca (Wardwell) Osgood; Samuel d. 16 Mar 1774. Samuel was first married to Dorothy Wardwell.

Samuel Osgood did not leave a will. His widow Elizabeth was administrator of the estate. The value of the estate was £1,085. The probate records contain the details of the portion that Elizabeth received but does not have the other distributions.[574] Elizabeth Osgood also did not leave a will and her estate entered probate 6 Nov 1792. The value of her estate was £42. Thomas Osgood was the administrator of Elizabeth's estate.[575]

Elizabeth Abbott and Samuel Osgood had eight children whose births are recorded at Andover.

    i   LYDIA OSGOOD, b. 31 May 1754; d. at Andover, 2 Oct 1816; m. 20 Dec 1791, as the second of his three wives, ABIEL FAULKNER, b. at Andover, 4 Sep 1755 son of Abiel and Mary (Poor) Faulkner; Abiel d. 26 Nov 1818. His first marriage was to Hannah Abbott who was Lydia Osgood's first cousin. Abiel's third

---

[574] *Essex County, MA: Probate File Papers, 1638-1881. Probate of* Samuel Osgood, 5 Jul 1774, *Case number* 20268.

[575] *Essex County, MA: Probate File Papers, 1638-1881. Probate of* Elizabeth Osgood, 6 Nov 1792, *Case number* 20192.

marriage was to Clarissa Dillaway. Lydia did not have children.

 ii ELIZABETH OSGOOD, b. 17 Dec 1755; d. 16 Sep 1764.

 iii SARAH OSGOOD, b. 14 Sep 1758; d. 21 Oct 1764.

877) iv JOSEPH OSGOOD, b. 5 Oct 1760; d. at Blue Hill, ME, after 1845; m. 31 May 1785, HANNAH BAILEY, b. at Andover, 21 Dec 1765 daughter of Nathan and Deborah (Johnson) Bailey.

878) v DORCAS OSGOOD, b. Mar 1763; d. at Blue Hill, ME, 27 Apr 1832; m. at Andover, 4 Oct 1791, THEODORE STEVENS, b. 12 Jul 1763 son of Benjamin and Hannah (Varnum) Stevens; Theodore d. 15 May 1820.

 vi JOHN OSGOOD, b. 7 Sep 1765; d. at Allenstown, NH, Dec 1829; m. Oct 1802, MARY SLATER daughter of Benjamin and Mary (Henley) Slater.[576] No children have been identified for this couple.

879) vii THOMAS OSGOOD, b. 11 Jun 1767; d. at Charlestown, MA, 21 Mar 1818; m. 15 Mar 1792, HANNAH STEVENS, b. at Andover, 23 May 1770 daughter of Bimsley and Rebecca (-) Stevens; Hannah d. 1 Sep 1830.

---

[576] Her father's name is given in a Massachusetts Supreme Court Case involving a property dispute, not directly involving Mary, but concerning a property of her father Benjamin (a seaman who was an alien and never naturalized). She is listed as a daughter of Benjamin, Mary the wife of John Osgood. Massachusetts Reports: Cases Argued and Determined in the Supreme Judicial Court of Massachusetts, Volume 32, p 346

880) viii CHRISTOPHER OSGOOD, b. 25 Apr 1769; d. at Suncook, 3 Oct 1841; m. 7 Nov 1793, his third cousin once removed, ANNA ABBOTT, b. Sep 1767 daughter of Zebadiah and Rebecca (Ballard) Abbott; Anna d. 26 Dec 1827. Anna Abbott is a descendant of both George Abbott of Andover and George Abbott of Rowley.

217) THOMAS ABBOT *(Thomas³, Thomas², George¹)*, b. 4 Apr 1729 son of Thomas and Elizabeth (Ballard) Abbott; d. at Andover 29 Mar 1775; m. 12 Feb 1756, LYDIA BLUNT, b. 6 Apr 1731 daughter of David and Lydia (Foster) Blunt; Lydia d. 16 Nov 1798.

Thomas was a farmer in Andover having inherited the homestead as the oldest son in his family of origin.

Thomas Abbot wrote his will 24 Mar 1775. The will includes a request that his honored mother be well provided for. Thomas's father died in 1774 and as executor of his father's estate, Thomas would have been charged with the care of his mother. In his will, Thomas bequeaths to eldest son Thomas £80 or that value in land when he reaches age 21. Son Joel receives £60. Daughters Lydia, Hannah, Betty, Ane, and Chloe each receive £40. Dearly beloved wife Lydia receives all the remainder of the estate trusting that she in the future will make a just distribution of the estate. Lydia is also named executor of the estate.[577]

Thomas and Lydia had seven children whose births are recorded at Andover. The Andover record transcriptions contain a baptism in November 1771 for a daughter "Eleanor" but this is the same month as the birth of daughter Chloe; as there is Chloe, but not

---

[577] *Essex County, MA: Probate File Papers, 1638-1881*. Probate of Thomas Abbot, 6 May 1776, Case number 141.

Eleanor, in the will, this is either an error in the records or there was a twin who died very young.

881) i LYDIA ABBOTT, b. 10 Apr 1757; d. at Deering, NH, 12 Nov 1826; m. at Andover, 4 May 1779, THOMAS ELIPHALET MERRILL, b. at South Hampton, NH, 25 Oct 1751 son of Eliphalet and Mary (Clough) Merrill; Thomas d. at Weare, NH, 19 Oct 1830.

882) ii HANNAH ABBOTT, b. 5 May 1759; d. 14 Nov 1789; m. at Andover, 16 Feb 1777, ABIEL FAULKNER, b. at Andover, 4 Sep 1755 son of Abiel and Mary (Poor) Faulkner; Abiel d. 26 Nov 1818.

883) iii THOMAS ABBOTT, b. 25 May 1761; d. at Providence, 11 Jun 1826;[578] m. at Providence, 5 Jan 1800, RUTH OWEN, b. 21 Feb 1766 daughter of Joseph and Mary (Tripp) Owen; Ruth d. 26 Apr 1849.

884) iv BETTE ABBOTT, b. 25 Jun 1763; d. at Temple, ME, 12 Feb 1842; m. 17 Dec 1789, JONATHAN BALLARD, b. May 1761; Jonathan d. 28 Nov 1830.

v JOEL ABBOTT, b. 22 Nov 1765; d. at Andover, Dec 1826. He does seem to have married and had a son Joel. The identity of his wife has not yet been found. There is not any specific information about the son Joel.

vi ANNA ABBOTT, b. 28 Feb 1769. The Abbot genealogy lists her as marrying Christopher Osgood of Pembroke, but they also list Anna Abbott born in 1767 the daughter of Zebadiah and Rebecca (Ballard) Abbott (Rowley line) as marrying Christopher Osgood of Pembroke, and I believe it is Anna born in

---

[578] *Rhode Island, Vital Extracts, 1636-1899.*

Generation Four

1767 that married Christopher.[579] A different marriage for Anna has not been located.

885) vii CHLOE ABBOTT, b. 4 Nov 1771; d. at Melbourne, Québec; m. 19 Jan 1799, PETER FRYE, b. about 1771; Peter d. at Melbourne, Québec, 29 Jul 1843.[580]

218) JABEZ ABBOTT *(Thomas³, Thomas², George¹)*, b. 18 Apr 1731 son of Thomas and Elizabeth (Ballard) Abbott; d. 7 Jan 1804 at Concord; m. 1st by 1756, his first cousin, PHEBE ABBOTT *(Edward³, Thomas², George¹)*, b. 13 Feb 1732 daughter of Edward and Dorcas (Chandler) Abbott; Phebe d. 6 Jan 1770. Jabez m. 2nd 8 Aug 1772, HEPHZIBAH STEVENS, b. 28 Feb 1739/40 daughter of Samuel and Hephzibah (Ingalls) Stevens.

Jabez participated in some civic duties in Concord including serving as a highway surveyor. He also signed a 1776 resolution related to pledging loyalty to the revolutionary cause: *We, the Subscribers, do solemnly engage and promise, that we will, to the utmost of our Power, at the Risque of our Lives and Fortunes, with ARMS, oppose the Hostile Proceedings of the British Fleet and Armies against the United American Colonies.*[581]

Jabez Abbott and Phebe Abbott had four children whose births are recorded at Concord.

i JOSEPH ABBOTT, b. 22 Apr 1757; d. 21 Nov 1758.

---

[579] Abbot and Abbot, *Genealogical Record of Descendants*, p 86 and p 156
[580] Ancestry.com, *Quebec, Canada, Vital and Church Records (Drouin Collection), 1621-1968* (Provo, UT, USA: Ancestry.com Operations, Inc., 2008), Institut Généalogique Drouin; Montreal, Quebec, Canada; Author: Gabriel Drouin, comp..
[581] Bouton, *History of Concord*, p 270

886) ii JOSEPH ABBOTT, b. 5 Aug 1759; d. at Boscawen, NH, 7 Oct 1837; m. at Salisbury, 3 Apr 1794, MOLLY MELOON, b. at Salisbury, 25 Jan 1769 daughter of Nathaniel and Bathsheba (Tucker) Meloon; Molly d. 17 Dec 1847.

887) iii PHEBE ABBOTT, b. 29 Oct 1762; d. at Boscawen, 14 Sep 1819; m. 29 Dec 1791, PAUL CLARK, b. at Newbury, 23 May 1762 son of Daniel and Mehitable (Hale) Clark;[582] Paul d. 11 Jan 1808.

888) iv NATHAN ABBOTT, b. 29 Jun 1765; d. at Concord, 19 Mar 1844; m. 24 Feb 1801, RHODA BRICKETT, b. at Newbury, MA, 24 Jul 1769 daughter of Thomas and Mary (Noyes) Brickett.

Jabez Abbott and Hephzibah Stevens had four children whose births are recorded at Concord.

889) i LYDIA ABBOTT, b. 10 Jun 1773; d, 23 Mar 1841; m. at Concord, 27 Oct 1796, CHRISTOPHER ROWELL, b. at Hampstead, 22 Aug 1769 son of Christopher and Ruth (Moors) Rowell.

ii HEPHZIBAH ABBOTT, b. 1 Feb 1780; d. at Concord, 23 Jan 1817. Hephzibah did not marry.

890) iii DYER ABBOTT, b. 18 Jun 1778; d. at Henniker, 8 Mar 1832; m. at Boscawen, 1 Oct 1807, SARAH ATKINSON, b. at Boscawen, 19 Jul 1785 daughter of Benjamin and Jane (Varney) Atkinson.

---

[582] Hale, *Genealogy of the Descendants of Thomas Hale*, p 248

891) iv ASENATH ABBOTT, b. 3 Oct 1781; d. at Pembroke, NH after 1850;[583] m. 24 Feb 1801, THOMAS BRICKETT, b. at Pembroke, 7 Aug 1778 son of Thomas and Mary (Noyes) Brickett; Thomas d. about 1855 (probate of estate 25 Sep 1855).

219) AARON ABBOTT (*Thomas³, Thomas², George¹*), b. 17 Feb 1732/3 son of Thomas and Elizabeth (Ballard) Abbott; d. at Concord 31 Dec 1812; m. his first cousin, LYDIA ABBOTT (*Edward³, Thomas², George¹*), b. 15 Jun 1737 daughter of Edward and Dorcas (Chandler) Abbott; Lydia d. 15 Dec 1811.

There are perhaps eight children (according to the Abbot genealogy) but only two survived childhood.[584] There were no records located for the six children who died in childhood, so they are just listed here: Betsey, Betsey2, Samuel, Samuel2, Joseph, and Thomas. The two children who lived to adult age are listed below. Both these children married other Abbotts.

    i LYDIA ABBOTT, b. 4 Apr 1771; m. at Concord, 17 Apr 1811, as his second wife, her first cousin, TIMOTHY ABBOTT, b. 12 Mar 1769 son of Edward and Deborah (Stevens) Abbott; Timothy d. 23 Jan 1819. Lydia and Timothy did not have children. Timothy was first married to Sarah Bradley.

892) ii AARON ABBOTT, b. at Concord, 11 Apr 1778; d. at Bethel, ME, 8 Sep 1856; m. 1 Jan 1800, his second cousin, SARAH ABBOTT, b. at Concord, 26 Jun 1780

---

[583] She and her husband Thomas Brickett are both listed in the 1850 U.S. Census living at Pembroke.
[584] Abbot and Abbot, *Genealogical Record of Descendants*, p 88

daughter of Stephen and Mary (Gile) Abbott; Sarah d. at Bethel, 1853.

220) NATHAN ABBOTT *(Thomas³, Thomas², George¹)*, b. 7 Feb 1736/7 son of Thomas and Elizabeth (Ballard) Abbott; d. at Concord, 18 Jan 1805; m. 1766, BETTY FARNUM, b. 1743 daughter of Joseph and Zerviah (Hoit) Farnum; Betty d. 11 Nov 1821

Nathan Abbott and Betty Farnum had ten children whose births are recorded at Concord.

      i   BETTY ABBOTT, b. 2 Jul 1767; d. 1774.

893) ii   JACOB ABBOTT, b. 16 Jan 1769; d. 13 Jan 1838; m. 1802, BETSEY KNAPP, b. 4 Mar 1782; Betsey d. at Rumford, ME, 18 Mar 1831.

     iii ASA ABBOTT, b. 11 Nov 1770; d. 11 Feb 1843. Asa did not marry.

894) iv DAVID ABBOTT, b. 22 Sep 1772. The Abbot genealogy reports he went to New York in 1794 and left no trace after that. He was a house-joiner. The Rutherford County Tennessee Historical Society suggests that this David Abbott made his way to Tennessee and died in Gibson County, TN in 1856. The historical society has prepared a summary on David and reports he married Elizabeth Cummins 15 Oct 1811.[585] David Abbott owned a mill and received a pension for service in the War of 1812.[586] There is

---

[585] Rutherford County Tennessee Historical Society, "Some of the Earliest People in Rutherford County by Their Date of Birth Prior to 1800," retrieved from http://rutherfordtnhistory.org/wp-content/uploads/2017/10/Pioneers-before-1800.pdf

[586] National Archives, War of 1812 Pension and Bounty Land Warrant Application Files, www.fold3.com/image/270301070?xid=1945

an 1850 U.S. Census Record for Fall Creek, Rutherford, TN which lists David Abbott born about 1772 in NH as head of the household.[587] He wrote a will in 1835 that was in probate in Gibson County, TN in 1857.[588]

895) v HENRY ABBOTT, b. 22 Sep 1774; d. at Rumford, ME, 1 Feb 1862; m. 1 Jun 1798, his second cousin once removed (and George Abbott descendant), SUSANNAH HALL, b. at Concord, 13 Nov 1781 daughter of Stephen and Patience (Flanders) Hall; Susannah d. 20 Mar 1867.

vi ANNA ABBOTT, b. 7 Jun 1776; died young.

vii BETTY ABBOTT, b. 19 Apr 1778; d. 24 May 1831; m. 3 Jun 1816, JEREMIAH EASTMAN. Betty and Jeremiah did not have children.

896) viii ANNA ABBOTT, b. 8 Jan 1781; m. Feb 1806, her third cousin once removed (and George Abbott descendant), EDMUND BLANCHARD, b. at Canterbury, NH, 27 Jan 1778 son of Jonathan and Hannah (Chadwick) Blanchard; Edmund d. in Vermont, 29 Nov 1836.[589]

897) ix CHLOE ABBOTT, b. 10 Jun 1783; m. 19 Dec 1809, ZEBADIAH FARNUM, b. at Concord, 4 Mar 1781 son of John and Sally (West) Farnum.

---

[587] Year: 1850; Census Place: Fall Creek, Rutherford, Tennessee; Roll: M432_894; Page: 164B; Image: 321
[588] Tennessee Wills and Probate Records, 1779-2008, Gibson County, TN, Will Books Vol D-F, 1846-1862, Will of David Abbott.
[589] *Vermont, Vital Records, 1720-1908*.

x   ESTHER ABBOTT, b. 19 May 1789; d. at Concord after 1850. At the 1850 U.S. Census she was living with her nephew Asa Blanchard in Concord.

Edward[3], Thomas[2], George[1]

221)   DORCAS ABBOTT *(Edward[3], Thomas[2], George[1])*, b. at Rumford 15 Feb 1728/9 daughter of Edward and Dorcas (Chandler) Abbott; d. at Concord, 28 Sep 1797; m. 17 Jun 1746, EBENEZER HALL, b. at Bradford, 19 Sep 1721 son of Joseph and Sarah (Kimball) Hall; Ebenezer d. 24 Apr 1801; Ebenezer was the brother of Joseph Hall who married Deborah Abbott [daughter of Thomas and Hannah (Gray) Abbott]. Ebenezer Hall was first married to Hephzibah Farnum.

Ebenezer Hall was a farmer in Concord and served as selectman. Dorcas Abbott is believed to be the "first white girl born in Concord."[590]

Ebenezer Hall wrote his will 8 June 1791. Beloved wife Dorcas receives the income from one-half of his real estate and one-half of the cattle during her natural life and all the household items. Beloved son Ebenezer receives a 60-acre lot in Warner. Beloved daughter Hephzibah Hazeltine receives £3. Well beloved son Obadiah receives six shillings. Beloved daughter Dorcas Carter receives £3. Beloved daughter Sarah Hazeltine also receives £3. Beloved sons Daniel, Timothy, and Abiel each receive six shillings. Daughter Lydia Cavis receives $8 as does daughter Deborah Barker. Beloved son Stephen receives the whole of the real estate in Concord. Son Stephen is also the sole executor of the estate. The 7 July 1801 inventory of the estate of Ebenezer Hall included real

---

[590] Hurd, *History of Merrimack and Belknap Counties*, Part 2, p 540

Generation Four

estate valued at $3,475.[591] The son Ebenezer Hall mentioned in the will is Ebenezer's son from his first marriage to Hephzibah Farnum.

Dorcas Abbott and Ebenezer Hall were parents to twelve children.

898) i HEPHZIBAH HALL, b. at Rumford, 29 Mar 1747; d. at Concord, 23 Nov 1817; m. about 1765, RICHARD HAZELTINE, b. 5 Apr 1742 son of Richard and Sarah (Barnes) Hazeltine; Richard d. 21 Apr 1817.

899) ii OBADIAH HALL, b. at Rumford, 13 Oct 1748; d. 24 Mar 1831; m. 3 Nov 1770, MARY PERHAM, b. 3 May 1749; Mary d. 27 Feb 1822. After Mary's death, Obadiah married Abigail Morrison.

900) iii DORCAS HALL; b. 13 Jan 1751; d. 5 Sep 1813 (or 1823); m. EPHRAIM CARTER, b. at Concord, 21 Oct 1746 son of Ezra and Ruth (Eastman) Carter.

901) iv SARAH HALL, b. at Rumford, 4 Feb 1753; d. May 1845; m. by 1774, WILLIAM HAZELTINE, b. at Rumford, 16 Jun 1744 son of Richard and Sarah (Barnes) Hazeltine; William d. at Canterbury, Jan 1826.

902) v DANIEL HALL, b. at Rumford, 13 Jan 1755; d. at Concord, 18 Feb 1835; m. 26 Sep 1775, DEBORAH DAVIS, b. at Concord, 15 Jul 1757 daughter of Robert and Sarah (Walker) Davis; Deborah d. 31 Oct 1822.

902a vi TIMOTHY HALL, b. at Rumford, 5 Jun 1757; d. at Irasburg, VT, 16 Jul 1832; m. at Concord, 15 Oct 1780,

---

[591] *New Hampshire Wills and Probate Records 1643-1982,* Probate of Ebenezer Hall, Rockingham, 5 May 1801, Case number 6818.

ANNA FOSTER of Bow, born about 1760; d. after 1850.[592][593]

903) vii STEPHEN HALL, b. at Concord, 13 May 1759; d. at Concord, 23 Nov 1808; m. PATIENCE FLANDERS, b. at Boscawen, 9 Oct 1758 daughter of Ezekiel and Sarah (Bishop) Flanders; Patience d. 17 Feb 1834.

904) viii ABIEL HALL, b. at Rumford, 31 May 1761; d. 13 Oct 1829 at Alfred, ME; m. 1st, MARY FARNUM, b. at Concord, 26 Aug 1764 daughter of Benjamin and Anna (Merrill) Farnum; Mary d. 23 Nov 1816. Abiel m. 2nd, 1819, ANNA FRANCIS (widow of Edward Grant); Anna d. 11 Dec 1857.

ix HANNAH HALL, b. 1 Nov 1764; d. 16 Nov 1765.

x HANNAH HALL, b. 2 Oct 1766; died young.

905) xi LYDIA HALL, b. at Concord, 10 Oct 1767; d. at Bow, NH, 30 Mar 1855; m. 5 Jan 1788, NATHANIEL CAVIS, b. 25 Dec 1761; Nathaniel d. 10 Sep 1842.

906) xii DEBORAH HALL, b. at Concord, 18 Sep 1769; d. 25 Oct 1791; m. at Hillsborough, 26 Oct 1787, DANIEL BARKER. Daniel perhaps married Anna Lathrop 19 Mar 1792.

222) EDWARD ABBOTT (*Edward³, Thomas², George¹*), b. 27 Dec 1730 son of Edward and Dorcas (Chandler) Abbott; d. 15 Sep 1801; m. about 1760 DEBORAH STEVENS, origins not certain but likely the Deborah born 1738 in Rumford, NH daughter of Aaron and Deborah (Stevens) Stevens. Aaron Stevens was an early settler at Concord. Deborah d. Nov 1817.

Edward Abbott and Deborah Stevens had nine children.

---

[592] Revolutionary War Pension and Bounty-Land Warrant Application Files
[593] Anna Hall was living with her daughter Judith Kellogg at the 1850 census.

Generation Four

907) i MARY ABBOTT, b. 1761; d. 1843; m. by 1780, THOMAS CAPEN, b. at Charlestown, 19 Apr 1762 son of Thomas and Mary (Wyman) Capen;[594] Thomas died at sea in 1808. This family settled in New Pennacook, Maine.

908) ii MEHITABLE ABBOTT, b. 23 Apr 1763; d. 16 Sep 1838;[595] m. by 1786, BENJAMIN LUFKIN, b. at Ipswich, 8 Apr 1763;[596] Benjamin d. at Roxbury, ME, Nov 1844.

909) iii SUSANNA ABBOTT, b. 1765; d. 25 Feb 1841; m. by 1786, JOHN WEEKS, b. at Portsmouth, NH, 23 Jun 1757; John d. at Concord, 6 Apr 1836.

iv EDWARD ABBOTT, b. about 1767; d. about 1784?

910) v TIMOTHY ABBOTT, b. 12 Mar 1769; d. 23 Jan 1819; m. 1st, SARAH BRADLEY daughter of Abraham and Sarah (-) Bradley; Sarah d. 1810.[597] Timothy m. 2nd, his first cousin, LYDIA ABBOTT, b. 4 Apr 1771 daughter of Aaron and Lydia (Abbott) Abbott. Aaron and Lydia Abbott are Family # 219.

911) vi SAMUEL ABBOTT, b. 8 Apr 1771; m. at Pembroke, 4 Mar 1792, MARY "POLLY" CURRIER, b. at Concord, 13 Oct 1776 daughter of William and Mary (Carter)

---

[594] Hayden and Tuttle, *The Capen Family*, p 137
[595] Mehitable Lufkin's death is reported in the records of the First Congregational Church of Concord. (Reed and Thorne, History and Manual of the First Congregational Church)
[596] Lapham, *History of Rumford*, p 369
[597] Ancestry.com, New Hampshire, Death and Disinterment Records, 1754-1947

Currier.⁵⁹⁸ Samuel was a carpenter and relocated to Buffalo, New York. Later, the family moved to Switzerland County, Indiana where both Samuel and Polly died in 1820.

    vii   DEBORAH ABBOTT, b. and d. 1773.

912) viii DEBORAH ABBOTT, b. at Concord, 29 May 1774; d. at Rumford, ME, 20 Apr 1861; m. PHINEAS HOWE, b. at Bolton, MA, 25 Mar 1769 son of Phineas and Experience (Pollard)⁵⁹⁹ Howe; Phineas d. 27 Dec 1847.

    ix   ESTHER ABBOTT, b. 1777; d. 1824; m. at Concord, 13 Mar 1800, TRUEWORTHY KILGORE. Esther and Trueworthy did not have children.

218) JABEZ ABBOTT *(Thomas³, Thomas², George¹)* and PHEBE ABBOTT *(Edward³, Thomas², George¹)*; JABEZ ABBOTT and HEPHZIBAH STEVENS. This is Family #218 covered above.

219) AARON ABBOTT *(Thomas³, Thomas², George¹)*, b. 17 Feb 1732/3 son of Thomas and Elizabeth (Ballard) Abbott; d. at Concord 31 Dec 1812; m. his first cousin, LYDIA ABBOTT *(Edward³, Thomas², George¹)*, b. 15 Jun 1737 daughter of Edward and Dorcas (Chandler) Abbott; Lydia d. 15 Dec 1811. This is Family #219 covered above.

223) BETSEY ABBOTT *(Edward³, Thomas², George¹)*, b. 25 Aug 1743 daughter of Edward and Dorcas (Chandler) Abbott; d. 2 Oct 1827 at Goffstown, NH; m. 1759, THOMAS SALTMARSH, b. at Watertown,

---

⁵⁹⁸ Currier and Currier, *The Genealogy of Richard Currier*, p 26. The Abbot and Abbot genealogy gives her name as Ruth Currier, but the Currier genealogy says Mary Currier and the marriage record says Polly Currier.

⁵⁹⁹ The division of William Pollard's estate in 1763 includes a disbursement to his daughter Elizabeth wife of Phineas Howe.

2 Mar 1736 son of Thomas and Mary (Hazen) Saltmarsh; Thomas d. at Goffstown, NH 8 May 1826.[600]

Betsey Abbott and Thomas Saltmarsh had ten children born in New Hampshire with some births recorded at Concord. Birth records for every child were not located and the Abbot genealogy was used to supplement information.[601]

913) i MEHITABLE SALTMARSH, b. at Concord, 12 Apr 1762; d. at Gilford, NH, 25 Oct 1814; m. at Goffstown, 9 Feb 1784, JAMES HOYT, b. at Kingston, 28 Mar 1762 son of Eliphalet and Mary (Peaslee) Hoyt; James d. 1834. After Mehitable's death, James married Abigail Whittier in 1815 and Huldah Fifield in 1822.

914) ii JOHN SALTMARSH, b. at Concord, 21 May 1764; d. after 1850 (living in Bedford at the 1850 U.S. Census); m. at Goffstown, 22 Nov 1785, SUSAN BURNHAM, b. at Ipswich, 1756 daughter of Samuel and Martha (Story) Burnham.

915) iii MARY "POLLY" SALTMARSH, b. at Concord, 28 Aug 1766; d. at Peterborough, 21 Apr 1848; m. at Goffstown, 31 Mar 1791, SAMUEL VOSE, b. at Bedford, 23 May 1759 son of Samuel and Phebe (Vickery) Vose; Samuel d. at Antrim, NH, 8 Aug 1830.

916) iv EDWARD ABBOTT SALTMARSH, b. 1768 likely at Goffstown; d. at Hookset, NH, 11 Mar 1851; m. at

---

[600] The graves of Elizabeth Abbott and Thomas Saltmarsh are in the Westlawn Cemetery at Goffstown with a gravestone that lists their names as Thomas Saltmarsh and Elisabeth Abbott, his wife. (accessed through findagrave.com)
[601] Abbot and Abbot, *Genealogical Record of Descendants*, p 101

Goffstown, 19 Oct 1791, SARAH "SALLY" STORY, b. 1773 (based on age at time of death) daughter of Nehemiah and Sarah (Gold) Story; Sally d. 19 May 1860.

917) v   THOMAS SALTMARSH, b. 1771; d. at Saco, ME, 1804; m. at Wolfeboro, 7 Jun 1799, BETSY EVANS, b. 21 May 1780 daughter of Benjamin and Lydia (Browne) Evans.

vi   SALLY SALTMARSH, b. 1773.

918) vii SAMUEL SALTMARSH, b. 1775; d. at Goffstown, 1844; m. 28 May 1800, BETSY BURNHAM, b. about 1780; Betsy d. at Goffstown, 1840.

919) viii CATHERINE SALTMARSH, b. 1777; d. after 1850 (still living at the 1850 U.S. Census); m. her first cousin, THOMAS SALTMARSH, b. at Bedford, MA, 22 Aug 1772 son of Seth and Ruth (Bowman) Saltmarsh; Thomas d. at Gilford, NH, 18 Sep 1823.

920) ix ISAAC SALTMARSH, b. 1779; d. at Antrim, NH, 13 Mar 1823; m. at Bradford, NH, 13 Nov 1805, PHEBE STRATTON, b. at Marlboro, MA, 27 Feb 1790 daughter of Jonathan and Abigail (Barnes) Stratton; Phebe d. 13 Sep 1872.

x   HAZEN SALTMARSH, b. 1781; d. 1805.

Deborah Abbott Hall[3], Thomas[2], George[1]

224) MARY HALL *(Deborah Abbott Hall[3], Thomas[2], George[1])*, b. 17 Mar 1743 daughter of Joseph and Deborah (Abbott) Hall; d. 12 Dec 1773; m. THOMAS WILSON who d. at Concord 23 May 1818. Thomas m. 2nd, Mary Hopkins Bancroft.

Thomas Wilson wrote his will 20 May 1818. In his will, he directs that his estate be divided equally among his five children (four children living and the children of his son Thomas who is deceased). First named is Mary Thorndike wife of John Thorndike. However, if John Thorndike brings any demand against the estate, that amount is to be deducted from Mary's share. Second named is daughter Eliza Flagg. Next named is daughter Rebecca Wilson. Then named are the children of his son Thomas. Lastly, is daughter Ruth Wilson who is to pay Eliza what she owes her.[602] Just the oldest child named, Mary Thorndike, is from Thomas's marriage to Mary Hall.

Mary Hall and Thomas Wilson had two children born at Concord.

    i   JEREMIAH HALL WILSON, b. at Concord 1770; d. 10 Apr 1775

921) ii MARY "MOLLY" WILSON, b. 23 Jul 1772; m. 1st, 25 Mar 1792, JOHN THORNDIKE, b. at Beverly, 30 Nov 1768 son of Larkin and Ruth (Woodbury) Thorndike. Dr. John Thorndike died at Concord, 1821. Mary m. 2nd, 27 Nov 1823, her third cousin, ABIEL WALKER, b. 5 Jul 1766 son of James and Ruth (Abbott) Walker. Abiel was first married to Judith Davis.

George³, Thomas², George¹ *and* Sarah⁴, Stephen³, John², George¹
[Families #225 through #228 are descendants by both paths given above.]

---

[602] *New Hampshire Wills and Probate Records 1643-1982,* Probate of Thomas Wilson, Rockingham, 20 May 1818, Case number 9739.

225) DANIEL ABBOT *(George³, Thomas², George¹* **and** *Sarah⁴, Stephen³, John², George¹)*, b. 7 Aug 1738 son of George and Sarah (Abbott) Abbott; d. 11 Jun 1804; m. 1st by 1761, his second cousin RACHEL ABBOTT *(Nathaniel³, Nathaniel², George¹)*, b. 7 Apr 1743 daughter of Nathaniel and Penelope (Ballard) Abbott; Rachel d. 13 Jun 1788. Daniel m. 2nd 1 Jan 1789 at Boscawen, MERCY "MARY" KILBURN whose origins are not fully verified, although she is likely the daughter of Jedediah and Hannah (Platts) Kilburn. She was born about 1758 based on the birth of her last child in 1799. Mercy was living in 1830 when she was listed as a head of household in the 1830 US Census of Concord (between age 60-70).

The will of Daniel Abbot has bequests for the following persons: beloved wife Mary, beloved sons Beriah, Jeremiah, Daniel, George, Thomas, Abiel, Peter Hazeltine, Benjamin, daughters Judith, Sarah, Hannah, Lois, Susanna, son Nathan Kilburn, and son Samuel who is appointed executor along with Thomas.[603]

Children of Daniel Abbot and Rachel Abbott were born at Concord. There are birth records for all the children except the oldest child Beriah.

922)   i   BERIAH ABBOTT, b. about 1758; d. at Pomfret, VT, 13 Mar 1832;[604] m. about 1785 the widow MARY ANDREWS FAIRFIELD. Mary d. 29 Jul 1813; Beriah m. 2nd, MARTHA GRISWOLD, b. about 1759 and d. at Randolph, VT, 28 Jan 1841.

         ii   SARAH ABBOTT, b. 19 Jul 1761; d. 21 Jan 1774.

---

[603] *New Hampshire Wills and Probate Records 1643-1982*, Probate of Daniel Abbott, Rockingham, 27 Aug 1804, Case number 7284.
[604] Ancestry.com, *Vermont, Vital Records, 1720-1908* (Provo, UT, USA: Ancestry.com Operations, Inc., 2013).

923)	iii	SAMUEL ABBOTT, b. 26 Mar 1764; d. at Concord, 1 Dec 1849; m. 17 Nov 1787, MARY T. "POLLY" STORY, b. 16 Oct 1764 daughter of Jeremiah and Mary "Polly" (Burnham) Story; Polly d. 21 Dec 1849.
924)	iv	JEREMIAH ABBOTT, b. 21 Feb 1766; d. at Pomfret, VT, 10 Feb 1811; m. 15 Jan 1795, CLARISSA PERRY, b. at Ashford, CT, 31 Mar 1770 daughter of Robert and Sarah (Hodges) Perry;[605] Clarissa d. 10 Oct 1826.
	v	DANIEL ABBOTT, b. 21 Feb 1768; d. 19 Sep 1769.
925)	vi	DANIEL ABBOTT, b. 7 Mar 1770; d. unknown; m. 29 Jan 1794, LUCY HARVEY, b. at Gilsum, NH, 15 Dec 1768 daughter of Thomas and Grace (Willey) Harvey; Lucy d. 8 Feb 1849.
926)	vii	GEORGE ABBOTT, b. 12 May 1772; m. BETSY EASTMAN.
927)	viii	THOMAS ABBOTT, b. 5 Jul 1776; d. at Concord, NH, 1845; m. 14 Apr 1801, ANNA EATON, b. in NH about 1781; d. at Concord after 1850 (living with her daughter Dorcas and her family at the 1850 census). Her parentage is not verified but she is *possibly* the daughter of Ephraim and Eunice (-) Eaton.
928)	ix	ABIEL ABBOTT, b. 19 Mar 1778; d. at Waldo, ME, 1 Aug 1836;[606] m. at Lincolnville, ME, 2 Feb 1809, SARAH COMBS,[607] "of Georgetown (ME)". She is

---

[605] Robert Perry was an early settler of Windsor County, Vermont. Aldrich and Holmes, *History of Windsor County, Vermont*, p 969
[606] Ancestry.com, Maine, Death Records, 1761-1922
[607] "Maine Marriages, 1771-1907," database, *FamilySearch* (https://familysearch.org/ark:/61903/1:1:F4DX-WLN: 10 February 2018), Abial

SARAH HINKLEY, b. at Georgetown, 14 Aug 1774 daughter of John and Hannah (Oliver) Hinkley[608] and the widow of Leonard Coombs. Sarah d. at Waldo, 4 Nov 1865 (age 91 years, 3 months at time of death).[609] The death record of daughter Harriet gives the maiden name of mother as Sarah Hinkley.

929) x PETER HAZELTINE ABBOTT, b. 28 Feb 1780; d. after 1860 (listed in the 1860 Census living with his son Asaph); m. 9 Mar 1815, his first cousin once removed, SARAH ABBOTT, b. 10 Sep 1781 daughter of Moses and Mary (Batchelder) Abbott; Sarah d. 10 Aug 1846.

930) xi BENJAMIN ABBOTT, b. 29 Mar 1782; m. ESTHER CURRIER, b. 5 Nov 1787 daughter of Nathaniel Currier.

931) xii JUDITH ABBOTT, b. 4 Apr 1784; d. 18 Apr 1831; m. JOHN CARPENTER.

xiii CHILD ABBOTT, b. and d. 12 Jun 1788.

Children of Daniel Abbott and Mercy Kilburn: In the 1850, 1860, and 1870 U.S. Census, Sarah, Lois, and Nathan were living together in Concord and it seems none of them married. Nathan is listed as single on his death record. Susannah also does not seem to have married.

Abbot and Sarah Combs, 02 Feb 1809; citing Lincolnville, Waldo, Maine, reference vol 1; FHL microfilm 11,351.
[608] "Maine Births and Christenings, 1739-1900," database, *FamilySearch* (https://familysearch.org/ark:/61903/1:1:F4HY-ZPV: 10 February 2018), Sarah Hinkley, 14 Aug 1774; citing GEORGETOWN, SAGADAHOC, MAINE; FHL microfilm 873,976.
[609] Maine State Archives; Cultural Building, 84 State House Station, Augusta, ME 04333-0084; Pre-1892 Delayed Returns; Roll Number: 1; Maine State death records 1761-1922

	i	SARAH ABBOTT, b. 4 Apr 1790; d. after 1870.[610]
932)	ii	HANNAH ABBOTT, b. 28 Oct 1791; d. 13 Sep 1876; m. 16 Mar 1815, her third cousin once removed, REUBEN ABBOTT, b. at Concord, 23 Oct 1790 son of Reuben and Zerviah (Farnum) Abbott; Reuben d. 27 Jun 1869.
	iii	LOIS ABBOTT, b. 31 Oct 1793; d. at Concord, 18 Dec 1881.
	iv	SUSANNAH ABBOTT, b. 23 May 1797; d. 22 Jun 1847.[611]
	v	NATHAN KILBURN ABBOTT, b. 30 Aug 1799; d. at Concord 14 Jun 1878.

226) JOSEPH ABBOTT *(George³, Thomas², George¹* **and** *Sarah⁴, Stephen³, John², George¹)*, b. 23 Oct 1741 son of George and Sarah (Abbott) Abbott; d. at Concord, NH, 19 Jan 1832; m. 25 Apr 1765, his third cousin once removed, PHEBE LOVEJOY *(Phebe Chandler Lovejoy⁴, John Chandler³, Hannah Abbott Chandler², George¹)*, b. 20 Sep 1735 daughter of Henry and Phebe (Chandler) Lovejoy; Phebe d. 4 Jan 1789. Joseph m. 2nd, ABIGAIL TYLER.

Joseph Abbott and Phebe Lovejoy had ten children born at Concord.

---

[610] She is listed in the 1870 US Census living with Lois Abbot and Nathan K. Abbot. There is no record of her after that.
[611] Abbot and Abbot, *Genealogical Record of Descendants*, p 105

Grandchildren of Thomas Abbott and Hannah Gray

933) i PHEBE ABBOTT, b. 22 Feb 1766; d. at Woodbury, VT, 31 May 1837;[612] m. her third cousin (and George Abbott descendant), JOSEPH BLANCHARD, b. at Dunstable, NH, 24 Nov 1761 son of John and Eleanor (Stevens) Blanchard; Joseph d. 19 Feb 1839.

934) ii MOLLY ABBOTT, b. 20 Jul 1767; d. at Concord, 15 Aug 1791; m. 22 May 1785, ISAAC HOUSTON, b. at Bedford, NH, 1760 son of James and Mary (Mitchell) Houston. Isaac m. 2nd, Ruth Gale. Isaac d. at Hanover, NH, 25 Mar 1833.

935) iii HANNAH ABBOTT, b. 3 Jan 1769; d. 31 Oct 1810; m. 10 Dec 1795, DAVID KIMBALL, b. at Rumford, 10 Oct 1757 son of Reuben and Miriam (Collins) Kimball.

936) iv SARAH ABBOTT, b. 3 Jan 1769; d. at Concord, 27 Jan 1857; m. Nov 1787, her second cousin (and George Abbott descendant), TIMOTHY CHANDLER, b. at Rumford, 25 Apr 1762 son of Timothy and Elizabeth (Copp) Chandler; Timothy d. 9 Aug 1848. This is the same as Family #259, child ii.

v LOIS ABBOTT, b. 29 Mar 1771; d. 14 Mar 1790.

937) vi RACHEL ABBOTT, b. 2 Mar 1773; d. at Fryeburg, ME, 2 Mar 1837; m. 29 Nov 1797, JONATHAN WARD, b. at Concord, 17 Aug 1774 son of Stephen and Elizabeth (Copp) Ward; Jonathan d. 5 Feb 1822. Jonathan's mother, Elizabeth Copp, was first married to Timothy Chandler who was Rachel Abbott's first cousin, once removed.

vii DORCAS ABBOTT, b. 20 Dec 1774; d. 6 Oct 1788.

---

[612] *Vermont, Vital Records, 1720-1908.*

	viii	ISAAC ABBOTT, b. 10 Apr 1777; d. Jan 1800.
938)	ix	NATHAN ABBOTT, b. 27 Aug 1779; d. 26 Aug 1839; m. ELIZABETH "BETSEY" COLBY, b. 1786 daughter of John and Ann (Carter) Colby; Betsey d. 14 Dec 1819.
	x	RUTH ABBOTT, b. 8 May 1782; d. after 1850. Ruth did not marry. She was living alone in Concord at the 1850 U. S. Census.[613]

227) STEPHEN ABBOTT *(George³, Thomas², George¹* **and** *Sarah⁴, Stephen³, John², George¹)*, 28 Oct 1746 son of George and Sarah (Abbott) Abbott; d. 12 May 1811;[614] m. 11 Apr 1778, MARY GILE, b. about 1755 (parentage not verified at this point); Mary d. Jan 1822.

Stephen Abbott and Mary Gile had seven children born at Concord.

	i	EPHRAIM ABBOTT, b. 5 Feb 1779; d. Jan 1822. Ephraim did not marry.
892)	ii	SARAH ABBOTT, b. 20 Jun 1780; d. at Bethel, ME, 1853; m. 1 Jan 1800, her second cousin, AARON ABBOTT, b. at Concord, 11 Apr 1778 son of Aaron and Lydia (Abbott) Abbott; Aaron d. 8 Sep 1856. This is the same as Family #219, child ii.
939)	iii	POLLY ABBOTT, b. at Concord, 26 Apr 1782; d. after 1850 at Bethel, ME (still living at the 1850 U.S.

---

[613] Year: 1850; Census Place: Concord, Merrimack, New Hampshire; Roll: M432_435; Page: 61A; Image: 124. Ruth Abbott, age 68, as the only member of the household.
[614] *New Hampshire, Death and Disinterment Records, 1754-1947.*

Census); m. about 1804, JOSEPH TWITCHELL, b. at Bethel, 28 Mar 1782 son of Eleazer and Martha (Mason) Twitchell; Joseph d. after 1870.

940) iv THEODORE ABBOTT, b. 23 Feb 1784; d at George's Mill, NH, 8 May 1855; m. at New London, NH, 25 Jun 1809, MARY "POLLY" BURPEE, b. 29 Sep 1791 daughter of Thomas and Sarah (Smith) Burpee.

v STEPHEN ABBOTT, b. 19 May 1786; d. likely at Portland, ME; m. at Portland, 11 Jul 1819, the widow ABIGAIL WEBB, b. about 1787; Abigail d. 26 Aug 1846. Stephen and Abigail did not have children.

941) vi LUCY ABBOTT, b. 24 Jan 1789; m. at Springfield, NH, 2 Oct 1816, BENJAMIN HASELITNE, b. about 1785 "of Wendell."

942) vii SAMUEL ABBOTT, b. 14 May 1791; d. at Montpelier, VT, 4 May 1861; m. 5 Mar 1813, JANE DAY, b. at Boscawen, 20 Jul 1794 daughter of Daniel and Jane (Cass) Day.

228) EZRA ABBOTT *(George³, Thomas², George¹* **and** *Sarah⁴, Stephen³, John², George¹)*, b. 22 Aug 1756 son of George and Sarah (Abbott) Abbott; d. 21 Feb 1837; m. 1st 21 Nov 1782, BETTY ANDREWS, b. 12 May 1762 daughter of Thomas and Mary (Burnham) Andrews; Betty d. 25 Aug 1794. Ezra m. 2nd, 10 May 1795, ANNER CHOATE, b. at Ipswich 12 Jan 1758 daughter of Thomas and Dorothy (Proctor) Choate; Anner d. 21 Mar 1798. Ezra m. 3rd, 15 Nov 1798, JANE JACKMAN, b. at Boscawen, 20 Dec 1767 daughter of Benjamin and Jane (Woodman) Jackman; Jane d. 2 May 1847.

Ezra Abbott served several campaigns during the Revolutionary War.[615] He was taken prisoner at Fort Cedars 19 May

---

[615] Bouton, *History of Concord*, p 623

1779. He was also at Ticonderoga in 1777 serving in the regiment of Colonel Thomas Stickney.

Ezra and his first wife Betty Andrews had four children whose births are recorded at Concord.

  i LUCY ABBOTT, b. 5 Apr 1784; d. at Warner, Nov 1869; m. 17 Feb 1835, OBADIAH/DIAH HUTCHINSON, b. 2 Nov 1776 son of Jonathan and Mehitable (Lovejoy) Hutchinson; Diah d. at Warner, NH, 22 Aug 1843. Lucy did not have any children.

943) ii HARRIET B. ABBOTT, b. 12 Apr 1786; d. at Hartford, VT, 1 Apr 1862; m. 20 Jun 1816, JOHN CHAMPION, b. at South Lyme, CT, 12 Dec 1792 son of Ezra and Lucretia (Tubbs) Champion;[616] John d. at Hartford, VT, 27 Oct 1879.

  iii ROBERT BURNHAM ABBOTT, b. 27 Apr 1791; d. at Concord, 22 Aug 1830; m. 1st, at Hopkinton, 25 Dec 1817, RACHEL BURNHAM, b. 2 Sep 1796; Rachel d. 19 Jun 1823. Robert m. 2nd, 11 May 1823, ELIZABETH FOX, b. 2 Jun 1794; Elizabeth d. 7 Apr 1840. Robert did not have children. His will leaves his estate to his wife Elizabeth and to his sister Champion, sister Lucy, and sister Rose Dimond.[617]

944) iv ROSE B. ABBOTT, b. 26 Oct 1796; d. after 1860 (still living at the 1860 U.S. Census, but deceased before 1870); m. 11 Dec 1816, JACOB DIMOND, b. at

---

[616] Trowbridge, *The Champion Genealogy*, p 121
[617] Probate Records, 1832-1972; Probate Indexes, 1823-1973; Author: New Hampshire Probate Court (Merrimack County): Probate Place: Merrimakc, New Hampshire. Will of Robert B. Abbott, 5 Jun 1830.

Concord about 1790 son of Reuben and Mary (Currier) Dimond; Jacob d. at Concord, 28 Apr 1879.[618]

Ezra and Anner Choate had one child.

    i   ANNER ABBOTT, b. 2 Mar 1798; d. 12 Jun 1798.

Ezra and his third wife Jane Jackman had six children whose births are recorded at Concord.

945)   i   BETSY ABBOTT, b. 9 Aug 1799; d. 8 Aug 1856; m. Apr 1822, AMOS HOIT, b. 20 Feb 1800 son of Joseph and Polly (Elliot) Hoit. Amos m. 2nd, 6 Apr 1858, Asaneth Swain widow of Henry Swain.

946)   ii   ANNER ABBOTT, b. 8 Feb 1801; d. 23 Jan 1872; m. 13 Jun 1827, SAMUEL RUNNELS, b. at Boxford, 6 Dec 1796 son of Samuel and Anna (Hardy) Runnels; Samuel d. at Concord, 22 Nov 1864.

947)   iii   GEORGE B. ABBOTT, b. 27 Jan 1803; d. 8 May 1887; m. 1st, 22 Aug 1836, ELIZA DIDO SPAULDING, b. 6 Dec 1807 daughter of John and Elizabeth (Wheeler) Spaulding; Eliza d. 11 Oct 1856. George m. 2nd, 31 Dec 1861, CLARISSA CARTER, b. about 1815; Clarissa d. 14 Mar 1882.

    iv   JANE WOODMAN ABBOTT, b. 15 Sep 1805; d. at Warner, 30 Nov 1891; m. 9 Oct 1850, as his second wife, STEPHEN SANBORN, b. 21 Jun 1807 son of Daniel and Betsey (Whitcomb) Sanborn; Stephen d. 24 Jul 1869. Jane did not have children.

948)   v   BENJAMIN JACKMAN ABBOTT, b. 4 Feb 1808; d. 4 Mar 1869; m. about 1833, DOROTHY TEWKSBURY,

---

[618] Ancestry.com, New Hampshire, Death and Burial Records Index, 1654-1949

b. about 1813 possibly the sister of Daniel who married Sarah, but no records have been located.

949) vi SARAH ABBOTT, b. 22 Jan 1815; d. at Stewartstown, 26 Feb 1889; m. DANIEL TEWKSBURY, b. at Warner, 1 Oct 1810 son of Stephen and Sally (Flanders) Tewksbury; Daniel d. 6 Mar 1874.

Benjamin³, Thomas², George¹ *and* Hannah Abbott Abbott⁴, Samuel³, John², George¹

[Families #229 and #230 are descendants by both paths above.]

229) HANNAH ABBOTT (*Benjamin³, Thomas², George¹* and *Hannah (Abbott) Abbott⁴, Samuel³, John², George¹*), b. 22 Jan 1743 daughter of Benjamin and Hannah (Abbott) Abbott; d. 22 Oct 1820; m. Sep 1783, JEREMIAH STORY (origins not fully verified, but perhaps the Jeremiah Story of Ipswich); d. at Concord, about 1806 based on the date of probate of his estate May 1806 with widow Hannah Story as administrator.

Jeremiah Story did not leave a will. His widow Hannah was administrator of the estate. The inventory of the estate gave a value of $1,000 for real estate which included a lot in Concord, a 36-acre wood lot in Hopkinton, and a 100-acre lot in Groton in Grafton County.[619]

Just two children have been identified in this family.

950) i HANNAH STORY, b. 6 Sep 1784; d. after 1850 likely at Concord; m. 1st, 27 Feb 1806, BENNING NOYES, b. at Bow, 9 Dec 1780 son of Benjamin and Hannah

---

[619] *New Hampshire Wills and Probate Records 1643-1982,* Probate of Jeremiah Story, Rockingham, 19 Mar 1806, Case number 7548.

(Thompson) Noyes; Benjamin d. 2 Nov 1814. Hannah m. 2nd, at Montague, 13 Apr 1816, as his second wife, EPHRAIM UPHAM, b. at Weston, 3 Nov 1778 son of Thomas and Martha (Williams) Upham; Ephraim d. 29 Mar 1844. Ephraim was first married to Hannah Cushman.

 ii SARAH STORY, b. May 1787; died young.

230) BENJAMIN ABBOT *(Benjamin³, Thomas², George¹* and *Hannah (Abbott) Abbott⁴, Samuel³, John², George¹)*, b. 10 Feb 1750 son of Benjamin and Hannah (Abbott) Abbott; d. at Concord, 11 Dec 1815; m. 29 Jan 1778, SARAH BROWN, b. at Kingston, NH, 13 Feb 1758 daughter of Daniel and Ruth (Morrill) Brown; Sarah d. 27 Sep 1801. Benjamin m. 2nd, 17 Jun 1805, HANNAH GREENLEAF who was still living at the time of Benjamin's death.

 Benjamin Abbot served in the Revolutionary War with the rank of Sargent under the commands of Captain Gordon Hutchins and Colonel John Stark.[620] He is reported to have been at the Battle of Bunker Hill.

 Benjamin Abbot wrote his will 19 October 1815. His beloved wife Hannah receives the improvements of one-third part of the real and personal estate. Son Ephraim Abbot and daughter Hannah Hall each receive one dollar. Daughter Ruth Morrill Hall receives two dollars as does daughter Sarah Noyes. Son Isaac receives ten dollars and daughter Abigail Baker receives five dollars. Daughter Permelia receives fifty dollars and son Theodore Thomas Abbot receives four dollars. Son Benjamin Abbot receives all the remainder of the estate and is also named executor.[621]

---

[620] Rolls of Soldiers in the Revolutionary War, Volume 14, p 63, 181, 186
[621] *New Hampshire Wills and Probate Records 1643-1982,* Probate of Benjamin Abbott, Rockingham, 17 Jan 1816, Case number 9209.

Generation Four

Benjamin Abbot and Sarah Brown had nine children whose births are recorded at Concord, although some of the births occurred elsewhere.

951) i   EPHRAIM ABBOTT, b. 28 Sep 1779; d. at Westford, MA, 21 Jul 1870; m. 1st, at Andover, 5 Jan 1814, MARY HOLYOKE PEARSON, b. 10 Mar 1782 daughter of Eliphalet and Priscilla (Holyoke) Pearson; Mary d. 15 Jul 1829. Ephraim m. 2nd, 21 Jan 1830, ABIGAIL WHITING BANCROFT, b. at Groton, 1797 daughter of Amos and Abigail (Whiting) Bancroft; Abigail d. at Groton, 17 May 1886.

952) ii   HANNAH ABBOTT, b. 9 Mar 1782; d. at Westford, MA, 5 Apr 1869; m. 15 Nov 1803, her second cousin once removed (and George Abbott descendant), EBENEZER HALL, b. 9 May 1778 son of Daniel and Deborah (Davis) Hall; Ebenezer d. 14 Oct 1853.

953) iii   RUTH MORRILL ABBOTT, b. 27 Jun 1784; d. after 1860 (living in Concord at the 1860 U.S. Census); m. 26 Nov 1805, her second cousin once removed (and George Abbott descendant), JAMES HALL, b. 1784 son of Daniel and Deborah (Davis) Hall.

954) iv   BENJAMIN ABBOTT, b. 23 Sep 1786; d. at Whiteside, IL, 28 Feb 1854; m. 17 Sep 1807, DORCAS NOYES, b. at Bow, NH, 22 Aug 1785 daughter of Enoch and Eunice (Kinsman) Noyes; Dorcas d. 17 Feb 1877.

955) v   SARAH ABBOTT, b. 3 Oct 1788; d. at Hartland, VT, 27 Jul 1878; m. 12 Sep 1805, STEPHEN NOYES, b. at

Bow, NH, 5 Jul 1783 son of Enoch and Eunice (Kinsman) Noyes; Stephen d. 27 Feb 1868.

956) vi ABIGAIL LAWRENCE ABBOTT, b. 20 May 1791; d. at Chicopee, MA, 5 Dec 1856; m. 9 Feb 1809, SETH BAKER, b. at Pembroke, 21 May 1783 son of Thomas and Ruth (Peabody) Baker; Seth d. 30 Apr 1865.

957) vii ISAAC ABBOTT, b. 3 Aug 1793; d. 12 Nov 1840; m. 7 May 1817, SUSAN ELA, b. at Hooksett, 7 Jan 1797 daughter of Israel and Zebiah (Martin) Ela.[622] Susan was still living in 1880 when she was living with her daughter Fanny and her husband Leonard Beard.[623]

958) viii PARMELIA ABBOTT, b. 1 Feb 1796; d. at Pewaukee, WI, 1872; m. 7 Nov 1816, NATHANIEL GOSS, b. at Greenland, NH, 3 Nov 1788 son of Nathaniel and Mary (Nye) Goss; Nathaniel d. at Pewaukee, 7 Jul 1855.

959) ix THEODORE THOMAS ABBOTT, b. 22 Mar 1799; d. at Lunenburg, MA, 23 Mar 1887; m. at Lowell, 7 Aug 1826, MEHITABLE FROST GREENOUGH, b. at Newburyport, 1 Jan 1800 daughter of John and Elizabeth "Betsy" (March) Greenough; Mehitable d. 28 Mar 1887.

---

[622] Ela, *Genealogy of the Ela Family*, p 17
[623] Year: 1880; Census Place: Lancaster, Coos, New Hampshire; Roll: 762; Page: 153C; Enumeration District: 040

Section IX: The Grandchildren of Nathaniel Abbott and Dorcas Hibbert

Mary Abbott Blanchard³, Nathaniel², George¹

231) MARY BLANCHARD *(Mary Abbott Blanchard³, Nathaniel², George¹)*, b. 6 Dec 1719 daughter of Benjamin and Mary (Abbott) Blanchard; m. at Andover, 11 Jan 1742/3, EDWARD TAYLOR.

Edward and Mary settled in Hollis where Edward was a farmer and had a property on the west side of Flint Hill. Three of his sons (Daniel, Joel, and Jacob) served in the Revolution.[624]

There are seven children of Mary Blanchard and Edward Taylor the first two born at Dracut and the remainder at Hollis.

960) i   EDWARD TAYLOR, b. at Dracut, 14 Jul 1744; d. at Plymouth, NH, 1777;[625] m. at Hollis, 14 Nov 1771, MARY WORCESTER daughter of Jesse and Patience (Pope) Worcester who were early settlers of Hollis. After Edward's death, Mary married Enoch Page.

  ii   MARY TAYLOR, b. at Dracut, 13 Aug 1746; died young.

  iii DANIEL TAYLOR, b. at Hollis, 24 Mar 1749

961) iv JOEL TAYLOR, b. at Hollis, 23 Aug 1752; d. at Thornton, NH, 29 Apr 1814; m. 9 Apr 1778, as her second husband, SARAH HOBART, b. at Hollis, 15 Jan 1745 daughter of David and Sarah (Parker)

---

[624] Spaulding, *An Account of Some Early Settlers of West Dunstable*, p 135
[625] Stearns and Runnels, *History of Plymouth, NH*, volume II, p 669

Hobart; Sarah d. 1 Jan 1827. Sarah was first married to Phineas Lovejoy who died about 1777.

962)   v   MARY TAYLOR, b. 19 Jun 1754; m., Dec 1778, JAMES HOPKINS.[626]

963)   vi   JACOB TAYLOR, b. 21 Aug 1756; d. at Groton, NH, 5 Aug 1838; m. 19 Nov 1781, BETTY BOYNTON, b. at Hollis, 26 Sep 1756 daughter of John and Lydia (Jewett) Boynton; Betty d. at Grafton, 7 Feb 1843.[627]

       vii   ANNA TAYLOR, b. 28 Aug 1757; no further record.

232)   BENJAMIN BLANCHARD *(Mary Abbott Blanchard[3], Nathaniel[2], George[1])*, b. 19 Mar 1720/1 son of Benjamin and Mary (Abbott) Blanchard; d. 7 Mar 1791 at Canterbury, NH; m. 1st, ELIZABETH HOLT, b. 12 Mar 1719/20 daughter of Moses and Elizabeth (Russell) Holt. Benjamin m. 2nd, 27 Dec 1744, KEZIAH HASTINGS, b. at Lexington, 7 Jul 1723 daughter of Thomas and Sarah (White) Hastings; Keziah d. before 1778. Benjamin m. 3rd, SARAH BURBANK, b. Sep 1758.

Benjamin first married Elizabeth Holt who died in 1744 following the birth of their only child. This son, Benjamin, died a few weeks later. His second marriage was to Keziah Hastings by whom he had fourteen children. Following Keziah's death, Benjamin married Sarah Burbank in 1778.

---

[626] Spaulding, *An Account of Early Settlers of West Dunstable*, p 135 reports Mary's spouse as James Hopkins. The History of Milford, p 623, has Jonathan Buxton marrying Mary Taylor born in 1754, and so it is not entirely clear who Mary married. But Spaulding's account has this listing as part of the Edward Taylor genealogy. Secomb's *History of Amherst* also has James Hopkins as her spouse. And Buxton Family Association of America states that Jonathan Buxton married Mary Taylor who was the daughter of Timothy. (Volume II, The Buxton Family, p 62)

[627] Ancestry.com, U.S., Revolutionary War Pension and Bounty-Land Warrant Application Files, 1800-1900. Death date of Jacob given in pension papers; the widow's pension was received until 1843.

This family includes sons Abiel (born 1751) and Abel (born 1761), and these two sons married sisters, Mary Eastman and Elizabeth Eastman, and both marriages were in 1784.

Children of Benjamin Blanchard and Keziah Hastings all born at Hollis:

964)	i	BENJAMIN BLANCHARD; b. 15 Nov 1745; d. 21 Dec 1789; m. 1st, PATTY GOODWIN who died about 1771. Benjamin m. 2nd, SARAH CURRY, b. 15 Nov 1752 daughter of William and Ann (MacFarland) Curry.[628]
	ii	KEZIAH BLANCHARD, b. 26 Mar 1747
	iii	ABIEL BLANCHARD, b. 9 Jan 1748/9; died young
965)	iv	JONATHAN BLANCHARD, b. 28 Jun 1750; d. in Vermont, 31 Dec 1837; m. 13 Oct 1772, HANNAH CHADWICK, b. at Bradford, 22 Jun 1752 daughter of James and Mary (Thurston) Chadwick.
966)	v	ABIEL BLANCHARD, b. 1 Dec 1751; d. at Peacham, VT, 4 Jan 1803; m. 19 Feb 1784, MARY EASTMAN, b. at Rumford, 6 Apr 1758 daughter of Nathaniel and Phebe (Chandler) Eastman; Mary d. 12 Sep 1831.
967)	vi	ISAAC BLANCHARD, b. 14 Apr 1753; m. MOLLY WHEELER. Isaac and Molly lived in Concord and there are records for six children there but have yet to locate information on the deaths of Isaac or Molly or Molly's parentage.
	vii	DORCAS BLANCHARD, b. 25 Feb 1755; died young.

---

[628] Lyford, *History of the Town of Canterbury*, p 28

968) viii PETER BLANCHARD, b. 17 Aug 1756; d. at Danville, VT, 25 May 1810; m. by 1786, his second cousin (and George Abbott descendant), SARAH CHANDLER, b. at Concord, 15 Jan 1768 daughter of Abiel and Judith (Walker) Chandler; Sarah d. 21 Nov 1836. This is the same as Family #270, child i.

ix DORCAS BLANCHARD, b. 25 Feb 1757

969) x JOEL BLANCHARD, b. 27 Aug 1759; d. at Peacham, VT, 23 Jul 1816; m. by 1790, REBECCA GEORGE. Joel died from a "wrestle with a neighbor at Peacham, VT."[629]

970) xi ABEL CHANDLER, b. 17 Feb 1761; d. at Peacham, VT, 12 Aug 1827; m. 1784, ELIZABETH EASTMAN, b. 5 Jun 1761 daughter of Nathaniel and Phebe (Chandler) Eastman.

971) xii REUBEN BLANCHARD, b. 1 Feb 1763; d. at Peacham, VT, 27 Jun 1832;[630] m. by 1790, MARY GRAY of Guy.

972) xiii BETTY BLANCHARD, b. 21 Jan 1765; d. about 1811 (husband remarried 1812); m. at Boscawen, 4 May 1783, ABNER HOYT, b. at Rumford, 15 Apr 1759 son of John and Abigail (Carter) Hoyt. Abner m. 2nd, the widow Mary Livingston Phillips. Abner d. at Wentworth, NH, 28 Dec 1852.

973) xiv SIMON BLANCHARD, b. 10 Apr 1766; d. at Peacham, VT, 22 Apr 1837; m. MARGARET GRAY or Guy, b. about 1768; Margaret d. at Peacham, 9 Aug 1824.

---

[629] Ancestry.com, Rhode Island, Vital Extracts, 1636-1899
[630] Ancestry.com, Vermont, Vital Records, 1720-1908

233) ANNE BLANCHARD *(Mary Abbott Blanchard³, Nathaniel², George¹)*, b. 22 Nov 1722 daughter of Benjamin and Mary (Abbott) Blanchard; d. at Hollis, before 1758 (when her second husband remarried); m. 26 Feb 1743, JONATHAN DANFORTH, b. at Billerica, 1 Nov 1714 son of Jonathan and Elizabeth (Manning) Danforth; Jonathan d. 1747 at Hollis, NH. Anne m. 2nd, STEPHEN MARTIN. After Anne's death, Stephen m. 21 Mar 1759, Patience Pope.

Anne Blanchard and Jonathan Danforth had three children whose births are recorded at Hollis.

974) i ANNA DANFORTH, b. 7 Feb 1744; d. at Westminster, MA, 5 Nov 1813; m. 7 Feb 1765, JAMES LAWS, b. at Billerica, 12 Mar 1741/2 son of James and Eunice (-) Laws; James d. Jul 1821.

975) ii JONATHAN DANFORTH, b. 20 Jul 1745; d. at Danville, 6 Feb 1839; m. 1770, HANNAH LEMAN, b. at Hollis, 1 Oct 1751 daughter of Abraham and Elizabeth (Hastings) Leman; Hannah d. 13 Sep 1815.

976) iii DAVID DANFORTH, b. 20 Jan 1746; d. at Washington, NH, 1 Mar 1815; m. by 1773, HANNAH PROCTOR, b. at Chelmsford, 2 Feb 1748 daughter of Israel and Sarah (Raymond) Proctor; Hannah d. 12 Jan 1842.

Anne Blanchard and Stephen Martin had two children whose births are recorded at Hollis. It is not known what became of these two sons. It is possible that Jesse married but it is not clear that the marriage was this Jesse. In any case, no children were located for either Stephen or Jesse in New Hampshire or Vermont.

    i   STEPHEN MARTIN, b. 1 Sep 1749[631]

    ii   JESSE MARTIN, b. 1 Aug 1754

234) JACOB BLANCHARD (*Mary Abbott Blanchard³, Nathaniel², George¹*), b. 11 May 1724 son of Benjamin and Mary (Abbott) Blanchard; d. at Groton, 26 Apr 1770; m. by 1753, REBECCA LAWRENCE, b. at Groton, 17 Apr 1724 daughter of Nathaniel and Anna (Scripture) Lawrence. Rebecca m. 2nd, John Sheple 8 Dec 1772; Rebecca's date of death is not known.

The estate of Jacob Blanchard entered probate 5 March 1771. Rebecca is the administrator of the estate. There is not a will or a distribution document. The inventory gives the total value of the estate as £96.[632]

Records for the births of five children were found at Groton. The birth of the oldest child, Jacob, was recorded at Groton but described as occurring at Hollis. There were no births of other children found at Hollis.

    i   JACOB BLANCHARD, b. 16 Feb 1753; d. 21 Dec 1769.

977) ii   REBECCA BLANCHARD, b. 22 Feb 1756; d. at Groton, 19 Sep 1826; m. 22 Mar 1774, DAVID LAKIN, b. at Groton, 10 Oct 1753 son of John and Lydia (Parker) Lakin; David d. 3 Mar 1846. David's death was attributed to the "decay of nature" at age 92.

    iii   LUCY BLANCHARD, b. 15 Dec 1757; died in early childhood.

---

[631] Hollis Town Records, 1739-1841, volume 1, image 175, Family Search
[632] *Middlesex County, MA: Probate File Papers, 1648-1871. Probate of* Jacob Blanchard, *1771, Case number 1878.*

978) iv NATHANIEL BLANCHARD, b. 29 May 1760; d.?; m. 28 Nov 1782, ANNA GREEN, b. 10 Oct 1762 daughter of Eleazer and Sarah (Parker) Green. There is an out-of-wedlock child born in Groton 14 Feb (the year missing) I believe may be a son of this Nathaniel. The child is named Nathaniel, the mother is Esther Nutting and "she saith" this is the child of Nathaniel Blanchard. Esther was born in 1759 so that would fit. I cannot find what happened to Nathaniel and Anna; there are births of two children recorded at Groton.

v LUCY BLANCHARD, b. 29 Apr 1762; d. 30 Sep 1843; m. 6 Apr 1778, ELEAZER GREEN, b. 15 Oct 1753 son of Eleazer and Sarah (Parker) Green; Eleazer d. 13 Oct 1824. Lucy and Eleazer did have had children.

235) JOSHUA BLANCHARD *(Mary Abbott Blanchard³, Nathaniel², George¹)*, b. 29 Mar 1726 son of Benjamin and Mary (Abbott) Blanchard; d. *perhaps* 1818 at Wilton, NH; m. 23 Dec 1747, SARAH BURGE, b. 30 May 1728 daughter of John and Sarah (Taylor) Burge.

Joshua Blanchard and Sarah Burge had six children all born at Hollis.

i SARAH BLANCHARD, b. 8 Nov 1748

979) ii JOSHUA BLANCHARD, b. 21 Oct 1750; d. 11 Jan 1776; m. 16 Feb 1775, LUCY FRENCH, b. at Hollis, 21 Apr 1755 daughter of Nicholas and Priscilla (Mooar) French. Lucy m. 2nd, 6 Mar 1781, BRAY WILKINS.

        iii   DAVID BLANCHARD, b. 10 Nov 1752; m. May 1776, SUSANNA CHENEY, b. at Ashburnham, 2 Nov 1759 daughter of Tristram and Margaret (Joyner) Cheney. No clear records were located for this couple after their marriage.

980)   iv   MOLLY BLANCHARD, b. 30 Aug 1754; d. at Deering, NH, 5 Oct 1826; m. about 1774, MAJOR MILES RALEIGH, b. at Sudbury, MA, 1749 son of Philip and Susannah (Joyner) Raleigh; Major Raleigh d. at Deering, NH 6 Jun 1838.

        v   JOHN BLANCHARD, b. 10 Sep 1757

981)   vi   LUCY BLANCHARD, b. 4 Jun 1760; d. about 1798; m. about 1785, ELIAS CHENEY, b. at Sudbury, 14 Oct 1760 son of Tristram and Margaret (Joyner) Cheney. Elias m. 2nd, 6 Jun 1799, Deborah Winchester. Elias d. at Concord, VT, 1816.

Nathaniel³, Nathaniel², George¹

236)   NATHANIEL ABBOTT *(Nathaniel³, Nathaniel², George¹)*, b. 10 Mar 1726/7 daughter of Nathaniel and Penelope (Ballard) Abbott; d. at Concord 4 Feb 1806; m. by 1749, MIRIAM CHANDLER, b. at Amesbury 24 Nov 1728 daughter of Nathaniel and Susannah (Rowel) Chandler; Miriam d. at Concord Jan 1811.

Nathaniel Abbott's father was a first settler of Concord receiving land at the Plantation of Penacook in 1726.[633] Nathaniel carried on in his father's footsteps maintaining a farm in Concord. Nathaniel and his wife Miriam raised a family of ten children. Four of the sons, Nathan Chandler, Moses, Philip, and Joshua, served in the Revolutionary War.[634]

---

[633] Bouton, *The History of Concord, NH*
[634] Abbot and Abbot, *Genealogical Record of Descendants*, p 118

Nathaniel and Miriam had ten children, the birth of the oldest child recorded at Rumford and the others recorded at Concord.

982) i NATHANIEL CHANDLER ABBOTT, b. 28 Jul 1750; d. at Rumney, NH; m. 20 Jul 1778, HANNAH FARRINGTON who origins are unknown at this time.

983) ii MOSES ABBOTT, b. 19 Jun 1752; d. 11 Jul 1837; m. by 1779, MARY BATCHELDER, b. about 1756; Mary d. at Concord 2 Jul 1833.

iii JOSEPH ABBOTT, b. 24 May 1754; d. 24 Jan 1774.

984) iv PHILIP ABBOTT, b. 4 Feb 1757; d. at Rumford, ME, 20 Mar 1841; m. 10 Feb 1791, EXPERIENCE HOWE, b. at Bolton, MA, 1 Apr 1771 daughter of Phineas and Experience (Pollard) Howe; Experience d. 1857.

985) v JOSHUA ABBOTT, b. 15 Jun 1759; d. at Bow Junction, NH, 4 Mar 1837; m. 1st, 1780, POLLY BROWN. Joshua m. 2nd, ANN MANNING, b. 1767; Ann d. at Bow Junction, 11 Sep 1850.

986) vi SUSANNA ABBOTT, b. 21 Jan 1762; d. at Concord, 24 Jun 1832; m. 29 Nov 1791, JOHN GARVIN, b. at Bow, NH, 14 Aug 1764 son of James and Deborah (-) Garvin; John d. 16 Dec 1826.

575) vii PHEBE ABBOTT, b. 8 Aug 1764; d. at Concord, 11 Aug 1854; m. by 1791, her third cousin, NATHAN ABBOTT, b. at Concord, 8 Aug 1765 son of Reuben and Rhoda (Whittemore) Abbott; Nathan d. 13 May 1849.

987) viii LEVI ABBOTT, b. 23 Sep 1767; d. 15 Dec 1825; m. 1st, 10 Jul 1791, his first cousin, ELSIE MOOR daughter of Ephraim and Hannah (Abbott) Moor; Elsie d. Apr 1795. Levi m. 2nd, MARY "POLLY" CARTER, b. 1770 daughter of Joseph Carter; Polly d. 24 Dec 1840.

988) ix DAVID ABBOTT, b. 8 Aug 1770; d. in Oxford County, ME, 30 Jun 1836; m. BETSEY COLSON, b. at Weymouth, 24 Aug 1780 daughter of Gideon and Elizabeth (White) Colson; Betsey d. at Roxbury, ME, 16 Sep 1821.

x JOSEPH ABBOTT, b. Jan 1774. Joseph did not marry.[635]

237) DORCAS ABBOTT (*Nathaniel³, Nathaniel², George¹*), b. 11 Nov 1728 daughter of Nathaniel and Penelope (Ballard) Abbott; d. probably at Concord date unknown; m. by 1749, MOSES MERRILL, b. at Haverhill 27 Sep 1727 son of John and Lydia (Haynes) Merrill; Moses d. 1767.

Six children of Dorcas and Moses are reported in the Abbot genealogy. Very little in the way of records have yet been located for this family.

i PENELOPE MERRILL, b. at Rumford, 13 Dec 1749; m. Hoit. There is a 1777 deed record in Exeter, New Hampshire for Penelope Hoyt of Concord, NH granddaughter of John Merrill.[636] Beyond that, there are no records for this couple.

ii MOSES MERRILL, b. at Concord, 19 Nov 1751; d. 10 Apr 1752.

---

[635] Abbot and Abbot, *Genealogical Record of Descendants*, p 118
[636] Hoyt, *Hoyt Family*, p 122

Generation Four 431

989) iii DORCAS MERRILL, b. about 1754; d. at Reading, 30 Mar 1841; m. 3 Mar 1778, WILLIAM BEARD, b. at Reading, 5 Sep 1745 son of Andrew and Elizabeth (Burnap) Beard; William d. 15 Nov 1809.

iv NEHEMIAH MERRILL, b. about 1757

v BETSEY MERRILL, b. about 1758; m. 30 Apr 1810, as his second wife, GIDEON PIPER; Gideon d. about 1814 (will 4 Apr 1814). Betsey did not have children.

990) vi LYDIA MERRILL, b. 10 Nov 1759; d. at Concord, 10 Jan 1839; m. SAMUEL DAVIS, b. at Concord, 17 Apr 1759 son of Robert and Sarah (Walker) Davis; Samuel d. about 1848.

238) REBECCA ABBOTT *(Nathaniel³, Nathaniel², George¹)*, b. 27 May 1731 daughter of Nathaniel and Penelope (Ballard) Abbott; d. after 1799 possibly at Thetford, VT; m. 1st by 1750 JOHN MERRILL, b. at Haverhill 25 Nov 1725 son of John and Lydia (Haynes) Merrill; John d. at Bow, NH about 1758. Rebecca m. 2nd JACOB DOYNE, b. about 1729; d. 1799 at Pembroke where his estate was probated with his widow Rebecca as administrator.

Rebecca Abbott and John Merrill had four children, the birth of the oldest child recorded at Rumford and the youngest three at Concord.

991) i REBECCA MERRILL, b. 16 Aug 1751; m. ABNER FARNUM, b. about 1748 possibly the son of Joseph Farnum; Abner d. at Concord, 2 Aug 1820.

ii LYDIA MERRILL, b. 19 Feb 1753

iii PENELOPE MERRILL, b. 5 Oct 1754

992) iv JOHN MERRILL, b. 14 Jun 1756; d. at Tunbridge, VT, 7 Apr 1814; m. at Pembroke, 14 Mar 1782, his third cousin once removed, SARAH "SALLY" ROBERTSON, b. at Bow, 18 Apr 1757 daughter of John and Elizabeth (Lovejoy) Robertson.[637]

Jacob Doyne's estate was valued at $529 and the real property was sold to pay the creditors. His five surviving children received a total of $148.[638]

Rebecca Abbott and Jacob Doyne had six children whose births are recorded at Pembroke. Two of their children married two children of James and Deborah (-) Garvin. A third child of James and Deborah Garvin, John Garvin, married Rebecca Abbott's niece, Susanna Abbott.

993) i JACOB DOYNE, b. 22 Apr 1759. Jacob seems to have had a complicated life and perhaps was a bigamist. One of his wives was Mercy Cribbs. He lived in Maine for a time. Jacob's son John married Sarah Tuck and later Lydia Dutton. John Doyne and Sarah Tuck were the parents of Dorcas Doyne, aka Helen Jewett who was murdered in New York in 1836.[639]

ii MARTHA DOYNE, b. 18 Dec 1760; d. 26 Feb 1776.[640]

---

[637] Some published histories/genealogies give Sarah's mother as John Robertson's first wife, Lydia Cales. However, *Bow, NH: The Town Book of Bow* identifies Elizabeth as the mother of all the children of John Robertson. *Bow, NH: The Town Book of Bow, New Hampshire, 1760-1877.* Manuscript. R. Stanton Avery Special Collections, New England Historic Genealogical Society, Boston, MA. (Online database. *AmericanAncestors.org*, New England Historic Genealogical Society, 2012.)

[638] Rockingham County Probate Records 1799-1800, (microfilm) 77, 185, 272, 330, NEHGS

[639] Cohen, P. C. (1993). The Mystery of Helen Jewett: Romantic Fiction and the Eroticization of Violence. *Legal Stud. F., 17,* 133.

[640] History of Pembroke, NH 1730-1893, p 70

994) iii SAMUEL DOYNE, b. 26 Feb 1764. Samuel completed a bounty-land warrant application for land in Maine[641] and died at Levant, ME about 1832. Samuel does marry but do not know who yet, perhaps a woman named Polly who died in Maine in 1832.

995) iv FRANCIS DOYNE, b. 17 Feb 1767; d. likely in Maine after 1830;[642] m. 7 Sep 1789, BETTY GARVIN, b. at Bow, 20 Dec 1770 daughter of James and Deborah (-) Garvin.

996) v NATHANIEL DOYNE, b. 17 Feb 1767; d. at Pembroke, 8 May 1841; m. DEBORAH SMITH.

997) vi HANNAH DOYNE, b. 1772; m. EBENEZER GARVIN, b. at Bow, 15 Sep 1768 son of James and Deborah (-) Garvin.

239) ELIZABETH ABBOTT (*Nathaniel³, Nathaniel², George¹*), b. 1 Jul 1733 daughter of Nathaniel and Penelope (Ballard) Abbott; d. at Concord 25 Jan 1834; m. by 1755, JOSEPH HAZELTINE, b. at Rumford 27 Dec 1731 son of Richard and Sarah (Barnes) Hazeltine; Richard d. 30 May 1798.

Joseph Hazeltine wrote his will 26 May 1798. Beloved wife Elizabeth receives improvements on one-half of the real estate. His daughters each receive $25 and they are Sarah Houghton, Anne Green, Susanna Moore, Hannah Stickney, and Betty Noyes. The daughters will divide one-half of the estate after the decease of their

---

[641] Ancestry.com, U.S., Revolutionary War Pension and Bounty-Land Warrant Application Files, 1800-1900

[642] He is perhaps the Francis Doyne listed in the 1830 Census at Avon, Somerset, Maine as the male age 60-69. 1830; Census Place: Avon, Somerset, Maine; Series: M19; Roll: 51; Page: 174; Family History Library Film: 0497947

mother. Beloved son Ballard Hazeltine receives one-half of the real estate. Ballard is also named sole executor of the estate.[643]

There are records for nine children of Elizabeth Abbott and Joseph Hazeltine, the first four birth at Rumford and the younger children at Concord.

998) i SARAH HAZELTINE, b. 24 Dec 1755; m. at Concord, 20 Jan 1777, NAHUM HOUGHTON, origin uncertain but perhaps the Nahum born in 1732 in Worcester County, MA; Nahum d. about 1800 as there is a guardianship case for his son Nahum in 1800 (son Nahum at 14 or above requests uncle Jacob Green as guardian). Sarah seems to have married 19 Jan 1812, EDMUND CARLETON.

ii ABIGAIL HAZELTINE, b. 3 Sep 1758; d. at Haverhill, NH, 17 Apr 1785; m. 29 Nov 1783, as his second wife, JOHN PAGE, b. at Rindge, 16 Jul 1741 son of Nathaniel and Mercy (Gould) Page. Abigail and John had one son who died at 2 days old. John had married first, Abigail Sanders with whom he had no children. John married third, Hannah Royce who was the widow of William Green.[644]

999) iii ANNA HAZELTINE, b. 19 May 1760; d. at Bow, 13 Nov 1838; m. at Concord, 26 Sep 1776, JACOB GREEN, b. at Worcester, MA, 18 Jan 1749/50 son of Nathaniel and Lucy (Gerfield) Green; Jacob d. 17 Apr 1815.

iv PETER HAZELTINE, b. 23 Sep 1762; d. 20 Nov 1779 by drowning.

---

[643] *New Hampshire Wills and Probate Records 1643-1982,* Probate of Joseph Hazeltine, Rockingham, 18 Jul 1798, Case number 6477.
[644] Witcher, *History of the Town of Haverhill, New Hampshire*, p 611

	v	SUSANNA HAZELTINE, b. 12 Sep 1765; m. at Bow, 21 Nov 1784, EPHRAIM MOORE. Nothing certain has been found for this family. Ephraim Moor and Hannah Abbott (Family #241) were living in Bow at this time and perhaps Ephraim is a child in that family. He may be the Ephraim Moore with an estate probated in 1830 in Beekmantown, NY with widow Susanna. Birth records for children have not been located.
1000)	vi	HANNAH HAZELTINE, b. 31 Aug 1767; m. 19 Apr 1787, JAMES STICKNEY, b. at Concord, 5 Dec 1766 son of Jonathan and Sarah (Webster) Stickney.
1001)	vii	BALLARD HAZELTINE, b. 4 Sep 1769; d. at Plattsburgh, NY, 1836; m. 19 Apr 1792, SALLY NOYES, b. at Bow, 17 Dec 1768 daughter of John and Mary (Fowler) Noyes.
1002)	viii	BETTY HAZELTINE, b. 3 Oct 1771; d. at Bow, 1801; m. at Pembroke, 18 Nov 1788, JOHN P. NOYES, b. at Bow, 27 Jun 1766 son of John and Mary (Fowler) Noyes; John d. in upstate New York, 1 Mar 1814 while in military service. John married second, MARTHA "PATTY" GREEN (Betty Hazeltine's niece and George Abbott descendant in the sixth generation), b. at Bow 14 Oct 1777 daughter of Jacob and Anna (Hazeltine) Green; Martha d. at Concord, 28 Jun 1843. Martha's parents and Family #995.
	ix	NATHANIEL HAZELTINE, b. 24 Aug 1774; d. 23 Feb 1796.

240) MARY ABBOTT *(Nathaniel³, Nathaniel², George¹)*, b. 7 Mar 1735 daughter of Nathaniel and Penelope (Ballard) Abbott; d. Mar 1795; m. by 1754, JOSEPH WALKER,[645] b. at Concord, 24 Apr 1732 son of Isaac and Sarah (Breed) Walker; Joseph d. at 1800 at Fryeburg, ME.

Joseph and Mary Walker were early settlers in Fryeburg. Joseph signed a petition in 1764 related to the opening of a road and another petition in 1776 requesting incorporation of the town.[646]

Mary Walker and Joseph Walker had eleven children at Fryeburg.[647] Three of the daughters in this family married three Stevens brothers (John, Samuel, and Ebenezer).

1003) i JOSEPH WALKER, b. 1754; m. 11 Dec 1776, JANE STERLING, b. at Conway, NH, 1755 daughter of Hugh and Isabel (Stark) Sterling.[648]

1004) ii NATHANIEL WALKER, b. 1757; d. at Fryeburg, 13 Jun 1839;[649] m. 18 Aug 1777, ABIGAIL CHARLES, b. 1758 (based on age at time of death); d. 5 Sep 1843.

1005) iii SARAH WALKER, b. 1759; m. JOHN AMES of unknown origins. Evidence of one child of this family, Jeremiah Walker Ames born at Chatham, NH has so far been located.

iv MARY WALKER, b. 1761; died in infancy.

574) v MARY WALKER, b. 1763; d. at Concord, 22 Sep 1852; m. her third cousin, EZRA ABBOTT, b. at

---

[645] Foster and Walker, "The Walkers of Woburn, Massachusetts", *Historical Bulletin*, volumes 6-9, pp 64-65
[646] Barrows, *Fryeburg, Maine: An Historical Sketch*
[647] Foster and Walker, "The Walkers of Woburn", pp 64-65
[648] Albert Sterling, 1909, The Sterling Genealogy, volume II, pp 1102-1103
[649] The members of this family who died at Fryeburg are buried in the West Fryeburg Cemetery, Oxford County, Maine. The various gravestones with death dates and ages can be found on Find A Grave.

Concord, 8 Aug 1765 son of Reuben and Rhoda (Whittemore) Abbott; Ezra d. 24 Apr 1839.

1006) vi ANNA WALKER, b. 1765; d. at Fryeburg, 11 Mar 1854; m. JOHN STEVENS, b. Mar 1764 (based on age at death) son of John Stevens who was perhaps born in England; John d. 30 Sep 1825.

1007) vii RUTH WALKER, b. Oct 1768; d. at Fryeburg, 19 Aug 1848; m. EBENEZER STEVENS, b. Oct 1767 son of John Stevens; John d. 1 Apr 1851.

viii JEREMIAH WALKER; b. 1771 and died in infancy.

ix NAMAH WALKER, b. 1772; died in infancy.

1008) x JEREMIAH BALLARD WALKER, b. 8 Dec 1777; d. at Whitefield, NH, 19 Oct 1841; m. his first cousin, HANNAH WALKER, b. 1781 daughter of Samuel and Hannah (Hazeltine) Walker; Hannah d. at Whitefield, 15 Jan 1855.

1009) xi NAMAH WALKER, b. Nov 1778; d. at Fryeburg, 3 Dec 1844; m. SAMUEL STEVENS, b. 11 Jun 1773 son of John Stevens; Samuel d. at Fryeburg, 7 Oct 1849.

241) HANNAH ABBOTT *(Nathaniel³, Nathaniel², George¹)*, b. 7 Mar 1736 daughter of Nathaniel and Penelope (Ballard) Abbott; d. after 1792 when dower rights were set off to her; m. EPHRAIM MOOR whose origin is not yet established but perhaps the son of James and Agnes (Colbreath) Moor;[650] Ephraim d. at Bow, NH about 1791 (when his estate was probated).

---

[650] According to Cutter, Volume 2, p 726 the parents of Ephraim were from Ireland and Ephraim was born in New Hampshire.

Ephraim Moor's estate entered probate 2 November 1791. Moses Moor was the administrator of his father's estate. The widow Hannah gave up her right to administer the estate and requested that her son Moses assume those responsibilities. The dower rights were set off to widow Hannah Moor. The estate had little value and there were multiple creditors.[651]

Published sources have conflicting information on this family. The Chandler and Abbot genealogies have Hannah Abbott as the wife of Ephraim Moor. The History of Pembroke (pp 230-231) states she is Hannah Rogers and that Ephraim had a second wife named Jennie Moore. However, as stated in his probate record, Ephraim's widow was Hannah. Ephraim Moor's brother William married someone named Hannah so perhaps Hannah Rogers was William's wife. One of the grandchildren of Ephraim Moor and Hannah Abbott was named Albert Abbott Moor which would support there being an Abbott connection. In addition, the published genealogies that give Ephraim's wife as Hannah Rogers have a birthdate for her of 7 March 1736 which is the birthdate of Hannah Abbott, and there is a birth record for Hannah Abbott daughter of Nathaniel and Penelope with the date 7 March 1736.

There is also discrepancy for the children in the family. The History of Pembroke and the Abbot genealogy have somewhat different lists of children. Some, but not all, the names are the same. What there does seem to be is a lack of much clear documentation for this family. There are no birth records for the children. The children given here are from the Abbot genealogy.

1010) i   JAMES MOOR, b. about 1760; d. at Waterville, ME, 27 Aug 1835; m. Nov 1779, ABIGAIL NOYES, b. at Bow, 28 Jan 1764 daughter of John and Mary (Fowler) Noyes.

---

[651] *New Hampshire Wills and Probate Records 1643-1982,* Probate of Ephraim Moor, Rockingham, 2 Nov 1791, Case number 5704.

Generation Four 439

	ii	ANNA MOOR m. (-) LONG whose identity is not known. There is no information on this family.
1011)	iii	MOSES MOOR (twin of Aaron), b. about 1762; m. 22 Nov 1788, ESTHER MOOR, b. at Pembroke, 6 Oct 1769 daughter of Robert and Ruhamah (Mitchell) Moor.
	iv	AARON MOOR (twin of Moses); b. about 1762; died young.
987)	v	ELSIE MOOR, b. estimate 1771; d. at Concord, Apr 1795; m. 1791, LEVI ABBOTT, b. at Concord, 23 Sep 1767 son of Nathaniel and Miriam (Chandler) Abbott. Levi m. 2nd, 1 Oct 1795, Mary "Polly" Carter. Levi d. 15 Dec 1825.
	vi	DAVID MOOR; according to the Abbot genealogy he married, but name of his wife was not given. One possibility to explore is Janet Ross who married a David Moor at Barnet, VT in 1792.
1012)	vii	HANNAH MOOR, b. at Pembroke, about 1772; d. 3 Jan 1828; m. about 1791, WILLIAM NEILSON, b. 1767 at Erskine, Renfrewshire, Scotland son of William and Jean (Stewart) Neilson; William d. at Lyman, NH, 19 Sep 1830. The father of William rewrote his will 29 Sep 1830 naming the children of William, who was then deceased, among his heirs.
	viii	POLLY MOOR; she is reported to have married, but name of her husband is not known.
1013)	ix	MARTHA "PATTY" MOOR, b. 1779 (based on age at time of death); d. at Barnet, VT, 7 May 1827; m. at Barnet, VT, 6 Nov 1801, ALEXANDER

BUCHANAN, b. in Scotland 4 Sep 1771 son of Peter and Anabel (Miller) Buchanan; Alexander d. at Barnet, 2 Oct 1853.[652] Alexander m. 2nd, Deborah.

1014) x DOLLY MOOR, b. about 1780; m. at Bow, 29 Jan 1801,[653] ELISHA UPTON, b. about 1779 son of Elisha and Sarah (Gilford) Upton; Elisha d. at Parishville, NY, 1854.[654][655]

xi Son who died as infant.

242) RUTH ABBOTT *(Nathaniel³, Nathaniel², George¹)*, b. 28 Jan 1738 daughter of Nathaniel and Penelope (Ballard) Abbott; d. 27 Feb 1817; m. by 1759, JAMES A. WALKER, b. at Concord 2 Sep 1739 son of Isaac and Sarah (Breed) Walker; James d. 9 Feb 1821.

James Walker wrote his will 7 December 1805 and his estate entered probate 3 May 1821. Son Bruce Walker receives $20 and a feather bed. Son John receives $80 and a feather bed. Daughter Hannah receives $150 and a feather bed as do sons James Walker and Peter Walker. Beloved wife Ruth ("in case she survives me") receives the use, occupation, and improvement of all the household goods for her natural life. These household goods will go to Hannah after her mother's decease. His wife also receives the privilege of a seat in his pew in the meeting house. Daughter Hannah also "the privilege of a seat in my pew in said meeting house so long as she remains single and unmarried." Son Abiel Walker receives a feather

---

[652] The graves of Martha and Alexander Buchanan are in Barnet Center Cemetery and the gravestones include dates of death and age at time of death. Alexander's gravestone includes that he was a native of Scotland (findagrave.com)
[653] *Bow, NH: The Town Book of Bow, New Hampshire, 1760-1877*, p 233 (americanancestors.org)
[654] Vinton, *The Upton Memorial*, p 224
[655] Year: 1850; Census Place: Parishville, Saint Lawrence, New York; Roll: M432_590; Page: 124A; Image: 517. Elisha Upton, age 71, living in a household headed by his son Guilford Upton. Dolly is apparently deceased.

Generation Four 441

bed and pew number 29 in the Concord meeting house. All the rest of the estate goes to Ruth. Son Abiel is named executor.[656]

Ruth Abbott and Bruce Walker had seven children whose births are recorded at Rumford/Concord.

1015) i BRUCE WALKER, b. at Rumford, 17 May 1760; d. at Hebron, NH, 27 Jul 1840; m. MEHITABLE CURRIER, b. at Concord, 26 Apr 1762 daughter of William and Mary (Carter) Currier; Mehitable d. 8 May 1849.

1016) ii JOHN WALKER, b. at Rumford, 8 May 1763; d. at Bethel, ME, 25 Feb 1825; m. ELIZABETH CALEF, b. at Kingston, NH, 1 Oct 1767 daughter of Joseph and Hannah (Pettingill) Calef;[657] Elizabeth d. at Bethel, 14 Nov 1829.

921) iii ABIEL WALKER, b. at Concord, 5 Jul 1766; d. 4 Apr 1855; m. 1st, 3 Feb 1807, JUDITH DAVIS; Judith d. 1 Apr 1808. Abiel m. 2nd, as her second husband, his third cousin (and George Abbott descendant), MARY "MOLLY" WILSON, b. 23 Jul 1772 daughter of Thomas and Mary (Hall) Wilson. Molly was first married to John Thorndike. This is the same as Family #224, child ii.

iv HANNAH WALKER, b. at Concord, 26 Feb 1770; d, at Concord, 10 Dec 1847; m. at Concord, 28 Nov 1819, as his second wife, WILLIAM FISK, b. at

---

[656] *New Hampshire Wills and Probate Records 1643-1982,* Probate of James Walker, Rockingham, 3 May 1821, Case number 10289.
[657] The 1810 will of Joseph Calef includes a bequest to his daughter Elizabeth Walker.

Wenham, MA, 20 Apr 1755 son of William and Susannah (Batchelder) Fisk. William d. at Amherst, 4 Jun 1831. William was married first to Eunice Nourse.[658] Hannah did not have children.

    v   RUTH WALKER, b. 12 Mar 1776; d. 17 May 1797.

1017) vi JAMES WALKER, b. 26 Jul 1778; d. at Milton, NH, 4 Sep 1826; m. ABIGAIL CHAPMAN, b. at Methuen, 29 Dec 1778 daughter of Eliphaz and Hannah (Jackman) Chapman; Abigail d. 3 Oct 1807. James m. 2nd, PATTY HEATH INGALLS,[659] b. 8 Aug 1786 daughter of Moses and Susan (Heath) Ingalls; Patty d. Dec 1865.[660]

1018) vii PETER WALKER, b. 6 Jul 1780; d. 2 Jun 1857; m. 3 Jan 1808, ABIGAIL SWAN, b. 15 Dec 1787 daughter of Joseph Greely and Elizabeth (Evans) Swan; Abigail d. 26 Jan 1861.[661]

243)   JOSHUA ABBOT *(Nathaniel³, Nathaniel², George¹)*, b. 24 Feb 1740 son of Nathaniel and Penelope (Ballard) Abbott; d. at Concord, NH, Mar 1815; m. at Bradford 23 Oct 1766, his third cousin once removed, ELIZA CHANDLER, b. at Bradford 20 Jul 1739 daughter of Josiah and Sara (-- Parker widow) Chandler; Eliza d. 27 May 1812.

    Joshua served as a Captain in the Revolutionary War marching on Bunker Hill, and additional periods of service in New York in 1776, and his company was present with Gerrish's regiment in September 1777 at Saratoga.[662]

---

[658] Secomb, *History of Amherst*, p 585
[659] Foster and Walker, "The Walkers of Woburn," p 108
[660] Burleigh, *Genealogy of the Ingalls Family*, p 96
[661] Evans, *Descendants of David Evans*, p 18
[662] Lyford, *History of Concord, New Hampshire*

Joshua Abbot wrote his will 3 March 1815 at Concord. The will includes bequests to the following persons: daughter Betsey Abbot of Hallowell, daughter Sally Dummer who is in Hallowell, son Joshua Abbot of Concord, granddaughter Elizabeth Chandler Abbot, granddaughter Mary Faulkner Abbot, grandson Thomas Faulkner Abbot, grandson John Sullivan Abbot, and son Nathaniel Abbot of Concord. Son Nathaniel Abbot is named executor of the estate.[663]

Joshua and Eliza had six children whose births are recorded at Concord.

    i   NATHANIEL ABBOT, b. 25 Aug 1767; d. 31 May 1769.

1019) ii NATHANIEL ABBOT, b. 28 Oct 1769; d. 25 Nov 1848; m. 10 Feb 1793, ELIZABETH DEARBORN, b. at Chester, 1 Feb 1772 daughter of John and Mary (Emerson) Dearborn; Elizabeth d. 7 Jun 1855.

1020) iii BETSY ABBOT, b. 6 Aug 1773; d. at Farmington, ME, 30 Jul 1846; m. at Hallowell, 8 Apr 1798, her second cousin, JACOB ABBOT, b. at Wilton, 20 Oct 1776 son of Jacob and Lydia (Stevens) Abbott; Jacob d. 21 Jan 1847. This is the same as Family #255, child v.

1021) iv SARAH "SALLY" ABBOT, b. 16 Dec 1775; d. at Hallowell, 1 Dec 1841; m. 29 Apr 1802, GORHAM DUMMER, b. at Hallowell, 27 Sep 1782 son of Nathaniel and Mary (Owen) Dummer; Gorham d. 2 Jan 1805.

---

[663] *New Hampshire Wills and Probate Records 1643-1982*, will of Joshua Abbot, 3 Mar 1815, Rockingham.

1022) v   JOHN SULLIVAN ABBOT, b. 20 Aug 1778; d. 10 Aug 1810; m. his second cousin once removed (and George Abbott descendant) MARY FAULKNER, b. 1781 daughter of Abiel and Hannah (Abbott) Faulkner; Mary d. 17 Jun 1840.

1023) vi   JOSHUA ABBOT, b. 8 Dec 1782; d. at Norfolk, VA of consumption while serving as a minister, 29 Sep 1821; m. 6 Nov 1808, ELIZA "BETSY" KIMBALL, b. 12 Jul 1787 daughter of Phineas and Lucy (Pearl) Kimball; Betsy d. at Concord 23 Jan 1870.[664]

225)   RACHEL ABBOTT *(Nathaniel³, Nathaniel², George¹)* and DANIEL ABBOTT *(George³, Thomas², George¹ and Sarah⁴, Stephen³, John², George¹)* This is Family #225 covered above.

244)   JEREMIAH ABBOTT *(Nathaniel³, Nathaniel², George¹)*, b. 17 Mar 1744 son of Nathaniel and Penelope (Ballard) Abbott; d. at Conway, NH 8 Nov 1823; m. ELIZABETH STICKNEY, b. at Rumford 7 Dec 1753 daughter of Thomas and Anna (Osgood) Stickney; Elizabeth d. about 1836.

    Jeremiah Abbott was a prominent early settler of Conway. He was involved in making additions to a store built by Harry Merrill, and this structure was ultimately known as the Pequawket Hotel. This building was also the site of the first post office in Conway, and for a time housed the jail under a trap door in the floor – a true multi-purpose building. This hotel had several notable guests in later years including President Grant and John Greenleaf Whittier.[665]

---

[664] Morrison and Sharples, *History of the Kimball Family in America, volume 1*, p 340

[665] Brian P. Wiggin, 2015, Conway's Early Inns, The Conway Daily Sun, https://www.conwaydailysun.com/news/conway-s-early-inns-part-i-grant-and-maybe-lincoln/article_395a7ed7-ce14-572d-ae0e-f84b9ba68905.html

Jeremiah was in the Battle of Bunker Hill serving in the company commanded by his brother Joshua. He also served at the Battle of Ticonderoga with the rank of Lieutenant. He also participated in the expedition against Canada.[666]

The Abbot genealogy lists ten children for this family.

1024) i ANNA ABBOTT, b. at Concord, 6 Jun 1770; m. 27 Dec 1789, RICHARD BUSWELL, b. at Kingston, 28 Mar 1761 son of Caleb and Mary (Badger) Buswell; Richard d. at Lebanon, NH, 22 Oct 1835.

ii RUTH ABBOTT; Ruth did not marry.

iii JAMES OSGOOD ABBOTT; died young.

iv JOHN ABBOTT; he was a seaman who died at Havana.

v JAMES OSGOOD ABBOTT; sea captain who died at Baltimore; he married but had no children.

vi MARY ABBOTT; died at Portland, ME; Mary did not marry.

1025) vii ELIZABETH "BETSY" ABBOTT, b. 1784; d. at Conway, NH, 26 Nov 1846; m. 22 Apr 1805, THOMAS ODELL, b. at Conway, 25 Apr 1775 son of Joseph and Sarah (Ingalls) Odell; Thomas d. 31 Jan 1865.

1026) viii JEREMIAH ABBOTT; m. BETSEY SMITH of Biddeford, ME.

1027) ix THOMAS STICKNEY ABBOTT, b. 24 Aug 1792; d. at Portland, ME, 12 Nov 1864; m. 1st, 28 Dec 1818, his

---

[666] Abbot and Abbot, *Genealogical Record of Descendants*, p 125

third cousin once removed (and George Abbott descendant), BETSEY LOVEJOY, b. at Conway, 19 Apr 1795 daughter of Jeremiah and Elizabeth (Spring) Lovejoy; Betsey d. 1828. Thomas m. 2nd, about 1829, MARY S. PRATT.

1028)   x   NATHANIEL ABBOTT, b. about 1797 (based on age at census records); d. after 1850; m. his third cousin once removed (and George Abbott descendant), NANCY LOVEJOY, b. about 1805 daughter of Jeremiah and Elizabeth (Spring) Lovejoy.

245)   DOROTHY ABBOTT *(Nathaniel³, Nathaniel², George¹)*, b. 28 Dec 1746 daughter of Nathaniel and Penelope (Ballard) Abbott; d. 27 Sep 1776; m. 29 May 1766, DAVID GEORGE of uncertain origins but perhaps the son of David George and Ann Cottle born in 1745 in Haverhill. There were several Haverhill families who migrated to Concord near the time of its first settlement. After Dorothy's death, David George married Hannah Colby about 1777 and they had eight children. David died at Littleton, NH about 1816.

David George was a tailor in Concord. He placed an advertisement in the newspaper giving the price for making a "genteel suit of superfine broadcloth" as three dollars and the price for an "ordinary suite of coarse cloth" as two dollars.[667] He also held several civil positions in the town.

In his will written 8 July 1811 (probate 5 November 1816), David George made bequests to the following persons: oldest son David George, George Thatcher the only son of daughter Hannah Thatcher, daughter Jane Virgin has already received her portion, daughter Dolly Morse, and daughter Betsey Martin. These first five bequests are to the children from his marriage to Dorothy Abbott. His children from his second marriage named in the will are Nanne

---

[667] Bouton, *History of Concord*, p 311

George, daughter Ruth Gridley, daughter Polly Gennes, son Jacob Rise George, son Christopher Columbus George, son Hector Temple George, daughter Laura C. George, and son George Washington Adams George.[668]

Dorothy Abbott and David George had five children all born at Concord.

1029) i DAVID GEORGE, b. 4 Jan 1767; d. at Concord, 1838; m. 30 Aug 1789, ELIZABETH EMERY, b. at Concord, 30 Apr 1771 daughter of Benjamin and Sarah (Bailey) Emery;[669] Elizabeth d. 6 Aug 1827.

1030) ii HANNAH GEORGE, b. 23 Jun 1768; likely died by the early 1790's assuming she had just the one child mentioned in her father's will; married a Mr. Thatcher whose identity has not been found.

1031) iii JANE GEORGE, b. 22 Apr 1772; d. after 1830 at Rumford, ME;[670] m. 6 Jun 1793, JEREMIAH VIRGIN, b. at Concord, 7 Sep 1765 son of William and Mehitable (Stickney) Virgin; Jeremiah died after 1830. Jeremiah Virgin and Jane Virgin were first members of the congregational church in Rumford which was organized in 1803.[671]

---

[668] *New Hampshire Wills and Probate Records 1643-1982,* Probate of David George, Grafton, 5 Nov 1816.
[669] The 1819 will of Benjamin Emery of Concord includes a bequest to his daughter Elizabeth George.
[670] There is an 1830 Census record for Rumford for Jeremiah Virgin that includes a male and female of the ages of Jeremiah and Jane Virgin. A census record from 1840 that would fit with them was not located.
[671] Lapham, *History of Rumford, Oxford County, Maine*, p 141

1032) iv DOLLY GEORGE, b. 8 Feb 1774; d. 20 Mar 1861 at Rumford, ME;[672] m. 5 Aug 1792, BENJAMIN MORSE, b. at Amherst, NH, 24 Jun 1771 son of Benjamin and Rachel (Webster) Morse; Benjamin d. at Rumford, 4 May 1849.

1033) v BETSEY GEORGE, b. 22 Jan 1776; d. at Rumford, ME, 2 May 1832; m. 1 Jul 1798, DANIEL MARTIN, b. at Concord, 16 Jul 1772 son of Henry and Esther (Kimball) Martin; Daniel d. 15 Jun 1861.

246) SARAH ABBOTT (*Nathaniel³, Nathaniel², George¹*), b. 3 Dec 1748 daughter of Nathaniel and Penelope (Ballard) Abbott; d. Jun 1842; m. 1 Dec 1764, SAMUEL FARNUM, b. at Concord, 10 Feb 1743 son of Zebadiah and Mary (Walker) Farnum.

There is little information on this family. Samuel was born in New Hampshire, may have spent some time in Corinth Vermont where some of their children were born, and later relocated to New York.

i SAMUEL FARNUM, b. 1767; d. 12 Feb 1813 at Reber, NY. His gravestone has age at death as 46.

1034) ii ZEBADIAH FARNUM, b. in Vermont, 31 Mar 1769; d. at Watkins, OH, 13 Oct 1854; m. JANE MCNINCH, b. 13 Oct 1763; Jane d. 18 Mar 1853.

iii SARAH FARNUM, b. 1773

iv DAVID FARNUM, b. 1775; lived in Pembroke, NH.

v LYDIA FARNUM, b. 1777

vi JOHN FARNUM, b. 1779

---

[672] Dorothy Morse, age 86, is listed in the 1860 U.S. Census for Rumford; she is the head of household with Clarissa Morse age 43 living with her.

Sarah Abbott Blanchard³, Nathaniel², George¹

247)   HANNAH BLANCHARD *(Sarah Abbott Blanchard³, Nathaniel², George¹)*, b. 8 Oct 1728 daughter of Joseph and Sarah (Abbott) Blanchard; d. likely at Hillsborough, NH; m. 19 May 1748, her third cousin, STEPHEN BLANCHARD, b. 9 Aug 1726 son of Stephen and Deborah (Phelps) Blanchard. Stephen had a second marriage to ELIZABETH POTTER. Stephen d. at Hillsborough between 1796 and 1802 (will written 4 Mar 1796 and proved 19 Oct 1802).

Stephen Blanchard of Milford, New Hampshire wrote his will 4 March 1796 and it was proved 19 October 1802. The will includes token bequests of one dollar to his children who have already received their full portions of the estate. The children named are son Jacob, son John, daughter Sarah, daughter Mary, and daughter Phebe. Other children receive more substantial bequests (some money or land bequests) including son Cyrus, son Joel, son James, and son Phineas. These last four sons are sons from his second marriage. He also mentions grandchildren, the sons of Stephen who is deceased, and to grandchildren the children of Hannah who is deceased. None of the last names of the daughters are given in the will nor are the names of the grandchildren. Beloved wife Elizabeth received the use of the East room and other material support for her maintenance.[673]

Hannah Blanchard and Stephen Blanchard had eight children whose births are recorded at Andover. There is one record discrepancy regarding the marriages of the children. The Batchelder

---

[673] *New Hampshire Wills and Probate Records 1643-1982,* Probate of Stephen Blanchard, Hillsborough, will 4 Mar 1796.

genealogy[674] states that Sarah Blanchard married Uziel Batchelder while there is a marriage transcription for a marriage of Mary Blanchard and Uziel. There are baptism records in Andover for two of Uziel's children that give the mother's name as Sarah. Finally, there is a Vermont death record for Sarah Batchelder wife of Uziel.

1035)   i   STEPHEN BLANCHARD, b. 4 Jan 1748/9; d. at Milford, 1789; m. by 1774, LUCY ADAMS, b. at Dunstable, NH, b. 8 May 1747 daughter of Ephraim and Thankful (Blodgett) Adams.

ii   PHINEAS BLANCHARD, b. 21 Jun 1750; d. at Milford, 18 Oct 1775. Phineas did not marry.

iii   HANNAH BLANCHARD, b. 20 Jul 1752. It is known from the will that she married and had children and died prior to 1796. However, no good information has been located that would shed light on the name of her husband.

1036)   iv   SARAH BLANCHARD, b. 27 Feb 1755; d. in Vermont, 2 Nov 1836; m. 18 Sep 1777, UZIEL BATCHELDER, b. at Beverly, 30 Oct 1755 son of Joseph and Judith (Ray) Batchelder.

1037)   v   JACOB BLANCHARD, b. 22 Jun 1758; d. at Guildhall, VT, 1806; m. at Holland, MA, 6 Apr 1784, ELIZABETH CRAWFORD, b. at Union, CT, 1860 daughter of John and Mary (Rosebrooks) Crawford.[675]

vi   MARY BLANCHARD, b. 9 Aug 1760; she was living at the time of her father's will in 1796.

---

[674] Pierce, *Batcheller Genealogy*, p 412
[675] Gould, *Early Families of Bradford*, p 43

1038) vii PHEBE BLANCHARD, b. 15 Dec 1762; d. at Wilton Center, NH, 20 Aug 1838; m. JEREMIAH BURNHAM, b. at Ipswich, 14 Sep 1763 son of Jeremiah and Mary (Burnham) Burnham; Jeremiah d. at Wilton Center, NH, 1 Nov 1844.

1039) viii JOHN BLANCHARD, b. 16 Feb 1767; d. at Chester, VT, 19 Apr 1855; m. SYBIL CRAWFORD, b. at Union, CT, about 1762 daughter of John and Mary (Rosebrooks) Crawofrd. This is confirmed by the will of John Blanchard as the children named in his will have birth and death records that name parents as John and Sybil. (This John is first cousin to John born in 1768 who married Dorcas Osgood.) Both John and Sybil appear to be living in 1840 in Andover, Vermont. At the 1850 Census, John Blanchard heads a household that includes his unmarried daughter Sybil who died in 1851.

248) JOSEPH BLANCHARD *(Sarah Abbott Blanchard³, Nathaniel², George¹)*, b. 9 Feb 1730/1 son of Joseph and Sarah (Abbott) Blanchard; d. 22 Mar 1776; m. 27 Feb 1753, his third cousin, DINAH BLANCHARD, b. 28 Dec 1731 daughter of Stephen and Deborah (Phelps) Blanchard. Dinah m. 2nd, as his second wife, REUBEN ABBOTT son of James and Abigail (Farnum) Abbott; Dinah d. at Concord, NH, 11 Mar 1826.

There are births of three children of Joseph and Dinah recorded at Andover. After Joseph's death, guardians were appointed for children Joseph and John. Mother Dinah was named guardian.

  i JOSEPH BLANCHARD, b. 20 May 1754; d. 3 Mar 1758.

1040) ii JOSEPH BLANCHARD, b. 10 Apr 1765; m. 27 Feb 1786, his second cousin once removed (and George Abbott descendant), HANNAH MOOAR, b. 6 Nov 1768 daughter of Benjamin and Hannah (Phelps) Mooar. Joseph served in the Revolutionary War. After Joseph's death (not yet found), Hannah married Nathan Cutler.[676] Hannah d. at Lewiston, ME, 12 Sep 1860.[677][678]

1041) iii JOHN BLANCHARD, b. 20 Feb 1768; d. at Boston, 6 Feb 1802 at age 32 or 34;[679] m. 27 Apr 1789, DORCAS OSGOOD, b. at Tewksbury, 27 Feb 1770 daughter of Stephen and Mary (Foster) Osgood. Dorcas m. 2nd, Daniel Hastings; Dorcas d. at Boston, 28 Oct 1813.

249) JEREMIAH BLANCHARD *(Sarah Abbott Blanchard[3], Nathaniel[2], George[1])*, b. Jun 1733 son of Joseph and Sarah (Abbott) Blanchard; d. at Weston, VT, 29 Jan 1826; m. 1st, 17 May 1759, DOROTHY SMITH who d. about 1770. Jeremiah m. 2nd, Aug 1772, SUSANNA MARTIN, b. 6 Apr 1743 daughter of John and Hannah(-) Martin.

  There are three children recorded for Jeremiah Blanchard and Dorothy Smith, all born at Andover.

---

[676] Hannah Cutler received a widow's pension for Joseph Blanchard. Ancestry.com. *U.S., Revolutionary War Pension and Bounty-Land Warrant Application Files, 1800-1900*
[677] Mooar, *Mooar Genealogy*, p 32
[678] Hannah is buried in Hillside Cemetery in Lisbon Falls, ME with an inscription that reads wife of Nathan Cutler, died Sept 12, 1860 age 92 years. Findagrave.com
[679] One record gives age at death as 32 and another as age 34.

1042) i   JEREMIAH BLANCHARD, b. 10 Oct 1759; d. at Newburyport, 4 Apr 1844; m. 20 Nov 1784, SUSANNA PEARSON; Susanna d. at Newbury, 4 Mar 1808.

ii   PETER BLANCHARD, b. 12 Aug 1767; d. in Vermont, 22 Nov 1858; m. at Royalston, MA, 6 Mar 1804, HANNAH HOLDEN, b. 1776 (based on age at time of death); Hannah d. at Weston, 14 Apr 1855. Peter and Hannah do not seem to have had children. In his 1856 will, Peter leaves his entire estate to Ivers Holden and his wife Rebecca. [Ivers Holden was married to Rebecca Craggin, so there is likely a connection to the bequest in Peter's brother Eber's will mentioned just below.]

iii   EBER BLANCHARD, b. 14 Jan 1769; d. at Weston, VT, 4 Feb 1842; m. MARY (last name unknown); Mary d. 4 Mar 1852. Eber and Mary do not seem to have had children. In his 1842 will, Eber leaves his entire estate to Mary, and after her death, the estate goes to her son-in-law (last name is Craggin and the first name is not readable but begins with an "A").

Jeremiah Blanchard and Susannah Martin had nine children, the first four baptized at Andover, and the youngest five recorded in New Hampshire (Wilton).[680]

---

[680] *New Hampshire: Births, Deaths and Marriages, 1654-1969.* (From microfilmed records. Online database: *AmericanAncestors.org*, New England Historic Genealogical Society, 2014.)

	i	HENRY BLANCHARD, baptized 25 Jul 1773; died young.
	ii	SARAH BLANCHARD, baptized 13 Nov 1774
	iii	DOROTHY BLANCHARD, baptized 3 Nov 1776
1043)	iv	JUDITH BLANCHARD, baptized 13 Jun 1779; d. at Wilton, NH after 1860 (living at the 1860 U.S. Census); m. 12 Feb 1801, her third cousin (and George Abbott descendant) BENJAMIN STEEL, b. at Wilton, 11 Jun 1776 son of Benjamin and Hannah (Lovejoy) Steel; Benjamin d. 18 Nov 1845. This is the same as Family #288, child iv.
1044)	v	HENRY BLANCHARD, b. 30 Mar 1781; d. at Raymondville, NY, 22 Oct 1824; m. at Billerica, 21 Jan 1807, MARY "POLLY" CROSBY, b. 1786 (based on age at time of death); Polly d. 2 Apr 1848.
1045)	vi	JOHN BLANCHARD, b. 26 Nov 1782; d. at Norfolk, NY, 28 Jan 1851; m. MARY; Mary d. 18 Aug 1848.
	vii	HANNAH BLANCHARD, b. 27 Mar 1785
1046)	viii	WILLIAM BLANCHARD, b. 10 Feb 1788; d. at Royalton, NY, 1861; m. ELIZABETH GILBERT, b. 1790; Elizabeth d. 10 Oct 1857.
1047)	ix	AARON BLANCHARD, b. 20 Jul 1791; perhaps married Sally and relocated to Norfolk, NY with his brother John. There is an Aaron of the right age with wife Sally and children in census records.

250) DANIEL BLANCHARD *(Sarah Abbott Blanchard³, Nathaniel², George¹)*, b. 15 Jul 1735 son of Joseph and Sarah (Abbott) Blanchard; d. 19 Mar 1776; m. 29 Sep 1757, JERUSHA EATON, b. 19 Sep 1737 daughter of Silas and Jerusha (Gould) Eaton.

Generation Four 455

The births of eight children are recorded at Andover for Daniel Blanchard and Jerusha Eaton.

1048) i DANIEL BLANCHARD, b. 20 Sep 1759; d. at Thetford, VT; m. at Salem, 26 Feb 1783, MARY BLANCHARD, b. 4 Feb 1762 daughter of Samuel and Ruth (Tenney) Blanchard.

ii JERUSHA BLANCHARD, b. 24 Jun 1761; d. 8 Aug 1779.

1049) iii ISAAC BLANCHARD, b. 14 Sep 1763; d. at Milford, NH, 26 Apr 1826; m. about 1786, OLIVE HOPKINS, b. at Milford, 1 Apr 1769 daughter of Ebenezer and Martha (Burns) Hopkins; Olive d. 13 Aug 1864.

1050) iv AMOS BLANCHARD, b. 22 Jan 1766; d. at Lynn 25 May 1842; m. 27 Jan 1789, LAVINA HOPKINS, b. at Milford, 1769 daughter of Benjamin and Anna (Powers) Hopkins; Lavina d. 1 Aug 1843.

v REBECCA BLANCHARD, b. May 1768; nothing else known.

1051) vi LUCY BLANCHARD, b. Jan 1771; d. at Milford, NH, 12 Feb 1855;[681] m. at Danvers, 27 Oct 1793, NATHAN PUTNAM, b. at Danvers, 18 Mar 1773 son of Nathan and Hannah (Putnam) Putnam; Nathan d. at Milford 12 Mar 1842.[682]

1052) vii ABIEL BLANCHARD, b. Mar 1773; m. 1st, 9 Apr 1795, HANNAH GRAY, b. at Wilton, 17 Jun 1773 daughter of Timothy and Hannah (Blanchard) Gray.

---

[681] Ramsdell and Colburn, *History of Milford*, vol 1, p 891
[682] Burial site is Union Street Cemetery, Milford, NH, Plot 47. Findagrave.com

Abiel m. 2nd, at Monkton, VT, 31 May 1808, PATIENCE VARNEY.

viii HANNAH BLANCHARD, b. 4 Feb 1776; m. 13 Jan 1803, ENOCH BROWN. There is no other information found for this couple.

251) JOHN BLANCHARD *(Sarah Abbott Blanchard³, Nathaniel², George¹)*, b. 19 Jul 1737 son of Joseph and Sarah (Abbott) Blanchard; d. at Concord, NH, 10 Feb 1823; m. 5 Feb 1761, ELEANOR STEVENS, b. 1739 daughter of Samuel and Phebe (Bodwell) Stevens; Eleanor d. 4 Dec 1799. After Eleanor's death, John married 9 Oct 1800 the widow Hannah Page.

John and Eleanor had six children, the birth of the oldest child at Dunstable, New Hampshire and the youngest five at Concord, New Hampshire.

933) i JOSEPH BLANCHARD, b. 24 Nov 1761; d. at Woodbury, VT, 19 Feb 1839; m. his third cousin once removed, PHEBE ABBOTT, b. at Concord, 22 Feb 1766 daughter of Joseph and Phebe (Lovejoy) Abbott; Phebe d. 31 May 1837.

1053) ii JOHN BLANCHARD, b. 11 Sep 1763; d. at Farmington, MI, 1844; m. HANNAH PERRIN.

1054) iii STEVENS BLANCHARD, b. 15 Sep 1765; d. at Concord, 1790; m. 16 Oct 1788, his third cousin once removed (and George Abbott descendant), SARAH HALL, b. at Canterbury, 3 Sep 1771 daughter of Obadiah and Mary (Perham) Hall; Sarah d. at Beekmantown, NY, 1824. Sarah m. 2nd, OBADIAH MOONEY.

1055) iv   SARAH BLANCHARD, b. 28 Sep 1769; d. at Concord, 11 Nov 1848; m. about 1797, EBENEZER FISK, b. at Tewksbury, 26 Jan 1766 son of Ephraim and Mehitable (Frost) Fisk; Ebenezer d. at Concord about 1857.

1056) v   DAVID BLANCHARD, b. 4 Dec 1771; d. at Concord, 10 Jan 1805; m. 4 Oct 1796, HANNAH EATON, b. 31 Jun 1772 daughter of William and Sarah (Farnum) Eaton.

1057) vi   MOSES BLANCHARD, b. 15 Oct 1783; d. at Stark, NH, 15 Oct 1858;[683] m. 24 Apr 1806, ELIZABETH WADLEIGH, b. about 1785; d, after 1850. Both Moses and Elizabeth were listed in the 1850 U.S. at Mexico, ME. Moses went to stay with his son Calvary in New Hampshire after the death of Elizabeth.

Joseph³, Nathaniel², George¹

252)   BATHSHEBA ABBOTT *(Joseph³, Nathaniel², George¹)*, b. 16 Sep 1735 daughter of Joseph and Deborah (Blanchard) Abbott; d. at Andover (at least buried at Andover), 8 Dec 1784; m. 2 Jul 1752, NATHAN BLANCHARD, b. 30 Mar 1730 son of Stephen and Deborah (Phelps) Blanchard; Nathan d. before 1784[684] probably at Wilton, NH.[685]

There is just one daughter recorded for this family at Andover. In 1763 they were dismissed from the church at Andover

---

[683] New Hampshire, Death and Burial Records Index, 1654-1949
[684] Bathsheba is listed as a widow on her death record.
[685] Livermore, *History of Wilton*, NH, p 318

to a new church at Wilton. But it is not clear what happened to them after that. There are no records in Wilton for any other children. However, Charlotte Helen Abbott, identifies three other children in this family, although no other records could be located for these children.[686] There are records in Wilton and Milford for the children of the daughter Bathsheba Blanchard and her husband Daniel Barker. A probate record was not located for Nathan Blanchard.

1058) i   BATHSHEBA BLANCHARD, b. at Andover, 20 Apr 1754; d. likely at Lyndeborough, NH; m. 1 Jul 1768 (intention listed, although seems very young), DANIEL BARKER, b. at Methuen, 30 May 1746 son of Zebadiah and Phebe (Merrill) Barker; Daniel is reported to have died during the Revolutionary War probably about 1784 (date of birth of youngest child).[687] Bathsheba may have remarried David Hardy in 1792.

    ii   MOSES BLANCHARD

    iii   STEPHEN BLANCHARD

    iv   LUCY BLANCHARD, b. 1776

253)   HANNAH ABBOTT (*Joseph³, Nathaniel², George¹*), b. 15 Jun 1742 daughter of Joseph and Deborah (Blanchard) Abbott; d. about 1770 at Wilton, NH (about this time her husband remarried); m. 15 Jan 1761, TIMOTHY DALE, b. at Danvers, 9 May 1733 son of John and Abigail (Putnam) Dale. Timothy m. 2nd Rebeckah (-); date of death of Timothy is not known. He was last taxed in Wilton in 1801.

Hannah Abbott and Timothy Dale had four children born at Wilton. It is known that the oldest son, Timothy, did marry and

---

[686] Charlotte Helen Abbott, *Blanchard Family*, retrieved from https://mhl.org/sites/default/files/files/Abbott/Blanchard%20Family.pdf
[687] Cochrane, *Families of Antrim*, NH, p 352

resided in Wilton off and on. This son received a fractured skull from a tree limb falling and was partially paralyzed as a result.[688]

	i	TIMOTHY DALE, b. 24 Mar 1762; d. at Wilton, 18 Sep 1830. Timothy is known to have married and had children, but there are no records of who these might be.
1059)	ii	HANNAH DALE, b. 22 Oct 1763; she is likely the Hannah Dale who married at Wilton, 26 Feb 1793, BARNABAS GIBSON, b. at Pelham, 12 Jul 1767 son of Barnabas and Elizabeth (-) Gibson; Barnabas d. at Pelham, 4 Feb 1852.
1060)	iii	JOSHUA DALE, b. 22 Jan 1765; d. at Weston, VT, 23 Mar 1845; m. at Andover, VT, 13 Apr 1789, RHODA PEASE, b. 11 May 1764 daughter of Ezekiel and Jemima (Markham) Pease; Rhoda d. at Andover, VT, 6 Jan 1821.
	iv	SAMUEL DALE, b. 23 Mar 1767. He might be living in Milford in the 1810 U. S. Census, in which case he married and had children, but no records have been located there. There is a Samuel Dale in Landgrove, VT who has several children at about the right time for this Samuel so perhaps Samuel went to Landgrove with his brother.

254) JOSEPH ABBOTT (*Joseph³, Nathaniel², George¹*), b. 2 Apr 1744 son of Joseph and Deborah (Blanchard) Abbott; d. at Wilton, NH

---

[688] Livermore, *History of Wilton, NH*, p 358

about 1792; m. about 1763 MARY BARKER whose parentage is uncertain.

There are records for the births of seven children, four recorded at Andover and three at Wilton.

1061) i JOSEPH ABBOTT, b. at Andover, 6 Nov 1763; d. at Keene, NH, 23 Nov 1790; m. 30 Jun 1785, BETSY KING, b. 26 Jun 1764 daughter of Richard and Lucy (Butterfield) King. Lucy m. 2nd, Thomas Baker.

320) ii JOSHUA ABBOTT, b. at Wilton, 5 Nov 1765; d. 30 Nov 1798; m. his third cousin, HULDAH ABBOTT, b. 21 Oct 1760 daughter of Joseph and Anna (Peabody) Abbott. Huldah m. 2nd, Gideon Phillips. This is the same as Family #66, child vi.

1062) iii JAMES ABBOTT, b. at Andover, 2 Feb 1768; d. at Billerica, Jul 1810; m. 20 Feb 1791, MEHITABLE HOLT, b. at Wilton, 11 Sep 1768 daughter of Daniel and Mehitable (Putnam) Holt; Mehitable d. at Pomfret, CT, 7 Mar 1857.

1063) iv ISRAEL ABBOTT, b. at Andover, 29 Jul 1771; d. at Charlestown, NH, 26 Feb 1840; m. at Nelson, NH, 1 May 1789, ALICE BAKER, b. at Littleton, 1 Oct 1770 daughter of Timothy and Mary (Dakin) Baker; Alice d. at Whitefield, NH, 13 Aug 1858.

1064) v MOLLY ABBOTT, b. at Andover, 18 Jun 1773; d. likely at Alstead, NH; m. at Nelson, NH, 30 Aug 1789, LEVI WARREN.

1065) vi LUCY ABBOTT, b. at Wilton, 18 Jul 1775; d. at Washington County, NY, 31 Jan 1839; m. 1st, 13 Sep 1792, PEPPERRELL SKINNER, b. at Mansfield, MA, 8 Jul 1773 son of Samuel and Martha (Grover)

Skinner;[689] Pepperrell d. at Whipple, NY, 16 Apr 1810. Lucy m. 2nd, Jonathan Pulman.

vii JEDEDIAH ABBOTT, b. at Wilton 20 Aug 1780. According to the Abiel Abbot genealogy, he was in Upper Canada and Smithville, NY. He married but it is not known to whom.

255) JACOB ABBOTT (*Joseph³, Nathaniel², George¹*), b. 9 Feb 1745/6 son of Joseph and Deborah (Blanchard) Abbott; d. 5 Mar 1820 at Brunswick, ME; m. 1 Dec 1767, LYDIA STEVENS, b. 3 May 1745 daughter of John and Lydia (Gray) Stevens; Lydia d. Jun 1821.

Jacob began his adult life as a farmer, but sold his farm in Wilton, New Hampshire to his brother in 1776. He lived in the town of Wilton involved in trade goods. He also built the first mills on the Souhegan River. He returned to Andover for a time and served on the board of Phillips Academy. He returned to New Hampshire and was later in Maine where he served on the board of Bowdoin College.[690]

Jacob and Lydia's grandson, Jacob Abbott (1803-1879), was a writer of children's books, the most well-known being the Rollo books.

Jacob and Lydia had ten children, five of whom died in childhood. A sixth child, John, graduated Harvard in 1801 but died in 1809.

   i LYDIA ABBOTT, b. and d. 1 Jun 1769

1066) ii LYDIA ABBOTT, b. 1 May 1771; d. at Franklin, ME, 20 Jun 1855; m. 10 Feb 1789, a fourth cousin,

---

[689] The Genealogical Exchange, volumes 1-7, 1906, p 11
[690] Abbot and Abbot, *Genealogical Record of Descendants*, p 131

THOMAS RUSSELL, b. at Andover, 5 Jun 1765 son of Thomas and Bethia (Holt) Russell; Thomas d. 9 Jul 1863.

iii HANNAH ABBOTT, b. 31 Jul 1772; d. 10 May 1786.

799) iv PHEBE ABBOTT, b. 25 Jun 1774; d. 18 Apr 1857 (buried at Andover); m. at Andover, 17 Jan 1793, her third cousin once removed, BENJAMIN ABBOTT, b. at Wilton, 17 Mar 1770 son of Abiel and Dorcas (Abbott) Abbott; Benjamin d. at Temple, ME, 10 Sep 1823.

1020) v JACOB ABBOTT, b. 20 Oct 1776; d. at Farmington, ME, 21 Jan 1847; m. at Hallowell, ME, 8 Apr 1798, his second cousin, BETSY ABBOTT, b. at Concord, NH, 6 Aug 1773 daughter of Joshua and Eliza (Chandler) Abbott; Betsy d. 30 Jul 1846. This is the same as Family #243, child iii.

vi DORCAS ABBOTT, b. 6 Sep 1778; d. 29 Dec 1778.

vii SALVA ABBOTT, b, 6 Sep 1778; d. 16 Sep 1778.

viii JOHN S. ABBOTT, b. 25 Sep 1779; d. 9 Jun 1809. John graduated from Harvard in 1801.

ix LUCY ABBOTT, b. 19 Apr 1781; d. at Grafton, NH, 1 Apr 1866; m. DANIEL CAMPBELL, born about 1777 whose origins are not yet known; Daniel d. Oct 1849. Lucy and Daniel did not have children. In his will, Daniel left his estate to his wife Lucy as long as she was his widow and also had bequests to his brothers.

x DORCAS HIBBERT ABBOTT, b. 21 Feb 1784; d. 14 Aug 1784.

256) NATHANIEL ABBOTT *(Joseph³, Nathaniel², George¹)*, b. 27 Oct 1751 son of Joseph and Deborah (Blanchard) Abbott; d. Mar 1791 at Wilton, NH;[691] m. 31 Aug 1773, SARAH STEVENS. The identity of Sarah is not clear. Charlotte Helen Abbot suggests she was Sarah born in Andover in 1742, but that seems unlikely particularly as the last child of Nathaniel and Sarah was born in 1791. There is a Sarah daughter of James born in 1752 who is a more appropriate age. But there are no probate records for any family members yet located that would shed any light on this.

Nathaniel was a shoemaker as well as a farmer. Nathaniel and Sarah relocated from Andover to New Hampshire. The Abbot genealogy book says they located in Wilton, but their children born in New Hampshire were born at Pelham. Nathaniel did serve in the Revolutionary War which perhaps accounts for the several years gap in the births of their children.

There are records for seven children of Nathaniel and Sarah, the oldest two recorded at Andover and the youngest five at Pelham, New Hampshire.

	i	NATHANIEL ABBOTT, b. 20 Jun 1774; d. 11 Jul 1774.
1067)	ii	SARAH ABBOTT, b. 12 Oct 1775; d. 17 Feb 1854 at Acworth, ME; m. 5 Oct 1799, ABIJAH KEYES, b. at Wilton, 30 Jun 1773 son of Simon and Lucy Wheeler Keyes; Abijah d. about 1845.
1068)	iii	PETER ABBOTT, b. 1 Jan 1782; d. at Plainfield, NH, Feb 1850; m. 6 Mar 1806, OLIVE READ born about

---

[691] This is the information given in the Abbot genealogy book and is also the information used by the DAR, but there do not seem to be any records that support this.

1780 and *possibly* the daughter of Elisha and Welthia (Kinney) Read; Olive d. 3 Mar 1855.

    iv   HANNAH ABBOTT, b. 9 Mar 1784; no further record located.

    v   DORCAS ABBOTT, b. 24 Dec 1786; d. 6 Jul 1811.

    vi   PHEBE ABBOTT, b. 3 Feb 1789; no further record located.

1069) vii   NATHANIEL ABBOTT, b. Nov 1791; d. at Somerville, MA, 18 Aug 1860;[692] m. at Jaffrey, 26 Mar 1823, ABIGAIL "ABI" BUTTERS, b. about 1800 (age based on census data) likely the daughter of Amos and Abi (Wilson) Butters; Abi d. after 1860 (living at the time of the 1860 census).

257)   REBECCA ABBOTT (*Joseph³, Nathaniel², George¹*), b. 19 Jun 1754 daughter of Joseph and Deborah (Blanchard) Abbott; d. 19 Apr 1795 at Wilton, NH; m. 6 Apr 1775, DANIEL BATCHELDER, b. 2 Oct 1751 son of Joseph and Judith (Rea) Batchelder. Daniel m. 2nd Sarah Kidder who was born at New Ipswich, NH; Daniel d. 23 Mar 1832.

Daniel was a farmer in Wilton. His first land holding in Wilton was 70 acres in lot seven of the first range. Over the years, he acquired other tracts of land. He served in the Revolutionary War.[693]

Rebecca and Daniel had eleven children born at Wilton.

1070) i   REBECCA BATCHELDER, b. 20 Dec 1775; d. 1805; m. 29 Jan 1799, her third cousin once removed,

---

[692] There is a death record at Somerville that includes his birthplace as Wilton, NH with parents Nathaniel and Sally and his age at death of 69 fits with this Nathaniel. This record also lists him as married.

[693] Livermore, *History of the Town of Wilton*, p 313

Generation Four

WILLIAM ABBOTT, b. at Wilton, 7 Jan 1779 son of William and Sara (Holt) Abbott. William m. 2nd, at Wilton, 29 Sep 1807, ABIGAIL SAWTELL; William d. at Malden, 15 Jan 1843.

1071) ii BETSY BATCHELDER, b. 4 Aug 1777; d. at Bethel, ME, 18 Nov 1864; m. 27 Jan 1799, her third cousin once removed, JONATHAN ABBOTT, b. at Andover, 11 Jun 1776 son of Jonathan and Mehitable (Abbott) Abbott; Jonathan d. 7 Jan 1843.

1072) iii JUDITH RAY BATCHELDER, b. 21 Jun 1779; d. at Wilton after 1850 (still living at 1850 U.S. Census); m. 24 Mar 1803, her third cousin once removed, JOEL ABBOTT, b. at Andover, 10 Oct 1776 son of Barachias and Sarah (Holt) Abbott; Joel d. at Wilton, 26 Mar 1863.

1073) iv DANIEL BATCHELDER, b. 15 May 1781; d. at Wilton, 28 May 1853; m. 1805, PERSIS MAYNARD, b. at Temple, 10 Apr 1782 daughter of Caleb and Elizabeth (Moore) Maynard.[694]

v JOHN BATCHELDER, b. 6 May 1783; died young.

1074) vi MARY "MOLLY" BATCHELDER, b. 11 Mar 1784; d. at Jaffrey, NH, 3 Jun 1859; m. 1806, JOHN CUTTER, b. 24 Oct 1780 son of Joseph and Rachel (Hobart) Cutter; John d. 15 Jan 1857.

vii JOSEPH BATCHELDER; b. 20 Mar 1786; d. 30 Aug 1788.

---

[694] The 1823 will of Caleb Maynard includes a bequest to his daughter Persis "now the wife of Daniel Batchelder." New Hampshire Will and Probate Records 1643-1982.

	viii	JOHN BATCHELDER, b. 17 Mar 1788; d. 5 Mar 1795.
1075)	ix	HERMAN BATCHELDER, b. 8 Aug 1790; d. at Clay, NY, 15 Aug 1876; m. 1812, POLLY BLOOD, b. at Temple, NH, about 1795 daughter of Francis and Rebecca (Parlin) Blood; Polly d. 1865 at Clay, NY.
1076)	x	HANNAH BATCHELDER, b. 2 May 1793; d. at Philadelphia, 2 May 1862; m. 1818, NATHANIEL RICHARDSON, b. at Weston, VT, 22 Aug 1798 son of Nathan and Hannah (Shattuck) Richardson; Nathaniel d. at Philadelphia, 17 Mar 1861.
1077)	xi	LYDIA BATCHELDER, b. 18 Mar 1795; d. 4 Mar 1886 at Oppenheim, NY; m. 1819, ABNER SHATTUCK, b. at Wilton, 18 Jan 1796 son of Abraham and Polly (Wright) Shattuck; Abner d. at Oppenheim, 20 Oct 1878.

Tabitha Abbott Chandler³, Nathaniel², George¹

258) JOHN CHANDLER *(Tabitha Abbott Chandler³, Nathaniel², George¹)*, b. 15 Aug 1730 son of John and Tabitha (Abbott) Chandler; d. at Concord, 1 Mar 1807; m. Oct 1751, MARY CARTER, b. 1729 (based on age at time of death) whose parents are unknown; Mary d. 9 Jun 1793.

John Chandler was a farmer in Concord and owned a tavern. Her served as a lieutenant in the militia. He also held the office of selectman in Concord. According to the Chandler genealogy, Mary died of an overdose of opium.[695]

John Chandler and Mary Carter had six children whose births are recorded at Concord.

---

[695] Chandler, *The Descendants of William and Annis Chandler*, p 323

1078) i JOHN CHANDLER, b. 11 Dec 1752; d. at Boscawen, NH, 24 Jan 1825; m. Mar 1780, NAOMI FARNUM, b. 20 Apr 1760 daughter of Ephraim and Judith (Hall) Farnum; Naomi d. 20 Mar 1832.

1079) ii NATHAN CHANDLER, b. 28 Apr 1754; d. 13 Apr 1781; m. 4 Mar 1775, SUSAN AMBROSE, b, at Chester about 1755 daughter of Robert Ambrose. Susan m. 2nd, Enoch Brown.

iii ISAAC CHANDLER, b. 18 Apr 1758; d. at Boscawen, NH, 25 Mar 1826; m. MARY KIMBALL. Isaac and Mary did not have children.

1080) iv JOSEPH CHANDLER, b. 18 Nov 1760; d. at Fryeburg, ME, 23 Apr 1826; m. about 1785, HANNAH FARRINGTON, b. at Andover, 9 Jul 1765 daughter of Daniel and Hannah (Farnum) Farrington; Hannah d. 29 Nov 1825.

1081) v JEREMIAH CHANDLER, b. 31 Mar 1763; d. at Lovell, ME, 12 Feb 1828; m. 3 Jun 1791, JUDITH FARNUM, b. 13 Jun 1764 daughter of Ephraim and Judith (Hall) Farnum.

1082) vi MOSES CHANDLER, b. 23 Nov 1765; d. at Fryeburg, 10 Sep 1822; m. 1st, 4 Feb 1794, SALLY GOODWIN, b. about 1770; Sally d. 24 Sep 1801. Moses m. 2nd, MARY LANGDON, b. 21 Mar 1782 daughter of Paul Langdon; Mary d. 10 May 1863.

259) TIMOTHY CHANDLER *(Tabitha Abbott Chandler³, Nathaniel², George¹)*, b. 15 Aug 1733 son of John and Tabitha (Abbott) Chandler;

d. at Concord, 24 Mar 1770; m. by 1760, ELIZABETH COPP, b. at Amesbury, 5 Apr 1740 daughter of Solomon and Elizabeth (Davis) Copp. Elizabeth m. 2nd, Stephen Ward; Elizabeth d. 20 Mar 1830.

Timothy and Elizabeth had four children born at Rumford/Concord.

1083) i TABITHA CHANDLER, b. 17 Jun 1761; d. at Randolph, VT, 22 Sep 1839; m. at Plymouth, NH, 17 Dec 1789, HUGH MCINTYRE, b. 11 May 1754 perhaps born in Scotland; Hugh d. 16 May 1837.

936) ii TIMOTHY CHANDLER, b. 25 Apr 1762; d. at Concord, 9 Aug 1848; m. Nov 1787, his second cousin, SARAH ABBOTT, b. 3 Jan 1769 daughter of Joseph and Phebe (Lovejoy) Abbott; Sarah d. 27 Jan 1857. This is the same as Family #226, child iv.

1084) iii ABIEL CHANDLER, b. 20 Oct 1765; d. at Bristol, NH, 5 Mar 1854; m. 25 Dec 1788, ABIGAIL THOMAS (whose origins are not yet verified; she seems to be living at the 1820 Census, but not in 1850).

iv ELIZABETH CHANDLER, b. 28 Jan 1768; d. 24 Jan 1791. Elizabeth did not marry.

260) DANIEL CHANDLER *(Tabitha Abbott Chandler[3], Nathaniel[2], George[1])*, b. 15 Feb 1735 son of John and Tabitha (Abbott) Chandler; d. at Concord, 25 Oct 1795; m. 1st, about 1755, SARAH EASTMAN, b. 14 Jul 1737 daughter of Ebenezer and Eleanor (-) Eastman; Sarah died by 1757 (after the birth of her only child). Daniel m. 2nd, by 1759, SARAH MERRILL, b. 24 Apr 1741 daughter of John and Lydia (Haynes) Merrill; Sarah d. at Chatham, NH, 1810.

Generation Four

Three of the daughters of Daniel Chandler married three Flanders brothers who were sons of Richard and Mary (Fowler) Flanders.

Daniel Chandler and Sarah Eastman had one child.

1085) i SARAH CHANDLER, b. at Concord, 15 Dec 1756; d. 26 Sep 1840 at Northfield, NH; m. 14 Aug 1773, ABNER FLANDERS, b. at South Hampton, 18 Nov 1754 son of Richard and Mary (Fowler) Flanders; Abner d. after 1840 (he was listed on the 1840 pensioners list in Northfield, NH age 85).[696] There is a gravestone in Williams Cemetery in Northfield with a death date given as 26 Nov 1843.[697]

Daniel Chandler and Sarah Merrill had nine children born at Concord.

i JOANNA CHANDLER, b. about 1759; this is a child listed in the Chandler genealogy book for whom there are no known records.

1086) ii MARY CHANDLER, b. 27 Jan 1760; d. at Concord, 1831;[698] m. 1st, about 1775, EBENEZER WEST, b. 25 Dec 1754 son of Nathaniel and Sarah (Burbank) West; Ebenezer d. about 1776. Mary m. 2nd, 20 Mar 1777, RICHARD FLANDERS, b. Mar 1752 son of Richard and Mary (Fowler) Flanders; Richard d, at Concord, 1841.

---

[696] Ancestry.com. *New Hampshire, Compiled Census and Census Substitutes Index, 1790-1890* [database on-line]. Provo, UT, USA: Ancestry.com Operations Inc, 1999.
[697] Findagrave.com memorial 151316433, Abner Flanders
[698] New Hampshire, Death and Disinterment Records, 1754-1947

1087) iii HANNAH CHANDLER, b. 19 Jun 1763; d. 31 Mar 1828 at Rumford, ME; m. 7 Jun 1787, JOSHUA GRAHAM, b. at Rumford, 7 Jun 1763 son of George and Azubah (-) Graham; Joshua d. at Rumford, ME, 15 Mar 1830.

1088) iv LYDIA CHANDLER, b. 22 Jun 1765; d. 21 Jun 1842 at North Chatham, NH; m. 22 Feb 1784, JONAS WYMAN, b. 1759 perhaps the Jonas Wyman born at Wilmington son of Reuben and Catherine (Wyman) Wyman; Jonas d. at Chatham, 10 Oct 1818.

1089) v ABIGAIL CHANDLER, b. 4 Jul 1767; d. 2 Jan 1841; m. 18 Jan 1784, OLIVER FLANDERS, b. 21 Apr 1765 son of Richard and Mary (Fowler) Flanders; Oliver d. at West Plymouth, NH, 31 Jan 1838.

1090) vi PAUL CHANDLER, b. 5 May 1769; d. 1815 at North Chatham, NH (guardians appointed for minor children 7 Jun 1815); m. about 1795, SUSAN HARDY, b. at Fryeburg, 21 Feb 1773 daughter of David and Molly (-) Hardy; Susan d. 27 Mar 1841.

1091) vii ANN CHANDLER, b. 1771; d. at Chatham, 7 Feb 1799; m. about 1794, RICHARD WALKER.

viii ABIEL CHANDLER, b. 26 Feb 1777; d. at Walpole, NH, 22 Mar 1851; m. 15 May 1827, DORCAS SARGENT, b. at Gloucester, 15 Oct 1787 daughter of Epes and Dorcas (Babson) Sargent; Dorcas d. 2 Feb 1837. Abiel and Dorcas did not have children. Abiel was educated at Fryeburg Academy, Exeter Academy, and Harvard College. He was a school teacher, including for a year in Baltimore. He became a merchant in Boston. His will left the bulk of his estate to Dartmouth College, the legacy being

Generation Four 471

used to found a scientific school at Dartmouth. Abiel and Dorcas did not have children.

1092) ix JOHN CHANDLER, b. 19 Mar 1781; d. at Chatham, 23 Apr 1815; m. 28 Nov 1805, MARY HARRIMAN, b. about 1783 daughter of Amos and Nancy (Church) Harriman. Mary m. 2nd, Nathaniel Hutchins. Mary d. 13 Jun 1844.

261) JOSHUA CHANDLER *(Tabitha Abbott Chandler³, Nathaniel², George¹)*, b. 9 Jun 1740 son of John and Tabitha (Abbott) Chandler; d. 3 Dec 1816; m. 1768, IRENE COPP, b. at Amesbury, 17 May 1745 daughter of Solomon and Elizabeth (Davis) Copp; Irene d. 7 Dec 1810.

Joshua and Irene Chandler had seven children born at Concord. Four of the children married children of Samuel and Anna (Hanson) Arlin.

1093) i DANIEL CHANDLER, b. 1 Sep 1768; d. Jun 1817; m. 3 Feb 1794, MEHITABLE ARLIN, b. 1770 daughter of Samuel and Anna (Hanson) Arlin. After the death of Daniel, Mehitable remarried Josiah Chandler.

ii RUTH CHANDLER, b. 20 Feb 1770; d. May 1792; m. 20 Mar 1791, GEORGE ARLIN, b. 1768 son of Samuel and Anna (Hanson) Arlin; George married Ruth's younger sister Sarah after Ruth's death. Ruth and George had one child who died as an infant.

	iii	RUHAMAH CHANDLER, b. 4 May 1772; d. after 1850 (living in Concord qt the 1850 U.S. Census);[699] m. JOHN SIMPSON 16 Feb 1824. Ruhamah did not have children.
1094)	iv	SARAH CHANDLER, b. 12 Feb 1774; d. after 1860 (living in Concord at the 1860 U.S. Census); m. 25 Aug 1792, GEORGE ARLIN, b. 1768 son of Samuel and Anna (Hanson) Arlin; George d. between 1850 and 1860.
	v	JOSHUA CHANDLER, b. 1776; d. at 16 months of age.
	vi	HANNAH CHANDLER, b. 2 Apr 1779; d. 18 Sep 1806. Hannah did not marry.
1095)	vii	JOSHUA CHANDLER, b. 4 Sep 1782; m. Aug 1802, NANCY ARLIN, b. 11 Mar 1783 daughter of Samuel and Anna (Hanson) Arlin; Nancy d. after 1870 (living in Concord at the 1870 U. S. Census).

Jeremiah[3], Nathaniel[2], George[1]

262) HANNAH ABBOTT (*Jeremiah[3], Nathaniel[2], George[1]*), b. 10 Oct 1735 daughter of Jeremiah and Hannah (Ballard) Abbott; d. 13 Sep 1819; m. 3 Jul 1766, OLIVER FARMER, b. 31 Jul 1728 son of Oliver and Abigail (Johnson) Farmer; Oliver d. 24 Sep 1814.

Oliver Farmer had first married Rachel Shed by whom he had six children. Hannah married Oliver when she was 31 years old. Oliver and Hannah had three children. Neither of them left a

---

[699] Year: 1850; Census Place: Concord, Merrimack, New Hampshire; Roll: M432_435; Page: 67A; Image: 136. Ruhamah Simpson, age 78, living in the household of George and Sarah Arlin aged 82 and 76

will that was located. The births of their three children are recorded at Billerica.

1096) i HANNAH FARMER, b. 17 Sep 1767; d. 21 Apr 1856; m. 10 Dec 1789, as his 2nd wife, WILLIAM ROGERS, b. 10 Dec 1789 son of Samuel and Rebeckah (Farmer) Rogers. William first married Susannah Pollard in 1787. William d. 17 Aug 1838.

ii REBECCA FARMER, b. 29 Nov 1768; d. 8 Jan 1792; Rebecca did not marry.

1097) iii JEREMIAH FARMER, b. 10 Apr 1771; d. 2 Mar 1836; m. 13 Oct 1816, CLARISSA FOSTER, b. 16 Apr 1785 daughter of Timothy and Sally (Crosby) Foster; Clarissa d. at Boston, 20 Feb 1873.

263) REBECCA ABBOTT (*Jeremiah³, Nathaniel², George¹*), b. 13 Jul 1741 daughter of Jeremiah and Hannah (Ballard) Abbott; m. 29 Oct 1761, RICHARD BOYNTON, b. at Tewksbury, 22 Mar 1741 son of Richard and Jerusha (Hutchins) Boynton.

Richard Boynton's father died in 1754. In 1756, Richard selected William Stickney of Billerica as his guardian.[700] William Stickney was Rebecca Abbott's step-father. Hannah Ballard Abbott married William Stickney in 1749 following the death of Rebecca's father Jeremiah Abbott.

According to the *History of the Boynton Family*, this family relocated to Milford, New Hampshire, then moved on to Rindge,

---

[700] *Middlesex County, MA: Probate File Papers, 1648-1871*. Online database. AmericanAncestors.org. New England Historic Genealogical Society, 2014. (From records supplied by the Massachusetts Supreme Judicial Court Archives. Digitized images provided by FamilySearch.org)

and ultimately settled in Weathersfield, Vermont. A death year of 1814 is also given by that source.[701]

Rebecca and Richard Boynton had ten children. Births of the first three children are recorded at Billerica. The other children were likely born in New Hampshire. Birth records were not located for all the children and record information was supplemented by information in *The Boynton Family: A Genealogy*.

1098) i JOHN BOYNTON, b. 14 Mar 1762; d. at Chester, VT, 4 Aug 1852; m. 7 Sep 1787, PHEBE MARTIN, b. at Andover, 14 Jul 1764 daughter of Jonathan and Phebe (Farnum) Martin; Phebe d. 27 Sep 1840.

1099) ii REBECCA BOYNTON, baptized 13 Nov 1763; d. 27 Apr 1833; m. 1785, NEHEMIAH ROUNDY, b. at Beverly, 10 May 1756 son of Robert and Abigail (Presson) Roundy; Nehemiah d. at sea, Sep 1804.

1100) iii RICHARD BOYNTON, b. 3 Oct 1765; d. at Redman, NY, Jul 1841; m. BETSEY WYMAN, b. at Pelham, 20 Jun 1764 daughter of Joseph and Mary (-) Wyman. Richard married second the widow Mrs. Allen and third Jerusha Bishop.

1101) iv HANNAH BOYNTON, b. 7 Jun 1767; d. 1841 at Spencer, NY; m. at Wilton, 23 Nov 1786, NATHAN MARTIN, b. at Rockingham, VT, 3 Apr 1763 son of Samuel and Elizabeth (Osgood) Martin; Nathan d. 27 Sep 1834.

v JERUSHA BOYNTON, b. Jul 1769; d. 1788.

1102) vi SARAH BOYNTON, b. 28 Aug 1770; m. 16 Jan 1793, DAVID KENNY; their first child was born at Wilton,

---

[701] Boynton, *The Boynton Family: A Genealogy*, p 122

but it is possible that this family resettled in Vermont.

1103) vii ORPHA BOYNTON, b. 10 May 1772; d. at Milford, 1851; m. about 1794, JOHN HOPKINS born at Milford about 1772 son of Ebenezer and Martha (Burns) Hopkins.

1104) viii BETSEY BOYNTON, b. 1774; d. at Wilton, 1819; m. at Amherst, NH, 31 Oct 1802, AARON FULLER, b. 1773; Aaron d. at Crown Point, NY, 4 Apr 1847.

1105) ix DAVID BOYNTON, b. 7 Mar 1776; d. at Rockingham, VT, 14 Dec 1813;[702] m. 1 Jun 1804, LYDIA NOURSE, b. at Jaffrey, NH, 6 Jun 1783 daughter of Peter and Lydia (Low) Nourse;[703] Lydia d. 16 Oct 1874 in New York.[704]

1106) x SUSANNAH BOYNTON, b. 25 Oct 1778; m. at Rockingham, VT, 12 Jun 1804, JOSHUA EATON, b. at Reading, 3 Jul 1778 son of Thomas and Abigail (Bancroft) Eaton; Joshua d. 16 May 1840. Their oldest child was born at Wilton, but the family seems to have moved on to Vermont.

264) WILLIAM ABBOTT (*Jeremiah³, Nathaniel², George¹*), b. 21 Jul 1746 son of Jeremiah and Hannah (Ballard) Abbott; d. after 1800 at Wheelock, VT; m. 28 Dec 1769, BRIDGET SPAULDING, b. 11 Mar 1748/9 daughter of David and Phebe (-) Spaulding; Bridget's death is

---

[702] Hayes, *History of the Town of Rockingham Vermont*, p 810
[703] Wells, *History of Newbury, Vermont: From the Discovery of the Coös Country*, p 645
[704] At the 1860 U.S. Census, she was living in Charlotte, New York with her daughter Elvira and her husband Daniel Lake.

not known but likely in Vermont; William married second, MEHITABLE SCOTT (according to the Abbot genealogy book).

William was a tanner and currier. William and Bridget wandered a bit in their life. They did have five children in Chelmsford, were then in Fitchburg, and then were a year in Townsend. They were warned out of Townsend, which was sometimes done by towns to encourage new arrivals who had no means of supporting themselves to leave the town. The concern was that these new arrivals might be a burden on the town for support.[705] There was this notice in Townsend: *To notify and warn out - William Abbit & Bridget his wife together with there Children named Bridget, Jedethan, Sarah, William, Joshua & David who came last from Fitchburg in the county of Worcester to Townshend the Twenty fifth of February 1783. Dated Twentyeth day of February 1784.*[706] From Townsend, the family seems to have made its way to Vermont with a stay in Swanzey, New Hampshire on the way.

William Abbott did serve in the Revolutionary War in various companies: Captain Pollard of Billerica and in the company of Captain Edward Farmer of Billerica. He had periods of service in 1775, 1778, and 1779. It is reported that marched to the alarm of 19 April 1775 and was at Bunker Hill.[707]

The Abbot genealogy reports that William had a second marriage to Mehitable Scott with two more children from that marriage, but no records have been located for that second family.[708]

Births of five children for William and Bridget are recorded at Chelmsford. Son David is known as he is included in the "warning out" of Townsend. There is a son Calvin attributed to this family in most published genealogies and in the listings for the SAR and DAR.

---

[705] Benton, *Warning Out in New England*
[706] Massachusetts: Vital Records, 1621-1850 (Online Database: AmericanAncestors.org, New England Historic Genealogical Society, 2001-2016).
[707] Massachusetts Soldiers and Sailors of the Revolution, volume 1, p 16 and p 21; volume 5, p 507
[708] Abbot and Abbot, *Genealogical Record of Descendants*, p 143

Generation Four

1107) i BRIDGET ABBOTT, b. 13 Dec 1770; d. at Westford, 16 Jun 1849; m. 17 Dec 1807, BENJAMIN READ, b. at Westford, 19 Jan 1779 son of Abel and Rebekah (Farrar) Reed; Benjamin d. 21 Jan 1850.

ii JEDATHAN ABBOTT, b. 9 Feb 1773; he does not seem to have married; death unknown.

1108) iii SARAH ABBOTT, b. 1 Oct 1775; d. at Hancock, NH, 17 Feb 1841; m. at Swanzey, NH, 5 Nov 1794, LOTAN GASSET, b. at Northborough, MA, 31 Oct 1771 son of Levi and Vashti (Brigham) Gasset; Lotan d. 28 Jul 1861.

1109) iv WILLIAM ABBOTT, b. Apr 1778; d. at Dansville, MI, 9 Jan 1849; m. SARAH "SALLY" WOODCOCK, b. at Swanzey, NH, 1 Mar 1782 daughter of Nathan and Lovina (Goodenow) Woodcock; Sally d. 26 Mar 1854.

v JOSHUA ABBOTT, b. Apr 1780; no further record after the "warning out" of Townsend.

vi DAVID ABBOTT, b. about 1782; no record after 1784.

1110) vii CALVIN ABBOTT, b. in New Hampshire, 3 Dec 1788; d. at Ogden, NY,[709] 19 Nov 1858; m. at Danville, VT, 4 Dec 1815, CHARLOTTE CLEMENT, b. at Danville, 12 Sep 1794 daughter of William and Abigail (Hill) Clement; Charlotte d. 12 Dec 1854.

---

[709] *1850 United States Federal Census*, Year: 1850; Census Place: Ogden, Monroe, New York; Roll: M432_529; Page: 83B; Image: 173. Calvin Abbott was living in Ogden in 1850.

The following are the children from the proposed second marriage to Mehitable Scott. The Abbot genealogy suggests that Mehitable was from Richmond, New Hampshire. No records have been located for these children or for a marriage of William and Mehitable.

    i   MEHITABLE ABBOTT, b. about 1797

    ii   JESSE ABBOTT, b. about 1799

265)   JEREMIAH ABBOTT (*Jeremiah³, Nathaniel², George¹*), b. 11 Aug 1748 son of Jeremiah and Hannah (Ballard) Abbott; d.?; m. 19 Jan 1769, SUSANNAH BALDWIN, b. 1746 (probably the daughter of Josiah Baldwin of Tewksbury); Susanna d. 9 Apr 1825.

Jeremiah and Susannah had nine children whose births or baptisms are recorded at Chelmsford.

    i   SUSANNAH ABBOTT, b. 12 Jun 1769; d. likely at Milford, NH, 1 Nov 1803; m. at Lyndeborough, 18 Oct 1795, ZADOC JONES, b. at Milford, 5 Jul 1773 son of Caleb and Deborah (Hopkins) Jones; Zadoc married second Susannah's sister Rebeckah; Zadoc d. at Milford, 31 Jul 1823. There are no children recorded for Susannah and Zadoc.

1111) ii   JEREMIAH ABBOTT, b. 26 Feb 1772; d. at Springfield, VT, 2 Oct 1850;[710] m. 30 May 1801, SALLY FARROR, b. at Chelmsford, 14 Apr 1776 daughter of Nathaniel and Rachel (Fletcher) Farror; Sally d. at Springfield, VT about 1815.[711]

---

[710] *Vermont, Vital Records, 1720-1908.*
[711] The 1810 U.S. Census for Springfield has a household for Jeremiah Abbott that includes a woman in the right age range; in the 1820 Census that older woman is no longer listed.

1112) iii HANNAH ABBOTT, b. 30 Jan 1774; d. perhaps at Vincennes, IN;[712] m. her third cousin once removed (and George Abbott descendant), DAVID CHANDLER, b. at Milford, 28 Jun 1775 son of David and Hannah (Peabody) Chandler.

iv JESSE ABBOTT, b. 22 Sep 1776; d. 26 Dec 1799.

1113) v REBECKAH ABBOTT, b. 26 Aug 1778; d. at Milford, 25 Mar 1864; m. about 1804, ZADOC JONES, b. 5 Jul 1773 son of Caleb and Deborah (Hopkins) Jones. Zadoc had first married Rebeckah's older sister Susannah. Zadoc d. at Milford, 31 Jul 1823.

1114) vi JONAS ABBOTT, b. 29 Apr 1781; d. 11 Sep 1839 at Lyndeborough; m. 18 Jan 1807, BETSEY PARKER, b. at New Ipswich, NH, 17 Mar 1783 daughter of Joseph and Susannah (Fletcher) Parker; Betsey d. 13 Dec 1857.

vii SILAS ABBOTT, baptized 25 Jul 1784. It is not certain what became of Silas, but he is possibly the Silas Abbott who died at Chelmsford 6 Aug 1856 at age 72. This Silas was single and lived frequently in the almshouse at Chelmsford. The only issue is that the death record lists his father as Nehemiah rather than Jeremiah. However, there is no other Silas Abbott in birth records of the right age other than the son of Jeremiah. Of course, it may well be there was another Silas whose birth record has not survived.

---

[712] Both the Abbot and the Chandler genealogy books list this family as going to Vincennes.

1115) viii WILLIAM ABBOTT, b. 3 Nov 1787; d. at Lyndeborough, 14 Jan 1824; m. EUNICE CRAM, b. at Lyndeborough, 31 Aug 1785 daughter of Uriah and Eunice (Ellingwood) Cram. Eunice m. 2nd, 25 Jul 1836, William Strafford; Eunice d. 29 Feb 1868.

1116) ix SALLY ABBOTT, b. Mar 1792; d. at Lyndeborough, 31 May 1857; m. 27 Dec 1817, JOSEPH CHAMBERLAIN, b. at Lyndeborough, 12 Dec 1789 son of Samuel and Naomi (Richardson) Chamberlain; Joseph d. 30 Aug 1862.

Elizabeth Abbott Mooar³, Nathaniel², George¹

266) JOHN MOOAR *(Elizabeth Abbott Mooar³, Nathaniel², George¹)*, b. Jun 1745 son of Timothy and Elizabeth (Abbott) Mooar; d. 1777 at Saratoga, NY during the Revolution; m. 28 Jul 1774, MARY BALLARD, b. 1754 daughter of William and Hannah (Howe) Ballard. Mary m. 2nd 13 Dec 1781, JONATHAN BOYNTON; Mary d. by 1795 when probate petition filed related to John Mooar's estate requesting administration of her widow's portion which reverted to creditors as she is deceased.

John Mooar did not leave a will; his estate entered probate 1 December 1777. Debts exceeded the value of the estate and it was deemed insolvent. Mary Mooar was administrator of the estate. One-third portion of the estate was set off to the widow for her support. She made an accounting of her expenses 1 October 1781 which was shortly before her remarriage to Jonathan Boynton. She maked another accounting in 1783 in which she is listed as Mary Mooar now Mary Boynton. On 5 May 1795, Samuel Phillips made a request of the Court to be named administrator of that portion of the estate that had been set out to the widow and now reverted to the estate as the widow is deceased. Timothy Mooar had expressed his unwillingness to assume the administration and there were no other close relatives known to be living in the state.[713]

There is in published genealogies a statement that the probate includes a provision for the support of children Jacob, Sarah, and Andrew. However, I did not find that in the probate record. There are birth records in Andover in this period for children Jacob, Sarah, and Andrew but each of those births are listed with parents Abraham and Martha Mooar. The only record for a possible child in this family was Hannah baptized 26 October 1783 described as daughter of John lately deceased. Of note is that this is the same baptismal date of Mary Boynton who is the daughter of Mary Ballard Mooar and her second husband Jonathan Boynton; this at least suggests these are girls from the same family group. It is possible there are four children in this family, but none for which there are firm records. In any case, there is no information about what became of these children. In 1795, there were no living relatives of John Mooar in the State, so if there were children, they were by 1795 deceased or out of the area.

267) ELIZABETH MOOAR (*Elizabeth Abbott Mooar³, Nathaniel², George¹*), b. 8 Mar 1747/8 daughter of Timothy and Elizabeth (Abbott) Mooar; d. 16 Mar 1818; m. 29 Jul 1766, MOSES BAILEY, b. at Bradford, 16 Jan 1743/4 son of Nathan and Mary (Palmer) Bailey; Moses d. 14 Mar 1842.

In his will, Moses makes bequests to son Moses, son John M. Bailey, son Timothy, daughters Elizabeth Downing, Sarah Ames, Hannah Abbott, Rebecca Abbott, and Rhoda Abbott, to the children of his son Joshua (deceased) namely Joshua, Hephzibah, and

---

[713] *Essex County, MA: Probate File Papers, 1638-1881*. Probate of John Mooar, 1 Dec 1777, Case number 18664.

Elizabeth, and son Nathan who receives the remainder of the estate and is the sole executor.[714]

Elizabeth Mooar and Moses Bailey had eleven children whose births are recorded at Andover. Of the ten children who married, seven of them married fellow George Abbott descendants, and son Nathan had two wives and they were both GA descendants. Three of the spouses were children of Bixby and Hephzibah (Ames) Abbott.

1117) i   MOSES BAILEY, b. 20 Oct 1766; d. 3 Jun 1846; m. 13 Sep 1787, MEHITABLE CHASE, b. at Andover, 12 Dec 1768 daughter of Emery and Mehitable (Mooar) Chase; Mehitable d. 9 Oct 1849.

1118) ii ELIZABETH BAILEY, b. 6 Jul 1768; d. at Minot, ME, 1830; m. 25 Aug 1789, SAMUEL DOWNING, b. 30 Jan 1765 son of Samuel and Abigail (Barnard) Downing; Samuel d. at Minot, 24 Jan 1836.

1119) iii JOSHUA BAILEY, b. 14 Aug 1770; d. 30 Oct 1820; m. 19 Feb 1795, his third cousin once removed, HEPHZIBAH ABBOTT, b. 17 Aug 1772 daughter of Bixby and Hephzibah (Ames) Abbott; Hephzibah d. 7 Aug 1813.

1120) iv SARAH BAILEY, b. 1 Nov 1772; d. 22 Mar 1857; m. 30 Mar 1790, her third cousin once removed (and George Abbott descendant), SIMEON AMES, b. 29 Mar 1772 son of Benjamin and Dorcas (Lovejoy) Ames; Simeon d. 29 Sep 1849.

v   NATHAN BAILEY, b. 2 Feb 1775; died in infancy.

---

[714] *Essex County, MA: Probate File Papers, 1638-1881. Probate of* Moses Bailey, 5 Apr 1842, *Case number* 31843.

1121) vi NATHAN BAILEY, b. 4 Feb 1777; d. 16 Jan 1862;[715] m. 1st, 23 Dec 1802, his third cousin once removed, BETSY ABBOTT, b. 18 Sep 1780 daughter of Bixby and Hephzibah (Ames) Abbott; Betsy d. 24 Oct 1817. Nathan m. 2nd, 4 May 1819, his third cousin once removed (and George Abbott descendant), CHLOE POOR, b. 14 May 1779 daughter of John and Chloe (Lovejoy) Poor; Chloe d. 8 Jun 1867.

1122) vii HANNAH BAILEY, b. 3 May 1779; d. at Concord, NH, 27 Dec 1867; m. 14 Nov 1799, her third cousin once removed, WILLIAM ABBOTT, b. 14 Jul 1774 son of Bixby and Hephzibah (Ames) Abbott; William d. at Greenfield, 13 Aug 1852.

1123) viii REBECCA BAILEY, b. 10 Apr 1781; d. likely at Concord; m. 14 May 1801, her third cousin, WILLIAM ABBOTT, b. 30 Oct 1772 son of Isaac and Phebe (Chandler) Abbott; William d. at Concord, 1856 (probate 24 Jun 1856). This is the same as Family #132, child iv.

1124) ix JOHN MOOAR BAILEY, b. 20 Jul 1784; d. 3 Apr 1836; m. 5 Dec 1811, his third cousin once removed (and George Abbott descendant), ELIZABETH BOYNTON, b. 18 Jan 1789 daughter of Thomas and Hannah (Ames) Boynton.

---

[715] Massachusetts: Vital Records, 1841-1910. (From original records held by the Massachusetts Archives. Online database: AmericanAncestors.org, New England Historic Genealogical Society, 2004.) The death record gives his age as 84 and parents as Moses Bailey and Elizabeth. He is listed as married at the time of his death.

1125) x   TIMOTHY BAILEY, b. 18 Oct 1786; d. 8 Jan 1875; m. 7 Jun 1827, SALLY POOR, b. 9 Apr 1794 daughter of Theodore and Sally (Dowling) Poor; Sally d. 21 Apr 1882.

1126) xi   RHODA BAILEY, b. 7 May 1789; d. at Amherst, NH, 1 Sep 1854; m. 17 Jan 1811, her third cousin once removed, HENRY ABBOTT, b. 5 Mar 1785 son of Bixby and Hephzibah (Ames) Abbott; Henry d. 28 Mar 1868.

268)   JOSHUA MOOAR *(Elizabeth Abbott Mooar³, Nathaniel², George¹)*, b. 3 Jun 1751 son of Timothy and Elizabeth (Abbott) Mooar; d. at Milford, NH, 10 Sep 1824; m. 17 Sep 1776, DEBORAH CHANDLER, b. 26 Apr 1757 daughter of Zebadiah and Deborah (Blanchard) Chandler; Deborah was still living in 1822 when Joshua wrote his will.

Note of the spelling of Mooar: At some point in this transition between generations, the spelling of Mooar became Moar. The name is also at times spelled Moor or Moore.

Joshua served as a drummer in Captain Benjamin Ames's company during 1775. The Mooar genealogy includes the transcript of a letter from Joshua to his brother Timothy written 28 August 1775 which recounts some of his experiences in the war zone: "... the Cannon bals flew Like Smoke the regulers killed two of our men belonging to Hamshere" and goes on the request that his brother John might come to where he is in about a fortnight and bring Joshua's cloak.[716]

In his will dated 14 November 1822, Joshua Mooar has the following bequests: wife Deborah receives improvements on one-third part of the estate; his two daughters will receive the household furnishings and the library of books following the decease of their

---

[716] Mooar, *Mooar (Moors) Genealogy*, p 31

mother. Sons Joshua, Stephen C., and Timothy each receive a token bequest of $2 to make up their full portions of the estate. His daughters are Betsy Jenkins wife of Micah Jenkins and Sarah Hutchinson wife of Luther Hutchinson. Luther Hutchinson is named executor.[717] His daughter Deborah died in 1805 and no heirs of hers are mentioned; she had one child who died young.

Joshua and Deborah had seven children whose births are recorded at Milford.

1127) i DEBORAH MOOAR, b. 20 Jul 1777; d. at Milford, 28 Aug 1805; m. 18 Nov 1800, SIMEON GUTTERSON, b. at Andover, 8 Dec 1769 son of Samuel and Lydia (Stevens) Gutterson. Samuel m. 2nd, Phebe Burnham. Deborah and Simeon had one son, Simeon, born two months before his mother's death; Simeon died young.

1128) ii JOSHUA MOOAR, b. 2 Nov 1778; d. at Milford, 20 Jul 1831; m. at Milford, 19 Nov 1805, BEULAH BLANCHARD, b. 13 Jun 1783 daughter of Benjamin and Sarah (Griffin) Blanchard; Beulah d. 20 Nov 1824.

1129) iii STEPHEN CHANDLER MOOAR, b. 17 Aug 1780; d. at Andover, 16 Mar 1861; m. 6 Nov 1804, ELIZABETH SAWYER CHASE, b. at Leominster, 5 Jul 1782 daughter of Enoch and Sarah (Sawyer) Chase; Elizabeth d. 25 Apr 1854.

iv TIMOTHY MOOAR, b. 9 Jan and d. 19 Jan 1783.

---

[717] *New Hampshire Wills and Probate Records 1643-1982,* will of Joshua Mooar, Hillsborough, 14 Nov 1822, Probate Records, Vol 34-35 1824-1827.

1130) v TIMOTHY MOOAR, b. 22 Mar 1784; d. at Nashua, 1855; m. BETSY HOPKINS, b. at Milford, 8 Sep 1792 daughter of Daniel and Hannah (-) Hopkins; Betsy d. at Nashua, 1852.

1131) vi SARAH MOOAR, b. 26 Oct 1786; d. at Milford, 6 Jan 1857; m. 1808, LUTHER HUTCHINSON, b. 2 May 1783 son of Benjamin and Susannah (Peabody) Hutchinson; Luther d. 5 Sep 1861.

1132) vii BETSY MOOAR, b. 25 Jan 1790; d. 1825; m. 20 Apr 1813, MICAH JENKINS, b. 26 Jul 1786 son of Joel and Patty (Carter) Jenkins.

269) MARY MOOAR *(Elizabeth Abbott Mooar³, Nathaniel², George¹)*, b. 26 May 1760 daughter of Timothy and Elizabeth (Abbott) Mooar; d. 2 Aug 1820; m. 30 Jul 1778, WILLIAM HARRIS whose origins are not pinned down; his death is unknown but was before Mary died in 1820. Mary Harris left a will in 1820 and she was a widow at that time.

Mary Harris wrote her will 15 May 1820 and entered probate 5 September 1820. At the time of his mother's death, John M. Harris was living in Watertown as he wrote a letter from that location agreeing to the probate court for the estate to be held in Ipswich. Mary's daughter Mary Holt was living in Andover as she communicated to the probate court related to the location of the court. The will includes a bequest of one dollar to daughter Mary Holt and son John M. Harris receives the remainder of the estate both real and personal.[718]

No birth records were located for the children of William and Mary; they are known through their mother's will. There is a marriage record for the daughter Mary (Polly) and birth records for

---

[718] *Essex County, MA: Probate File Papers, 1638-1881. Probate of* Mary Harris, 5 Sep 1820, *Case number* 12519.

three of Polly's children including a son named William Harris Holt. Son John Moore Harris also has little in the way of records. There is a newspaper notice of his death in Watertown in 1832 at age 48. No marriage record was located, but in the 1820 and 1830 U. S. Census, there is in Watertown a John M. Harris.

1133) i MARY "POLLY" HARRIS, b. about 1779; date of death unknown but after 1820; m. at Andover, 12 Jan 1797, LOAMMI HOLT, b. 23 Jul 1775 son of Simeon and Sarah (Read) Holt; Loammi d. at Andover, 11 Jan 1827 at the almshouse.

ii JOHN MOORE HARRIS, b. about 1784; d. at Watertown, 1832. He perhaps married and had children, but no records have been located (other than census records that show a John M. Harris in Watertown with what appears to be wife and children). It is also possible that the others in the census record are his sister and her children as she was widowed in 1827.

Rebecca Abbott Chandler³, Nathaniel², George¹ *and* Amos⁴, James³, William², George¹

[The next group of families are descendants by the two paths above.]

270) ABIEL CHANDLER *(Rebecca Abbott Chandler³, Nathaniel², George¹)*, b. 11 May 1744 son of Abiel and Rebecca (Abbott) Chandler; d. 27 Aug 1776 at Long Island, NY; m. about 1766, JUDITH WALKER, b. at Rumford, 21 Dec 1744 daughter of Timothy and Sarah (Burbeen) Walker; Judith m. 2ⁿᵈ Nathaniel Rolfe; Judith d. at Concord 1806

Abiel and Judith lived in Concord. Abiel Chandler served as a captain in the Revolutionary War and died of smallpox while serving in New York. He earlier had been at Bunker Hill serving in John Abbott's company. The inventory of his estate was completed July 1777. Timothy Walker, Jr. was administrator of the estate. The final settlement of the estate (payment to creditors) occurred in 1806 following the death of Judith. There were total claims on the estate of $1,484.74 and there was $118.61 available to pay the claims.[719]

Abiel Chandler and Judith Walker had three children born at Concord.

968) i SARAH CHANDLER, b. 15 Jan 1768; d. at Danville, VT, 21 Nov 1836; m. by 1786, her second cousin (and George Abbott descendant), PETER BLANCHARD, b. at Hollis, 17 Aug 1756 son of Benjamin and Keziah (Hastings) Blanchard; Peter d. 25 May 1810.

1134) ii JUDITH CHANDLER, b. 9 Oct 1770; d. at Concord, 28 Dec 1852; m. 12 Jun 1794, TIMOTHY CARTER, b. at Concord, 6 Mar 1767 son of Ezra and Phebe (Whittemore) Carter; Timothy d. 7 Feb 1843.

iii REBECCA CHANDLER, b. 17 Dec 1773; Rebecca did not marry.

271) AMOS ABBOT (*Rebecca Abbott Abbott³, Nathaniel², George¹* **and** *Amos⁴, James³, William², George¹*), b. 15 Jul 1754 son of Amos and Rebecca (Abbott) Abbott; d. at Concord 11 Oct 1834; m. JUDITH MORSE, b. at Newburyport, 1 Mar 1766 daughter of Moses and Sarah (Hale) Morse.

Amos Abbot wrote his will 23 February 1830. He bequeathed to his wife Judith his clock and all the household

---

[719] *New Hampshire Wills and Probate Records 1643-1982,* Probate of Abiel Chandler, Rockingham, 27 Nov 1777, Case number 4401.

furnishings except two beds. Judith also receives the income from one-third part of the farm and use of half the dwelling house. Daughter Sarah Hale Abbot receives $300 to be paid within one year of his death. Sons John Abbot and Simeon Abbot receive all the real estate. Sons John and Simeon are named executors.[720]

A marriage record for Amos and Judith was not located but they seem to have married later in life as their first child was born in 1805. Three children of Amos Abbott and Judith Morse were born at Concord.

        i   JOHN ABBOT, b. at Concord, 15 Nov 1805; d. at Concord, 18 Mar 1886.[721] John does not seem to have married. At the 1850 U.S. Census, he was living with his brother Simeon and his family in Concord.

1135) ii   SIMEON ABBOT, b. at Concord, 3 Aug 1807; d. at Concord, 22 Feb 1895; m. 8 Feb 1837, MARY FARNUM, b. 25 Jun 1814; Mary d. 26 Apr 1898.

1136) iii   SARAH HALE ABBOT, b. at Concord, 27 Jun 1809; d. 8 Sep 1884; m. 18 Dec 1839, her fourth cousin, DAVID ABBOTT *(Nathan⁵, Jabez⁴, Thomas³, Thomas², George¹)*, b. 12 Jul 1809 son of Nathan and Rhoda (Brickett) Abbott; David d. at Concord, 12 Apr 1882.

272)   REBECCA ABBOTT *(Rebecca Abbott Abbott³, Nathaniel², George¹* **and** *Amos⁴, James³, William², George¹)*, b. 26 Sep 1760 daughter of Amos and Rebecca (Abbott) Abbott; d. at Loudon, NH, 24 Dec 1846; m. 9 Oct 1781, MOSES CHAMBERLAIN, b. at Hopkinton, 5

---

[720] *New Hampshire Wills and Probate Records 1643-1982*, will of Amos Abbot, 23 Feb 1830, Merrimack.
[721] New Hampshire, Death and Burial Records Index, 1654-1949, John Abbot, age 80, parents Amos Abbot and Judith Morse.

Oct 1757 son of Samuel and Martha (Mellen) Chamberlain; Moses d. 21 Oct 1811.

Rebecca Abbott Chamberlain wrote her will 7 August 1843. She left to her sons William, Moses, and John A. Chamberlain who are now living, and to the heirs of her two sons Amos and Samuel Chamberlain who are deceased, all her property that is in her possession at the time of her decease as well as one share in the Federal Bridge. The remainder of her estate to be divided among her heirs-at-law but these heirs are not named. Her son John A. Chamberlain is named executor. She does not specifically mention any of her daughters or their heirs in the will.[722]

1137) i REBECCA CHAMBERLAIN, b. 15 Mar 1783; d. 31 Jan 1868; m. 8 Feb 1805, SHADRACH CATE, b. at Loudon, 10 Aug 1779 son of Stephen and Annie (Griffin) Cate; Shadrach d. 9 Oct 1842. Rebecca m. 2nd Nathaniel True in 1852.

1138) ii JUDITH CHAMBERLAIN, b. at Loudon, 20 Apr 1785; d. at Pataskala, OH, 1843[723]; m. 16 Jun 1807, SAMUEL ELLIOT, b. at Boscawen, 13 Mar 1778 son of Jonathan and Molly (Conner) Elliot; Samuel d. 1851.

iii PATTY CHAMBERLAIN, b. at Loudon, 31 May 1786; d. at Loudon, 11 Sep 1816.

1139) iv AMOS CHAMBERLAIN, b. 24 Apr 1788; d. at Loudon, 24 Oct 1818; m. 20 Jan 1812, BETSY WOOD. Betsy m. 2nd, Joseph Baker.

1140) v WILLIAM CHAMBERLAIN, b. 3 Apr 1790; d. at Keene, 13 Apr 1860; m. 9 Nov 1820, MARY ANN

---

[722] *New Hampshire Wills and Probate Records 1643-1982*, will of Rebecca Chamberlain, 7 Aug 1843, Merrimack.
[723] Gravestone reads Judith C. Elliot wife of Samuel Elliot 1785-1843, grave at Pataskala Cemetery. Findagrave.com

Generation Four

BAKER, b. at Loudon, 1805 daughter of Joseph and Anna (Hook) Baker; Mary Ann d. at Fitchburg, 10 Jan 1873.

1141) vi MOSES CHAMBERLAIN, b. 7 Feb 1792; d. at Three Oaks, MI, 12 Feb 1866; m. 18 Jun 1817, MARY "POLLY" FOSTER, b. at Canterbury, 1 Jan 1797 daughter of Abiel and Susanna (Moore) Foster; Polly d. 18 Jun 1870.

1142) vii JOHN ABBOT CHAMBERLAIN, b. at Loudon, 12 Feb 1794; d. at Concord, 28 Feb 1853; m. 10 Dec 1817, POLLY CLOUGH, b. at Canterbury, 16 Jun 1798 daughter of Jeremiah and Martha (Foster) Clough; Polly d. 11 Sep 1856.

1143) viii BETSY CHAMBERLAIN, b. 31 Aug 1796; m. 3 Oct 1815, JOSHUA EMERY, b. 16 May 1788 son of Thomas and Dolly (Sargent) Emery; Joshua d. at Loudon, 21 Jan 1870. Joshua m. 2nd Betsy Abbott and m. 3rd, Eliza Eastman.[724] Betsy Chamberlain's date of death is not clear. There is a death record for Betsy Emery for 1825, but that may be Joshua's second wife as he married his third wife in 1826.

1144) ix SAMUEL CHAMBERLAIN, b. 16 Jun 1799; d. at Loudon, 3 Nov 1838; m. 20 Nov 1823, MARTHA GERRISH, b. at Boscawen, 26 Nov 1809 daughter of Jacob and Sarah (Ames) Gerrish. Martha m. 2nd, 10 Nov 1839, Reuel Walker. Martha d. 1867.

---

[724] Emery, *Genealogical Records of Descendants of John and Anthony Emery*, p 79

Section X: The Grandchildren of Elizabeth Abbott and Nathan Stevens

Nathan Stevens³, Elizabeth Abbott Stevens², George¹

273) MARY STEVENS (*Nathan Stevens³, Elizabeth Abbott Stevens², George¹*), b. Apr 1716 daughter of Nathan and Hannah (Robinson) Stevens; d.?; m. 3 May 1742, SAMUEL PARKER, b. at Bradford, 6 Oct 1716 son of Daniel and Anne (Morse) Parker; Samuel d. 4 Oct 1796.

The births of five children of Mary Stevens and Samuel Parker are recorded at Bradford.

	i	ABIGAIL PARKER, b. 13 Nov 1742; d. 23 Aug 1762.
1145)	ii	MOLLY PARKER, b. 18 Oct 1743; d. at Bradford, 21 Feb 1842; m. by 1768, JOHN CURTIS, b. 19 Apr 1743 whose parentage in unclear;[725] John d. at Bradford 3 Apr 1826.
1146)	iii	ANNA PARKER, b. 28 May 1747; d. at Haverhill, 30 Sep 1824; m. 20 Sep 1770, NATHAN PARKER, b. 14 Jul 1740 son of Nathan and Hannah (Stevens) Parker; Nathan d. 1779 (date of probate 1 Feb 1779).
1147)	iv	SAMUEL PARKER, b. 28 Jul 1753; d. at Bradford, 12 Jun 1822; m. 27 Mar 1777, ANNA GREENOUGH, b. at Bradford, 30 Apr 1754 daughter of William and Hannah (Atwood) Greenough; Anna d. 1 Oct 1830.
	v	EDMUND PARKER, b. 1 Nov 1757; d. 7 Sep 1762.

---

[725] 1743 is the year of birth based on age at time of death. The 19 Apr 1743 date is used by the DAR.

274) HANNAH STEVENS *(Nathan Stevens³, Elizabeth Abbott Stevens², George¹)*, b. about 1721 daughter of Nathan and Hannah (Robinson) Stevens; d. at Brookfield, 17 Nov 1789; m. 11 Feb 1741/2, ABNER TYLER of Boxford, b. 15 Feb 1708/9 son of John and Anna (Messenger) Tyler; Abner d. 8 Dec 1777 at Brookfield

There is another Hannah Stevens of similar age in Andover (Hannah daughter of Benjamin), but that Hannah married Aaron Gage as confirmed by Benjamin's 1748 probate record which includes a disbursement to Hannah Stevens "alias Gage."

Abner Tyler wrote his will 29 September 1773. He made a bequest to his wife Hannah including provisions for her continued maintenance. His eldest son John received all the estate, personal, real, and moveable aside from what is given in other bequests. Sons Gideon, Moses, and Joshua are to receive £100 each when they are of legal age. Daughter Hannah received a token bequest of five shillings over and above what she has received and his three other daughters, Molly, Martha, and Abigail, received bequests of £33. Son John was named sole executor.[726]

Hannah Tyler did not leave a will, but her estate entered probate 19 November 1789.[727] The value of the estate after the deduction of administrative fees from the inventory value was about £48.

Hannah Stevens and Abner Tyler had nine children, the two oldest born at Boxford and the seven younger children at Brookfield.

---

[726] *Worcester County, MA: Probate File Papers, 1731-1881, Probate of* Abner Tyler, 1778, *Case number* 60333.
[727] *Worcester County, MA: Probate File Papers, 1731-1881, Probate of* Hannah Tyler, 1789, *Case number* 60374.

	i	NATHAN TYLER, b. Nov 1742; died in 1759 of smallpox while returning from the French and Indian War.
1148)	ii	JOHN TYLER, b. Mar 1744/5; d. at Bakersfield, VT, 17 Feb 1813; m. at Brookfield, Apr 1771, RACHEL CROSBY, b. at Billerica, 15 Sep 1751 daughter of David Crosby;[728] Rachel d. at Brookfield, MA, 6 Apr 1817.
1149)	iii	GIDEON TYLER, b. 8 Jul 1747; d. at Brookfield, 1832; m. 1 Dec 1766, ESTHER HILL daughter of Peter and Sarah (Woodbury) Hill.[729]
1150)	iv	HANNAH TYLER, b. 15 Feb 1749; d. at Gorham, NY, 21 May 1815; m. 27 Feb 1769, THOMAS TUFTS, b. 1749; Thomas d. 21 Jul 1811.
1151)	v	MARY "MOLLY" TYLER, b. 1 Sep 1753; d. at Chesterfield, NH, 16 Dec 1842; m. 9 May 1775, SAMUEL HAMILTON who was born in Ireland about 1752;[730] Samuel d. at Chesterfield, 12 Feb 1810.
1152)	vi	MOSES TYLER, b. 16 Mar 1756; d. at Brookfield, 8 Mar 1825; m. REBECCA TRUANT, b. about 1760; d. 17 Feb 1817. Rebecca's parents are not known. She is likely from the Trouant family of Plymouth County, the Trouants being early settlers in Marshfield.
1153)	vii	JOSHUA TYLER, b. 12 Aug 1758; d. at Chesterfield, NH, 11 Jun 1807; m. 1780, JUDITH AYERS, b. 12 Jan 1763 daughter of Onesiphorus and Anna (Goodale) Ayers; Judith d. 11 Aug 1854.

---

[728] Brigham, *Tyler Genealogy, the Descendants of Job Tyler*, p 118
[729] Temple, *History of North Brookfield*, p 625
[730] Bolton, *Immigrants to New England 1700-1775*, p 81

1154)	viii	MARTHA "PATTY" TYLER, b. 13 Jan 1761; m. at Brookfield, 3 Jun 1781, JOHN HUBBARD, b. at Leicester, 14 Mar 1761 son of Daniel and Elizabeth (Lynde) Hubbard; John d. at Batavia, NY 4 Jan 1850.
1155)	ix	ABIGAIL TYLER, b. 5 Dec 1763; m. at Brookfield, 14 Sep 1783, JESSE AYERS, b. at Brookfield, 8 Oct 1763 son of Moses and Sarah (Converse) Ayers.

275) ELIZABETH STEVENS *(Nathan Stevens³, Elizabeth Abbott Stevens², George¹)*, b. 2 Jul 1722 daughter of Nathan and Hannah (Robinson) Stevens; m. 11 Jul 1744, SAMUEL AMES, b. 1719 son of Samuel and Abigail (Spofford) Ames.

The births of nine children of Elizabeth Stevens and Samuel Ames are recorded at Andover.

	i	ELIZABETH AMES, b. 14 Jan 1744/5
1156)	ii	SAMUEL AMES, b. 19 Sep 1746; d. at Epsom, NH, 1792; m. at Andover, 10 Jul 1770, his second cousin once removed, ABIGAIL STEVENS, b. at Andover, 28 Oct 1752 daughter of David and Abigail (Martin) Stevens.
	iii	STEPHENS AMES, b. 24 Aug 1749
1157)	iv	SPOFFORD AMES, b. 23 Mar 1752; d. at Pembroke, 1835; m. 18 Apr 1780, MARY WHITE, b. 1759 daughter of John and Abigail (Bowen) Wight;[731] Mary d. at Pembroke, 6 Jul 1832.
	v	SOLOMON AMES, b. 21 Apr 1754

---

[731] Wight, "John Wight of Bristol, M.A."

1158)　vi　ABIGAIL AMES, b. 1756; m. 1775, DANIEL NOYES, b. at Pembroke, 24 Nov 1748 son of John and Abigail (Poor) Noyes; Daniel d. at Pembroke, 13 Jan 1822.[732]

vii　SIMON AMES, b. 28 Oct 1761

810)　viii　PHINEAS AMES, b. 7 Sep 1764; m. 24 Dec 1787, his third cousin, BRIDGET ABBOTT, b. about 1761 daughter of Daniel and Hannah (Chandler) Abbott. This is the same as Family #199, child iv.

ix　LYDIA AMES, b. 22 Aug 1767

Elizabeth Stevens Pearl³, Elizabeth Abbott Stevens², George¹

276)　TIMOTHY PEARL *(Elizabeth Stevens Pearl³, Elizabeth Abbott Stevens², George¹)*, b. 24 Oct 1723 son of Timothy and Elizabeth (Stevens) Pearl; d. at Willington, 19 Oct 1789; m. 6 Nov 1746, DINAH HOLT, b. at Windham, 17 Mar 1725/6 daughter of Joshua and Keturah (Holt) Holt; Dinah d. at Willington, 25 Sep 1806.

There are some double-birth records at Windham which have children (Hannah, Phineas) of the same names and birthdates with one attributed to Timothy and Dinah and one attributed to Timothy's father Timothy and his second wife Mary. [Phineas, s. of Timothy and Mary, b. 2 Aug 1753; Phineas, s. of Timothy and Dinah, b. 2 Aug 1753.] These children are all named in the will of the elder Timothy. Also, they are recorded at Windham and Timothy and Dinah were at Willington soon after their marriage. Therefore, they are not included here as it seems more likely they are the children of Timothy and Mary. There are births of nine children recorded for Timothy and Dinah, the oldest at Windham and the rest of the children at Willington.

---

[732] Noyes and Noyes, *Descendants of Nicholas Noyes*, p 82

	i	ALICE PEARL, b. 6 Sep 1747; d. 10 Sep 1747.
1159)	ii	ALICE PEARL, b. 6 Jul 1748. The birth transcription says 6 Jul 1743, but this seems an error and Durrie's Holt genealogy says 1748; her age at death in 1826 was 76. Alice d. Dec 1826; m. at Willington, 10 Oct 1767, ELEAZER SCRIPTURE, b. at Willington, 10 May 1742 son of John and Hannah (Wells) Scripture; Eleazer d. 18 Aug 1815.
675)	iii	OLIVER PEARL, b. 9 Oct 1749; d. 4 Nov 1831; m. 1st, 1 Jan 1772, MERCY HINCKLEY; Mercy d. 15 Nov 1781. Oliver m. 2nd, 24 Apr 1782, his second cousin (and George Abbott descendant), HANNAH HOLT, b. 14 Mar 1756 daughter of Abiel and Mary (Downer) Holt; Hannah d. 20 Nov 1832. This is the same as Family #159, child i.
1160)	iv	JOSHUA PEARL, b. 15 Sep 1752; d. at Vernon, 11 Oct 1837; m. 14 Jan 1773, DEBORAH MARSHALL, b. at Bolton, 1755 daughter of John and Eunice (Kingsbury) Marshall; Deborah d. at Vernon, 11 May 1818.
1161)	v	LOIS PEARL, b. 21 Apr 1753; d. at Willington, 15 Jul 1788; m. 6 Aug 1771, SAMUEL DUNTON, b. at Wrentham, MA, 10 Nov 1748 son of Samuel and Sarah (Bennet) Dunton; Samuel d. at Willington, 1 May 1813. After Lois's death, Samuel married Lovina Marcy.
1162)	vi	ELIZABETH PEARL, b. 15 Jan 1756; d. 8 Jan 1779; m. 6 Aug 1771, ZOETH ELDRIDGE, b. at Willington, about 1751 son of Jesse and Abigail (Smith)

Eldridge; Zoeth d. at Willington, 18 Mar 1828. Zoeth m. 2nd, Bethiah Hinkley.733

1163) vii SARAH PEARL, b. 16 Nov 1758; d. 11 Oct 1826; m. 17 Nov 1776, SAMUEL JOHNSON, b. 1751 (based on age 92 at time of death); Samuel d. at Willington, 22 Mar 1843. Samuel is likely the son of Daniel and Keziah (Dodge) Johnson born at Lebanon 10 Jun 1751.

1164) viii TIMOTHY PEARL, b. 6 Jun 1760; d. at Willington, 2 Jul 1834; m. 9 Jan 1783, LOIS CROCKER, b. 9 Dec 1763 daughter of Joseph and Anne (Fenton) Crocker; Lois d. 24 Sep 1850.

1165) ix PHEBE PEARL, b. 27 Nov 1765; d. at Willington, 10 Apr 1816; m. 24 Mar 1785, ZEBADIAH MARCY, b. at Woodstock, 2 Jul 1761 son of Zebadiah and Priscilla (Morris) Marcy; Zebadiah d. 24 Sep 1851.

277) NATHAN PEARL *(Elizabeth Stevens Pearl³, Elizabeth Abbott Stevens², George¹)*, b. 22 Nov 1727 son of Timothy and Elizabeth (Stevens) Pearl; d.?; m. 7 Mar 1748, ELIZABETH UTLEY, b. 22 Apr 1729 daughter of James and Annah (-) Utley.

The births of seven children are recorded for Nathan and Elizabeth, the oldest two at Windham and the youngest five at Ashford.

i STEPHEN PEARL, b. 29 Apr 1749; d. at Burlington, VT, 21 Nov 1816; m. 1st at Stockbridge, ELECTA WOODBRIDGE, b. 1 Apr 1754 daughter of Timothy and Abigail (Day) Woodbridge; Electa d. at Bennington, VT, 13 Jan 1781. Stephen m. 2nd

---

733 Eldredge, *Eldredge Genealogy*, p 8

ABIGAIL EDWARDS, b. about 1758, d. at Burlington, 21 Nov 1816. Stephen may not have had any children as there are no children named in his will.

ii   JAMES PEARL, b. 27 Oct 1750; died young.

1166) iii   TIMOTHY PEARL, b. 20 Apr 1752; d. at Grand Isle, VT, 15 Sep 1839; m. SARAH SWIFT, b. 18 Feb 1755 daughter of Reuben and Hannah (Dexter) Swift; Sarah d. 24 Jul 1843.

1167) iv   ELIZABETH PEARL, b. 6 Jul 1757; d. unknown; m. 9 Mar 1781; SAMUEL KIMBALL, b. at Windham, 1 Feb 1761 son of Samuel and Ann (Mudge) Kimball. It is not known where this family located. There are births of four children at Ashford. Nearly all Elizabeth's siblings went to Vermont.

1168) v   ANNA PEARL, b. 1 Aug 1758; d. at Plattsburgh, NY, about 1830;[734] m. ABEL BRISTOL, b. at Newtown, CT, 5 May 1755 son of Ebenezer and Sarah (Lake) Bristol; Abel d. at Plattsburgh about 1830.

1169) vi   AZUBAH PEARL, b. 10 Oct 1762; d. at South Hero, VT, 19 Jun 1840; m. DANIEL WADSWORTH, b. at Hartford, 4 Jan 1761 son of Hezekiah and Millicent (Seymour) Wadsworth; Daniel d. at South Hero, 7 Jan 1806.

vii   NATHAN PEARL, b. 8 Mar 1764; d. Nov 1764.

---

[734] This is the date used by DAR

278) **ELIZABETH PEARL** *(Elizabeth Stevens Pearl³, Elizabeth Abbott Stevens², George¹),* b. Jan 1729/30 daughter of Timothy and Elizabeth (Stevens) Pearl; d. not known but living at the probate of her husband's estate 1805; m. 24 May 1749, JOHN HIBBARD, b. 9 Dec 1727 son of John and Martha (Durkee) Hibbard; John d. at Royalton, VT, 31 Dec 1804.

John Hibbard was one of the original grantees of Royalton, Vermont.[735] John Hibbard wrote his will 10 October 1789 with the following bequests: well-beloved daughter Abigail Hutchins, five shillings; well-beloved sons James, John, and Timothy Hibbard each receive five shillings; and well-beloved wife Elisabeth Hibbard receives the whole of the estate, "moveables and immoveables, real and personal." Elizabeth was also named executor of the estate. The will was presented to the probate court 17 January 1805.[736]

The births of seven children are recorded at Canterbury, Connecticut.

1170) i ABIGAIL HIBBARD, b. 8 May 1749; d. likely at Cherry Valley, NY; m. 22 Aug 1769, JOSHUA HUTCHINS, b. at Plainfield, 24 Feb 1747 son of Benjamin and Prudence (-) Hutchins.

ii TIMOTHY HIBBARD, b. 5 Sep 1750; d. 9 Dec 1750.

iii ELIZABETH HIBBARD, b. 25 Oct 1751; d. 25 Sep 1754.

1171) iv JAMES HIBBARD, b. 30 Jul 1753; d. at Royalton, VT likely after 1820 (he seems to be in Royalton in the 1820 census); m. 15 Aug 1773, SUSAN SHEPARD.

---

[735] Lovejoy, *History of Royalton, Vermont: With Family Genealogies,* 1769-1911, Part 2, p 820

[736] Vermont Wills and Probate Records, 1749-1999, will of John Hebbard, 13 Oct 1789, Windsor, Probate Records, Vol 1-3 1783-1809.

1172) v   JOHN HIBBARD, b. 15 Sep 1755; d. at Royalton, VT, 18 Jul 1800; m. 17 Mar 1777, ABIGAIL CLEVELAND, b. at Canterbury, 6 Aug 1758 daughter of Samuel and Ruth (Darbe) Cleveland.

       vi   TIMOTHY HIBBARD, b. 31 Dec 1757; d. 4 Mar 1758.

1173) vii TIMOTHY HIBBARD, b. 4 Jan 1759; d. in Quebec about 1841; m. by 1780, JERUSHA LAWRENCE whose origins are unknown. There are children born in Vermont, but some vital records for the children in Quebec. Timothy received a land grant in Quebec in 1832.[737]

279)   PHEBE PEARL *(Elizabeth Stevens Pearl³, Elizabeth Abbott Stevens², George¹)*, b. 12 May 1732 daughter of Timothy and Elizabeth (Stevens) Pearl; d. at Yarmouth, Nova Scotia, date unknown; m. 29 Nov 1750, PHINEAS DURKEE, b. 16 Sep 1730 son of Stephen and Lois (Moulton) Durkee; Phineas d. at Yarmouth, Nova Scotia, 5 Nov 1801.[738]

There are births for twelve children recorded in Hampden County, Massachusetts, some recorded at Wales and some at Brimfield. Additional information related to marriages for this family obtained from Brown's Yarmouth, Nova Scotia Genealogies. There is a second set of transcriptions for the Wales birth records and those transcriptions have slightly different information for the children, although that set of records has some obvious errors [e.g., attributing Moses Paine Durkee to Phineas although he was the son of Robert and Mehitable (Paine) Durkee]. The information presented

---

[737] Ancestry.com, Quebec, Canada, Land Grants, 1763-1890, Letters Patent Book: L Grants; Page: 424; County Index Volume: 1; Page: 166
[738] Brown, *Yarmouth, Nova Scotia, Genealogies* [database on-line]. (ancestry.com)

here are the children from Brown's Yarmouth, Nova Scotia Genealogies.

Phineas Durkee wrote his will 19 November 1800. Loving wife Phebe receives all the household items and furniture including the looms. Phebe also receives the farming tools and the livestock. She also receives one and one-half acres marsh land in Yarmouth. She also receives other land bequests of about 200 acres. Phebe also receives all the hay and the produce. Son Pearl Durkee receives one lot of land in the third division at Yarmouth which contains 202 acres. His daughters Phebe Bancroft, Elizabeth Hayse, and Hannah Kinney each receive lots of 60 acres out of the lot numbered 114. Grandsons Phineas Allen and Nathan Bancroft receive 35 acres each.[739] The bequests to his children are to the four youngest children in the family and it may well be that all the older children have received their portions of the estate previously. The will describes one of the land bequests being land that adjoins Amasa Durkee's land who is one of the older sons.

1174) i LOIS DURKEE, b. at Wales, 26 Sep 1752; d. at Yarmouth, Nova Scotia; m. 25 Mar 1770, SOLOMON LUFKIN, b. at Ipswich, 25 Sep 1747 son of Solomon and Mary (Knowlton) Lufkin; Solomon d. by 1780. Lois m. 2nd, 5 Mar 1780, DANIEL ALLEN, b. at Manchester, 15 Mar 1758 son of Jeremiah and Eunice (Gardner) Allen.

1175) ii AMASA DURKEE, b. at Brimfield, 6 Jul 1754; d. at Yarmouth, Nova Scotia, 1827; m. 21 Nov 1776, RUTH ROBBINS, b. about 1757; Ruth d. at Yarmouth, 1824. Amasa married the widow Mary Shurtliffe after Ruth's death.

---

[739] Nova Scotia Probate Records 1760-1993, Yarmouth, will books 1794-1859, volume 1, image 18-19, familysearch.org.

Generation Four

1176) iii OLIVE DURKEE, b. 18 Jul 1756; d. at Yarmouth, Nova Scotia, 4 Jan 1846; m. 9 Nov 1775, SAMUEL TRASK, b. 27 Dec 1753 son of Elias and Abigail (Woods) Trask;[740] Samuel d. 25 Dec 1829.

1177) iv ELEANOR DURKEE, b. at Brimfield, 11 May 1758; d. at Yarmouth, 8 Mar 1817; m. about 1780; THOMAS DALTON, Thomas d. about 1809 (year of probate).[741] Eleanor m. 2nd, THOMAS RICKER.

v JOHN DURKEE, b. 1 Nov 1760; d. 30 Mar 1761.

vi PHINEAS DURKEE, b. 19 Jun 1762; died young.

1178) vii ROBERT DURKEE, b. at Wales, 22 Feb 1765; m. 1st, ABIGAIL ROGERS daughter of Cornelius and Abigail (Holmes) Rogers; Abigail d. 1817 in Nova Scotia. Robert m. 2nd, LYDIA ALLEN.

1179) viii STEPHEN DURKEE, b. 22 Sep 1766; d. at Yarmouth, Nova Scotia, 1845; m. at Yarmouth, 26 Apr 1787, LYDIA LOVITT, b. at Yarmouth, 9 Jul 1769 daughter of Andrew and Lydia (Thorndike) Lovitt; Lydia d. 6 Nov 1857.

1180) ix PEARL DURKEE (m), b. 25 May 1769; d. at Baltimore, MD, 25 Jan 1826; m. 1st, MARY HANKEY who was "of Baltimore"; Mary d. about 1812. Pearl m. 2nd, 7 Nov 1817, CHARLOTTE ROSE.

1181) x PHEBE DURKEE, b. 28 Apr 1771; d. at Carleton, Yarmouth, 16 Apr 1856; m. 31 Aug 1786, SAMUEL BANCROFT.

---

[740] The New England Historical and Genealogical Register, Volume 56, p 397
[741] Nova Scotia Probate Records 1760-1993, Will Books 1794-1859, volumes 1-2, p 59 (familysearch.org)

1182) xi ELIZABETH DURKEE, b. 22 Oct 1774; d. at Cornwallis, Nova Scotia; m. 17 Dec 1790, JOHN HAYSE "of Long Island"; John d. at Cornwallis, 17 Dec 1848.

1183) xii HANNAH DURKEE, b. 27 Jun 1781; d. at Yarmouth, Nova Scotia, 1857; m. NATHAN KINNEY, b. 1778; Nathan d. 1856.

280) LYDIA PEARL *(Elizabeth Stevens Pearl³, Elizabeth Abbott Stevens², George¹)*, b. 31 Jul 1734 daughter of Timothy and Elizabeth (Stevens) Pearl; d. Sep 1819; m. 27 Nov 1753, DANIEL DENISON, b. 5 Sep 1730 son of Daniel and Hannah (Crocker) Denison; Daniel d. at Hampton, 4 Aug 1823.[742]

There are just three births recorded for Lydia and Daniel at Windham. The 1822 will of their son Daniel makes mention of his bond to care for his parents and so in his will includes a provision that a gravestone be placed on the grave of his mother and an equally suitable stone placed on the grave of his father after his father's decease.[743]

1184) i DANIEL DENISON, b. 25 Jan 1755; d. at Hampton, 10 Nov 1822; m. at Norwich, 24 Apr 1788, LUCY CLARK, b. 1763 (based on age of 80 at time of death);[744] d. at Hampton, 8 Dec 1843.

---

[742] Ancestry.com, *Connecticut, Hale Collection of Cemetery Inscriptions and Newspaper Notices, 1629-1934* (Provo, UT, USA: Ancestry.com Operations, Inc., 2012), Connecticut State Library; Hartford, Connecticut; The Charles R. Hale Collection of Connecticut Cemetery Inscriptions.
[743] *Connecticut Wills and Probate, 1609-1999*, Probate of Daniel Denison, Jr, Hartford, 1822, Case number 1095.
[744] Ancestry.com, Connecticut, Deaths and Burials Index, 1650-1934

640) ii HANNAH DENISON, b. 18 Mar 1757; d. 17 Jan 1784[745]; m. 1 Jan 1778 as his first wife, her third cousin, JAMES ABBOTT, b. at Windham, 9 Mar 1753 son of Abiel and Abigail (Fenton) Abbott; James m. 2nd at Kingston, PA, 17 Jan 1798, PHEBE HOWE; James d. at Cornell, NY, 2 May 1830.[746] This is the same as Family #151, child ii.

iii DYER DENISON, b. 25 Oct 1767; d. 13 Jan 1772.

Hannah Stevens Ames³, Elizabeth Abbott Stevens², George¹

281) BENJAMIN AMES *(Hannah Stevens Ames³, Elizabeth Abbott Stevens², George¹)*, b. 6 Jun 1724 son of Samuel and Hannah (Stevens) Ames; d. at Andover, 10 Jan 1809; m. 1st 4 Dec 1746, his second cousin, HEPHZIBAH CHANDLER, b. 7 Apr 1726 daughter of Timothy and Hephzibah (Harnden) Chandler; Hephzibah d. 19 Jan 1768. Benjamin m. 2nd, about 1770, his second cousin once removed, DORCAS LOVEJOY *(Lydia Abbott Lovejoy⁴, Henry³, George², George¹)*, b. 18 Aug 1749 daughter of Joshua and Lydea (Abbott) Lovejoy; Dorcas d. 25 Jun 1843.

Captain Benjamin Ames was the captain of Ames's Company which served in the Revolutionary War including service at Bunker Hill. His company was part of the regiment of Colonel James Frye. Benjamin Ames first saw military service in 1757 as a private in one of Andover's militia companies.[747]

---

[745] Ancestry.com, Connecticut Town Death Records, pre-1870 (Barbour Collection)
[746] Gravesite located at Stahl Brothers Cemetery in Steuben County, NY, findagrave.com
[747] Memorial Hall Library, Andover Answers, "Benjamin Ames," retrieved from https://answers.mhl.org/Benjamin_Ames

Benjamin Ames was active in the civic affairs of Andover serving as Warden and Surveyor of Highways in 1777 and served on the building committee for the new meeting house in South Parish in 1787.

The will of Benjamin Ames includes bequests to the following persons: Dorcas dearly beloved wife and Simeon is the son charged with her care; Simeon receives the lands, buildings, and husbandry utensils. The other heirs named are Benjamin Ames, Timothy Ames, Hannah Boynton wife of Thomas Boynton, heirs of daughter Hephzibah formerly the wife of Bixby Abbot, Dorcas wife of Isaac Phelps, and Abigail wife of David Johnson.[748]

There are records for nine children of Benjamin Ames and Hephzibah Chandler born at Andover.

        i   CHANDLER AMES, b. 14 Nov 1747; d. 24 Sep 1766

1185) ii   BENJAMIN AMES, b. 9 Nov 1749; d. 23 Nov 1813; m. 30 Apr 1772, his second cousin once removed (and George Abbott descendant), PHEBE CHANDLER, b. 18 Oct 1754 daughter of Nathan and Phebe (Abbott) Chandler; Phebe d. 19 Jun 1798. The grave of Phebe Chandler Ames has the following inscription: *While o'er the grave you walk or weep, Remember here all flesh must sleep; Slender's the thread whence life depends, Begins this hour, the next it ends.*[749]

1186) iii   HANNAH AMES, b. 26 Nov 1751; d. 20 Dec 1831; m. 16 Jun 1772, THOMAS BOYNTON, b. 29 Nov 1747 son of David and Mary (Stickney) Boynton; Thomas d. 10 Mar 1833.

---

[748] *Essex County, MA: Probate File Papers, 1638-1881.* Probate of Benjamin Ames, 4 May 1809, Case number 573.
[749] The Essex Antiquarian, 1898, Andover Inscriptions, Old South Burying Ground

Generation Four 507

        iv   RICHARD AMES, b. 16 Sep 1754; d. 6 Oct 1754

1187) v   HEPHZIBAH AMES, b. 3 Nov 1755; d. 20 May 1796; m. 9 Jan 1772, her third cousin, BIXBY ABBOTT, b. 24 Nov 1750 son of William and Experience (Bixby) Abbott. Bixby m. 2nd Mary Johnson; Bixby d. at Greenfield, NH, 1813.

        vi   RICHARD AMES, b. 16 Aug 1758; d. 8 Sep 1758.

        vii   ELIZABETH AMES, b. 8 Aug 1760; d. 1 Nov 1760.

        viii BETHIAH AMES, b. 22 Jul 1762; d. 11 Aug 1762.

1188) ix   TIMOTHY AMES, b. 26 Sep 1765; d. at Peterborough, NH, 14 May 1835; m. 21 Mar 1787, SALLY KNEELAND, b. 1769 (based on age at time of death) who parentage is uncertain; Sally d. 13 Nov 1861.

Four children are recorded for Benjamin Ames and Dorcas Lovejoy.

1120) i   SIMEON AMES, b. 29 Mar 1772; d. 29 Sep 1849; m. 30 Mar 1790, his third cousin, once removed, SARAH BAILEY, b. 1 Nov 1772 daughter of Moses and Elizabeth (Mooar) Bailey; Sarah d. 22 Mar 1857.

        ii   DORCAS AMES, b. 25 Jul 1773; d. 28 Sep 1775.

1189) iii   DORCAS AMES, b. 31 Jul 1776; d. after 1855; m. 31 Oct 1799, ISAAC PHELPS, b. 21 Jun 1772 son of Thomas and Mary (Shattuck) Phelps; Isaac d. after 1850 (listed in the 1850 U. S. Census). Dorcas is listed in the 1855 Massachusetts census in the Andover almshouse, age 77, described as insane.[750]

1190) iv ABIGAIL AMES, b. 4 Oct 1779; d. after 1850 at Bradford, VT;[751] m. 15 Dec 1796, DAVID JOHNSON whose parents are not clear are there are several David Johnsons of the right age in Andover; d. after 1830 at Bradford, VT.

282) NATHAN AMES *(Hannah Stevens Ames³, Elizabeth Abbott Stevens², George¹)*, b. Apr 1729 son of Samuel and Hannah (Stevens) Ames; d. at Groton 7 Mar 1791; m. 19 Apr 1763, DEBORAH BOWERS, b. at Groton, 2 Sep 1746 daughter of Samuel and Deborah (Farnsworth) Bowers; Deborah d. 8 Apr 1782. Nathan m. 2nd by 1783, LYDIA GREEN, b. 19 Aug 1765 daughter of Jonas and Jemima (Holden) Green; d. 24 Feb 1834 at age 67. After Nathan's death, Lydia married Jeremiah Chaplin.

Nathan Ames and Deborah Bowers were married and had nine children whose births are recorded at Groton. Deborah died in 1782. After the death of Deborah, Nathan married Lydia Green in 1783. Nathan Ames died in March 1791 at age 61. The estate of Nathan Ames entered probate April 1791 with his widow Lydia as the administrator of the estate. There was no will. The current available probate papers include the inventory, but not the distribution. There are also guardianship cases for the minor children.[752] After she turned 14 years old, Anna Ames (mother

---

[750] Ancestry.com, Massachusetts, State Census, 1855
[751] In the 1850 U.S. Census, Abigail Johnson age 79 is living in Bradford, Vermont in a household that includes Abigail Dearborn who is her daughter. *United States 1850 Census*. Online database. AmericanAncestors.org. New England Historic Genealogical Society, 2014. (Original index: *United States Census, 1850*. FamilySearch, 2014.)
[752] *Middlesex County, MA: Probate File Papers, 1648-1871*. Probate of Nathan Ames, 1791, Case number 389. The guardianship cases for the children are cases 390, 391, and 392.

Deborah) selected her brother-in-law Nathan Gray Baker as guardian. Simeon Ames (mother Deborah) selected Nathan Ames of Carlisle; it is not clear who this Nathan Ames is, but possibly his oldest brother. After he was 14 years old, Moses Ames selected Jeremiah Chaplin as his guardian.

Moses Ames, the son of Nathan and Lydia, did not marry, but he left a will in 1820. At that time, his mother was Lydia Chaplin having married Jeremiah Chaplin in 1796. Moses names several sisters in his will who were daughters of Nathan Ames and Lydia Green and then his Chaplin sisters, the daughters of Lydia and Jeremiah Chaplin. He names none of the children of Nathan and Deborah in the will. This raises the question of why he would include his half-siblings by his mother's last marriage, but not his half-siblings from his father's first marriage. Perhaps they were all adults and so not of concern. As they were adults (for the most part) at the time of Lydia's marriage to Nathan, he was not reared with them.

The age difference between Nathan Ames and Lydia Green is a concern in terms of feeling completely confident that all these relationships are correct. In 1783, Lydia had just turned 18 and Nathan was 54. Although not an impossible age difference, it was not the usual pattern. Perhaps for this family that was not so unusual, as Lydia's father, Jonas Green, married a woman 25 years younger than him when he remarried after the death of Lydia's mother.

Two of the sons of Nathan and Deborah went to Providence and two of the daughters of Nathan and Lydia went to Providence.

Nathan Ames and Deborah Bowers had nine children whose births were recorded at Groton.

	i	NATHAN AMES, b. 6 Feb 1764; d. at Groton 23 Mar 1851; he is listed as a bachelor on the death record. He *perhaps* married Lydia Goodhue in 1788, but there are no children recorded from that marriage.
1191)	ii	SAMUEL AMES, b. 7 Feb 1766; d. at Providence, RI, 16 Feb 1830; m. at Boston, 8 Sep 1801, ANNE CHECKLEY, b. at Philadelphia, 13 Aug 1785 daughter of John Webb and Anne (Wicker) Checkley; Anne d. 15 Jun 1868.
1192)	iii	DEBORAH AMES, b. 6 Apr 1768; d. at Andover 7 Dec 1819; m. 1st 21 Sep 1786, HENRY GRAY BAKER, b. 1 Apr 1767 son of Symonds and Lydia (Gray) Baker; Henry d. 10 Mar 1802. Deborah m. 2nd 18 Nov 1802, as his second wife, CALEB ABBOTT son of Asa and Elizabeth (Abbott) Abbott; Caleb d. 12 Apr 1837. The is the same as Family #80, child iv.
1193)	iv	LYDIA AMES, b. 29 Mar 1770; d. at Andover 24 Jun 1843; m. 21 Jul 1796, her third cousin once removed (and George Abbott descendant), ABBOTT WALKER, b. at Chelmsford, 24 Jul 1770 son of Benjamin and Abiel (Abbott) Walker; Abbott Walker d. 2 Aug 1831.
1194)	v	ASA AMES, b. 6 May 1772; d. at Providence, RI, 21 Jan 1838; m. REBECCA BRATTELL, b. 1 Jan 1776 daughter of Robert and Rebecca (Pierce) Brattell; Rebecca d. 17 Apr 1824.
	vi	BENJAMIN AMES, b. 22 Aug 1774; d. 24 Dec 1787.
	vii	ANNA AMES, b. 29 Jul 1776; she was still living in 1793 when she selected Henry Gray Baker of Andover as her guardian. She is perhaps the Anna Ames who married Peter Hutchinson in Andover in

1807, but that cannot be verified. Her sisters Deborah and Lydia had gone to Andover, so this might make sense but cannot be established. There is one child recorded for Peter and Anna Hutchinson (Lyman born in 1808) but was not tracked after that.

  viii JEPHTHAH AMES, b. 29 Jun 1779; d. 30 Jun 1786.

1195) ix SIMEON AMES, b. 13 Sep 1781; d. at Sterling, CT 11 Feb 1863; m. 17 Apr 1826, BETSEY GILMORE, b. about 1809; Betsey was still living in 1870 at the time of the US Census.

Nathan Ames and Lydia Green had three children whose births are recorded at Groton.

  i MOSES AMES, b. 1 Nov 1783; d. 11 Dec 1820. Moses did not marry.

1196) ii AMELIA AMES, b. 9 Apr 1788; d. at Providence, RI, 6 Apr 1874; m. 11 Oct 1812, JOSEPH WHEELOCK, b. at Westborough, 25 Jun 1788 son of Moses and Lydia (Bond) Wheelock; Joseph d. 16 May 1857.

1197) iii JEMIMA GREEN AMES, b. 14 Mar 1791; d. at Providence, RI, 11 Aug 1839; m. 10 Feb 1824, WILLIAM ALMY, b. at Westport, 23 Sep 1788 son of William and Mary "Polly" (Millett) Almy; William d. at Newport, RI aboard ship in the harbor, 16 Sep 1830.

283) AMOS AMES (*Hannah Stevens Ames[3], Elizabeth Abbott Stevens[2], George[1]*), baptized 20 Jan 1733/4 son of Samuel and Hannah

(Stevens) Ames; d. at Groton, 4 Aug 1817; m. 27 Oct 1757, ABIGAIL BUCKLEY, b. at Concord, MA, 28 Oct 1733 daughter of John and Abigail (-) Buckley; Abigail d. 20 Aug 1809.

The oldest sons in the family, Amos, Moses, and Simeon, all served in the Revolutionary War. All three were captured and were prisoners for a time on a prison ship at Halifax. Two of the brothers escaped and the third brother was later exchanged.[753]

The births of ten children are recorded at Groton.

1198) i AMOS AMES, b. 15 Apr 1758; d. at Sullivan, ME after 1810; m. 1st by 1784, MARY "POLLY" ORDIANE, parentage unknown, d. 29 Jul 1787. Amos next had an out-of-wedlock relationship with DEBORAH LAWRENCE with daughter recorded.[754] Amos m. 2nd MARY "POLLY" BRAGDON daughter of Ebenezer Bragdon; Polly Bragdon d. 1806.

ii MOSES AMES, b. 14 Nov 1759; d. 23 May 1783.

iii SIMEON AMES, b. 25 Sep 1761; d. 25 Sep 1784.

1199) iv ABIGAIL AMES, b. 28 Nov 1763; d. at Ashby, 11 Aug 1848; m. 10 Mar 1785, WILLIAM GREEN, b. at Pepperrell, 19 Jan 1755 son of William and Ruth (Colburn) Green; William d. 1 May 1843.

1200) v ELI AMES, b. 4 May 1765; reported to have gone to Virginia and perhaps Georgia;[755] m. at NH, 27 Nov 1788, EUNICE PARKER, b. Apr 1761 and d. 1843. This family was in Groton for a time and in New Ipswich, NH as the births of several children are recorded there.

---

[753] Green, *Groton Historical Series*, volume 3, p 159
[754] A., d. Deborah Laurence and Amos Ames "as She Saith," Oct. 6, 1788. Massachusetts Vital Records for Groton
[755] The DAR gives his place of death as Georgia.

1201) vi PETER AMES, b. 7 Nov 1767; d. Jun 1823; m. 7 Oct 1799, SALLY CHILD, b. at Groton, but of uncertain parentage but possibly the daughter of Abraham Child; Sarah d. 28 Feb 1838.

1202) vii HANNAH AMES, b. 30 Jan 1770; d. 22 Aug 1840; m. 7 Jun 1789, IMLAH PARKER, b. at Groton, 12 Jan 1765 son of Nathaniel and Eunice (Lakin) Parker; Imlah d. 4 Apr 1828.

1203) viii BUCKLEY AMES, b. 20 Jul 1772; d. 22 Jan 1836; m. 22 Sep 1799, LYDIA PRESCOTT, b. at Westford, 8 Jan 1780 daughter of Ebenezer and Lydia (Wood) Prescott; Lydia d. 15 Feb 1848.

ix ABEL AMES, b. 3 Sep 1774; d. 14 Aug 1775.

1204) x BETSEY BUCKLEY AMES, b. 10 Dec 1776; d. 28 Jul 1861; m. 21 Apr 1799, WILLIAM LIVERMORE, b. at Shirley 23 Jun 1770 son of Oliver and Catherine (Bond) Livermore; William d. 2 Mar 1846.

284) ROBERT AMES *(Hannah Stevens Ames³, Elizabeth Abbott Stevens², George¹)*, baptized 1737 son of Samuel and Hannah (Stevens) Ames; d.?; m. 1st 2 Dec 1762, SARAH WOODS, b. 19 Aug 1742 daughter of Isaac and Abigail (Stevens) Woods; Sarah d. 23 Nov 1774. Robert m. 2nd 29 Apr 1777, SUSANNA GREEN (widow of Abijah Warren), b. 20 Mar 1746 daughter of Isaac and Martha (Boyden) Green.

There are three probate records for men named Robert Ames in Massachusetts between 1786 and 1825 but none of those is this Robert. No death or probate record for Robert or Susanna was found in Massachusetts, New Hampshire, or Vermont. Robert's children scattered to further west in Massachusetts and up to New Hampshire and Vermont.

There are five births recorded at Groton for Robert Ames and Sarah Woods.

1205) i ROBERT AMES, b. 12 Oct 1763; d. 15 Nov 1789; m. 27 Mar 1783, RUTH LAWRENCE, b. 3 Jan 1758 daughter of Benjamin and Rebecca (-) Lawrence; Ruth d. at Groton 3 Jul 1825.

1206) ii SARAH AMES, b. 27 May 1765; d. at Bridport, VT, 13 Jul 1836; m. 18 Jun 1787, EPHRAIM STONE, b. at Groton, 11 Jan 1763 son of Benjamin and Prudence (Farnsworth) Stone; Ephraim d. 6 Jun 1841.[756]

1207) iii PRUDENCE AMES, b. 29 Dec 1767; d. at Ashby, MA, 6 Nov 1821;[757] m. 27 Dec 1786, ISAAC GREEN "of Ashby," b. about 1757 who parentage is uncertain; Isaac d. at Ashby 7 Nov 1821. One of Prudence's cousins married a Green from Pepperrell; there is an Isaac Green from Groton who was the much younger brother of Susanna Green who was Robert Ames's second wife.

1208) iv BETHIAH AMES, b. 30 Nov 1770; d. at Peterborough, NH, 15 Feb 1852;[758] m. 18 Feb 1788, JOHN SCOTT, b. at Dublin, NY about 1765; John d. 27 Dec 1847.

v MOLLY AMES, b. 5 Dec 1772; d. 6 Aug 1775.

---

[756] Ancestry.com, *Vermont, Vital Records, 1720-1908* (Provo, UT, USA: Ancestry.com Operations, Inc., 2013).
[757] This is the date engraved on her gravestone. Findagrave.com
[758] Ancestry.com, *New Hampshire, Death and Burial Records Index, 1654-1949* (Provo, UT, USA: Ancestry.com Operations, Inc., 2011).

Two children are recorded at Groton of Robert Ames and Susanna Green. No further record was found for either of these children.

    i   SAMUEL AMES, b. 9 Dec 1781

    ii   MOLLY AMES, b. 23 Feb 1786

Phebe Stevens Steel³, Elizabeth Abbott Stevens², George¹

285)   PHEBE STEEL *(Phebe Stevens Steel³, Elizabeth Abbott Stevens², George¹)*, b. 27 Sep 1735 daughter of Nicholas and Phebe (Stevens) Steel; d. unknown but still living in 1783; m. 22 Nov 1776, as his second wife, JOHN ABBOTT (of the George Abbott of Rowley line), b. 10 Mar 1724/5 son of Uriah and Sarah (Mitchell) Abbott; John d. of smallpox 3 Jan 1779.

John Abbott had seven children with his first wife, Sarah Carleton. John and Phebe had one daughter born at Andover.

1209)   i   HANNAH ABBOTT, b. 15 Oct 1777; d. at Haverhill, 25 Nov 1853;[759] m. 27 Feb 1810 as his second wife, JOHN JOHNSON whose parentage is not yet certain, but likely the son of John and Hannah (Abbott) Johnson born in Andover 8 Dec 1777. John Johnson died 1814 (probate of estate 4 Aug 1814 with widow Hannah declining administration). John Johnson was first married to Lydia Kimball who died 1808. The 1826 will of John Kimball (Lydia's

---

[759] At the 1850 US Census she is listed as living with Leonard Johnson who is her son. There is a probate record for her from 1854 in which Leonard Johnson, the sole heir, is also the administrator of the estate.

father) has a bequest for grandson Edward Johnson, who was the son of John and Lydia. John Johnson who married Hannah Abbott (of the Rowley Abbott line) was married second to Abigail Abbott of the Andover line.

286) ELIZABETH STEEL *(Phebe Stevens Steel³, Elizabeth Abbott Stevens², George¹)*, b. 21 Feb 1737 daughter of Nicholas and Phebe (Stevens) Steel; date of death not known but she appears to be the Elizabeth Ingalls in Andover in the 1810 US Census; m. 9 Sep 1760, JOSHUA INGALLS, b. 13 Aug 1732 son of Joseph and Phebe (Farnum) Ingalls; Joshua d. 1785, his will probated 5 Jul 1785.

The will of Joshua Ingalls has bequests for the following persons: beloved wife Elizabeth, son Simeon, daughter Phebe Ingalls, and son Stephen.[760] The births of five children are recorded at Andover.

1210) i STEPHEN INGALLS, b. 17 Jun 1761; d. about May 1794 (will written 4 Apr 1794 and probate 3 June 1794); m. 21 Sep 1786, LYDIA KIMBALL, b. 9 Mar 1761 daughter of Andrew and Esther (Barker) Kimball; Lydia d. at Andover, 16 Dec 1831.

ii ELIZABETH INGALLS, b. 2 Sep 1762; d. before 1785.

1211) iii SIMEON INGALLS, b. 3 Sep 1764; m. 16 Jan 1787 the widow ELIZABETH FISH. The identity of Elizabeth is unknown, but she is possibly Bette Fisk who married David Fish in Andover in 1777 but just a wild guess at this point.

iv PETER INGALLS, b. 14 Jan 1766; d, before 1785.

---

[760] *Essex County, MA: Probate File Papers, 1638-1881. Probate of* Joshua Ingalls, 5 Jul 1785, *Case number* 14535.

1212) v PHEBE INGALLS, b. 30 Dec 1768; d. at Pelham, NH, 20 Jul 1847; m. 3 Jun 1790, ELIJAH BRADSTREET, b. 4 Jul 1767 son of Samuel and Ruth (Lampson) Bradstreet; Elijah d. at Pelham, 2 Dec 1850.

287) RACHEL STEEL *(Phebe Stevens Steel^3, Elizabeth Abbott Stevens^2, George^1)*, b. 1 Jul 1739 daughter of Nicholas and Phebe (Stevens) Steel; death before 1796 when her second husband married his third wife; m. 11 Dec 1767, DUDLEY FOSTER, b. at Boxford, 21 Feb 1737/8 son of Zebadiah and Margaret (Tyler) Foster; Dudley d. by 1787 when widow Rachel Foster married James Frye (1731-1804). Rachel married James Frye in 1787 as his second wife.

There are records for four daughters in this family. For three of the daughters, the only record is the baptism and all four of the girls were baptized on the same day. There is a birth record for only one of the girls. There is marriage for one of the daughters that can be confirmed. For two of the girls, there seem to be no marriage records. Daughter Rachel was unmarried in 1801 (will written in 1801 but probate in 1804) when she receives a bequest from her stepfather James Frye with whom she has lived.[761] There is uncertainty about the daughter Mary. As there is a birth record for only one daughter, the order of birth is not known.

1213) i MEHITABLE FOSTER, b. 17 Sep 1772; d. at North Andover, 16 Aug 1859; m. 3 Mar 1791, her third cousin, NATHANIEL HOLT, b. 6 Apr 1769 son of

---

[761] *Essex County, MA: Probate File Papers, 1638-1881.* Online database. AmericanAncestors.org. New England Historic Genealogical Society, 2014. (From records supplied by the Massachusetts Supreme Judicial Court Archives.)

Nathaniel and Elizabeth (Stevens) Holt; Nathaniel d. 24 May 1829.

    ii   MARY FOSTER, baptized 14 Dec 1777

    iii   PHEBE FOSTER, baptized 14 Dec 1777; no further record.

    iv   RACHEL FOSTER, baptized 14 Dec 1777; still living but unmarried in 1801.

288)   BENJAMIN STEEL *(Phebe Stevens Steel³, Elizabeth Abbott Stevens², George¹)*, b. 25 Jan 1741 son of Nicholas and Phebe (Stevens) Steel; d. at Wilton, NH 14 Nov 1817; m. 16 Jun 1768, HANNAH LOVEJOY, b. 1748 (parentage uncertain); Hannah d. at Wilton, 31 Aug 1812.

There are records for the births of seven children in this family, the two oldest born at Andover and the other five children at Wilton, New Hampshire.[762] There are no further records for the daughters in this family.

    i   HANNAH STEEL, b. 13 Dec 1768; died young.

    ii   HANNAH STEEL, b. 24 Dec 1770; no further record.

    iii   PHEBE STEEL, b. 28 Mar 1774; no further record.

1043) iv   BENJAMIN STEEL, b. 11 Dec 1776; d. 18 Nov 1845; m. 12 Feb 1801, his third cousin, JUDITH BLANCHARD, baptized at Andover 13 Jun 1779 daughter of Jeremiah and Susanna (Martin) Blanchard; Judith d. after 1860 (still living at the

---

[762] *New Hampshire, Births and Christenings Index, 1714-1904* (Provo, UT, USA: Ancestry.com Operations, Inc., 2011).

Generation Four

1860 US Census).⁷⁶³ This is the same as Family #249, child iv.

    v   SARAH STEEL, b. 2 Jun 1779; no further record.

    vi   LYDIA STEEL, b. 19 Apr 1781; no further record.

1214) vii WILLIAM LOVEJOY STEEL, b. 28 Jun 1784; d. at Wilton, 4 Mar 1860; m. by 1820, DOLLY TARBELL, b. at Mason, NH, 3 May 1798 daughter of Samuel and Anna (Heldrick) Tarbell;⁷⁶⁴ Dolly d. 30 Aug 1861.

---

⁷⁶³ Year: 1860; Census Place: Wilton, Hillsborough, New Hampshire; Roll: M653_673; Page: 388; Family History Library Film: 803673

⁷⁶⁴ Parentage confirmed by the 1824 will of Samuel Tarbell which includes a bequest to daughter Dolly Steel. Probate Records, 1771-1921; Indexes to Probate Records, 1771-1859, 1885-1961; Author: New Hampshire. Probate Court (Hillsborough County); Probate Place: Hillsborough, New Hampshire

Grandchildren of Elizabeth Abbott and Nathan Stevens

Master List of Families

1)	George Abbott and Hannah Chandler
2)	John Abbott and Sarah Barker
3)	Hannah Abbott and John Chandler
4)	George Abbott and Dorcas Graves
5)	William Abbott and Elizabeth Geary
6)	Sarah Abbott and Ephraim Stevens
7)	Benjamin Abbott and Sarah Farnum
8)	Timothy Abbott and Hannah Graves
9)	Thomas Abbott and Hannah Gray
10)	Nathaniel Abbott and Dorcas Hibbert
11)	Elizabeth Abbott and Nathan Stevens
12)	John Abbot and Elizabeth Harnden
13)	Joseph Abbot and Hannah Allen
14)	Stephen Abbot and Sarah Stevens
15)	Sarah Abbott and Zebadiah Chandler
16)	Ephraim Abbot and Sarah Crosby
17)	Joshua Abbott and Rebeckah Shed Joshua Abbott and Dorcas Whiting
18)	Ebenezer Abbot and Hannah Turner
19)	John Chandler and Hannah Frye
20)	Abiel Chandler and Hephzibah Harnden
21)	Hannah Chandler and Daniel Abbott
22)	Sarah Chandler and Joseph Wright
23)	Hannah Abbott and John Osgood
24)	Elizabeth Abbott and Benjamin Abbott
25)	George Abbott and Mary Phillips
26)	Henry Abbott and Mary Platts
27)	Isaac Abbott and Phebe Lovejoy
28)	Elizabeth Abbott and Joseph Phelps
29)	James Abbott and Abigail Farnum

30)	Paul Abbott and Elizabeth Gray
31)	Philip Abbott and Abigail Bigford
32)	Hannah Abbott and Abiel Holt
33)	Caleb Abbott and Elizabeth Paine
34)	Elizabeth Stevens and John Robinson
35)	Hannah Stevens and Robert Swan
36)	Mary Steven and James Ingalls
37)	Mehitable Stevens and Ebenezer Holt
38)	Deborah Stevens and Samuel Carleton
39)	Benjamin Abbott and Mary Carleton Benjamin Abbott and Abigail Abbott
40)	Jonathan Abbott and Zerviah Holt
41)	David Abbott and Hannah Danforth
42)	Timothy Abbott and Mary Foster
43)	Hannah Abbott and John Lane
44)	Dorcas Abbott and Nicholas Holt
45)	Thomas Abbott and Elizabeth Ballard
46)	Edward Abbott and Dorcas Chandler
47)	Deborah Abbott and Joseph Hall
48)	George Abbott and Sarah Abbott
49)	Benjamin Abbott and Hannah Abbott
50)	Mary Abbott and Benjamin Blanchard
51)	Nathaniel Abbott and Penelope Ballard
52)	Sarah Abbott and John Blanchard
53)	Joseph Abbott and Deborah Blanchard
54)	Tabitha Abbott and John Chandler
55)	Jeremiah Abbott and Hannah Ballard
56)	Elizabeth Abbott and Timothy Mooar
57)	Rebecca Abbott and Abiel Chandler Rebecca Abbott and Amos Abbot
58)	Nathan Stevens and Hannah Robinson
59)	Elizabeth Stevens and Timothy Pearl
60)	Hannah Stevens and Samuel Ames
61)	Phebe Stevens and Nicholas Steel
62)	John Abbot and Phebe Fiske

Master List of Families

63)	Barachias Abbot and Hannah Holt
64)	Elizabeth Abbot and Asa Foster
65)	Joseph Abbot and Hannah Abbott
66)	Joseph Abbot and Anna Peabody
67)	Ephraim Abbott and Hannah Phelps
68)	Mary Abbott and Joseph Holt
69)	Stephen Abbot and Mary Abbott
70)	Samuel Abbot and Elizabeth Wyman
71)	Sarah Chandler and Joshua Chandler
72)	Joanna Chandler and Joseph Shattuck
73)	Priscilla Chandler and Samuel Phelps
74)	Mehitable Chandler and Caleb Lovejoy
75)	Elizabeth Chandler and David Lovejoy
76)	Sarah Abbott and Samuel Gray
77)	Ephraim Abbott and Mary Abbott Ephraim Abbott and Mary Kneeland
78)	Mary Abbott and Robert Read
79)	Joshua Abbott and Phebe Ingalls
80)	Elizabeth Abbott and Asa Abbot
81)	Josiah Abbott and Hannah Hobbs
82)	Ebenezer Abbott and Lydia Farrington
83)	Peter Abbott and Elizabeth Damon widow
84)	Martha Abbott and Archelaus Towne
85)	John Abbott and Hannah Richardson
86)	Sarah Abbott and Christopher Osgood Sarah Abbott and James Goodwin
87)	Mary Abbott and Henry Jefts
88)	Hannah Abbott and Phineas Osgood
89)	Elizabeth Abbott and Robert Walker
90)	Joshua Abbott and Sarah Stearns
91)	Oliver Abbott and Joanna French Oliver Abbott and Abigail Hall
92)	David Abbott and Hannah Ellis

	David Abbott and Huldah Paine
93)	Mary Abbott and Joseph Chandler
	Mary Abbott and Isaac Blunt
94)	Isaac Abbott and Susanna Farnum
95)	Phebe Abbott and James Griffin
96)	James Abbott and Lydia Coburn
97)	Nathan Chandler and Priscilla Holt
98)	Hannah Chandler and Timothy Ballard
99)	Phebe Chandler and Henry Lovejoy
100)	Lydia Chandler and Hezekiah Ballard
101)	Abial Chandler and David Chandler
102)	Dorcas Abbott and Thomas Chaffee
103)	Joseph Abbott and Abigail Cutler
104)	Elizabeth Abbott and Matthew Murray
105)	Phebe Abbott and Ebenezer Holmes
106)	Nathan Abbott and Anna Leach
107)	John Abbott and Mary Wright
108)	Sarah Abbott and Jabez Corbin
109)	George Abbott and Mary Whitney
110)	Joseph Wright and Abigail Chaffee
	Joseph Wright and Mary
111)	Sarah Wright and Edmund Chamberlain
112)	Hannah Wright and Beamsley Peters
113)	Elizabeth Wright and John Carpenter
114)	Hephzibah Wright and Enos Bartholomew
115)	Abigail Wright and Abijah Corbin
116)	Dorothy Wright and Penuel Bacon
117)	Hannah Osgood and Samuel Chickering
118)	John Osgood and Martha Carleton
	John Osgood and Huldah Frye
119)	Elizabeth Osgood and James Frye
120)	Joseph Osgood and Margaret Binney
121)	Dorcas Osgood and Thomas March
122)	Mary Osgood and William Allen
123)	Sarah Abbott and James Holt

124)	George Abbott and Hannah Lovejoy
125)	Elizabeth Abbott and Benjamin Abbott – same as #200
126)	Sarah Abbott and Nathan Holt
127)	Hannah Abbott and William Foster
128)	Lydea Abbott and Joshua Lovejoy
129)	Henry Abbott and Phebe Abbott
130)	Dorcas Abbott and Benjamin Butler
131)	Mary Abbott and Thomas Hovey
132)	Isaac Abbott and Phebe Chandler
133)	Sarah Abbott and Timothy Abbott
134)	Elizabeth Phelps and Benoni Barrett
135)	Hannah Phelps and Samuel Lawrence
136)	Abigail Abbott and John Kidder
137)	James Abbott and Sarah Bancroft
138)	Reuben Abbott and Rhoda Whittemore
139)	Phebe Abbott and Thomas Merrill
140)	Rebecca Abbott and Enoch Eastman
141)	Sarah Abbott and Job Abbott Sarah Abbott and Richard Eastman
142)	Mary Abbott and Adonijah Tyler
143)	Nathan Abbott and Eunice Marsh
144)	William Abbott and Jerusha Stowell
145)	Benjamin Abbott and Mary Ann Andrews
146)	Mary Abbott and Joshua Holt
147)	Sarah Abbott and Joseph Ingalls
148)	Isaac Abbott and Mary Barker
149)	Darius Abbott and Mary Holt
150)	Elizabeth Abbott and Joseph Phelps
151)	Abiel Abbott and Abigail Fenton
152)	Stephen Abbott and Freelove Burgess
153)	Hannah Abbott and Samuel Utley
154)	Mary Abbott and Stephen Fuller
155)	Joseph Abbott and Elizabeth Stedman

	Joseph Abbott and Olive Pearce
156)	John Abbott and Alice Fuller
157)	Hannah Holt and William Holt
158)	Elizabeth Holt and Francis Fenton
159)	Abiel Holt and Mary Downer
	Abiel Holt and Eunice Kingsbury
160)	Caleb Holt and Mary Merrick
161)	Nathan Holt and Abigail Merrick
	Nathan Holt and Bathsheba Williams
	Nathan Holt and Lydia Kingsbury
162)	Anna Holt and Joseph Merrick
163)	Isaac Holt and Sarah Orcutt
164)	Timothy Holt and Rebecca Chamberlain
165)	Mary Holt and Joseph Persons
166)	James Holt and Esther Owens
	James Holt and Luce Sawins
167)	Hannah Abbott and John Hendrick
168)	Sarah Abbott and Jonathan Burk
169)	Samuel Abbott and Rachel Ward
170)	William Abbott and Mary Coy
	William Abbott and Esther Green
171)	Joseph Robinson and Mehitable Eams
172)	Isaac Robinson and Dorothy Poor
173)	Samuel Robinson and Sarah Barker
174)	Ephraim Robinson and Hannah Kimball
175)	Elizabeth Swan and Nathaniel Lovejoy
176)	Robert Swan and Elizabeth Farnum
177)	Ephraim Swan and Sarah Poole
178)	Hannah Swan and Peter Parker
179)	James Ingalls and Mary Frye
180)	Ephraim Ingalls and Mary Sharp
181)	Zebadiah Ingalls and Esther Goodell
182)	Abiah Ingalls and Nathaniel Rogers
183)	Ebenezer Holt and Lydia Peabody
184)	Mehitable Holt and James Holt

185)	Ezekiel Holt and Mary Stewart
186)	Reuben Holt and Lydia Small
187)	Samuel Carleton and Eunice Hunt
188)	Hannah Carleton and Jacob Crowninshield
189)	Mary Carleton and John Bowditch
190)	William Carleton and unknown Palfrey
191)	Daniel Abbott and Lucy Parker
192)	Mary Abbott and Nehemiah Barker
193)	Abigail Abbott and John Abbott
194)	Abiel Abbot and Phebe Ballard
195)	Elizabeth Abbott and Ebenezer Cummings Elizabeth Abbott and Thomas Merrill
196)	Anna Abbott and Ephraim Burge
197)	Dorcas Abbot and Abiel Abbot
198)	Jonathan Abbott and Martha Lovejoy
199)	David Abbott and Hannah Chandler
200)	Zerviah Abbott and Ephraim Blunt
201)	Samuel Abbott and Miriam Stevens
202)	Sarah Abbot and Robert Hildreth Sarah Abbott and John Lane
203)	David Abbot and Prudence Sheldon
204)	Solomon Abbot and Hannah Colbe
205)	Jonathan Abbot and Mary Chandler
206)	Hannah Abbott and Joseph Parker
207)	Nathan Abbott and Jane Paul
208)	Sarah Abbott and Edward Farmer
209)	Lydia Abbott and Thomas Farnum
210)	Phebe Abbott and William Dane
211)	Samuel Lane and Elizabeth Fitch
212)	Timothy Holt and Elizabeth Holt
213)	Dorcas Holt and Thomas Holt
214)	Joshua Holt and Phebe Farnum
215)	Daniel Holt and Hannah Holt

216)	Elizabeth Abbott and Samuel Osgood
217)	Thomas Abbott and Lydia Blunt
218)	Jabez Abbott and Phebe Abbott
	Jabez Abbott and Hephzibah Farnum
219)	Aaron Abbott and Lydia Abbott
220)	Nathan Abbott and Betty Farnum
221)	Dorcas Abbott and Ebenezer Hall
222)	Edward Abbott and Deborah Stevens
223)	Betsey Abbott and Thomas Saltmarsh
224)	Mary Hall and Thomas Wilson
225)	Daniel Abbott and Rachel Abbott
	Daniel Abbott and Mercy Kilburn
226)	Joseph Abbott and Phebe Lovejoy
227)	Stephen Abbott and Mary Gile
228)	Ezra Abbott and Betty Andrews
	Ezra Abbott and Anner Choate
	Ezra Abbott and Jane Jackman
229)	Hannah Abbott and Jeremiah Story
230)	Benjamin Abbott and Sarah Brown
231)	Mary Blanchard and Edward Taylor
232)	Benjamin Blanchard and Keziah Hastings
233)	Anne Blanchard and Jonathan Danforth
	Anne Blanchard and Stephen Martin
234)	Jacob Blanchard and Rebecca Lawrence
235)	Joshua Blanchard and Sarah Burge
236)	Nathaniel Abbott and Miriam Chandler
237)	Dorcas Abbott and Moses Merrill
238)	Rebecca Abbott and John Merrill
	Rebecca Abbott and Jacob Doyne
239)	Elizabeth Abbott and Joseph Hazeltine
240)	Mary Abbott and Joseph Walker
241)	Hannah Abbott and Ephraim Moor
242)	Ruth Abbott and James A. Walker
243)	Joshua Abbott and Eliza Chandler
244)	Jeremiah Abbott and Elizabeth Stickney

245)	Dorothy Abbott and David George
246)	Sarah Abbott and Samuel Farnum
247)	Hannah Blanchard and Stephen Blanchard
248)	Joseph Blanchard and Dinah Blanchard
249)	Jeremiah Blanchard and Dorothy Smith Jeremiah Blanchard and Susanna Martin
250)	Daniel Blanchard and Jerusha Eaton
251)	John Blanchard and Eleanor Stevens
252)	Bathsheba Abbott and Nathan Blanchard
253)	Hannah Abbott and Timothy Dale
254)	Joseph Abbott and Mary Barker
255)	Jacob Abbott and Lydia Stevens
256)	Nathaniel Abbott and Sarah Stevens
257)	Rebecca Abbott and Daniel Batchelder
258)	John Chandler and Mary Carter
259)	Timothy Chandler and Elizabeth Copp
260)	Daniel Chandler and Sarah Eastman
261)	Joshua Chandler and Irene Copp
262)	Hannah Abbott and Oliver Farmer
263)	Rebecca Abbott and Richard Boynton
264)	William Abbott and Bridget Spaulding William Abbott and Mehitable Scott
265)	Jeremiah Abbott and Susannah Baldwin
266)	John Mooar and Mary Ballard
267)	Elizabeth Mooar and Moses Bailey
268)	Joshua Mooar and Deborah Chandler
269)	Mary Mooar and William Harris
270)	Abiel Chandler and Judith Walker
271)	Amos Abbott and Judith Morse
272)	Rebecca Abbott and Moses Chamberlain
273)	Mary Stevens and Samuel Parker
274)	Hannah Stevens and Abner Tyler
275)	Elizabeth Stevens and Samuel Ames

276)	Timothy Pearl and Dinah Holt
277)	Nathan Pearl and Elizabeth Utley
278)	Elizabeth Pearl and John Hibbard
279)	Phebe Pearl and Phineas Durkee
280)	Lydia Pearl and Daniel Denison
281)	Benjamin Ames and Hephzibah Chandler Benjamin Ames and Dorcas Lovejoy
282)	Nathan Ames and Deborah Bowers
283)	Amos Ames and Abigail Buckley
284)	Robert Ames and Sarah Woods Robert Ames and Susanna Green
285)	Phebe Steel and John Abbott
286)	Elizabeth Steel and Joshua Ingalls
287)	Rachel Steel and Dudley Foster
288)	Benjamin Steel and Hannah Lovejoy

Families numbered 289 and higher are in Generation Five to be covered in Volume II.

Data Sources

The vital records and wills used for documentation are provided in brief form in the footnotes, but full reference information is provided here. Vital records and wills were obtained through databases available through NEHGS (americanancestors.org), ancestry.com, and familysearch.org.

Ancestry.com. *1851 Census of Canada East, Canada West, New Brunswick, and Nova Scotia* [database on-line]. Provo, UT, USA: Ancestry.com Operations Inc, 2006. Original data: *Census of 1851 (Canada East, Canada West, New Brunswick, and Nova Scotia)*. Library and Archives Canada, Ottawa, Canada. *Census of Nova Scotia, 1851*. Halifax, Nova Scotia, Canada: Nova Scotia Archives and Records Management (NSARM): Nova Scotia Board of Statistics, 1851.

Ancestry.com. *Connecticut, Church Record Abstracts, 1630-1920* [database on-line]. Provo, UT, USA: 2013. Original data: Connecticut. Church Records Index. Connecticut State Library, Hartford, Connecticut.

Ancestry.com. *Connecticut, Hale Collection of Cemetery Inscriptions and Newspaper Notices, 1629-1934* [database on-line]. Provo, UT, USA: Ancestry.com Operations, Inc., 2012. Original data: *The Charles R. Hale Collection. Hale Collection of Connecticut Cemetery Inscriptions*. Hartford, Connecticut: Connecticut State Library.

Ancestry.com. *Connecticut Town Birth Records, pre-1870 (Barbour Collection)* [database on-line]. Provo, UT, USA: Ancestry.com Operations Inc, 2006. Original data: White, Lorraine Cook, ed. *The Barbour Collection of Connecticut Town Vital Records. Vol. 1-55.* Baltimore, MD, USA: Genealogical Publishing Co., 1994-2002.

Ancestry.com. *Connecticut Town Death Records, pre-1870 (Barbour Collection)* [database on-line]. Provo, UT, USA: Ancestry.com Operations Inc, 2006. Original data: White, Lorraine Cook, ed. *The Barbour Collection of Connecticut Town Vital Records. Vol. 1-55.* Baltimore, MD, USA: Genealogical Publishing Co., 1994-2002.

Ancestry.com. *Mayflower Births and Deaths, Vol. 1 and 2* [database on-line]. Provo, UT, USA: Ancestry.com Operations, Inc., 2013. This collection was indexed by Ancestry World Archives Project contributors. Original data: Roser, Susan E. *Mayflower Births and Deaths: From the Files of George Ernest Bowman at the Massachusetts Society of Mayflower Descendants.* Volumes 1 & 2. Baltimore, MD: Genealogical Publishing Company, Inc., 1992.

Ancestry.com. *Michigan, Homestead and Cash Entry Patents, Pre-1908* [database on-line]. Provo, UT, USA: Ancestry.com Operations Inc, 1997. Original data: United States, Bureau of Land Management. *Michigan Pre-1908 Homestead & Cash Entry Patent and Cadastral Survey Plat Index.* General Land Office Automated Records Project, 1994.

Ancestry.com. *New Hampshire, Birth Index, 1659-1900* [database on-line]. Provo, UT, USA: Ancestry.com Operations. Inc., 2013. Original data: "New Hampshire, Birth Records, through 1900." Online index and digital images. *New England Historical Genealogical Society.* Citing New Hampshire Bureau of Vital Records, Concord, New Hampshire.

Ancestry.com. *New Hampshire, Death and Disinterment Records, 1754-1947* [database on-line]. Provo, UT, USA: Ancestry.com Operations, Inc., 2013. Original data: "New Hampshire, Death and Disinterment Records, 1754–1947." Online index and digital images. *New England Historical Genealogical Society.* Citing New Hampshire Bureau of Vital Records, Concord, New Hampshire.

Ancestry.com. *New Hampshire, Marriage Records Index, 1637-1947* [database on-line]. Provo, UT, USA: Ancestry.com Operations, Inc.,

2011. Original data: "New Hampshire Marriage Records 1637–1947." Index. FamilySearch, Salt Lake City, Utah, 2011. "New Hampshire Statewide Marriage Records 1637–1947," database, FamilySearch, 2009. New Hampshire Bureau of Vital Records. "Marriage Records." New Hampshire Bureau of Vital Records and Health Statistics, Concord.

Ancestry.com. *New Hampshire, Wills and Probate Records, 1643-1982* [database on-line]. Provo, UT, USA: Ancestry.com Operations, Inc., 2015. Original data: New Hampshire County, District and Probate Courts.

Ancestry.com. *New York, Wills and Probate Records, 1659-1999* [database on-line]. Provo, UT, USA: Ancestry.com Operations, Inc., 2015. Original data: New York County, District and Probate Courts.

Ancestry.com. *Quebec, Canada, Vital and Church Records (Drouin Collection), 1621-1968* [database on-line]. Provo, UT, USA: Ancestry.com Operations, Inc., 2008. Original data: Gabriel Drouin, comp. *Drouin Collection*. Montreal, Quebec, Canada: Institut Généalogique Drouin.

Ancestry.com. *Rhode Island, Wills and Probate Records, 1582-1932* [database on-line]. Provo, UT, USA: Ancestry.com Operations, Inc., 2015. Original data: Rhode Island, District and Probate Courts.

Ancestry.com. *Tennessee, Wills and Probate Records, 1779-2008*. Provo, UT, USA: Ancestry.com Operations, Inc., 2015. Tennessee County, District and Probate Courts.

Ancestry.com. U.S. Federal Census Collection.

Ancestry.com. *U.S., Newspaper Extractions from the Northeast, 1704-1930* [database on-line]. Provo, UT, USA: Ancestry.com Operations,

Inc., 2014. This collection was indexed by Ancestry World Archives Project contributors. Original data: Newspapers and Periodicals. American Antiquarian Society, Worcester, Massachusetts.

Ancestry.com. *U.S., Revolutionary War Pension and Bounty-Land Warrant Application Files, 1800-1900* [database on-line]. Provo, UT, USA: Ancestry.com Operations, Inc., 2010. Original data: Revolutionary War Pension and Bounty-Land Warrant Application Files (NARA microfilm publication M804, 2,670 rolls). Records of the Department of Veterans Affairs, Record Group 15. National Archives, Washington, D.C.

Ancestry.com. *Vermont, Vital Records, 1720-1908* [database on-line]. Provo, UT, USA: Ancestry.com Operations, Inc., 2013. Original data: State of Vermont. Vermont Vital Records through 1870. New England Historic Genealogical Society, Boston, Massachusetts.

Ancestry.com. *Vermont, Wills and Probate Records, 1749-1999* [database on-line]. Provo, UT, USA: Ancestry.com Operations, Inc., 2015. Original data: Vermont County, District and Probate Courts.

Ancestry.com. *Web: Delaware County, Ohio, Burial Index, 1784-2011* [database on-line]. Provo, UT, USA: Ancestry.com Operations, Inc., 2013. Original data: *Delaware County Burials*. Delaware County Genealogical and Historical Societies. http://www.rootsweb.ancestry.com/~ohdchs/cemetery/burials.htm?cj=1&o_xid=0000584978&o_lid=0000584978: accessed 3 April 2012.

Andover Historic Preservation. https://preservation.mhl.org/

Essex County, Massachusetts, Probate Records and Indexes 1638-1916; Author: *Massachusetts. Court of Insolvency (Essex County);* Probate Place: *Essex, Massachusetts*

Family Tree Samplers, 1759-1894. Online database. AmericanAncestors.org. New England Historic Genealogical Society, 2013. (From the collection of Dan and Marty Campanelli.)

Findagrave.com

"Maine Marriages, 1771-1907." Database. *FamilySearch*. http://FamilySearch.org: 14 June 2016. Index based upon data collected by the Genealogical Society of Utah, Salt Lake City.

Massachusetts: Grand Lodge of Masons Membership Cards, 1733-1990. Online database. *AmericanAncestors.org.* New England Historic Genealogical Society, 2010. (From records held by the Grand Lodge of Ancient Free and Accepted Masons of Massachusetts.)

Massachusetts: Legislators of the General Court, 1691-1780 (Online database: *AmericanAncestors.org*, New England Historic Genealogical Society, 2002).

Massachusetts Vital Records Project. http://ma-vitalrecords.org/

Middlesex County Deeds, 1792-1827, volumes 110-112, Images 85-86, Familysearch.org.

New Hampshire: Births, Deaths and Marriages, 1654-1969. (From microfilmed records. Online database: *AmericanAncestors.org*, New England Historic Genealogical Society, 2014.)

"New Hampshire Revolutionary War Records, 1675-1835." Database with images. *FamilySearch*. http://FamilySearch.org: accessed 2018. Citing Archives and Records Management, Concord.

"Nova Scotia Probate Records, 1760-1993." Images. *FamilySearch*. http://FamilySearch.org: 14 June 2016. County courthouses, Nova Scotia.

Probate Records 1648--1924 (Middlesex County, Massachusetts); Author: *Massachusetts. Probate Court (Middlesex County)*; Probate Place: *Middlesex, Massachusetts*

Suffolk County (Massachusetts) Probate Records, 1636-1899; Author: *Massachusetts. Probate Court (Suffolk County)*; Probate Place: *Suffolk, Massachusetts*

References

Abbot, Abiel. 1829. *History of Andover: From its Settlement to 1829.* Andover, MA: Flagg and Gould.

Abbot, Abiel, and Ephraim Abbot. 1847. *Genealogical Record of the Descendants of George Abbot of Andover, George Abbot of Rowley, Thomas Abbot of Andover, Arthur Abbot of Ipswich, Robert Abbot of Branford, CT, and George Abbot of Norwalk, CT.* Boston: James Munroe and Company.

Abbott, Charlotte Helen. n.d. "Abbott Genealogies." http://www.mhl.org/abbott-genealogies.

Abbott, Lemuel Abijah. 1906. *Descendants of George Abbott of Rowley, Mass., of His Joint Descendants of George Abbott, Sr., of Andover, Mass...* Boston: Published by the compiler, T. R. Marvin Printing.

Abbott, Margaret T. 1952. "Ten Generations of Abbotts in America." Unpublished manuscript. https://www.mhl.org/sites/default/files/files/Abbott/Abbott%20Family.pdf.

Abbott, Stanley Hale. 1961. *The Family Tree of Ezra Abbot.* Hastings, NE: Stanley Hale Abbott.

Adams, John Quincy, and Charles Francis Adams. 1903. *Life in a New England Town, 1787, 1788: Diary of John Quincy Adams While a Student in the Office of Theophilus Parsons at Newburyport.* Newburyport, MA: Little, Brown.

Aldrich, Lewis Cass, and Frank R. Holmes. 1891. *History of Windsor County, Vermont.* Syracuse, NY: D. Mason and Co.

American Series of Popular Biographies. 1901. *Biographical Skethces of Representative Citizens of the Commonwealth of Massachusetts.* Boston, MA: Graves and Steinbarger.

Bailey, Abigail Abbot. 1815. *Memoirs of Mrs. Abigail Bailey, Who Had Been the Wife of Major Asa Bailey.* Boston: Samuel T. Armstrong.

Bailey, Sarah Loring. 1880. *Historical Sketches of Andover: Comprising the Present Towns of Andover and North Andover.* Boston: Houghton.

Barbour, Lucius Barnes, and Case Brainard Newton. 1914. *Vital Records of Woodstock, 1686-1854.* Hartford: The Case, Lockwood, and Brainard Co.

Barker, Elizabeth Frye. 1920. *Frye Genealogy; Adrian of Kittery, Me., John of Andover, Mass., Joshua of Virginia, Thomas of Rhode Island.* New York: T. A. Wright.

Barrows, John Stuart. 1938. *Fryeburg, Maine: An Historical Sketch.* Fryeburg, ME: Pequawket Press.

Belknap, Henry Wyckoff. 1918. *The Lambert Family of Salem, Massachusetts.* Salem, MA: Essex Institute.

Benton, Josiah Henry. 1911. *Warning Out in New England 1656-1817.* Boston: W. B. Clarke.

Blair, Williams T., and Jacob I. Shoemaker. 1924. *The Michael Shoemaker Book : (Schumacher).* Scranton, PA: International Textbook Press.

Blake, Francis E. 1915. *History of the Town of Princeton in the County of Worcester and the Commonwealth of Massachusetts.* Princeton, MA: Published by the town.

Bolton, Ethel Stanwood. 2009. *Immigrants to New England, 1700-1775.* Heritage Books.

Bouton, Nathaniel. 1856. *The History of Concord from Its First Grant in 1725 to the Organization of the City Government in 1853.* Concord, NH: Benning W. Sanborn.

Boynton, John Farnham, and Caroline Harriman Boynton. 1897. *The Boynton Family. A Genealogy of the Descendants of William and John Boynton, who Emigrated from Yorkshire, England, in 1638, and Setted at Rowley, Essex County, Massachusetts.* Groveland, MA.

Bradsby, Henry C. (Ed.). 1893. *History of Luzerne County, Pennsylvania, with Biographical Selections.* Chicago: S. B. Nelson.

Brigham, Willard. 1912. *The Tyler Genealogy; the Descendants of Job Tyler, of Andover, Massachusetts, 1619-1700.* Plainfield, NJ: C. B. Tyler.

Brown, George Stayley. 1993. *Yarmouth, Nova Scotia, Genealogies: Transcribed from the Yarmouth Herald.* Genealogical Publishing Company.

Browne, George Waldo. 1921-22. *The History of Hillsborough, New Hampshire, 1735-1921.* Manchester, NH: John B. Clarke.

Burleigh, Charles. 1903. *The Genealogy and History of the Ingalls Family in America.* Malden, MA: G. E. Dunbar.

Carter, Nathan Franklin, and Trueworthy Ladd Fowler. 1895. *History of Pembroke, N. H. 1730-1895.* Concord, NH: Republican Press Association.

Caulfield, Ernest. 1950. "The Pursuit of a Pestilence." *Pocessdings of the American Antiquarian Society* 60 (1): 21-52.

Chaffee, William Henry. 1909. *The Chaffee Genealogy.* New York: Grafton Press.

Chandler, George. 1883. *The Descendants of William and Annis Chandler who Settled in Roxbury, Mass., 1637.* Worcester: Press of C. Hamilton.

Chapman, George T. 1867. *Sketches of the Alumni of Dartmouth College, from the First Graduation in 1771 to the Present Time, with a Brief History of the Institution.* Cambridge, MA: Riverside Press.

Chapman, Leonard Bond. 1907. *Monograph on the Southgate Family of Scarborough, Maine: Their Ancestors and Descendants.* Portland, ME: H. W. Bryant.

Chase, Benjamin. 1869. *History of Old Chester.* Auburn, NH: Published by the author.

Coburn, Silas Roger. 1922. *History of Dracut, Massachusetts, Called by the Indians Augumtoocooke and before Incorporation, the Wildernesse North of the Merrimac. First Permanment Settlement in 1669 and Incorporated as a Town in 1701.* Lowell, MA: Press of the Courier-Citizen.

Cochrane, Warren Robert. 1880. *History of the Town of Antrim, New Hampshire, from its Earliest Settlement to June 27, 1877, with a*

Brief Genealogical Record of all the Antrim Families. Manchester, NH: Mirror Steam Printing Press.

Cochrane, Warren Robert, and George K. Wood. 1895. *History of Francestown, N. H., from its Earliest Settlement April, 1758, to January 1, 1891: With a Brief Genealogical Record of all the Francestown Families.* Nashua, NH: Published by the town.

Cogswell, Elliott C. 1878. *History of Nottingham, Deerfield, and Northwood, Comprised Within the Original Limits of Nottingham, Rockingham County, N.H., with Records of the Centennial Proceedings at Northwood, and Genealogical Sketches.* Manchester, NH: J. B. Clarke.

Cogswell, Leander Winslow. 1880. *History of the Town of Henniker, Merrimack County, New Hampshire, from the Date of the Canada Grant by the Province of Massachusetts, in 1735, to 1880; with a Genealogical Register of the Families of Henniker.* Concord, NH: Republican Press Association.

Currier, Harvey Lear, and John McNabb Currier. 1910. *Genealogy of Richard Currier of Salisbury and Amesbury, Massachusetts (1616--1686-7) and Many of His Descendants.* Newport, VT: Orleans County Historical Society.

Cushing, James Stevenson. 1905. *The Genealogy of the Cushing Family, an Account of the Ancestors and Descendants of Matthew Cushing, Who Came to America in 1638.* Montreal: Perrault Printing Co.

Cutter, William Richard. 1915. *New England Families, Genealogical and Memorial; a Record of the Achievements of Her People in the Making of Commonwealths and the Founding of a Nation, Volumes 1-4.* New York: Lewis Historical Publishing Co.

Daniel Hovey Association. 1914. *The Hovey Book: Describing the English Ancestry and American Descendants of Daniel Hovey of Ipswich, Massachusetts.* Ipswich, MA: Lewis R. Hovey.

Darling, Nancy. 1913. "History and Anniversary of Hartland, Vermont." *The Vermonter, Volume 18.*

Dodge, Joseph Thompson. 1894. *Genealogy of the Dodge Family of Essex County, Mass. 1629-1894.* Madison, WI: Democrat Printing Co.

Donovan, Dennis. 1906. *The History of the Town of Lyndeborough, New Hampshire.* Tufts College Press.

Durrie, Daniel S. 1864. *A Genealogical History of the Holt Family in the United States More Particularly the Descendants of Nicholas Holt of Newbury and Andover, Mass.* Albany: Munsell.

Ela, David Hough. 1896. *Genealogy of the Ela Family: Descendant of Israel Ela, of Haverhill, Mass.* Manchester, CT: Elwood S. Ela, Printer.

Eldredge, Zoeth Skinner. 1896. *Eldredge Genealogy.* Boston: D. Clapp Printers.

Emery, Rufus. 1890. *Genealogical Records of Desendants of John and Anthony Emery, of Newbury, Mass. 1590-1890.* Salem, MA: Emery Cleaves.

Evans, Simeon Adams. 1893. *Descendants of David Evans of Charleston, Massachusetts: To which is Appended Partial Records of Certain Families Connected with Them by Marriage.*

Farnham, Russell Clare. 1999. *The New England Descendants of the Immigrant Ralph Farnum of Rochester, Kent County, England, and Ipswich, Massachusetts.* Peter Randall Publishing.

Fernald, Natalie R. 1906. "Corrections and Additions to Thomas Skinner's Descendants." *The Genealogical Exchange,* June: 9-11.

Floyd, C. Harold. 1912. "Some Descendants of Joel Jenkins of Braintree and Malden, Mass." *New England Historical and Genealogical Register* 268 ff.

Foster, E. W., and Philip Walker. 1905. "The Walkers of Woburn, Massachusetts." *Historical Bulletin, Volumes 6-9* 64-65.

Fuess, Claude Moore. 1959. *Andover: Symbol of New England: The Evolution of a Town.* Andover, MA: Andover Historical Society.

Fuller, William Hyslop. 1919. *Genealogy of Some Descendants of Thomas Fuller of Woburn.* Palmer, MA: C. B. Fiske.

Goodhue, Jonathan Elbridge. 1891. *History and Genealogy of the Goodhue Family : In England and America to the Year 1890.* Rochester, NY: E. R. Andrews.

Gould, Sherry L, and Kathleen C. Beals. 2004. *Early Families of Bradford, NH.* Bradford, NH: Bradford Historical Society.

Green, Samuel Abbott. 1893. *Groton Historical Series: A Collection of Papers Relating to the History of the Town of Groton, Massachusetts, Volume 3.* Cambridge, MA: John Wilson and Son.

Greven, Philip. 1970. *Four Generations: Population, Land, and Family in Colonial Andover, Massachusetts.* Ithaca: Cornell University Press.

Griggs, Susan Jewett. 1950. *Early Homesteads of Pomfret and Hampton.* Abington, CT.

Hale, Robert Safford. 1889. *Genealogy of Descendants of Thomas Hale of Walton, England, and of Newbury, Mass.* Albany, NY: Weed, Parsons, and Co.

Harvard University. 1905. *Quinquennial Catalogue of the Officers and Graduates of Harvard University.* Cambridge, MA: Harvard University.

Haskell, T. H. 1875. *The New Gloucester Centennial.* Portland, ME: Hoyt, Fogg, and Donham.

Hatch, Louis C. 1920. *History of Bowdoin College.* Portland, ME: Loring, Short, and Harmon.

Hayden, Charles Albert, and Jessie Hale Tuttle. 1929. *The Capen Family: Descendants of Bernard Capen of Dorchester, Mass.* Minneapolis, MN: Augsburg Publishing House.

Hayes, Lyman Simpson. 1907. *History of the Town of Rockingham, Vermont, Including the Villages of Bellows Falls, Saxtons River, Rockingham, Cambridgeport and Bartonsville, 1753-1907, with Family Genealogies.* Bellows Falls, VT: Published by the town.

Hazen, Henry Allen. 1883. *History of Billerica, Massachusetts, with a Genealogical Register.* Boston: A. Williams and Co.

Hodgman, Edwin Ruthven. 1883. *History of the Town of Westford, in the County of Middlesex, Massachusetts, 1659-1883.* Lowell, MA: Morning Mail Co.

Holt Association of America. 1930. *The First Three Generations of Holts in America.* Newburgh, NY: Moore Printing Company.

Howard, Cecil Hampden Cutts. 1892. *Genealogy of the Cutts Family in America.* Albany, NY: Munsell.

Howe, Gilman Bigelow. 1890. *Genealogy of the Bigelow Family of America, from the Marriage in 1642 of John Biglo and Mary Warren to the Year 1890.* Worcester, MA: Charles Hamilton.

Hoyt, David Webster. 1857. *Hoyt Family: A Genealogical History of John Hoyt of Salisbury, and David Hoyt of Deerfield, (Massachusetts,) and Their Descendants: With Some Account of the Earlier Connecticut Hoyts.* Boston, MA: C. Benjamin Richardson.

Hurd, Duane Hamilton (Ed.). 1885. *History of Merrimack and Belknap Counties, New Hampshire.* Philadelphia: J. W. Lewis.

Hyde, Charles McEwan. 1879. *Historical Celebration of the Town of Brimfield, Hampden County, Mass.* Springfield, MA: C. W. Bryan.

King, Marquis Fayette. 1903. *Annals of Oxford, Maine.* Hebron, ME: New England History Press.

Kingsbury, Frank B. 1925. *History of the Town of Surry, Cheshire County, New Hampshire: From Date of Severance from Gilsum and Westmoreland, 1769-1922, with a Genealogical Register and Map of the Town.* Surry, NH: Published by the town.

Kneeland, Stillman Foster. 1897. *Seven Centuries in the Kneeland Family.* New York: Published by the author.

Lapham, William Berry. 1890. *History of Rumford, Oxford County, Maine, from Its First Settlement in 1779, to the Present Time.* Augusta, ME: Press of the Maine Farmer.

Lawson, Harvey Merrill. 1905. *History and Genealogy of the Descendants of Clement Corbin of Muddy River (Brookline), Mass. and Woodstock, Conn. with Notices of Other Lines of Corbins.* Hartford, CT: Hartford Press.

Littlefield, Peter F., and Karl Pfister. 2001. *Genealogies of the Early Settlers of Weston, Vermont, Second Edition.* Weston, VT: Weston Historical Society.

Livermore, Abiel Abbot, and Putnam Sewall. 1888. *History of the Town of Wilton, Hillsborough County, New Hampshire, with a Genealogical Register.* Lowell, MA: Marden and Rowell.

Lord, Charles Chase. 1890. *Life and Times in Hopkinton, N.H.* Concord, NH: Republican Press.

Lovejoy, Clarence Earle. 1930. *The Lovejoy Genealogy with Biographies and History.* New York: Published by the author.

Lovejoy, Mary Elevyn Wood. 1911. *History of Royalton, Vermont, with Family Genealogies, 1769-1911.* Burlington, VT: Free Press Printing Company.

Lyford, James Otis. 1912. *History of the Town of Canterbury, New Hampshire, 1727-1912.* Concord, NH: Rumford.

McKeen, Phebe Fuller. 1880. *Annals of Fifty Years: A History of Abbot Academy, Andover, Mass., 1829-1879.* Andover, MA: W. F. Draper.

Meriam, Rufus N. 1892. "John and Thomas Totman and Their Descendants." *Proceedings of Worcester Society of Antiquity for the Year 1891, Volume XIII* 45-75.

Merrill, Samuel. 1917-1928. *A Merrill Memorial: An Account of the Descendants of Nathaniel Merrill, an Early Settler of Newbury, Massachusetts.* Cambridge, MA.

Mooar, George. 1901. *Mooar (Moors) Genealogy: Abraham Mooar of Andover, and His Descendants.* Boston: Press of David Clapp.

—. 1903. *The Cummings Memorial: A Genealogical History of the Descendants of Isaac Cummings, an Early Settler of Topsfield, Massachusetts.* New York: B. F. Cummings.

Moriarty, G. Andrews. 1931. "Ancestry of George Abbott of Andover." *New England Historic and Genealogical Register* 85: 79-86.

Morrison, Leonard Allison. 1893. *The History of the Alison, or Allison Family in Europe and America, A.D. 1135 to 1893; Giving an Account of the Family in Scotland, England, Ireland, Australia, Canada, and the United States.* Boston, MA: Damrell & Upham.

Morrison, Leonard Allison, and Stephen Paschall Sharples. 1897. *History of the Kimball Family in America, from 1634 to 1897 : and of its Ancestors the Kemballs or Kemboldes of England; with an Account of the Kembles of Boston, Massachusetts.* Boston: Damrell & Upham.

Moyer, Paul B. 2006. "A Dangerous Combination of Villains: Pennsylvania's Wild Yankees and the Social Context of Agrarian Resistance in Early America." *Pennsylvania History: A Journal of Mid-Atlantic Studies* 73 (1): 37-68.

Nourse, Henry S. 1993. *The Birth, Marriage, and Death Register, Church Records and Epitaphs of Lancaster, Massachusetts, 1643-1850.* Heritage Books.

Noyes, Henry E., and Harrlette E. Noyes. 1904. *Genealogical Record of Some of the Noyes Descendants: Volume I, Descendants of Nicholas Noyes.* Boston, MA.

Osgood, Ira. 1894. *A Genealogy of the Descendants of John, Christopher and William Osgood, Who Came from England and Settled in New England Early in the Seventeenth Century.* Salem, MA: Salem Press.

Otten, Marjorie Wardell. 2000. "The Two George Abbot Families of Andover, Massachusetts." *The Essex Genealogist* 20: 19-23.

Perley, Sidney (Ed.). 1897. "Abbot Genealogy." *Essex Antiquarian* 1 (3): 35-42.

Peters, Eleanor Bradley. 1903. *Peters of New England: A Genealogy, and Family History.* Knickerbocker Press.

Pierce, Frederick Clifton. 1898. *Batchelder, Batcheller genealogy. Descendants of Rev. Stephen Bachiler, of England ... Who Settled the Town of New Hampton, N.H., and Joseph, Henry, Joshua and John Batcheller of Essex Co., Mass.* Chicago: W. B. Conkey.

Poore, Alfred. 1913. "A Genealogical-Historical Visitation of Andover, Mass. in the Year 1863." *Essex Institute Historical Collections* 49: 50-64.

Ramsdell, George Allen, and William P. Colburn. 1901. *The History of Milford, Volume 1.* Milford, NH: Rumford Press.

Rix, Guy Scoby. 1901. *History and Genealogy of the Eastman Family of America: Containing Biographical Sketches and Genealogies of both Males and Females.* Concord, NH: I. C. Evans.

Secomb, Daniel F. 1883. *History of the Town of Amherst, Hillsborough County, New Hampshire.* Concord, NH: Evans, Sleeper, and Woodbury.

Shattuck, L'emuel. 1855. *Memorials of the Descendants of William Shattuck, the Progenitor of the Families in America that Have Borne His Name.* Boston: Dutton and Wentworth, printed for the family.

Smith, Charles James. 1907. *History of the Town of Mont Vernon, New Hampshire.* Boston: Blanchard Printing Company.

Spaulding, Charles S. 1915. *An Account of Some of the Early Settlers of West Dunstable, Monson and Hollis, N. H.* Nashua, NH: Telegraph Press.

Spofford, Charles B. 1896. *Grave Stone Records: Rrom the Ancient Cemeteries in the Town of Claremont, New Hampshire, with Historical and Biographical Notes.* Claremont, NH: G. I Putnam.

Sprague, William Buell. 1859. *Annals of the American Pulpit, Volume 1.* R. Carter and Brothers.

Stearns, Ezra S., William F. Witcher, and Edward E. Parker. 1908. *Genealogical and Family History of the State of New Hampshire: A Record of the Achievements of Her People in the Making of a Commonwealth and the Founding of a Nation.* New York: Lewis Publishing.

Stearsns, Ezra Scollay, and Moses Thurston Runnels. 1906. *History of Plymouth, New Hampshire: Vol. I. Narrative--vol. II. Genealogies.* Plymouth, NH: Printed for the town by University Press.

Sterling, Albert Mack, and Sterling Edward Boker. 1909. *The Sterling Genealogy, Vol II.* New York: Grafton Press.

Temple, Josiah Howard. 1887. *History of North Brookfield, Massachusetts: Preceded by an Account of Old Quabaug, Indian and English Occupation, 1647-1676; Brookfield Records, 1686-1783.* Boston: Rand Avery Company.

The Essex Antiquarian. 1898. "Andover Inscriptions Old South Burying Ground." August.

Trask, William Blake. 1902. "Captain William Trask and Some of HIs Descedants." *New England Historical and Genealogical Record* 56: 397-401.

Trowbridge, Francis Bacon. 1891. *The Champion Genealogy: A History of the Descendants of Henry Champion, of Saybrook and Lyme,*

Connecticut, Together with Some Account of Other Families of the Name. New Haven, CT: Printed for the author by Tuttle, Morehouse & Taylor.

Trussell, John B. B. 1976. "The Battle of Wyoming and Hartley's Expedition." *Historical Pennsylvania Leaflet, No. 40*. Harrisburg: Pennsylvania Historical and Museum Commission.

Vinton, John Adams. 1874. *The Upton Memorial: A Genealogical Record of the Descendants of John Upton, of North Reading, Mass. ... Together with Short Genealogies of the Putnam, Stone and Bruce Families*. E. Upton and Sons.

Ward, Robert Leigh. 1999. "The Footloose Joshua Whitney (1687-1771) and Some of His Descendants." *The American Genealogist* 74: 197-208.

Weaver, William L. 1867. *A Genealogy of the Fenton Family : Descendants of Robert Fenton, an Early Settler of Ancient Windham, Conn. (Now Mansfield)*. Willimantic, CT.

Webster, Kimball, and George Waldo Browne. 1913. *History of Hudson, N.H.: Formerly a Part of Dunstable, Mass., 1673-1733, Nottingham, Mass., 1733-1741, District of Nottingham, 1741-1746, Nottingham West, N.H., 1746-1830, Hudson, N.H., 1830-1912*. Manchester, NH: Granite State Publishing.

Wells, Frederic Palmer. 1902. *History of Newbury, Vermont, from the Discovery of the Coös Country to Present Time. With Genealogical Records of Many Families*. St. Johnsbury, VT: The Caledonian Company.

Wiggin, Brian P. 2015. "Conway's Early Inns, Part I: Grant (and Maybe Lincoln) Slept Here." *The Conway Daily Sun*,

September 9. https://www.conwaydailysun.com/news/conway-s-early-inns-part-i-grant-and-maybe-lincoln/article_395a7ed7-ce14-572d-ae0e-f84b9ba68905.html.

Wight, William Ward. 1888. "John Wight, of Bristol, M.A." *New England Historical and Genealogical Record* 42: 91-93.

—. 1890. *The Wights: A Record of Thomas Wight of Dedham and Medfield and His Descendants 1635-1890*. Milwaukee: Swain and Tate Printers.

Witcher, William. 1919. *The History of the Town of Haverhill, NH*.

Worcester Society of Antiquity. 1881. *Proceedings of the Worcester Society of Antiquity for the Year 1880, Volume XIII*. Published by the Society.

Worcester, Samuel T. 1879. *History of the Town of Hollis, New Hampshire, from its First Settlement to the Year 1879: with Many Biographical Sketches of its Early Settlers, Their Descendants, and Other Residents*. Boston: A. Williams.

Name Index

A

ABBOTT/ABBOT
Aaron 1714-1730 · 22
Aaron 1733-1812 · 98, 100, 397
Aaron 1778-1856 · 397, 413
Abiel 1716-1739 · 31
Abiel 1726-1772 · 69, 280
Abiel 1735-1764 · 86, 351
Abiel 1741-1809 · 87, 130, 356
Abiel 1745-1795 · 140
Abiel 1749-1831 · 135
Abiel 1754-1838 · 281
Abiel 1756-1812 · 207
Abiel 1761-1828 · 351
Abiel 1765-1859 · 350, 357
Abiel 1770-1828 · 350
Abiel 1778-1836 · 409
Abigail 1699-1753 · 18, 84
Abigail 1715-1737 · 64, 253
Abigail 1731-1733 · 86
Abigail 1734-1807 · 86, 130, 348
Abigail 1746- · 254
Abigail 1751-1841 · 132
Abigail 1753- · 363
Abigail 1756-1781 · 157
Abigail 1757-1845 · 262
Abigail 1762-1844 · 289
Abigail 1763-1843 · 281
Abigail 1764-1790 · 291
Abigail 1764-1841 · 350
Abigail 1766-1823 · 207
Abigail 1774-1816 · 178
Abigail 1779-1812 · 358
Abigail Lawrence 1791-1856 · 420
Abner 1751-1758 · 144
Abner 1761- · 145
ALice 1763-1809 · 291
Amos 1726-1821 · 25, 46, 65, 118
Amos 1754-1834 · 118, 488
Amos 1772-1852 · 208
Amy 1757-1777 · 164
Anna 1740-1810 · 87, 354
Anna 1748-1791 · 267
Anna 1749-1788 · 137
Anna 1758-1775 · 277
Anna 1765-1846 · 281
Anna 1767-1827 · 393
Anna 1769- · 394
Anna 1770- · 445
Anna 1776- · 399
Anna 1781-1806 · 399
Anner 1798-1798 · 416
Anner 1801-1872 · 416
Asa 1721-1796 · 39, 92, 161
Asa 1743-1754 · 68
Asa 1749-1763 · 162
Asa 1756-1834 · 269, 287
Asa 1765- · 378
Asa 1770-1843 · 398
Asa 1770-1850 · 250
Asa 1774-1775 · 277
Asenath 1781- · 397
Bancroft 1757-1829 · 255
Barachias 1707-1784 · 30, 130
Barachias 1734-1738 · 131
Barachias 1739-1812 · 131, 231
Bathsheba 1735-1784 · 112, 457

552 Index

Benjamin 1661-1703 · 4, 16
Benjamin 1686-1716 · 18
Benjamin 1686-1748 · 11, 56, 84
Benjamin 1710-1794 · 22, 33, 103
Benjamin 1723-1771 · 57, 85, 235, 345
Benjamin 1724-1807 · 67, 268
Benjamin 1743-1753 · 91
Benjamin 1748-1748 · 236
Benjamin 1749-1838 · 236
Benjamin 1750-1815 · 105, 418
Benjamin 1753-1754 · 268
Benjamin 1760-1765 · 167
Benjamin 1762-1849 · 349
Benjamin 1763-1821 · 351
Benjamin 1764-1829 · 269
Benjamin 1768-1856 · 369
Benjamin 1770-1823 · 358, 462
Benjamin 1770-1835 · 374
Benjamin 1782- · 410
Benjamin 1786-1854 · 419
Benjamin Jackman 1808-1869 · 416
Beriah 1758-1832 · 408

Beriah 1759-1759 · 177
Bethiah 1768- · 210
Betsey 1743-1827 · 100, 404
Betsey 1786-1839 · 331
Betsy 1773-1846 · 443, 462
Betsy 1780-1817 · 483
Betsy 1799-1856 · 416
Bette 1763-1842 · 394
Betty 1762-1765 · 167
Betty 1766- · 167
Betty 1767-1774 · 398
Betty 1778-1831 · 399
Bixby 1750-1813 · 507
Blaney 1772-1855 · 179
Bridget 1761- · 496
Bridget 1761-1787 · 362
Bridget 1770-1849 · 477
Caleb 1704-1778 · 14, 73
Caleb 1731-1776 · 73
Caleb 1738-1738 · 93
Caleb 1751-1837 · 162, 510
Caleb 1774-1851 · 311
Calvin 1788-1858 · 477
Calvin Holt 1771-1841 · 277

Catherine 1710-1744 · 22
Celinda 1766-1854 · 291
Charles 1769-1853 · 292
Chloe 1760-1835 · 275
Chloe 1771-1799 · 395
Chloe 1783-1809 · 399
Cloe 1737-1809 · 130
Daniel 1688-1731 · 9, 11, 47
Daniel 1715-1741 · 49
Daniel 1724-1761 · 38
Daniel 1725-1793 · 85, 345
Daniel 1738-1804 · 102, 109, 408
Daniel 1740- · 200
Daniel 1754-1776 · 163
Daniel 1757-1827 · 345
Daniel 1762- · 157
Daniel 1762-1765 · 167
Daniel 1768-1769 · 409
Daniel 1768-1812 · 207
Daniel 1769-1854 · 164
Daniel 1770- · 409
Daniel 1777-1853 · 250
Daniel Colby 1766-1842 · 371
Darius 1734-1817 · 68, 276

David 1689-1718 · 18
David 1689-1753 · 89
David 1716-1777 · 88, 360
David 1728-1798 · 90, 366
David 1729-1801 · 42, 178
David 1758-1827 · 207
David 1760-1761 · 178
David 1764-1823 · 374
David 1766-1847 · 369
David 1770-1804 · 179
David 1770-1836 · 430
David 1772- · 398
David 1775-1855 · 371
David 1782- · 477
David 1809-1882 · 489
Deborah 1704-1801 · 21, 100
Deborah 1732-1736 · 112
Deborah 1740-1745 · 112
Deborah 1745- · 143
Deborah 1773-1773 · 404
Deborah 1774-1806 · 276
Deborah 1774-1861 · 404
Delano 1774-1852 · 290
Dolly · 371
Dorcas 1698-1758 · 21, 95
Dorcas 1713-1798 · 48, 198
Dorcas 1724-1810 · 41
Dorcas 1728- · 108, 430
Dorcas 1729-1789 · 59, 243
Dorcas 1729-1797 · 99, 400
Dorcas 1735- · 93
Dorcas 1744-1829 · 87, 130, 356
Dorcas 1748-1749 · 113
Dorcas 1752- · 157
Dorcas 1755-1821 · 138
Dorcas 1758-1844 · 139, 144, 360
Dorcas 1764- · 177
Dorcas 1766-1841 · 234, 389
Dorcas 1773-1850 · 369
Dorcas 1774-1788 · 412
Dorcas 1774-1846 · 358
Dorcas 1778-1778 · 462
Dorcas 1786-1811 · 464
Dorcas Hibbert 1784-1784 · 462
Dorothy 1746-1776 · 110, 446
Dorothy 1762-1848 · 136
Dorothy 1774-1802 · 276
Dorothy 1778-1858 · 183
Dyer 1778-1832 · 396
Ebenezer 1689-1761 · 7, 42
Ebenezer 1721-1721 · 43
Ebenezer 1723-1725 · 43
Ebenezer 1731-1771 · 39, 165
Ebenezer 1751- · 363
Ebenezer 1753- · 136
Ebenezer 1757-1803 · 165
Ebenezer 1760- · 182
Ebenezer 1771- · 186
Edmund 1758-1765 · 167
Edward 1668- · 5
Edward 1702-1759 · 21, 99
Edward 1730-1801 · 99, 402
Edward 1767-1784 · 403
Elias 1757-1847 · 256
Elizabeth 1673-1750 · 5, 25
Elizabeth 1683-1762 · 13, 62

Elizabeth 1690-1718 · 11, 56
Elizabeth 1711-1758 · 30, 132
Elizabeth 1713-1799 · 24, 116
Elizabeth 1718- · 64
Elizabeth 1719-1785 · 49, 201
Elizabeth 1719-1803 · 41, 174
Elizabeth 1721-1786 · 34
Elizabeth 1726-1727 · 57
Elizabeth 1726-1736 · 67
Elizabeth 1726-1819 · 39, 92, 161
Elizabeth 1727- · 57, 85, 235, 345
Elizabeth 1727-1792 · 97, 391
Elizabeth 1733-1742 · 73
Elizabeth 1733-1753 · 91
Elizabeth 1733-1834 · 109, 433
Elizabeth 1737-1828 · 68, 278
Elizabeth 1738-1789 · 86, 351
Elizabeth 1740-1780 · 131, 149
Elizabeth 1746- · 135
Elizabeth 1747-1802 · 162
Elizabeth 1751-1836 · 236
Elizabeth 1754- · 368
Elizabeth 1755-1815 · 146
Elizabeth 1755-1821 · 233
Elizabeth 1756- · 160
Elizabeth 1757-1813 · 266
Elizabeth 1758-1769 · 267
Elizabeth 1761-1784 · 289
Elizabeth 1763- · 277
Elizabeth 1766- · 358
Elizabeth 1766-1833 · 145
Elizabeth 1766-1853 · 350
Elizabeth 1779-1852 · 178
Elizabeth 1784-1846 · 445
Elizabeth D. 1768-1856 · 371
Elizabeth Kneeland 1783-1812 · 243
Ellinor 1747- · 205
Enos 1769- · 380
Ephraim 1682-1748 · 7, 36
Ephraim 1710-1745 · 33, 138
Ephraim 1718-1775 · 37, 92, 155
Ephraim 1739-1739 · 139
Ephraim 1742-1827 · 156
Ephraim 1743-1809 · 139
Ephraim 1752-1778 · 105
Ephraim 1759-1834 · 165
Ephraim 1764- · 167
Ephraim 1778-1870 · 419
Ephraim 1779-1822 · 413
Esther 1755- · 157
Esther 1768- · 275
Esther 1777-1824 · 404
Esther 1784- · 312
Esther 1789- · 400
Eunice 1746- · 266
Ezra 1689-1712 · 13
Ezra 1722-1741 · 64
Ezra 1737-1760 · 130
Ezra 1756-1837 · 103, 414
Ezra 1759- · 255
Ezra 1760-1844 · 349
Ezra 1763-1824 · 364
Ezra 1765-1839 · 257, 436
Ezra 1765-1842 · 255, 257
Ezra 1772-1847 · 358
Ezra 1785-1871 · 359
Fidelia 1770- · 275
George 1617-1681 · 1
George 1655-1736 · 4, 10
George 1687-1690 · 13
George 1691-1691 · 13
George 1692-1768 · 12, 57
George 1706-1785 · 22, 33, 102
George 1724-1775 · 57, 232
George 1730-1772 · 50, 210
George 1740-1791 · 103

George 1748-1784 · 232
George 1755- · 210
George 1755-1818 · 236
George 1756- · 144
George 1770- · 210
George 1772- · 409
George B. 1803-1887 · 416
Gideon 1748-1754 · 266
Hannah · 25
Hannah 1650-1741 · 3, 8
Hannah 1684-1774 · 11, 54
Hannah 1695-1769 · 20
Hannah 1700-1746 · 21
Hannah 1701-1752 · 14, 70
Hannah 1712-1734 · 48
Hannah 1716-1786 · 22, 33, 103
Hannah 1717/1753 · 173
Hannah 1717-1753 · 41
Hannah 1721-1722 · 90
Hannah 1721-1805 · 31, 43, 134
Hannah 1723-1813 · 90
Hannah 1726- · 93, 376
Hannah 1730-1801 · 69, 283
Hannah 1733-1820 · 58, 238
Hannah 1734-1798 · 139
Hannah 1734-1813 · 74, 308
Hannah 1735-1736 · 66
Hannah 1735-1819 · 115, 472
Hannah 1736- · 109, 437
Hannah 1737-1738 · 169
Hannah 1737-1812 · 131
Hannah 1739- · 200
Hannah 1741-1763 · 68
Hannah 1741-1783 · 170
Hannah 1742-1770 · 112, 458
Hannah 1743- · 361
Hannah 1743-1802 · 135
Hannah 1743-1820 · 104, 417
Hannah 1749-1784 · 191, 233
Hannah 1750-1754 · 266
Hannah 1751-1785 · 132
Hannah 1752-1816 · 165
Hannah 1753-1769 · 144
Hannah 1755-1784 · 164
Hannah 1757- · 370
Hannah 1757-1837 · 146
Hannah 1758- · 210
Hannah 1758-1847 · 275
Hannah 1759- · 269
Hannah 1759-1789 · 394
Hannah 1762-1832 · 255, 257
Hannah 1762-1856 · 368
Hannah 1765-1775 · 277
Hannah 1769-1810 · 412
Hannah 1769-1857 · 186
Hannah 1772-1786 · 462
Hannah 1774- · 479
Hannah 1776- · 293
Hannah 1776-1840 · 375
Hannah 1776-1844 · 208
Hannah 1777-1853 · 515
Hannah 1778-1803 · 278
Hannah 1782-1869 · 419
Hannah 1784- · 464
Hannah 1791-1876 · 411
Harriet 1740-1740 · 68
Harriet B. 1786-1862 · 415
Henry 1696-1776 · 12, 58

Henry 1724-1805 ·
  59, 60, 241
Henry 1746-1749 ·
  268
Henry 1749-1807 ·
  268
Henry 1754-1797 ·
  206
Henry 1761- · 277
Henry 1770-1770 ·
  243
Henry 1771-1776 ·
  243
Henry 1774-1862 ·
  399
Henry 1777-1862 ·
  243
Henry 1785-1868 ·
  484
Hephzibah 1772-
  1813 · 482
Hephzibah 1780-
  1817 · 396
Huldah 1760- · 460
Huldah 1760-1830 ·
  138
Isaac 1699-1784 ·
  12, 60
Isaac 1728- · 43, 181
Isaac 1732-1800 ·
  68, 274
Isaac 1745-1746 ·
  104
Isaac 1745-1836 ·
  60, 189, 247
Isaac 1747-1799 ·
  104
Isaac 1762-1861 ·
  182
Isaac 1766-1831 ·
  275
Isaac 1768-1806 ·
  248
Isaac 1777-1800 ·
  413

Isaac 1793-1840 ·
  420
Isaack 1716-1745 ·
  22
Israel 1771-1840 ·
  460
Jabez 1731-1804 ·
  97, 99, 395
Jacob 1737-1760 ·
  86
Jacob 1746-1820 ·
  113, 461
Jacob 1760-1815 ·
  237
Jacob 1768-1802 ·
  358
Jacob 1769-1838 ·
  398
Jacob 1771-1772 ·
  350
Jacob 1776-1847 ·
  443, 462
James 1695-1778 ·
  13, 63
James 1717- · 253
James 1717-1803 ·
  64
James 1736- · 44,
  184
James 1750-1814 ·
  254
James 1753-1830 ·
  281, 505
James 1768-1810 ·
  460
James 1770-1859 ·
  183
James Osgood · 445
Jane Woodman
  1805-1891 · 416
Jedathan 1773- · 477
Jedediah 1780- · 461
Jemima 1746-1746 ·
  100

Jemima 1748-1748 ·
  100
Jeremiah · 445
Jeremiah 1709-1748
  · 24, 115
Jeremiah 1733-1755
  · 89
Jeremiah 1738-1740
  · 115
Jeremiah 1743-1825
  · 130
Jeremiah 1744-1823
  · 110, 444
Jeremiah 1745-1745
  · 116
Jeremiah 1748- ·
  116, 478
Jeremiah 1757-1816
  · 364
Jeremiah 1766-1811
  · 409
Jeremiah 1772-1850
  · 478
Jeremiah 1776-1835
  · 369
Jesse 1740-1740 · 98
Jesse 1741-1808 · 98
Jesse 1776-1799 ·
  479
Jesse 1799- · 478
Jethro 1761-1764 ·
  166
Joanna 1753-1753 ·
  177
Joanna 1775- · 177
Job 1724- · 65, 89
Job 1724-1765 · 261
Job 1742-1815 · 361
Job 1755-1805 · 262
Joel 1742-1743 · 87
Joel 1757-1806 · 236
Joel 1765-1826 · 394
Joel 1776-1863 · 465
John · 445

John 1648-1721 · 3, 5
John 1674-1754 · 6, 29
John 1703-1703 · 30
John 1704-1793 · 30, 129
John 1713-1791 · 40, 169
John 1724-1740 · 69
John 1725-1779 · 127, 515
John 1726-1806 · 50, 206
John 1735-1818 · 86, 130, 348
John 1741-1778 · 70, 290
John 1743-1804 · 170
John 1751-1782 · 207
John 1751-1798 · 136
John 1752- · 361
John 1756-1779 · 118
John 1759-1843 · 348
John 1784-1859 · 290
John 1805- · 489
John Lovejoy 1757-1837 · 234
John S. 1779-1809 · 462
John Sullivan 1778-1810 · 444
Jonas 1781-1839 · 479
Jonathan 1687-1770 · 18, 87
Jonathan 1714-1794 · 34, 87, 359
Jonathan 1739-1817 · 91, 189, 372
Jonathan 1740-1821 · 139, 144, 360
Jonathan 1760-1830 · 373
Jonathan 1772- · 346
Jonathan 1776-1843 · 465
Joseph 1649-1650 · 3
Joseph 1652-1676 · 4
Joseph 1676-1757 · 6, 31
Joseph 1680- · 11
Joseph 1705-1787 · 23, 112
Joseph 1716- · 49, 200
Joseph 1719-1790 · 31, 43, 134
Joseph 1724-1766 · 31, 136
Joseph 1734-1758 · 98
Joseph 1735-1814 · 288
Joseph 1735-1815 · 70
Joseph 1740-1741 · 112
Joseph 1741-1832 · 103, 192, 411
Joseph 1742- · 135
Joseph 1743-1813 · 200
Joseph 1744-1792 · 113, 459
Joseph 1754-1774 · 429
Joseph 1757-1758 · 395
Joseph 1758-1835 · 138
Joseph 1759-1837 · 396
Joseph 1763-1790 · 460
Joseph 1766-1834 · 290
Joseph 1767-1778 · 185
Joseph 1771-1829 · 208
Joseph 1772- · 161
Joseph 1774- · 430
Joshua 1685-1769 · 7, 40
Joshua 1712- · 24
Joshua 1722-1772 · 38, 159
Joshua 1722-1807 · 41, 175
Joshua 1734-1736 · 112
Joshua 1739-1739 · 112
Joshua 1740-1815 · 109, 442
Joshua 1747-1752 · 176
Joshua 1750-1752 · 170
Joshua 1754- · 160
Joshua 1759-1837 · 429
Joshua 1765-1798 · 138, 460
Joshua 1772-1795 · 178

Joshua 1774-1775 · 375
Joshua 1780- · 477
Joshua 1782-1821 · 444
Joshua 1784-1784 · 375
Josiah 1728-1777 · 39, 163
Josiah 1735-1753 · 91
Josiah 1759- · 164
Josiah 1759-1837 · 368
Judah 1760-1845 · 207
Judith 1753-1806 · 255
Judith 1755- · 363
Judith 1784-1831 · 410
Kneeland 1748- · 157
Lemuel 1764-1841 · 164
Lemuel 1768-1846 · 290
Levi 1767-1825 · 430
Lois 1771-1790 · 412
Lois 1793-1881 · 411
Louisa 1762-1806 · 269
Lucy 1755- · 283
Lucy 1759-1790 · 182
Lucy 1775-1839 · 460
Lucy 1781-1866 · 462
Lucy 1784- · 415
Lucy 1789- · 414
Luther 1773-1773 · 277
Luther 1778- · 277

Lydea 1723-1807 · 59, 240
Lydia 1732-1748 · 42
Lydia 1733-1816 · 93, 379
Lydia 1735-1736 · 100
Lydia 1737-1811 · 98, 100, 397
Lydia 1743-1749 · 98
Lydia 1745-1829 · 132
Lydia 1753-1826 · 137
Lydia 1754-1775 · 165
Lydia 1754-1788 · 177
Lydia 1757-1826 · 394
Lydia 1761-1840 · 364
Lydia 1762-1767 · 185
Lydia 1769-1769 · 461
Lydia 1771- · 371, 397, 403
Lydia 1771-1855 · 461
Lydia 1773-1841 · 396
Lydia 1775- · 292
Mariam 1771-1820 · 365
Martha 1682-1683 · 11
Martha 1733-1733 · 39
Martha 1737-1773 · 39, 167
Martha 1750-1842 · 360
Martha 1755-1842 · 170

Martha 1764-1798 · 234
Martha 1771- · 378
Mary · 445
Mary 1687-1688 · 7
Mary 1698- · 106
Mary 1698-1718 · 23
Mary 1713-1748 · 33, 140
Mary 1717-1800 · 41, 172
Mary 1718-1718 · 92
Mary 1720- · 38, 157
Mary 1723-1792 · 34, 57, 88, 142, 359
Mary 1724-1744 · 37, 92, 155
Mary 1725-1760 · 43, 179
Mary 1727-1734 · 59
Mary 1729-1769 · 67, 270
Mary 1732-1780 · 66, 263
Mary 1732-1798 · 86, 346
Mary 1732-1803 · 70, 285
Mary 1735-1795 · 109, 436
Mary 1737-1813 · 59, 245
Mary 1739- · 74
Mary 1741- · 156
Mary 1744-1820 · 143
Mary 1748- · 254
Mary 1751-1752 · 233
Mary 1753-1790 · 207
Mary 1753-1820 · 233

Mary 1754-1755 · 236
Mary 1754-1811 · 268
Mary 1757-1849 · 271, 275
Mary 1759-1835 · 289
Mary 1761-1843 · 403
Mary 1762-1797 · 237
Mary 1762-1845 · 373
Mary 1768-1769 · 242
Mary 1769- · 378
Mary 1776- · 292
Mary 1779- · 312
Mary 1780- · 278
Mehitable 1728-1728 · 34
Mehitable 1736-1777 · 139, 360
Mehitable 1762- · 362
Mehitable 1763-1838 · 403
Mehitable 1797- · 478
Mercy 1780-1863 · 186
Metylda 1764- · 275
Micah 1766-1767 · 183
Micah 1774-1825 · 183
Molly 1762- · 210
Molly 1764-1765 · 185
Molly 1767-1791 · 412
Molly 1773- · 460
Moses 1735-1826 · 131
Moses 1752-1837 · 429
Nancy 1779- · 278
Nathan 1682- · 11
Nathan 1691-1713 · 13
Nathan 1719-1798 · 88, 124
Nathan 1721- · 66, 265
Nathan 1723- · 49, 203
Nathan 1729- · 93, 377
Nathan 1737-1805 · 98, 398
Nathan 1744- · 360
Nathan 1744-1794 · 266
Nathan 1748-1749 · 103
Nathan 1752-1758 · 103
Nathan 1753-1801 · 195, 261
Nathan 1756-1840 · 163
Nathan 1757-1758 · 206
Nathan 1760- · 210
Nathan 1761- · 378
Nathan 1763-1836 · 207
Nathan 1765-1844 · 396
Nathan 1765-1849 · 257, 429
Nathan 1767- · 378
Nathan 1768- · 374
Nathan 1779-1839 · 413
Nathan Kilburn 1799-1878 · 411
Nathaniel · 446
Nathaniel 1671-1749 · 5, 22
Nathaniel 1700-1770 · 23, 107
Nathaniel 1727-1806 · 108, 428
Nathaniel 1737-1740 · 112
Nathaniel 1751-1791 · 113, 463
Nathaniel 1766-1815 · 185
Nathaniel 1767-1769 · 443
Nathaniel 1769-1848 · 443
Nathaniel 1774-1774 · 463
Nathaniel 1791-1860 · 464
Nathaniel Chandler 1750- · 429
Nehemiah 1727-1727 · 43
Nehemiah 1731-1808 · 190
Nehemiah 1757-1823 · 234
Nehemiah 1759- · 185
Nehemiah 1776-1776 · 311
Nehemiah 1781-1869 · 312
Obediah 1749-1750 · 113

Olive 1749-1784 · 205
Olive 1756-1828 · 182
Olive 1770-1834 · 369
Olive 1772- · 276
Olive 1772-1776 · 290
Oliver 1727-1796 · 42, 176
Oliver 1756-1757 · 177
Oliver Whiting 1757-1758 · 177
Orinda 1786- · 312
Parmelia 1796-1872 · 420
Paul 1697-1752 · 14, 66
Paul 1753-1754 · 266
Paul 1759- · 378
Paul 1767- · 277
Paul 1783-1831 · 312
Persis 1781-1859 · 359
Peter 1734-1774 · 39, 166
Peter 1758-1825 · 167
Peter 1762- · 161
Peter 1782-1850 · 463
Peter Hazeltine 1780- · 410
Phebe 1721- · 49, 202
Phebe 1727-1754 · 65, 257
Phebe 1732-1770 · 97, 99, 395
Phebe 1732-1805 · 44, 183

Phebe 1733-1812 · 129, 188
Phebe 1737- · 93, 380
Phebe 1746-1833 · 59, 60, 241
Phebe 1749-1809 · 132
Phebe 1750- · 160
Phebe 1756- · 136
Phebe 1759-1760 · 256
Phebe 1760-1777 · 256
Phebe 1762-1819 · 396
Phebe 1763-1826 · 234
Phebe 1764-1854 · 257, 429
Phebe 1766-1837 · 412, 456
Phebe 1766-1848 · 374
Phebe 1766-1852 · 242
Phebe 1767-1772 · 248
Phebe 1768-1852 · 350
Phebe 1774-1857 · 358, 462
Phebe 1788-1825 · 359
Phebe 1789- · 464
Philip 1699-1748 · 14, 68
Philip 1751-1834 · 280
Philip 1753-1776 · 282
Philip 1757-1841 · 429
Polly 1782- · 413

Priscilla 1691-1791 · 8
Priscilla 1720-1771 · 34
Priscilla 1743- · 132
Priscilla 1770-1830 · 249
Priscilla 1780-1862 · 375
Prudence 1757-1839 · 368
Rachel 1720- · 64
Rachel 1742-1742 · 100
Rachel 1743-1788 · 102, 109, 408
Rachel 1761-1844 · 185
Rachel 1768-1854 · 365
Rachel 1773-1837 · 412
Rebecca 1717-1803 · 25, 46, 65, 117
Rebecca 1730- · 65, 259
Rebecca 1731- · 108, 431
Rebecca 1739-1785 · 170
Rebecca 1741- · 473
Rebecca 1741-1761 · 116
Rebecca 1754-1795 · 113, 464
Rebecca 1760-1846 · 118, 489
Rebeckah 1711-1761 · 40
Rebeckah 1778-1864 · 479
Relief 1759-1817 · 136
Relief 1778- · 186

Reuben 1723-1822 ·
64, 111, 256, 451
Reuben 1752-1752 ·
256
Reuben 1754-1834 ·
256
Reuben 1774- · 292
Reuben 1774-1863 ·
283
Reuben 1790-1869 ·
411
Rhoda 1741-1821 ·
139
Rhoda 1747-1775 ·
132
Rhoda 1755-1839 ·
256
Rhoda 1761- · 267
Rhoda 1784-1853 ·
359
Robert Burnham
1791-1830 · 415
Rone 1773-1778 ·
186
Rose B. 1796- · 415
Rufus 1759-1760 ·
267
Ruth · 445
Ruth 1738-1817 ·
109, 440
Ruth 1764-1764 ·
257
Ruth 1782- · 413
Ruth Morrill 1784- ·
419
Sally 1792-1857 ·
480
Salva 1778-1778 ·
462
Samuel 1694-1762 ·
19

Samuel 1725-1725 ·
97
Samuel 1726-1758 ·
34, 145
Samuel 1727- · 89,
363
Samuel 1732-1812 ·
58
Samuel 1743-1761 ·
103
Samuel 1743-1825 ·
74, 310
Samuel 1750-1836 ·
363
Samuel 1753-1794 ·
236
Samuel 1759-1759 ·
234
Samuel 1760-1792 ·
234
Samuel 1763-1769 ·
145
Samuel 1764-1833 ·
368
Samuel 1764-1849 ·
409
Samuel 1765-1840 ·
346
Samuel 1777-1782 ·
358
Samuel 1786-1839 ·
359
Samuel 1789- · 312
Samuel 1791-1861 ·
414
Sarah 1659-1711 · 4,
15
Sarah 1679-1679 ·
11
Sarah 1680-1754 · 7,
9, 34

Sarah 1702-1757 ·
23, 110
Sarah 1711-1769 ·
22, 33, 102
Sarah 1715-1798 ·
40, 170
Sarah 1716- · 155
Sarah 1716-1736 ·
37
Sarah 1718-1778 ·
56, 95, 230
Sarah 1726-1814 ·
90, 365
Sarah 1728-1802 ·
50, 208
Sarah 1730- · 65, 89,
261
Sarah 1730-1797 ·
58, 95, 237
Sarah 1730-1811 ·
67, 272
Sarah 1731- · 93,
378
Sarah 1733-1809 ·
190
Sarah 1736-1761 ·
74, 309
Sarah 1737-1831 ·
139
Sarah 1743- · 254
Sarah 1747-1824 ·
144
Sarah 1748- · 201
Sarah 1748-1842 ·
110, 448
Sarah 1750-1835 ·
61, 162, 249
Sarah 1751-1811 ·
157
Sarah 1751-1820 ·
137

562 Index

Sarah 1751-1854 · 142, 261
Sarah 1752-1754 · 160
Sarah 1759- · 364
Sarah 1761- · 371
Sarah 1761-1761 · 105
Sarah 1761-1774 · 408
Sarah 1761-1848 · 161
Sarah 1762-1846 · 275
Sarah 1762-1848 · 234
Sarah 1765- · 210
Sarah 1765-1856 · 166
Sarah 1769-1857 · 412, 468
Sarah 1771-1772 · 311
Sarah 1773-1849 · 309, 311
Sarah 1773-1870 · 164
Sarah 1775-1841 · 443, 477
Sarah 1775-1854 · 463
Sarah 1778- · 293
Sarah 1778-1860 · 375
Sarah 1780-1853 · 397, 413
Sarah 1781-1846 · 410
Sarah 1783-1858 · 250
Sarah 1788-1878 · 419
Sarah 1790- · 411
Sarah 1815-1889 · 417

Sarah Hale 1809-1884 · 489
Sibyl 1774- · 186
Silas 1784- · 479
Silence 1760-1760 · 177
Silent 1761-1761 · 177
Simeon 1724-1741 · 64
Simeon 1764-1851 · 183
Simeon 1807-1895 · 489
Solomon 1731-1797 · 91, 370
Solomon 1759-1842 · 371
Solomon 1772-1840 · 374
Stephen 1678-1766 · 7, 32
Stephen 1718-1768 · 34, 57, 142
Stephen 1728-1801 · 69, 281
Stephen 1746-1811 · 103, 413
Stephen 1749-1813 · 144
Stephen 1751-1754 · 268
Stephen 1757-1813 · 330
Stephen 1759- · 160
Stephen 1767-1770 · 292
Stephen 1771-1853 · 292
Stephen 1778-1792 · 276
Stephen 1786- · 414
Susanna 1754-1827 · 182

Susanna 1762-1832 · 429
Susanna 1765-1841 · 403
Susannah 1752-1815 · 282
Susannah 1763- · 255
Susannah 1769-1803 · 478
Susannah 1797-1847 · 411
Tabitha 1707- · 24, 45, 113
Tamison 1769-1850 · 235
Theodore 1759-1778 · 105
Theodore 1763-1764 · 166
Theodore 1784-1855 · 414
Theodore Thomas 1799-1887 · 420
Thomas 1666-1728 · 5, 21
Thomas 1699-1774 · 21, 97
Thomas 1729-1775 · 97, 393
Thomas 1754-1773 · 105
Thomas 1761-1826 · 394
Thomas 1776- · 409
Thomas Stickney 1792-1864 · 445
Timothy 1663-1730 · 4, 19
Timothy 1693-1766 · 20, 92
Timothy 1719-1745 · 92
Timothy 1739-1814 · 100

Timothy 1745-1826 · 61, 162, 249
Timothy 1747-1772 · 132
Timothy 1762-1831 · 378
Timothy 1769-1819 · 397, 403
Timothy 1774-1777 · 250
Tryphena 1760-1835 · 269
Tryphena 1769-1836 · 277
William 1657-1713 · 4, 12
William 1685-1713 · 13
William 1719-1741 · 64
William 1723-1805 · 67, 267
William 1730-1730 · 31
William 1741-1768 · 60
William 1745- · 360
William 1745-1832 · 74, 311
William 1746- · 116, 475
William 1748-1793 · 130, 191
William 1752-1806 · 267
William 1755-1807 · 255
William 1760- · 345
William 1761-1764 · 164
William 1765-1838 · 365, 377
William 1766-1766 · 164
William 1772-1856 · 249, 483
William 1774-1852 · 483
William 1778-1849 · 477
William 1779-1843 · 465
William 1787-1824 · 480
William 1792-1819 · 312
Zebadiah 1706- · 14
Zebadiah 1709-1745 · 22
Zebadiah 1731-1731 · 70
Zebadiah 1739-1793 · 194
Zebadiah 1750- · 206
Zerviah 1722- · 88, 362

ABELL
Zerviah 1780-1845 · 307

ADAMS
John · 386
Lucy 1747- · 450
Lucy 1753-1834 · 252
Thomas 1757- · 268

AINSWORTH
Candace · 215
Grace 1743-1788 · 213

ALDEN
Irena 1772-1858 · 301

Joanna 1782-1849 · 303

ALLEN
Aaron 1761-1766 · 229
Aaron 1766- · 229
Amasa 1752-1821 · 328
Benjamin 1758- · 229
Christopher 1763-1763 · 229
Christopher 1765-1819 · 229
Daniel 1758- · 502
Dorcas 1754-1785 · 228
Elizabeth 1752-1850 · 228
Hannah 1690-1755 · 6, 31
Jeremiah 1769- · 229
John 1756-1834 · 228
Joseph 1747- · 228
Lydia · 503
Mary 1746-1746 · 228
Mary 1748- · 228
Nathaniel Coit 1759- · 229
Peter 1764- · 168
Samuel 1771-1846 · 229
William 1717- · 56, 227
William 1750-1826 · 228

ALLISON
Sarah 1770-1837 · 164

ALMY

Index

William 1788-1830 · 511

AMBROSE
Hannah 1750- · 258
Mary 1755-1815 · 258
Nathaniel 1752-1835 · 154
Susan 1755- · 467

AMES
Abel 1774-1775 · 513
Abigail 1722-1812 · 88, 124
Abigail 1756- · 496
Abigail 1763-1848 · 512
Abigail 1779- · 508
Alice · 355
Amelia 1788-1874 · 511
Amos 1734-1817 · 125, 511
Amos 1758- · 512
Anna 1776- · 510
Asa 1772-1838 · 510
Benjamin 1724-1809 · 125, 241, 505
Benjamin 1749-1813 · 506
Benjamin 1774-1787 · 510
Bethiah 1762-1762 · 507
Bethiah 1770-1852 · 514
Betsey Buckley 1776-1861 · 513
Buckley 1772-1836 · 513
Chandler 1747-1766 · 506
Deborah 1768-1819 · 162, 510
Dorcas 1773-1775 · 507
Dorcas 1776-1855 · 507
Eli 1765- · 512
Elizabeth 1745- · 495
Elizabeth 1760-1760 · 507
Hannah 1722- · 125
Hannah 1751-1831 · 506
Hannah 1770-1840 · 513
Hephzibah 1755-1796 · 507
Jemima Green 1791-1839 · 511
Jephthah 1779-1786 · 511
John · 436
Lydia 1770-1843 · 510
Molly 1772-1775 · 514
Molly 1786- · 515
Moses 1759-1783 · 512
Moses 1783-1820 · 511
Nathan 1729-1791 · 125, 508
Nathan 1764-1851 · 510
Peter 1767-1823 · 513
Phineas 1764- · 362, 496
Prudence 1767-1821 · 514
Richard 1754-1754 · 507
Richard 1758-1758 · 507
Robert 1737- · 125, 513
Robert 1763-1789 · 514
Ruth 1776-1844 · 275
Samuel 1696-1784 · 26, 124
Samuel 1719- · 121, 495
Samuel 1746-1792 · 495
Samuel 1766-1830 · 510
Samuel 1781- · 515
Sarah 1765-1836 · 514
Simeon 1741-1760 · 126
Simeon 1761-1784 · 512
Simeon 1772-1849 · 482, 507
Simeon 1781-1863 · 511
Simon 1761- · 496
Solomon 1754- · 495
Spofford 1752-1835 · 495
Stephens 1749- · 495
Timothy 1765-1835 · 507

AMIDON
Jonathan 1759-1838 · 271

ANDREWS
Betty 1762-1794 · 103, 414
Mary Ann 1727-1788 · 67, 268

APPLETON
William 1765-1822 · 235

ARLIN
George 1768- · 471, 472

Mehitable 1770- ·
471
Nancy 1783- · 472
ASHLEY
Abner 1754-1829 ·
269
Sarah 1752-1811 ·
272
ATKINSON
Sarah 1785- · 396
ATWOOD
Mehitable 1765-
1855 · 300
AYERS
Jesse 1763- · 495
Judith 1763-1854 ·
494

B

BACON
Penuel 1726- · 52,
216
Pinias 1747- · 217
BADGER
Hannah 1742-1768 ·
133
Mary · 144
BAILEY
Asa 1745- · 254
Elizabeth 1768-1830
· 482
Hannah 1765- · 392
Hannah 1779-1867 ·
483
John Mooar 1784-
1836 · 483
Joshua 1770-1820 ·
482
Moses 1744-1842 ·
117, 481

Moses 1766-1846 ·
482
Nathan 1775- · 482
Nathan 1777-1862 ·
483
Rebecca 1781- · 249,
483
Rhoda 1789-1854 ·
484
Samuel 1705-1798 ·
93
Sarah 1772-1857 ·
482, 507
Timothy 1786-1875 ·
484
BAKER
Alice 1770-1858 ·
460
Henry Gray 1767-
1802 · 510
Mary · 228
Mary Ann 1805-
1873 · 491
Seth 1783-1865 ·
420
Thomas · 460
BALCH
Deborah 1780-1862
· 164
BALDWIN
Patty 1764-1822 ·
355
Susannah 1746-1825
· 116, 478
Thomas 1755-1810 ·
288
BALLARD
Anna 1762-1805 ·
262
Dorcas 1757-1775 ·
195
Dorothy 1757- · 191

Elizabeth 1701-1782
· 21, 97
Elizabeth 1746- · 190
Hannah 1714-1789 ·
24, 115
Hannah 1733-1824 ·
188
Hannah 1736-1778 ·
190
Hannah 1748-1838 ·
147, 188, 195
Hezekiah 1720-1801
· 46, 193
Hezekiah 1762-1848
· 195
John 1734-1736 ·
190
John 1739- · 190
Jonathan 1761-1830
· 394
Joseph 1741-1747 ·
190
Joseph 1749-1819 ·
191, 233
Joshua 1753-1755 ·
195
Lois 1746-1836 ·
150, 194
Lucy 1760-1827 ·
195
Lydia 1742-1813 ·
194
Mary 1732-1803 ·
190
Mary 1751-1835 ·
150, 195
Mary 1754-1795 ·
117, 480
Nathan 1744-1835 ·
190
Penelope 1705- · 23,
108

Phebe 1738-1815 ·
  86, 95, 351
Phebe 1752-1846 ·
  130, 191
Rebecca 1744-1821 ·
  194
Sarah 1755-1825 ·
  195, 261
Timothy 1702-1773 ·
  46, 189
Timothy 1730-1768 ·
  190
Timothy 1757-1828 ·
  239
BANCROFT
  Abigail Whiting
    1797- · 419
  Samuel · 503
  Sarah 1722- · 64,
    254
BANNISTER
  Lazarus · 310
BARKER
  Abigail 1762-1793 ·
    347
  Daniel · 402
  Daniel 1746- · 458
  Dorcas 1770-1840 ·
    347
  Esther 1776-1857 ·
    312
  Gilbert 1774-1853 ·
    375
  Joanna (-) · 3
  Joel 1764-1832 · 347
  Mary · 68, 113, 274,
    460
  Mary 1766-1766 ·
    347
  Mary 1767-1824 ·
    347
  Nehemiah 1734-
    1810 · 86, 346
  Phebe 1750- · 317
  Richard · 3

Richard 1775- · 375
Samuel 1692-1770 ·
  76, 316
Sarah 1647-1729 · 3,
  6
Sarah 1747-1763 ·
  317
BARNARD
  John 1728-1802 ·
    149
  Mary 1739-1804 ·
    148
BARR
  James 1755-1848 ·
    338
BARRELL
  Judith 1763- · 310
BARRETT
  Benoni 1718-1755 ·
    63, 251
  Elizabeth 1743- · 252
  James 1754-1776 ·
    252
  Joseph 1742- · 251
  William 1751-1838 ·
    252
BARTHOLOMEW
  Enos 1714- · 52, 214
  Hannah 1737- · 215
  John · 9
  John 1742-1798 ·
    215
  Mary 1746- · 215
  Mercy 1744- · 215
  Sarah 1737-1797 ·
    215
BARTLET
  Jean 1766- · 207
BARTLETT
  Ebenezer 1779-1854
    · 186
BATCHELDER
  Betsy 1777-1864 ·
    465

Daniel 1751-1832 ·
  113, 464
Daniel 1781-1853 ·
  465
Hannah 1793-1862 ·
  466
Herman 1790-1876 ·
  466
John 1783- · 465
John 1788-1795 ·
  466
Joseph 1748-1826 ·
  388
Joseph 1786-1788 ·
  465
Judith Ray 1779- ·
  465
Lydia 1795-1886 ·
  466
Margaret 1784-1867
  · 389
Mary 1756-1833 ·
  429
Mary 1784-1859 ·
  465
Rebecca 1775-1805 ·
  464
Uziel 1755- · 450
BAYFORD
  Annis · 1
BEARD
  William 1745-1809 ·
    431
BENNET
  Lois 1757- · 136
  Polly 1771- · 285
BERRY
  Susannah 1767-1854
    · 380
BIDLACK
  James 1750-1779 ·
    287
  Sarah 1756- · 269,
    287
BIGFORD

Abigail · 14, 68
BINGHAM
  Lucretia 1766-1835 · 290
  Mary 1778-1852 · 290
BINNEY
  Margaret 1719-1797 · 55, 225
BIRGE
  Aby 1774- · 333
BIXBY
  William 1779-1862 · 353
BLANCHARD
  Aaron 1791- · 454
  Abiel 1737-1739 · 107
  Abiel 1741-1743 · 107
  Abiel 1749- · 423
  Abiel 1751-1803 · 423
  Abiel 1773- · 455
  Amos 1766-1842 · 455
  Anne 1722-1758 · 106, 425
  Bathsheba 1754- · 458
  Benjamin 1693- · 23, 106
  Benjamin 1721-1791 · 106, 422
  Benjamin 1745-1789 · 423
  Betty 1765-1811 · 424
  Beulah 1783-1824 · 485
  Daniel 1735-1776 · 111, 454
  Daniel 1759- · 455
  David 1732-1739 · 107
  David 1740-1740 · 107
  David 1752- · 428
  David 1771-1805 · 457
  Deborah 1712-1773 · 23, 112
  Deborah 1727-1799 · 147
  Dinah 1731-1826 · 111, 256, 451
  Dorcas 1730-1739 · 107
  Dorcas 1755- · 423
  Dorcas 1757- · 424
  Dorothy 1776- · 454
  Eber 1769-1842 · 453
  Edmund 1778-1836 · 399
  Elizabeth 1726-1728 · 111
  Elizabeth 1734- · 107
  Hannah 1728- · 111, 449
  Hannah 1752- · 450
  Hannah 1776- · 456
  Hannah 1785- · 454
  Henry 1773- · 454
  Henry 1781-1824 · 454
  Isaac 1753- · 423
  Isaac 1763-1826 · 455
  Jacob 1724-1770 · 107, 426
  Jacob 1753-1769 · 426
  Jacob 1758- · 450
  Jeremiah 1733-1826 · 111, 452
  Jeremiah 1759- · 453
  Jerusha 1761-1779 · 455
  Joel 1759-1816 · 424
  John 1737-1823 · 111, 456
  John 1757- · 428
  John 1763-1844 · 456
  John 1767-1855 · 451
  John 1768-1802 · 452
  John 1782-1851 · 454
  Jonathan 1728-1739 · 107
  Jonathan 1750-1837 · 423
  Joseph 1701- · 23, 110
  Joseph 1731-1776 · 111, 451
  Joseph 1754-1758 · 452
  Joseph 1761-1839 · 412, 456
  Joseph 1765- · 452
  Joshua 1726-1818 · 107, 427
  Joshua 1750-1776 · 427
  Judith 1779- · 454, 518
  Keziah 1747- · 423
  Lucy 1757- · 426
  Lucy 1760-1798 · 428
  Lucy 1762-1843 · 427

Lucy 1771-1855 ·
455
Lucy 1776- · 458
Mary (-) -1848 · 454
Mary (-) -1852 · 453
Mary 1719- · 106,
421
Mary 1760- · 450
Mary 1762- · 455
Molly 1754-1826 ·
428
Moses · 458
Moses 1783-1858 ·
457
Nathan 1730- · 112,
457
Nathaniel 1760- ·
427
Peter 1756-1810 ·
424, 488
Peter 1767-1858 ·
453
Phebe 1741-1749 ·
111
Phebe 1762-1838 ·
451
Phineas 1750-1775 ·
450
Rebecca 1754- · 144
Rebecca 1756-1826 ·
426
Rebecca 1768- · 455
Reuben 1763-1832 ·
424
Rhoda 1762-1800 ·
368
Sarah 1723-1729 ·
110
Sarah 1748- · 427
Sarah 1755- · 450
Sarah 1769-1848 ·
457
Sarah 1774- · 454
Simon 1766-1837 ·
424

Stephen · 458
Stephen 1726-1802 ·
111, 449
Stephen 1749-1789 ·
450
Stevens 1765-1790 ·
456
William 1788-1861 ·
454

BLOOD
Polly 1795-1865 ·
466
BLUNT
Elizabeth 1752-1801
· 181
Ephraim 1721- · 88,
362
Ephraim 1747- · 362
Ephraim 1754-1829 ·
362
Hannah 1758- · 181
Isaac 1712-1798 ·
43, 179
Isaac 1757-1757 ·
181
John 1756-1836 ·
181
Lydia 1731-1798 ·
97, 393
Mary 1747- · 180
Sarah 1750-1841 ·
181
Zerviah 1759-1860 ·
362
BODWELL
Henry 1729-1816 ·
314
Parker 1750-1795 ·
370
Ruth -1790 · 368
BOND
Ephraim 1746- · 205
BOWDITCH
Deborah 1767-1823
· 343

Ebenezer 1771- ·
343
Hannah 1761-1825 ·
343
John 1732-1793 · 83,
341
John 1764-1793 ·
343
Mary 1760-1829 ·
342
Samuel 1769-1791 ·
343
Sarah 1770- · 343
BOWEN
Elizabeth 1765-1808
· 207
BOWERS
Deborah 1746-1782
· 125, 508
Fanny 1773-1828 ·
389
Francis 1775-1835 ·
390
Jonathan 1761-1804
· 177
Rachel 1763-1845 ·
371
BOYD
Mary Southgate
1797-1861 · 354
BOYDEN
John 1736-1819 ·
223
BOYNTON
Abel 1755- · 237
Betsey 1774-1819 ·
475
Betty · 422
David 1776-1813 ·
475
Dorcas 1715-1775 ·
140
Elizabeth 1789- · 483
Hannah 1767- · 474

Index

Jerusha 1769-1788 · 474
John 1762-1852 · 474
Jonathan 1753- · 117, 480
Orpha 1772-1851 · 475
Rebecca 1763-1833 · 474
Richard 1741- · 116, 473
Richard 1765-1841 · 474
Sarah 1770- · 474
Susannah 1778- · 475
Thomas 1747-1833 · 506

BRADFORD
Benjamin · 158

BRADLEY
Hannah 1768-1851 · 246
Martha 1774-1825 · 247
Sarah -1809 · 403
Timothy 1743-1811 · 134

BRADSTREET
Elijah 1767-1850 · 517

BRAGDON
Mary -1806 · 512

BRAGG
Ingalls 1753-1808 · 224

BRANDON
Elizabeth 1750-1788 · 319

BRATTELL

Rebecca 1776-1824 · 510

BRETT
Sybil 1756- · 212

BRICKETT
Rhoda 1769- · 396
Thomas 1778-1855 · 397

BRISTOL
Abel 1755-1830 · 499

BROCK
Thomas 1745-1811 · 255

BROWN
Abraham 1753-1824 · 244
Ebenezer 1773-1860 · 186
Enoch · 456
Hannah · 67
Hannah 1742-1779 · 171
Hephzibah 1727-1790 · 66, 265
James · 275
Joseph 1762-1829 · 240
Mary · 222
Molly -1836 · 364
Polly · 429
Sarah 1758-1801 · 105, 418

BUCHANAN
Alexander · 440

BUCKLEY
Abigail 1733-1809 · 125, 512

BURGE
Abial 1775-1775 · 355

Anna 1762-1794 · 355
Benjamin 1782-1815 · 356
Ephraim 1738-1784 · 87, 354
Ephraim 1764-1853 · 355
Jacob 1768-1809 · 355
Josiah 1766-1790 · 355
Samuel 1779-1824 · 356
Sarah 1728- · 107, 427
Sarah 1777-1825 · 355
Susannah 1773-1816 · 355

BURGESS
Freelove 1731- · 69, 282
Stephen 1751- · 282

BURK
Abigail 1761-1801 · 310
Jonathan 1733-1775 · 74, 309
Jonathan 1756- · 310
Joseph 1758-1829 · 310

BURNHAM
Betsy 1781-1840 · 406
Jeremiah 1763-1844 · 451
Lucy 1738-1826 · 104
Rachel 1796-1823 · 415
Sarah 1750- · 268

Susan · 405
BURPEE
  Mary 1791- · 414
BURT
  Experience 1776-1833 · 301
BUSWELL
  Elizabeth 1761-1832 · 256
  Richard 1761-1835 · 445
BUTLER
  Benjamin 1729-1804 · 59, 184, 243
  Benjamin 1757-1757 · 244
  Benjamin 1758-1759 · 244
  Dorcas 1766-1857 · 245
  Henry 1754-1808 · 244
  James Platt 1766-1766 · 245
  Jemima 1766-1766 · 245
  Mary 1760-1846 · 244
BUTTERS
  Abi 1800-1860 · 464
BUTTS
  James 1748- · 284

C

CALEF
  Eliza · 441
CAMPBELL
  Daniel 1777-1849 · 462
  Phebe · 224
CAPEN
  John · 74

Thomas -1808 · 403
CARLETON
  Benjamin 1736- · 83
  Benjamin 1765-1820 · 339
  Deborah 1729- · 82
  Deborah 1759-1831 · 339
  Edmund · 434
  Edward 1762-1825 · 350
  Elizabeth 1773- · 339
  Ephraim 1739- · 83
  Eunice 1754-1838 · 338
  Ezekiel 1742-1831 · 224
  Hannah 1734-1824 · 83, 339
  Hannah 1762-1842 · 339
  John 1741- · 83
  John 1770-1847 · 339
  Martha 1722-1755 · 55, 220
  Mary · 326
  Mary 1700-1726 · 18, 84
  Mary 1738-1805 · 83, 341
  Mary 1767-1814 · 339
  Samuel 1696-1767 · 16, 82
  Samuel 1731-1804 · 83, 337
  Samuel 1757- · 338
  William 1744-1791 · 83, 344
  William 1771-1805 · 344
CARPENTER
  Aaron 1763-1836 · 271

Beamsley 1743- · 214
Jemima 1743- · 251
John · 410
John 1713- · 52, 214
John 1740-1809 · 214
Joseph 1752- · 214
Simeon 1783-1862 · 303
CARR
  Naomi · 277
CARTER
  Clarissa 1815-1882 · 416
  Ephraim 1746- · 401
  Ezra 1746-1827 · 181
  Mary 1729-1793 · 114, 466
  Mary 1770-1840 · 430
  Timothy 1767-1843 · 488
CASH
  Mary P. 1775- · 288
CATE
  Shadrach 1779-1842 · 490
CAVIS
  Nathaniel 1761-1842 · 402
CHADWICK
  Betty 1756-1818 · 316
  Hannah 1752- · 423
CHAFFEE
  Abigail 1715- · 51, 210
  Dorcas 1744-1746 · 199
  Dorcas 1747- · 199
  Francis Green 1745-1786 · 200

Jemima 1741-1818 · 199
Rhoda 1751-1834 · 200
Thomas 1716-1753 · 48, 198

CHAMBERLAIN
Abiel 1737-1818 · 213
Amos 1788-1818 · 490
Betsy 1796-1825 · 491
Edmund 1702-1779 · 51, 212
Edmund 1743-1824 · 213
Irena 1765- · 207
John Abbot 1794-1853 · 491
Joseph 1789-1862 · 480
Judith 1785-1843 · 490
Moses 1757-1811 · 119, 489
Moses 1792-1866 · 491
Patty 1786-1816 · 490
Rebecca 1730-1809 · 72, 304
Rebecca 1783-1868 · 490
Samuel 1745-1812 · 164
Samuel 1799-1838 · 491
William 1734-1739 · 213
William 1741- · 213

William 1790-1860 · 490
Zerviah 1736- · 213

CHAMPION
John · 415

CHANDLER
Abel 1761-1827 · 424
Abial 1711-1780 · 47, 196
Abiel 1687-1711 · 9, 47
Abiel 1717-1752 · 25, 46, 117
Abiel 1742-1742 · 118
Abiel 1744-1776 · 118, 487
Abiel 1760-1833 · 374
Abiel 1765-1854 · 468
Abiel 1777-1851 · 470
Abigail 1767-1841 · 470
Ann 1771-1799 · 470
Daniel 1735-1795 · 114, 468
Daniel 1768-1817 · 471
David 1698- · 47, 196
David 1724-1776 · 190
David 1775- · 479
Deborah 1757- · 117, 484
Dorcas 1705-1748 · 21, 99
Dorcas 1727-1727 · 47

Eliza 1739-1812 · 109, 442
Elizabeth 1721- · 36, 152
Elizabeth 1768-1791 · 468
Hannah 1630-1711 · 1
Hannah 1690-1755 · 9, 11, 47
Hannah 1710-1784 · 46, 189
Hannah 1724- · 88, 360
Hannah 1728-1728 · 114
Hannah 1735-1791 · 147, 188
Hannah 1744- · 115
Hannah 1755- · 198
Hannah 1763-1828 · 470
Hannah 1779-1806 · 472
Hephzibah 1726-1768 · 125, 505
Hephzibah 1743-1810 · 197
Huldah 1740- · 197
Isaac 1725-1725 · 46
Isaac 1732-1817 · 188
Isaac 1754-1832 · 231
Isaac 1758-1826 · 467
Jeremiah 1763-1828 · 467
Joanna 1710-1791 · 35, 147
Joanna 1759- · 469

Index

John 1655-1721 · 3, 8
John 1677-1679 · 9
John 1679-1741 · 9
John 1680-1741 · 45
John 1702-1775 · 24, 45, 113
John 1722- · 138
John 1730-1807 · 114, 466
John 1752-1825 · 467
John 1759-1819 · 191
John 1781-1815 · 471
Joseph 1720-1745 · 43, 179
Joseph 1743-1834 · 180
Joseph 1753-1827 · 138
Joseph 1760-1826 · 467
Joshua 1705-1734 · 35, 45, 146
Joshua 1732-1807 · 147, 188, 195
Joshua 1740-1816 · 114, 471
Joshua 1776-1777 · 472
Joshua 1782- · 472
Judith 1770-1852 · 488
Lydia 1720-1803 · 46, 193
Lydia 1746- · 197
Lydia 1765-1842 · 470
Mary 1712-1728 · 46
Mary 1734- · 196
Mary 1740-1824 · 91, 189, 372
Mary 1760-1831 · 469
Mary 1764-1834 · 196
Mehitable 1717-1786 · 35, 150
Miriam 1728-1811 · 108, 428
Moses 1765-1822 · 467
Nathan 1708-1784 · 45, 187
Nathan 1730-1786 · 130, 188
Nathan 1754-1781 · 467
Nathan 1756-1837 · 195
Paul 1769-1815 · 470
Peter 1747-1776 · 118
Phebe 1715-1805 · 46, 191
Phebe 1742-1800 · 60, 189, 247
Phebe 1754-1798 · 506
Priscilla 1713-1778 · 35, 149
Priscilla 1768-1831 · 374
Rebecca 1773- · 488
Rhoda 1775-1853 · 374
Ruhamah 1772- · 472
Ruth 1770-1792 · 471
Samuel 1717-1717 · 46
Samuel 1723-1723 · 46
Sarah 1693-1737 · 10, 50
Sarah 1707-1768 · 35, 45, 146
Sarah 1749- · 118
Sarah 1751- · 131, 149
Sarah 1756-1840 · 469
Sarah 1768-1836 · 424, 488
Sarah 1774- · 472
Tabitha 1761-1839 · 468
Timothy 1733-1770 · 114, 467
Timothy 1738- · 197
Timothy 1762-1848 · 412, 468
William · 1
Zebadiah 1683-1766 · 7, 9, 29, 34
Zebadiah 1729-1775 · 147

CHAPMAN
Abigail · 442
William -1792 · 208

CHARLES
Abigail 1758-1843 · 436
John 1744-1831 · 182
Joseph 1773-1846 · 183
Samuel 1754-1843 · 182

CHASE
Elizabeth Sawyer 1782-1854 · 485
Mehitable 1768-1849 · 482

CHECKLEY
Anne 1785-1868 · 510

CHENEY
Elias 1760-1816 · 428

Index 573

Susanna 1759- · 428
CHICKERING
　Dorcas 1742-1807 ·
　219
　Elizabeth 1737-1767
　· 219
　Hannah 1730- · 218
　John 1744- · 219
　Mary 1750-1820 ·
　219
　Phebe 1751- · 219
　Samuel 1704-1787 ·
　55, 218
　Samuel 1732-1814 ·
　218
　Sarah 1735- · 218
　Susanna 1739- · 219
　Zachariah 1747- ·
　219
CHILD
　Sally -1838 · 513
CHILDS
　Asa 1743-1826 · 202
CHOATE
　Anner 1758-1798 ·
　103, 414
CHUBB
　Molly 1754- · 206
CILLEY
　Jonathan 1762-1807
　· 245
CLARK
　Abijah 1742-1818 ·
　165
　Lucy 1763-1843 ·
　504
　Lydia · 190
　Paul 1762-1808 ·
　396
CLEMENT
　Charlotte 1794-1854
　· 477

CLEMENTS
　Benjamin 1760-1853
　· 184
CLEVELAND
　Abigail 1758- · 501
CLOUGH
　Betsey 1770-1861 ·
　260
　Polly 1798-1856 ·
　491
COBURN
　Hezekiah 1748-1816
　· 323
　Jonathan 1757- · 185
　Lydia · 44
　Lydia 1739- · 185
　Mary 1745- · 211
　Patience 1768-1830
　· 371
COCHRAN
　Jane 1766-1844 ·
　154
CODMAN
　William 1748-1813 ·
　157
COLBE
　Hannah 1735- · 91,
　370
COLBURN
　Marcella 1760-1815
　· 203
　Martha 1765- · 345
COLBY
　Elizabeth 1786-1819
　· 413
　Moses 1751-1790 ·
　259
COLLINS
　Josiah 1749-1812 ·
　269
COLSON

Betsey · 430
COMBS
　Sarah Copps -1865 ·
　410
CONE
　Achsah 1789-1882 ·
　290
CONVERSE
　Sally 1781- · 307
COOK
　Elizabeth 1747- · 180
　Polly 1760-1844 ·
　343
COOKE
　Elizabeth · 344
COPP
　Elizabeth 1740-1830
　· 114, 468
　Irene 1745-1810 ·
　114, 471
CORBIN
　Abigail 1759- · 216
　Abijah 1722-1808 ·
　52, 216
　Alice 1766- · 216
　Daniel 1768- · 216
　Esther 1755- · 216
　Hannah 1750- · 216
　Jabez 1724-1774 ·
　50, 208
　Jonathan 1760- · 209
　Sarah 1764-1852 ·
　209
CORTWRIGHT
　John 1774-1822 ·
　292
COTENEY
　George · 215
COTTON
　Elizabeth 1768-1837
　· 346

COY
  Mary -1776 · 74, 311
CRAM
  Eunice 1785-1868 · 480
CRAWFORD
  Elizabeth 1760- · 450
  Sybil · 451
CROCKER
  Lois 1763-1850 · 498
  Stephen 1760- · 304
  Zebulon 1757- · 295
CROSBY
  Hannah 1773- · 371
  Mary 1786-1848 · 454
  Rachel 1751-1817 · 494
  Sarah 1694-1760 · 7, 36
CROSS
  Uriah · 254
CROWELL
  Robert · 265
  Sarah 1750-1805 · 144
CROWNINSHIELD
  Benjamin 1758-1836 · 341
  Hannah 1764-1832 · 341
  Jacob 1733-1774 · 83, 339
  John 1762-1786 · 341
CUMMINGS
  Abigail 1763-1801 · 353
  Bridget 1765-1786 · 353
  Ebenezer 1735-1778 · 86, 352
  Ebenezer 1761-1842 · 352

Elizabeth 1759-1812 · 352
Jacob Abbot 1772-1820 · 353
Jonathan · 240
Lucy 1767-1854 · 353
Lydia 1769-1813 · 236
Mary 1770-1856 · 353
Mary 1775-1852 · 389
Phebe 1770-1843 · 185
Polly 1767- · 237
Sarah 1775- · 353
CUMMINS
  Elizabeth · 398
CURRIER
  Esther 1787- · 410
  Mary 1776- · 403
  Mehitable · 441
  Reuben -1827 · 318
CURRY
  Sarah 1752- · 423
CURTIS
  John 1743-1826 · 492
  William 1774-1860 · 303
CUSHING
  John 1749-1833 · 225
CUTLER
  Abigail 1711- · 49
  Abigial 1711- · 200
CUTTER
  John 1780-1857 · 465
CUTTS
  Mary 1763-1796 · 234

D

DALE
  Hannah 1763- · 459
  Joshua 1765-1845 · 459
  Samuel 1767- · 459
  Timothy 1733- · 113, 458
  Timothy 1762-1830 · 459
DALTON
  Thomas · 503
DAMON
  Elizabeth (-) · 39, 166
DANE
  Dorcas 1769-1854 · 146
  Dorcas 1771- · 381
  Francis · 1
  Hannah 1776- · 381
  John · 36
  John 1779- · 381
  Joseph 1723-1807 · 145
  Lydia 1769- · 381
  Mary 1733-1824 · 218
  Phebe 1767- · 381
  Philemon 1742-1816 · 150
  Timothy 1773- · 381
  William 1728- · 93, 380
DANFORTH
  Anna 1744-1813 · 425
  David 1746-1815 · 425
  Hannah 1698-1788 · 18, 89
  Jonathan 1714-1747 · 106, 425

Jonathan 1745-1839 · 425

DARLING
  Benjamin 1728-1783 · 141

DAVIS
  Abigail -1831 · 153
  Deborah 1757- · 401
  Judith -1808 · 441
  Samuel 1759-1848 · 431

DAY
  Elizabeth 1773-1857 · 183
  Jane 1794- · 414
  Mary 1768-1840 · 183

DEARBORN
  Elizabeth 1772-1855 · 443
  Henry -1829 · 221

DENISON
  Daniel 1730-1823 · 123, 504
  Daniel 1755-1822 · 504
  Dyer 1767-1772 · 505
  Hannah 1757-1784 · 281, 505
  Sarah · 292

DIMOND
  Jacob · 416

DODGE
  Amos 1769- · 169

DOOLITTLE
  Joel 1752-1829 · 172

DOUGLAS
  William 1761-1827 · 350

DOUGLASS
  William · 368

DOWNER
  Mary -1766 · 71, 294
  Sarah · 14

DOWNING
  Samuel 1765-1836 · 482

DOYNE
  Francis 1767- · 433
  Hannah 1772- · 433
  Jacob 1729-1799 · 108, 431
  Jacob 1759- · 432
  Martha 1760-1776 · 432
  Nathaniel 1767-1841 · 433
  Samuel 1764-1832 · 433

DRESSER
  Stephen 1754-1829 · 262

DUMMER
  Gorham 1782-1805 · 443

DUNTON
  Levinia · 298
  Samuel 1749-1813 · 497

DURKEE
  Amasa 1754-1827 · 502
  Eleanor 1758- · 503
  Elizabeth 1774- · 504
  Hannah 1781-1857 · 504
  Henry 1749-1820 · 294
  John 1760-1761 · 503
  John 1762-1838 · 271

Lois 1752- · 502
Olive 1756-1846 · 503
Pearl 1769-1826 · 503
Phebe 1771-1856 · 503
Phineas 1730-1801 · 123, 501
Phineas 1762- · 503
Robert 1765- · 503
Stephen 1766-1845 · 503
Wilkes 1768-1844 · 288

DUTTON
  Lucy 1781-1851 · 277

E

EAMES
  Sarah -1858 · 181

EAMS
  Mehitable 1713-1782 · 75, 313
  Nathan 1738 · 315

EASTMAN
  Abiather 1745-1815 · 258
  Abigail 1759-1836 · 259
  Betsy · 409
  Cyrus 1767- · 263
  Daniel 1766-1844 · 262
  Elizabeth 1761- · 424
  Enoch 1725- · 65, 259
  Enoch 1752-1756 · 259

Enoch 1757- · 259
Esther 1761-1846 · 165
Ezra 1754- · 259
Ezra 1764-1816 · 260
James 1775-1778 · 263
Jeremiah · 399
Jeremy 1771-1846 · 263
Joseph 1768-1823 · 260
Lucy 1763-1816 · 260
Mary 1758-1831 · 423
Mehitable 1707- · 21, 99
Rebeckah 1762- · 260
Richard 1712-1807 · 65, 261
Samuel 1760- · 260
Sarah 1737-1757 · 114, 468
Sarah 1761-1828 · 284
Sarah 1771- · 261
Simeon 1755- · 259
Susannah 1769-1770 · 263
Tamison 1766- · 260

EATON
Anna · 409
Hannah · 457
Jerusha 1737- · 111, 454
Joshua 1778-1840 · 475
Molly 1769-1825 · 260
Thomas 1771- · 261

EDMUND
Hannah -1808 · 67, 267

EDWARDS
Abigail 1758-1816 · 499

EELS
Patty 1787- · 312

ELA
Susan 1795- · 420

ELDRIDGE
Zoeth · 498

ELLIOT
Samuel 1778-1851 · 490

ELLIS
Hannah 1727-1767 · 42, 178

ELLSWORTH
Daniel 1758-1798 · 289

ELWELL
Henry Butler 1746- · 323

EMERY
Dorcas · 228
Elizabeth 1771-1827 · 447
Hannah Tracy 1771-1793 · 349
Joshua 1788-1870 · 491
Susannah 1759-1842 · 320

ENDICOTT
Robert 1756-1819 · 238

ERSKINE
Deborah 1755-1843 · 212

EVANS
Betsy · 406

EVERDEN
John · 160

F

FAIRCHILD
Mary Andrews -1813 · 408

FARLEY
Thomas 1769-1832 · 355

FARMER
Caleb 1767- · 379
Edward · 93, 378
Hannah 1767-1856 · 473
Jeremiah 1771-1836 · 473
Lydia 1763- · 379
Mary · 83, 344
Molly 1760- · 379
Oliver 1728-1814 · 115, 472
Phebe 1761- · 379
Rebecca 1768-1792 · 473
Sarah 1758- · 379
Timothy 1765- · 379

FARNSWORTH
William 1737- · 197
William 1766- · 333

FARNUM
Abigail 1692- · 13, 63
Abigail 1767- · 161
Abner 1748-1820 · 431
Betty 1743-1821 · 98, 398
David 1775- · 448
Dorcas 1766- · 380
Elizabeth 1711-1780 · 78, 319
Isaac 1742-1823 · 221
Israel 1758- · 380
John 1779- · 448
Judith 1764- · 467

Lydia 1756- · 379, 385
Lydia 1777- · 448
Mary 1764-1816 · 402
Mary 1770-1809 · 380
Mary 1814-1898 · 489
Naomi 1760-1832 · 467
Phebe · 361
Phebe 1731-1806 · 96, 386
Phebe 1762- · 380
Samuel 1743- · 110, 448
Samuel 1767-1813 · 448
Sarah 1661-1726 · 4, 17
Sarah 1764- · 380
Sarah 1773- · 448
Susanna · 43, 182
Susannah 1772- · 380
Theodore 1749-1789 · 193
Thomas 1734- · 93, 379
Timothy 1759- · 380
Zebadiah 1769-1854 · 448
Zebadiah 1781- · 399
Zerviah 1752-1818 · 256
FARRAR
Mary 1747-1815 · 170
FARRINGTON
Affa 1756-1788 · 320

Hannah · 429
Hannah 1765-1825 · 467
Lydia 1735- · 39, 165
Martha 1741- · 321
Thomas 1736-1808 · 223
FARROR
Sally 1776-1815 · 478
FAULKNER
Abiel 1755-1818 · 391, 394
Mary 1781-1840 · 444
FELLOWS
Eleazer 1772- · 303
FENTON
Abigail 1730-1776 · 69, 280
Francis 1718- · 71, 294
Francis 1751- · 294
Mary 1749-1822 · 294
FISH
Elizabeth (widow) · 516
FISK
Ebenezer 1766-1857 · 457
William · 442
FISKE
Hephzibah 1773-1800 · 248
Isabella 1757-1808 · 244
Jonathan · 144
Phebe 1712-1802 · 30, 129
FITCH

Elizabeth 1739-1807 · 94, 381
Samuel 1736-1809 · 140
FLANDERS
Abner 1754-1843 · 469
Oliver 1765-1838 · 470
Patience 1758-1834 · 402
Richard 1752-1841 · 469
FLETCHER
Phineas 1757-1833 · 355
FLINT
Lucy 1767-1839 · 269
FOLANSBEE
Judith 1782-1864 · 243
FORD
Abraham 1764-1813 · 273
Ella 1775-1857 · 274
FOSTER
Abiel 1735-1806 · 133
Asa 1710-1787 · 30, 132
Asa 1733-1814 · 133
Benjamin 1747- · 134
Clarissa 1785-1873 · 473
Daniel 1737-1833 · 133
David 1740-1740 · 134
David 1741-1810 · 134

Dudley 1738- · 127, 517
Elizabeth 1744-1775 · 134, 319
Hannah 1754-1794 · 231
Hannah 1756-1830 · 239
Isaac 1751- · 388
John · 326
Jonathan 1747-1818 · 134
Mary · 518
Mary 1698-1784 · 20, 92
Mary 1763-1834 · 239
Mary 1797-1870 · 491
Mehitable 1772-1859 · 517
Obadiah 1741- · 195
Phebe · 518
Rachel · 518
Sarah 1750-1825 · 134
Sarah 1750-1830 · 134
Sarah 1765-1807 · 240
Sarah 1774-1820 · 347
William 1730-1803 · 58, 238
William 1758-1843 · 239
FOWLE
  Jacob 1749- · 135
  Jacob -1774 · 34
FOX
  Elizabeth 1794-1840 · 415
FRANCIS
  Anna -1857 · 402
FRANKLIN
  John 1749-1831 · 287
FRENCH
  Joanna 1729-1768 · 42, 176
  Lucy 1755- · 427
  Samuel 1762-1799 · 260
FROST
  Dorcas · 33
  Samuel -1796 · 184
  William 1754-1836 · 237
FRYE · 45
  Dorcas 1750-1821 · 224
  Elizabeth 1735-1807 · 223
  Elizabeth 1767-1841 · 364
  Hannah 1683-1727 · 9, 45
  Hannah 1744-1824 · 224
  Huldah 1737- · 55, 220
  James 1710-1776 · 55, 222
  James 1731-1804 · 218
  James 1741-1826 · 223, 314
  Johanna 1737-1767 · 223
  Jonathan 1742-1793 · 224
  Lucy 1778- · 374
  Mary 1725-1797 · 79, 324
  Molly 1752-1796 · 224
  Peter 1771-1843 · 395
  Samuel 1729-1819 · 223
  Sarah 1739-1785 · 223
  Theophilus 1753-1830 · 241
FULLER
  Aaron 1773-1847 · 475
  Abigail 1752-1834 · 287
  Alice 1741-1816 · 70, 290
  Hannah 1772-1817 · 288
  John 1762-1817 · 288
  Joseph 1739-1805 · 270
  Josiah 1764-1835 · 271
  Mary 1759- · 287
  Reuben 1769-1837 · 288
  Stephen 1730-1813 · 70, 285
  Stephen 1755-1778 · 287
  Thomas 1757-1778 · 287
FURBUSH
  Anna 1768- · 368

G

GARDNER
  Stephen · 291
GARVIN
  Betty 1770- · 433
  Ebenezer 1768- · 433
  John 1764-1826 · 429
GASSET
  Lotan 1771-1861 · 477

Index

GAYLORD
Mary -1809 · 312
GEARY
Elizabeth 1661-1712 · 4, 12
GEORGE
Betsey 1776-1832 · 448
David 1745-1816 · 110, 446
David 1767-1838 · 447
Dolly 1774-1861 · 448
Hannah 1768- · 447
Jane 1772- · 447
Rebecca · 424
GERRISH
Martha 1809-1867 · 491
GIBSON
Barnabas 1767-1852 · 459
GILBERT
Elizabeth 1790-1857 · 454
GILE
Mary 1755-1822 · 413
Mary -1822 · 103
GILMORE
Betsey 1809- · 511
Esther · 223
GLAZIER
Daniel 1776-1852 · 303
GOLDSMITH
Benjamin 1755-1817 · 146
GOODALE
Chloe 1755-1833 · 294
Lois 1764-1842 · 299
Sally -1831 · 298
GOODELL
Esther 1735-1778 · 79, 329
Esther 1776- · 309
Lucy · 328
Zedekiah 1769-1863 · 309
GOODWIN
James 1714-1776 · 41, 170
John 1753-1801 · 172
Patty -1771 · 423
Rebecca 1751- · 172
Sally 1770-1801 · 467
Tabitha 1756-1825 · 172
GORDON
Bethiah · 182
GOSS
Nathaniel 1788-1855 · 420
Peter 1737- · 156
GOULD
Sarah · 309
Sarah 1760- · 264
GRAFFAM
Peter · 228
GRAHAM
Azubah · 193
Joshua 1763-1830 · 470
GRAVES
Dorcas 1655-1740 · 4, 10
Gideon 1758- · 333
Hannah 1657-1726 · 4, 19
Sarah 1765- · 165
GRAY
Elizabeth 1700-1765 · 14, 66
Hannah 1675-1763 · 5, 21
Hannah 1773- · 455
Margaret 1768-1824 · 424
Mary · 424
Mary 1743-1775 · 155
Samuel 1711- · 37
Samuel 1711-1769 · 155
Samuel 1737-1737 · 155
Sarah 1739-1740 · 155
Sarah 1741-1746 · 155
GREELEY
Bridget · 159
Samuel 1752-1798 · 159
GREEN
Abigail 1728- · 320
Anna 1762- · 427
Eleazer 1753-1824 · 427
Esther 1753-1839 · 74, 311
Isaac 1757-1821 · 514
Jacob 1750-1815 · 434
John 1736-1799 · 171
Lydia 1765-1834 · 508

Susanna 1746- · 126, 513
William 1755-1843 · 512
GREENLEAF
Hannah · 105, 418
GREENOUGH
Anna 1754-1830 · 492
Mehitable Frost 1800-1887 · 420
GRIFFIN
Abigail 1764-1860 · 184
Elizabeth 1758- · 184
Hannah 1754- · 184
James -1815 · 44, 183
Mary 1768- · 184
Phebe 1751- · 183, 243
Sarah 1764- · 184
GRIGGS
Sarah 1776- · 208
GRISWOLD
Martha · 408
GROSVENOR
Joshua 1758-1838 · 328
Olive 1760-1782 · 327
GUTTERSON
Simeon 1769- · 485

H

HADLEY
Enos · 379
Enos 1755-1838 · 379
HALE
Rebekah 1781-1860 · 358

HALL
Abiel 1761-1829 · 402
Abigail 1734-1804 · 42, 176
Benjamin · 325
Daniel 1755-1835 · 401
Deborah 1769-1791 · 402
Dorcas 1751-1813 · 401
Ebenezer 1721-1801 · 99, 400
Ebenezer 1778-1853 · 419
Hannah 1740-1746 · 101
Hannah 1764-1765 · 402
Hannah 1766- · 402
Hephzibah 1747-1817 · 401
James 1784- · 419
Jeremiah 1746-1770 · 101
Joseph 1707-1784 · 22, 100
Joseph 1737-1807 · 101
Lydia 1767-1855 · 402
Mary 1743-1773 · 101, 406
Obadiah 1748-1831 · 401
Sarah 1738-1746 · 101
Sarah 1753-1845 · 401
Sarah 1771-1824 · 456
Stephen 1759-1808 · 402

Susannah 1781-1867 · 399
Timothy 1757- · 402
HAMILTON
Samuel 1752-1810 · 494
HAMMOND
Jerusha · 223
HANKEY
Mary -1812 · 503
HARDY
Benjamin 1768-1834 · 381
Susan 1773-1841 · 470
HARE
Stephen 1755- · 284
HARNDEN
Elizabeth 1672-1756 · 6, 7, 29
Hephzibah 1688-1783 · 9, 47
HARRIMAN
Mary 1783-1844 · 471
HARRINGTON
Nathan 1762-1818 · 279
HARRIS
John Moore 1784-1832 · 487
Mary 1779- · 487
Rachel · 327
Sarah · 260
William · 117, 486
HARTSHORN
Aaron 1754-1799 · 363
William 1753-1831 · 82
HARVEY
Lucy 1768-1849 · 409
HASELITNE

Benjamin · 414
HASTINGS
  Keziah 1723- · 106, 422
  Moses -1815 · 264
HATHORNE
  Sarah 1761-1829 · 341
HAWKS
  Sarah · 332
HAYS
  David · 228
HAYSE
  John -1848 · 504
HAZELTINE
  Abigail 1758-1785 · 434
  Anna 1760-1838 · 434
  Ballard 1769-1836 · 435
  Betty 1771- · 435
  Hannah 1767- · 435
  Joseph 1731-1798 · 109, 433
  Nathaniel 1774-1796 · 435
  Peter 1762-1779 · 434
  Richard 1742-1817 · 401
  Samuel 1745- · 173
  Sarah 1755- · 434
  Susanna 1765- · 435
  William 1744- · 401
HEACOCK
  David · 268
HEATON
  Irene 1774-1840 · 264
HELME

Hugh -1792 · 339
HENDRICK
  Caleb 1767-1837 · 309, 311
  Elizabeth 1775-1857 · 309
  Ezra 1762-1770 · 308
  Ezra 1772-1799 · 309
  Hannah 1770-1843 · 309
  John 1722-1810 · 74, 308
  John 1764-1826 · 308
  Mary 1765- · 308
HENFIELD
  Lydia (-) · 38
HERRICK
  Benjamin 1752-1782 · 137
HEWETT
  Anna 1754-1796 · 280
HIBBARD
  Abigail 1749- · 500
  Daniel · 325
  Elizabeth 1751-1754 · 500
  James 1753- · 500
  John 1727-1804 · 123, 500
  John 1755-1800 · 501
  Timothy 1750-1750 · 500
  Timothy 1757-1758 · 501
  Timothy 1759- · 501
HIBBERT

Dorcas 1675-1743 · 5, 22
HIDDEN
  Mehitable · 255
HILDRETH
  Benjamin 1754-1754 · 366
  Robert 1713-1760 · 90, 365
HILL
  Esther · 494
  Judith 1779-1813 · 337
  Mary · 226
  Timothy 1776-1850 · 337
HINCKLEY
  David 1754-1835 · 300
  Mercy -1781 · 497
HINKLEY
  Sarah 1774-1865 · 410
HOBART
  Sarah 1745-1827 · 421
HOBBS
  Hannah · 39
  Hannah 1729- · 163
HOIT
  Amos 1800- · 416
HOLBROOK
  Calvin 1758-1845 · 330
HOLDEN
  Hannah 1776-1855 · 453
HOLMAN
  Elizabeth 1762-1801 · 339
HOLMES

582 Index

Chandler 1750-1755 · 203
Dorothy 1745- · 203
Ebenezer 1721-1794 · 49, 202
Ebenezer 1748-1810 · 203
Huldah 1756-1853 · 203
Joanna 1765-1828 · 351
Phebe 1743-1828 · 203

HOLT
Abel 1770- · 296
Abiah 1761-1841 · 388
Abiel 1698-1772 · 14, 70
Abiel 1727-1785 · 71, 294
Abiel 1746-1824 · 241
Abiel 1748-1811 · 142, 261
Abiel 1762-1829 · 296
Abiel 1765- · 390
Abiel 1780-1826 · 307
Abigail 1758-1824 · 231
Abigail 1767- · 299
Abigail 1767-1821 · 386
Alice 1747-1814 · 293
Andrew 1768-1853 · 296
Anna (-) -1797 · 296
Anna 1735-1806 · 72, 300
Anna 1762- · 304
Anne 1784-1855 · 303

Asa 1768- · 184
Asenath 1786-1813 · 303
Bathsheba 1770-1790 · 300
Benjamin 1741- · 361
Bethiah 1764-1833 · 296
Caleb 1729-1810 · 71, 297
Caleb 1759-1826 · 298
Chloe 1775-1849 · 390
Clarissa 1775-1840 · 307
Dane 1740-1818 · 194
Daniel 1733-1796 · 96, 390
Daniel 1744-1813 · 153
Daniel 1761-1830 · 390
Daniel 1767-1854 · 168
David 1792- · 336
Dinah 1726-1806 · 122, 496
Dinah 1750-1826 · 270
Dorcas 1727- · 96, 384
Dorcas 1753- · 386
Dorcas 1756-1778 · 231
Dorcas 1767-1800 · 271
Ebenezer 1705- · 16, 80
Ebenezer 1730-1805 · 81, 334
Ebenezer 1778- · 337

Elijah 1757-1817 · 298
Elizabeth 1718-1776 · 95, 383
Elizabeth 1725-1753 · 71, 294
Elizabeth 1743-1838 · 131
Elizabeth 1751-1777 · 231
Elizabeth 1756- · 298
Elizabeth 1773- · 336
Elizabeth 1777- · 303
Ephraim 1769-1836 · 389
Esther 1774- · 307
Eunice 1772- · 297
Ezekiel 1741- · 81, 336
Ezekiel 1782-1845 · 336
Ezra 1762- · 381
Hannah 1709-1775 · 30, 130
Hannah 1723-1751 · 71, 293
Hannah 1739-1831 · 96, 390
Hannah 1745-1754 · 293
Hannah 1745-1818 · 190
Hannah 1749- · 82
Hannah 1756-1832 · 295, 497
Hannah 1764-1855 · 271
Hannah 1769-1857 · 238, 388
Hannah 1771- · 302
Hannah 1771-1842 · 389
Hephzibah 1748-1851 · 82

Isaac 1738-1822 · 72, 301
Isaac 1763-1813 · 302
Jacob 1739-1816 · 139
James 1723-1812 · 56, 86, 95, 230, 351
James 1733- · 81, 335
James 1746-1818 · 72, 306
James 1749-1800 · 231
James 1764-1766 · 298
James 1770-1856 · 306
Jedediah 1744-1790 · 317
Jeremiah 1734- · 131
Jesse 1755- · 335
Joel 1753-1755 · 231
John 1765-1835 · 234, 389
John 1774-1776 · 300
John 1776-1841 · 307
Joseph 1716-1754 · 33, 140
Joseph 1744- · 141
Joseph 1766-1791 · 386
Joseph 1770-1816 · 306
Joshua 1729-1791 · 67, 270
Joshua 1730-1810 · 96, 386

Joshua 1758-1835 · 388
Joshua 1763-1790 · 298
Keturah 1729-1805 · 123
Keturah 1758-1839 · 271
Lemuel 1756-1836 · 271, 275
Leonard 1782-1857 · 303
Loammi 1775-1827 · 487
Lois 1760- · 386
Luce 1778-1847 · 307
Lydia 1767-1825 · 389
Lydia 1781- · 337
Mary 1739-1787 · 68, 276
Mary 1742-1823 · 72, 305
Mary 1745-1814 · 141
Mary 1752-1824 · 270
Mary 1758- · 386
Mary 1759-1760 · 295
Mary 1759-1819 · 388
Mary 1760- · 296
Mary 1761-1850 · 238
Mary 1773-1861 · 303
Mary 1775- · 336
Mehitable 1733-1767 · 81, 335

Mehitable 1768-1857 · 460
Mercy 1741-1799 · 293
Moses 1765-1819 · 302
Nathan 1725-1792 · 58, 95, 237
Nathan 1733-1800 · 71, 298
Nathan 1761-1820 · 299
Nathan 1767-1778 · 390
Nathaniel 1769-1829 · 517
Nicholas 1683-1756 · 21, 95
Oliver 1775-1869 · 303
Paul 1743-1827 · 270
Peter 1763-1851 · 238, 388
Phebe 1756-1849 · 388
Priscilla 1709-1803 · 45, 187
Priscilla 1737 · 81
Rachel 1737-1737 · 81
Rachel 1741- · 81
Rachel 1776-1860 · 337
Rebecca 1752-1782 · 334
Reuben 1744-1836 · 81, 336
Reuben 1775-1836 · 337
Ruth 1765- · 145
Sara 1746- · 360

Sarah 1746- · 142
Sarah 1747-1808 · 131, 231
Sarah 1748-1777 · 294
Sarah 1757- · 295, 334
Sarah 1758-1841 · 237
Sarah 1761-1813 · 271
Sarah 1769-1836 · 302
Sarah 1772-1851 · 337
Sarah 1775-1833 · 284
Sarah 1780- · 336
Solomon 1768-1830 · 389
Solomon 1772-1838 · 307
Stephen 1773-1868 · 389
Susanna 1760-1760 · 231
Thomas 1712-1776 · 96, 384
Thomas 1750- · 379, 385
Timothy 1721-1801 · 95, 383
Timothy 1739-1807 · 72, 304
Timothy 1765-1850 · 304
Timothy 1767-1856 · 389
Uriah 1754-1828 · 271
William 1720-1793 · 71, 293
William 1743-1815 · 293
William 1763- · 386
William 1783-1811 · 337
Zela 1738- · 132
Zerviah 1689-1768 · 18, 87

HOPKINS
Betsy 1792-1852 · 486
James · 422
John · 475
Lavina 1769-1843 · 455
Olive 1769-1864 · 455

HORTON
Mary 1759-1833 · 273

HOUGHTON
Jonas -1791 · 201
Nahum -1800 · 434

HOUSTON
Isaac 1760-1833 · 412

HOVEY
Benjamin 1775-1866 · 247
Elizabeth 1771-1845 · 247
Henry Abbott 1764-1830 · 246
James Platts 1767-1831 · 246
John 1765- · 246
Joseph 1784-1860 · 247
Joshua 1778-1804 · 247
Mary 1769-1837 · 246
Mary 1781- · 247
Rebeckah 1777-1853 · 246
Ruth 1754-1832 · 281
Samuel 1773- · 247
Thomas 1736-1826 · 59, 245
Thomas 1762-1812 · 246

HOWARD
Abigail 1771-1852 · 159

HOWE
Experience 1771-1857 · 429
Phebe 1763-1842 · 281, 505
Phineas 1769-1847 · 404

HOYT
Abner 1759-1852 · 424
James 1762-1834 · 405
Naomi · 16

HUBBARD
Joel 1784- · 312
John 1761- · 495
Susan · 236

HUNT
Eunice 1730-1827 · 83, 338
Lewis 1746-1797 · 343
Thomas · 36

HUTCHINS
Joshua 1747- · 500

HUTCHINSON
Eleazer 1745-1824 · 205
Jonathan 1747- · 151
Luther 1783-1861 · 486
Obadiah/Diah -1843 · 415
Thomas · 219

I

ILSLEY
  Enoch 1730-1811 · 322

INGALLS
  Abiah 1731- · 79, 331
  Alfred 1765-1843 · 326
  Alice 1764-1838 · 330
  Allethiah 1774- · 331
  Asa 1756-1775 · 272
  Calvin 1760-1830 · 273
  Charles 1763-1812 · 326
  Charles 1768-1772 · 328
  Chester 1762-1842 · 273
  Chloe · 331
  Darius 1754-1824 · 272
  Deborah 1722-1752 · 79
  Deborah 1753-1779 · 325
  Deborah 1757-1811 · 328
  Dorcas 1751-1821 · 325
  Dorcas 1755-1764 · 327
  Dorcas 1772-1774 · 329
  Dorcus 1754- · 272
  Edmund 1770-1850 · 328
  Elizabeth 1762- · 516
  Ephraim 1695-1767 · 16
  Ephraim 1723-1725 · 79
  Ephraim 1725-1805 · 326
  Ephraim 1725-1809 · 79
  Ephraim 1764- · 328
  Esther 1762-1851 · 266, 330
  Francis 1694-1759 · 27
  Hannah 1748-1811 · 325
  Hannah 1759-1838 · 388
  Hannah 1769-1791 · 273
  Harvey 1775-1833 · 274
  Isaac 1733- · 197
  James 1695-1767 · 78
  James 1720-1804 · 79, 324
  James 1747-1748 · 325
  James 1755-1775 · 325
  James 1760-1813 · 330
  John 1776-1777 · 331
  Joseph 1723-1790 · 67, 272
  Joseph Royall 1764- · 273
  Joshua 1732-1785 · 127, 516
  Joshua 1757-1759 · 325
  Joshua 1759-1761 · 325
  Lemuel 1755-1839 · 330
  Luther 1758-1855 · 273
  Lydia 1767-1810 · 326
  Mary 1727-1751 · 79
  Mary 1745-1811 · 325
  Mary 1752-1764 · 327
  Mary 1768-1839 · 330
  Molly 1766- · 328
  Olive 1766- · 330
  Olive 1772- · 331
  Oliver 1770-1815 · 331
  Peter 1752-1808 · 272
  Peter 1766- · 516
  Phebe 1725- · 38
  Phebe 1725-1772 · 159
  Phebe 1750-1759 · 272
  Phebe 1768-1847 · 517
  Rhoda 1759-1764 · 328
  Sarah 1761-1849 · 325
  Sarah 1762-1807 · 328
  Sarah 1766-1833 · 273
  Silvanius 1759-1776 · 330
  Simeon 1736-1753 · 80

Simeon 1754-1827 · 327
Simeon 1764- · 516
Stephen 1761- · 516
Zebadiah 1729-1800 · 79, 329
Zebadiah 1757-1779 · 330
INGERSOLL
John 1756-1840 · 343
Josiah · 273

J

JACKMAN
Jane 1767-1847 · 103, 414
JACKSON
Jeremiah 1739-1802 · 201
JAQUITH
Judith 1777-1843 · 250
JEFTS
Alice 1756- · 173
Elizabeth 1746- · 173
Henry 1717-1772 · 41, 172
Henry 1748- · 173
John 1744-1750 · 173
Mary 1750- · 173
JENKINS
Lois 1767-1846 · 247
Micah 1786- · 486
JENKS
John 1751-1817 · 234
JENNE
Lot 1760- · 309
JEWELL

Asahel 1744-1790 · 212
Thomas -1753 · 52
JEWETT
Joseph 1740-1814 · 170
JOHNSON
Amos · 172
Anna 1737- · 148
David · 508
John -1814 · 515
John -1833 · 132
Jonathan 1753-1820 · 256
Samuel · 498
JONES
David 1741- · 370
Ebenezer 1757-1819 · 146
Elizabeth · 386
Joel · 278
Mary · 390
Nathan 1767-1804 · 380
Zadoc 1773-1823 · 478, 479
JUDKINS
Jemima -1853 · 151

K

KELLEY
John 1764- · 365
KENNEDY
James 1775-1864 · 293
KENNEY
Thomas -1814 · 198
KENNY
David · 474
KEYES
Abijah 1773-1845 · 463

KIDDER
Ephraim 1766-1807 · 178
John 1709- · 64, 253
John 1735- · 253
KILBURN
Mercy · 102, 408
KILGORE
Betsey 1776-1873 · 263
Trueworthy · 404
KIMBALL
Daniel 1755-1843 · 388
David 1757- · 412
Eliza · 151
Eliza 1787-1870 · 444
Hannah 1731- · 76, 317
Lydia 1761 · 516
Mary · 467
Sally Welch 1786-1850 · 239
Samuel 1761- · 499
Thomas 1753-1825 · 154
William -1813 · 182
KING
Betsy 1764- · 460
Lucy 1760-1842 · 138
Ruth 1779- · 296
KINGSBURY
Eunice 1733-1784 · 71, 295
Lydia 1737-1776 · 72, 299
KINGSLEY
Elizabeth 1747-1835 · 213
KINNEY
Nathan 1778-1856 · 504

Index

KITTREDGE
  Hannah 1742- · 133
KNAPP
  Betsey 1782-1831 · 398
KNEELAND
  John 1748-1831 · 249
  Mary 1720- · 37
  Mary 1721- · 156
  Sally 1769-1861 · 507
KNIGHT
  Susanna Noyes 1770-1851 · 182

L

LADD
  John 1755-1835 · 151
LAKEMAN
  Amos 1762-1850 · 154
LAKIN
  David 1753-1846 · 426
LAMBERT
  Mary 1760-1851 · 341
LAMSON
  Jonathan 1756- · 334
LANE
  David 1759-1842 · 383
  Dorcas 1771-1849 · 383
  Ephraim 1767-1837 · 371

  Hannah 1734-1769 · 94
  Hannah 1765-1848 · 366, 382
  John 1691-1763 · 20, 94
  John 1720-1789 · 90, 365
  Jonathan 1763-1808 · 366, 382
  Josiah 1762-1762 · 366
  Mary 1776-1815 · 383
  Phebe 1773-1838 · 383
  Samuel 1737-1822 · 94, 381
  Sarah 1765-1849 · 366
LANGDON
  Mary 1782-1863 · 467
LATHROP
  Seth 1762-1831 · 281
LAWRENCE
  Deborah · 512
  Jerusha · 501
  Joseph 1745-1775 · 253
  Rebecca 1724- · 107, 426
  Ruth 1758-1825 · 514
  Samuel · 63, 252
LAWS
  James 1742-1821 · 425
LEACH
  Anna · 50, 204
  Mary · 26

  Mary 1719-1790 · 122
  Robert · 215
LEAVITT
  Jeremiah 1749-1818 · 181
LEE
  Lodema 1757- · 272
LEMAN
  Hannah 1751-1815 · 425
LEONARD
  Dorothy 1759-1796 · 333
LIVERMORE
  Jonathan 1770-1845 · 358
  William 1770-1846 · 513
LOVEJOY
  Abiel 1737-1817 · 192
  Abigail 1750-1833 · 153
  Betsey 1795-1828 · 446
  Caleb 1716-1781 · 35, 151
  Caleb 1749-1821 · 151
  Catherine · 347
  Chandler 1742-1827 · 193
  Chandler 1744-1810 · 153
  Chloe 1753-1843 · 241
  David 1715- · 36, 152
  David 1767-1819 · 154
  Dorcas 1739- · 192

Dorcas 1749-1843 · 125, 241, 505
Dorcas 1758- · 154
Elizabeth 1738- · 151
Elizabeth 1742-1815 · 153
Esther 1764- · 154
Hannah 1724-1813 · 57, 232
Hannah 1748-1812 · 127, 518
Hannah 1749-1809 · 193
Henry 1714-1793 · 46, 191
Henry 1744- · 193
Henry 1746-1747 · 193
Henry 1753- · 352
Henry 1781-1863 · 359
Jerusha 1753-1841 · 151
Jonathan 1748-1758 · 319
Joshua 1719-1812 · 59, 240
Joshua 1744-1832 · 240
Lucy 1755-1802 · 241
Lucy 1757-1802 · 162
Lydia 1747- · 241
Martha 1720-1768 · 87, 359
Martha 1752- · 154
Martha 1755- · 152, 376
Mary 1745-1826 · 240
Mehitable 1745-1835 · 151
Molly 1748-1813 · 153
Moses 1751- · 386
Nancy · 446
Nathaniel 1699-1768 · 77
Nathaniel 1699-1769 · 318
Nathaniel 1744-1812 · 134, 319
Obadiah 1756- · 152
Olive 1756-1843 · 154
Phebe 1715-1751 · 12, 60
Phebe 1735-1789 · 103, 192, 411
Phebe 1754-1804 · 154
Priscilla 1746-1832 · 153
Samuel 1750-1801 · 137
Sarah 1752-1815 · 193
Sarah 1765- · 160
LOVITT
Lydia 1769-1857 · 503
LUCE
Polly · 285
LUFKIN
Benjamin 1763-1844 · 403
Solomon 1747-1780 · 502
LUMMUS
Samuel 1751-1810 · 233
LYON
Robert 1743-1809 · 293

M

MANN
Sarah 1764-1841 · 135
MANNING
Ann 1767-1850 · 429
Jesse 1745-1825 · 162
Priscilla 1733-1804 · 232
MANSFIELD
Mary · 41
MANVILLE
Urania 1775-1848 · 292
MARBLE
Isaac 1740-1780 · 221
Phebe 1744-1805 · 322
MARCH
Dorcas 1746-1820 · 227
Thomas 1745- · 227
Thomas -1752 · 55, 226
MARCY
Zebadiah 1761-1851 · 498
MARSH
Eunice 1724-1760 · 66, 265
Mary · 225
MARSHALL
Deborah 1755- · 497
MARTIN
Daniel 1772-1861 · 448
Jacob 1770-1830 · 265
Jesse 1754- · 426
Nathan 1763-1834 · 474

Index

Phebe 1764-1840 · 474
Stephen · 106, 425
Stephen 1749- · 426
Susanna 1743- · 111, 452
MASON
　Margaret 1754-1817 · 271
MASSEY
　Rebecca 1772-1795 · 346
MAY
　Anna 1787-1817 · 356
MAYNARD
　Persis 1782- · 465
MCADAMS
　Mary · 158
MCCONNELL
　Betsy 1774-1866 · 265
MCDOLE
　Alexander 1760-1814 · 369
MCINTYRE
　Hugh 1754-1837 · 468
MCKEEN
　David 1750-1824 · 326
MCKINLEY
　Sarah 1789-1869 · 371
MCNINCH
　Jane 1763-1853 · 448
MELOON
　Molly 1769-1847 · 396
MERRICK

Abigail 1737-1765 · 71, 298
Anne 1756-1809 · 300
Caleb 1767-1822 · 301
Constant 1772-1830 · 301
Elizabeth 1774-1824 · 301
Hannah 1769-1842 · 301
Joseph 1733-1787 · 72, 300
Joseph 1764-1814 · 301
Mary 1726-1790 · 71, 297
Thomas 1763-1840 · 300
Timothy 1760-1810 · 300
MERRILL
　Amos 1752-1840 · 258
　Benjamin 1784-1847 · 354
　Betsey 1758- · 431
　Dorcas 1754-1841 · 431
　Elizabeth 1781-1867 · 353
　Enoch 1750- · 258
　John 1725-1758 · 431
　John 1725-1760 · 108
　John 1756- · 432
　John 1782-1855 · 354
　Lydia 1753- · 431

Lydia 1759-1839 · 431
Moses 1727-1767 · 108, 430
Moses 1751-1752 · 430
Nehemiah 1757- · 431
Penelope 1749- · 430
Penelope 1754- · 431
Phebe 1753-1839 · 258
Rebecca 1751- · 431
Sarah 1741-1810 · 114, 468
Thomas 1724-1788 · 65, 87, 257, 352
Thomas 1748- · 258
Thomas Eliphalet 1751-1830 · 394
William 1749- · 258
MERRITT
　Mabel · 281
MILLS
　Benjamin 1755- · 154
MINCHEN
　Richard -1776 · 254
MOOAR
　Benjamin 1743-1828 · 150
　Betsy 1790-1825 · 486
　Deborah 1777-1805 · 485
　Elizabeth 1748-1818 · 117, 481
　Hannah 1768- · 452
　John 1745-1777 · 117, 480

Joshua 1751-1824 · 117, 484
Joshua 1778-1831 · 485
Mary 1760-1820 · 117, 486
Sarah 1786-1857 · 486
Stephen Chandler 1780-1861 · 485
Timothy 1713-1787 · 24, 116
Timothy 1742-1817 · 116
Timothy 1783-1783 · 485
Timothy 1784-1855 · 486

MOONEY
Obadiah · 456

MOOR
Aaron · 439
Anna · 439
David · 439
Dolly · 440
Elsie -1795 · 430, 439
Ephraim · 109
Ephraim -1791 · 437
Esther · 439
Hannah 1772-1828 · 439
James · 438
Moses · 439
Patty · 439
Polly · 439
Robert 1760-1810 · 136

MOORE
Ephraim · 435
Martha 1752- · 172

MORGAN
Jeremiah 1741-1819 · 153
Mercy · 214

MORIARTY
Thomas -1790 · 343

MORRILL
John 1759-1849 · 365
Nathaniel 1761-1832 · 364

MORSE
Benjamin 1771-1849 · 448
Judith 1766- · 118, 488
Samuel 1759- · 371

MOSHER
Mary 1762-1827 · 296

MOULTON
Mary 1775-1851 · 249

MULBERRY
Sarah 1727-1815 · 58

MURRAY
Elizabeth 1741-1790 · 202
James 1737-1739 · 201
James 1743- · 202
John 1753- · 202
Matthew -1788 · 49, 201
Phebe 1739- · 201
Sarah 1746- · 202

N

NARRIMORE
Joseph 1735-1808 · 211

NASON
Dorcas · 145

NEEDHAM
Daniel -1801 · 296

NEILSON
William 1767-1830 · 439

NEWELL
Lydia 1754-1836 · 226

NICHOLS
Aaron 1757-1821 · 161
Timothy 1756-1846 · 168

NILES
James 1747-1822 · 294

NOBLE
Charlotte 1771-1805 · 301
Joanna 1769-1860 · 300

NOONING
Betsey (-) -1854 · 369

NOURSE
Lydia 1783-1874 · 475

NOYES
Abigail · 439
Benning 1780-1814 · 417
Daniel 1748- · 496
Dorcas 1785-1877 · 419
John P. 1766-1814 · 435
Sally 1768- · 435
Stephen 1783-1868 · 419
Susanna · 318

NUTTING
Ebenezer · 236
Esther · 427

NYE
Samuel 1773-1837 · 301

Index 591

O

ODELL
  Thomas 1775-1865 · 445
ORCUTT
  Mehitable 1769-1851 · 302
  Sarah 1740-1816 · 72, 302
ORDIANE
  Mary -1787 · 512
ORDWAY
  Benjamin -1849 · 260
  Enoch 1762-1843 · 164
  Martha 1753- · 362
OSGOOD
  Alfred 1773-1847 · 221
  Charlotte 1767-1783 · 221
  Christopher 1712-1748 · 40, 170
  Christopher 1743- · 171
  Christopher 1769-1841 · 393
  Dorcas 1721-1749 · 55, 226
  Dorcas 1752-1810 · 221
  Dorcas 1763-1832 · 392
  Dorcas 1770-1813 · 452
  Elizabeth 1714-1756 · 55, 222
  Elizabeth 1755-1764 · 392
  Enoch 1775-1848 · 222
  George 1758-1823 · 226
  Hannah 1710-1761 · 55, 218
  Hannah 1743- · 174
  Hannah 1748-1754 · 221
  John 1683-1765 · 11, 54
  John 1711-1775 · 55, 220
  John 1748- · 225
  John 1748-1749 · 172
  John 1750-1754 · 221
  John 1754-1820 · 226
  John 1765-1829 · 392
  John 1770-1840 · 221
  John George 1742-1754 · 226
  Joseph 1718-1797 · 55, 224
  Joseph 1746-1812 · 225
  Joseph 1760-1845 · 392
  Lydia 1754-1816 · 391
  Margaret 1760-1762 · 226
  Martha 1747-1830 · 220
  Mary 1726-1806 · 56, 227
  Mary 1740-1761 · 171
  Mary 1753-1820 · 221
  Mehitable 1749-1788 · 225
  Moses 1766-1801 · 328
  Phineas 1714-1756 · 41, 173
  Phineas 1739-1752 · 174
  Rebeckah 1746-1749 · 172
  Samuel 1714-1774 · 97, 391
  Sarah 1738-1805 · 171
  Sarah 1758-1764 · 392
  Thomas 1756-1771 · 226
  Thomas 1767-1818 · 392
OTIS
  Elizabeth 1760-1802 · 226
OWEN
  Ruth 1766-1849 · 394
OWENS
  Esther 1747-1774 · 72, 306

P

PAGE
  Abigail 1768-1795 · 326
  John 1741- · 434
PAIGE
  Susan 1786-1865 · 264

Index

PAINE
  Elizabeth 1710-1772 · 14, 73
  Huldah -1797 · 42, 178
  Polly · 207

PALFREY
  Unknown -1777 · 83, 344

PARKER
  Aaron 1759-1857 · 368
  Abigail 1742-2762 · 492
  Anna 1747-1824 · 492
  Benjamin -1801 · 90, 365
  Betsey 1783-1857 · 479
  Betsy 1775-1814 · 306
  Daniel · 190
  Daniel 1777- · 307
  Dolly 1779- · 346
  Dorcas 1769-1853 · 365, 377
  Edmund 1757-1762 · 492
  Eunice 1761-1843 · 512
  Hannah 1736-1742 · 322
  Hannah 1743-1746 · 323
  Hannah 1747-1782 · 323
  Hannah 1758-1762 · 376
  Imlah 1765-1828 · 513
  Isaac 1749-1814 · 323
  James -1801 · 240
  John 1760-1825 · 152, 376
  Jonathan 1738- · 316
  Joseph 1726- · 93, 376
  Joseph 1726-1777 · 197
  Joseph 1756-1762 · 376
  Lucy 1732- · 85, 345
  Lydea 1752-1849 · 323
  Mary 1734- · 322
  Mary 1761-1834 · 323
  Molly 1743-1842 · 492
  Molly 1766- · 377
  Nathan 1739-1819 · 322
  Nathan 1740-1779 · 492
  Peter 1714-1795 · 78, 322
  Peter 1741-1822 · 322
  Phebe 1757-1759 · 324
  Robert 1745-1818 · 323
  Samuel 1716-1796 · 121, 492
  Samuel 1753-1822 · 492
  Sarah -1816 · 369
  Simeon 1754- · 323

PARMENTER
  John Newton 1742-1828 · 135

PAUL
  Jane -1772 · 93, 377
  Margaret 1727-1806 · 73
  William · 216

PEABODY
  Anna 1723-1766 · 31, 137
  Ephraim 1776-1861 · 359
  Lydia 1731- · 81, 334
  Moses 1755-1842 · 334

PEARCE
  Olive 1738-1822 · 70, 288

PEARL
  Alice 1747-1747 · 497
  Alice 1748- · 497
  Anna 1758-1830 · 499
  Azubah 1762-1840 · 499
  Elizabeth 1730- · 123, 500
  Elizabeth 1756-1779 · 497
  Elizabeth 1757- · 499
  James 1750- · 499
  John 1726- · 123
  Joshua 1752-1837 · 497
  Lois 1753-1788 · 497
  Lydia 1734-1819 · 123, 504
  Nathan 1727- · 123, 498
  Nathan 1764-1764 · 499
  Oliver 1749-1831 · 295, 497
  Phebe 1732- · 123, 501
  Phebe 1765-1816 · 498
  Sarah 1758-1826 · 498
  Stephen 1749-1816 · 498

Timothy 1695-1773 · 26, 122
Timothy 1723-1789 · 122, 496
Timothy 1752-1839 · 499
Timothy 1760-1834 · 498
PEARSON
  Mary Holyoke 1782-1829 · 419
  Moses · 386
  Susanna · 453
PEASE
  Rhoda 1764-1821 · 459
PEAVEY
  Peter 1762-1836 · 353
PERHAM
  Mary 1749-1822 · 401
PERKINS
  Mary 1769-1863 · 349
  Sarah 1744- · 240
PERRIN
  Amos -1811 · 199
  Hannah · 456
  Lydia 1752-1829 · 363
  Persis 1742-1817 · 200
PERRY
  Clarissa 1770-1826 · 409
PERSONS
  Joseph -1812 · 72, 305
PETERS
  Beamsley 1710- · 51, 213
  Benjamin 1728- · 218
  Hannah 1730-1815 · 133
  Hannah 1735- · 214
PHELPS
  Elisha 1771-1823 · 279
  Elizabeth 1712-1787 · 63, 251
  Elizabeth 1765-1835 · 279
  Hannah 1709-1781 · 33, 138
  Hannah 1715-1747 · 63, 252
  Hannah 1745-1826 · 150
  Hannah 1769-1853 · 374
  Henry 1740-1807 · 150, 195
  Isaac 1772- · 507
  Joseph 1689-1773 · 13, 62
  Joseph 1724-1802 · 278
  Joseph 1724-1820 · 68
  Joshua 1738-1798 · 150, 194
  Lydia 1767-1834 · 279
  Polly 1775-1778 · 280
  Priscilla 1748-1799 · 150
  Samuel 1713-1795 · 35, 149
  Samuel 1736-1756 · 150
  Samuel 1773-1778 · 280
  Sarah 1717- · 63
  Thomas 1739-1795 · 149
  Tryphena 1769-1818 · 279
PHILLIPS · 57
  Gideon · 138, 460
  Mary 1694-1785 · 12, 57
PICKMAN
  Elizabeth 1782-1850 · 250
PIERCE
  Merrill 1764- · 347
PIKE
  Abigail 1791-1873 · 336
  Benjamin · 157
PIPER
  Gideon -1814 · 431
  Mehitable · 259
  Sibyl 1793- · 337
PITSON
  Hannah 1740- · 135
PLATTS
  Edna 1737- · 31, 137
  Mary 1700-1784 · 12, 59
POOL
  Mary 1770-1853 · 306
POOLE
  Sarah 1713- · 78, 321
POOR
  Chloe 1779-1867 · 483

Daniel 1740-1814 · 224
Dorothy 1716-1801 · 75, 314
Enoch 1736-1780 · 220
Hannah 1770-1861 · 349
John 1754-1823 · 241
Joseph 1748-1815 · 233
Lydia 1751-1788 · 139
Sally 1794-1882 · 484
Sarah 1750- · 219
PORTER
  Jonathan 1745-1817 · 242
  Sarah 1777-1858 · 221
  William 1761-1847 · 275
POTTER
  Elizabeth · 449
POWERS
  Sampson -1823 · 236
PRATT
  Mary S. · 446
PRESCOTT
  John 1752-1842 · 170
  Lydia 1780-1848 · 513
PRESTON
  Mary 1699-1754 · 19
  Samuel 1763- · 269
PRINCE
  Martha 1773 · 229
PROCTOR
  Hannah 1748-1842 · 425

Lucy 1746-1779 · 170
PULMAN
  Jonathan · 461
PUTNAM
  Eliphalet 1766-1826 · 358
  Nathan 1773-1842 · 455
  Phebe 1770-1827 · 390
PUTNEY
  James 1761- · 260

R

RALEIGH
  Major Miles · 428
READ
  Lemuel 1746 · 158
  Mary 1748-1792 · 158
  Olive 1757-1811 · 159
  Olive 1780-1855 · 463
  Robert 1720-1803 · 38, 158
  Robert 1748- · 158
  William 1754-1834 · 158
REED
  Benjamin 1779-1850 · 477
REYNOLDS
  Sarah · 202
RICHARDSON
  Ebenezer 1754- · 175
  Hannah 1714-1795 · 40, 169
  Josiah 1751- · 175

Nathaniel 1798-1861 · 466
RICKER
  Thomas · 503
ROBBINS
  Ruth 1757-1824 · 502
ROBERTSON
  John 1732-1816 · 151
  Sarah · 432
ROBINSON
  Daniel 1750-1771 · 316
  Dolly 1747-1767 · 316
  Elizabeth 1707-1723 · 75
  Elizabeth 1727- · 76
  Elizabeth 1746-1777 · 314
  Elizabeth 1760-1762 · 318
  Elizabeth 1768- · 318
  Ephraim 1723- · 76, 317
  Hannah 1695-1753 · 26, 120
  Hannah 1744- · 316
  Hannah 1755- · 318
  Isaac 1715-1804 · 75, 314
  Isaac 1741- · 315
  Jeremiah 1754-1780 · 314
  John 1739-1810 · 314
  John 1758-1807 · 316
  Jonathan 1753-1838 · 316
  Joseph 1678-1763 · 16, 75
  Joseph 1710-1777 · 75, 313

Joseph 1751- · 318
Mary 1737-1811 · 314
Mehitable 1742-1787 · 223, 314
Naomy 1758-1762 · 318
Naomy 1763- · 318
Nathan 1734-1736 · 314
Nathan 1756-1762 · 316
Phebe 1717-1738 · 76
Phebe 1742- · 315
Reuben 1753-1839 · 310
Sarah 1716- · 76, 316
Sarah 1753- · 318
Sarah 1766- · 318
ROGERS
　Abiah · 333
　Abigail -1817 · 503
　Abishai 1762-1831 · 332
　Anna (-) 1765-1849 · 333
　Deborah · 333
　Elias 1759- · 332
　James Augustus 1765-1837 · 333
　Lucy 1748-1830 · 134
　Mary 1745-1813 · 133
　Molly 1757- · 332
　Moses -1808 · 333
　Nathaniel · 80, 332
　Nathaniel 1755-1799 · 332

Oren 1770-1853 · 333
Simeon 1762-1848 · 333
Timothy 1745-1814 · 239
William 1789-1838 · 473
ROLFE
　Nathaniel · 118
ROOT
　Jemima · 333
ROSE
　Charlotte · 503
ROUND
　Nathaniel · 208
ROUNDY
　Nehemiah 1756-1804 · 474
ROWELL
　Christopher 1769- · 396
　Hannah 1766-1831 · 264
RUDD
　Elizabeth 1765-1848 · 332
RUGGLES
　Mary · 171
RUNNELLS
　Esther · 219
RUNNELS
　Samuel 1796-1864 · 416
RUSSELL
　Cynthia 1769-1801 · 326
　John 1746-1830 · 132
　Tabitha 1749-1832 · 206

Index 595

Thomas 1765-1863 · 462
Uriah 1743-1822 · 132
William 1763- · 279

S

SAFFORD
　Sarah (widow) · 140
SALTMARSH
　Catherine 1777- · 406
　Edward Abbott 1768-1851 · 405
　Hazen 1781-1805 · 406
　Isaac 1779-1823 · 406
　John 1764- · 405
　Mary 1766-1848 · 405
　Mehitable 1762-1814 · 405
　Sally 1773- · 406
　Samuel 1775-1844 · 406
　Thomas 1736-1826 · 100, 404
　Thomas 1771-1804 · 406
　Thomas 1772-1823 · 406
SANBORN
　Stephen 1807-1869 · 416
SARGENT
　Dorcas 1787-1837 · 470
　Moses 1738- · 219
SAWIN

Isaac 1748-1776 · 294
SAWINS
  Luce 1740-1824 · 72, 306
SAWTELL
  Abigail · 465
SAWYER
  Nathaniel 1750-1807 · 368
SCALES
  Sarah 1743- · 98
SCARBOROUGH
  Ebenezer 1743-1813 · 289
SCOTT
  John 1765-1847 · 514
  Mehitable · 116, 476
SCRIPTURE
  Esther 1765-1841 · 304
SEARLE
  Abigail 1779-1842 · 292
SEATON
  James · 76
SEAVEY
  Joseph 1762-1812 · 353
SHARP
  Mary 1733-1809 · 79, 326
SHARPE
  Benjamin 1714-1782 · 79
SHATTUCK
  Abiel 1741-1742 · 149
  Abner 1796-1878 · 466
  Elizabeth -1747 · 149
  Elizabeth 1749-1753 · 149
  Hannah 1729- · 148
  Isaac 1734-1822 · 148
  Joseph 1707-1772 · 35, 147
  Joseph 1731-1778 · 148
  Joseph 1757-1847 · 374
  Mary 1743- · 149
  Nathaniel · 156
  Sarah 1739-1832 · 149
  Zebadiah 1736-1826 · 131, 148
SHAW
  Amy 1766-1834 · 288
SHED
  Rebeckah 1685-1720 · 7, 40
SHELDON
  Phebe · 380
  Prudence 1732- · 90, 366
SHEPARD
  Susan · 500
SHEPLE
  John · 107, 426
SHORT
  John 1741- · 219
SIBLEY
  Martha 1776-1846 · 303
SIBSON
  Elizabeth · 241
  Elizabeth -1764 · 59
SILL
  Mary · 285
SIMMONS
  Molly 1754-1814 · 298
SIMPSON
  John · 472
SKINNER
  Anna · 208
  Huldah 1777-1848 · 207
  Pepperrell 1773-1810 · 460
SLATER
  Mary · 392
SMALL
  Lydia 1745- · 336
  Lydia 1745-1795 · 81
SMITH
  Betsey · 445
  Deborah · 433
  Dorothy -1770 · 111, 452
  Hannah 1775-1855 · 296
  Mary 1778-1855 · 222
  Miriam 1770-1819 · 378
  Molly -1773 · 191
  Sarah 1765- · 378
  Zilpha · 255
SNOW
  Hannah 1754- · 267
  John 1774- · 369
  Mary 1773-1857 · 283
SPAULDING
  Bridget 1749-1795 · 116, 475
  Eliza Dido 1807-1856 · 416
  Jacob 1767-1838 · 347
SPRATT
  Phebe -1846 · 167
STANELY
  Jacob 1761- · 264
STANLEY
  Betsey · 157
STARETT

Deborah 1782- · 356
STEARNS
    Elizabeth 1751- · 173
    John 1765-1836 · 383
    Sarah 1726-1803 · 41, 176
    Timothy 1763-1816 · 366
STEDMAN
    Elizabeth 1739-1766 · 70, 288
STEEL
    Benjamin 1741-1817 · 127, 518
    Benjamin 1776-1845 · 454, 518
    Elizabeth 1737- · 127, 516
    Hannah 1743-1827 · 128
    Hannah 1768- · 518
    Hannah 1770- · 518
    Lydia 1745-1748 · 128
    Lydia 1781- · 519
    Nicholas · 27, 126
    Phebe 1735- · 127, 515
    Phebe 1774- · 518
    Rachel 1739- · 127, 517
    Sarah 1779- · 519
    William Lovejoy 1784-1860 · 519
STEPHENS
    Elkanah 1736- · 215
STERLING
    Jane 1755- · 436
STEVENS
    Abigail 1726-1736 · 121

Abigail 1752- · 495
Benjamin 1729- · 121
David 1761-1834 · 166
Deborah · 99
Deborah 1704-1748 · 16, 82
Deborah -1817 · 402
Ebenezer 1767-1851 · 437
Eleanor 1739- · 111
Eleanor 1739-1799 · 456
Elizabeth 1683-1763 · 16, 75
Elizabeth 1697-1736 · 26, 122
Elizabeth 1722- · 121, 495
Ephraim 1649-1718 · 4, 15
Ephraim 1698-1702 · 16
Hannah 1685-1773 · 16, 76
Hannah 1701-aft 1782 · 26, 123
Hannah 1721-1789 · 121, 493
Hannah 1770-1830 · 392
Hephzibah 1740- · 98, 395
John 1764-1825 · 437
Joseph 1750-1803 · 144
Lydia 1706-1790 · 27
Lydia 1745-1821 · 113, 461

Mary 1694-1773 · 16, 78
Mary 1716- · 121, 492
Mehitable 1691- · 16
Mehitable 1700- · 16, 80
Miriam · 89, 363
Nathan 1665-1740 · 5, 25
Nathan 1693-1741 · 26, 120
Nathan 1724- · 121
Phebe 1704- · 27, 126
Phineas 1731- · 122
Rachel 1720-1738 · 121
Samuel · 228
Samuel 1730-1810 · 148
Samuel 1773-1849 · 437
Sarah · 113, 157, 463
Sarah 1681-1750 · 7, 32
Sarah 1734-1738 · 122
Sarah 1741- · 122
Sylvia 1763- · 273
Theodore 1750- · 137
Theodore 1763-1820 · 392
STEWART
    Mary 1749- · 81, 336
STICKNEY
    Anna 1741-1815 · 192
    Elizabeth 1753-1836 · 110, 444
    James 1766- · 435

William · 24
William 1704-1781 · 115
William 1743- · 175
STILES
  Dorothy 1740- · 156
  Stephen 1741- · 197
STIMSON
  Lydia 1703-1791 · 12, 60
STODDARD
  John 1761-1831 · 308
  Judith 1749- · 266
STONE
  Ephraim 1763-1841 · 514
  Lydia (-) -1825 · 74, 310
STORY
  Hannah 1784- · 417
  Jeremiah -1806 · 104, 417
  Mary T. 1764-1849 · 409
  Sarah 1773-1860 · 406
  Sarah 1787- · 418
STOWELL
  Jerusha 1721-1768 · 67, 267
  Seth 1742-1798 · 270
STRATTON
  Phebe 1790-1872 · 406
SUMMER
  Dorothy 1759-1851 · 330
SWAN
  Abigail · 442
  Benjamin 1738-1739 · 320

Benjamin 1743- · 320
Caleb 1749- · 325
Elizabeth 1710-1770 · 77, 318
Elizabeth 1739-1742 · 320
Ephraim 1713-1777 · 78, 321
Ephraim 1739-1777 · 321
Hannah 1716-1761 · 78, 322
Jonathan 1732-1783 · 320
Joseph 1734-1760 · 320
Joshua 1745- · 325
Phineas 1752-1829 · 320
Richard 1746- · 320
Robert 1686-1771 · 16, 76
Robert 1712-1752 · 78, 319
Robert 1749-1832 · 320
Sarah 1742-1812 · 321
SWETLAND
  Artemas · 292
SWIFT
  Nathaniel 1778-1840 · 250
  Sarah 1755-1843 · 499
SYMONDS
  Hannah 1733-1775 · 133

T

TARBELL

Dolly 1798-1861 · 519
TAY
  Rhoda 1770-1841 · 279
TAYLOR
  Anna 1757- · 422
  Daniel 1749- · 421
  Edward · 106, 421
  Edward 1744- · 421
  Jacob 1756- · 422
  Joel 1752-1814 · 421
  Mary 1746- · 421
  Mary 1754-1834 · 422
  Reuben 1759-1849 · 292
TERRINGTON
  Catherine · 273
TEWKSBURY
  Daniel 1810-1847 · 417
  Dorothy · 416
THAYER
  Catherine 1779-1843 · 358
THOMAS
  Abigail · 468
THORNDIKE
  John -1821 · 407
THURSTON
  Stephen 1770-1833 · 355
TOWN
  David 1762-1828 · 369
TOWNE
  Abigail 1765-1832 · 168
  Archelaus 1734-1779 · 39, 167
  Archelaus 1760-1818 · 168

Israel 1761-1848 · 275
Martha 1771-1845 · 168
Mary 1771- · 169
Moses 1739-1824 · 155
Peter 1749-1830 · 165
Sarah 1758- · 168
Susannah 1762-1840 · 168

TRASK
Samuel 1753-1829 · 503

TRUANT
Rebecca 1760-1817 · 494

TRUE
Nathaniel · 490

TRUESDELL
Darius 1752-1808 · 200

TUBBS
Sarah · 332

TUCKER
Zephaniah 1756-1817 · 203

TUFTS
Thomas 1749-1811 · 494

TURNER
Hannah 1694-1788 · 7, 42

TUTTLE
Naomi 1764-1833 · 236
Stephen 1772-1854 · 337

TWISS
Samuel · 157

TWITCHELL
Joseph 1782- · 414

TYLER
Abigail 1763-1783 · 495
Abigail -1826 · 192, 411
Abner 1709-1777 · 121, 493
Adonijah 1738-1812 · 66, 263
Gideon 1747-1832 · 494
Hannah 1749-1815 · 494
James 1760-1855 · 264
Jeremiah 1766-1844 · 264
John 1745-1813 · 494
Joshua 1758-1807 · 494
Martha 1761- · 495
Mary 1753-1842 · 494
Mary 1773-1839 · 265
Miriam 1764-1840 · 264
Moses 1756-1825 · 494
Moses 1770-1857 · 265
Nathan 1742-1759 · 494
Rachel 1762-1843 · 264
Sarah 1758-1840 · 316
Sarah 1775-1839 · 265

Simeon 1768-1855 · 264

U

UPHAM
Ephraim 1778-1844 · 418

UPTON
Elisha 1779-1854 · 440

UTLEY
Abigail 1749-1774 · 284
Amos 1764-1810 · 291
Anna 1755- · 284
Antipas 1770- · 285
Cyrus 1767- · 285
Elijah 1778-1825 · 285
Elizabeth 1729- · 123, 498
Elizabeth 1757-1825 · 284
Hannah 1753-1778 · 284
Joseph · 281
Lucy 1760-1831 · 273
Philip 1751-1754 · 284
Philip 1760-1832 · 284
Rufus 1773- · 285
Samuel 1723-1782 · 69, 283
Samuel 1759-1801 · 284
Samuel 1762-1841 · 284

Index

Timothy 1765- · 284

V

VALPY
   Abraham 1766-1848 · 145
VANCE
   James 1769-1864 · 186
VARNEY
   Patience · 456
VARNUM
   Anna 1767- · 185
VINTON
   John 1742-1814 · 203
   Ralph 1740-1832 · 203
VIRGIN
   Ebenezer 1735- · 192
   Jeremiah 1765- · 447
   Miriam 1744- · 193
VOSE
   Samuel 1759-1830 · 405
VOSS
   Sarah · 226

W

WADLEIGH
   Elizabeth 1785- · 457
WADSWORTH
   Daniel · 499
WAKELEE
   Elihu 1789-1833 · 312
WALDRON
   Jacob 1743- · 254
WALES
   Eunice 1772-1831 · 350
WALKER
   Aaron 1776-1815 · 307
   Abbott 1770-1831 · 510
   Abiel 1766- · 407
   Abiel 1766-1855 · 441
   ABigail 1746-1818 · 175
   Anna 1765-1854 · 437
   Benjamin 1741-1775 · 140
   Bruce 1760-1840 · 441
   Elizabeth 1745- · 174
   Hannah 1756- · 175
   Hannah 1770-1847 · 441
   Hannah 1781-1855 · 437
   James 1778-1826 · 442
   James A. 1739-1821 · 109, 440
   Jeremiah 1771- · 437
   Jeremian Ballard 1777-1841 · 437
   Joel 1750- · 175
   John 1763- · 441
   Joseph 1732-1800 · 109, 436
   Joseph 1754- · 436
   Judith 1744-1806 · 118, 487
   Lydia 1752- · 175
   Mary 1742-1777 · 197
   Mary 1761- · 436
   Mary 1763-1852 · 257, 436
   Namah 1772- · 437
   Namah 1778-1844 · 437
   Nathaniel 1757-1839 · 436
   Peter 1780- · 442
   Rebeckah 1754-1782 · 175
   Reuel · 491
   Richard · 470
   Robert -1757 · 41, 174
   Ruth 1768-1848 · 437
   Ruth 1776-1797 · 442
   Samuel 1748- · 175
   Sarah 1756- · 175
   Sarah 1759- · 436
WALLACE
   Anna · 368
   John 1764-1834 · 277
WARD
   Jonathan 1774-1822 · 412
   Lucretia 1748-1809 · 225
   Rachel 1748-1774 · 74, 310
   Stephen · 114
WARDWELL
   Jeremiah 1748-1817 · 153
   Nathan 1741-1769 · 197
WARREN
   Levi · 460
WASHER
   Hannah 1767-1837 · 352
WEBB
   Abigail 1787-1846 · 414
WEBSTER

Betsey · 263
David 1749-1828 · 181
Sarah 1748- · 219
Tryphena 1754-1843 · 320
WEEKS
John 1757-1836 · 403
WELMAN
Anna 1770- · 343
WEST
Ebenezer 1754-1776 · 469
Jonathan 1749-1826 · 193
Laura 1781-1853 · 290
WESTON
Esther 1763-1850 · 168
WHEELER
Esther 1778- · 381
Eunice 1756-1807 · 327
Jeremiah 1745-1827 · 364
Molly · 423
WHEELOCK
Joseph 1788-1857 · 511
WHEET
Hannah 1772-1842 · 311
WHITE
Dorothy 1774- · 328
Lydia 1763-1853 · 255
Mary · 495
Nathan · 383
WHITING

Dorcas 1692-1765 · 7, 40
Moses -1823 · 246
Oliver 1750-1829 · 360
Sarah 1762-1806 · 262
Timothy 1732-1799 · 171
WHITMAN
Samuel 1753-1810 · 289
WHITNEY
Mary 1732- · 50, 210
WHITTEMORE
Benjamin 1750- · 363
Esther 1752-1803 · 101
Philip Whittemore 1766-1855 · 279
Rhoda 1729-1785 · 64, 256
WHITTIER
William · 137
Whittlesey
Mabel 1757-1836 · 255
WIGHT
Abigail 1757-1825 · 209
Levi 1761-1831 · 209
WILKINS
Bray · 427
Mary · 132
WILLEY
Alice 1778-1858 · 183
John · 157
Lois 1760-1855 · 258
WILLIAMS

Bathsheba 1737-1769 · 71, 299
Eleazer 1764-1841 · 330
John 1761-1813 · 136
Sarah 1760-1831 · 330
WILSON
David 1770- · 186
Jeremiah 1770-1775 · 407
Margaret 1760-1841 · 163
Mary 1772- · 407, 441
Thomas -1818 · 101, 406
WINCHESTER
Deborah · 428
WINSHIP
Simon 1749-1813 · 177
WISE
Lucy 1723- · 132
WOOD
Betsy · 490
Mary 1748- · 322
Rebecca 1744-1810 · 314
Ruth 1753-1825 · 323
WOODBRIDGE
Benjamina 1772- · 319
Dudley 1733-1799 · 227
Electa 1754-1781 · 498
WOODCOCK
Sarah 1782-1854 · 477

WOODS
  Betty · 223
  Sarah 1742-1774 · 125, 513
WORCESTER
  Mary · 421
WORTHEN
  Jacob · 115
WORTHLEY
  Rachel 1764- · 228
WRIGHT
  Abiel 1726-1737 · 52
  Abiel 1739- · 211
  Abigail 1728- · 52, 216
  Abigail 1741- · 211
  Abigail 1750- · 212
  Anna 1758- · 136
  Benjamin 1753-1839 · 212
  Dorcas 1732- · 52
  Dorothy 1730- · 52, 216
  Ebenezer · 207
  Elizabeth 1719- · 52, 214
  Hannah 1717-1796 · 51, 213
  Hannah 1747-1812 · 212
  Hephzibah 1720-1797 · 52, 214
  John 1734-1734 · 53
  John 1756- · 175
  Joseph 1693- · 10, 50
  Joseph 1713-1785 · 51, 210
  Lemuel 1757-1846 · 212
  Mary 1722- · 52
  Mary 1730-1811 · 50, 206
  Samuel 1745-1786 · 211
  Sarah 1715- · 51
  Sarah 1715-1783 · 212
  Sarah 1737- · 211
  Sarah 1763- · 236
WYMAN
  Betsey 1764- · 474
  Elizabeth 1730-1778 · 145
  Elizabeth -1778 · 34
  Jonas 1759-1818 · 470

Y

YOUNG
  Hezekiah · 364

Made in the USA
Middletown, DE
24 November 2018